Kenya Handbook

Lizzie Williams

Kenya's landscapes are varied: from rolling savannah and mountain forests to stony parched deserts and a tropical coastline. It is these habitats that harbour some of Africa's most incredible animals and a safari, meaning 'journey' in Kiswahili, is a highlight for many visitors.

The principal draw card is the Big Five: lion, leopard, elephant, rhino and buffalo, but there are numerous other interesting species. Some of the game parks and reserves, such as the Masai Mara and Amboseli, are world famous for their plains game, while thousands of flamingos live on the Rift Valley lakes, and the verdant woodlands are home to primates and a profusion of African birds. Along the coast, the azure Indian Ocean offers exotic palm-fringed and pearly-white beaches that lie in wait of the sun-worshipping crowd, while the coral reefs team with life and colour.

Kenya's is also known for its diversity of people: the majestic Masai and Samburu still stalk the plains dressed in their trademark red and purple robes, while the legacies of the European white settlers who came in search of pristine farming land and hunting trophies can still be seen.

Kenya's two major cities – the high-altitude colonial-built capital Nairobi and the steamy trading port of Mombasa – have a vibrant urban feel. On the coast, ruins of once-sophisticated cities with their old mosques, Arabian-style houses and coral palaces remain, while places like Lamu or Old Mombasa are living testaments to the Swahili tradition that has survived for thousands of years.

THIS PAGE The Great Rift Valley at Poro near Maralal
PREVIOUS PAGE The elegant and photogenic giraffe is included in Kenya's 'Big Nine'

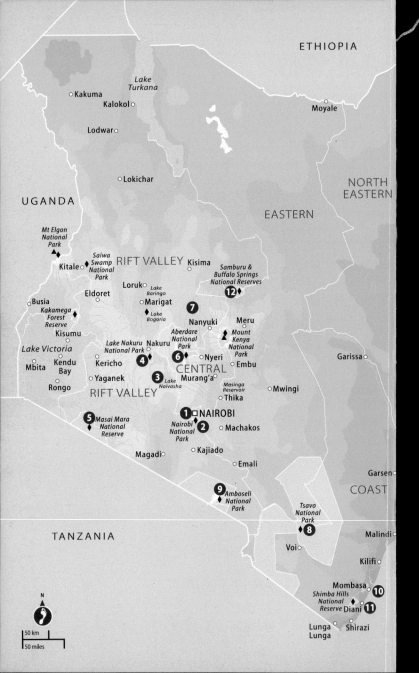

Ramu

El Wako

SOMALIA

Mokowe _Pate Island_
○ _Manda_
Lamu Island
Island

Indian Ocean

Women carry *makuti* (coconut palm fronds used for roofing) on a Mombasa beach

Don't miss... See colour maps at end of book

The best time of day to spot animals is early morning or late afternoon

Itineraries for Kenya

Straddling the equator and with a temperate climate, Kenya offers a bewildering choice of destinations and experiences. Most people visit to go on safari and, whilst the journey may be rough on the parks' bumpy roads, there is no denying that there are some spectacular locations to see the full complement of African animals. Also well known for its birdlife, Kenya has a huge number of species in the highland forests and Rift Valley lakes.

Ideally, a safari should be combined with some time on the coast where there are palm-fringed, white-sand beaches and coral reefs that are home to a spectrum of marine species. Those with more time can also explore Nairobi's interesting wildlife sanctuaries, the pretty forests in Western Kenya, the arid northern deserts, the enchanting old town of Lamu or stately Mount Kenya.

Nairobi is also the obvious gateway to neighbouring countries, and visits to Kenya can easily be extended south to the northern parks of Tanzania, which include the world-famous Serengeti and Ngorongoro Crater, or to climb Africa's tallest mountain, Kilimanjaro. Another option is to head west from Kenya to see the rare mountain gorillas in their fabled forests in Uganda or Rwanda. In short, an international flight to Kenya opens up inexhaustible opportunities for exploring East Africa.

Kenya is one of the world's top birding destinations

ITINERARY ONE (1-2 weeks)
Nairobi & the Big Five

All of Kenya's best parks and reserves are just a few hours' drive away from Nairobi, the closest being Nairobi National Park, which has the city as its backdrop and can easily be visited on a half-day tour. A one-week safari from Nairobi can be organized to the Masai Mara, Amboseli, Tsavo, the Aberdares and Lake Nakuru and the other Rift Valley lakes; how many you visit and how long you stay in each depends on personal preference and there are any number of combinations. A popular circuit from Nairobi is two to three days in the Masai Mara, with an additional couple of days to see Lake Naivasha and Lake Nakuru National Park. Another option is to spend two to three days in both Amboseli and Tsavo. It's worth allowing at least a day to

TRAVEL TIP
On safari in Kenya, you can camp, stay in a mid-range safari lodge or an exclusive luxury tented camp, and drive or fly between destinations.

explore Nairobi itself as there are some very interesting wildlife centres and attractions on the edge of the city, including the Giraffe Centre, the David Sheldrick Wildlife Trust and the Karen Blixen Museum. In the city itself, you can spend half a day at the newly revamped Nairobi National Museum to learn about Kenya's flora and fauna and its rich cultural history. Nairobi also has other urban distractions and a gin-and-tonic on the terrace of the historic colonial Norfolk Hotel or a gut-busting meal at the famous Carnivore restaurant are on most tourists' itineraries.

ITINERARY TWO (1-2 weeks)
Safari & the Indian Ocean

After a safari from Nairobi, Kenya offers a wonderful opportunity for relaxing on the beach, and transport links between Nairobi and the coast are very good. You could easily spend a week at one of the affordable beach resorts, which offer a range of facilities including diving and snorkelling, or choose to self-cater at a peaceful beachside cottage. From the resorts you can take day trips along the coast to see attractions, such as Wasini Island to the south, the old town of Mombasa itself, or the marine parks along the northern beaches. Not far from the beach, the Shimba Hills National Reserve is a very popular day trip with an excellent chance of spotting elephant. Tsavo East and West national parks are also within a two-hour drive, so if you have arrived in Kenya directly at the international airport in Mombasa, a beach holiday could be combined with one or two nights in a game lodge. There is also the possibility of heading north up the coast for a night or two on the island of Lamu (but see travel warning, page 293) to experience its wonderfully friendly ancient stone town with its intriguing narrow alleyways, superb museum and Arabic houses.

TRAVEL TIP

The warm water, clear visibility and exceptional marine life makes Kenya an ideal destination to learn scuba-diving and all the resorts have dive schools.

A traditional outrigger canoe sails close to the shore at Diani Beach

ITINERARY THREE (2-3 weeks)
Highlands, forests & deserts

With more time you can explore more of the Rift Valley, enjoy Naivasha's peaceful lakeshore accommodation, walk amongst game in Hell's Gate National Park, or head for lakes Bogoria and Baringo for some of Kenya's best birdwatching. If you want to climb Mount Kenya, allow four or five days and then, north of the mountain, a few days could easily be spent enjoying the varied safari activities on a private ranch on the Laikipia Plateau, an applauded conservation effort by ranch owners to use their land for the protection and, in many cases, breeding of wildlife. Other options include heading to the highlands of Western Kenya and Lake Victoria. While the provincial towns here won't keep your interest for long, the countryside is extraordinarily pretty, especially the Kakamega Forest and the verdant tea plantations around Kericho. Northern Kenya is a wild and untamed region of parched deserts, razor-sharp mountains, and the spectacular turquoise waters of Kenya's largest lake, Turkana. However, travel in this region is challenging and difficult, and has in recent years been marred by security problems, so it's best to explore this region on an organized tour.

TRAVEL TIP
To get off the beaten track in Kenya it's useful to have your own vehicle; otherwise tour operators in Nairobi can organize tailor-made tours.

Snow-capped Mount Kenya, Africa's second highest mountain

A Turkana woman makes the final ties to the framework of her home

Late afternoon light in the Masai Mara National Reserve of southern Kenya

Contents

Contents

Essentials

Planning your trip

Best time to visit Kenya

Thanks to its location on the equator, Kenya has a moderate climate and long sunny days for most of the year, though there are variations depending on topography and elevation. Daytime temperatures average between 20°C and 25°C, but it is cooler in the highlands and hotter along the coast. Humidity varies, being low in the interior highlands but much higher along the coastal strip, though high temperatures are cooled by ocean breezes so it is rarely overpoweringly hot. Away from the coast, it is much drier and the rains are a little more moderate. On peaks above 1500 m the climate is cooler with permanent snow on the highest points, such as Mount Kenya, where night-time temperatures drop to below zero. There are two rainy seasons in the country: the long rains fall March to May and the short rains fall November to December. Even in these months, however, there is an average of four to six hours of sunshine each day. Bear in mind that malaria peaks during the rainy seasons, when mosquitoes are prolific. Travelling by road, especially in the more remote areas or through the national parks, is easier during the dry months, as road conditions deteriorate significantly in the rainy seasons.

High season along the coast is from September to January and it gets especially busy around the Christmas and New Year period. High season in the safari regions is during the dry months of July to November, especially in the Masai Mara as this is when the wildebeest have arrived from the Serengeti in Tanzania on their annual migration. For sheer numbers of birds, the best time for birdwatching is October to April when over 120 migrant species arrive from the northern hemisphere, mostly from the Palearctic but with some African migrants too. As Kenya is on the equator, the times of sunrise and sunset hardly change throughout the year – sunrise is generally 0700-0800 and sunset 1800-1900.

What to do in Kenya

Ballooning

The Masai Mara is the top spot for a gentle float over the animals in a balloon and, for many, this excursion is the highlight of a visit to the reserve (albeit expensive). Most of the lodges and camps offer this activity, and watching the balloon inflate is part of the experience. Once the balloon rises, passengers can watch the dawn high above the plains and, when the sun comes up, it turns the grasslands from blue to gold. This is a spectacular experience, especially during the wildebeest migration; the price includes a bush breakfast with champagne. Details of local operators are listed in the relevant chapters.

Birdwatching

With over 1100 species of bird recorded, Kenya is one of the world's top birding destinations and has over 12% of the world's listed species. Serious twitchers should head for the Rift Valley lakes, the Arabuko Sokoke Forest on the coast, Kakamega Forest in the Western Highlands, and the Ngong and Karura forests just outside Nairobi. **Nature Kenya**, Nairobi, www.naturekenya. org, runs regular birding trips from Nairobi. The website www.kenyabirds.org.uk is an excellent resource and lists the region's birding hotspots and has extensive bird lists.

Climbing and hiking

Point Lenana (4985 m) on Mount Kenya is the country's most popular climb, and organized treks take 4-6 days. Africa's highest mountain, Kilimanjaro (5895 m), shares Kenya's southern border with Tanzania, although treks depart from the Tanzanian town of Moshi which is only a half-day's drive from Nairobi. Other multi-day treks in Kenya include the Cherangani Hills and Mount Elgon, while day hike destinations include Hell's Gate National Park, Menengani Crater and Mount Longonot in the Rift Valley. There are many small reserves and forests around the country which have nature trails and are ideal for birdwatching, and many safari lodges offer guided game walks. Details of local operators are listed in the relevant chapters. The **Mountain Club of Kenya**, www.mck.or.ke, is an excellent resource for climbing Mount Kenya.

Diving and snorkelling

Kenya has long fringing coral reefs that stretch along the entire coastline and surrounding islands, and there are some spectacular coral gardens and drop-offs. Most of the coast is protected in a number of marine parks and none of the dive sites is more than a 30-min boat ride away from the beaches. There is an abundance of tropical reef fish as well as large pelagic fish and, if lucky, you will encounter barracuda, manta rays, whale and reef sharks, hawksbill and green turtles and schools of dolphins. The best time to dive in Kenya is between Oct and Apr, when the average water temperature is 27°C and visibility ranges from 10 to 30 m. Non-divers can explore the reefs by snorkelling or, if you don't want to get wet, from glass-bottomed boats. Details of local operators are listed in the relevant chapters.

Fishing

There is excellent deep-sea fishing in the Pemba Channel off the Kenyan coast, and the larger game species include marlin, tuna, sailfish, shark, swordfish and yellowfin. The best places to head for are Watamu, Shimoni, Malindi and Kilifi. Lake Victoria attracts big-game fishermen after the weighty Nile perch that reach up to 100 kg, though the fishing camps around the lake are only in the top price category. Details of local operators are listed in the relevant chapters.

Golf

Because of Kenya's colonial legacy, there are over 40 golf courses in Kenya. Six are in Nairobi, the oldest being the Royal Nairobi Golf Club which opened in 1906. Most allow visitors to play with a temporary membership and hire out golf clubs. An advantage of playing golf in Nairobi or at the highlands courses above 1500 m is that the ball travels some 10 m further at high altitude than it would do at sea level. **Kenya Golf Union**, www.kenyagolfnetwork.co.ke, has information on courses and events.

Kiteboarding

With its cross-shore winds, wide flat sandy beaches, shallow waves and virtually no obstructions, this is the latest craze on the coast, particularly at Diani and Nyali beaches where there are centres that offer lessons and courses. Details of local operators are listed in the relevant chapters.

Riding

There are many horse and camel treks on offer on the game ranches of the Laikipia Plateau (www.laikipiatourism.com) and in Northern Kenya, from short out-rides to multi-day safaris. On horseback it's possible

Packing for Kenya

Before you leave home, send yourself an email to a web-based account with details of traveller's cheques, passport, driving licence, credit cards and travel insurance numbers. Be sure that someone at home also has access to this information.

A good rule of thumb is to take half the clothes you think you'll need and double the money. Laundry services are generally cheap and speedy in Kenya so you shouldn't need to bring too many clothes. A backpack or travelpack (a hybrid backpack/suitcase) rather than a rigid suitcase covers most eventualities and survives the rigours of a variety of modes of travel. A lock for your luggage is strongly advised – there are cases of pilfering by airport baggage handlers the world over.

Light cotton clothing is best, with a fleece or woollen clothing for evenings. Also pack something to change into at dusk – long sleeves and trousers (particularly light coloured) help ward off mosquitoes, which are at their most active in the evening. During the day you will need a hat, sunglasses and high-factor sun cream for protection against the sun. Modest dress is advisable for women, particularly on the coast, where men too should avoid revealing shoulders. Kenya is a great place to buy sarongs – known in East Africa as *kikois*, which in Africa are worn by both men and women and are ideal to cover up when, say, leaving the beach. Footwear should be airy because of the heat: sandals or canvas trainers are ideal. Trekkers will need comfortable walking boots, and ones that have been worn in if you are climbing Mount Kenya. Those going on camping safaris will need a sleeping bag, towel and torch, and budget travellers may want to consider bringing a sleeping sheet in case the sheets don't look too clean in a budget hotel.

to get very close to wildlife, as animals do not have an inherent fear of horses. Camels are usually used as pack animals off the beaten track into some real wilderness areas. These excursions mostly use local guides, especially the Samburu.

Water sports

As well as diving and snorkelling, many hotels and resorts on the coast organize windsurfing, jet skiing, parasailing, sea-kayaking and all types of boats from inflatable banana-boats or glass-bottomed boats, to catamaran sailing and a sunset cruise on a traditional white-sailed dhow. A very popular day excursion is the dhow trip to Wasini Island to the south of Diani Beach for snorkelling, a delicious seafood lunch and the opportunity to spot dolphins. Details of local operators are listed in the relevant chapters.

Whitewater rafting

The base for **Savage Wilderness Safaris** (www.whitewaterkenya.com) is on the Tana River on the road around Mount Kenya. It offers whitewater rafting on the Tana and, while most of the route is on fairly calm water, there are some Grade II and III sections of rapids and 2 Grade IV drops; a day trip from Nairobi costs US$100. They also arrange longer 3-day, 65-km rafting trips on the Athi River on the border of Tsavo National Park, which is excellent for game-viewing and birdwatching; 2 nights are spent camping on sandbanks.

Going on safari

No visit to Kenya is complete without going on safari, and there are a number of national parks and game reserves, some owned by the government and administered by the **Kenya Wildlife Services** (KWS), and some in the private sector such as local ranches in local communities. These offer visitors the chance of seeing splendid African landscapes and wildlife including the Big Five (elephant, buffalo, rhinoceros, lion and leopard), along with countless other animals and innumerable bird species. Along with wildlife, some of the parks have been gazetted to preserve the vegetation, such as Kakamega Forest, or unique locations, such as Mount Kenya, and marine-life is protected in the marine parks off Malindi, Watamu and Kisite. Some of the parks and reserves are world famous, such as the **Masai Mara** and **Amboseli**, and have excellent facilities and receive many visitors, while others rarely see tourists and have few amenities.

The best time of day to spot animals is early in the morning and late in the afternoon, as many animals sleep through the intense midday heat. Animals can most easily be seen during the dry season when the lack of surface water forces them to congregate around rivers and waterholes. However, the rainy seasons, from October to November and March to May, are when the animals are in the best condition after feeding on the new shoots, and there are chances of seeing breeding displays and young animals. The disadvantage of the wet season is that the thicker vegetation and the wider availability of water mean that the wildlife is more spread out and more difficult to spot; also, driving conditions are far harder in deep mud as none of the park roads are paved. However, prices for lodges can be up to a third lower during the rainy seasons. Driving around endlessly searching for animals is not usually the best way to view animals, and drives can be broken up by stops at waterholes, picnic sites and hides. Time spent around a waterhole with your engine switched off gives you an opportunity to listen to the sounds of the bush and experience the rhythms of nature as game moves to and from the water. Kenya's game parks and reserves are well organized; following the few park rules will ensure an enjoyable stay.

Organizing a safari

Most people visit the parks and reserves on an organized safari, which involves staying at a safari lodge or tented camp or, at the cheaper end of the scale, at a campsite, and going out on game drives in a specially adapted vehicle with a guide; however, it's still a good idea to take along some wildlife and bird identification books. You can pre-book a safari from your home country, or there are a huge number of safari companies in Kenya; these are listed in the relevant chapters. Ensure that the company is properly licensed and is a member of the **Kenya Association of Tour Operators (KATO)** ⓘ www.katokenya.org, which represents over 350 of Kenya's tour operators and is a good place to start when looking for a safari. Costs vary enormously depending on duration, season, where you stay and how many are in a group. At the very top end of the scale, staying in the most exclusive tented camps and flying between destinations, expect to pay in excess of US$500 per person per day; for larger mid-range lodges with buffet meals, around US$200-250 per person per day (more if you opt for air transfers); and for camping safaris using the basic national park campsites and the services of a safari cook, about US$140-180 per person per day.

Transport

It is worth emphasizing that most parks are some way from departure points. If you go on a three-day safari by road, you will often find that at least one day is taken up with

Kenya Wildlife Services conservation fees

In total **Kenya Wildlife Services (KWS)** administers 30 national parks and five marine reserves. Most conservation fees are taken at the gates on entry, but admission to the most popular parks – Nairobi, Nakuru, Amboseli, Tsavo East and West, and Aberdare national parks – is by an electronic ticketing system known as Safari Card. If you are on an organized safari your tour operator will arrange these, but if you are visiting the parks independently, you need to purchase and 'load' a Safari Card at the gates of these parks. If you prefer, and you know how many parks you are going to visit and roughly how much your park entry fees, vehicle costs and camping fees are going to be, you can purchase and pre-load one at the KWS headquarters at the Main Gate of Nairobi National park on Langata Road in Nairobi (page 57). Anyone over the age of 18 must have their own Safari Card, and under 18s can be paid for with a parent's. Money on the cards is not refundable, but you can always top it up at the gates as needs be. Note: National Reserves, such as the Masai Mara and the Samburu-Buffalo Springs-Shaba complex, are not administered by KWS and are managed by local councils who set their own entry fees. These are paid for on arrival at the main gates or lodges in cash, or will be included in the price of an organized safari.

Prices as of 1 January 2012. Children's fees apply from age 3 to 18; under 3s go free. Entry is per 24 hours or part thereof. For further details contact **KWS**, Nairobi, T020-600 0800, www.kws.org.

Amboseli and **Lake Nakuru**
Normal season (April-June, November-December) US$60 adults; US$30 children.
High season (January-March, July-October) US$75 adults; US$40 children.

Tsavo East, Tsavo West, Meru
Normal season (April-June, November-December) US$50 adults; US$25 children.
High season (January-March, July-October) US$60 adults; US$30 children.

Aberdare
US$50 adults; US$25 children.

Mount Elgon, Hell's Gate
US$25 adults; US$15 children.

Marsabit, Shimba Hills, Arabuko Sokoke Forest, Kakamega Forest, Chyulu Hills, Oldonyo Sabuk, Mwea, Ruma, Saiwa Swamp, South Turkana, Mount Longonot, Sibiloi, Central and South Island, Ndere Island
US$20 adults; US$10 children.

Urban safaris
Nairobi National Park
US$40 adults; US$20 children.
Nairobi Safari Walk
US$20 adults; US$10 children.
Nairobi Animal Orphanage and Kisumu Impala Sanctuary
US$15 adults; US$10 children.

Mountain climbing
Mount Kenya National Park
US$55 adults; US$25 children.
(Residents' rates apply to Kenyan porters and guides.)
Mount Kenya National Park (climbing for the first three days, includes accommodation in KWS mountain huts)
US$150 adults; US$70 children.

Marine parks and reserves
Kisite-Mpunguti
US$20 adults; US$10 children.
Mombasa, Malindi, Watamu, Kiunga
US$15 adults; US$10 children

Kenya Wildlife Services

The Kenyan government has long been aware that the principal attraction of the country to tourists is its wildlife and, since 1989, has been keen to ensure it is available in abundance for tourists to see. During the 1970s and 1980s Kenya's parks suffered at the hands of poachers, and whole populations of wildlife – particularly rhino and elephant – were all but wiped out. But thanks to gallant efforts by the well-organized Kenya Wildlife Services (KWS) and many private ranch owners, today the many species of animal, bird, marine and plant life are far better protected. When the country gained Independence in 1963, there were an estimated 170,000 elephants but by 1989 they numbered just 16,000. In 1989, 12 tons of confiscated ivory was burnt in Nairobi National Park (page 57), where today a mound of ash and an information board marks the spot. The fire was lit by then-president Moi and was a symbolic gesture that declared war on poachers and an end to the mass slaughter of elephants in Kenya. The event, televised across the world, contributed to the CITES international ban on ivory trading and the establishment of the KWS in 1990, headed up by Richard Leakey. Poaching patrols that were well trained and well equipped with Land Rovers and guns were put in place and extremely stiff penalties for anyone caught poaching were established. All employees of KWS are still armed and there's a shoot-to-kill policy against poachers. The present elephant population in Kenya is around 37,000 and, thanks to the anti-poaching efforts by KWS employees, numbers of many more species of large animal have recovered significantly. If visiting the Nairobi National Park, in the car park at the Main Gate look out for the Conservation Heroes Monument, which lists all the names of KWS employees who have died in the line of duty since the KWS was established.

Nevertheless, while the 1989 CITES global ban on the ivory trade briefly halted the elephants' demise and elephant numbers across Africa are much healthier today, it's initial success has been undermined by Asia's booming demand for ivory. In 2011, there was another burning of ivory; this time 6.5 tons at the KWS Field Training School at Manyani in Tsavo, and the torch was lit by President Kibaki. The ivory – most of which was thought to have originated in Zambia – was seized in Singapore in 2002 and arrived in Kenya in 2004; the KWS were considered to be the best custodians of the confiscated ivory. Although the event took place in Kenya, it was carried out by the Lusaka Agreement Task Force – a group of the wildlife conservation bodies of seven African countries that work together to prevent the illegal trade in Africa's flora and fauna. Again, as in 1989, the cache was burnt as a symbolic gesture to publicize the senseless slaughter of Africa's elephants.

travelling to and from the park, often on bad, bumpy and dusty roads – leaving you with less time on safari in the park itself. The easiest option, which is of course the most expensive, is to fly; most parks and reserves have a good network of airstrips with daily flights. If you are confident about driving on the poorly maintained tracks within the parks and are prepared to camp, you can also self-drive. In some parks there is the option to hire a guide from the park HQ to accompany you in your own vehicle. Some of the parks are better for driving than others. For example, Lake Nakuru and Nairobi national parks are easily negotiable in a car and are a pleasure to drive around, whilst others, such as the

Masai Mara or Tsavo, have rough roads and remote areas where you certainly do not want to get stuck in the event of a breakdown or emergency. On your own safari remember that you will need to budget for vehicle, camping and entry fees, and load your Safari Card with the relevant costs (see box, page 9).

Getting to Kenya

Air

Kenya is well served by many international airlines, so is usually the cheapest country in East Africa to get to by air and, consequently, is a good place to start off a tour of the region. The main point of arrival is Nairobi's **Jomo Kenyatta International Airport (JKIA)**, 15 km southeast of the city off the Mombasa road (page 42), though there are also a substantial number of regional flights, plus charter flights from Europe, to Mombasa's **Moi International Airport (MBA)**, 10 km west of the city centre on the mainland (page 229). Airport information can be found at www.kenyaairports.co.ke. Nairobi is a nine-hour flight from London and Mombasa is about 11 hours. Because of the proximity of the Northern Circuit national parks in Tanzania, many visitors going on safari to Northern Tanzania also fly into Nairobi as it is closer than Tanzania's capital Dar es Salaam.

The cheapest plane tickets are in the 'off season' from February to June and again from October to early December. If you do have to go during peak times, book as far in advance as you can, particularly if you aim to get there in mid-December when flights get full very quickly. If you are short of time, a package holiday to the coast could well be a useful option, particularly if you go out of the peak season when you can get excellent deals. Beach holidays are far cheaper than safaris. It is a good idea to find out as much as you can about the hotel in the package deal before going, although you can always stay elsewhere if necessary. Once on the coast there is then the option to book a short overnight safari to one of the parks.

From Europe
Airlines with daily direct services from London to Nairobi include the national carrier **Kenya Airways**, which also flies from Amsterdam, Paris and Rome; **British Airways**, and **Virgin Atlantic**. **Air France** has direct flights between Paris and Nairobi; **KLM** between Amsterdam and Nairobi, and **Lufthansa**, from Frankfurt and Munich. Non-direct flights from Europe may work out economical: **Egypt Air** flies to Nairobi via Cairo; **Emirates** via Dubai; **Qatar Airways** via Doha, and **Turkish Airlines**, via Istanbul. **Ethiopian Airlines** flies from Europe via Addis Ababa to Nairobi and Mombasa.

Jet lag is not an issue if flying from Europe to Kenya as there is only a minimal time difference.

From North America
There are no direct flights from the USA to Kenya. Americans have to change flights in Europe or the Middle East depending on which carrier they choose. It is usual to fly via London, Amsterdam or Dubai if travelling from the USA. Alternatively, **Delta Airlines** has a code-share agreement with **South African Airways**, who run daily direct flights from New York and Atlanta to Johannesburg, from where there are connections to Nairobi.

From Australia, New Zealand and Asia

There are no direct flights between Australia/New Zealand and Kenya, but a number of indirect routes. **Kenya Airways** flies between Nairobi and Mauritius, where it connects with the **Air Mauritius** flight to/from Perth. Otherwise flights go via the Middle East (below) or South Africa. Between them **Qantas** and **South African Airways**, on a code-sharing agreement, fly between Perth and Johannesburg and some flights continue to and from Sydney. **Singapore Airlines** offers flights between Sydney and Johannesburg via Singapore, and has a code-sharing agreement with **Air New Zealand** (which means that flights from Wellington to Johannesburg have two stops). **Air Malaysia** has regular flights from Perth, Melbourne, Sydney and Darwin in Australia and Auckland in New Zealand to Kuala Lumpur, connecting with a flight to Johannesburg. **Cathay Pacific** flies from Hong Kong to Johannesburg. From Johannesburg there are daily connections to Nairobi on both **Kenya Airways** and **South African Airways**. To and from East Asia, **Kenya Airways** flies direct between Nairobi and Bangkok, Hong Kong and Guangzhou.

From Africa and the Middle East

From South Africa both **Kenya Airways** and **South African Airways** have daily flights between Johannesburg and Nairobi. Just about all of the African airlines serve Nairobi, and some serve Mombasa, so Kenya is a good hub to travel to and from other African cities. From the Middle East, Nairobi is served by **Gulf Air**, which also touches down in Mombasa, **Emirates** and **Qatar Airways**. **Kenya Airways** has a direct flight between Nairobi and Dubai, and Nairobi and Muscat. **RwandAir** flies from Kigali in Rwanda via Nairobi and Mombasa to Dubai.

Airlines

Air France, www.airfrance.com.
Air Malaysia, www.malaysia-airlines.com.
Air Mauritius, www.airmauritius.com.
Air New Zealand, www.airnewzealand.com.
British Airways, www.britishairways.com.
Cathy Pacific, www.cathaypacific.com.
Delta, www.delta.com.
Egypt Air, www.egyptair.com.
Emirates, www.emirates.com.
Ethiopian Airlines,
www.ethiopianairlines.com.

Gulf Air, www.gulfair.com.
Kenya Airways, www.kenya-airways.com.
KLM, www.klm.com.
Lufthansa, www.lufthansa.com.
Qantas, www.qantas.com.au.
Qatar Airways, www.qatarairways.com.
RwandAir, www.rwandair.com.
Singapore Airlines, www.singaporeair.com.
South African Airways, www.flysaa.com.
Turkish Airlines, www.turkishairlines.com.
Virgin Atlantic, www.virgin-atlantic.com.

Road → *See box, opposite, for border crossing information.*

Bus

There are international long-distance bus services between Nairobi and **Kampala** in Uganda, which take around 13 hours; Nairobi and **Dar es Salaam** in Tanzania, about 14 hours, which also stop in **Arusha** and **Moshi**; and Nairobi and **Musoma** and **Mwanza** on Lake Victoria in northwestern Tanzania, around 13½ hours. There are also services between Mombasa and **Tanga** in Tanzania, which connect with buses to and from **Dar es Salaam**. Although there are several companies, **Akamba**, www.akambabus.com, and **Scandinavia Express**, www.scandinaviagroup.com (an equally good Tanzanian company), are the most reliable for long-distance cross-border services. See Nairobi Transport

Border crossings

Kenya has numerous borders with its neighbouring countries; crossings are detailed in the relevant chapters.

Kenya–Ethiopia

Moyale, page 345.

The only crossing to and from Ethiopia is at Moyale on the A2, 508 km north of Isiolo, from where the road heads north 775 km to Addis Ababa. There is no public transport north of Isiolo, but on the Ethiopian side there are buses from Moyale to Addis Ababa.

Kenya–Somalia

Because of Somali militant activity in the border regions between Somalia and Kenya, the borders between these two countries at Liboi, 275 east of Garissa, and Mandera, 370 km northeast of Wajir, are currently closed.

Kenya–South Sudan

Lokichoggio, page 323.

Lokichoggio, the border with newly proclaimed South Sudan, is on the A1, 216 km north of Lodwar, although there is no public transport on this route. From the border it's 375 km to Juba, South Sudan's capital.

Kenya–Tanzania

Isebania, page 141; **Namanga**, page 220; **Taveta**, page 220; **Lunga Lunga**, page 249.

The main road crossing is at Namanga 162 km south of Nairobi on the A104, which is roughly midway between Nairobi and Arusha in Tanzania and, as this border receives thousands of tourists each week en route between the Kenyan and Tanzanian parks, it is open 24 hours and is quick and efficient. The most popular way to get between the two cities is by shuttle bus (see box, page 14 and Nairobi Transport, page 81). A cheaper alternative is to do the journey in stages by taking a minibus from Ronald Ngala Road in Nairobi to Namanga, crossing the border on foot, and then catching another minibus to Arusha, but this takes a lot longer than the shuttle. Other crossings are at Lunga Lunga, on the A14 between Mombasa and Tanga, and there are daily through buses between the two cities. Slower public buses and minibuses frequent the quieter border crossings at Taveta, on the A23 between Voi and Moshi, and at Isebania, on the A1 between Kisii and Mwanza. Visas for both Tanzania and Kenya are available at all the borders. The Sand River border crossing between the Masai Mara National Reserve and the Serengeti National Park is currently closed.

Kenya–Uganda

Malaba, page 151; **Busia**, page 151.

There are two border crossings between Kenya and Uganda at Malaba, on the A104, 127 km west of Eldoret, and Busai, on the B1, 112 km northwest of Kisumu; both are open 24 hours and procedures are quick and efficient. Daily through buses run between Nairobi and Kampala (see Nairobi Transport, page 81).

(page 80) or the relevant chapters for more details. Further afield, Scandinavia Express also operates a service between Dar es Salaam and **Lusaka** in Zambia, so die-hard fans of African bus travel can go all the way from Kampala in Uganda to Lusaka in Zambia with Scandinavia Express. In addition to the long-distance bus companies, there are daily shuttle bus services to and from Nairobi and **Arusha** (for Tanzania's Northern Circuit parks) and **Moshi** (to climb Kilimanjaro), see box, page 14.

Kenya–Tanzania shuttle services

Shuttle buses run daily between Kenya and Tanzania on the following route: Nairobi (city centre)–Nairobi Jomo Kenyatta International Airport–Arusha (via the Namanga border post)–Kilimanjaro International Airport–Moshi. Arusha is the springboard town for safaris to Tanzania's Northern Circuit parks and Moshi is the town where you can organize and begin a climb of Mount Kilimanjaro. From both, you can also get onward buses to Dar es Salaam. The shuttle operators utilize 20- to 30-seat buses with comfortable, individual seating, and drivers assist passengers through the Namanga border crossing. There is an early morning and early afternoon departure. Expect to pay about US$30 for Nairobi to Arusha, US$40 for Nairobi to Moshi, and US$20 from Kilimanjaro International Airport to Arusha or Moshi. The journey time from Nairobi to Arusha is 5½ hours, and it's another 1½ hours to Moshi via Kilimanjaro International Airport. The company websites have booking facilities, timetables, prices and information about where to meet the buses, and they can also be booked at the company town offices, or by hotels or local tour operators.

AA Shuttles, www.aashuttles.com.
Impala Shuttles, www.impalashuttle.com.
Regional Luxury Shuttle, www.regionalluxuryshuttle.com.
Riverside Shuttles, www.riverside-shuttle.com.

Car

If you are driving, border crossings between Kenya and its neighbours can be laborious or simple, depending on your preparation and the state of your vehicle's paperwork. If in a private car, you must have a registration document, a driving licence printed in English with a photograph and, for a foreign-registered vehicle, a Carnet de Passage issued by a body in your own country (such as the Automobile Association) You will also be required to take out third party insurance for Kenya from one of the insurance companies who have kiosks at the border posts. Most car hire companies will not allow you to take a rented vehicle out of the country, but some may consider it if you only want to go to Tanzania. (See page 17 for information about hiring a car in Kenya). If crossing the border into Kenya in a car registered in Tanzania, you'll be issued with a temporary import permit.

Overland trucks

Overland truck safaris are a popular way of exploring East Africa by road. They demand a little more fortitude and adventurous spirit from the traveller, but the compensation is usually the camaraderie and life-long friendships that result from what is invariably a real adventure, going to places the more luxurious travellers will never visit. The standard overland route most commercial trucks take through East Africa (in either direction) is from Nairobi: a two-week circuit into Uganda to see the mountain gorillas via some of the Kenya national parks, then crossing into Tanzania to Arusha for the Ngorongoro Crater and Serengeti, before heading south to Dar es Salaam, for Zanzibar. If you have more time, you can complete the full circuit that goes from Tanzania through Malawi and Zambia to Livingstone to see the Victoria Falls, and then another three weeks from there to Cape Town in South Africa via Botswana and Namibia. There are several overland companies and there are departures almost weekly from Nairobi, Livingstone and Cape Town throughout the year.

Overland truck safari operators

Acacia Africa, www.acacia-africa.com.
Africa Travel Co, www.africatravelco.com.
Dragoman, www.dragoman.com.

Exodus Travels, www.exodus.co.uk.
Kumuka Worldwide, www.kumuka.com.
Oasis Overland, www.oasisoverland.co.uk.

Transport in Kenya

Kenya has an efficient transport network linking its towns and cities. There are regular flights between Nairobi and the larger towns and coast, and further afield to Tanzania and Zanzibar. There are overnight train services between Nairobi and Mombasa and Nairobi and Kisumu that are a fairly enjoyable, if slow experience, and in recent years there have been great improvements in the standards of the bus and *matatu* (minibus) services. It is quite feasible for a visitor to move around by public transport, which is cheap and efficient, but be aware of petty theft not only on the vehicles but in the bus stands and stations.

Air

Regular daily flights connect the major towns and cities and some of the safari destinations, all of which can be reached within a couple of hours' flying time from each other. The introduction of 'no-frills' airlines has introduced competition and flights are very affordable. Many of these airlines run services in circuits and flights may involve intermediate stops as the plane drops passengers at different airstrips on each circuit and may often return on the same route. For example, a flight to the Masai Mara may actually 'drop down' at several safari lodges. All tickets can be booked online or can be bought directly from the airline desks at the airports.

Air Kenya, T020-391 6000, www.airkenya.com, flies between Nairobi's Wilson Airport and Amboseli, Lamu, Lewa Downs, Malindi, Masai Mara, Meru, Mombasa, Nanyuki and Samburu. It also code shares with Regional Air in Tanzania and offer flights from Nairobi to Kilimanjaro, where they connect with flights to the lodges in the Serengeti and other Northern Circuit parks.

Kenya Airways, T020-327 4747,www.kenya-airways.com, flies between Nairobi's Jomo Kenyatta International Airport and Kisumu, Malindi, Lamu and Mombasa, plus regional destinations.

Fly 540, T0722-540 540, www.fly540.com, flies between Nairobi's Jomo Kenyatta International Airport and Eldoret, Kakamega, Kisumu, Kitale, Lamu, Lodwar, Malindi and Mombasa. Regionally they fly between Nairobi and Entebbe in Uganda, Juba in South Sudan, and Dar es Salaam and Zanzibar in Tanzania. From Nairobi's Wilson Airport they have flights to Amboseli, Masai Mara, Nanyuki and Samburu.

Mombasa Air Safaris, T0734-400 400, www.mombasaairsafari.com, operate a circuit between Mombasa and Amboseli, Tsavo and the Masai Mara.

Safarilink, T020-600 777, www.flysafarilink.com, flies between Nairobi's Wilson Airport and Amboseli, Kiwayu, Lamu, Lewa Downs, Masai Mara, Nanyuki, Samburu and Tsavo. It code shares with Air Excel in Tanzania so has flights from Nairobi to Kilimanjaro.

Rail

Nairobi Railway Station ① *T020-221 0885*, is to the south of Haile Selassie Avenue, at the very end of Moi Avenue. For details of the train services between Nairobi and Mombasa and Nairobi and Kisumu, see box, page 18. It is essential to make reservations in advance and this can be done at the stations or through a tour operator.

Road

Bus and matatu

There is an efficient network of privately run buses and *matatus* across the country. The *matatu*, the most popular form of public transport in Kenya, has become a national icon and a large part of Kenyan modern culture. A *matatu* is a minibus, usually a Nissan or Toyota, with a three-tonne capacity, hence the name *matatu – tatu* means 'three' in Kiswahili. On good, sealed roads, buses and *matatus* cover 50-80 km per hour, but on unsealed or poorly maintained roads they may average only 20 km per hour. Fairly new regulations of public transport in Kenya mean that standing is no longer permitted: everyone gets their own seat, every vehicle is fitted with seat belts and it is law for passengers to buckle up – police issue on-the-spot fines to passengers who haven't got seat belts on. Larger buses are considerably more comfortable than *matatus*, have more space for luggage and are to be recommended on safety grounds; the vehicles tend to be better maintained and driven a little less recklessly. The larger buses cover the long-distance routes and you will be able to reserve a seat a day in advance at kiosks run by the bus companies at the bus stations. The *matatus* do the shorter distances and link the major towns; they usually go when full. If you have problems locating the bus station (alternatively called bus stand or bus stage in Kenya), or finding the right bus in the bus station, just ask around and someone will direct you. In Nairobi and Mombasa city buses operate on set routes with formal bus stops, while *matatus* follow the same routes and can be flagged down anywhere.

Car

Driving is on the left side of the road. The key roads are in good condition, and a normal saloon car is adequate in Nairobi, along the coast as far north as Malindi, around the Rift Valley lakes, the loop around Mount Kenya and in Western Kenya. However, some of the tarred roads are in poor shape: cracked and littered with small and not-so-small potholes, and on some steep hills, heavy vehicles with hot tyres curve the tar into deep ridges, making the roads very bumpy. Added to this are Kenya's ubiquitous speed bumps (hardly necessary when the potholes do a fine job slowing traffic down). Away from the main highways the minor roads of unmade gravel with potholes can be rough going and they deteriorate further in the rainy season. Road conditions in the reserves and national parks of Kenya are extremely rough and, during the rainy season, many are passable only with 4WD vehicles. A 4WD, or at the very least a vehicle with high clearance, is essential if you are going off the tarred roads or into the game parks. If you break down, it is common practice in Kenya to place a bundle of leaves 50 m or so in front and behind the vehicle to warn oncoming motorists. Fuel is available along the main highways and towns, but if you're going way off the beaten track, consider taking a couple of jerry cans with extra fuel. Also ensure the vehicle has a jack and possibly take a shovel to dig it out of mud or sand. Note that when parking in the towns, you pay a small fee to a parking official who will give you a ticket to display in the window.

Car hire   Most people visit the parks and reserves on an organized safari, but if you're confident driving in Kenya, there is also the option to hire a car. Most companies can also organize drivers for an additional fee. You generally need to be over 23, have a full driving licence (it does not have to be an international licence, your home country one will do – with English translation if necessary), and a credit card. Always take out the collision damage waiver premium as even the smallest accident can be very expensive. Costs vary between the different car hire companies and are from around US$50-80 per day for a normal saloon car, and US$80-150 for a 4WD. Deals can be made for more than seven days' car hire. It is important to shop around and ask the companies what is and what is not included in the rates and what the provisions are in the event of a breakdown. Things to consider include whether you take out a limited mileage package or unlimited mileage depending on how you many kilometres you think you will drive. Finally, 16% VAT is added to all costs. For car hire companies in Nairobi, some of which can also organize car hire in Mombasa and Malindi, see page 81.

Taxi

Hotels and town centres are well served by taxis, some good and some very run-down but serviceable. Hotel staff, even at the smallest locations, will rustle up a taxi even when there is not one waiting outside. If you visit an out-of-town location, it is wise to ask the taxi to wait – it will normally be happy to do so for the benefit of the return fare. Very few taxis have meters; you should establish the fare (*bei gani?* – how much?) before you set off. Prices are generally fair as drivers simply won't take you if you offer a fare that's too low. A common practice is a driver will set off and then go and get petrol using part of your fare to pay for it, so often the first part of a journey is spent sitting in a petrol station. Also be aware that taxi drivers never seem to have change, so try and accumulate some small notes for taxi rides.

Boda boda   A *boda boda* is a bicycle taxi with one padded seat on the back. They were first popular in the border towns to transport people across no man's land between the border posts of East Africa and the cyclist would shout out '*boda boda*' offering his services. They are very popular along the coast and in the smaller towns, although not in Nairobi and Mombasa, and cost next to nothing. The driver/cyclist does an excellent job of cycling and keeping the bike balanced with you on the back of it, although you are still advised to hang on to the seat. A word of warning to the ladies, however, if you are wearing a skirt you will have to sit side saddle, which makes the bike far more wobbly. In some places, there are more comfortable and faster motorbike *boda bodas*.

Tuk-tuk   These motorized three-wheel buggies are starting to feature in many African cities and are cheap and convenient. The driver sits in the front whilst two or three passengers can sit comfortably on the back seat. They offer a service that is at least half the price of regular taxis. They do not, however, go very fast, so for longer journeys, stick to taxis.

Hitchhiking

In the Western sense (standing beside the road and requesting a free ride) hitchhiking is not generally an option in Kenya, although truck drivers and many private motorists will often carry you if you pay, and if you are stuck where there is no public transport; on that basis you can approach likely vehicles. Nevertheless, hitchhiking is not generally recommended. Women alone should be very wary of hitchhiking. If there is no other

The Iron Snake

The Uganda Railway was built by the colonialists to link the Indian Ocean at Mombasa to Lake Victoria in Kenya and Uganda. At the time it was built, it was referred to as the Iron Snake by Africans and, because of its incredible cost, the Lunatic Line by the British parliament. Construction began in Mombasa in 1896, and by 1898 the line had reached the Tsavo River. Here, construction was held up for several months by two man-eating lions, who attacked the railway camp and killed scores of African and Asian workers, before being eventually hunted down and shot by Captain John Patterson (who later wrote the famed book, *Man-eaters of Tsavo*). This was not the last time lions were to disrupt the line. In 1899, an engineer was dragged from his tent near Voi and killed, and in 1900, at Kima station, a police superintendent was sleeping in an observation carriage and was killed by a lion which dragged the body through a window and off into the bush (this carriage is now at the Nairobi Railway Museum, see page 52). By 1899, nearly 500 km of track had been laid and the line had crossed the Athi plains to an area of swampy ground at the foot of the Kenya Highlands. A major depot was built, the railway's administrative offices were moved from Mombasa, and the settlement grew quickly into Nairobi.

The railway then crossed the Rift Valley and finally reached Lake Victoria, 930 km from Mombasa, on 19 December 1901 at a point called Port Florence (later to become Kisumu), which was named after Florence Preston, wife of the chief foreman platelayer. At a cost of £5 million, and five years, 43 stations, 1200 bridges and countless lost lives later, the railway line was completed and opened up East Africa to the rest of the world.

Today, there are two train services on the line: between Nairobi and Mombasa and Nairobi and Kisumu. The journey between Nairobi and Mombasa especially, remains one of the world's most evocative rail journeys and is well worth doing if you have the time. In the Mombasa direction, you can wake at dawn as the train passes through Tsavo National Park and there is a high possibility of spotting game from your bunk. Note though, that in the other direction from Mombasa, it will be dark when you pass through Tsavo, but the scenery is still quite spectacular during daylight hours. On the Kisumu line, immediately on departing from Nairobi the train passes through the vast Kibera slum (see page 50) and then there are great views of the Rift Valley as the railway winds through the escarpment down to the base of Mount Longonot, and passes close to lakes Naivasha and Nakuru.

option (say if your vehicle has broken down or there is no public transport), be aware of who you are accepting a lift from; a car with a family or couple is usually the best option or, in rural areas, opt for vehicles (such as trucks) that are carrying local people. In some remote regions there are even touts who will approach you to sell you 'a lift'.

Maps

The best map and travel guide store in the UK is **Stanfords**, 12-14 Longacre, Covent Garden, London WC2 9LP, T020-7836 1321, www.stanfords.co.uk, with branches in Manchester and Bristol. The **Michelin Map of Africa**, Central and South, www.michelintravel.com, covers

Travelling by train in Kenya is certainly a great experience; however, in saying that, chronic under investment in recent years means that the railway today suffers from dilapidated rolling stock and frequent breakdowns (not necessarily by the passenger trains, but by other freight trains which subsequently block the line). Do not expect any degree of luxury and do not arrange onward travel arrangements too close to the scheduled arrival times.

The Mombasa train departs Nairobi at 1900 on Monday, Wednesday and Friday and (in theory) arrives in Mombasa at 0930. In the other direction it departs Mombasa on Saturday, Tuesday and Thursday at 1900 and arrives in Nairobi at 0930. First class is in cabins that sleep two people in bunks and includes bedding and a washbasin; second class is for four people in bunks with bedding and a washbasin; and third class is seating in carriages that take up to 80 people. First class is the best bet as some of the other rickety carriages are almost 90 years old and lights and washbasins may not always function. There is a restaurant car – complete with sun-bleached red leather seats, pristine white tablecloths, silver cutlery and uniformed staff – where first- and second-class passengers can have dinner and drinks and the following morning a cooked breakfast, though you may want to bring additional drinks and snacks with you to last for a much longer than scheduled journey. The set meals are adequate (sponge and custard for dessert is certainly a throwback to the colonial days) and there's a choice for vegetarians. Tickets: First class, adults US$65, children (3-11) US$45, including dinner and breakfast; second class, US$54, children (3-11) US$34 including dinner and breakfast; and third class, US$21.

The Kisumu service is almost identical though more basic and the carriages are even older. It departs Nairobi at 1830 on Monday, Wednesday and Friday and (in theory) arrives in Kisumu at 0800. In the other direction it departs Kisumu on Saturday, Tuesday and Thursday at 1830 and arrives in Nairobi at 0800. Tickets: first class, adults US$40, children (3-11) US$30, including dinner and breakfast; second class, US$30, children (3-11) US$25 including dinner and breakfast; and third class, US$18. It is essential to make reservations in advance and this can be done at the stations, or for an extra administration fee and by credit card, through a tour operator who can also arrange delivery of tickets to your hotel – for a list of these in Nairobi, see page 77, and Mombasa, page 240.

Kenya in detail. In South Africa, **Map Studio**, T+27 (0)21-460 5400, www.mapstudio.co.za, produces a wide range of maps covering much of Africa; these are available to buy online or there are shops in Johannesburg and Cape Town. In Kenya, **The Stanley Bookshop**, on Kenyatta Avenue in Nairobi, next to the Thorn Tree Café, T020-212 776, has a good selection of maps, as do the bookshops in the large shopping malls. **Kenya Wildlife Services (KWS)**, Langata Road, next to the Main Gate of Nairobi National Park, T020-600 0800, www.kws. org, produce some maps for the parks, which are also available at the individual park gates. Some of these are fairly simple and hand drawn, though there are exceptionally good ones such as the map for the Nairobi National Park that has numbered junctions which correspond to junction numbers on sign posts within the park.

Where to stay in Kenya

There is a wide range of accommodation on offer. At the top end are game lodges and tented camps that charge US$300-1000 per couple per day; mid-range safari lodges and beach resorts with self-contained double rooms with air conditioning charge around US$150-250 per room; standard small town hotels used by local business people cost around US$50-100 per room; and basic board and lodgings used by local travellers are under US$20 a day. At the top end, Kenya now boasts some accommodation options that rival the luxurious camps in southern Africa – intimate safari camps with an amazing standard of comfort and service in stunning settings. The beach resorts too have improved considerably in recent years, and there are some luxurious and romantic options in commanding positions next to the Indian Ocean.

Generally, accommodation booked through a European agent will be more expensive than if you contact the hotel or lodge directly, and most of Kenya's hoteliers have websites. Hotels in the towns and cities usually keep the same rates year-round, but safari lodges and beach resorts have seasonal rates depending on weather, periods of popularity of overseas (especially European) visitors, and events like the wildebeest migration in the Masai Mara, for example. Low season in East Africa is generally around the long rainy season from the beginning of April to the end of June, when most room rates drop considerably and it may be possible to negotiate rates, especially if you plan to stay a few days. Some establishments even close during this period, though the resorts on the coast remain open throughout the year. 'Resident' and 'non-resident' rates operate for more expensive hotels, airlines, game park entrance and camping fees, whereby tourists are charged approximately double the rate locals are charged. Most upmarket hotels will publish non-resident rates in US dollars – but these can be paid in Kenyan shillings as well as foreign currency. This really makes no difference but check the exchange rates and make a fuss if you're not being charged a fair rate. Credit cards are widely accepted at the larger establishments, but may attract a surcharge of around 5%. VAT at 16% is added to all service charges, though this is usually included in the bill.

Hotels

A few international hotel chains, such as **Hilton** and **Inter-Continental** among others, have hotels in Nairobi. Quality of local town and city hotels varies widely, and some tend to be bland with poor service and dated decor, while others are newly built with good amenities; there are a number of characterful hotels that have been around since the colonial days, such as **The Norfolk** in Nairobi or the **Country Club** in Naivasha. Some of the beach hotels are resorts, which can either be tired-looking concrete blocks that were built in the 1980s when package holidays first became popular on the Kenyan coast or, much more appealingly, built sensitively to blend in with the coastal forest in low-lying timber-and-thatch structures. Most resorts have a range of watersports and activities where guests stay for their entire holiday, and while they will appeal to those who enjoy the all-inclusive holiday experience, they may not appeal to more independent travellers. However, also on the coast is some small, simple beach-cottage type accommodation, which is mostly in good locations and is excellent value. At the budget end there's a fairly wide choice of cheap hotels. A room often comprises a simple bed, basic bathroom, mosquito net and fan, but may have an irregular water or electricity supply; it is always a good idea to look at a room first to ensure it's clean and everything works. It is also imperative to ensure that

Accommodation price codes

$$$$ over US$300 $$$ US$100-300
$$ US$50-100 $ under US$50

Unless otherwise stated, prices refer to the cost of a double room, not including service charge or meals.

your luggage will be locked away securely for protection against petty theft, especially in shared accommodation. At the very bottom of the budget scale are numerous basic board and lodgings in all the towns that cost under US$10. For this you get a bare room with a bed and a door that may or may not lock. They are generally not recommended and are often simply rooms attached to a bar that, more often than not, are rented by the hour. The word hotel (or in Kiswahili, *hoteli*) means food and drink, rather than lodging. It is better to use the word guesthouse (in Kiswahili, *guesti*).

Self-catering and homestays

In the national parks, **Kenya Wildlife Services (KWS)** offer a number of simple self-catering accommodation options which are generally not booked as part of an organized safari. These are in *bandas*, which are also referred to as *guesthouses*. Most are located in fairly peaceful and remote locations – on the lower slopes of Mount Kenya or in Kakamega Forest, for example – and some have resident caretakers. Many are conveniently located near the park HQ at the gate, while others are further into the parks and a 4WD may be necessary. They can be fairly old and basic, but are good value for a family or group and are sufficiently equipped with kitchen and utensils; some means of cooking either on a stove or open fire; bed linen, mosquito nets and towels, though at some you may need to bring your own drinking water and firewood. Not all have electricity; hot water is usually heated by a donkey boiler over a fire and kerosene lamps are provided, but you may want to bring torches and candles. For more information contact **Kenya Wildlife Services (KWS)** ① *T020-600 0800, www.kws.org*.

Renting a private property or homestay is a good way to gain a new perspective on Kenya and relax on your own. The homestays are often surprisingly good value if you intend to stay for a while. They vary from rustic cottages in the bush or historic Swahili mansions on the coast, to serviced city apartments; very few are near the game parks. Often assistance with cleaning and cooking is available. For more information contact **Kenya Holiday Villas** ① *www.kenyaholidayvillas.com*, or **Langata Link Holiday Homes** ① *www.holidayhomeskenya.com*. Each website has a full description, including photos of each property.

Hostels

There are only a handful of hostels around the country, affiliated with the Youth Hostelling Association, YMCA and YWCA, and most are clean, safe and very cheap. Nevertheless, they tend to be very spartan and generally cater for long-term residents such as students or church groups.

Camping

Away from the campsites in the national parks and game reserves (see Safari options, below), camping in Kenya is fairly limited and there are only a few formal private campsites (most notably around the lakes in the Rift Valley; there are none on the coast). The ones that do exist are generally in shady locations and have good facilities with clean ablution blocks with plenty of hot water, and some also have simple sleeping huts, guards for tents and vehicles, and possibly a restaurant and bar. However, you should always have your own tent and basic equipment as these cannot be hired, and bring adequate supplies of fresh water and food. If you are going off the beaten track and planning to bush or free camp outside of official or designated campsites, seek local advice in advance. The land on which you are planning to camp may be privately owned or be traditional lands under the control of a nearby village. In some instances, advance permission and/or payment is required. Do not rely on local water supplies or rivers and streams for potable water. Any water taken from a stream should be filtered or boiled for several minutes before drinking. Never bush camp on the side of a busy road or near a town; it's an invitation to be robbed in the middle of the night.

Safari options

All safari companies offer basically the same safari but at different prices, which is reflective of what accommodation is booked. For example, you could choose a two-day safari of the Masai Mara and the options would be camping (the companies provide the equipment) or a lodge safari, making it considerably more expensive. For those that want to spend more, there is the option of adding flights between destinations or staying at one of the luxury private tented camps. Everyone is likely to have the same sort of game-viewing experiences, but the level of comfort you want on safari depends on where you stay and how much you spend.

Hotels and lodges These vary and may be either typical hotels with rooms and facilities in one building or individual *bandas* or *rondavels* (small huts) with a central dining area. Standards vary from the rustic to the modern, from the simply appointed to the last word in luxury. Efforts are usually made to design lodges that blend into their environment, with an emphasis on natural local building materials and use of traditional art and decoration. Most lodges serve meals and have lounges and bars, sometimes swimming pools. They often have excellent views or overlook waterholes or salt licks that attract game.

Campsites There are campsites in most national parks. They are extensively used by camping safari companies. Vehicles, guides, tents and equipment, as well as food and a cook, are all provided. They are often most attractively sited, perhaps in the elbow of a river course but always with plenty of shade. Birds are plentiful and several hours can be whiled away birdwatching. Some campsites have attached to them a few *bandas* or huts run by the park where you may be able to shower. Toilet facilities can be primitive – the 'long drop', a basic hole in a concrete slab, being very common. Most camps are guarded but despite this you should be careful to ensure that valuables are not left unattended. If you are camping on your own, you will almost always need to be totally self-sufficient with all your own equipment. The campsites usually provide running water and firewood. Camping should always have minimal impact on the environment. All rubbish and waste matter should be buried, burnt or taken away with you. Do not leave food scraps or containers where they may attract and harm animals, and be careful about leaving items outside your tent. Many campsites have troupes of baboons nearby that can be a nuisance and a hyena can chew through something as solid as a saucepan.

Tented camps A luxury tented camp is really the best of both worlds: the comfort of extremely high facilities and service combined with sleeping closer to the animals. They are usually built with a central dining and bar area, are in stunning well-designed locations, and each tent will have a thatched roof to keep it cool inside, proper beds, a veranda and a small bathroom at the back with solar-heated hot water. The added benefit is that the camps are usually fairly small with just a few tents, so the safari experience is intimate and professional. Tented camps can be found in most of Kenya's national parks and game reserves, as well as on private game ranches and sanctuaries.

Food and drink in Kenya

Food

Traditional Kenyan food reflects the many different lifestyles of the various groups in the country, as well as historical international influences dating back to the 15th century when the Portuguese introduced maize, cassava and (a little-known fact) bananas and pineapples to East Africa. Later culinary influences include, Middle Eastern from the period of Arabian trade, British during the colonial times and Indian when indentured labour was brought to Kenya to build the railway. Kenyans are largely big meat eaters and a standard meal is *nyama choma* – roasted beef or goat meat, usually served with a spicy relish, although some like it with a mixture of raw peppers, onions and tomato known as *kachumbari*. Inland, *tilapia*, a freshwater fish from Lake Victoria, is also popular. It is usually served with the main staple or starch in Kenya, *ugali*, a mealie meal porridge eaten all over Africa. In Kikuyu areas you will also find *irio*: potatoes, peas and corn mashed together.

Small town hotels and restaurants tend to serve either traditional Kenyan fare or a limited amount of bland processed food, omelette or chicken and chips, and, perhaps, a meat stew but not much else. Indian food is extremely good in Kenya and cheap, and an important option for vegetarians travelling in the country. In Nairobi and in the upmarket coastal resorts, you'll also find other international cuisines, and Nairobi in particular has an excellent choice for eating out. Food on the coast is much more varied, and the Swahili style of cooking features aromatic curries using coconut milk, fragrant steamed rice, grilled fish and calamari and delicious bisques made from lobster and crab. Some of the larger beach resorts and safari lodges offer breakfast, lunch and dinner buffets for their all-inclusive guests, some of which can be excellent while others can be of a poor standard and there's no real way of knowing what you'll get. The most important thing is to avoid food sitting around for a long time on a buffet table, so ensure it has been freshly prepared and served. Restaurant prices are low; it is quite possible to get a plate of hot food in a basic restaurant for US$3 and even the most expensive places will often not be more than US$30 per person with drinks. The quality, standard and variety of food depends on where you are and what you intend to pay.

Various items can be can be bought at temporary roadside stalls from **street vendors** who prepare and cook over charcoal, which adds considerably to the flavour. It's pretty safe, despite hygiene being fairly basic, because most of the items are cooked or peeled. Snacks include chips, omelettes, barbecued beef on skewers (*mishkaki*), roast maize, samosas, hard-boiled eggs, roast cassava (looks like white, peeled turnips) and *mandazi* (a kind of sweet or savoury doughnut). Fruits include oranges (peeled and halved), pineapples, bananas, mangoes (slices scored and turned inside-out), paw-paw (papaya) and watermelon. These items are very cheap and are all worth trying, and when travelling, are indispensable.

Most food produce is purchased in open-air markets. In the larger towns and cities these are held daily and, as well as selling fresh fruit and vegetables, sell eggs, bread and meat. In the smaller villages, a market will be held on one day of the week when the farmers come to sell their wares. Markets are very colourful places to visit and just about any fruit or vegetable is available. Other locally produced food items are sold in supermarkets, often run by Asian traders, whilst imported products are sold in the few upmarket supermarkets in the larger cities, such as Nakumatt.

Drink

Sodas (soft drinks) are available everywhere and are very cheap; they are sold in refundable 300 ml bottles. On the coast, especially Lamu, freshly squeezed fruit juices are delicious. Bottled water is fairly expensive, but is available in all but the smallest villages. Tap water is reputedly safe in many parts of the country, but is only really recommended if you have a fairly hardy traveller's stomach. Popular throughout the country is *chai* (tea), which up-country is served milky and sweet and, on the coast, black in little glasses. Both are surprisingly refreshing. **Coffee**, although grown in Kenya, is often instant powder but this is not bad, especially the local brand **Africafe**. For freshly ground Kenyan coffee look out for **Nairobi Java House** and **Dorman's**, coffee shop chains in Nairobi.

Kenyan beer is very good: *Tusker*, *White Cap* and *Pilsner* are the main brands, sold in 700 ml refundable bottles. Imported **wines** are on the expensive side, but there's a good choice in the more upmarket restaurants, and Nakumatt supermarkets sell South African wines.

Imported **spirits** are widely available; local alternatives that are sold in both bottles and sachets of one tot include some rough vodkas and whiskies, *Kenya Cane*, a type of rum, and the sweet *Kenya Gold* coffee liqueur. In the beach resorts, cocktails are popular, and a favourite is a *dawa* – vodka, crushed ice, sugar and lime served with a stick coated with honey; it means 'medicine' in Kiswahili.

Shopping in Kenya

Kenya has many types of crafts and curios on offer including wood and soapstone carvings, musical instruments, baskets made from leather and sisal, and textiles. Masai crafts such as beaded jewellery, decorated gourds and spears are available to buy in southern Kenya as well as the distinctive red checked Masai blankets. Brightly coloured sarongs called *kangas* are worn by women all over Kenya and Tanzania; they're sold in pairs and emblazoned with a traditional proverb. Woven with vertical stripes, *kikois* are similar but are traditionally worn by the men of the Swahili coast as wrap-around sarongs. These are made into other items including clothes, cushion covers and bags.

Most tourist areas have numerous places to buy these items: Nairobi and Mombasa city centres are dotted with curio shops, the roads on safari routes to and from the parks and reserves have plenty of roadside stalls where safari minibuses can conveniently pull in, and stalls line the coast roads behind the beach resorts. Prices in tourist shops are largely fixed, though in the depths of the quiet low season, can be negotiable. Prices at roadside stalls or markets are always negotiable. See page 28 for tips on bargaining.

Festivals in Kenya → See also Holidays, page 32.

June

KCB Safari Rally, www.safarirally.net. This tough car rally has been going since 1953 when it was held to celebrate the queen's coronation. It runs for 3 days over an on- and off-road course of 720 km on the plains between Nairobi and Namanga on the Tanzania border.

Rhino Charge, Laikipia Plateau, www.rhino charge.co.ke. This is an off-road 4WD motor rally and fund-raising event that was established in 1989 to raise money for the fencing of the Aberdare National Park. Now this has been completed, funds go towards its maintenance including solar power to electrify it. The winner is the car that visits all of the 13 control points along the course and has the lowest mileage within the allocated 10 hrs of driving time. Spectators are welcome (and can camp) but the venue is kept secret until as late as possible to prevent cheating by the participants.

Safaricom Marathon, Lewa Wildlife Conservancy, Laikipia Plateau, www.lewa.org. This is a fund-raising event, and both the half and full marathons attract more than 1000 runners from all over the world, including many world-class Kenyan long-distance runners. They are hard runs at altitude and the course is held within the game conservancy. Helicopters are used to keep an eye out for elephant and predators along the course. It is a unique experience! You can take part or watch.

August

Maralal International Camel Derby, Maralal, see box, page 336. Operating since 1990, this is a fun weekend with a 10-km camel race around the town (amateurs get help from camel handlers), plus cycle races, food and craft stalls, and traditional dancing, which is performed by the local Samburu.

September

Africa Concours d'Elegance, Ngong Racecourse, Ngong Rd, Nairobi, www.concourskenya.com. This is a classic car and motorbike show with vehicles from across East Africa on display, some dating to the early colonial times. A fun family day out with entertainment, food stalls and children's activities, and spectators can watch the vehicles drive past the judges from the racecourse's grandstand.

Responsible travel

The tourism industry in Kenya is very important for the country's economy, and creates thousands of jobs. Many national parks and game reserves, valuable archaeological sites and museums are funded by visitor entry fees, which in turn promote their protection. Additionally, some of the tour operators, private reserves and lodges fund conservation and community projects. By earning from tourism, the poorer people who rely on the land for their livelihoods are more likely to protect their environments for the benefit of tourism and these projects are well worth supporting.

10 ways to be a responsible traveller

There are some aspects of travel that you have to accept are going to have an impact, but try to balance the negatives with positives by following these guidelines to responsible travel.

• **Cut your emissions** Plan an itinerary that minimizes carbon emissions whenever possible. This might involve travelling by train, hiring a bike or booking a walking or canoeing tour rather than one that relies on vehicle transport. See opposite page for details of carbon offset programmes. Visit www.seat61.com for worldwide train travel.

• **Check the small print** Choose travel operators that abide by a responsible travel policy (if they have one it will usually be posted on their website). Visit www.responsibletravel.com.

• **Keep it local** If travelling independently, try to use public transport, stay in locally owned accommodation, eat in local restaurants, buy local produce and hire local guides.

• **Cut out waste** Take biodegradable soap and shampoo and leave excess packaging, particularly plastics, at home. The countries you are visiting may not have the waste collection or recycling facilities to deal with it.

• **Get in touch** Find out if there are any local schools, charities or voluntary conservation organizations that you could include in your itinerary. If appropriate, take along some useful gifts or supplies; www.stuffyourrucksack.com has a list of projects that could benefit from your support.

• **Learn the lingo** Practice some local words, even if it's just to say 'hello', 'thank you' and 'goodbye'. Respect local customs and dress codes and always ask permission before photographing people – including your wildlife tour guide. Once you get home, remember to honour any promises you've made to send photographs.

• **Avoid the crowds** Consider travelling out of season to relieve pressure on popular destinations, or visit a lesser-known alternative.

• **Take only photos** Resist the temptation to buy souvenirs made from animals or plants. Not only is it illegal to import or export many wildlife souvenirs, but their uncontrolled collection supports poaching and can have a devastating impact on local populations, upsetting the natural balance of entire ecosystems. CITES, the Convention on International Trade in Endangered Species (www.cites.org) bans international trade in around 900 animal and plant species, and controls trade in a further 33,000 species.

Several organizations, including WWF, TRAFFIC and the Smithsonian Institution have formed the Coalition Against Wildlife Trafficking (www.cawtglobal.org).

• **Use water wisely** Water is a precious commodity in many countries. Treating your own water avoids the need to buy bottled water which can contribute to the build-up of litter.

• **Don't interfere** Avoid disturbing wildlife, damaging habitats or interfering with natural behaviour by feeding wild animals, getting too close or being too noisy. Leave plants and shells where you find them.

Code green for hikers
• Take biodegradable soap, shampoo and toilet paper, long-lasting lithium batteries and plastic bags for packing out all rubbish.
• Use a water filter instead of buying bottled water and save fuel at remote lodges by ordering the same food at the same time. Only take a hot shower if the water has been heated by solar power.
• If no toilet facilities are available, make sure you are at least 30 m from any water source.
• Keep to trails to avoid erosion and trampling vegetation. Don't take short cuts, especially at high altitude where plants may take years to recover.

Code green for divers and snorkellers
• Help conserve underwater environments by joining local cleanups or collecting data for Project AWARE (www.projectaware.org).
• Choose resorts that properly treat sewage and wastewater and support marine protected areas.
• Choose operators that use mooring buoys or drift diving techniques, rather than anchors that can damage fragile marine habitats such as coral reefs.
• Never touch coral. Practice buoyancy control skills in a pool or sandy area before diving around coral reefs, and tuck away trailing equipment.
• Avoid handling, feeding or riding on marine life.
• Never purchase marine souvenirs.
• Don't order seafood caught using destructive or unsustainable practices such as dynamite fishing.

How should I offset my carbon emissions?
Carbon offsetting schemes allow you to offset greenhouse gas emissions by donating to various projects, from tree planting to renewable energy schemes. Although some conservation groups are concerned that carbon offsetting is being used as a smoke-screen to delay the urgent action needed to cut emissions and develop alternative energy solutions, it remains an important way of counterbalancing your carbon footprint.

For every tonne of CO_2 you generate through a fossil fuel-burning activity such as flying, you pay for an equivalent tonne to be removed elsewhere through a 'green' initiative. There are numerous online carbon footprint calculators (such as www.carbonfootprint.com). Alternatively, book with a travel operator that supports a carbon offset provider like TICOS (www.ticos.co.uk) or Reduce my Footprint (www.reducemyfootprint.travel).

It's not all about tree-planting schemes. Support now goes to a far wider range of climate-friendly technology projects, ranging from the provision of energy-efficient light bulbs and cookers in the developing world to large-scale renewable energy schemes such as wind farms.

Essentials A-Z

Accident and emergency

Police, fire and ambulance T999.

Bargaining

Whilst most prices in shops are set, the exception are curio shops where a little good-natured bargaining is possible, especially if it's quiet or you are buying a number of things. Bargaining is very much expected in the street markets whether you are buying an apple or a Masai blanket. Generally traders will attempt to overcharge tourists who are unaware of local prices. Start lower than you would expect to pay, be polite and good humoured, and if the final price doesn't suit – walk away. You may be called back for more negotiation, or the trader may let you go, in which case your price was too low. Ask about the prices of taxis, excursions, souvenirs and so on at your hotel.

Children

Kenya has great appeal for children because of the animals, and safaris are very exciting for children (and their parents) when they catch their first glimpse of an elephant or lion. However, small children may get bored driving around a hot park all day if there is no animal activity. It's a good idea to get children enthused about safaris by providing them with checklists for animals and birds and perhaps giving them their own binoculars and cameras. Pick one of the parks or reserves where animals are easily spotted; Nairobi or Amboseli National Parks are ideal. Some safari lodges do not permit children at all, whereas others are completely child-friendly and are aimed at families. **Heritage Hotels** (www.heritage-east africa.com) run the excellent Adventurer's Club for children aged 4 to 12 and have several family-orientated lodges in the parks. There are considerable discounts on accommodation at the beach for children, especially in the family-orientated resorts, which have either specific family rooms or adjoining rooms suitable for families, and often extra amenities for children. Items such as disposable nappies, formula milk powders and puréed foods are only available in the major cities and they are expensive, so you may want to bring enough with you. It is important to remember that children have an increased risk of gastroenteritis, malaria and sunburn and are more likely to develop complications, so care must be taken to minimize risks. See Health, page 29, for more details.

Customs and duty free

The official customs allowance for visitors over 18 years includes 200 cigarettes, 50 cigars, 250 g of tobacco, 2 litres of wine, 1 litre of spirits, 50 ml of perfume and 250 ml of eau de toilette. There is no duty on any equipment for your own use (such as laptops or cameras).

Disabled travellers

Wheelchairs are not accommodated on public transport, so Kenya would need to be visited on an organized tour or in a rented vehicle. Wheelchair access in hotels and safari lodges has improved over the last few years; there are several options in Nairobi and on the coast and most of the popular parks and reserves have at least one lodge with good access, or consider a camping or tented camp safari which provides easy access to a tent at ground level. Most tour operators are accommodating and should be able to make special arrangements for disabled travellers. Specialist operators include:
Go Africa Safaris & Travel, Nairobi, T020-235 3883, www.go-africa-safaris.com. Organizes

tailor-made safaris in vehicles adapted for wheelchairs and selects accommodation with disabled facilities, also has some specialist equipment such as hoists, plus can cater for visually and hearing-impaired clients.

Southern Cross Safaris, Mombasa, T041-243 4600, www.southerncrosssafaris.com. A safari option from Mombasa, which has vehicles specially adapted for wheelchairs and also runs its own tented camp in Tsavo East.

Victoria Safaris, Nairobi, T020-225 2015, www.victoriasafaris.com. Organizes tailor-made safaris for wheelchair-users and the visually and hearing impaired, can arrange professional nurses if required, and books hotels with disabled rooms.

Dress

Travellers are encouraged to show respect by adhering to a modest dress code in public places, especially in the predominantly Muslim areas like Mombasa or Lamu. In the evening at social functions there is no particular dress code, although hosts will feel insulted if you arrive for dinner in shorts, sandals or bare feet, and you will be expected to dress up a little in the more upmarket lodges and hotels. On safari, clothes in muted brown and khaki colours are the best. This is certainly true of the more remote parks where seeing unexpected bright colours may startle the animals. But in the Masai Mara, the animals here are so used to seeing hordes of tourists each day, it is not so important.

Drugs

The use of *bhangi* (cannabis) and *miraa* (a mild stimulant) is relatively widespread, but both are illegal, punishment is severe and your embassy is unlikely to be sympathetic. In some rural areas, locally distilled alcohol is available, but it can be dangerous to the uninitiated and should be avoided.

Embassies and consulates

For embassies and consulates of Kenya, see http://embassy.goabroad.com.

Gay and lesbian travellers

Homosexuality is illegal in Kenya and is considered a criminal offence, so extreme discretion is advised. There are no specific gay clubs or bars. Nevertheless, Kenyans generally have the attitude that, while being gay is considered 'un-African', non-Africans may be gay.

Health

See your GP or travel clinic at least 6 weeks before your departure for general advice on travel risks and vaccinations. Make sure you have travel insurance, get a dental check, know your own blood group and, if you suffer from a long-term condition such as diabetes or epilepsy, make sure someone knows or that you have a Medic Alert bracelet/necklace (www.medicalert.co.uk). If you wear glasses, take a copy of your prescription. Specialist advice should be taken on the best anti-malarials to use.

Vaccinations
Basic vaccinations recommended include polio, tetanus, diphtheria, typhoid, and hepatitis A. You may well be asked for a yellow fever vaccination certificate on arrival if you have come from (or transited through) an infected country, and most certainly if you are coming from Tanzania. If you arrive at the airports without one, you'll be required to get a vaccination at the airport before being permitted entry.

Health risks
Altitude sickness
Altitude sickness can strike above 3000 m and is a response to the lack of oxygen in the air. The best way of preventing altitude sickness is a relatively slow ascent when trekking

to high altitude and spending some time walking at medium altitude to acclimatize to the rarefied air. There are no specific factors such as age, sex or physical condition that contribute to the condition – some people get it and some people don't. Symptoms include headache, lassitude, dizziness, loss of appetite, nausea and vomiting. If the symptoms are mild, the treatment is rest, painkillers (preferably not aspirin-based) for the headaches and anti-sickness pills for vomiting. If the symptoms are severe, it is best to descend to a lower altitude immediately – the symptoms disappear very quickly.

Cholera
There are occasional outbreaks of cholera in the north of the country. The main symptoms of cholera are profuse watery diarrhoea and vomiting, which may lead to severe dehydration. However, most travellers are at extremely low risk of infection and the disease rarely shows symptoms in healthy well-nourished people. The cholera vaccine is only recommended for certain high-risk individuals, such as health professionals or volunteers.

Diarrhoea
Diarrhoea can refer either to loose stools or an increased frequency of bowel movement, both of which can be a nuisance, but symptoms should be relatively short lived. Adults can use an antidiarrhoeal medication to control the symptoms but only for up to 24 hrs. In addition, keep well hydrated by drinking plenty of fluids and eat bland foods. Oral rehydration sachets taken after each loose stool are a useful way to keep well hydrated. These should always be used when treating children and the elderly. Bacterial traveller's diarrhoea is the most common form; if there are no signs of improvement the diarrhoea is likely to be viral and not bacterial and antibiotics may be required. Also seek medical help if there is blood in the stools and/or fever.

The standard advice to prevent problems is to be careful with water and ice for drinking. If you have any doubts then boil the water or filter and treat it. Food can also transmit disease. Be wary of salads (what were they washed in, who handled them), re-heated foods or food that has been left out in the sun having been cooked earlier in the day. There is a simple adage that says 'wash it, peel it, boil it or forget it'. Also be wary of unpasteurized dairy products as these can transmit a range of diseases.

Hepatitis
Hepatitis means inflammation of the liver. Viral causes of the disease can be acquired anywhere in the world. The most obvious symptom is a yellowing of your skin or the whites of your eyes. However, prior to this, all that you may notice is itching and tiredness. Pre-travel hepatitis A vaccine is the best bet. Hepatitis B (for which there is a vaccine) is spread through blood and unprotected sexual intercourse; both of these can be avoided.

HIV/AIDS
Africa has the highest rates of HIV and AIDS in the world. Efforts to stem the rate of infection have had limited success, as many of the factors that need addressing, such as social change, poverty and gender inequalities, are long-term processes. Visitors should be aware of the dangers of infection from unprotected sex and always use a condom. If you have to have medical treatment, ensure any equipment used is taken from a sealed pack or is freshly sterilized. If you have to have a blood transfusion, ask for screened blood.

Malaria
There is a medium to high risk of malaria in the low-lying regions of Kenya. Nairobi and the highlands above 2500 m are considered low risk. Malaria can start as something just resembling an attack of flu. You may feel tired, lethargic, headachy, feverish; or, more seriously, develop fits, followed by coma and then death. Have a low index of suspicion

because it is very easy to write off vague symptoms, which may actually be malaria. If you have a temperature, go to a doctor as soon as you can and ask for a malaria test. On your return home, if you suffer any of these symptoms, get tested as soon as possible.

To prevent mosquito bites wear clothes that cover arms and legs and use effective insect repellents. Rooms with a/c or fans also help ward off mosquitoes at night. If your doctor or travel clinic advises you to take anti-malarials, ensure you finish the recommended course.

Rabies
Avoid dogs and monkeys that are behaving strangely. Bats also carry rabies in Kenya. If you are bitten by a domestic or wild animal, do not leave things to chance: scrub the wound with soap and water and/ or disinfectant, try to at least determine the animal's ownership, and seek medical assistance at once. The course of treatment depends on whether you have already been satisfactorily vaccinated against rabies.

Sun
Protect yourself adequately against the sun. Apply a high-factor sunscreen (greater than SPF15) and also make sure it screens against UVB. Prevent heat exhaustion and heatstroke by drinking enough fluids throughout the day (your urine will be pale if you are drinking enough). Symptoms of heat exhaustion and heatstroke include dizziness, tiredness and headache. Use rehydration salts mixed with water to replenish fluids and salts and find somewhere cool and shady to recover. If you suspect heatstroke rather than heat exhaustion, you need to cool the body down quickly (cold showers are particularly effective).

Other diseases and risks
If you are unlucky (or careless) enough to be bitten by a venomous snake, spider, scorpion or sea creature, try to identify the culprit, without putting yourself in further danger. Victims should be taken to a hospital or a doctor without delay. Fresh water can be a source of diseases such as bilharzia. Lake Victoria and many smaller lakes are infected and it's always wise to ask locally about swimming.

If you get sick
There are plenty of private hospitals in Nairobi and along the coast, which have 24-hr emergency departments and pharmacies, and have a very high standard of healthcare. In other areas facilities range from government hospitals to rural clinics, but these can be poorly equipped and under staffed. In the case of emergency, always try to get to the main cities, preferably Nairobi. If you are planning to travel in more isolated areas, consider the **Flying Doctors' Society of Africa**, based at Wilson Airport. For an annual tourist fee of US$50, it offers free evacuation by air to a medical centre or hospital. This may be worth considering if you are visiting remote regions, but not if visiting the more popular parks as adequate provision is made in the case of an emergency. The income goes back into the service and the **African Medical Research Foundation** (AMREF) behind it. You can contact them in advance on T020-699 3000, www.amref.org. It is essential to have travel insurance, as hospital bills need to be paid at the time of admittance, so keep all paperwork to make a claim.

Useful websites
www.btha.org British Travel Health Association.
www.cdc.gov US government site that gives excellent advice on travel health and details of disease outbreaks.
www.fco.gov.uk British Foreign and Commonwealth Office travel site has useful information on each country, people, climate and a list of UK embassies/consulates.
www.fitfortravel.scot.nhs.uk A-Z of vaccine/health advice.
www.travelhealth.co.uk Independent travel health site with advice on vaccination, travel insurance and health risks.

Holidays

All along the coast and in the northeast the Islamic calendar is followed and festivals are celebrated. These include the beginning and end of **Ramadan** (variable); **Islamic New Year** (Jun) and the **Prophet's birthday** (Aug). On Lamu the Islamic **Maulidi Festival** is held each year (see box, page 299).

1 Jan New Year's Day
Mar/Apr Good Friday; Easter Monday
1 May Labour Day
1 Jun Madaraka Day
10 Oct Kenyatta Day
20 Oct Jamhuri (Independence) Day
25 Dec Christmas Day
26 Dec Boxing Day

Insurance

Before departure, it is vital to take out comprehensive travel insurance. There are a wide variety of policies to choose from, so shop around. At the very least, the policy should cover medical expenses, including repatriation to your home country in the event of a medical emergency. If you are going to be active in Kenya, ensure the policy covers trekking or diving, for example. There is no substitute for suitable precautions against petty crime, but if you do have something stolen whilst in Kenya, report the incident to the nearest police station and ensure you get a police report. You will need these to make any claim from your insurance company.

Internet

Internet cafés are plentiful in the major towns and range from the upmarket hotels, cybercafés with fast connections to small shops and business centres that may just have a single computer. The **Kenya Post Office** offers access in most of its branches even in the small towns. Costs are little more than US$1 per hr. Wi-Fi is available at the **Jomo Kenyatta International Airport**, in some of the hotels in Nairobi and on the coast, and increasingly in the coffee shop chains in Nairobi.

Language → *See also page 378.*

Kenya is a welcoming country and the first word that you will hear and come to know is the Kiswahili greeting *Jambo* – 'hello', often followed by *Hakuna matata* – 'no problem'! There are a number of local languages but most people in Kenya, as in all of East Africa, speak Kiswahili and some English. Kiswahili is the official language of Kenya and is taught in primary schools. English is generally used in business and is taught in secondary schools. Only in the remote rural regions will you find people that only speak in their local tongues. A little Kiswahili goes a long way, and most Kenyans will be thrilled to hear visitors attempt to use it. Since the language was originally written down by the British colonists, words are pronounced just as they are spelt.

Media

Newspapers and magazines

Kenya has several English-language newspapers and each one has good online news. The most popular are the *Daily Nation* (www.nation.co.ke) and the *East African Standard* (www.eastandard.net). *The East African* (www.theeastafrican.co.ke) is a weekly newspaper sold throughout Kenya, Tanzania and Uganda and provides the most objective reporting on East African issues and has in-depth coverage of international news. There are also a number of newspapers published in Kiswahili. International newspapers from the US, UK and Europe are regularly available in Nairobi (although a day or so late). Most newspapers and magazines are available from street stalls, which can be found on every street in Nairobi.

Radio

Kenya Broadcasting Corporation (KBC) broadcasts in Kiswahili, English and some local languages. There are several popular FM stations that can be picked up in the cities such as **Capital FM** and **Kiss 100 FM**. BBC World Service is broadcast to Kenya; check www.bbc.co.uk/worldservice.

Television

There are 3 television channels: **Kenya Broadcasting Corporation (KBC)** broadcasts in Kiswahili and English with a considerable number of imported foreign programmes; **Nation TV** is the station of the newspaper of the same name and broadcasts news and imported shows from the US; and **Kenya Television News** is based on CNN material. Many hotels have South African **DSTV** (Digital Satellite Television), which offers international programming of news, sport, entertainment and movie channels.

Money

Currency

→ *US$1=84KSh, £1=132KSh, €1=109KSh (Feb 2012)*

The currency in Kenya is the Kenyan shilling (the written abbreviation is either KSh or using /= after the amount, ie 500/=). Notes are 50, 100, 200, 500 and 1000KSh, coins are 5, 10, 50 cents and 1KSh. As it is not a hard currency, it cannot be brought into or taken out of the country, however there are no restrictions on the amount of foreign currency that can be brought into Kenya. The easiest currencies to exchange are US dollars, UK pounds and euros. If you are bringing US dollars cash, try and bring newer notes – because of the prevalence of forgery, many banks and bureaux de changes do not accept bills printed before 2005. Sometimes lower denomination bills attract a lower exchange rate than higher denominations.

Changing money Kenya's main banks are **Barclays Bank**, **Kenya Commercial Bank**, and **Standard Chartered Bank**. There are plenty of banks with ATMs and bureaux de change (known as forex bureaux) in the cities and at both Nairobi and Mombasa airports, and most small towns have at least one bank. Forex bureaux are open longer hours and offer faster service than banks and, although the exchange rates are only nominally different, the bureaux usually offer a better rate on traveller's cheques. Visitors should never change money on the black market, which is illegal.

Credit cards

Credit cards are widely accepted by many upmarket hotels, tour operators, safari companies and restaurants. However, there may be a surcharge of up to 5%, so check first if paying a sizeable bill. Banks in Kenya can advance cash on credit cards, and most now have ATMs. In Nairobi and Mombasa, many shopping malls and petrol stations also have ATMs. Visa, MasterCard, Plus and Cirrus are accepted; Diners Club and American Express are, however, limited. It is quite feasible to travel around Kenya with just a credit card, although it is always a good idea to bring some cash as a back-up.

Traveller's cheques

The major advantage of traveller's cheques (TCs) is that if they are lost or stolen there is a relatively efficient system for replacement. Make sure you keep a full record of the cheques' numbers and value and always keep the receipts separate from the cheques. The drawback is that replacement cheques can usually only be collected from banks in major cities. Another disadvantage in Kenya is the time it takes to cash them and the commission charged, which ranges from 2% to 5%.

Opening hours

Banks Mon-Fri 0830-1330, Sat 0830-1100. Forex bureaux are open longer hours 7 days a week; at Jomo Kenyatta and Moi international airports 24 hrs. **Post offices** Mon-Fri 0800-1700, Sat 0900-1300. **Shops** Generally Mon-Sat 0800-1700 or 1800. Larger branches of the supermarkets stay open until late in the evening and are open on Sun morning. In Muslim areas, shops may close early on Fri.

Post

The **Kenya Post Office**, www.posta.co.ke, has branches across the country, even in the smallest of towns. Sending post out of the country is cheap and efficient, and letters to Europe and the US should take no more than a few days. If you are sending home souvenirs, surface mail is the cheapest method but will take at least 6 weeks. Parcels must be wrapped in brown paper with string. There is no point doing this before getting to the post office as you will be asked to undo it to be checked for export duty. It's probably best to use registered mail for more valuable items so that you can track their progress. The post office has its own domestic and international courier service, **EMS**, www.emskenya.co.ke. The main international companies are also represented; check the websites for the nearest branch: **DHL**, www.dhl.co.ke: **Fedex**, www.fedex.co.za.

Safety

Because of Somalian unrest and militant activity in the region, the British Foreign Office (FCO) strongly advise against travel in Northeast Kenya along the Somali border (the route from Garissa to Wajit and Mandera, and the coastal area immediately north of Lamu Island which includes the other islands in the Lamu Archipelago). There is a problem with *shiftas* (bandits) attacking vehicles on roads in Northern Kenya, and vehicles on the route between Isiolo and the Ethiopian border at Moyale are required to travel in an organized convoy (see the Northern Kenya chapter for details of this).

The majority of the people you will meet in Kenya are honest and ready to help you so there is no need to get paranoid about your safety. However, Nairobi and Mombasa do have reputations for street crime, especially bag-snatching. Basically, you just have to be sensible and not carry expensive cameras, open bags or valuable jewellery and be careful about carrying large sums of money. Waist pouches are very vulnerable as the belt can be cut easily. Day packs have also been known to be slashed, with their entire contents drifting out on to the street without the wearer knowing. Carry money and any valuables in a slim belt under clothing. Do not automatically expect your belongings to be safe in a tent on safari. You also need to be vigilant of thieves on buses and trains and guard your possessions fiercely. Avoid walking around after dusk, particularly in the more run-down urban areas – take a taxi; walking alone at night, even on beaches, is dangerous. In built-up areas, lock your car, and if there is an *askari* (security guard) nearby, pay him a small sum to watch over it. Also be wary of someone distracting a driver in a parked vehicle, whilst an accomplice gets into the car on the opposite side. Always keep car doors locked and windows wound up, and lock room doors at night as noisy fans and a/c can provide cover for sneak thieves. Crime and hazardous road conditions make travel by night dangerous.

It's not only crime that may affect your personal safety; you must also take safety precautions when visiting the game reserves and national parks. If camping, it is not advisable to leave your tent or *banda* during the night. Wild animals wander around the camps freely in the hours of darkness, and a protruding leg may seem like a tasty take-away to a hungry hyena. This is especially true at organized campsites, where the local animals have got so used to humans that they have lost much of their inherent fear. Exercise care during daylight hours too – remember wild animals can be unpredictable and potentially dangerous.

Telephone

→ *Country code +254.*
Generally speaking, the telephone system is very good. You can make international calls from public coin or card phones on the street or at post offices – the latter are found in even the smallest towns where you can buy

phonecards. Most hotels and lodges offer international telephone services, though they will usually charge double. In larger towns, private shops also offer international services, usually with additional internet. Calls between Kenya and Tanzania and Uganda are charged at long-distance local rates rather than international. If you have a mobile phone with roaming, you can make use of Kenya's cellular networks, which cover most larger towns, the length of the coast and the Mombasa to Uganda road and the tourist areas but not some of the parks and reserves or the north of Kenya away from the towns. Sim and top-up cards for pay-as-you-go mobile providers are available almost everywhere; in the towns and cities these often have their own shops, but you can buy cards from roadside vendors anywhere, even in the smallest of settlements. Mobile phones are now such a part of everyday life in Kenya that many establishments have abandoned the local landline services and use the mobile network instead. You will see from listings such as hotels and restaurants in this book, mobile numbers (starting with T07) are sometimes provided instead of landline numbers. Indeed, if you find a taxi driver or tour guide you like, get their mobile number as this is the best way to reach them.

Time

GMT+3.

Tipping

It is customary to tip around 10% for good service, which is greatly appreciated by hotel and restaurant staff, most of whom receive very low pay. You can make individual tips, or most large hotels and beach resorts have tip boxes in reception for you to make a contribution at the end of your stay which is shared amongst all staff. Taxi drivers don't need tipping since the price of a fare is usually negotiated first. How much to tip the guide/driver on safari (on a camping trip the

cook too) is tricky. It is best to enquire from the company at the time of booking what the going rate is. As a very rough guide you should allow US$8-20 per person per day. Always try to come to an agreement with other members of the group and put the tip into a common kitty. The tip is per recipient per day, not per traveller/client per day. For example, if you are in a group of four that would like to tip US$20 per day, each would contribute US$5 per day to the tip kitty, and the member of staff's total tip at the end of a 7-day safari would be US$140.

Tour operators

If you plan to book an organized tour from your own country, the best bet is to locate a travel agent with links to tour companies in Kenya as they will probably be able to get you the best deals. Within Kenya there is a bewildering array of tour operators offering safaris in Kenya and East Africa, with most having offices in Nairobi (see page 77) or Mombasa (see page 240). There is no reason why you cannot deal with them directly and they may often be cheaper and better informed than travel agents in your home country.

UK and Ireland
Abercrombie & Kent, T0845-070 0600, www.abercrombiekent.co.uk.
Acacia Africa, T020-7706 4700, www.acacia-africa.com.
Africa Explorer, T020-8987 8742, www.africa-explorer.co.uk.
Africa Travel Centre, T0845-450 1520, www.africatravel.co.uk.
Africa Travel Resource, T01306-880 770, www.africatravelresource.com.
Aim 4 Africa, T0114-255 2533, www.aim4africa.com.
Expert Africa, T020-8232 9777, www.expertafrica.com.
Explore, T0870-333 4001, www.explore.co.uk.
Global Village, T0844-844 2541, www.globalvillage-travel.com.

Odyssey World, T0845-370 7733, www.odyssey-world.co.uk.
Okavango Tours and Safaris, T020-8347 4030, www.okavango.com.
Rainbow Tours, T020-7226 1004, www.rainbowtours.co.uk.
Safari Consultants Ltd, T01787-888590, www.safari-consultants.co.uk.
Somak, T020-8423 3000, www.somak.co.uk.
Steppes Africa, T01285-880980, www.steppestravel.co.uk.
Tim Best Travel, T020-7591 0300, www.timbesttravel.com.
Wildlife Worldwide, T0845-130 6982, www.wildlifeworldwide.com.

Australia
African Wildlife Safaris, T+61 (0)3-9249 3777, www.africanwildlifesafaris.com.au.
Classic Safari Company, T+61 2 9327 0666, www.classicsafaricompany.com.au.
Peregrine Travel, T+61 (0)3-8601 4444, www.peregrine.net.au.

North America
Adventure Centre, T1 800-228 8747, T+1 51-0654 1879, www.adventure-centre.com.
Africa Adventure Company, T+1 954-491 8877, www.africa-adventure.com.
Bushtracks, T+1 707-433 4492, www.bushtracks.com.

South Africa and Tanzania
Go2Africa, T+27-(0)21-4814900, www.go2africa.com.
Predators Safari Club, T+255(0)27-250 6471, www.predators-safari.com.
Pulse Africa, T+27 (0)11-325 2290, www.pulseafrica.com.
Wild Frontiers, T+27 (0)72-927 7529, www.wildfrontiers.com.

Tourist information

The head office of the **Kenya Tourist Board** is on Ragati Rd in Nairobi, T020-271 1262, www.magicalkenya.com, but this is not a

drop-in office. However, they will send you brochures on request and the website is excellent. **Kenya Wildlife Services (KWS)**, Langata Road, next to the Main Gate of Nairobi National Park, T020-600 0800, www.kws.org, 0900-1730, is very helpful with advice about visiting the parks and also has a shop here that sells some useful brochures and maps. **Kenya Tourism Federation**, also at the KWS complex in Nairobi, offers a 24-hr tourist helpline, T020-800 1000, www.ktf.co.ke, and a safety and communication centre, which advises tourists on most things including road conditions and emergency help. If you want to go off the beaten track, get advice from them first. There are several useful publications for sale at the bookshops in Nairobi. These include the annual *Visitors' Guide Kenya*, which is published by Yellow Pages Kenya and lists attractions, shops, restaurants and services, and the similar *Go Places*, which comes out bi-monthly.

Tourist offices overseas

Australia, 5/68 Alfred St, Milsons Point, New South Wales 2061, T+61 (0)2 9959 4277, arobertsbrown@aviareps.com. **Canada**, Suite 2601, 2 Bloor St West, Toronto, Ontario M4W 3E2, T+41 (0)6 935-1896, kenya@voxtm.ca. **UK**, Colechurch House, 1 London Bridge Walk, London SE1 2SX, T+44 (0)20-7367 0931, kenya@hillsbalfoursynergy.com.

USA, Suite 300, 1334 Parkview Av, Manhattan Beach, CA, 90266, T+1 310 545 3047, kenya@myriadmarketing.com

Useful websites

www.eatout.co.ke Useful restaurant guide for Nairobi and the coast.
www.ecotourismkenya.org Website for the Ecotourism Society of Kenya, which provides support for small community ecotourism projects.
www.katokenya.org Website for the Kenyan Association of Tour Operators.
www.kenyalogy.com General tourism information.
www.kenyatravelideas.com Comprehensive all-round information about Kenya.
www.kenyabuzz.com Lists nightlife, entertainment and events in Nairobi.
www.kenya.go.ke Website for the Kenyan government.
www.kws.org Kenya Wildlife Services (KWS).
www.magicalkenya.com Official website of the Kenya Tourist Board.

Visas and immigration

Almost all visitors require a visa, with the exception of some African countries. A transit visa valid for 7 days costs US$20 per person; a single-entry visa valid for 3 months costs US$50; a multi-entry visa valid for 12 months costs US$100. Visas are issued at Jomo

Kenyatta International Airport in Nairobi, Moi International Airport in Mombasa and all the road border crossings. Visas can be paid for in US dollars, euros or pounds sterling. Multi-entry visas are not available on arrival but only through embassies. As long as your single-entry visa remains valid you are allowed to move freely between Kenya, Tanzania and Uganda without the need for re-entry permits. If you want to get an extension you can stay a maximum of 6 months in the country fairly easily, but at extra cost. In Nairobi this can be done at Nyayo House, corner of Kenyatta Av and Uhuru Highway, T020-222 022, Mon-Fri 0830-1230 and 1400-1530; it can also be done at the Provincial Commissioner's Offices in Embu, Garissa, Kisumu, Mombasa and Nakuru. Do check your visitor's pass, as it has been known for people who have overstayed their time in the country to be fined quite heavily. Your passport must be valid for a minimum of 6 months after your planned departure date from Kenya; this is a requirement whether you need a visa or not. For more information visit www.immigration. go.ke. Incidentally, if passengers are transiting through Nairobi and have a couple of hours to kill, they are allowed out of the airport on their transit visas, so there is no reason at all why they can't grab a taxi and go to Nairobi National Park for a game drive.

Voltage

220-240 volts AC at 50 Hz. Square 3-pin British-type sockets. Travellers with round-pin plugs will require adaptors. Hotels usually have 2-pin round sockets for razors, phones, etc.

Weights and measures

Metric. In country areas items are often sold by the piece.

Women travellers

Women do have to be more wary than men, although Kenya seems to be a more pleasant place for lone women travellers than many other countries. If you are hassled, it is best to totally ignore the person, whatever you feel, as expressions of anger are often taken as acts of encouragement. Kenyan women will generally be very supportive if they see you are being harassed and may well intervene if they think you need help, but the situation is very rarely anything more than a nuisance. You are more likely to be approached at the coast, as the number of women coming to Kenya for sexual adventure has encouraged this type of pestering. The key is to keep patient and maintain a sense of humour. Women in Kenya dress very decorously, and it is wise to follow suit particularly in small towns and rural areas. In Lamu in particular, it is important for both men and women to dress modestly as it's a fairly conservative Muslim community.

Working in Kenya

Whilst there is a fairly large expatriate community in Nairobi and Mombasa working in construction, telecommunications and the import/export industry, there are few opportunities for travellers to obtain casual paid employment in Kenya and it is illegal for a foreigner to work there without an official work permit. A number of NGOs and voluntary organizations can arrange placements for volunteers, especially teachers and HIV/Aids educators, for periods ranging from a few weeks to 6 months, visit www.volunteerkenya.org or www.volunteerafrica.org. The **Kenya Voluntary and Community Development Project**, www.kvcdp.org, is a good grass-roots organization that puts volunteers in a number of placements, especially those involving Kenya's needy children.

Contents

Nairobi

At a glance

◉ **Getting around** On foot in the city centre; tours, bus or self-drive to the outlying attractions.

◉ **Time required** A minimum of 2 days to see the sights in the city centre and suburbs; half a day in Nairobi National Park.

◉ **Weather** Moderate temperatures year round of 15-25°C but often cloudy.

◉ **When not to go** Mar-May are the wettest months when the streets get flooded and muddy.

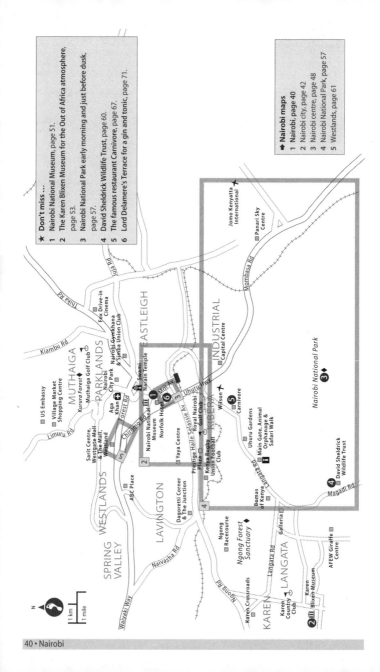

★ Don't miss ...

1 Nairobi National Museum, page 51.
2 The Karen Blixen Museum for the Out of Africa atmosphere, page 53.
3 Nairobi National Park early morning and just before dusk, page 57.
4 David Sheldrick Wildlife Trust, page 60.
5 The famous restaurant Carnivore, page 67.
6 Lord Delamere's Terrace for a gin and tonic, page 71.

Nairobi, capital of Kenya, is a lively, cosmopolitan and bustling city that sits at 1870 m above sea level. The centre is modern and prosperous; services are well organized and efficient. Businessmen and women talking on mobile phones walk the pavements alongside Masai warriors with long, ochre-stained hair; tourists mingle with busy traders and commuters; markets sell traditional handicrafts in the shadow of office towers, and life goes on at a frenetic pace. The city never stops moving, and the streets throng with pedestrians, cars, *matatus* and *mkokoteni* (hand-drawn carts used to carry goods to market). However, the combination of Kenya's rising population and migration to the towns has resulted in the size of Nairobi increasing at an enormous rate, and the population today is officially estimated at just over three million – it was only around 300,000 at Independence in 1963. Housing and other facilities have failed to keep up, and shanty towns in the outskirts are the inevitable result. By contrast, there are leafy upmarket suburbs and modern shopping malls, and the city is home to a wide international community of multinational companies, embassies and NGOs, and is Africa's coordinating base for the United Nations. Unfortunately Nairobi has also attracted fame for its high crime rate, and visitors should at all times exercise caution. Nevertheless, there are many interesting things to do and see. Nairobi is home to some of the best restaurants and shops in East Africa, Nairobi National Park is within sight of the city and there are a number of other wildlife attractions just a stone's throw away. It's worth making time for Nairobi at the beginning or end of a trip to Kenya.

Arriving in Nairobi → *Colour map 1, A/B4. Phone code: 020. Population: 2.9 million.*

Getting there

Air Nairobi is the most important air transport hub for East Africa. International and domestic flights touch down at **Jomo Kenyatta International Airport** ① *15 km southeast of the city off the Mombasa Rd, T020-661 1000, www.kenyaairports.co.ke.* Although the untidy old building is in desperate need of refurbishing and is far too small for the amount of traffic it now gets, airport facilities are adequate. There are cafés and snack bars (but no proper restaurants), several banks (with longer banking hours than the rest of the country), ATMs, a left-luggage desk (US$5 per item for 24 hours), hotel booking, tour-operator and car-hire desks, and air-side, several duty free and souvenir shops and a branch of the excellent **Nairobi Java House** coffee shop, which also sells coffee beans for those wanting to take a lasting taste of Kenyan coffee home with them.

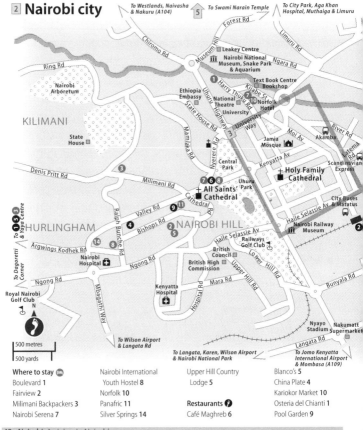

2 **Nairobi city**

Where to stay		Nairobi International	Upper Hill Country	Blanco's 5
Boulevard 1		Youth Hostel 8	Lodge 5	China Plate 4
Fairview 2		Norfolk 10		Kariokor Market 10
Milimani Backpackers 3		Panafric 11	**Restaurants** 🍴	Osteria del Chianti 1
Nairobi Serena 7		Silver Springs 14	Café Maghreb 6	Pool Garden 9

Outside the international and domestic arrivals halls are desks for the **Airport Taxi Operators Association**; a taxi from the airport into the centre should cost around US$30. Pay at the desk, where they'll give you a receipt to show the driver. Ignore any individual taxi drivers who start to badger you; these are not registered to operate at the airport. You will need Kenyan shillings to pay for a taxi and you can change money at the banks and bureaux de change in the airport or use an ATM. Most hotels and tour operators provide transport or at the very least can arrange a shuttle bus. There is also a bus service (No 34, every 30 minutes, 0600-1800, US$0.50) to and from the airport and the bus stand outside the **Hilton Hotel** in the city centre. The journey time is 40 minutes depending on traffic and time of day, although buses are best avoided if you have a lot of luggage as they get crowded nearer the city. If you arrive after dark, the sensible option is to take a taxi. Remember that rush hour in Nairobi runs from 0800 to 1000 in the morning and 1600 to 1900 in the evening and traffic is very congested on the way to and from the airport – allow plenty of time.

Nairobi's second airport is **Wilson Airport** ⓘ *6 km south of the city on the Langata Rd, T020-603 260, www.kenyaairports.com.* This airport is used for domestic scheduled and charter flights by the light aircraft airlines, as well as being the base for **AMREF** – the flying doctor service (see page 31). There is no main terminal, but rather a string of individual airline's buildings. A taxi into the city centre should cost US$15-20.

Rail The railway station is at the southern end of Moi Avenue near the roundabout with Haile Selassie Avenue. It is easily spotted thanks to the coloured lights around the main entrance. There are passenger rail services between Nairobi and Mombasa and Kisumu (see box, page 18).

Road There are good road connections into the city from all directions. The long-distance bus station is on Landhies Road from where there are daily departures to most destinations. **Akamba Bus** is one of the better organized and safer of the many bus services travelling long distance within Kenya and to neighbouring countries. Their terminus is in Lagos Road. There are also several shuttle bus companies offering a daily service to/from Arusha and Moshi in Tanzania. ▸▸ *See Transport, page 79.*

Orientation
Central Nairobi is bounded by Uhuru Highway to the west, Nairobi River to the

---

Map labels:
To Thika (A2)
Muranga Rd
Park Rd
Ring Road Ngara
Kariokor ⑩
Racecourse Rd
KBS
KARIOKOR
Matatus
City Buses
Long-distance Bus Station
Nairobi River
Landies Rd
Jogoo Rd
City Stadium
Factory St
Go Down Arts Centre
Lusaka Rd
[4]

➡ **Nairobi maps**
1 Nairobi, page 40
2 Nairobi city, page 42
3 Nairobi centre, page 48
4 Nairobi National Park, page 57
5 Westlands, page 61

Railway 2   Lord Delamare's Terrace 7

Bars & clubs 🍸
Aksum Bar 8
Casablanca 3

north and east and the railway to the south. Across the Uhuru Highway is **Uhuru Park** and **Central Park**. In the southwest of this central triangle of about 5 sq km is the crop of high-rise buildings where most of the government buildings, offices, banks, hotels and shops are located. In the northern section the buildings are closer together and there are many less expensive shops and restaurants, while to the east of the triangle is the poorer section where there are cheaper hotels and restaurants, shops and markets. This is the area around **River Road**, which is very lively, full of character and has the authentic atmosphere of the African section of a great city (although it is an area in which visitors should take care over their safety).

Southeast of the city centre around the **Mombasa Road** is the concentrated industrial area that peters out near the airport. By contrast, to the south of here is the 117 sq km **Nairobi National Park**, which makes up about one fifth of the city's area. To the west of the city centre and hemmed in by the Langata and Ngong roads is the congested **Kibera slum** (see page 50), and beyond here and past the Main Gate to Nairobi National Park are the affluent suburbs of **Langata** and **Karen** where many of the sights are located. Much of this area was sold for development by Karen Blixen, the Danish authoress, when she left Kenya in 1931, and these leafy suburbs are isolated from the rest of Nairobi by the **Ngong Forest Sanctuary**. There is a semi-rural atmosphere, with seemingly more dogs and horses than human residents. This is changing, however, as clusters of homes are being built on what were once large plots with single dwellings, and estates of houses occupy former farmland.

Getting around

Walking around central Nairobi is relatively straightforward, as the city centre is small and accessible. Taxis are widely available, convenient and are parked on just about every street corner. Any make of car can serve as a taxi, although most Nairobi taxis are white and marked with a yellow line along each side. There is also a large fleet of London black taxis operating within the city. **Taxis** are not metered, and a price should be agreed with the driver before departure. Expect to pay in the region of US$5 for a short hop across the city centre rising to US$15-20 for a ride to outlying areas. Ask locally or at your hotel for correct rates.

City **buses** are numbered and operate on set routes throughout the city. They can be boarded at any stop, and tickets are purchased on board. You can catch buses as far as Karen and beyond, and the main city bus terminal is located at the end of River Road. There are also main bus stands outside the Hilton Hotel on Moi Avenue, outside Nation House on Tom Mboya Street, outside the Railway Station at the end of Moi Avenue, and outside the General Post Office on Kenyatta Avenue. **Matatus** (minibuses) also operate on set routes and are the most popular form of local public transport. Again, like taxis, most are white with a yellow stripe. Their destination is clearly written on the side. There are countless *matatu* stands throughout Nairobi, with continuous arrivals and departures throughout the day.

Most tour operators are able to arrange **tours** of Nairobi, which is a very useful way of familiarizing yourself with the layout of the city, as well as seeing some of the sights that are further out. City centre tours last around three hours and usually include a trip to the City Market, the Parliament buildings, the Kenyatta International Conference Centre, the August 7th Memorial Gardens and the Nairobi National Museum. In reality there's no reason why you can't walk around and visit these places yourself. More useful half-day tours take in the Nairobi National Park or combine the sights in the western suburbs, such as the Karen Blixen Museum, Giraffe Centre and David Sheldrick Wildlife Trust. For tour operators, see page 77. You can also hire a **car** for a day or two to explore on your own, but only do so if you have had some experience of manic, congested traffic typical of an African city, although the suburbs, such as Karen, and the Nairobi National Park, are easy to negotiate by road. ▸▸ *See Transport, page 79.*

Maps The best maps of Nairobi are the *City of Nairobi: Map and Guide*, published by the Survey of Kenya in English, German and French. If you want more detail or are staying for a while, it may be worth getting *A to Z Guide to Nairobi*, by RW Moss (Kenway Publications), which is clear and easy to use. There are several other maps on offer, so it's just a case of finding one that suits you. Try the bookshop in the **Stanley Hotel**, or the bookshops in the shopping malls, which all have a good selection.

Best time to visit
Nairobi lies 145 km south of the equator but it's far from hot. The city is at 1870 m, so temperatures are a moderate 15-25°C year-round and rarely reach over 30°C. September to April are the hottest months, with maximum temperatures averaging 24°C but falling at night to around 13°C. May to August is cooler, with a maximum average of 21°C and minimum of 11°C at night. The main rainy seasons are March to May and October to December, when it gets slightly humid and the streets may become flooded and muddy.

Tourist information
There is no tourist information centre in Nairobi, but the tour operators will be able to help, see page 77. For details of **Kenya Wildlife Services** and the **Kenya Tourism Federation**, see page 36. For listings and restaurant and nightlife reviews, **Kenya Buzz** ① *www.kenya buzz.com*, is a good source of information.

Safety
Historically, crime in Nairobi has been well documented with frequent muggings, bag snatchings, car-jackings and robberies. These can certainly be a problem if you are not extremely sensible, and if you walk around with a camera hanging from your neck, an obviously expensive watch, jewellery or a money belt showing, then you are very vulnerable. If you are at all unsure, take a taxi that you should lock from the inside if possible, and make it a rule to always do so at night. Places definitely to avoid walking around are River Road and its neighbouring streets; as a rule of thumb do not wander casually much farther west than Moi Avenue. Some thieves specialize in jostling, robbing and snatching from new arrivals on buses and *matatus* and on these **do not** take items to eat offered by strangers, as they may have been drugged to aid robbery. Despite all this, things have improved in central Nairobi since the mid-1990s. The Nairobi Central Business District Association (NCBDA) has worked with police to provide better policing of the streets and CCTV cameras have been installed, resulting in a marked decline in petty theft. Nevertheless it is always wise to exercise caution when walking around Nairobi, avoid walking around the city centre on Sundays as businesses are shut and the streets are virtually empty, and never walk around at night. If driving, be wary of car hijacking, especially at traffic lights in the suburbs. It's a good idea to travel with the windows closed and the doors locked. Remember, almost all car-jackers are armed and will use their weapons when faced with resistance.

Background

The name Nairobi comes from the Masai *'enkare nyarobe'* meaning sweet (or cold) water, for, originally, this was a watering hole for the Masai and their cattle. Just 110 years ago Nairobi hardly existed. It began life in 1896 as a railway camp during the building of the Uganda Railway from the coast to the highlands. The location was chosen due to its central position between Mombasa and Kampala, just before the railway was to make its difficult descent and ascent of the walls of the Rift Valley. It was also chosen because its rivers could supply the camp with water. It grew steadily and, by 1907, had become a town sufficient in size to take over from Mombasa as capital of British East Africa. Its climate was considered healthier than that of the coast, as its temperature was too cool for the malaria mosquito to survive, and its position was ideal for developing into a trading centre for the settlers who farmed the fertile land around Nairobi and beyond into Western Kenya, referred to as the White Highlands, which attracted some 80,000 European settlers between the 1920s and 1950s. These 'intrepid adventurers' included Karen Blixen of *Out of Africa* fame – her house is now a museum on the outskirts of the city. Nairobi's famous **Norfolk Hotel** opened in 1904 and was once the social meeting place for this privileged community; today you can still enjoy a gin and tonic in the bar. The local Kikuyu who were losing their land to these white settlers and were dispersed further by the Mau Mau rebellion in the 1950s (see page 355), moved into Nairobi and the city swelled. It became a municipality in 1919, received city status in 1950 and, after Independence in 1963, became capital of the republic.

The euphoria inspired by Independence brought with it a wave of construction in the city centre, which resulted in the many not terribly attractive 1960-1970s blocks that still stand today among the more modern gleaming skyscrapers. With 19 floors, the Hilton Hotel became the city's tallest building in 1969 before it was superseded by the Kenyatta International Conference centre with 33 floors in 1972, which in turn was overtaken by the New Central Bank Tower in 2000, which with 38 floors is currently the tallest building in Nairobi. Westlands pioneered the under-one-roof shopping mall when the Sarit Centre was built in 1983, and now modern shopping malls feature in almost every fairly affluent neighbourhood with more being built all the time.

Like many African cities, Nairobi today has bustling markets, alarming *matatu* drivers, potholed roads, shanty towns and leafy suburbs. As well as being the seat of government and commerce for Kenya, it is also the most important city in East Africa and is home to many diplomatic agencies, NGOs and multinationals and is an important base for the UN. Over the years it has also attracted many of Kenya's rural poor seeking employment in the big city, which has resulted in large slums developing around the city centre. Nevertheless it's a lively African city, which boasts a generally good infrastructure, amazingly friendly, interesting and intelligent people from all walks of life, and excellent facilities for tourists.

Places in Nairobi

Nairobi has an interesting cross-section of sights that explore both its colonial past and Kenya's unique wildlife and cultural heritage, and at least a couple of days are warranted here before or after a longer safari. It's also the best place to buy souvenirs in the good curio shops and markets, or modern shopping malls. It has the best restaurants and nightlife in the country, and Kenyans themselves like to go out and socialize, especially at the weekends when nightclubs are pumping and families enjoy picnics in the parks or long lazy lunches around hotel swimming pools. ▸▸ *For listings, see pages 61-83.*

Nairobi centre

The Norfolk

Anyone with an interest in the growth of the city from its early colonial days should visit this hotel on Harry Thuku Road, a place that played a vital role in Nairobi's history. This was the city's first hotel, built to house new arrivals to the colony, and when it first opened on Christmas Day 1904, the Savoy Hotel in London was five years old and the London Ritz still a year away. The Norfolk became an important meeting point and watering hole for settlers, adventurers and travellers from all over the world; American President Theodore Roosevelt, Lord Baden-Powell, the Earl of Warwick, Lord and Lady Cranworth, and the Baron and Baroness von Blixen have all been part of the hotel's history. It once looked out across sweeping plains and is now in the heart of the bustling city, but the mock Tudor façade and colonial opulence remains intact. The **Lord Delamere's Terrace** (see page 71)is a good place for a drink and is the place where early Nairobi colonial society enjoyed their gin and tonics in the evening. In 1980 a bomb went off and extensively damaged the hotel, killing 20 people and injuring more. At the time, responsibility for the attack was claimed by an Arab group that said it was seeking retaliation for Kenya allowing Israeli troops to refuel in Nairobi during the raid on Entebbe Airport in Uganda four years earlier to rescue hostages from an El-Al hijacked aircraft. The hotel consequently went through a major refit and it was refurbished again in 2008. ▸▸ *See also Where to stay, page 61.*

Kenyatta Avenue

Kenyatta Avenue is the main multi-laned artery in the middle of the city centre, which is bordered by flowering trees and has a concrete 'island' in the middle of it, which was originally designed to be wide enough for a full team of oxen to turn around in. The tower block at the eastern end is another hotel with a place in history: the **Stanley**, which started life as a boarding house on Victoria Street (later Tom Mboya street) in 1902, was built on its present site in 1913 and was named after the great African explorer. Some of its most revered guests have included authors Elspeth Huxley and Ernest Hemmingway. A central landmark on Kenyatta Avenue, its reputation as an important stopover for African travellers was cemented in 1961, with the creation of its famous **Thorn Tree Café**. Here, a single acacia tree in the centre of the café became a noticeboard for travellers, who would leave notes, letters and messages for fellow travellers pinned to the trunk. This tradition became so popular that the thorn tree became a symbol for African travel. Eventually notice boards were erected to protect the tree. The original tree died a natural death and has been replaced by a sapling, but the café remains popular.

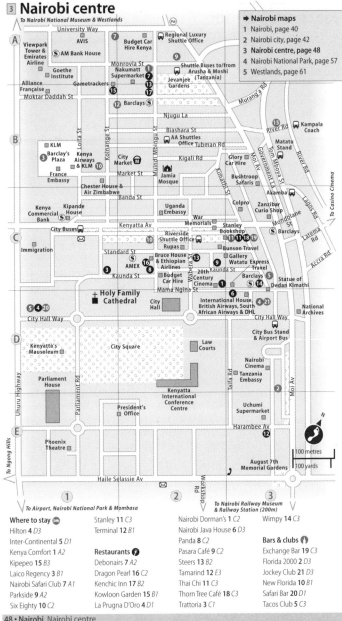

To Nairobi National Museum & Westlands

→ **Nairobi maps**
1 Nairobi, page 40
2 Nairobi city, page 42
3 **Nairobi centre, page 48**
4 Nairobi National Park, page 57
5 Westlands, page 61

University Way

A
Viewpark Tower & Emirates Airline
AVIS
AM Bank House
Goethe Institute
Budget Car Hire Kenya
Regional Luxury Shuttle Office
Monrovia St
Nakumatt Supermarket
Shuttle Buses to/from Arusha & Moshi (Tanzania)
Jevanjee Gardens
Alliance Française
Gametrackers
Moktar Daddah St
Barclays

B
KLM
Barclay's Plaza
Kenya Airways & KLM
France Embassy
Chester House & Air Zimbabwe
Kenya Commercial Bank
Kipande House
City Market
Jamia Mosque
Banda St
Uganda Embassy
Njugu La
Biashara St
AA Shuttles Office
Tubman Rd
Kigali Rd
Glory Car Hire
Bushtrop Safaris
Colpro
Zanzibar Curio Shop
Akamba
Murang'a Rd
River Rd
Kampala Coach
Matatu Stand
Gov ernment Ln
Moi Av
Tom Mboya St
Kirinyaga Rd
Lagos Rd
To Casino Cinema

C
City Buses
Immigration
Kenyatta Av
War Memorials
Standard St
Riverside Shuttle Office
Rupas
Stanley Bookshop
Bunson Travel
Bruce House & Ethiopian Airlines
AMEX
Budget Car Hire
20th Century Cinema
Kaunda St
Mama Ngina St
Gallery
Watatu Express Travel
Barclays
Statue of Dedan Kimathi
International House, British Airways, South African Airways & DHL
Mondolane St
Laremu Rd
Accra Rd
Barclays

D
Holy Family Cathedral
City Hall
City Hall Way
Kenyatta's Mausoleum
City Square
Parliament House
President's Office
Law Courts
Kenyatta International Conference Centre
Nairobi Cinema
Tanzania Embassy
Uchumi Supermarket
City Bus Stand & Airport Bus
National Archives
Taifa Rd
Moi Av

E
Phoenix Theatre
Harambee Av
August 7th Memorial Gardens
Haile Selassie Av
Uhuru Highway
Parliament Rd
Workshop Rd
To Ngong Hills
To Airport, Nairobi National Park & Mombasa
To Nairobi Railway Museum & Railway Station (200m)

100 metres
100 yards
N

Other colonial-era monuments include a pair of twin **War Memorials**, dedicated to the fallen members of the Carrier Corps and the King's African Rifles from the two World Wars. Opposite the post office is **Kipande House**, a historic building with a striking clock tower and now a branch of Kenya Commercial Bank, where Kenyans were once required to be registered and issued with identification cards known as *Kipande*.

Jevanjee Gardens, Biashara Street and around

The small Jevanjee Gardens, off Moi Avenue north of the city market, were named after AM Jevanjee, one of Nairobi's first Indian businessmen. A railway contractor by trade, he was also a philanthropist and donated the land to the city after the small bazaar it housed was burned down. In 1906 a statue of Queen Victoria was unveiled here by her son, the Duke of Connaught. Today the park is a popular place with preachers and each lunchtime people come to sing evangelical hymns. This area is bordered by Biashara Street, still a stronghold of Asian enterprise. The influence of Nairobi's Indian community, the descendants of the original colonial railway labourers and merchants, is undeniable. They play a major role in the economic and social life of the city, and there are a number of Indian shops along this street, many of which sell Kenya's colourful textiles. There are several Hindu and Sikh temples throughout Nairobi, one of the most impressive being the **Swami Narain Temple** on Forest Road in Parklands, a massive temple complex with fine statuary and an impressive interior of intricately carved wood, which was built in 1999 from 350 tonnes of stone mined near Rajasthan in India and shipped to Kenya. At the centre of the city on Banda Street near the market is the large **Jamia Mosque** with attractive twinned minarets and silver domes.

National Archives

ⓘ *T020-222 8959, www.kenyarchives.go.ke, Mon-Fri 0815-1615, Sat 0815-1300, US$2.20.*
This is much more interesting than it might sound. The building (1906) originally served as the **Bank of India** and is located on Moi Avenue opposite the Hilton Hotel. On the ground floor it contains various exhibitions of arts and crafts, including some superb tribal artefacts gathered from across Africa, which were part of the private collection of avid art collector and former vice-president (1966) Joseph Murumbi. His collection, which also included 8000 rare, pre-1900 books, was bequeathed to the National Archives after his death in 1990. Upstairs there's a fascinating gallery of photographs covering Kenya's history from the building of the Uganda Railway to the present day, as well as the library of archives housing hundreds of thousands of documents.

Statue of Dedan Kimathi

On a triangle traffic island at the end of Kimathi Street and close to the Hilton Hotel is this new statue of Field Marshall Dedan Kimathi, one of the Mau Mau Rebellion's most influential leaders who was captured and executed by the British in 1957. The statue was unveiled in 2007, 50 years to the day of his death, by President Kibaki and Kimathi's widow, with some of the surviving Mau Mau soldiers attending the ceremony. The life-sized bronze statue features him in army fatigues sporting the famous Mau Mau dreadlocks, which were a feature of the Mau Mau fighters, and carrying a home-made gun and a sword.

August 7th Memorial Gardens

ⓘ *Corner of Moi Av and Haile Selassie Av, T020-341 062, www.memorialparkkenya.org, Mon-Sat 0900-1800, Sun 1300-1800, US$1.20, children (under 16) US$0.60.*

Kibera

Driving out of the city centre southwest towards Langata and the Nairobi National Park, you cannot fail to miss the sight of the densely packed brown tin roofs of the Kibera slum, which is hemmed in between Langata and Ngong roads. The name is a Nubian word for 'forest' or 'jungle'. Although no one really knows for sure how many people live here, it has a population of perhaps one million and, covering just 2.5 sq km, is the densest slum in East Africa. The site was first settled in 1918 by soldiers returning from the First World War and has, over time, grown haphazardly and informally into a heaving, cramped grid of home-made shacks with few basic amenities or services. It is home to Nairobi's poorest people, many who have come from rural regions looking for work in the city. So many people living on top of each other as well as poor sanitation results in many social problems and health risks. Kibera's residents represent all of Kenya's major ethnic groups, with some areas being specifically dominated by people of one ethno-linguistic group. At times this has sparked spats between the ethnic groups, including violence over the disputed 2007 elections. Across Nairobi, the government is addressing the problem of slum-living, and 2009 saw the beginning of a long-term scheme to re-house Kibera's people; some have now been relocated to newly built high-rise apartments. Schools, markets, playgrounds and other facilities are also planned. Additionally, local NGOs and the **United Nations Human Settlements Programme (UN–HABITAT)**, which has its international HQ in Nairobi, are on a constant mission to improve the standard of life for Kibera's inhabitants.

Several NGOs in Nairobi offer fascinating and eye-opening walking tours of Kibera. Try **Kibera Tours**, T072-366 9218, www.kiberatours.com, or **Explore Kibera**, T072-025 7421, www.explorekibera.com. These are led by guides who are residents and profits are channelled back into the community. Tours may visit an orphanage, school, informal market or self-help project like a craft-making cooperative. Costs are in the region of US$6-8 per person and further donations are encouraged (the companies will advise on other suggested items apart from cash). Pickups from the city centre and hotels can be arranged.

On 7 August 1998, Nairobi was rocked by a terrorist attack on the US Embassy, which resulted in the death of 213 people and seriously injured thousands more. Simultaneously, there was an attack on the US Embassy in Dar es Salam in Tanzania that killed 11 people. The attacks were linked to local members of Al Qaeda and brought the organization and its leader, Osama bin Laden, to international attention for the first time, resulting in the FBI placing Bin Laden on its 10-most-wanted list. On that fateful day in Nairobi, explosives were loaded on to the back of a truck, which was intended to be driven into the embassy's basement car park, but the vehicle was stopped at the gate, where the terrorists detonated the bombs. The explosion, which could be heard and felt 10 km away, ripped through the embassy and the building behind it and killed the 40 people inside the embassy including 12 Americans and many more ordinary Kenyans on the street. It was thought East Africa was chosen as a target by the terrorists because of its proximity to the US's activities in Sudan and because Nairobi was one of Africa's most important bases for both the CIA and the FBI. After the attack the remainder of the buildings had to be demolished, and the memorial gardens were opened on 7 August 2001. They feature a museum that documents what happened on the day, which includes a National Geographic documentary film, **Seconds from Disaster**, and some rather harrowing photographs, a granite wall with a plaque of the names of all those who died and a statue made up from debris collected after the attack. The gardens themselves are a peaceful green space where Kenyans still come to contemplate and remember the loved ones that they lost.

Minor Basilica Holy Family Cathedral
Nairobi's population is predominantly Christian, and there are countless churches throughout the city. In the city centre near the City Square is the large Catholic Minor Basilica Holy Family Cathedral, built in the 1960s. It doesn't have any particular architectural merit but is the largest church in Nairobi, with a capacity for 4000 people, and is the seat of the Archbishop of Nairobi. Also of interest is **All Saints' Cathedral**, on Kenyatta Avenue near the Nairobi Serena Hotel, a Gothic-style Anglican church that was founded in 1917 and consecrated in 1952.

Parliament House and City Square
Parliament House on Parliament Road is recognizable by its clock tower and was built in the 1950s. When Parliament is in session you can watch the proceedings from the public gallery, otherwise you can usually arrange to be shown around the building – ask at the main entrance. Directly beside Parliament the republic's first president, Jomo Kenyatta, rests in a respectfully landscaped mausoleum. Other government buildings, such as the Law Courts, President's office and City Hall, flank the City Square, a popular place at lunchtime with office workers and dominated by a large statue of Jomo Kenyatta sitting regally in his gowns with his trademark fly swat in his hand.

Kenyatta International Conference Centre
ⓘ *T020-326 1000, www.kicc.co.ke, Mon-Fri 0900-2000, Sat-Sun 0900-1800, US$4.50.*
The Kenyatta International Conference Centre overlooks a large amphitheatre, built in the traditional shape of an African hut, with a central plenary hall that resembles the ancient Roman Senate. This building is the second tallest in the city with 33 floors and was built in 1972. You can go up to the viewing level from where you can take photos – ask at the information desk on the ground floor for the guide to take you up. There are fantastic views to the city limits in all directions as well as a bird's-eye view down on to the streets of the CBD. The contrast between building styles and greenery in the different suburbs of the city is very evident, and you can make out the large parks and golf courses and Nairobi National Park. You can also see planes landing and taking off from Jomo Kenyatta and Wilson airports.

Nairobi National Museum
ⓘ *On Museum Hill off Chiromo Rd, T020-374 1424-4, www.museums.or.ke, 0830-1730, museum US$9, children (under 16) US$4.50, snake park US$9, children (under 16) US$4.50, combined ticket US$13, children (under 16) US$6.50.*
This museum presents an overview of Kenya's history, culture and natural history. Construction on the present site began in 1929 after the government set aside the land for it and in the 1950s the late Doctor Louis Leakey made a public appeal for funds to enlarge the Museum's galleries. The result was the construction of all the present galleries to the right of the main entrance. The Leakey Memorial building was opened in 1976 and houses the administration, archaeology and palaeontology departments. In 2005 the museum closed for an extensive refurbishment and re-opened again in early 2008 to critical acclaim. Outside, the grounds have been attractively landscaped and are now decorated

with some interesting sculptures, including a map of Kenya and a mosaic garden made by Kitengela Glass (see page 74), and there's a new row of upmarket shops and cafés. Inside, the first gallery is the Kenya Hall, which has some interesting contemporary exhibits, the most spectacular of which is the gourd tower that is cleverly built from dozens of different sized gourds from Kenya's various ethnic groups and dominates the centre of the room. Gourds have a number of traditional uses such as to store water or grain, keep bees and are even used as suitcases. Also of note is the colourful map of Kenya made up of hundreds of butterflies. Beyond here are some stuffed animals and many thousands of East Africa's birds, a hall dedicated to the history of evolutionary finds in Kenya, which is particularly strong with exhibits of archaeological findings made so famous by the work of the Leakeys, and a display about the history of the museum itself that includes some old display cabinets and a larger-than-life bronze statue of Louis Leakey sitting on a rock. Upstairs are displays of traditional artefacts, a hall dedicated to ancient rock art all over Africa and two excellent galleries with photographs of Masai ceremonies and contemporary life in Nairobi, and a striking collection of photographs of Kenya's animals. The excellent museum shop stocks some fine upmarket Kenyan art and souvenirs and a comprehensive range of books on Kenya, and enthusiastic guides are on hand throughout to talk visitors through the exhibits.

Snake Park and Aquarium

Set within the grounds of the museum, this place houses examples of most of the snake species found in Kenya as well as crocodiles and tortoises. There are many live snakes including puff adders and black and green mambas. The staff here help with the removal of snakes from residential premises in Nairobi. To the right of the Snake Park follow the path down the hill through the pleasant gardens a short distance and you'll come across a view of the narrow Nairobi River as it tumbles over some rocks. The gardens are also a good spot for birdwatching; look out for sunbirds, flycatchers and bee-eaters.

Nairobi Railway Museum

ⓘ *In the rail compound at the corner of Haile Selassie Av and Uhuru Highway, 200 m west of the railway station on Station Rd (an alternative route to avoid the chaotic matatu stand at the station is by turning onto Workshop Rd from Haile Selassie near City Square Post Office, then turn right on to Station Rd), T020-340 049, 0800-1645, US$4.50, children (under 16) US$2.25.*

This is the best place to come and learn the history of the Uganda Railway, on which the colony of Kenya was effectively founded. Among the outside exhibits are a number of the old steam trains from the colonial era. One of the best known is the carriage that was used during the hunt for the Man-eater of Kima in 1900. A lion halted the construction of the line with repeated attacks on the labour camps. A colonial officer, Captain Charles Ryall, and some other men positioned themselves in a rail carriage one night in an effort to shoot the man-eater. Unfortunately they all fell asleep, and the lion slipped into the carriage under cover of darkness, took Ryall into his mouth and sprang through a window. The inside of the museum is stuffed to the gills with railway memorabilia, original construction equipment, maps and old photographs. Look out for the bench seat that could be fitted to a locomotive's footplate at the front to allow distinguished travellers on the line, one of which was Theodore Roosevelt, unsurpassed views of the scenery and wildlife. There are also some marine exhibits including a model of *MV Liemba*, the German-built vessel that still plies Lake Tanganyika in Tanzania.

Nairobi Arboretum

ⓘ *Arboretum Rd, off State House Rd from Uhuru Highway, T020-272 5471, www.naturekenya. org, sunrise-sunset, free.*

Surrounded by buildings, the Nairobi Arboretum covers 32 ha and is home to many indigenous plant species, some 350 species of tree and over 100 species of bird, as well as Sykes and vervet monkeys and butterflies. There are picnic places, jogging trails and nature trails, and at the entrance you can buy a booklet on tree identification. It was originally established in 1907 as a trial area to see if fast-growing non-indigenous trees (needed to fuel steam locomotives) could survive Nairobi's climate. Many did, and went on to be grown commercially, but there is also a sizeable collection of Kenya's indigenous trees here.

Nairobi City Park

ⓘ *between Limuru and Forest roads, Parklands, the main entrance is opposite the Aga Khan hospital on Limuru Rd, sunrise-sunset, free.*

Declared a public park in 1925 and covering 60 ha, as parks go in the city, Nairobi City Park stands above the rest for its rich biodiversity. It has pathways through some attractive landscaped gardens, as well as tracts of forest with a number of tree species that are endemic to Kenya. About 100 species of bird are present including black-capped social weavers that nest in the acacia trees along the main entrance drive. Butterflies are prolific, and Sykes monkey are easily spotted thanks to the seemingly confident way they approach picnicking visitors for titbits. The Nairobi City Council's Environment Department is based here and has a tree and plant nursery in the park where members of the public can buy plants, and there's a kiosk for snacks and drinks.

Around Nairobi city

Uhuru Gardens

ⓘ *Near Wilson Airport, on Langata Rd, 0930-1800, free.*

Uhuru Gardens are Nairobi's largest memorial to the struggle for Independence and were built on the spot where freedom (*Uhuru*) from colonial rule was declared at midnight on 12 December 1963. The monument is a 24-m-high triumphal column, supporting a pair of clasped hands and the dove of peace, high over a statue of a group of freedom fighters raising the flag. Across the car park is a less interesting granite and black marble structure with a disused fountain put up in 1988 to mark 25 years of Independence.

Karen Blixen Museum

ⓘ *Karen Rd, Karen, from Nairobi take the No 24 bus from in front of the railway station, T020-800 2139, www.museums.or.ke, 0930-1800, US$9, children (under 16) US$4.50, guided tours are available, shop selling curios and books.*

The museum is in the house of Karen Blixen (Isak Dinesen), in the suburb of Karen, about 10 km from the city centre. Many people who have read her books or seen *Out of Africa* will want to savour the atmosphere. The house was originally a coffee plantation out in the country (she wrote, "I had a farm in Africa, at the foot of the Ngong Hills ...") but now finds itself on the outskirts of Nairobi. The quiet, tree-lined roads and older homes with large yards make this a pleasant place. The author lived in the house known as *Bogani* from 1914 until 1931. Efforts have been made to decorate all of the rooms of the house in their original style, and it is furnished with a mixture of original decor and props from the 1985 film production that was filmed here. Exhibits include many photographs of Karen Blixen, Denys

Beryl Markham

Beryl Markham was a champion horse trainer, record-breaking aviator, author and celebrated beauty, who counted two members of the British royal family among her lovers. Her style was formed by a childhood that embraced both traditional African and European ways of life.

Beryl was born in Leicestershire in 1902 and, when she was two, the family sold up and sailed for East Africa where her father took a job as dairy manager for Lord Delamere at Equator Ranch near Njoro in Kenya. Home was a rondavel – a mud hut with a thatched roof and sacking covering the windows.

Beryl grew up with local Nandi house servants and farm workers and their children with whom she formed a bond, going barefoot, eating with her hand and wearing a *shulen*, an African shirt. Kiswahili was Beryl's first language.

At nine she was sent to board at Nairobi European School, but ran away after less than a year, returning to Njoro, the stables and her Kipsigis companions.

Ten years later Beryl began training horses, first for a neighbour, Ben Birkbeck, and then for Delamere at his nearby estate, Soysambu.

In 1928, Kenyan society was in a frenzy of anticipation for the visit of Edward, Prince of Wales, and his younger brother Henry, Duke of Gloucester. Beryl and her then husband, the sophisticated, very well-off but rather frail Mansfield Markham, took up residence for the duration at the Muthaiga Club. In next to no time Beryl had secured both royal trophies.

When the royal tour ended at the end of November, cut short by the illness of King George V, Beryl, although six months pregnant, travelled to London where the Duke of Gloucester met her on the quay side and installed her in a suite at the Grosvenor Hotel, close to Buckingham Palace. When the Duke was out of town she would tryst with the Prince of Wales. Mansfield Markham came from Kenya for the birth of Gervaise Markham in February.

In the London of 1929 flying became a very fashionable pastime. Both of Beryl's royal lovers became aviators and Beryl took some flying lessons before returning to Kenya in 1930. Karen Blixen's coffee farm was failing and about to be sold, and Denys Finch-Hatton, adored lover of both Karen Blixen and Beryl, was killed when his plane crashed at Voi.

This tragedy did not deter Beryl, and under the tutelage of her instructor and lover, Tom Campbell-Black, she gained a pilot's licence in July 1931. In 1933 she got her 'B' licence, which allowed her to work as a commercial pilot – the first woman in Kenya to do so.

One evening in the bar of the White Rhino in Nyeri a wealthy local flying enthusiast JC Carberry dared Beryl to fly solo across the Atlantic from east to west, 'against the wind'. Carberry offered to bankroll the flight. The feat had never been achieved in 39 previous attempts. Beryl ordered the recently designed Percival Vega Gull, a single-engined monoplane, from De Havillands at Gravesend. At the end of 1935 she flew to London in her Leopard Moth, hopping across Africa and Europe with Bror Blixen, a former lover and white hunter husband of Karen, as passenger. The *Daily Express* bought exclusive rights to Beryl's story and the audacity of the attempt allied to Beryl's beauty created a fever of interest as she waited patiently for fair weather. On 4 September the winds had dropped. Beryl, in a white leather flying suit and helmet, squeezed into the cramped cockpit with five flasks of coffee, some cold meat, dried fruit, nuts and fruit pastilles and a hip flask of brandy. There was no room for a life jacket. Edgar Percival, the plane's designer, swung the propeller. With a wave, Beryl rumbled down the runway and climbed slowly into the air. It was close to twilight, just before 1900. Edgar Percival shook his head and observed to onlookers: "Well, that's the last we shall see of Beryl".

After a flight of over 21 hours Beryl saw land, but she was on the last tank of fuel and the engine began to splutter. She selected a landing field but ditched in a Nova Scotia bog.

The Atlantic flight made Beryl a sensation in America – a crowd of 5000 awaited her flight to New York – there were press conferences, radio interviews, banquets and guest spots on comedy shows. This was all cut short when she learned that Tom Campbell-Black, her flying instructor, had been killed in a flying accident. Beryl sailed back to England. She filled in time with an affair with Jack Doyle, the Irish heavyweight boxer.

In 1937 she returned to America to do some screen tests for a film of her epic flight – which were not a success. While in California she met Raoul Schumacher, five years younger than Beryl, tall, born in Minneapolis, comfortably off and good company, who was working as a writer in Hollywood. They produced *West with the Night*, a memoir of Beryl's childhood and transatlantic flight. Although Beryl was credited as author, it seems clear that Raoul provided the structure and style. It was published in 1942 to excellent reviews and was on the best-seller lists. Ernest Hemingway judged it a 'bloody wonderful book'.

Raoul and Beryl married in 1942 but Beryl took a string of lovers and, in 1946,

Raoul moved out. Beryl continued to amuse herself in her accustomed manner, had a farewell fling with the singer Burl Ives, and in 1949 moved back to Kenya.

She stayed in the guest cottage of Forest Farm near Nanyuki, owned by the Norman family. Forest Farm was managed by a Dane, Jorgen Thrane, who became Beryl's lover. Beryl bought a small farm nearby and Jorgen managed that as well.

A trip to see her father in South Africa got her in the mood for training horses again. Back in Kenya she set to with a purpose, and over the next 15 years she was outstandingly successful, training winners for all the Kenyan Classic Races, and winning the Derby four times.

In 1965, the relationship with Jorgen waning, Beryl found a property in South Africa going for a song and she relocated her training stables there, but the move was not a success. Returning to Kenya in 1970, Beryl managed to get her trainer's licence back and she had some triumphs including a fifth Derby win. She carried on training until 1983, although the latter part of this period was marred by continual squabbles with jockeys, owners and the stewards.

The Jockey Club made her an honorary member and allocated her a cottage on the Ngong Racecourse. Interest in her book was revived and a reissue in 1983 sold over a million copies. Beryl enjoyed a revival of her fame as a celebrity and she was the subject of considerable television and newspaper interest. Greeting well-wishers with a cigarette in one hand and a tumbler of vodka in the other, however, she could be less than gracious to visitors.

Beryl died in 1986 and her ashes were scattered at Cemetery Corner on Ngong Racecourse.

Finch Hatton and various agricultural implements used to grade and roast coffee beans. The house was bought by the Danish government in 1959 and presented to the Kenyan government at Independence, along with the nearby agricultural college. The house is surprisingly small and dark but the gardens are quite special. Just up the road **Karen Blixen Coffee Gardens** (see page 64) are centred around the house of Blixen's farm manager.

Ngong Forest Sanctuary

ⓘ *Off Ngong Rd, 6 km from the city centre, the main gate is off Kibera Rd near the racecourse; there's another gate just after the Bomas of Kenya (below), T020-211 3358, www.ngongforest. org, 0800-1800, US$10, children (under 16) US$5.*

This sanctuary is a 620-ha piece of forest carved out of the larger Ngong forest characterized by indigenous trees interspersed with grassy patches, dams and streams. Here there are 120 bird species, 35 species of small mammal and numerous insects and reptiles. Because of its proximity to the Kibera slum (see box, page 50), there was a problem of trees being cut down by local people for firewood, but the sanctuary is now fenced with an electric fence and patrolled by KWS wardens. You can also visit on one of the free two-hour guided group forest walks held on Tuesday and Thursday; meet outside the restaurant at the Ngong Racecourse at 0900.

Bomas of Kenya

ⓘ *Forest Edge Rd, off Langata Rd, 2 km past the Main Gate of Nairobi National Park on the right, from Nairobi take the No 24 bus from the front of the railway station towards Karen, T020-891 391, www.bomasofkenya.co.ke, shows Mon-Fri 1430-1600, Sat-Sun 1530-1715, US$6.50, children US$3.25.*

A *boma* is a traditional homestead. Here programmes based on traditional dances of the different tribes of Kenya are presented. They are not in fact performed by people of the actual tribe but by a professional group called the **Harambee Dancers**. The dancers are colourfully dressed in full regalia and finish with a lively display of acrobatics and tumbling. The *bomas* form an open-air museum that shows the different lifestyles of each tribe. There is also a bar and a restaurant that serves *nyama choma* (grilled meat).

AFEW Giraffe Centre

ⓘ *Koitobus Rd, off South Langata Rd, Langata, from Nairobi take the No 24 bus from the front of the railway station towards Karen; it's a short walk from the top of the road, T020-891 658, www.giraffecenter.org, 0900-1730, US$8, children (3-12) US$3.60. The No 24 bus drops at the top of the road then follow the signs; you may walk into a giraffe as they cross the road to get to the nature reserve.*

Set in 6 ha of indigenous forest, this centre is 20 km out of the city near the **Hardy Estate Shopping Centre**. It is funded by the African Foundation for Endangered Wildlife and houses a number of Rothschild's giraffes. To date, the centre has rescued, hand-reared and released about 500 orphaned giraffes back into the wild. The Rothschild's giraffe is no longer threatened with imminent extinction having tripled in number and been successfully reintroduced to four of Kenya's national parks. Money raised by ticket sales is used to fund an education centre promoting conservation, visited by school children from all over Kenya. There is information about the giraffes on display, designed to be interesting to children. The young visitors' artistic interpretations of East African wildlife adorn the walls. You can watch and feed the giraffes pellets from a raised wooden structure, and children in particular will enjoy this experience. The centre is also an excellent spot for birdwatching and there is a short trail in a nature reserve across the road where you may well come across a giraffe.

Nairobi National Park

ⓘ *T 020-600 0800, www.kws.org, 0600-1800, entry is by Safari Card which can be obtained and loaded at the main gate, US$40, children (3-18) US$20. The main point of entrance is through Main Gate, at the Safari Walk and Animal Orphanage on the Langata Rd, although there are four other gates through which visitors can access the park: East Gate on the northeast of the park on the Embakasi Plain; Cheetah Gate at the far eastern edge of the park; Banda Gate on the western edge of the park; and Masai Gate at the south of the park near the Oloonjua Ridge.* Facilities at the Main Gate include an information centre, an office where you can buy and load Safari Cards for this and other parks, a shop selling drinks, snacks, souvenirs and an excellent map that corresponds to the road markers within the park, as well as the headquarters of KWS and the office of the safety and communication centre (see page 45). Almost all roads are navigable in a normal car or see page 77 for details of guided tours from Nairobi. Staff at the gate will advise on where there has been recent animal activity, especially lion and cheetah, which are monitored closely, and it takes three to four hours to get around. There is a picnic site and nature trail at Hippo Pools in the southeast of the park, where you can get out of your vehicle as there is an armed KWS ranger stationed here. The Animal Orphanage and the Safari Walk at the Main Gate can both be visited independently from the park.

④ Nairobi National Park

➔ **Nairobi maps**
1 Nairobi, page 40
2 Nairobi city, page 42
3 Nairobi centre, page 48
4 **Nairobi National Park, page 57**
5 Westlands, page 61

N
2 km
2 miles

Where to stay 🛏
Nairobi Campsite 1
Nairobi Tented Camp 2
Ole Sereni 3
Osoita Lodge 4

Restaurants 🍴
Carnivore 1
Haveli 2
Mister Wok 3
Pampa Churrascarius 4

Rangers 5

Bars & clubs 🍸
Simba Saloon 6

Nairobi National Park is so close to Kenya's capital city, it's not unusual to take a photo of a rhino browsing peacefully amongst the acacia thorn with a background of high-rise office buildings. The park covers 117 sq km, was established in 1946 and is the oldest in the country. It's only 7 km or a 20-minute drive from the city centre and most of its fences border Nairobi's suburbs with only the southern perimeter unfenced where some of the animals migrate into Masai grazing areas. Despite its proximity to the city, it is home to over 100 recorded species of mammal. Animals include the Big Five, except for elephant – the park is too small to sustain them, though you can see baby elephants at the David Sheldrick Wildlife Trust at the edge of the park (see page 60). You are also very likely to see zebra, giraffe, baboons, buffalo, ostrich, vultures, hippos and various antelope. This is one of the best parks for spotting black rhinos: the area is not remote enough for poachers, and the Park has proved to be one of the most successful rhino sanctuaries in Kenya.

The concentration of wildlife is greatest in the dry season when areas outside the park have dried up. Water sources are greater in the park as small dams have been built along the Mbagathi River. There are also many birds, up to 500 permanent and migratory species. To the south of the national park is the Kitengela Game Conservation Area and Migration Corridor leading to the Athi and Kaputiei plains. The herbivores disperse over these plains following the rains and return to the park during the dry season.

Apart from wildlife watching, the other point of interest is just a kilometre or two into the park from the Main Gate. The **Ivory Burning Site** is to the left of the road and is where on 18 July 1989 12 tons of confiscated ivory was burnt (see box, page 10). A mound of ash and an information board mark the spot. Back at the Main Gate, in the car park, look out for the Conservation Heroes Monument, which lists all the names of KWS employees who have died in the line of duty since the KWS was established in 1990. Some died in accidents, when they were relocating animals for example, while others died during armed battles with poachers or bandits.

Animal Orphanage ① *at the Main Gate of the Nairobi National Park, T020-600 0800, www.kws.org, 0900-1730, US$15, children (3-18) US$10.* Opened in 1963, this facility cares for orphaned and sick animals, which are brought from all over Kenya. Whenever possible they are released back into the wild, or, if that's not possible, relocated to the more spacious Safari Walk (see below), or if they are severely injured remain in the care of the orphanage for the rest of their lives. The centre is most popular at about 1430 when it is feeding time. When it was built, enclosures were quite cramped, but in response to criticism, the animals are now housed in more spacious accommodation in a more natural environment. If there are resident cheetah or lion cubs, visitors may be permitted to go into the enclosures for a close-up photograph.

Elephants never forget

David Sheldrick Wildlife Trust was established in 1977 and was named after the late naturalist who created Kenya's vast Tsavo East National Park. It is administered by his pioneering wife Daphne who developed the first elephant formula milk (within 24 hours of becoming orphaned, a calf less than two years old will die without milk). It took years for Daphne to perfect the formula, which has proved to be a massive success and brought new hope of survival for Kenya's vulnerable milk-dependent calves. Most of the infants that are brought to the nursery are between a few days and three months old. Some arrive severely traumatized and confused, often having witnessed the killing or trapping of their mother by poachers or farmers, or having been deserted by the herd, or else suffering from drought or sunburn. They go through an intense period of grieving for many months and are known to suffer depression and even cry. Survival depends on an individual's personality and willpower, but it is essential that the elephant, like any baby, is happy and feels safe and cared for.

It's not easy to hand-rear an elephant; they are complex feeders and it's difficult to duplicate a natural mother's nurturing and support. It takes endless patience by the keepers at the orphanage to teach a baby to suckle (the very young ones need to suckle every 12 minutes). These keepers become mother substitutes, providing all the care and attention a baby elephant needs whilst growing up. The calves are bottle-fed on demand, and the keeper provides a back or arm for the baby to rest its trunk while feeding. They also need to be taught how to use their trunks and ears, roll in the dust, bathe and cover their stools. (They have to learn to control their bowels, which can move up to 300 times a day!) In the wild the herd shelters the baby from the elements, but keepers provide hanging blankets for shade and as something warm to rub up against as if it was a mother's belly. They even apply sunscreen when necessary.

These foster parents are employed for the full two years that it takes a calf to be weaned off milk and remain with the babies 24 hours a day and provide a close physical relationship and constant companionship. The extraordinary dedication and amount of time it takes to raise an elephant by these people is remarkable. When the calves are no longer dependent on milk they are transported to Tsavo National Park and gradually released back into the wild. (Nairobi National Park is too small to accommodate elephant.) In the beginning the keepers remain nearby, keeping a safe distance so the elephants can return to them at any time. Elephants are naturally sociable animals and integrate well both with the wild herds and the ex-orphans, many of which have gone on to give birth in Tsavo.

Daphne Sheldrick has been involved in elephant conservation for over 30 years. Not only has she developed the milk formula, but recognized the sophisticated, almost human-like emotions and social needs of the calves. All her elephants now in Tsavo still recognize and retain a deep fondness for her and the keepers who acted as a foster family in their childhood. It seems that it is true when they say 'an elephant never forgets'.

"Animals are indeed more ancient, more complex, and in many ways more sophisticated than man ... perhaps the most respected and revered should be the elephant, for not only is it the largest land mammal on earth, but also the most emotionally human." – Daphne Sheldrick

Safari Walk ① *at the Main Gate of the Nairobi National Park, T020-600 0800, www.kws. org, 0900-1730, US$20, children (3-18) US$10.* This is a lovely 1.5-km walk through 18 ha of indigenous trees and vegetation full of birds and butterflies. It's completely wheelchair friendly, everything is well labelled and there are a number of interesting boards about Kenya's flora and fauna, conservation issues and the conflicts animals have with the environment and humans. The beginning of the walk begins on a concrete pathway, and this eventually rises on to an elevated boardwalk that goes to the edge of Nairobi National Park and overlooks a natural waterhole. Animals are housed not in cages, but on grassy mounds separated by moats so it's not zoo-like at all. Residents include lion, cheetah, leopard, pygmy hippo, rhino, plains game, hyena, ostrich, monkey, buffalo, two unusual albino zebras and the rare bongo antelope. It's a perfect introduction to Kenya's wildlife and children especially enjoy it. Attached is the **Rangers Restaurant** (see page 68).

David Sheldrick Wildlife Trust
① *Access via the Mbagathi Gate, Nairobi National Park (also signposted as staff/maintenance gate), Magadi Rd, T020-230 1396, www.sheldrickwildlifetrust.org, 1100-1200, US$3.50.*
On the edge of the Nairobi National Park lies this remarkable rescue centre for lost, abandoned and orphaned elephants run by Daphne Sheldrick, see box, page 59. The morning trip to the sanctuary involves watching the baby elephants, which are brought into an enclosure for perhaps a bath or a play with each other. It is an endearing experience and thoroughly recommended. It is a real treat to see a baby elephant trot along, trunk and ears flopping this way and that as they discover what they are supposed to do with them. It is like watching a playground full of kids – tearing around, chasing each other, playing, arguing and even standing in a corner and visibly sulking! Visitors are encouraged to adopt an elephant and souvenirs are sold in the shop.

Ngong Hills
① *Ngong, 25 km southwest of Nairobi, follow Ngong or Langata roads from the city centre, and the path into the hills starts about 1 km after the Ngong Police Station, where you can park. Alternatively, you can get a bus or matatu to Ngong, and once there, a boda-boda (motorbike taxi) to the police station.*
These undulating hills with four peaks, said to resemble knuckles, commonly numbered one to four (north to south) are located about 25 km to the southwest of Nairobi on the edge of the Great Rift Valley. Masai legend has it that the hills were created from a handful of earth that a giant clutched after falling over Mount Kilimanjaro. Partly wooded, the hills are no longer rich in animals, but zebra, giraffe and bush-buck maybe seen. Although steep in places, you can hike along the four peaks (allow three to four hours). Security can be an issue, and muggings have occurred here in the past, so it is advisable to go in a group. From the top you can look back from where you have come to see the skyline of Nairobi. The city centre with its skyscrapers is clearly visible and gradually peters out to the suburbs and farms. On a very clear day you can see Mount Kenya. Looking over in the other direction, towards the Great Rift Valley, you can see as far as 100 km.

Karura Forest Reserve
① *Kiambu Rd, 300 m after the turning to Muthaiga Golf Club; there's another entrance on Limuru Rd just after the Belgian Embassy, www.karurafriends.org, 0600-1830, US$6.50, children (under 16) US$2.20.*

Bordering the suburbs of Runda, Gigiri and Muthaiga about 5 km north of the city centre, this public urban forest opened in 2011, after a lengthy and much publicized conservation campaign led by tireless environment champion Wangari Maathai (see box, page 166), to stop the land being turned over to housing developments. The 1063 ha indigenous forest has nature trails and picnic sites, and is home to Syke's and vervet monkey, which are fairly easily seen, and other far more secretive forest species such as bushbuck, duiker, bush pig, genet and civet. Some 200 species of bird have been recorded, including the African crowned eagle, crested crane, silvery-cheeked hornbill, Hartlaub's turaco and numerous species of owl, dove and weaver. A bird list can be bought at the entrance gates. One of the more interesting walks is to the **Karura Caves and Waterfall**, which are well signposted. The caves near the Gitathuru River are reputed to have been used as a hideout by the Mau Mau during the fight for Independence, while a little further on, the 50-m falls cascade prettily over three shelves of rock.

5 Westlands

Nairobi maps
1 Nairobi, page 40
2 Nairobi city, page 42
3 Nairobi centre, page 48
4 Nairobi National Park, page 57
5 Westlands, page 61

Where to stay
Pride Inn 2
Sankara 3
Southern Sun Mayfair Nairobi 1
Pepper's 1
Phoenician 8
Tamambo 15

Restaurants
Addis Ababa 5
Alan Bobbe's Bistro 3
Bangkok 7
China Plate 6
Haandi 4
Mediterraneo 14

Bars & clubs
Gipsy 10
Havana 12
Hidden Agenda 9
Klub House 1 2
Mercury Lounge 11
Soho's 13

Nairobi listings

For sleeping and eating price codes and other relevant information, see pages 20-24.

Where to stay

There is an enormous range of hotels in Nairobi from luxury international chains with all the facilities to the most basic board and lodgings. Although numerous and cheap, the latter are best avoided as they are mostly in insalubrious city-centre locations, are not wholly clean and often double up as brothels. Nevertheless, there are a few good budget options in the city centre that are used to hosting international visitors and some backpackers' accommodation and campsites in the suburbs. The hotels out of town are more peaceful than those in the centre.

Nairobi centre *p47, maps p42 and p48*
$$$$ Inter-Continental, City Hall Way and Uhuru Highway, T020-320 0000, www.ichotelsgroup.com. A 5-star offering with 376 rooms on 7 floors, with a/c, satellite TV and internet, 4 restaurants and several

bars (some of which are listed below), casino, gym, sauna, jacuzzi and a 15-m swimming pool.

$$$$ Nairobi Serena, Kenyatta Av and Nyerere Rd, close to All Saints' Cathedral, T020-282 2000, www.serenahotels.com. Set in beautiful gardens, the **Serena** has a good reputation and is generally considered the finest hotel in central Nairobi, with 184 a/c rooms with Wi-Fi, satellite TV and great city views, a heated swimming pool, spa, shops, and 6 fine restaurants.

$$$$ The Norfolk, Harry Thuku Rd, T020-226 5555, www.fairmont.com/norfolkhotel. Built in 1904 and one of Nairobi's original buildings, this is a world-famous hotel with a lot of history (see page 47) and, as a result, many people who cannot afford to stay, drop in for a drink or afternoon tea. It has 165 luxury rooms, 6 restaurants and bars including the famous **Lord Delamere's Terrace**, see page 71, a heated pool and spa, all set in established tropical gardens.

$$$ Boulevard, Harry Thuku Rd, T020-222 7567, www.hotelboulevardkenya.com. A popular mid-range option, though the decor is now very old-fashioned and it could do with a refit, but in a great location only 500 m from the city centre and near the museum and Norfolk Hotel. The 70 rooms have balconies, fans and satellite TV, and there's a swimming pool, gardens, bar, restaurant and internet room. Virtually all the overland companies begin and end their tours here.

$$$ Fairview, Bishops Rd, Nairobi Hill, T020-288 1000, www.fairviewkenya.com. Peaceful and good value and makes a change from the larger tower block chain hotels, set in 2 ha of extensive tropical gardens, 100 rooms with satellite TV and Wi-Fi, the **Pango Brasserie** is an excellent terrace restaurant with its own underground winebar, café, large pool and gym.

$$$ Hilton, Mama Ngina St, T020-279 0000, www1.hilton.com. The circular 287-room Hilton is a landmark in the city centre. All rooms have a/c, satellite TV, Wi-Fi, and are soundproofed against the traffic noise.

Facilities include 4 restaurants, 1 pub with live entertainment, a heated pool, gym, sauna, steam bath and massage.

$$$ Laico Regency, Loita St, city centre, T020-221 1199, www.laicoregencyhotel. co.ke. A profusion of marble and gilt, with 194 rooms in a 12-storey block, with a/c, satellite TV, Wi-Fi, 3 restaurants, including the very good Indian **Sitar**, as well as bars, gym, swimming pool and a shopping arcade.

$$$ Nairobi Safari Club, Lillian Towers, University Way, city centre, T020-282 1000, www.nairobisafariclub.com. The foyer is palatial with marble, fountains and lots of greenery, and there are 2 restaurants, a popular 1st-floor bar, a heated pool, sauna and gym. The furnishings are becoming slightly worn, but the 147 rooms are nevertheless comfortable with satellite TV, and great city views from the top floors.

$$$ Panafric, Kenyatta Av, Nairobi Hill, T020-271 4444, www.sarova.com. A modern practical hotel, with 157 rooms with satellite TV and Wi-Fi. There's a swimming pool, spa and shop; the popular **Flame Tree** restaurant has a leafy terrace, and the café by the pool has a popular Sun brunch (see page 66).

$$$ Silver Springs, junction of Argwings Kodhek and Valley rds, Hurlingham, T020-272 2451, www.silversprings-hotel.com. A bit out of the way from the city centre but good mid-range option with 160 brightly decorated a/c rooms with satellite TV and Wi-Fi, Indian and Chinese dishes from the **Flagship** restaurant, bar with satellite TV for sports, gym, spa and pool.

$$$ Stanley, corner of Kenyatta Av and Kimathi St, T020-275 7000, www.sarova.com. This modern 8-storey tower block has a long history (see page 47). The celebrated outdoor **Thorn Tree Café** is found here, as is the good **Stanley Bookshop**. The 217 rooms have all mod cons and are attractively decorated. Facilities include valet parking, gym, a 5th-floor heated pool, bars and restaurants (see pages 66 and 67).

$$$-$$ Six Eighty, Muindi Mbingu St, T020-315 680, www.680-hotel.co.ke.

Very central with an unprepossessing appearance. 370 tired-looking but clean rooms, those at the back are the best option away from the noise from a disco across the road, shops, 2 restaurants, bar, casino, coffee shop. The staff are helpful and there are security guards on each floor.

$$$-$$ Upper Hill Country Lodge, T020-288 1600, www.countrylodge.co.ke. Next door to and run by the **Fairview** and sharing the same facilities, this is more modern and cheaper but has smaller and simpler rooms (a single starts from US$100 B&B) with satellite TV and Wi-Fi.

$$-$ Kenya Comfort Hotel, corner of Muindi Mbingu/Monrovia streets, T0722-608 866, www.kenyacomfort.com. Good location in one of the quieter sections of the city centre opposite Jevanjee Gardens; the Arusha/Moshi shuttle bus pickup/drop-off is across the road (see page 14). Friendly set-up and well used to budget travellers with 95 simple en suite, single, double, triple and quad rooms, plus 2 male and female dorms sleeping 6 in each, 1st-floor restaurant, bar (excellent cappuccinos), internet café and rooftop deck with good city views. Rates are either with or without a hot breakfast,

$$-$ Hotel Kipepeo, River Rd, T020-212 1528, www.hotelkipepeo.com. Newly built budget hotel on the slightly less busy part of River Rd close to the Akamba bus stand, with 56 rooms, reasonable modern

furnishings, satellite TV, hot showers, soundproofed windows, good security with CCTV in the public areas, restaurant and bar. Simple, clean and cheap, and much better than the numerous other board and lodgings in the area.

$ Milimani Backpackers, Milimani Rd, Nairobi Hill, T020-272 4827, www.milimani backpackers.com. Good and friendly set-up in an old 1940s stone house, with neat, clean dorms and doubles, good shared bathrooms, and parking and camping in the garden, where there are also a couple of permanent tents if you don't have your own, bar with open fire, BBQ area, meals available. The staff can book buses to Kampala and the Arusha shuttle, and organize Nairobi day tours. Also a good place to hook up with other travellers for budget safaris to the parks.

$ Nairobi Youth Hostel, 3 km out of town on Ralph Bunche Rd (which runs between Ngong Rd and Valley Rd), buses 28, 36, 40, and 42 from the Hilton drop off at the traffic police headquarters on Ngong Rd, then cross over and walk down Ralph Bunche Rd for about 500 m, T020-277 8046, www.yhak.org. You must be a member of the International Youth Hostels Association but can join here (US$11 per year). There are simple dorms or double bunk rooms and the shared bathrooms have sporadic hot water. It's reasonably safe, with café, lounge with TV, internet access, lockers, luggage storage and communal kitchen, but not wholly clean.

$ Parkside, Monrovia St, T020-333 348. Overlooking the Jevanjee Gardens in a relatively quiet part of the city, the 57 basic single, double and triple rooms have bathrooms with hot water. It's friendly and clean but there's no elevator so you may struggle with luggage up to the 3rd floor. There's a 1st-floor restaurant and bar for simple meals and beers, and an internet café. Usefully, the shuttle buses to/from Arusha/Moshi (see page 14) drop off across the road.

$ Terminal, Moktar Daddah St, T020-222 8817. Bare-bones basic but popular, central, reasonably secure, friendly staff, and rooms have clean bathrooms with hot water. As it's just off Koinange St, it can be noisy at night so ask for one of the back rooms, no breakfast but it's opposite Nakumatt supermarket which is open 24 hrs.

Around Nairobi *p53,*
maps p42, p57 and p61

$$$$ Giraffe Manor, Koitobos Rd, off South Langata Rd, Langata, reservations T020-251 3166, www.giraffemanor.com. Lovely 1930s red-brick, ivy-covered English country manor house, set in woodland and gardens next to the Giraffe Centre (see page 56). 6 beautifully decorated rooms with antiques and art deco bathrooms. It is perhaps the only place in the world where you can feed giraffe from your 1st-floor bedroom window, over the lunch table and at the front door. A double starts from US$720 and includes all meals prepared by a gourmet chef.

$$$$ House of Waine, Masai Lane, Karen, T020-891 820, www.houseofwaine.com. Boutique hotel 2 km from the Karen Blixen Museum set in 1 ha of gardens with heated swimming pool. There are 11 elegantly furnished rooms complete with 4-poster beds, Persian rugs and marble bathrooms, a comfortable lounge and bar with fireplace. Gourmet food includes rich afternoon teas and well-presented 3-course dinners.

$$$$ Karen Blixen Coffee Garden and Cottages, 336 Karen Rd, Karen, T020-882 138, www.karenblixencoffeegarden.com. Just up the road from the Karen Blixen Museum and set in gardens of indigenous trees and flowering bushes on an old settler's farm dating to 1906. The comfortable 1- to 2-bedroomed cottages have high ceilings, fireplaces, stone floors, pretty verandas, satellite TV and internet. There's a swimming pool and the **Tamambo** restaurant and garden bar (see page 68).

$$$$ Nairobi Tented Camp, Nairobi National Park, guests are transferred from the Main Gate, T020-260 3337, www.nairobitented camp.com. The first and only accommodation within Nairobi National Park and a typical safari-style tented camp set in a tranquil tract of forest in the middle of the park, with 8 comfortable en suite tents with veranda, lit by hurricane lamps. Hot water comes from a wood-burning stove, there's a central mess tent for meals and drinks are taken around a campfire. Excellent reports and a good option for families. Half-board rates start from US$610 for 2 including game drives.

$$$$ Ngong House, Induvo Lane, Karen, T020-891 856, www.ngonghouse.com. Set in woodland with views of the Ngong Hills, beautifully decorated rooms in 6 treehouses raised 5 m from the ground, plus 2 cottages for families and 1 room in the main house suitable for the elderly or disabled. Good 4-course dinners are eaten with the family in the thatched rondavel with fireplace. Penny Winter is an acclaimed fashion designer with a boutique in the garden.

$$$$ Sankara, Woodvale Grove, Westlands, T020-420 8000, www.sankara.com. Nairobi's new 5-star luxury hotel in the heart of Westlands just across from the Sarit Centre with 156 rooms, super plush decor and all mod cons. Special features include rain showers, DVD players and pillow 'menu', gym, international **Angsana** spa, stunning heated pool with wooden deck, gourmet food in 3 restaurants, deli and winebar, and a rooftop bar with great city views.

**$$$$ The Tribe – The Village Market
Hotel**, The Village Market, Limuru Rd, Gigiri,
T020-720 0000, www.tribe-hotel.com.
Award-winning contemporary and very
stylish addition to Nairobi and adjacent
to the **Village Market**. Chic decor with
African touches, 142 a/c rooms with Wi-Fi
and all mod cons, mood lighting and floor-
to-ceiling mirrors. The 24-hr **Epic** restaurant
serves continental cuisine, bars, pool, gym
and luxury spa.

**$$$$-$$$ Windsor Golf and Country
Club**, 9 km north of the city centre,
Ridgeways Rd off the Kiambu road, T020-
856 2300, www.windsorgolfresort.com.
Built in 1991 and modelled on a Victorian-
style English country hotel, 130 luxury rooms
with a/c, satellite TV, 4-poster beds, Wi-Fi,
some have fireplaces, extensive facilities
include a number of restaurants and bars,
health club, 18-hole golf course (in a forest),
squash and tennis courts and horse riding.

$$$ Macushla House, Nguruwe Rd, off
Gogo Falls Rd, Langata, T020-891 987,
www.macushla.biz. A small intimate and
friendly guesthouse within walking distance
of the **Giraffe Centre**. Just 6 rooms nicely
decorated with Afghan rugs and animal-
print fabrics, some have 4-poster beds, set
in pretty gardens with a pool and some
interesting modern sculptures, and there's
an excellent restaurant.

$$$ Ole Sereni, Mombasa Rd, 5 km before
Jomo Kenyatta International Airport,
T020-503 6000, www.ole-serenihotel.com.
Newly built hotel in a useful location
between the airport and city centre. The
134 rooms have all mod cons and views
towards the city or the Nairobi National Park,
but are quite small. Contemporary African
decor, restaurant, bar, gym, heated rooftop
pool. Mixed opinions so far and possibly
better suited to the business traveller.

$$$ Osoita Lodge, Nazarene University Rd,
1 km off the Magadi road, Ongata Rongai,
which is 7 km south of the turn-off from
Langata Rd, T020-263 3107, www.osita
lodge.com. On the edge of Nairobi National

Park and near the David Sheldrick Trust,
this fairly new lodge is a rustic and peaceful
out-of-town option and has 16 rooms
with balconies, satellite TV and Wi-Fi, in
an impressive double-storey stone and
thatched structure in gardens full of birds
and vervet monkeys. Pleasant restaurant
with outside tables and an extensive Indian
menu, bar popular for watching sports,
swimming pool, children's playground,
and BBQs are held here at the weekends.
Doubles from US$120.

$$$ Pride Inn, Westlands Rd, Westlands,
T020-374 0920, www.prideinn.co.ke.
Excellent value considering its Westlands
location; a double starts from US$125.
Smart rooms with satellite TV and a/c,
good range of facilities for a 3-star hotel
including large pool, bar, Wi-Fi in public
areas, and **The Royal Kitchen** has an
astonishingly long menu of Chinese,
Indian and continental dishes.

$$$ Safari Park Hotel & Casino, 15 km
north of the city centre in Kasarani on the
Thika Rd, T020-363 3000, www.safaripark-
hotel.com. A retreat for British army officers
during the colonial period and now
marketing itself as an inland resort with
204 rooms, 4-poster beds, satellite TV,
a/c and balconies with a view, 7 restaurants,
3 bars, casino, shops, gym and spa, pool
with an artificial beach, all set in 50 ha of
leafy grounds.

$$$ Southern Sun Mayfair Nairobi,
Parklands Rd, Parklands, T020-374 0920,
www.southernsun.com. Good offering from
quality South African chain in smart mock-
Tudor buildings in 12 ha of landscaped lush
gardens. 171 rooms with satellite TV, Wi-Fi
and classy furnishings, some with patios,
restaurant, poolside terrace café and bar, not
far from shops and restaurants in Westlands.

$ Karen Camp, Marula Lane, off Karen Rd,
Karen, T020-883 3475, www.karencamp.
com. Run by Dougie, an ex-overland driver,
with a good and lively bar, home-cooked
food, comfortable doubles in the main
house with or without bathrooms, dorms

with shared bathrooms in the outside buildings, plenty of grass for camping and overland vehicles in the 2 ha of gardens, excursions to the local attractions can be arranged.

$ Nairobi Campsite, Magadi Rd, Langata, T020-892 261. Excellent budget facilities set in a well-signposted secure compound not far from the turning off Langata Road with dorms and doubles in outbuildings with good hot showers and laundry facilities, internet, rustic thatched bar with pool table and food like burgers and chicken and chips, camping on well-kept lawns and parking for overland vehicles.

🍴 Restaurants

All the hotels have restaurants and bars, which are also very popular with non-guests. There are a number of superb individual restaurants but most of these tend to be out in the upmarket suburbs so you will need to take a taxi. For cheap eats in the city centre there are numerous food kiosks around River Rd and Tom Mboya St selling African and Indian food and snacks, and around the business district of the city between Kenyatta Av and City Hall Way there are plenty of coffee bars. There are also branches of quality South African fast-food chains dotted around the city centre and at petrol stations in the suburbs. **Debonairs** serves pizza and salads, while **Steers** offers burgers, ribs and chips. There are also a number of **Wimpys** and several branches of local **Kenchic Inn** for good chicken and chips costing around US$2.

Nairobi centre *p47, maps p42 and p48*
$$$ Café Maghreb, Nairobi Serena Hotel, see page 62. Open 1230-1500, 1900-2400. Popular hotel restaurant serving buffet and à la carte menus with stunning Moroccan decor, tables next to the swimming pool, and good city views. It's particularly busy on Fri evenings for its seafood buffet and for other themed buffet evenings include Mongolian

stir fries, Kenyan specialities and pasta. Coffee is poured from giant copper urns.
$$$ La Prugna D'oro, Inter-Continental Hotel, see page 61. Mon-Sat 1900-2230. Superb Italian cuisine from Italian chefs with a pricey but full menu of pasta, meat and seafood dishes, lovely decor with drapes and paintings, white tablecloths and fine china, and small outdoor terrace.
$$$ The Tamarind, National Bank building on Harambee Av, T020-251 1811, www. tamarind.co.ke/nairobi. Mon-Sat 1200-1400, 1830-2200. Nairobi's finest seafood restaurant (seafood is flown up from the coast daily) and best known for its lobster, giant crab claws and prawns, but fish like red snapper is also a good bet. Non-seafood eaters can opt for steak, duck, ostrich or quail. Set in a beautiful formal dining room with high ceilings and stained glass, with excellent ambience and service.
$$$ Thai Chi, at the Stanley Hotel, see page 62. Open 1200-1400, 1830-2200, no lunch on Sat. Nairobi's best Thai restaurant with traditional decor of Asian art, sculptures and Buddhas on the 1st floor of the **Stanley**, with very authentic food prepared by a Thai chef using plenty of lemongrass and coconut milk.
$$ Panda, 1st floor, Fedha Towers, Kaunda St, T020-340 855. Mon-Sat 1200-1500, 1800-2200. One of the best Chinese restaurants in the city, tasty food especially the Peking duck, lots of vegetarian options, elegant dining room with Chinese pottery and lattice screens. Not well signposted, you need to look up for the sign.
$$ Pool Garden, Panafric Hotel, see page 62. Open 1000-2300. Varied Kenyan buffet of traditional local food such as grilled tilapia fish, beef and *matoke*, offal and *kachumbari*, sautéed spinach and sweet potatoes. International dishes also available, next to the swimming pool, popular with families especially for Sun lunch.
$$ Trattoria, Kaunda St, T020-340 855, www.trattoria.co.ke. 0730-2400. Long-established Italian spread over 2 spacious

floors, with traditional decor, checked tablecloths, buzzing atmosphere and professional service. The menu of antipasti, soups, salads, grills, pasta, pizza and gooey desserts is huge, and there's a good selection of Italian wine and a deli counter.

$$-$ Dragon Pearl, Bruce House, Standard St, T020-251 1483. Open 1200-1430, 1830-2230. Rightly popular and one of the oldest Chinese restaurants in Nairobi with a full range of dishes including seafood, duck, lamb and pork, and attentive chefs who make dishes on request. The hot and sour soup is very good.

$ Kariokor Market, Racecourse Rd. Good and cheap local African food can be found at numerous stalls here, you eat with your hands, although utensils are provided on request. A specimen menu is goat's ribs, *ugali*, chopped spinach, *irio* made with peas, potatoes and sweetcorn, and the meat and fish is freshly cooked on charcoal grills.

$ Kowloon Garden, 2nd floor, Nginyo Towers, Koinange St, T020-318 885. Open 1100-1530, 1800-2230. Typical decor of hanging lanterns, round tables and fake flowers, standard but authentic food, try the Peking duck or steamed chicken; nothing fancy but it's cheap and close to the budget hotels around Mundi Mbingu St.

Cafés

Nairobi Dorman's, Jubilee Exchange building, Mama Ngina St, T020-253 299, www.dorman.co.ke. 0700-2000. Great coffee shop chain with branches at the Yaya Centre, Sarit Centre, Village Market, Westgate Mall, Karen Crossroads, Capital Centre and The Junction. The interiors are modern and they serve an excellent range of Kenyan and Tanzanian coffee, plus smoothies, shakes, sodas, sandwiches and pastries.

Nairobi Java House, Mama Ninga St, T020-313 564, www.nairobijavahouse.com. Mon-Sat 0700-2100, Sun 0800-2000. Similar to Dorman's (above), a chain of coffee houses with 10 other branches around Nairobi in the shopping malls and one at the airport,

serving excellent Java brand Kenyan coffee and tea in a modern bistro atmosphere. The menu offers generous portions of chilli con carne, salads, omelettes and burgers, and the breakfasts of bagels, pancakes and French toast are excellent.

Pasara Café, Lonrho House, Kaunda St, T020-225 0013. Mon-Fri 0730-1800. Good downtown venue for lunch where you can build your own sandwiches from baguettes and pittas, plus pastries, coffee, soups and some hot meals. Newspapers and magazines are available.

Railway Restaurant, at the station. 0700-2000. Cheap African food and basics like chicken and chips but the setting is everything. Decor as it always has been in a run-down sort of way with red linen tablecloths and silver-plated cutlery, and the atmosphere when a train is getting ready to depart is fantastic.

Thorn Tree Café, at the Stanley Hotel, see page 62. Open 24 hrs. Popular pavement bistro-style café famous for its message tree (see page 47). Varied menu with trendy coffees, sandwiches, pizzas, pastas and continental dishes, sometimes has live music in the evenings.

Around Nairobi p53,
maps p42, p57 and p61

$$$ Alan Bobbe's Bistro, 24 Riverside Dr, Westlands, T020-425 2000. Daily 1200-1530, Mon-Sat 1830-2200. Named after the original chef who established the restaurant in 1962, this is a Nairobi institution and a number of celebrities have eaten here over the years, including Barack Obama. It specializes in gourmet French cuisine and very good wines, the food and atmosphere are both excellent, very personalized service, lovely garden terrace.

$$$ Carnivore, Langata Rd, past Wilson Airport, T020-600 5933, www.tamarind.co.ke/carnivore. 1200-1430, 1900-2230, much later for the bars. This is a hugely popular complex of bars, restaurants and dance floors that's been going strong since

1980 and is on most tourists' itineraries to Nairobi. It specializes in meat, including game (warthog, antelope and crocodile), which is grilled on Masai spears over a huge charcoal fire; the waiters keep carving the various meats until you say stop by lowering the little white flag of surrender that is placed on the table. There's also a vegetarian menu. A fun night out and also a drinking venue and a nightclub (see Bars and clubs, page 71).

$$$ China Plate, Mpaka Centre, Westlands, T020-444 6144, and Chancery Building, Valley Rd, Nairobi Hill, T020-271 9194. Open 1230-1500, 1900-2230. Expensive but very good food and wine, with authentic Chinese decor and attentive service. They have been operating for almost 30 years and are best known for Szechwan cuisine and seafood, such as crab, calamari, langoustine, lobster and scampi; they also serve continental dishes.

$$$ Lord Erroll, 89 Ruaka Rd, off Limuru Rd, Runda Estate, T020-712 2433, www.lord-erroll.com. Tue-Sun 1200-1430, 1900-2130. Taking its name from the famous unsolved murder in colonial times of the 22nd Lord Erroll, this smart restaurant offers an exceptional garden setting and gourmet food such as Mongolian stir fry or BBQ prepared at your table, Italian and Oriental dishes, and the cheese fondue is a firm favourite. A pianist performs on Sun when there is a good-value buffet lunch for US$23. Among the most atmospheric places to eat in Nairobi with fine champagnes, wines and coffees, cranes stalk the grass, the bar is full of colonial memorabilia.

$$$ Nyama Choma, Safari Park Hotel & Casino, about 15 km north of the city centre in Kasarani on the Thika Rd, T020-363 3000, www.safaripark-hotel.com. 1900-2300. A similar concept to Carnivore (see above), and popular with tour groups, this is an all-you-can-eat grilled meat buffet served at your table, including game meat, with African-inspired decor, and entertainment from the colourful Safari Cats band and a nightly acrobatic show at 2100.

$$$ Rangers, Main Gate, Nairobi National Park, Langata Rd, Langata, T020-235 7470, www.rangersnairobi.com. 0700-2230. Set on the edge of the park in an ingenious wood and glass structure, this restaurant offers diners the opportunity to spot animals in the Safari Walk (see page 60) as they eat, and the Twiga Terrace overlooks a waterhole which is floodlit in the evenings. Good nyama choma plus Western dishes and BBQs, and popular with tour groups.

$$$ Tamambo, The Mall, Westlands, T020-444 8064, www.tamarind.co.ke/tamambo. Mon-Fri 1030-2230, Sat 1200-2230, Sun 1100-2230. Part of the acclaimed Tamarind restaurant group, this has very high standards and is stylishly decorated in African antiques and warm, earthy colours. The very good gourmet food includes baked local tilapia fish, seafood and African dishes, such as Moroccan tagines and Swahili curries.

$$$ Tamambo Karen Blixen Coffee Garden, up the road from the Karen Blixen Museum, 365 Karen Rd, T071-934 6349, www.tamarind.co.ke/tamambo-karen. 0600-2200. Charming restaurant set in what was Blixen's farm manager's house, oozing with colonial atmosphere. There's a formal dining room and bar, and at lunchtime, tables are laid out in the pretty grounds next to the fish pond. Very good service and food – a combination of the menus from the Tamarind in the city centre and the Westlands branch of Tamambo (see above) – and there's accommodation in garden cottages, see page 64.

$$$-$$ Haandi, The Mall, Westlands, T020-444 8294, www.haandi-restaurants.com. 1200-1430, 1900-2230. Excellent northern Indian cuisine, each dish is cooked to order and prepared with the utmost attention and you can watch the chefs in the glass-fronted kitchen. One of the best Indian restaurants in Kenya with branches in Kampala and London.

$$ Addis Ababa, Woodvale Place off Woodvale Grove, Westlands, T020-444 7321.

Mon-Sat 1200-1500, daily 1800-2300. Locally known as 'Das', an upmarket Ethiopian restaurant, with traditional decor of stools around low tables, personable service and regular live music and dancing (patrons are encouraged to participate). Stews and vegetable dishes are eaten off a woven platter and scooped up with *injera*, a sponge-like bread used as your eating utensil.

$$ Bangkok, Amee Arcade, Parklands Rd, Westlands, T020-375 1312. Open 1100-1500, 1800-2230. Very authentic Chinese, not Thai as the name suggests, specializing in seafood, the ginger garlic crab and pepper sautéed prawns are especially good. There's a full bar and takeaway service and it's deservedly popular.

$$ Blanco's, Timau Plaza, just off Argwings Khodek Rd, Hurlingham, T020-386 4670, www.blancos.co.ke. Mon-Sat 1200-1500, 1700-2300. Smart modern decor and popular with local business people for lunch, the menu here is traditionally Kenyan but with a modern twist, such as *tilapia* fish cooked in coconut sauce, oxtail or char-grilled lamb chops with mint sauce, served with chapattis, cassava and maize meal, and relishes like *kachumbari*. There's a good choice of imported wine.

$$ Haveli, Capital Centre, Mombasa Rd, T020-531 607. Open 1200-1430, 1800-2200. Sister restaurant to the excellent Haandi in Westlands, with a large venue, some outside seating and plenty of parking. The food is excellent quality and very authentic, all cooked from scratch by Indian chefs.

$$ Mediterraneo, The Junction, Ngong Rd, Dagoretti Corner, T020-387 8608, and Pamstech House, Woodvale Grove, Westlands, T020-444 7494, www.mediterraneo restaurant.co.ke. 1200-2300. Modern decor, outside tables and good service from staff in bow ties, with a long Italian menu, antipasti using imported parma ham and cheese, home-made pasta, pizza, seafood and meat, and desserts including (naturally) tiramisu.

$$ Osteria del Chianti, Nyangumi Rd, off Lenana Rd, Hurlingham, T020-272

3173. Open 1200-1600, 1900-2400. Well-regarded Italian with elegant decor, friendly atmosphere, some outside tables in the garden where fires are lit in the evening. There's a vast range of food from melon and parma ham or fish carpaccio to start, followed by pasta or pizza, and excellent home-made ice-cream. It's next door to **Casablanca** (see page 70).

$$ Pampa Churrascarias, Panari Sky Centre, Mombasa Rd, T020-820 601, www. pampagrillkenya.com. 1200-1500, 1800-2300. A *churrascaria* is a meat-roasting house in southern Brazil, and this serves all-you-can-eat cuts of meat grilled over open flames, plus a buffet of hot vegetables and salads which is suitable for vegetarians. Brazilian wines are on offer too.

$$ Phoenician, Karuna Rd, behind the Sarit Centre, Westlands, T020-374 4279. Mon-Fri 1030-1500, 1800-2300, Sat-Sun 1030-2300. Lebanese and continental dishes, pitta bread and pizzas cooked in a wood-burning oven, plenty of vegetarian options, mezzes with olives, hummus and the like and (oddly) a very good sushi bar.

$$-$ Pepper's, Parklands Rd, opposite the **Southern Sun Mayfair Hotel**, Westlands, T020-375 5267. Mon-Fri 1200-1500, 1800-2300, Sat-Sun 1200-2300. Specializes in Indian Tawa and Tandoor cuisine, but also has a chicken rotisserie and *shwarma* machine, and continental and Chinese dishes on the menu. You can eat in or outside the big house, it's a great family option with a kids' menu, indoor crèche and outdoor playground and sandpit.

$ Mister Wok, Capital Centre, Mombasa Rd, T020-559 376, www.misterwok.net. 1100-2200. Stylish, with simple black and red decor and Chinese lanterns, and close to the cinema in the Capital Centre. Good food that you can watch being cooked in woks in the open kitchen; try the fish in hot garlic sauce or Schezuan lamb, and lots of vegetarian choices.

$ Village Market Food Court, Limuru Rd, Gigiri, T020-712 2538, www.villagemarket-kenya.com. 0900-2000. Most of the shopping malls have food courts; the one at **Village Market** has numerous outlets for quality international and African cuisine, from German sausages and sauerkraut or Thai fishcakes, to Italian ice cream and Kenyan *nyama choma*. Communal tables are set out in the middle, fully licensed and popular at the weekends. There's an equally good set up at **Westgate Mall** (see Shopping, page 75).

♫ Bars and clubs

Nairobi

p42, maps p42, p48, p57 and p61
Eating, drinking and dancing are the most popular evening entertainments in Nairobi. There are a number of popular bars and clubs, many of which serve food if they're open during the day or in the early evenings, and many have stages for live music, but single men should expect a lot of attention from girls and prostitutes. There are numerous and very dodgy 'all day and night bars' around the River Rd area, where *miraa* chewing is common to liven up hard-core drinkers and fights are frequent. For sleeker and more sophisticated nightlife, head to Westlands. As with most establishments in Kenya, dress is casual with the exception of bars in the upmarket hotels. For the places with dance floors or live music, expect to pay a cover charge of US$3-7.
Aksum Bar, Nairobi Serena Hotel, Kenyatta Av, city centre, see page 62. Open 0800-2400. Upmarket cocktail bar with stunning Ethiopian decor and soothing lighting, offering savoury snacks and pastries, cocktails and specialist coffees, salsa sessions on Sat night and live jazz on Thu evening. Suited to a quieter, older crowd.
Casablanca, Nyangumi Rd, off Lenana Rd, Hurlingham, T020-272 3173. Open 1700-late. Bar and club with Moroccan-inspired decor and hookah pipes. Pricey but excellent cocktails, including a good Margarita, large dance floor that teems at the weekends,

good music. Outside the ground is covered in sand and there's a large bonfire. It's next door to the excellent **Osteria del Chianti** Italian restaurant (see page 69).
Cats Club, at the **Safari Park Hotel & Casino**, 15 km north of the city centre in Kasarani on the Thika Rd, see page 65. Open 1930-0300. A pub, disco, beer garden, karaoke bar, pool room and a snack bar, with a range of music from hip hop to R&B and rock and roll. Specials on most nights – airline crews get half-price drinks on Tue, for example.
CluBarn, at the **Ngong Racecourse**, Ngong Rd, T020-434 7508, www.clubarn.com. 1700-late. Large venue and part of the Nairobi Jockey Club at the racecourse, with indoor and outdoor bars, dance floor and stage, large-screen TVs for sports events, and snacks like pizza and *nyama choma*.
The Exchange Bar, **Stanley Hotel**, corner of Kenyatta Av and Kimathi St, city centre, see page 62. Open 0930-late. Comfortable lounge with leather sofas and elaborate drapes, plasma TVs and a wide range of drinks. The Nairobi Stock Exchange operated from here for 37 years from 1954 and there are early photos and memorabilia on the walls.
Gipsy Bar, Woodvale Grove, opposite Barclays Bank, Westlands, T020-444 0964, www.gipsybar.com. 1200-1500, 1800-late. There are 4 back-to-back bars here, decorated in a Spanish theme and consistently popular, especially with expats. Lots of atmosphere, infectious Latin and flamenco music, delicious tapas, packed on weekend nights, a DJ plays on Fri.
Havana Bar, Woodvale Grove, Westlands, T020-445 0653, www.havana.co.ke. 1200-late. Lively bar and restaurant with a bright red interior and Latin theme, with Latin and Brazilian music, snacks and cigars, occasional live bands, and long cocktail menu, including a good Mojito.
Hidden Agenda, Sarit Centre, Westlands, T020-374 3872. Open 1000-late. Cosy laid-back bar with comfortable lounge areas, the menu features continental dishes and grills,

including good flame-grilled steaks, and there's an extensive choice of drinks.

Jockey Club, Hilton Hotel, Mama Ngina St, city centre, see page 62. Mon-Sat 1200-2400, Sun 1600-2400. Very popular British-style pub with dark wood, booths, paintings of jockeys and horses on the walls, beer on tap and a pub menu of sandwiches, steaks, burgers and savoury snacks.

Klub House 1, Ojijo Rd, Parklands, T020-374 9870, www.klubhouse.co.ke. 0800 till the early hours. In a striking double-storey timber building, K1 has pool tables upstairs, and dance floors and bars downstairs, and is also a popular spot for watching football on the large-screen TVs. It regularly hosts bands.

Library Bar, Windsor Golf Hotel & Country Club, 9 km north of the city centre on Garden Estate Rd, see page 65. Open 0700-late. Elegant upmarket wood-panelled hotel bar that's open until the last person leaves, with barmen in black ties, occasional live music and a dance floor, and an excellent selection of cocktails, aged malt whiskies and cigars.

Lord Delamere's Terrace, The Norfolk, Harry Thuka Rd, city centre, see page 62. Open 0600-2300. A popular spot for Kenya's white settlers from 1904, who used to come to the terrace bar for gin and tonics. Named after Lord Delamere, one of the earliest and unofficial leader of the white settlers, whose reputed party trick was riding into **The Norfolk** on horseback and shooting down bottles off the bar. A man of honour, he would have any damages added to his bill. Very atmospheric, continental food served, and the **Tea Room** is also a fine place for an afternoon cuppa.

Mercury Lounge, ABC Place, Waiyaki Way, Westlands, T020-445 0378, www.mercury lounge.co.ke. Mon-Thu 1230-0200, Fri-Sun 1700-0200. Tasteful, modern and spacious bar, with fabric-covered walls and moody lighting, tapas-style snacks, martinis and cocktails, and a DJ plays later in the evening.

The New Florida, Koinange St, T020-221 5014, and **Florida 2000**, Commerce House, Moi Av, T020-222 9036, www.floridaclubskenya. com. Both of these city-centre clubs have been going strong now for more than 30 years and literally heave at the weekends. They have excellent sound systems and lights and stay open until 0600, and the all-night restaurants serve Kenyan and Chinese food. These are fun places to visit and are certainly real eye-openers, but it is best to visit in a group and don't take anything valuable with you. Prostitutes abound and think nothing of putting hands in trousers, and have been known to rob tourists. **The Florida** is probably where the term 'the Nairobi handshake' comes from (use your imagination)! Rather amusingly, security is run by the FBI (Florida Bouncers International).

Safari Bar, Inter-Continental Hotel, City Hall Way, city centre, see page 61. Open 1700-0100. Comfortable pub atmosphere with good service and a dance floor, different music each night, very popular Salsa nights on Wed and Fri with a Latino band and a DJ on Sun.

Simba Saloon, Carnivore, Langata Rd, T020-501 709, www.tamarind.co.ke/simba-saloon. Wed-Sun 2100-0400. A huge club with numerous bars, a massive dance floor with stage for live bands, and an outside concert venue in the gardens, where well-known African music stars and US rappers can play to over 15,000 people. A fun night out after eating at the restaurant (see page 67), check the website to see what's on. A **Carnivore** must-do is to try a *dawa* – vodka, crushed ice, sugar and lime served with a stick coated with honey; it means 'medicine' in Kiswahili.

Soho's, Maua Close, Westlands, T020-374 5710. Open 1800-late. Stylish bar/club with bright, yellow, orange and purple decor, popular with an expat crowd, good selection of wines and cocktails, shisha pipes, Mexican snacks, dance floor downstairs and a VIP lounge upstairs.

Tacos Club, Kimathi St. 1000-late. Simple downtown bar that is popular with business people for quick cheap lunches and the informal upstairs bar. Has a balcony that overlooks the traffic and a TV showing sport. Serves shakes and juices as well as booze. In the evening the tables are pushed aside for dancing.

☻ Entertainment

Nairobi *p42, maps p42, p48, p57 and p61*
Nairobi has a good range of entertainment, and the arts scene has particularly come into its own in recent years. To find out what's on, check the local papers, especially the *Daily Nation*, or visit the excellent website of *Nairobi Now*, www.nairobinow.wordpress.com, which is a useful blog on arts and cultural events around the city. *Kenya Buzz*, www.kenyabuzz.com, is another good source of information.

Arts centres
The Go Down Arts Centre, Dunga Rd, industrial area next to **CMC Motors**, T020-555 770, www.thegodownartscentre.com. Home of the **Kuona Trust** (www.kuonatrust.org), a non-profit organization that supports and promotes the arts in marginalized communities in Kenya. This centre brings together visual and the performing arts under one roof and has a theatre, a puppet workshop, rehearsal space for dancers, an acrobat school, a recording studio, a web-design school, a number of studios for artists and exhibition space. Check the website or local press for what's on, which can be anything from poetry recitals, hip hop competitions, art, sculpture or photography exhibitions, dance, a battle of local bands or lectures. This is an excellent venue and gives the opportunity to see Kenya's contemporary side of art and culture; a far cry from the usual trinkets seen in the touristy souvenir shops or 'traditional' dancing shows in the coastal hotels.

Casinos
There are several places advertising themselves as casinos dotted around the city centre, but many of these are just seedy slot-machine joints. The nicest proper casinos with gaming tables, waiter service and bars, are the **RKL Casino**, in the Inter-Continental, on City Hall Way, and the **Paradise Casino**, in the Safari Park on Thika Rd. These open about 1200 for the slot-machines and from 1700 for the gaming tables and stay open until 0300 or 0400. Passports are required for entry and US$ cash and credit cards are accepted.

Cinemas
Movie listings can be found in the *Daily Nation*. Tickets cost around US$7. **20th Century**, Mama Ngina St, city centre, T020-338 070; **Century Cinemax**, Prestige Plaza, Ngong Rd, Kilimani, T020-802 2073; **Fox**, Thika Rd, Ruaraka, T020-85602 3293, a drive-in; Capital Centre, Mombasa Rd, T020-201 7101, and the Sarit Centre, Westlands, T020-375 3025, www.foxtheatres.co.ke; Nairobi, Uchumi House, Moi Av, city centre, T020-241 614; **Nu Media**, Westgate Mall, Westlands, and Village Market, Gigiri, T072-062 1111.

Theatre
Check the Thu and Fri editions of the *Daily Nation* and the websites above for what's on. The **Kenya National Theatre**, opposite the **Norfolk Hotel**, Harry Thuku Rd, T020-222 0536, has productions, but the best option is the **Phoenix Players**, Phoenix Theatre, Parliament Rd, T020-222 5506, www.phoenixtheatre.co.ke, who are the most active theatrical company in the city. They produce a range of drama of a very high standard and perform something new about every 3 weeks at their 120-seat theatre. The **Alliance Française**, see page 83, also hosts performances.

○ Shopping

Nairobi *p42, maps p42, p48, p57 and p61*
Bookshops
As well as the bookshops listed below, the museum shops in both the **Nairobi National**

Museum (page 51) and the **Karen Blixen Museum** (page 53) have an excellent range of books on East Africa including the classic stories like *Out of Africa* and *Man-eaters of Tsavo*. There are also a couple of decent bookshops at the airport selling books that will appeal to tourists.

Books First, Ukay Centre in Westlands, and in most branches of the larger **Nakumatt** stores across the city. An excellent bookshop chain, with a good selection of imported books, and cafés with decent coffee, alcoholic drinks and internet access.

Legacy Books, Yaya Centre, Hurlingham, The Mall, Westlands, and on the ground floor of the Kenya International Conference Centre, city centre,www.legacybookshop. net. A comprehensive range of books including a good selection of East African fiction and books covering development issues, plus CDs of Kenyan music. The flagship store at the Yaya Centre also has a café with Wi-Fi.

Silverbird Media Stores, The Junction, Dagoretti Corner, Ngong Rd, and Westgate Mall, Westlands. A wide range of books, DVDs, CDs and computer games.

The Stanley Bookshop, entrance not from the hotel but on Kenyatta Av, T020-212 776. A good selection of fiction and non-fiction, as well as maps, guidebooks and coffee-table books. Staff are helpful.

Text Book Centre, Kijabe St, city centre, Sarit Centre, Westlands, and Galleria Mall, Langata Rd, www.textbookcentre.com. As the name suggests, sells text books but also has a good range of other books, cards and stationery. It sponsors the biannual **Jomo Kenyatta Award for Literature**, which is open to Kenyan writers.

Clothing

Visitors might want to take home the all-purpose lengths of cotton cloth called *kikoys* and *kangas*. The *kikoy* is striped and comes from the coast, while the *kanga* has patterns and mottos in Kiswahili printed on the hems. They are sold all over Kenya, but there is a

good selection in the cluster of shops selling material on Biashara St, quite close to the City Market. Here you can also watch tailors on their foot-propelled machines sewing clothes, cushions, etc and stitching some of the most elaborate embroidery at amazing speed. *Kikoys* are now marketed by the **Kikoy Company**, www.kikoy.com. As well as being used as sarongs, they have fashioned the material into other items of clothing, including bikinis, bags, cushions and other accessories, which can be bought at Kenya's upmarket curio shops and online; **Kenya Airways** also carries some products in their duty free selection. There are lots of places that will kit you out in traditional safari gear. **Colpro**, Balfour House, Kimathi St, city centre, T020-222 4430, is recommended as good quality and reliable.

Curios and crafts

There are a huge number of souvenir shops in Nairobi and they vary enormously in terms of price and quality. Be sure to have a good look – wood that may look like ebony may in fact just have been polished with black shoe polish. Also cracks may appear in the wood (particularly when placed in a central-heated room), if it has not been properly seasoned. At stalls you will be able to bargain the prices down to between a third and a half of the original asking price. In the city centre there are a number of very similar curio shops on Muindi Mbingu St and the other streets around the City Market, while more specialist shops are in the outlying suburbs and can be visited on the way to one of the sights, such as the **Karen Blixen Museum**.

African Art Shoppe, Hilton Hotel Shopping Arcade, Mama Ngina St, city centre, T020-222 2074, www.allthingsafrican.com. 0900-1900. An upmarket shop with a fine selection of antiques, oil and watercolour paintings, carvings, batiks and sculptures. Expensive but of the highest quality.

African Heritage, at the **Carnivore** restaurant (see page 67), T020-530 054, www.africanheritage.net. Mon-Sat 0900-1700, Sun 1000-1600. A vast collection of original works of art and tribal sculptures from all parts of Africa, and authentic artefacts from Kenya. There are 6 lines of jewellery and hand-painted beads, and it also has shops in Zanzibar and Paris.

Collectors Den, Hilton Hotel Shopping Arcade, Mama Ngina St, city centre, T020-226 990, www.collectorsdenkenya.com. 0800-1800. A good selection of wooden and soapstone carvings, batiks, engraved glass – wine glass sets with the Big Five on them for example – and just about every other kind of Kenyan souvenir.

Gallery Watatu, 1st floor, Lonhro House, Standard St, city centre, T020-221 5321, www.gallerywatatu.com. Mon-Fri 1000-1700. Showcases contemporary African paintings and has changing exhibitions in the spacious and well-lit formal art gallery and plenty of pieces for sale at the back.

House of Treasures, 70 Dagoretti Rd, Karen, T020-388 3224, www.treasureskenya.com. 0930-1730. Despite its distance from the city centre, African art lovers should head here for the carefully chosen pieces from all over Africa, including antique tribal items, such as bridal corsets and Ashanti stools from Ghana, cowrie shell baskets from Ivory Coast, and ceremonial masks from the Congo. There's also a wide selection of Africana books.

Kazuri Beads, branches at the Capital Centre, Mombasa Rd, Galleria Mall, Langata Rd, Village Market, Gigiri, The Junction, Dagoretti Corner, Ngong Rd, Westgate Mall, Westlands, and on the coast in the Diani Shopping Centre, head office T020-232 8905, www.kazuri.com. This company has been going since 1975 and from the outset has provided jobs for women in need, especially single mothers with no other source of income. Clay is purchased from small farmers in the highland region of Muranga, northwestern Kenya, and the women make it not only into colourful beads, but also a stunning range of hand-thrown pottery and ceramics.

Kitengela Glass, on the edge of Nairobi National Park, beyond the David Sheldrick Wildlife Trust, 9 km off Mgadi Rd, T020-675 0602, www.kitengela-glass.com. Mon-Sat 0800-1700, Sun 1100-1600. It's well worth coming out here for this beautiful sculpture garden, riddled with mosaic pathways leading to the artists' studios, who turn recycled glass and other materials into statues, vases, jewellery and homeware. There are some wonderful items for sale in the shop. Also branches at Village Market, Gigiri, and The Junction, Dagoretti Corner, Ngong Rd.

Matbronze, Langata South Rd, Langata, T020-891 251, www.matbronze.com, phone for an appointment. A fine-art foundry and gallery selling unique bronze wildlife statues by acclaimed sculpture artist Denis Mathews.

Rupas, Uganda House, Standard St, city centre, T020-222 4417. Mon-Sat 0900-1730. An outstanding selection of gift purchases, good quality, courteous staff and competitive prices.

Zanzibar Curio Shop, York House, Moi Av, city centre, T020-222 2704. Open 0800-1800. Crammed from floor to ceiling with curios, and prices are reasonable, but as they are marked, there's no haggling. Established in 1936, it sells batiks, jewellery, safari wear, Arabian chests, sisal baskets, ebony carvings and African semi-precious stones.

Markets

City Market, Muindi Mbingu St, Mon-Sat 0700-1800. Located in a greying and, in some parts, crumbling art-deco building, this sells fruit and vegetables, fish, meat and flowers, and the many curio stalls stock armies of wooden giraffes amongst other crafts. Around the market and the Jamia Mosque, other stalls sell baskets, wooden and soapstone carvings, bracelets and lots of other souvenirs. Be prepared to bargain and go in late afternoon, as prices are lowest just before they close.

Kariakor Market, Racecourse Rd, Ngara. A huge sprawling congested market selling everything imaginable from fresh produce to household goods; it is perhaps the best place to buy sisal baskets. Watch out for pick-pockets here.

Masai Market, Tue, Westgate Mall, Westlands; Wed, Capital Centre, Mombasa Rd; Fri, Village Market, Limuru Rd, Gigiri; Sat, outside the Law Courts in City Square, city centre; Sun, Safari Park Hotel, Thika Rd, Kasarani, and Yaya Centre, Argwings Kodhek Rd, Hurlingham, Gigiri, 0800-1800. This is an open-air market that rotates between the car parks of shopping malls and other locations with more than 350 traders and artists selling contemporary as well as traditional crafts, such as trendy beaded sandals, handbags, cushions, etc. Prices are reasonably low and bargaining is expected.

Shopping malls

Opening hours are listed for shops; restaurants and other facilities stay open longer in the evening.

Capital Centre, Mombasa Rd, T020-556 176, www.capitalcentre.co.ke. Mon-Sat 0930-1730, Sun 1000-1700. Good range of shops, including an **Uchumi** hypermarket, plus a cinema, restaurants and a food court.

Galleria, Langata Rd, T020-444 8085, www.galleria.co.ke. Mon-Sat 0930-1730, Sun 1000-1700. A smart new mall just after the Magadi road turning and close to the Bomas of Kenya (see page 56) with restaurants, a food court, banks and 80 shops, including a branch of **Nakumatt**.

The Junction, Dagoretti Corner, Ngong Rd, T020-387 2881. Mon-Fri 0830-1800, Sat 0900-1700, Sun 1000-1600. Pleasant shopping centre that has become a social hub in Nairobi with some good restaurants and coffee shops, a cinema, a **Nakumatt** supermarket, and a number of small gift shops and boutiques.

Karen Crossroads, junction of Langata and Ngong rds, Karen. Mon-Fri 0830-1800,

Sat 0830-1600, Sun 1000-1300. Small mall serving the upmarket Karen and Langata communities, with a **Nakumatt** supermarket, restaurants and coffee shops, curio and clothes shops and banks.

Sarit Centre, Parklands Rd, Westlands, T020-374 7408/9, www.saritcentre.com. Mon-Fri 0800-2000, Sat 0900-1700, Sun 1000-1600. Vast shopping complex on 3 floors with an exhibition hall hosting regular trade fairs, shows and other events, a food court, internet cafés, a branch of **Uchumi** supermarket, a cinema, and the biggest community notice board in the city.

Village Market, Limuru Rd, Gigiri, T020-712 2488, www.villagemarket-kenya.com. Mon-Sat 0900-1800, Sun 0900-1600. Nairobi's glitziest mall has been laid out to resemble (as the name suggests) a village, with over 160 shops, an **Uchumi** supermarket, another supermarket where diplomats can buy duty-free goods, and a central food court with outside seating (see page 69), which is phenomenally popular at the weekends and is a local haunt for UN people, as the UN HQ is just around the corner. Recreational facilities include a 12-lane 10-pin bowling alley, a cinema, a pool hall, an outside playground and curly waterslides for kids.

Westgate Mall, Mwanzi Rd, off Waiyaki Way, Westlands, T020-374 6172, www.westgate. co.ke. 0800-2000. Nairobi's most modern mall with 80 shops, including international brands and South African chain stores, as well as a 24-hr **Nakumatt** supermarket, plus banks, restaurants and a food court, and within walking distance of the Sarit Centre.

Yaya Centre, Argwings Kodhek Rd, Hurlingham, T020-271 3360/1, www.yaya-centre.co.ke. Mon-Sat 0930-2000, Sun 1000-1800. Smart mall on 4 floors with specialist food shops, restaurants, food court, an internet café, bookshops, several clothes and gift shops, and the useful **Xtreme Outdoors** shop that sells camping and outdoor equipment like binoculars, thermal underwear and backpacks.

Supermarkets

Nakumatt, www.nakumatt.net. Kenya's largest supermarket chain. The hypermarket branches sell just about everything from household goods, furniture and books, to electronics, camping equipment, and clothes. As well as the ones already mentioned in the shopping malls above, there is also a branch between Monrovia and Moktar Daddah streets near the **Kenya Comfort Hotel** in the city centre, and another on Uhuru Highway opposite the Nyayo Stadium. Both are open 24 hrs.

Uchumi, www.uchumi.com. This is the other supermarket chain with branches in the Sarit Centre, Capital Centre and the Village Market among numerous other locations.

⏾ What to do

Nairobi *p42, maps p42, p48, p57 and p61*
Athletics
The **Nairobi Marathon**, www.nairobi marathon.com, is in Oct. Established in 2003, every year it gets more popular and now attracts some 20,000 participants from Kenya and all over the world. There's a full and half marathon for runners and wheelchair users, plus shorter family runs, and for spectators it's a marvellous opportunity to see Kenya's famed runners. The marathon starts at **Nyayo National Stadium** and goes along Uhuru Highway, turns at the University Way roundabout into Kenyatta Av, follows Harambee Av and Haile Selassie Av, back to Mombasa Rd and finishes inside the stadium.

Cricket
Nairobi Gymkhana and Simba Union Club, next to each other off Forest Rd, Parklands, T020-374 1310. For details of fixtures, visit www.cricket-kenya.com. The Gymkhana pitch is Kenya's main cricket venue, seating 7000, and is home to the national team. The cricket season is Jun-Feb.

Go-karting
GP Karting, near the **Carnivore** restaurant, T020-600 8444, www.gpkarting.co.ke. Tue-Sun 1000-1900, US$15 for 10 mins. Helmets and suits are provided and there's a computerized timing system plus a sports bar on site.

Golf
There are a number of very well-kept golf courses in the suburbs of Nairobi. Most welcome visitors and a round costs in the region of US$25-30; clubs and caddies can be hired. Information about all of Kenya's 40 golf courses can be found on the **Kenya Golf Union**'s website: www.kenyagolf network.co.ke. An advantage of playing golf in Nairobi is that, because of the high altitude, the ball travels some 10 m further than it would do at sea level.

Karen Country Club, Karen Rd, Karen, T020-388 2802, www.karencountryclub. org. This is famous for its beautiful 18-hole, 72-par championship course and colonial clubhouse with lawn terrace. The flowering indigenous bushes and trees along the fairways give the course the look of a lovingly cared-for garden. It was founded in 1933 by the Karen Estates Company Ltd.

Kenya Railways Golf Club, Lower Hill Rd, Nairobi Hill, T020-272 1859. This 9-hole course was established in 1922 for the staff of the Uganda Railway and is a fun course to play, especially if you are lucky enough to have your game coincide with a train passing through the course.

Muthaiga Golf Club, Kiambu Rd, Karura Forest, 10 km to the northeast of the city centre, T020-376 1253, www.muthaiga golfclub.com. This 71-par, 18-hole golf course was first laid out in 1912, and is today home to the Kenya Golf Union and plays host to the most prestigious golfing event in the country, the Kenya Open.

Royal Nairobi Golf Club, Kibera Rd, off Ngong Rd, T020-272 5768, www.royal nairobigc.com. Established in 1906, the club got its royal prefix when King George V played a round of golf here in 1936. The 72-par 18-hole course is one of the longest in Kenya.

Windsor Golf and Country Club, 9 km north of the city centre on Garden Estate Rd, T020-856 2300, www.windsorgolfresort. com. Another stunning well-tended course, the upmarket resort is best suited to people on specific golfing holidays. For accommodation here, see page 65.

Horse racing

Ngong Racecourse, Ngong Rd, T020-387 3944, www.jockeyclubofkenya.com. The Jockey Club of Kenya holds meetings most Sun except in Aug. This is a wonderful setting as well as being a great place to observe all sections of Nairobi society. It's also good for children, with extra activities including face painting, camel rides and bouncy castles, and there's a good choice of food from *nyama choma* to a buffet restaurant. There's also a 9-hole golf course in the middle of the racetrack (T020-240 5125, daily 0630-1800), with a pro-shop where clubs can be hired.

Rugby

Kenya Rugby Union Football Club, Ngong Rd, Jamhuri, T020-237 0360, www.kenya rfu.com. The club was established in 1923 and today hosts the Safari Sevens in Nov, a major international competition and one of the most popular rugby sevens in the world. It's also a major event on the Nairobi social calendar.

Swimming

Most of the big hotels have swimming pools that can also be used by non-residents for a daily fee of about US$3, or for free if eating at one of the poolside restaurants.

Ten-pin bowling

Superbowl, The Village Market, Limuru Rd, Gigiri, T020-712 2488, www.villagemarket-kenya.com, 0830-2200, US$3.

Tours and tour operators

There are a number of minibus tours for either a morning or an afternoon, arranged by any of the tour companies in Nairobi and they pick up from hotels. City centre tours last around 3 hrs, while half-day tours take in the Nairobi National Park, or combine the sights in the western suburbs such as the Karen Blixen Museum, Giraffe Centre and David Sheldrick Wildlife Trust. The cost can vary, but averages around US$60-70, and US$100-120 for Nairobi National Park. For walking tours of Kibera, see box, page 50.

For longer safaris, there are numerous tour operators based in Nairobi. It is important to find an operator that you like, which offers good service and does not pressurize you into booking something that is not what you are looking for. You can find more at **Kenya Association of Tour Operators**, www.katokenya.org. See below for recommended companies.

Acacia Safaris, 4th floor, College House, corner of University Way and Koinange St, city centre, T020-341 997, www.acacia safaris.co.ke. Offers a full range of lodge and camping safaris with regular departures, plus day trips around Nairobi.

Adventure Penfam Tours & Travel, Summit House, Moi Av, city centre, T020-374 1299, www.penfamtours.com. Broad selection of lodge and camping safaris including birdwatching tours.

AustralKen Tours & Travel, 8th floor, Sonalux House, Moi Av, city centre, T020-243 3508, www.australken.com. Nairobi day trips and lodge and camping safaris from 2-14 days.

Best Camping Tours and Safaris, 1st floor, I & M, Towers, corner of Kenyatta Av and Muindu Mbingu St, T020-374 9661, www. bestcampingkenya.com. Well-established company offering a half-day trip to Nairobi National Park, plus camping and lodge safaris and tailor-made packages.

Bike Treks, T020-214 1757, www.biketreks. co.ke. Organizes good value walking/cycling tours, supported by a back-up vehicle, including a 3-day Rift Valley lakes safari.

Breakaway Expeditions Africa, Thika Rd, T020-811 004, www.breakawayexpedition. com. Nairobi excursions, day trips to Amboseli and Nakuru, and longer safaris to the parks.

Bunson Travel, Pan Africa House, Standard St, city centre, T020-222 1992, www.bunsontravel.com. Good, reliable, well-established travel and tour agent. Offers flight and rail bookings, car hire, safaris and hotel bookings, as well as a number of day trips in and around Nairobi.

Bush and Beyond/Bush Homes of East Africa, T020-600 457, www.bush-and-beyond.com and www.bush-homes.co.ke. Reservations for some of the more exclusive camps, including in the Masai Mara and Laikipia Plateau, all in excess of US$500 per person per night.

Bushtroop Safaris, Sonalux House, Moi Av, T020-316 645, www.bushtroop-safaris. com. Nairobi excursions including a day trip to Lake Nakuru, park safaris using Serena/ Sarova/Sopa lodges. They can also arrange car hire and book Arusha shuttle buses.

Call of Africa Safaris, 3rd floor, Uganda House, Kenyatta Av, city centre, T020-229 729, www.call-of-africa-safaris.com. Tailor-made safaris using top-end lodges including the Serena chain, can finish in Mombasa.

Cheli and Peacock Safaris, T020-60 3090, www.chelipeacock.com. Represents some of the most upmarket small lodges and tented camps and can arrange 8-10 tailor-made flying safaris between them.

Dallago Tours and Safaris, T020-387 2845, www.dallagotours.com. Park safaris using mid-range lodges and Mt Kenya climbs, can also book flights and hotels.

Express Travel, ground floor, Vedic House, Mama Ngina St, city centre, T020-222 0908, airport T020-822 348, www.expresstravel. co.ke. General travel agent with an office in the arrivals hall at Jomo Kenyatta International Airport. Also an agent for

Europcar, and can organize tailor-made road and flying safaris for a minimum of 2 people.

Gametrackers, 5th floor, Nginyo Towers, Moktar Daddah St, city centre, T020-222 2703, www.gametrackersafaris.com. Well-established company organizing camping safaris with both vehicles and camels to Lake Turkana and the Ndoto mountains, as well as biking and walking safaris. The 8- and 10-day trips to Northern Kenya are probably the best and most affordable on offer. They go to the Kalacha Desert, Lake Turkana and Maralal, including a camel safari. They also offer a number of Nairobi day trips.

Gamewatchers, Village Market, Gigiri, T020-712 3129, www.porini.com. A good selection of short road or flying safaris to the parks using tented camps.

Going Places, Westlands Centre, Mapaka Rd, Westlands, T020-444 2312, www.going placeskenya.com. General agent for booking tailor-made safaris and beach holidays.

Hoopoe Safaris, inside Wilson Airport, T020-604 303-4, www.hoopoe.com. Consistently recommended and has an excellent commitment to the local communities and conservation. Offers a range of luxury safaris, climbs and unusual trekking itineraries in Kenya, Tanzania and Uganda.

Kenya One Tours, 84, Riverside Dr, Westlands, T020-445 3318, www.kenya onetours.com. Good all round tailor-made tour operator that can arrange all accommodation, safaris and flights. Kenyan and German run.

Malaika Tours, Ukulima Cooperative House, Haile Selassie Av, city centre, T020-215 7732, www.malaikaecotourism.com. Day tours around Nairobi and longer tours to the parks with cultural experiences included, such as visiting a Masai *manyatta*.

Menengai Holidays, Bunyala/Lower Hill Rd, Upper Hill, T020-273 3702, www.menengai holidays.com. Offers a range of tours from Nairobi excursions to longer camping and lodge safaris and mountain-climbing trips.

Mountain Rock Kenya, Jubilee Insurance House, junction of Wabera St and Kaunda St, city centre, T020-224 2133, www. mountainrockkenya.com. As the name suggests, organizes mountain climbs and hikes including Mt Kenya and the Abedares.
Origins Safaris, T020-229 009, www.origin safaris.info. A special-interest safari operator with 40 years' experience based in Kenya but covering much of East Africa. Main areas of expertise are safaris and cultural expeditions using a combination of private lodges and camps and its own mobile tented camps.
Savage Wilderness Safaris Ltd, Sarit Centre, Westlands, T020-712 1590, www.whitewater kenya.com. Whitewater rafting and kayaking on several Kenyan rivers, including a day trip from Nairobi to the Tana River for around US$100 (see page 176 for more details).
Savuka Tours and Safaris, Pan Africa House, 4th floor, Kenyatta Av, city centre, T020-221 5256, www.savuka-travels.com. Good-value budget camping safaris and mid-range lodge safaris to all the parks plus Nairobi ½-day tours and a Lake Nakuru day trip.
Shoor Safaris, Corner Plaza, Parklands Rd, Parklands, T020-374 5690, www.shoortravel. com. Excellent well-established tour operator, offering a variety of safaris, all of which can be customized. Also offer a full hotel-booking service in Kenya, Tanzania and Zanzibar. Also has a branch in Nakuru.
Somak Safaris, T020-535 508, www.somak-nairobi.com. Safaris using Serena lodges, Nairobi ½-day trips and a full-day Nakuru/Naivasha tour.
SunTrek Tours and Travel, Safari Centre, Waiyaki Way, Westlands, T020-444 2982, www.suntreksafaris.com. Excellent tour operator that organizes tailor-made lodge safaris, plus adventure activities such as trekking, including Mt Kenya climb and scuba diving on the coast, also can combine with safaris to Tanzania.
Tobs Golf Safaris, T020-271 0825, www. kenya-golf-safaris.com. Golf specialist that combines hotel accommodation with bookings and transfers to golf courses.

UNIGLOBE Let's Go Travel, 1st floor, ABC Place, Waiyaki Way, Westlands, T020-444 7151, Karen Crossroads, Karen, T020-388 2505 (as well as offices in Uganda), www.uniglobeletsgotravel.com. A well-run company that organizes travel all over East Africa, it acts as agent for several other companies and publishes price and information lists of hotels, camps and lodges as well as car hire.
Victoria Safaris, www.victoriasafaris.com. Good choice of day tours to the usual city sights, plus the Bomas of Kenya, Kibera and Ngong Forest.

⊙ Transport

Nairobi *p42, maps p42, p48, p57 and p61*
Nairobi is fairly central to Kenya and unless you are flying directly to the coast for a beach holiday, most people pass through the city. It's also popular for getting to the parks of the Northern Circuit in Tanzania, as Nairobi is closer than the airport at Dar es Salaam and there are regular transport links between Nairobi and Arusha in northern Tanzania. For getting around the city there are plenty of cheap buses, *matatus* and taxis.

Air
The main airport is **Jomo Kenyatta International Airport**, T020-661 1000, www.kenyaairports.co.ke, 15 km southeast of the city, connected by a good dual carriageway. It costs US$0.75 per car to get into the airport (included in the price of a taxi). There is also **Wilson Airport**, 6 km south of the city, on Langata Rd, T020-501 943, www.kenyaairports.co.ke, from which smaller planes, including many internal charter flights, leave. See page 42 for further details including transport to and from the airports.

The following airlines offer daily scheduled flights. Specific schedules are detailed under each relevant chapter. For details of international airlines serving Nairobi, see page 11.

All tickets can also be bought directly from desks at the airports. **Kenya Airways** has daily flights from Jomo Kenyatta International Airport to **Kisumu**, **Malindi**, **Lamu** and **Mombasa**, as well as a number of regional destinations. **Fly 540** has flights from Jomo Kenyatta International Airport to **Eldoret**, **Kakamega**, **Kisumu**, **Kitale**, **Lamu**, **Lodwar**, **Malindi**, **Mombasa**, and **Entebbe** in Uganda, and **Dar es Salaam** in Tanzania. From Nairobi to **Zanzibar** flights go via either Dar or Mombasa. From Wilson Airport they have flights to **Amboseli**, **Masai Mara**, **Nanyuki** and **Samburu**.

Air Kenya has flights from Wilson Airport to **Amboseli**, **Lamu**, **Lewa Downs**, **Malindi**, **Masai Mara**, **Meru**, **Mombasa**, **Nanyuki** and **Samburu**. They also fly to **Kilimanjaro** in Tanzania, and from here code share with Tanzania's **Regional Air** for flights to the lodges in the Serengeti and other Northern Circuit parks.

Safarilink has flights to **Amboseli**, **Kiwayu**, **Lamu**, **Lewa Downs**, **Masai Mara**, **Nanyuki**, **Samburu** and **Tsavo**, and to **Kilimanjaro** in Tanzania.

Airline offices

Air Kenya, Wilson Airport, T020-391 6000, www.airkenya.com. Air Uganda, 5th floor, Jubilee Insurance House, Wabera St, T020-313 933, www.air-uganda.com. Air Zimbabwe, Chester House, Koinanage St, T020-339 522, www.airzimbabwe. com. British Airways, International House, Mama Ngina St, T020-327 7000, www. britishairways.com. Emirates, 20th floor, Viewpark Towers, Monrovia St, T020-329 0000, www.emirates.com. Ethiopian Airlines, Bruce House, Muindi Mbingu St, T020-311 649, www.ethiopianairlines. com. Fly 540, Laico Regency Hotel, Loita St, city centre, T020-243 211, ABC Place, Westlands, T020-445 3252, airport T020-827 521, www.fly540.com. Kenya Airways, 5th floor, Barclays Plaza, Loita St, city centre, T020-327 4747, airport T020-642 2000, www.kenya-airways.com. KLM, Barclays Bank Plaza, Loita St, T020-327 4210, www. klm.com. Safarilink, Wilson Airport, T020-600 777, www.flysafarilink.com. South African Airways, International House, Mama Ngina St, T020-224 7342, www.flysaa.com.

Bus
Local

Most city buses are run by **Kenya Bus Service (KBS)**, T020-222 3235, www.kenya bus.net. The main city bus terminal is located at the end of River Rd and there are main bus stands outside the Hilton Hotel on Moi Av, outside Nation House on Tom Mboya St, outside the Railway Station at the end of Moi Av, and outside the General Post Office on Kenyatta Av. The buses cover all the routes and operate as early as 0600 and as late as 2400, and each bus has an assigned route number. Useful numbers are: **34** to the airport from the Hilton stop, **24** to Karen via Langata Rd past the main gate of Nairobi National Park and the Bomas of Kenya, and **111** to Karen and on to Ngong via Ngong Rd past Dagoretti Corner, both from the Hilton stop and from in front of the Railway Station. Most buses are pale blue, but increasingly newer green City Hoppers are appearing on the streets. Fares are US$0.25 for a short hop to US$1 to the furthest outlying suburbs.

Long distance

The long-distance bus station is on Landhies Rd from where buses go from Nairobi to all the upcountry towns, Western Kenya and Mombasa. There are at least daily departures to almost every destination, but generally buses from here can't be pre-booked and go when full so you will have to arrive at 0700 or earlier, and wait until the bus fills up and departs. There are also a number of coach companies with scheduled timetables; there is a clutch of offices along and around Accra Rd to the east of the National Archives. These include **Coastline**, **Goldline**, **Guardian Coach**, **Kensilver Express**, **Easy Coach** and **Cross Road Travellers**, but recommended for long-distance journeys is **Akamba Bus**, Lagos Rd, T020-222 5488, www.akambabus.com, a private company offering a very good level of service and you can pre-book tickets. It is not the cheapest option but the buses are fairly well maintained and they have a good safety record. Timetables can be found on the website; for example buses to Mombasa depart daily at 0900 and 2100 and take 9 hrs and cost around US$12. The area around River Rd where the bus station and offices are located is unsafe. Beware of robbery and look after your luggage at all times.

There are also daily services to neighbouring countries. **Akamba Bus** has 3 departures to **Kampala** (Uganda) US$23, at 0700, 1930 and 2130, taking 13 hrs. **Akamba** also operate a Royal Service on this route, where the buses carry fewer passengers, have slightly bigger seats and are generally more comfortable, which departs at 0715 and costs US$30. The buses cross the border at Busia or Malaba where immigration procedures are completed, see page 151 for further details. **Scandinavia Express**, River Rd, T020-242 523, www.scandinaviagroup. com (an equally good Tanzanian company), also operates on the Nairobi– Kampala route, with daily departures at 2130. **Kampala Coach**, River Rd, T0718-703 300, www.kampalacoach.com, is the best of the Ugandan companies on the Nairobi– Kampala route, with daily departures at 0700, 0900, 1000, 1300 and 1930.

Akamba and Scandinavia Express depart Nairobi daily at 0630 for **Dar es Salaam** (Tanzania) via **Arusha** and **Moshi** and arrive in Dar at around 2030, US$35-45. The border at Namanga is efficient and visas can be purchased, see page 220 for further details. Akamba and Scandinavia Express also run services to **Musoma** and **Mwanza** on Lake Victoria in northwestern Tanzania via **Nakuru** (3 hrs), US$22, departing Nairobi daily at 2130 and taking 13½ hrs.

Shuttle There are daily shuttle services to and from Nairobi and **Arusha** (for Tanzania's Northern Circuit parks) and **Moshi**

(to climb Kilimanjaro), from where you can get onward buses to **Dar es Salaam**. See Essentials, page 14, for more details of these services. The operators utilize 20- to 30-seat buses with comfortable individual seating, and drivers assist passengers through the Namanga border crossing. They pick up at the major hotels or the airport by prior arrangement or meet the bus outside the Parkside Hotel (see page 64), on Monrovia St at least 15 mins before departure, especially if you have bulky luggage. They depart Nairobi each day at 0800 and 1400, and take about 5½ hrs to Arusha (US$30), and 6½ hrs to Moshi (US$40). These services can be arranged through hotel receptions, through a tour operator or directly through the downtown offices or websites: **AA Shuttles**, 2nd floor, Trust Mansion House, Tubman Rd (opposite the City Market), T020-213 6332, www. aashuttles.com; **Regional Luxury Shuttle**, 4th floor, Windsor House, corner University Way and Muindi Mbingu St, T020-356 9048, www. regionalluxuryshuttle.com; **Riverside Shuttle**, Pan Africa Insurance House, Kenyatta Av, T020-229 618, www.riverside-shuttle.com.

Car
Cars can be rented easily in Kenya, with or without a driver. You will usually need to be over 23 years of age and have a driver's licence. Driving in Nairobi is a bit of an art and you will have to get used to lots of roundabouts with rather bizarre lane systems. The right of way is usually (but not always) given to traffic already on the roundabout. Be prepared for a lot of hooting, traffic-light jumping and the odd pothole, and watch for *matatus* as they can break very suddenly to pick up passengers. Away from the city centre, driving in the suburbs where there is a lot less traffic is very straightforward. Parking is a problem in the centre and you will be pestered by parking boys but there is no need to pay them to ensure the safety of your vehicle. However on some downtown streets, there may be council parking attendants

during business hours who will charge a few shillings per hour and write a ticket to display in your windscreen. There are several multi-storey car parks around the city centre including at the **Inter-Continental Hotel** (around US$3 per hr).

Car hire

Rates vary, so shop around for the best deals. For more information see Getting around, page 17.

Active Car Hire, 4th floor, Standard Building, Wabera St, city centre, T020-221 0531, www.activecarhire.com.

Avis, College House, University Way, city centre, T020-316 061, airport, T020-338 6420, www.avis.com.

Budget, Travel House, opposite **Six Eighty Hotel**, Muindi Mbingu St, T020-496 1200, airport, T020-822 370, www.budget.com.

Budget Car Hire Kenya, Kingsway Nairobi Centre, University Way, city centre, T020-358 1027, www.budgetcarhirekenya.com.

Bushtroop Safaris, Sonalux House, Moi Av, T020-316 645, www.bushtroop-safaris.com.

Central Hire a Car, Six Eighty Hotel, Muindi Mbingu St, city centre, T020-222 8888, www.carhirekenya.com.

Cruising Cruisers, corner of Ngong and Karen roads, Karen, T0736-219 639, www.cruisingcruisers.com.

Europcar, airport, T020-822 625, www.europcar.com.

Glory Car Hire, Glory House, Moi Av, city centre, T020-231 3564, www.glorykenya.com.

Rent A Fine Car, Nyangumi Rd, off Lenana Rd, Hurlingham, T020-271 1288, www.rentafinecar.com.

Shoor Safaris, Corner Plaza, Parklands Rd, Parklands, T020-374 5690, www.shoortravel.com.

UNIGLOBE Let's Go Travel, 1st floor, ABC Place, Waiyaki Way, Westlands, T020-444 7151, Karen Crossroads, Karen, T020-388 2505, www.uniglobeletsgotravel.com. Acts as agent for several other companies and has comprehensive car hire information on the website.

Matatu
Local

Matatus are assigned to set routes within the city and are usually 14-seater minibuses. They collect as many passengers as possible from the outset and along the way, and passengers board and alight wherever they choose. *Matatus* normally have a crew of 2; a driver and a 'tout' who tries to encourage as many passengers as possible to board, and collects their fares. The vehicles are mostly white with a yellow stripe and their destination painted along the side. Also, although it is often flaunted, they are legally only permitted to carry a maximum of 14 passengers on seats with seat belts. They tend to be driven recklessly and drivers will think nothing about driving over central reservations and along pavements to get somewhere quicker. Most *matatu* rides within Nairobi cost around US$0.40.

Long distance

Matatus run to destinations such as **Nakuru**, **Naivasha** and the **Namanga** border with Tanzania; the main long-distance *matatu* stage is between Tom Mboya St and River Rd. There are regular departures and they go when full. For longer distances you need to swap *matatus* in the regional centres to get any further. They are driven recklessly, road accidents are common and there's the added problem of petty theft, so only use these as a last resort. There are regular shuttle buses to **Arusha**, see page 81; it's cheaper to do the journey in stages by *matatu* but takes a lot longer and is not advised if you've got luggage (see above).

Taxi

Taxis park up outside shopping malls, restaurants, hotels and at official taxi stands; they are easy enough to find on street corners and any hotel can get one for you. It is recommended that you should always take a taxi to get around at night. A taxi to the airport costs approximately US$20. Although some taxis are metered, they may not always work, so it's best to agree a price with the driver before setting off. Although they start with a higher price, they don't intentionally try to rip you off, and if you offer a price that's too low, they simply won't accept the fare. A short journey within the city centre should cost around US$5, and a longer journey to the suburbs US$15-20. Like *matutus*, most Nairobi taxis are marked with a yellow line along each side. There is also a fleet of large black London taxis. There are also several taxi companies that you can order by phone and these tend to have more modern vehicles and can pre-arrange airport transfers (although all hotels will do this). Alternatively, if you find a taxi driver you like, take his cell phone number.

Train
Nairobi Railway Station, T020-221 0885, is to the south of Haile Selassie Av, at the very end of Moi Av. For details of the train services between Nairobi and Mombasa and Nairobi and Kisumu, see box, page 18. It is essential to make reservations in advance and this can be done at the stations or through a tour operator. You need to check in at least an hour before. There's a left luggage office at the station (US$1.40 per item) and you can wait at the Railway Restaurant (see page 67).

Tuk-tuk
The 3-wheeled auto-rickshaws or tuk-tuks of southeast Asia are becoming increasingly popular as taxis in Nairobi. Like taxis, fares need to be negotiated in advance. They cost around US$3 for a short journey, but as they are open, there is the added disadvantage of getting a lung full of traffic fumes, and they don't go very fast so are only suitable for the shortest journeys.

ⓘ Directory

Nairobi *p42, maps p42, p48, p57 and p61*
Cultural centres
Regular films, concerts and talks are on offer, and in some, libraries and language courses. The Alliance Française and the Italian Cultural

Centre are particularly good venues for the arts. Alliance Française, Loita St, city centre, T020-340 054, www.afkenya.or.ke; British Council, Upper Hill Rd, Nairobi Hill, T020-283 6000, www.britishcouncil.org; Goethe Institute, Maendeleo House, Monrovia St, city centre, T020-222 4640, www.goethe.de/ins/ke/nai; Italian Cultural Institute, Woodvale Grove, off Waiyaki Way, Westlands, T020-445 1226, www.iicnairobi.esteri.it.

Embassies and consulates
For foreign embassies and consulates in Nairobi, see http://embassy.goabroad.com.

Immigration
Nyayo House, Kenyatta Av, T020-222 022, www.immigration.go.ke, Mon-Fri 0830-1230 and 1400-1530.

Medical services
Hospitals The 2 main private hospitals both have world-class facilities: Nairobi Hospital, Argwings Kodhek Rd, Nairobi Hill, T020-284 5000, www.nairobihospital.org; Aga Khan Hospital, Parklands Av, Parklands, T020-374 2531, www.agakhanhospitals. org. The Kenyatta Hospital, on Hospital Rd, Nairobi Hill, T020-726 300, is well equipped, but as a public hospital, has long queues.
Pharmacies These are found all over downtown Nairobi and in all shopping malls but are generally expensive. The major hospitals have 24-hr pharmacies.

Police
Police emergency T999; Central Police Station, University Way, city centre, T020-225 685; other police stations can be found on www.kenyapolice.go.ke. Always inform the police of any incidents – you will need a police statement for any insurance claims.

Tourist helpline
Run by the Kenya Tourism Federation at the Kenya Wildlife Services (KWS) complex at the main gate of the Nairobi National Park, Langata Rd, T020-800 1000, www.ktf.co.ke.

Contents

At a glance

◉ **Getting around** Safaris from Nairobi to the parks and lakes; self-drive; buses and *matatus* link the towns; fly-in or drive-in safaris to the Masai Mara.

◉ **Time required** From Nairobi 1 week for the lakes and parks at Naivasha, Nakuru, Bogoria and Baringo; at least 2 nights in the Masai Mara.

◉ **Weather** Overall, the climate is gentle with temperatures rarely above 25°C. Cool season is May-Sep.

◉ **When not to go** Possible all year round, but roads in the Masai Mara deteriorate rapidly in the wet seasons (Nov-Dec, Mar-May).

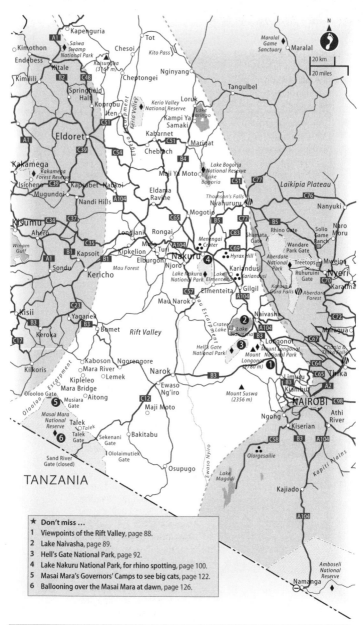

★ **Don't miss ...**
1 Viewpoints of the Rift Valley, page 88.
2 Lake Naivasha, page 89.
3 Hell's Gate National Park, page 92.
4 Lake Nakuru National Park, for rhino spotting, page 100.
5 Masai Mara's Governors' Camps to see big cats, page 122.
6 Ballooning over the Masai Mara at dawn, page 126.

The Great Rift Valley is one of the most dramatic features on earth, stretching some 6000 km from the Dead Sea in Jordan down to Mozambique in the south. In Kenya, the Rift Valley starts at Lake Turkana in the north, and runs right through the centre of the country. Up to 100 km wide in places, the floor is littered with the famous Rift Valley lakes, such as Nakuru, Naivasha, Baringo and Bogoria, which are surrounded by fascinating cliffs, escarpments, rivers and arid plains. These support an enormous diversity of wildlife, birds, trees and plants. The valley floor rises from around 200 m at Lake Turkana to about 1900 m above sea level at Lake Naivasha to the south.

In the south of the region the Masai Mara, bordering the Serengeti in Tanzania, is one of the most exciting game parks in the world, teeming with wildlife and the site of the quite spectacular wildebeest migration. It is also the most likely place in Kenya to see lions.

No visit to Kenya is complete without spending some time in the Rift Valley. The scenery here is wonderful, with Mount Kilimanjaro acting as the perfect backdrop to miles of arid savannah plains covered with fragile grasslands and scrub bush. Evaporation has left a high concentration of alkaline volcanic deposits in the remaining water. The algae and crustaceans that thrive in the soda lakes are ideal food for flamingos and many of these beautiful birds are attracted here, forming a truly spectacular display.

Naivasha and around

Lake Naivasha is a popular weekend destination from Nairobi, which is 90 km away or about a 90-minute drive, and there are some excellent accommodation options around its shores. The drive there is very pleasant too, with good views of the Rift Valley, and Moi South Lake Road runs through pretty countryside and flower farms. In recent years, wildlife numbers in the region have increased, thanks to better protection and some re-stocking projects on the private sanctuaries and reserves. It's also a region where there are no large predators, so walking is an option in Hell's Gate National Park and Crescent Island Game Sanctuary. To stroll among zebra and giraffe is a delightful experience. ▸▸ *For listings, see pages 94-97.*

Nairobi to Naivasha → *For listings, see pages 94-97.*

Getting there

The road that connects Nairobi and Naivasha is the **A104**. It is tarred, although potholed, and can be very busy with trucks, since it's the main artery between the country's capital, the Rift Valley and ultimately Uganda. This heavy traffic makes it a dangerous route with a high accident rate, so take care if driving. The A104 is the starting route for many safaris, so many of visitors get their first sight of the Kenyan landscape from here. Your first glimpse of the huge Rift Valley emptiness is likely to be from the **viewpoints** just past Limuru, at the top of the escarpments of the valley. Below, the acacia-scattered Kedong Valley bed conveys a neat and archetypal snapshot of the African landscape. Further away, you get a glimpse of Mount Longonot, Hell's Gate National Park and Lake Naivasha, while the plains seem to sweep on forever to the south. To the north of Naivasha, the A104 continues on to Nakuru.

From the old Nairobi–Naivasha road (**B3** – the more westerly road), which forks to the left at Rironi, the road continues in a northwesterly direction for approximately 6 km then turns left on a sealed tarmac road in a southwesterly direction around Mount Longonot. It then leads to the small town of Narok, see page 117, the main access point to the Mara. Some interesting diversions along this route are listed below.

Mount Suswa

From Nairobi, after a drive of about 17 km, a small dirt road leads to the south towards Mount Suswa, 2357 m, an easily accessed volcano in the heart of Masai country only 50 km outside Nairobi. It is not as well known as Mount Longonot to the north. The outer crater has been breached on the southern and eastern sides by volcanic eruptions, and numerous lava flows are visible. This whole area is honeycombed with lava caves and there are many examples of obsidian pebbles and rocks. One of the caves, over 20 km long, is believed to be the longest in Kenya. The caves are home to several small mammals including bats, snake owls, rock hyrax and squirrels, and birds. If you visit the caves, take care as there are some concealed drops in the cave floor.

With a 4WD, it is possible to drive up to the outer of the two craters, approximately 10 km in diameter. The caldera floor is richly covered with grasses, from which the volcano takes its name. The Masai graze their cattle in this peaceful enclosure, also home to a variety of game. The ring-shaped inner crater has a diameter of approximately 5 km and is covered with dense vegetation. There is a large central lava plug. The inner crater edge offers a good ridge walk of about 1½ hours to the main summit, **Ol Donyo Onyoke**. Circumnavigation of the crater rim is possible, but can take up to eight hours because of the difficulty going over the sharp lava blocks and fields in the southeast section of the crater. It is possible to camp in the caves, but you must bring all supplies, including water, with you.

Kiambu and Limuru → *Colour map 1, A4.*

An indirect route to Naivasha, which need not add more than an hour to your overall journey time (if in your own car), is via Kiambu, a one-way commuter town, and **Limuru**, a lively market town. The drive to Kiambu is hilly but smooth, through corridors of high trees and past the **Windsor Golf and Country Club**. Although neither town is particularly attractive, the Kiambu–Limuru road provides a quite beautiful 30-minute drive through lush, fertile land full of rich tea and coffee plantations, and dotted with the elegant, umbrella-like thorn trees.

This area is on the lower slopes of the Aberdares, and the soil and climate are ideal for growing coffee, which was introduced in 1902. The action of water from many streams flowing southeast from the Kinangop Mountain (3900 m) to join the Athi River has divided the area into sheer ridges and deep valleys. There are several waterfalls in the higher areas.

It is also the centre of one of the main Kikuyu clans (the other is based on Nyeri). The Kiambu Kikuyu were particularly powerful during the presidency of Jomo Kenyatta, who came from this clan. Many displaced Masai refugees settled in this area after the Masai civil wars at the end of the 19th century, and in time intermarried with the Kikuyu people.

Naivasha → *Colour map 1, A4. Phone code: 050.*

Naivasha is a small trading centre just off the main road from Nairobi to Nakuru and is well equipped with banks and ATMs, shops and petrol stations. It was traditionally used as grazing land by Masai, until they were displaced by European settlers at the turn of the 20th century. The most likely reason for stopping in Naivasha town is en route to either Lake Naivasha or Hell's Gate. There are few accommodation options in town and it is far nicer to stay near the lake, where there are resorts, campsites and hotels catering to all budgets. The best reason to stop is for the excellent **Belle Inn**, for fruit juices and pastries.

Lake Naivasha and around → *For listings, see pages 94-97. Colour map 1, A4.* *Phone code: 050.*

Lake Naivasha is one of the few freshwater lakes in the Rift Valley. It is 170 sq km in size, about 1890 m above sea level and is a lovely place to come for a weekend if you are staying in Nairobi, as it is only a 1½-hour drive away. Strong afternoon winds cause the lake to get suddenly very rough; the local Masai called the lake *Nai'posha* meaning 'rough water', which the British later misspelled as Naivasha. Much of the lake is surrounded by forests of the yellow-barked acacia tree, full of birds and black and white colobus monkeys. Acacia were once called 'yellow fever trees', after explorers who camped under them caught malaria. The lake has no apparent outlet, but it is believed to drain underground, and is quite picturesque with floating islands of papyrus. There are hippos that come out onto the shore at night to graze, and there are many different types of waterbirds. The lake is dominated by the overshadowing **Mount Longonot** (2780 m), a partially extinct volcano in the adjacent national park (52 sq km; see page 93). On the southern lakeshore, the road goes through a major flower-growing area. Owned by Brooke Bond among other flower growers, it is an important exporter and employs thousands of local people. The flowers are cut, chilled and then air freighted to Europe from the international airport at Eldoret.

Getting there and around

The Moi South Lake Road is tarred and in good condition. Beyond the village of Kongoni it meets the back road to Nakuru or Moi North Lake Road where it turns into a dirt track that is sometimes only suitable for 4WD vehicles. If you are in a saloon car, you will have to turn back from here and backtrack to the main Nairobi–Nakuru road. It is possible to come to spend a day at one of the lakeside hotels without staying the night (there may be a small charge or it may be free if you eat there). The lake itself is best explored by boat, and a number of the hotels listed rent vessels out for hire. A motorboat can be hired for around US$15 per person per hour to go and see the pods of hippo, and there are fish eagle nests near the yacht club. The twin-hulled launch from the Country Club on its 'ornithological cruise' often tries to entice the birds with fish. The evening cruise at about 1800 is a good time to see them. Alternatively, you could work your way around the shore by bicycle, and there are a few places that rent out bikes.

Background

The region was first settled in the 1930s by the notorious British 'Happy Valley' set who bought all the neighbouring farmland – much of which is still owned by white Kenyans. The Lake Naivasha Country Club opened in 1937 and, from then until 1955, the lake was used as the staging post for Imperial Airways' flying boats from Durban to London, which used to land on the water. Even today, when the water is low, you can see the wooden posts that mapped out the runway, and the foundations of the customs shed can be seen on Crescent Island. The lake is about 13 km across, but its waters are shallow with an average depth of 5 m. At the beginning of the 20th century, Naivasha inexplicably completely dried up and the land was farmed, until heavy rains a few years later caused the lake to return.

Around Lake Naivasha

Crescent Island Game Sanctuary ⓘ *T050-202 1030, www.crescentisland.co, US$25 per person plus boat across the lake.* Morning and evening walks can be made here, a protected private reserve where you can walk amongst zebra, antelope and giraffe that come to the water's edge to drink. The shores host abundant birdlife especially huge numbers of pelicans, cormorants and fish eagles. It is located on the eastern shore of the lake, near the Lake Naivasha Country Club, and it is not actually an island, as it is connected to the mainland by a sliver of land. There are no predators, so this is one of the few places in Kenya offering the opportunity to walk amongst the animals. Trips can be arranged from all the hotels along the southern lakeshore including the **Lake Naivasha Country Club**, **Fisherman's Camp**, **Simba Lodge** and **Sopa Lodge**.

Elsamere ⓘ *Moi South Lake Rd, 22 km from Naivasha, T050-202 1055, www.elsatrust.org, daily 1500-1800, US$8 includes copious amounts of tea.* A few metres past **Fisherman's Camp** and **Fish Eagle Inn** is Elsamere, the former home of George and Joy Adamson (see box, page 194). It is easy to miss, so look out for the sign to the Olkaria Gate of Hell's Gate; it is a few hundred metres further on the right-hand side. There is a small **museum** with first editions of Joy's books, her typewriter, her dress that she wore for the premier of *Born Free* in London and a selection of her paintings (although the best of her paintings of the various tribes of Kenya hang in the State House in Nairobi). The Landrover in which George was shot dead as he drove from his camp in Kora National Park to rescue a guest who had been captured by Somali bandits, is on view outside. The gardens are very pleasant, with lots of birds and black and white colobus monkeys flying among the trees, though in recent years some of the giant acacia trees have had to be felled because of disease. It is open daily in the afternoon for tea and a video. The aged film shows the life (and death) of Joy. Beware though, it lasts for well over an hour, but is worth sitting through for the tea – tables in the house are laden with scones, jam and cream, dainty sandwiches, home-made cookies, slices of cake and pots of tea and coffee. See also Where to stay, page 95.

Lake Naivasha & Hell's Gate

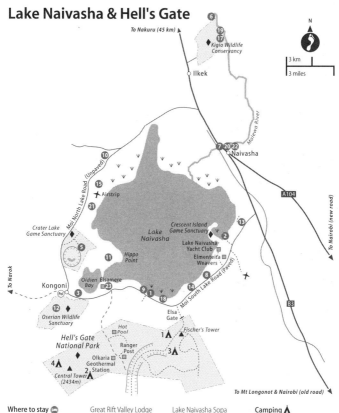

Where to stay 🛏

Belle Inn **20**
Camp Carnelleys **18**
Chui Lodge **3**
Crater Lake Camp **5**
Elsamere **23**
Enashipia Resort & Spa **13**
Fish Eagle Inn **9**
Fisherman's Camp **1**

Great Rift Valley Lodge
  & Golf Resort **10**
Hippo Point **11**
Kiangazi House **12**
Kigio Wildlife Camp **19**
Lake Naivasha Country
  Club **2**
Lake Naivasha Simba
  Lodge **14**

Lake Naivasha Sopa
  Lodge **8**
Loldia House **15**
Malewa Ranch House **6**
Malewa Wildlife Lodge **17**
Oleria & Sirocco Houses **21**
Silver **22**
Vash **7**

Camping ⛺

Naiburta **1**
Narasha **2**
Ol Dubai **3**
Ol Karia **4**

Oserian Wildlife Sanctuary ① *Moi South Lake Rd, 30 km from Naivasha, T050-202 0792, www.oserianwildlife.com, access is only for guests of the lodges.* Further southwest of Elsamere the road passes around Oidien Bay, a bottleneck in the extreme southwest corner of the lake, and reaches the village of Kongoni and the turn-off to **Chui Lodge** and **Kiangazi House** (see Where to stay, page 94). For a few kilometres before Kongoni, the road passes through the Oserian Game Corridor, which allows game to move from Hell's Gate to the lakeshore and is part of the private Oserian Wildlife Sanctuary, where the fences on the private land have been removed allowing the game in the area to move freely. If you are not staying, you are likely to see zebra and antelope from the road. The Oserian Wildlife Sanctuary is a private reserve that was created in 1996 on what was formerly a dairy and beef ranch of 1420 ha, where wildlife was present but numbers were declining. There are two upmarket accommodation options within the conservancy, and the profits generated by these go towards conservation of the area. In recent years several species have been introduced, including Grevy zebra, Beisa oryx and greater kudu, which all came from their native Northern Kenya, and wildebeest and topi were translocated from the Masai Mara. In 1996, six white rhino were introduced and have bred successfully; numbers on the conservancy are presently 14. The owners of the sanctuary also own the nearby Oserian Flower farm, which among other blooms grows roses and carnations and is the biggest flower-growing operation on the lakeshore.

Crater Lake Game Sanctuary ① *Moi North Lake Rd, 38 km from Naivasha, US$2.* West of Lake Naivasha, one hour's walk from Kongoni and approximately 17 km past **Fisherman's Camp** is Crater Lake. Its often jade-coloured waters are quite breathtaking and it is held in high regard by the local Masai who believe its water helps soothe ailing cattle. There is a pleasant two-hour nature trail to the lake, you are allowed to walk around by yourself and it's easy to see the rare black and white colobus monkey. Besides the impressive 150 bird species recorded here, giraffe, zebra and other plains wildlife are also regular residents, but if walking, remember that buffaloes lurk in the woods. It is possible to cycle to the game park, although the soft, dusty track after Kongoni is hard going.

Hell's Gate National Park → *Colour map 1, A4.*
① *Access is through Elsa Gate, Moi South Lake Rd, 20 km from Naivasha, T050-50407, www.kws.org, 0600-1800, US$25, children (3-18) US$15.*
This 68-sq-km park is one of the few in Kenya that you are allowed to explore on foot; bicycles and motorcycles are allowed too. The flora is mainly grasslands and shrubland, with several species of acacia. It is famous for its water geysers, as well as being a breeding area for Verreaux's eagles and Ruppell's vultures. Although very rare, lammergeyers have also been spotted hovering over the dramatic cliffs of Hell's Gate Gorge. A feature of this landscape is the lustrous acid-resistant volcanic glass, called obsidian, formed from cooled molten lava.

The 12-km route through the park (you return along the same route) is spectacular, leading through a gorge lined with sheer red cliffs and containing two volcanic plugs – **Fischer's Tower** and **Central Tower**. The park is small and, although there is a wide variety of wildlife – including eland, giraffe, zebra, impala and gazelle – you may not see many of them as they are few in number. What you will see though is the incredibly tame hyrax, which looks like a type of guinea-pig but is actually more closely related to the elephant, and a host of different birds of prey.

Within the park is the substantial **Olkaria Geothermal Station** generating power from underground – lots of large pipes and impressive steam vents in the hills. Near Central Tower is a smaller lower gorge that extends out of the park to the south. Here is a ranger post where water and sodas can be purchased, and a 2-km path that descends steeply into the gorge. The path skirts along the river in the bottom into which hot springs in the cliffs flow, and then climbs back to the ranger post. While in the gorge you can branch off into an even smaller gorge that has high, water-eroded walls that are so narrow in places that the sky is almost blocked out. After about 700 m there is a high wall that will force you to turn back, but on your return you will get a great view of Central Tower rising up.

Kigio Wildlife Conservancy
ⓘ *15 km north of Naivasha off the A104, www.kigio.com, access only to guests at the lodges.*
This is another former cattle and dairy farm that now operates as a private wildlife conservancy. Located in the hills to the northeast of Naivasha off the road to Nakuru, it covers 1420 ha and has breathtaking views of the Rift Valley, Mount Longonot and Lake Naivasha. Guests can walk or cycle amongst the wildlife and birds, or enjoy a splash in the Malewa River that runs through the conservancy.

The last remaining giraffe in the Naivasha region died as a result of poaching in 1996. Following an application by the management to the Kenya Wildlife Service, the request to relocate Rothschild's giraffe to the conservancy was granted, provided the property was fenced. Funding for this was sourced amongst others, from the European Union and the Born Free Foundation. With these facilities in place, eight Rothschild's giraffe were relocated from Lake Nakuru in 2002. The entire event was filmed by the BBC for the *Born to be Wild* series. The giraffe settled very well and the population now numbers over 30. The conservancy also has around 300 identified bird species, including the reputedly largest population of grey crested helmet shrikes in the world, and is home to 45 different mammals, including leopard, topi, hippo, spotted hyena, most of the plains game and a 200-strong herd of buffalo. In 1996, the large mammal count was only about 100, but today it is up to 3500, so the conservancy has been an exceptional success.

Mount Longonot National Park → *Colour map 1, A4.*
ⓘ *T050-50407, www.kws.org, 0600-1800, US$20, children (3-18) US$10.*
This 52-sq-km park encompasses Mount Longonot, which is a dormant volcano standing at 2886 m. The name is derived from the Masai word 'Oloonong'ot', meaning mountains of many spurs or steep ridges. The mountain cone is made up of soft volcanic rock that has eroded into deep clefts, v-shaped valleys and ridges. There is little vegetation on the stony soil. However, the crater is very lush and green, with fairly impenetrable trees. There are fine views over the Rift Valley on one side and into the enormous crater on the other. To climb Mount Longonot you need to get to Longonot village, about 12 km south of Naivasha town along the old road; from there it is about 6 km to the base of the mountain. There is a marked gate, where there is a secure parking area and Kenya Wildlife Services office. You can be escorted up by Kenya Wildlife Service rangers and the fairly straightforward climb takes about an hour, but be prepared for the last section which is quite steep. A wander round the rim of the mountain takes a further two to three hours.

For sleeping and eating price codes and other relevant information, see pages 20-24.

⊙ Where to stay

There is plenty of excellent accommodation in this popular and expanding weekend retreat for Nairobians, although there is little of attraction in Naivasha itself except for Belle Inn; its far nicer to stay near the lakeshore. Some of the accommodation is exceptional and, thanks to the conservation projects the region, increased game numbers has caused a mushrooming of game lodges. Many of the more upmarket hotels and lodges in the region can arrange transfers to and from Nairobi.

Lake Naivasha is home to thousands of hippos. At the lakeshore hotels, lodges and campsites, be very wary of the hippos that feed in the grounds at night. There have been accidents, including fatalities from people getting too close, so take heed of local advice.

Naivasha *p89, map p91*
$$ Belle Inn, Moi Av, T050-202 1007, labelleinn@kenyaweb.com. Old colonial hotel with several spacious rooms but old fashioned and basic, although the beds are reasonably comfortable and have mosquito nets. Rates include a huge and very good breakfast (fresh fruit juice, croissants, home-made jam, butter, bacon, eggs and lots of coffee). This is an institution in Kenya, and the large terrace restaurant and bar is an excellent place to stop for a break from driving for the selection of pastries, sandwiches, pies, cakes and full meals (many vegetarian, which is unusual for Kenya).
$ Silver Hotel, Kenyatta Av, T050-202 0580. Above the café, basic but clean and comfortable rooms with hot water, serving African staples and beer.
$ Vash Hotel, Posta Lane next to the post office, just up from Moi Av, T050-203 1503, www.kenvashhotel.com. The best of the basic hotels in an enormous white building, the tallest in town, with 65 spacious and comfortable rooms including some triples with balconies and TV, and friendly staff, a good, cheap restaurant and lively bar.

Lake Naivasha *p89, map p91*
$$$$ Chui Lodge, Oserian Wildlife Sanctuary, T050-202 0792, www.oserian wildlife.com. Exclusive lodge overlooking a waterhole with the dramatic Mau Escarpment as a backdrop, crafted from simple bush stone, local acacia and olive woods, with a heated swimming pool and excellent food using home-grown produce. The 8 individual and well-spaced cottages each has a veranda with its own view, log fire, marble bathroom, 4-poster beds and African antiques.
$$$$ Hippo Point, at Hippo Point to the southwest of the lake, T050-202 1295, www.hippopointkenya.com. One of the most expensive and luxurious places to stay on the lake, with 2 private homes built in 1933: the unusual needle-like 35-m-high Dodo's Tower, which has room for 9 guests on 8 floors, and the 1930s Manor House, an old colonial house that sleeps up to 17 guests. The cuisine is superb, game drives are included, horse riding, mountain-biking, water-skiing and day trips are also available, and there's a spa and stunning 25-m swimming pool.
$$$$ Kiangazi House, Oserian Wildlife Sanctuary, T050-202 0792, www.oserian wildlife.com. Delightful gardens, rolling lawns, swimming pool, private country house with 3 rooms in the house and 2 in garden cottages, satellite TV lounge and library, tennis court and gourmet food in the dining room. A salt lick and waterhole are excellently located at the bottom of the garden and attract the local game, and game drives are included in the rates.

$$$$ Loldia House, Moi North Lake Rd near the airstrip, reservations Nairobi T020-273 4000, www.governorscamp.com. A prestigious Governor's Camp and among Kenya's oldest farms, with lush lawns that run down to the lakeshore, en suite rooms in the main house or in garden cottages, colonial style with original furniture. Very atmospheric; you'll experience the life of Kenya's early settlers – the ranch was established by a family who trekked by ox-wagon from South Africa a century ago, and the property is still owned by their descendants. Inclusive rates from US$540 for a double.

$$$$ Oleria and Sirocco Houses, Moi North Lake Rd near the airstrip, reservations Nairobi T020-334 868, www.olerai.com. Oleria and Sirocco are the homes of Iain Douglas-Hamilton and his wife Oria. Iain is a leading conservation specialist who has been instrumental in protecting elephants in Kenya for decades (see also Elephant Watch Safari Camp at Samburu on page 332). The houses have been the family's home for many years. Accommodation is in very tranquil garden cottages decked with crawling vines and flowers, or in superbly luxurious rooms in the main houses. All-inclusive rates are from US$300 per person per day. Activities include *pirogue* trips on Lake Naivasha with the Masai.

$$$$-$$$ Great Rift Valley Lodge and Golf Resort, about 11 km from Naivasha on the northern lakeshore road, best accessed from the main Nairobi–Nakuru road, reservations through **Heritage Hotels**, Nairobi, T020-444 6651, www.heritage-eastafrica.com. Perched on the panoramic shoulder of the Eburu Escarpment overlooking Lake Naivasha and home to Kenya's newest championship 18-hole golf course, with private airstrip, 2 clay tennis courts, swimming pool; activities include walking and horse-riding safaris and fishing. Accommodation is in 30 rooms with private balconies, 4-poster beds, luxurious furnishings, 2 bars, very good buffet meals.

$$$$-$$$ Lake Naivasha Simba Lodge, Moi South Lake Rd, reservations Nairobi, T020-434 3960, www.marasimba.com. A large modern lodge built in expansive grounds full of giant acacia trees, 70 rooms in several blocks of stone buildings with slate roofs, disabled rooms, heated swimming pool, restaurant and pub, bike hire, tennis courts and a health club with gym, massage and sauna. A good set-up but primarily a conference venue, so give it a miss if there is a large conference on.

$$$ Crater Lake Camp, Crater Lake Game Sanctuary, reservations though **Merica Hotels**, Nairobi, T020-316 696, www.mericagrouphotels.com. This small camp is a little bit old fashioned and faded but has a great position on the shores of the lake and is near the grave of Lady Diana Delamere. The 8 simple double tents sit in secluded clearings in the lakeside forest with sweeping views, and there are 2 additional family *bandas* with bunk beds. Good food in the thatched restaurant, and rates are full board, a fully stocked bar, guided walks on offer and overall a relaxing spot.

$$$ Elsamere, Moi South Lake Rd, 22 km from Naivasha, T050-202 1055, www.elsatrust.org. Joy and George Adamson's house (see page 194). The conservation centre provides fairly simple but comfortable accommodation for 16 people in 4 cottages set in the gardens around the main house. The rooms are bright and attractive and all have en suite bathrooms. Dinner is hosted each night and is the perfect opportunity to get to know other guests, many of whom may be visiting researchers and conservationists, no bar but guests are invited to bring their own alcohol.

$$$ Enashipia Resort & Spa, Moi South Lake Rd, T050-213 0000, www.enashipai.com. Newly opened resort and excellent reports so far, with 46 rooms with satellite TV, Wi-Fi, contemporary decor with a nod at African colours, some have showers with open roofs. There's a full range of facilities, including restaurant, 2 bars, curio shop, gym, a large heated pool with a bridge over it, and beautifully designed spa set in tranquil gardens. A good family option with supervised children's activities, and boat trips and day excursions are on offer.

$$$ Lake Naivasha Country Club, Moi South Lake Rd, T020-234 5458, www.sun africahotels.com. This historic 22-ha property boasts green lawns shaded by giant mature acacias that stretch down to the lakeshore. Although the 50 rooms are overdue a refurbishment (which may have started by the time you read this), it's one of the cheaper options on the lakeshore at around US$250 for a double. There's a swimming pool, lounge with massive fireplace and a billiards room; boat trips are on offer and you can hire bicycles. Day visitors are welcome, there's an excellent buffet lunch on Sun (on lawns if the weather is good) – eat as much as you like for around US$14.

$$$ Lake Naivasha Sopa Lodge, Moi South Lake Rd, reservations Nairobi T020-375 0235, www.sopalodges.com. Part of the popular Sopa safari lodge group, this is a large lakeside resort with 84 very attractive rooms built in a crescent of cottages, some interconnecting and 1 with disabled facilities. The stunning lobby and bar has high ceilings, wrought-iron chandeliers and 3 fireplaces, the restaurant opens up to the manicured gardens and there's a lovely swimming pool.

$$-$ Camp Carnelleys, Moi South Lake Rd, 19 km from Naivasha, T050-50004, www.campcarnelleys.com. Excellent budget set up with simple en suite *bandas* spread out under the trees sleeping 2-6 or some with dorm bunks, with blankets, mosquito nets and lamps, plenty of space for camping with cooking shelters and hot showers, great rustic **Lazy Bones** bar and restaurant with pool table, lots of plants, big cushions and hammocks, good food including pizza, barbecue buffets at the weekends, plus smoothies and cocktails. Boat trips can be organized. *Bandas* from US$35 for 4 people, camping US$7 per person.

$$-$ Fish Eagle Inn, Moi South Lake Rd, 20 km from Naivasha, T050-273 7956, www.fisheagleinn.com. Decent en suite rooms and cottages sleeping 2-4 and camping facilities; you can hire tents, mattresses and blankets. There's a steam room, sauna and gym available at extra cost and an excellent swimming pool which day visitors can also use for a fee. Hippos come out of the water at night and graze a stone's throw away and staff can organize boat rides and bicycle hire. There's a good and affordable terrace restaurant and bar.

$$-$ Fisherman's Camp, next door to Fish Eagle Inn, T050-203 088, www.fishermans camp.com. Set in beautiful surroundings, shaded by huge acacia trees, with *bandas* sleeping up to 4 with reasonable facilities including showers, bed linen and electricity, and camping on springy grass with showers in tin sheds and a communal washing-up area, tents, mattresses and blankets can be hired. Across Moi South Lake Rd up the hill are 7 more simple self-catering cottages sleeping up to 6 and a swimming pool. Bar and simple meals in a rustic thatched shed or eat next door, and boat trips to Crescent Island can be arranged.

Hell's Gate National Park *p92, map p91*

There are a few campsites within the park: Narasha, Naiburta, Ol Dubai, and Ol Karia, see map. Each has water and pit latrines. Contact the warden, T050-50407, or KWS, Nairobi, T020-600 0800, www.kws.org.

Kigio Wildlife Conservancy *p93, map p91*

$$$$ Kigio Wildlife Camp, reservations Nairobi T020-374 8369, www.kigio.com. Luxury camp built along the Malewa River, with 11 very spacious thatched suites (72 sq m) set well apart from each other on the forested riverbank with broad balconies, 1 has 2 bedrooms for families and the honeymoon suite has an outside bathtub. The bar, lounge and dining area is in a glade overlooking a towering red cliff that houses colonies of bee-eaters. Rates are full board and night drives and cycling are on offer.

$$$$ Malewa Ranch House, reservations Nairobi T020-353 5878, www.malewaranch. com. To the northeast of the lake off the road to Nakuru, this is small exclusive 10-bed ranch house with a tin roof that can be rented as a whole with country-style floral decor and Persian rugs on wooden floors. There's a large sitting room, open fire, spacious veranda, bar and dining area with views over the Malewa River. Rates from US$545 for a double, though rates come down the larger the group and include all meals and game activities.

$$$$ Malewa Wildlife Lodge, reservations Nairobi T020-374 8369, www.kigio.com. A small exclusive 'eco-friendly' lodge set 2 km from **Kigio Wildlife Camp** (above), with 5 cottages nestled in the shade of huge acacia trees, and 4 river suites built on stilts over the Malewa River. Rates are full board with very good cuisine, and walking or cycling are on offer. The beds, tables and chairs are constructed using the timbers from old fencing posts taken from the former cattle ranch that was on the conservancy.

⑦ Restaurants

All the hotels have their own restaurants, which are also open to passing trade; many are extremely good. In Naivasha itself, **Belle Inn** is easily the best place to eat whatever your budget. There is a stall opposite that sells fresh fish and crayfish. See Where to stay, above, for more information.

⊙ Shopping

Elmenteita Weavers, Moi South Lake Rd at the turn-off to the Lake Naivasha Yacht Club,

just after Lake Naivasha Country Club, T050-202 3011, www.elmenteitaweavers.com. 0900-1700. A workshop specializing in hand-woven crafts, including wool rugs and cotton *kikois*, tablemats, throws and cushion covers. Much higher quality than those found at the usual curio stalls.

⊖ Transport

Mount Suswa *p88*
Matatus serve the B3 Narok Rd, but there is little traffic and few hitching opportunities along the last 12 km south on rough unmade roads. The road skirts the northeast flank of the mountain until it reaches a crossroad. Turn right here along a rough track until you reach a group of *manyattas* (Masai villages) that extend over a distance of 1.5 km. From here a rough track leads up to the caldera. The only identifying marks are the deeply grooved water channels lying to the sides of the track. The distance to the caldera is approximately 7 km. Turn left for the caves or right to reach the inner crater, a distance of another 8 km.

Lake Naivasha *p89, map p91*
There is regular public transport between Naivasha, **Nairobi** and **Nakuru** (1½ hrs from Naivasha). Buses and *matatus* arrive and depart at the bus stand on Kariuki Chotara Rd in Naivasha. There are also regular *matatus* from the centre of town along the southern lakeshore road as far as **Kongoni**.

There is bike hire available from various places from around US$10 a day, greatly increasing your options for exploration, particularly to Hell's Gate National Park. Try **Fisherman's Camp** and **Fish Eagle Inn**, or the stall at the turn-off to the Elsa Gate of Hell's Gate National Park.

Nakuru and around

Nakuru is the largest town in the Rift Valley lakes region and is a good place to stock up on provisions and browse in the good curio market. It's also on the edge of the Lake Nakuru National Park, which is one of Kenya's most popular parks to visit, thanks to its accessibility and proximity to Nairobi. The chances of seeing animals, such as rhino and leopard, are much better here than in other parks and reserves, and the flamingos on the lake itself and on other lakes in the region are a spectacular sight. ▶ *For listings, see pages 105-110.*

Lake Elmenteita → *Colour map 1, A3/4.*

From Naivasha the road continues towards Nakuru, a 1½-hour drive, via the uninspiring town of **Gilgil**. The small 18-sq-km lake is the notable attraction on this route. Elmenteita lies in the shadow of an impressively peaked hill known locally by the Masai as the

Nakuru

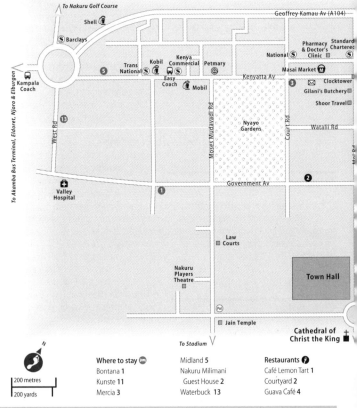

Where to stay	Midland 5	Restaurants
Bontana 1	Nakuru Milimani	Café Lemon Tart 1
Kunste 11	Guest House 2	Courtyard 2
Mercia 3	Waterbuck 13	Guava Café 4

'Sleeping Warrior' and is roughly halfway between Naivasha and Nakuru, just off the main road. It is a shallow soda lake, similar to Lake Nakuru, although it does not attract such enormous numbers of flamingos, which apparently fled due to encroachment by pelicans; Elmenteita is now one of Kenya's main breeding grounds for the great white pelican. Other birds include the great egret, great crested grebe, maccoa duck, and in total about 450 species of bird live in and around the lake. It was designated as a **RAMSAR** wetland of international importance in 2005. (The **RAMSAR** treaty, signed in 1971, ensures the conservation of wetlands.) As it is not a national park, you can walk around it and you don't have to pay. Most of the safaris covering the trip from Naivasha to Nakuru only stop at the viewpoint overlooking the lake on the main road.

Apart from the lodges, there are few facilities at the lake, but it is an easy day trip from Nakuru with direct *matatus* (one hour) or 30 minutes from Gilgil. It is an easy walk from the main road down to the edge of the lake, but fairly steep coming back up. Be very wary of driving too close to the lake down this track, as it's easy to get a vehicle stuck in the ground.

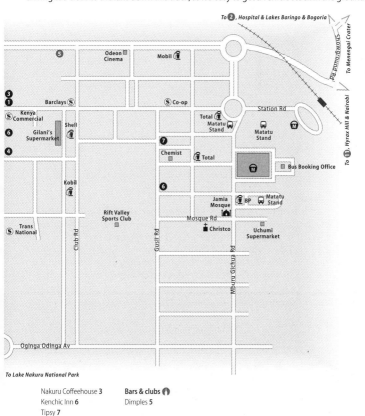

Nakuru Coffeehouse **3**
Kenchic Inn **6**
Tipsy **7**

Bars & clubs 🎷
Dimples **5**

Kariandusi ① *www.museums.or.ke, 0930-1800, US$5.50, children (under 16) US$2.75*, is a prehistoric site of the Acheulean period to the right of the Naivasha–Nakuru road (A104), discovered by Dr L Leakey in 1928 and excavated from 1929 to 1947. Studies suggest that it was not an area of permanent habitation, and the findings indicate that the people who lived here were of the genus *Homo erectus*. There is a small museum housing obsidian knives, Stone Age hand axes and a molar of the straight-tusked elephant, a variety that roamed in Northern Europe before extinction. The nearby diatomite (a type of algae) mine produces a white substance used for paints, insulation and as a face paint by the Masai.

Nakuru → *For listings, see pages 105-110. Colour map 1, A3. Phone code: 051.*

The next major town along from Naivasha and 156 km from Nairobi, Nakuru is Kenya's fourth-largest town and is in the centre of some of the country's best farming land. It is a pleasant, slightly dusty agricultural town with many supermarkets and shops mostly selling farming equipment and supplies; the main crops grown around town include coffee, barley, maize and wheat. Indeed, the name derives from a Masai word meaning 'place of dust'. Although its history can be dated back to the prehistoric period, thanks to archaeological findings at **Hyrax Hill**, modern Nakuru came into existence in 1900, when the building of the railway opened up access to the surrounding lush countryside attracting hundreds of white settlers to the area. Lord Delamere, one of the most famous figures in colonial times, collected around 600 sq km of land here and developed wheat and dairy farming.

Arriving in Nakuru

There are frequent buses and *matatus* from just about everywhere in the highlands region of Kenya to and from Nakuru. The main road from Nairobi passes by Naivasha and Gilgil and Lake Elmenteita on the way. Nakuru town itself is compact enough to walk around, though *boda bodas*, regular taxis and the odd tuk-tuk are available to get around. Many of the more upmarket hotels and lodges in the region can arrange transfers to and from Nairobi.

Places in Nakuru

The only notable building in town is the **Rift Valley Sports Club** ① *T051-221 2085*. This was formerly the Nakuru Club, first built in 1907, burnt down in 1924 and then restored. A patio restaurant looks out over the cricket pitch. The cricket pavilion has photos of past teams, and the ground is prettily surrounded by jacarandas and mango trees. In the Men's Bar (women still not allowed) there are sporting prints and etchings. Tennis, squash and a small swimming pool are available, as well as cricket nets for a small fee for non-members.

Lake Nakuru National Park → *For listings, see pages 105-110. Colour map 1, A3.*

① *T051-266 4071, www.kws.org, 0600-1800, Jan-Mar, Jul-Oct US$75, children (3-18) US$40, Apr-Jun, Nov-Dec US$60/30, vehicle US$3.25.*
This national park is just 4 km south of Nakuru town in central Kenya and 140 km northwest of Nairobi. It was established in 1960 as the first bird sanctuary in Africa to protect the flamingos and the other birds in the hills and plains around the lake. It covers 188 sq km, and the lake is fringed by swamp and surrounded by dry savannah. The upper areas within the national park are forested. The lake itself is in the centre of the park surrounded by huge white salt crusts, whose surface area varies from five to 40 sq km.

Arriving in Lake Nakuru National Park

Game viewing is very easy and rewarding here, and the whole park can be driven around in half a day. You will need to be in a vehicle, although you are allowed to get out at the picnic and camp sites. If you don't have your own car, the most logical way of exploring is by picking up a taxi in Nakuru and negotiating a price for half a day, which obviously can be shared among a group. Alternatively, arrange an excursion through **Shoor Travel** on Moi Road. The most popular way of accessing the park is through the **Main Gate**, 4 km south of Nakuru centre, next to the park's headquarters, where you can also obtain and reload your Safari Card. From Kenyatta Avenue, take Moi Road and turn left to Stadium Road, which will lead you right to the gate. Here there is also a map on a board showing the spots of the latest animal sightings. If you come from Nairobi and you want to avoid Nakuru altogether, you can enter the park through **Lanet Gate**, although this is not very well signposted off the main road. The turn-off is about 3 km before you reach town. Finally, **Nderit Gate** lies at the east side of the park, close to **Lake Nakuru Lodge**. This is a suitable way for visitors arriving from Mau Narok or Lake Elmenteita on the back road. However, you cannot get a Safari Card at these Lanet or Nderit gates, so you will have to already have one that has been pre-loaded. The park's tracks are usually well kept, although you may find some mud during the rains. The main road circles the lake completely. The north drive is very busy and is hence less interesting for wildlife viewing. The biggest stretch of land in the park is located south of the lake. There is a track network here which is much less visited and where you will have the chance to see some of the park's herbivores, such as Rothschild's giraffe, black and white rhino and eland.

Lake Nakuru National Park

Where to stay 🛏
Flamingo Hill
  Tented Camp **3**
Kunste **4**
Lake Nakuru Lodge **1**
Maili Saba Camp **5**
Mbweha Camp **7**
Naishi House **6**

Sarova Lion Game Lodge **2**

Camping ⛺
Backpackers' **1**
Kampi ya Nyati **2**
Kampi ya Nyuki **3**
Makalia **4**
Njoro **5**

Around Lake Nakuru National Park

The blue-green algae *Spirulina platensis* flourishes in the alkaline waters and is a primary food source for the flamingo population. Both the lesser and greater flamingo is present. In 1958 alkaline-tolerant *Tilapia grahami* were introduced to the lake to try to curb the problem of malaria in the nearby town. **Fish eagles** appeared in this area shortly afterwards, thanks to the abundant supply of these fish. There is a wide variety of wildlife: bat, colobus monkey, spring hare, otter, rock hyrax, hippo, buffalo, waterbuck, lion, hyena and giraffe, but the most popular reason for visiting is the wonderful sight of hundreds of thousands of flamingos. At one time there were thought to be around two million flamingos here, about one third of the world's entire population, but the numbers have considerably diminished in recent years. Now, the number of flamingos varies from several thousand to a few hundred, depending on the water level and their frequent migration to the other lakes in the Rift Valley. Usually, the lake recedes during the dry season and floods during the wet season, and in recent years, there have been wide variations between the dry and wet seasons' water levels. It's suspected that this is caused by increasing watershed conversion to intensive crop production and urbanization, both which reduce the capacity of soil to absorb water, recharge groundwaters and increase seasonal flooding. This has caused the flamingos to migrate to other lakes, namely Elmenteita, Simbi Nyaima and Bogoria.

The best viewing point is from the **Baboon Cliffs** on the western shores of the lake. There are also more than 450 other species of bird here. Thousands of both little grebes and white-winged black terns are seen, as are stilts, avocets, ducks and, in the European winter, the migrant waders. Another highlight is the very healthy population of black and white rhino; Nakuru was declared a sanctuary for the protection of these endangered animals in 1987. Both black and white rhino have been reintroduced, and the park has become the most successful refuge for rhino in East Africa – you'll literally trip over them here. There are quite a few leopard too, which are often, and unusually, spotted during the day in the acacia forest at the entrance to the park. Lion favour the savannah area to the south of the lake. In 1974 the endangered Rothchild's giraffe was introduced from the Soy plains of Eldoret where they have bred successfully. There are also a fair number of pythons, which may be seen crossing roads or dangling from trees. Because of its proximity to Nakuru town, the park is fenced, to stop the animals wandering into town and, previously, to stop poachers wandering into the park. It's so close to the city that it's not out of the ordinary to be watching a lion within the park and, at the same time, watching a woman doing her washing outside her house beyond the fence! The advantage of being so close is that local people get to know the wildlife – the park buses in local school children for game drives.

Hyrax Hill prehistoric site → *Colour map 1, A4.*

ⓘ *Just off the Nairobi Rd, T051-221 7175, www.museums.or.ke, 0930-1800, US$5.50, children (under 16) US$2.75. Take a matatu heading for Gilgil and ask to be dropped off at the turning for Hyrax Hill. It is about 1 km from here to the museum. You can camp here.*

About 4 km from Nakuru, Hyrax Hill contains Neolithic and Iron-Age burial pits and settlements, first investigated by the Leakeys in the 1920s; work has been going on there, periodically, ever since. The excavations have found evidence of seasonal settlements from 3000 years ago, and there are signs of habitation here up until about 300 years ago. The presence of beach sands is an indicator that Lake Nakuru may have extended right to the base of the hill in former times, turning Hyrax Hill into a peninsula or even an island. It is possible that 9000 years ago this vast prehistoric lake extended as far as Lake Elmenteita. The hill was given its name during the early part of the 20th century, reflecting the abundance of hyraxes in the rocky fissures of the hill.

The northeast village has some enclosures where the digging was carried out, although only one is not overgrown. It dates back about 400 years, and the finds have been pieced together and are exhibited in the museum. There is no evidence of human dwelling, suggesting this may have been used for livestock.

Up at the top of Hyrax Hill are the remains of a stone-walled fort and, on the other side of the hill, you can see the position of two huts in a settlement that has been dated back to the Iron Age. A series of burial pits with 19 skeletons were found, most of them decapitated, dating back to the same time. The remains are all in a heap and all appear to be young men suggesting they were buried in a hurry – possibly the remains of the enemy after a battle. On the path back to the museum, a *bau* board has been carved into the rock. One very curious find was six Indian coins dating back 500 years – no one knows how they got here.

Underneath the Iron Age site, a Neolithic site was found, and the Neolithic burial mound has been fenced off as a display, the stone slab which sealed the mound having been removed. Nine female skeletons were found at the site. Unlike the male remains, the female remains have been buried with grave goods including dishes, pestles and mortars. No one can be sure why the women were buried with grave goods and not the men, but it could indicate that women were more politically powerful. Oral history in the region suggests this may have been the case. Why the Iron Age burial site is directly on top of the Neolithic one also remains a mystery. Hyrax Hill was gazetted a National Monument in 1943. The **museum**, which contains artefacts from the site, was previously a farmhouse. Guides are on hand to take you around.

Rongai → *Colour map 1, A3.*

Rongai is a small, pretty village about 25 km west of Nakuru in the valley of the Rongai River, which rises in the Elburgon Hills. Originally the area was inhabited by the Tugen and Njembs tribes, before they were driven out by the Masai. But the Masai never settled and there is no record of their ever constructing *manyatta* (Masai villages) in the valley.

Arriving in Rongai
Rongai is a short diversion off the A104 Nakuru–Eldoret road. Numerous *matatus* go from Nakuru along the A104 past the turning to Rongai. Here you can swap for another going from the turn off to Rongai. From Nakuru there are also several direct *matatus* each day in both directions.

Background
The land was part of the great tract leased to Lord Delamere, who then rented it out to settlers. In the colonial period Rongai grew to prominence as a maize-growing area. This crop was first introduced to Kenya by the Portuguese, but it did not do well. Then an American variety was used to develop a hybrid known as Kenya White, which flourished. The land was tilled by teams of oxen, maize was being exported by 1910 and, by 1917, there were 3000 ha under maize around Rongai. The railway arrived in 1926 as part of the line onward from Nairobi to Uganda. A branch line was built from Rongai northeast to Solai, now disused, although you can still see the tracks. The branch went entirely through settler country and, as there was no 'native land' along the route, it was criticized as an example of the colonial administration favouring the interests of the settlers over those of the Africans.

Places in Rongai
One notable feature of Rongai is the number of churches. **Africa Inland Church** has arched windows in pairs, glazed in yellow, green and orange, with sunrise airbricks above each

pair. The walls are of grey volcanic stone, and it has a tin roof. The **Catholic Church of St Mary** is a modern, neat, functional structure of grey stone with timber panelling. **Heart of Christ Catholic Seminary**, dates from 1986, but is cloistered and quiet, with well-tended flower beds, run by Italian Fathers.

The prettiest of the churches, and a testament to the determination of the settlers to reproduce rural England on the equator, is **St Walstan's**, built in 1960. It is an exact replica of an early English (1016) country church at Bawburgh, 6 km east of Norwich in the UK. St Walstan is known as the 'Layman's Saint'. He came from a wealthy land-owning family, was fond of farm animals, and he insisted on working in the fields with the farm labourers. He collapsed and died while working one day, and a spring bubbled up on the very same spot. The church building has a square tower with battlements, pointed windows and a shingle (wooden tile) roof. In the vestibule is a piece of flint from the church in Bawburgh. Inside there is a tiny gallery with steps up to it cut into the wall. The saints are depicted in orange, yellow and blue stained-glass windows. The roof is supported by timber beams and there is a small bell. The approach to the church is bordered by jacarandas that carpet the path with fallen blue blossoms when the trees are in flower.

Menengai Crater → For listings, see pages 105-110. Colour map 1, A3.

This extinct volcano on the northern side of Nakuru is 2490 m high and is the second-largest surviving volcanic crater in the world, about 12 km across and 500 m deep with a surface area of 90 sq km. However, it is not easy to see it from the town. A sign erected at the highest point by the Rotary Club shows the distances and general directions of several places worldwide. The crater is 8 km from the main road and is surrounded by a nature reserve. As you ascend, the views over Lake Nakuru are excellent, although it is not visible from the top; on the other side, there are views of Lake Bogoria. If walking, leave from the Crater Climb Road, then Forest Road (it takes a couple of hours but is pleasant enough). However, recent reports of robberies makes this a less safe option, and an alternative is to drive along Menengai Drive out through the suburbs. It is fairly well signposted. There is no public transport from the town to the Menengai Crater and, as few people visit it, there is scant hope of hitching a lift.

In the 19th century the Menengai Crater was the site of a bloody battle between different Masai clans, vying for the pastures of the Rift Valley slopes and Naivasha. The Ilaikipiak Moran (warriors) were defeated by their southern neighbours the Ilpurko Masai, who reputedly threw the former over the crater edge. According to legend the fumaroles rising from the crater bed are the souls of the vanquished seeking to find their way to heaven. The Maa word *Menenga* means 'the dead'.

Nyahururu and Thomson's Falls → For listings, see pages 105-110. Colour map 1, A4.
Phone code: 065.

The small town of Nyahururu is 65 km north of Nakuru on the good and picturesque B5 and can easily be visited on a day trip from Nakuru. It also provides access to the Laikipia Plateau (page 188); the B5 continues on to Nyeri on the western side of Mount Kenya (page 164). Nyahururu lies at high altitude (2360 m) with a splendid climate and is Kenya's highest town, surrounded by pretty tracts of forest and agricultural land; the region benefits from high rainfall. The surrounding plateau is highly cultivated with maize, beans and sweet potatoes, which are well represented in Nyahururu's lively market. It originally served the colonial settler farmers in the area and was boosted when a branch line of the railway reached the town in 1929. This still runs, but only carries freight. In the post-war period the town was prosperous enough to boast a racecourse. Lately, flower farming has brought new life to Nyahururu. Although only a few kilometres north of the equator, nights can be cold, with occasional frosts in the early months of the year. Samuel Wanjiru, the long-distance runner and now Olympic marathon record holder as the first Kenyan to win the marathon at the Olympics in Beijing in 2008, calls Nyahururu home.

An explorer, Joseph Thomson, came across the waterfall to the north of the town in 1883, which he named **Thomson's Falls** after his father. He was the first European to walk from Mombasa to Lake Victoria. The cascade plunges 75 m and is a pretty area to walk around. A stony path of sorts leads down to the bottom of the ravine. Do not attempt to go down any other way, as the rocks on the side of the ravine are very loose. It's more commonly known as 'T-falls'. Upstream on the **Ewaso Narok River** is found one of Kenya's highest altitude hippo pools in an area of marshy bogland, about 2 km from the falls.

◉ Nakuru and around listings

For sleeping and eating price codes and other relevant information, see pages 20-24.

◉ Where to stay

Lake Elmenteita *p98*
There is a balloon at Lake Elmenteita; these lodges can organize early morning flights (see What to do, page 109, for more information).
$$$$ Serena Lake Elmenteita Camp, 28 km south of Nakuru, reservations Nairobi T020-284 2400, www.serenahotels.com. Newly opened in 2011 by the Serena group, this luxury camp is set under the shade of giant acacia trees and has 24 tents and verandas with lovely lake views, colonial-themed decor, attractive central lounge, bar and dining canvas structure, swimming pool, massages available, balloon rides, game day/night drives and walks on offer, and birdwatchers will particularly enjoy the 4 bird hides right on the water's edge.
$$$$-$$$ Sunbird Lodge, 30 km south of Nakuru, T0715-555 777, www.sunbirdkenya.com. This is a fairly new eco-lodge with 10 thatched chalets overlooking the lake with wide wooden verandas, and 1 king size and 1 single bed in each room. The restaurant has sliding glass doors and fireplaces, buffet meals are included in the rates, swimming

pool, local guided walks can be arranged and the balloon is based here.
$$$ Lake Elmenteita Lodge, 30 km south of Nakuru, T050-50836, www.jacaranda hotels.com. Built in 1916 as a ranch house, with 33 rooms in cottages, modestly decorated but comfortable with patios and fireplaces, pleasant lounges and dining room, lush tropical gardens, wide terrace with lake views, but it's some distance from the lakeshore. Activities include bird walks and the balloon safari. Rates are full or half board.
$$-$ Pink Lake Man's Ecolodge, 30 km south of Nakuru, T0721-842 811, www.pink lakeman.com. This is another new eco-lodge with 3 lovely wooden cottages set in a lush tract of woodland; each is surrounded by earthenware pots of flowering shrubs, and there's a pleasant campsite with hot showers. Bar and restaurant decorated with African touches, solar power, and locally managed by the affable Francis.

Nakuru *p100, maps p98 and p101*
Nakuru has a crop of basic board and lodgings, which are fairly dirty and dingy and best avoided as they are in the rough part of town on the of streets around Mosque Rd. Consider staying in Lake Nakuru

National Park or one of the better, larger hotels listed here instead.

In town

$$$ Bontana Hotel, Government Av, T051-221 0134, www.bontanahotel-nakuru.com. A modern 5-storey hotel in a fairly quiet part of town with 88 comfortable rooms, all with balconies overlooking the gardens, spacious public areas, lovely heated pool with sun loungers, restaurant, bar and coffee shop, business centre with internet, secure car park. A reasonable mid-range option for around US$120 a double, but avoid if there's a conference on.

$$$ Nakuru Milimani Guest House, Statehouse Rd, off Showground Rd near the golf club, T0753-616 263, www.nakuru milimaniguesthouse.com. Unusual for Kenya, guesthouse accommodation in a fairly modern house set in mature gardens full of birds in a quiet suburb, 7 rooms with satellite TV, DVD player, Wi-Fi and homely decor, pleasant lounge with fireplace, breakfast included, dinner on request. Doubles from US$110.

$$ Mercia Hotel, Kenyatta Av, T051-221 6013, www.merciagrouphotels.com. On first appearance quite a surprise for dusty little Nakuru, a modern block with an atrium-style lobby where all the doors to the rooms look inward on several storeys and are reached by glass elevators, but the 93 rooms could do with a touch up and it's in a noisy part of town. They do have satellite TV and Wi-Fi, the restaurant is reasonable, plus there's a bar, gym and nice swimming pool at the rear.

$$ Midland, Geoffrey Kamau Av, T051-221 2125, www.midlandhotelnakuru.com. Old-fashioned building (parts of it date back to the original Nakuru Railway Hotel), but with 63 comfortable, well-appointed rooms with satellite TV (the ones in the new block are nicer), doubles from US$80, good breakfast included, car washing for a small tip, newspapers in the morning, 2 bars with giant TVs and good restaurant (see Restaurants, page 108).

$ Waterbuck, West Rd, T051-221 5672. Modern budget hotel with good facilities, but, although the brightly coloured lobby with touches of African decor is impressive, the rooms are a little neglected but clean and spacious, and some have balconies. The restaurant is reasonable and the swimming pool here is popular with Kenyan families at the weekend.

Out of town

$$$$ Deloraine, 33 km from Nakuru on the A104 (6 km northwest of the turning to Rongai), T062-31081, www.offbeatsafaris. com. On the Deloraine Estate, this is an exclusive homestay in a classic colonial house built in the 1920s on the lower slopes of Londianin Mountain, set on a 2000-ha farm, with 9 double rooms, either in the main house or a garden cottage. All meals are taken in the dining room and guests are expected to be part of the family in a house party atmosphere. Swimming pool and croquet, lawn tennis and horse-riding safaris. Rates from US$350 per person.

$$-$ Kembu Cottages and Campsite, 40 km west of Nakuru, T0722-361 102, www.kembu.com. Take the main A104 road from Nakuru towards Eldoret and after a few kilometres turn off to the C56 to Njoro, and then take the Molo road; the farm is 8 km beyond Njoro. *Matatus* from Nakuru to Molo will drop you off at the turning to the farm. The cottages and campsite are located on a large 364-ha working farm, children can help feed horses, calves and chickens, and activities include mountain biking and horse riding, you can play football with the farm team or visit the local school, and day excursions can be arranged. Accommodation is in en suite cottages (one of which was built in 1915 and was a former home of Beryl Markham), rooms in the family house and in 1 unique treehouse with double bedroom only, for which guests use toilets and showers in the campsite. The campsite itself is a fantastic swathe of springy green grass surrounded by bushes full of chameleons. There's a lovely rustic bar and restaurant with wood fire and superb farm cuisine.

$$-$ Kunste, about 2 km out on the Nairobi road, T051-221 2140, www.kunstehotel.com. Large spacious hotel with secure parking, outside bar with kids' playground, restaurant, 105 comfortable rooms, singles, doubles and triples, the bigger suites also have TV, old-fashioned decor but well run with friendly staff. A double with breakfast starts at US$40.

Lake Nakuru National Park p100, map p101

The rates for accommodation within the park do not include park entrance fees.

$$$$ Lake Nakuru Lodge, reservations Nairobi, T020-243 0707, www.lakenakuru lodge.com. Medium-sized lodge situated to the southeast of the park near the Nderit Gate, with pleasant gardens and pool overlooking the park. Space for 180 people in double, triple and family cottages, *bandas* and suites. Friendly service, bar and dining room, and 24-hr room service. The original house was part of Kenya pioneer Lord Delamere's estate.

$$$$ Sarova Lion Hill Game Lodge, close to eastern shore of lake, access from Lanet Gate, T051-208 5455, www.sarovahotels. com. Popular with tour groups, each of the 67 chalet-style rooms and suites are positioned to have excellent views of the lake and park from the patios. Buffet meals and traditional dancing at dinner, swimming pool, sauna, massages and curio shop and special activities for children. Full board rates from US$290 for a double.

$$$$-$$$ Flamingo Hill Tented Camp, 1 km from the Main Gate, reservations Nairobi T0727-741 883, www.flamingo hillcamp.com. A new camp with 25 double and family tents under thatched roofs spread in a long line, with wrought-iron 4-poster beds, natural wood furnishings and verandas, central bar, restaurant, library and curio shop, rates are full board with good buffet meals. The drawback, however,

is it's right on the edge of the park near the town and next to some ugly overhead power lines.

$$$$-$$$ Mbweha Camp, off the road to the village of Elmenteita, access from the A104 near Hyrax Hill, reservations Nairobi T020-445 0035, www.atua-enkop. com. Not in the park but on a private conservancy on the southern boundary. You can see the majority of the plains game here. 10 spacious and peaceful stone-and-thatch cottages, 2 for families, lovely contemporary furnishings in earthy colours, restaurant and sunken thatched bar with a view of a waterhole at eye-level. Mountain-biking, game walks and day/night drives on the property and extended game drives into the park, as well as the balloon safari at Elmenteita (see page 109) can be arranged. Full board rates start from US$280 for a double.

$$$ Naishi House, 18 km from the Main Gate, KWS, Nakuru Warden, T051-266 4071, Nairobi, T020-600 800, www.kws.org. KWS self-catering accommodation in the south of the park, near **Makalia Campsite**. The house is furnished with rugs and paintings and has a fully equipped kitchen, lounge, 2 bedrooms, each with a double and a single bed, and 2 single rooms in an adjacent cottage. Bring all food, firewood and drinking water; electricity is provided by generator 1900-2200. The whole house rents for US$200, including the cottage, but other arrangements may be possible.

Camping

There are 2 public campsites within the park, **Backpackers'** and **Makalia**, which cost US$25, children (3-18) US$20, plus 3 'special' campsites, which cost US$40, children (3-18) US$20, reservations through the warden, T051-266 4071, www.kws.org, or simply book and pay for camping when you arrive at the Main Gate.

Backpackers' Campsite, just inside the Main Gate with basic facilities, including a communal tap and cold showers, in a good location under shady yellow acacias, but the monkeys and baboons can be bothersome so look after your stuff. You can camp here even if you do not have a vehicle, and there is no entry fee to the park. However, the park cannot be explored on foot, so to go on a game drive you would have to hitch from the Main Gate and, if you were lucky enough to get a lift (remember safari companies are unlikely to pick up non-paying passengers), then you would have to pay park entry fees. **Kampi ya Nyati** (Buffalo) and **Kampi ya Nyuki** (Bee), both lead down to quiet viewpoints on the lakeshore and are near the northeast entrance.

Makalia Campsite is by the southern boundary of the park and close to the waterfall – exercise caution, lions are often spotted here.

Njoro Campsite, is about 1 km into the park on the northwest side of the lake.

Menengai Crater *p104, map p101*
$$ Maili Saba Camp, turn left at **Hotel Kunste**, 2 km outside Nakuru and the camp is 11 km, T050-50845, www.mailisabacamp. com. Just 10 comfortable permanent en suite tents set under thatched roofs with wooden decks on the lower slopes of the Menengai Crater with excellent views. Well-stocked bar, restaurant serving Western and Swahili dishes, which is atmospherically lit at night with oil lamps, swimming pool. Can organize local excursions to Lake Nakuru National Park and Thomson's Falls.

Nyahururu and Thomson's Falls *p104*
$ Kianjata Springs Camp, 5 km south of town towards Gilgil, you can get here by *matatu* from outside the Baron Hotel in Nyahururu, T0722-635 149, www.sports camp-hostel.com. A simple but cool spot in well-tended gardens affiliated to the **Kenya Youth Hostel Association**, with 6 en suite *bandas*, dorm beds in an old double-decker bus and a campsite, hot showers, self-catering kitchen, dining hall and local meals are available. It's used by athletes wanting

to train at high altitude and has 4 km of running tracks.
$ Thomson's Falls Lodge, T065-22006, www.thomsonsfallslodge.com, just off the road out of town toward Nyeri and Nanyuki. Built in 1931 and set in pleasant gardens next to the waterfall, with a charming colonial atmosphere. 32 double and triple rooms in the main building or cottages and a grassy campsite with hot showers and free firewood. Most people visit to see the falls and have a drink at the bar, but the rooms are well furnished and all have fireplaces, the restaurant is good and the staff are friendly.

⑦ Restaurants

Nakuru *p100, map p98*
The best restaurants are attached to hotels and represent the limited choices after dark. There are a number of places for cheap snacks, the best of which is the branch of Kenyan fast-food chain **Kenchic Inn**, on Moi Rd, for good chicken and chips. The many supermarkets also sell pies and samosas.
$$-$ Courtyard, Government Av, T051-221 1585. Open 1200-2200. You can choose to eat inside, on the terrace at the front, or in the lovely courtyard decked with plants to the rear. Offers a wide choice of salads, Indian food, pizza or grills, and not unreasonably priced. The pan-fried chicken with coconut cream and chilli is rather good. Full bar including some wines.
$$-$ Midland Hotel, Geoffrey Kamau Av, see Where to stay, page 106. Open 1200-2200. Comfortable candlelit dining room that offers an excellent and affordable choice of hot and cold starters, pizza, steaks, pork chops, fresh tilapia fish, vegetarian choices and some South African wine. The garden bar serves delicious barbecued chicken and sports are shown on TV.
$ Tipsy Restaurant, Gusii Rd. 0730-1700. Popular with local people in a fast-food atmosphere with typical Kenyan dishes, such as chapattis, *ugali* and *nyama choma*, and *githeri* – a combination of beans and

corn, which was traditionally a Kikuyu dish and now features in many poorer Kenyan's diet as a good source of protein.

Cafés

Café Lemon Tart, corner of Moi Rd and Kenyatta Av, T051-221 3208. Open 0800-1700. Excellent breakfasts and light snacks, simple café environment conveniently next to the curio market, good freshly ground filter and espresso coffee.
Guava Café, Watalii Rd, T0722-433 054. Open 0830-1700. Serves sandwiches, salads, cakes and more substantial dishes like lamb chops and beef stews, plus coffee, fresh fruit juices and smoothies. Reasonable modern decor and service, and the best thing is it has (sporadic) free Wi-Fi.
Nakuru Coffeehouse, Moi Rd, T051-221 4596. Open 0730-1700. Serves very good Kenyan coffee, snacks and ice cream, although the café is a little dim inside and seating is on plastic bucket chairs. You can buy fresh coffee beans here and they will grind them for you in a wonderful old-fashioned grinder.

⋂ Bars and clubs

Nakuru *p100, map p98*
Dimples, upstairs in Dimu House at the western end of Kenyatta Av near the roundabout. Popular local bar and disco that seems to be open all of the time, with *nyama choma* and snacks, pool tables, strobe lights and a dark dance floor. A little ropey but the nearest thing to a nightclub in Nakuru and sometimes has live music.

⊙ Shopping

Nakuru *p100, map p98*
There are several well-stocked supermarkets around town including **Gelani's** on Club Rd, with a cafeteria serving affordable and generous portions of fresh juices, pastries and some Indian curries; it also has a good butchery 1 block back on Moi Rd that sells

some dairy produce such as yoghurt and cheese. Surprisingly for such a large town, there isn't a branch of **Nakumatt** but there is a branch of **Uchumi** on Mosque Rd. The **market** has an excellent selection of fresh fruit and vegetables but be wary of petty thieves here. For souvenirs, an obligatory stop for anyone passing through Nakuru is at the **Masai Market** in the car park near the clock tower, where there is fine selection of items from all over Kenya. The traders are well used to tour groups and don't hassle you too much.

❶ What to do

Lake Elmenteita *p98*
Go Ballooning Kenya, based at Sunbird Lodge (see Where to stay, page 105), T0715-555 777, www.goballooningkenya. com. 1-hr sunrise balloon rides including champagne breakfast, US$420, pick-ups from the lodges daily except May-Jun.

Nakuru *p100, map p98*
Nakuru Golf Club, 2 km northwest of town on the lower slopes of the Menengai Crater, T057-224 0391. This is the only uphill course in Kenya and was opened in 1929 and extended to 18 holes in 1935. Lake Nakuru can be seen from the 8th and 18th tees. Visitors are welcome, and there's an attractive clubhouse with restaurant and bar.
Shoor Safaris, Moi Rd, T051-221 1408, www.shoortravel.com. Excellent well-established tour operator, offering a variety of safaris and a full hotel-booking service in Kenya, Tanzania and Zanzibar. If you haven't arranged tours to lakes Baringo and Bogoria or Lake Nakuru National Park by the time you get to Nakuru, head here. Also has an office in Nairobi.

⊖ Transport

Nakuru *p100, map p98*
The main bus and *matatu* stand is on the eastern edge of town and vehicles are

clustered around the market. There is regular transport to Nairobi and all the upcountry towns. Recommended is **Easy Coach**, which has a separate terminal at the Kobil petrol station on Kenyatta Av, and has services to **Nairobi**, **Eldoret** and **Kakamega**. Akamba, terminal on the A104/Kisumu road about 500 m west of the roundabout, T051-221 3775, www.akambabus.com, has similar services and their Nairobi–Kampala bus stops in Nakuru. The other long-distance bus companies that stop in Nakuru on the Nairobi–Kampala route include **Kampala Coach**, on the A104/Kisumu road about 100 m west of the roundabout, T0716-283 901, www.kampalacoach.com. Buses generally stop in Nakuru 2 hrs after or before Nairobi (see Transport in Nairobi, page 80, for more details of these services).

Nyahururu and Thomson's Falls *p104*
There are regular buses and *matatus* linking to **Nakuru** (1¼ hrs) to the west and **Nyeri** (2 hrs) to the east. Less plentiful are services to **Naivasha** (1½ hrs) and **Nanyuki** (2 hrs). Several early-morning buses also serve **Nairobi** (3 hrs). If you are driving north from here, fill up on petrol, as it is much pricier in Mararal.

❶ Directory

Nakuru *p100, map p98*
Medical services Nakuru Provincial General Hospital is off Showground Rd to the north of town T051-221 580; **Valley Hospital**, Government Av, T051-221 4503, is a private hospital near the Waterbuck Hotel. There is a well-stocked **pharmacy** next to a doctor's clinic near the Standard Chartered Bank.

Northern Rift Valley

The Rift Valley lakes of Baringo and Bogoria are not far from Nakuru and make an interesting diversion away from the game parks. The lakes are in attractive settings, with Bogoria being best known for its hot springs and flamingos, and Baringo for its large pods of hippos and excellent birdlife. Serious twitchers should head to this region as it offers some of the best birding in East Africa. Mosquitoes are a problem in this region, so sleep under nets and use plenty of repellent. ▸▸ *For listings, see pages 115-117.*

Lake Bogoria National Reserve → *For listings, see pages 115-117. Colour map 3, C6.*
Phone code: 037.

ⓘ *Administered jointly by Baringo County Council and KWS, 0700-1900, entry fees are paid at Loboi Gate, US$20, children (3-18) US$10, US$2.50 per vehicle and US$5 per person for camping, get to the gate in plenty of time if you intend to camp.*

This reserve, which covers an area of 107 sq km in the Rift Valley, is 40 km south of Lake Baringo and 80 km north of Nakuru, and is mainly bushland with small patches of riverine forest. The main reason people visit Lake Bogoria is to see the thermal areas, with steam jets and geysers, and the large number of flamingos that live here.

Arriving in Lake Bogoria National Reserve
It is an easy drive from Nakuru taking less than one hour along the B4 Baringo road. Motorbikes are allowed into the park and the road is paved up to the hot springs, after which it becomes very rough. It is not possible to drive all around the lake as the road is closed on the east side between just north of **Fig Tree Camp** to just east of Loboi Gate. There are three gates, all accessible from by-roads off the B4 main road leading to Baringo. The main gate is **Loboi Gate**, at the lake's north end; the detour eastward from the B4 is 4 km south of Marigat, where a paved road, the E461, heads for Loboi and the gate after a 21-km stretch. The other two gates are to the south of the reserve. Take the east turn-off the B4 at Mogotio, 59 km south of Marigat. This road covers some 20 km up to Mugurin. One kilometre ahead, the road splits into two. The left track heads on for some 20 km until a right turn-off which leads you to **Maji Moto Gate**, close to the hot springs. The other track at the right is badly damaged and quite steep at some stretches and covers 14 km before reaching **Emsos Gate**, the southernmost gate, at the reserve's forest area. ▸▸ *See Transport, page 117.*

Around Lake Bogoria National Reserve
There are now thought to be over two million flamingos, predominantly the lesser flamingo, that feed on *Spirulina platensis*, the blue-green algae. Many of the flamingos have moved here from Lake Nakuru, possibly because the water level there fell so dramatically. Lake Bogoria's geysers are located mostly on the western side of the lake. There are pools with foul-smelling sulphurous steam bubbles, some of which send up boiling hot water spumes several metres high. Take care, the water is very hot and you can get badly burnt.

This is the least-visited of all Kenya's Rift lakes, but it can conveniently be included in a visit to Lake Baringo and the Kerio Valley, all of which are in this extremely hot area of the Rift Valley. The lake itself lies at the foot of the Laikipia Escarpment, and its bottle-green waters reflect woodlands to the east. It is a shallow soda lake, between 1 m and 9 m in depth, and the shoreline is littered with huge lava boulders, surrounded by grassland.

On the eastern side of the lake are found a number of greater kudu; they can best be seen in the evening when they come down to the lake to drink. The northern and eastern shoreline is swampy and attracts many waders. Along the eastern end of the lake you can see the northernmost part of the Aberdares. Trees, including wild fig and acacia, grow densely alongside the dry river beds, and this is the best place for birdwatching. A total of about 375 bird species have been recorded here.

Lake Baringo → *For listings, see pages 115-117. Colour map 3, C6.*

ⓘ *Administered by Baringo County Council, a community fee is paid at the council barrier at Kampi ya Samaki, US$2.20, children (3-18) US$0.50, US$1 per vehicle.*

Lake Baringo, 20 km north of Marigat, is a peaceful and beautiful freshwater lake covering about 168 sq km at an altitude of about 1000 m. It is a shallow lake (maximum depth is 12 m) and, like Lake Naivasha, Lake Baringo appears to have no outlet. It's thought it drains to the north through an underground series of fissures, possibly re-appearing at Kapedo, 80 km away, where steaming water tumbles over a 10-m cliff. This part of Kenya used to be heavily populated with game, but rinderpest greatly reduced the wildlife numbers in the early part of the 20th century. Nevertheless, in 2002, on their way from the Kerio Valley to the Laikipia Plateau, a herd of elephant swam across Lake Baringo, an event never seen before.

Arriving at Lake Baringo
Some 30 km past Nakuru on the B3 is the right turn-off to the B4, toward **Kampi Ya Moto**, **Bogoria**, **Marigat** and **Kampi Ya Samaki**, the latter town being at the lakeshore 2 km away from the main road. The road is tarmac up to the north tip of the lake. From Eldoret, take the C51 heading northward to Cherangani Hills. Some 33 km ahead, at the town of

Lakes Bogoria & Baringo

To Kapedo Springs, Silali
Volcano & Lake Turkana ▲

▲ Karosi
Volcano
(1449m)

Lake
Baringo

Samatian
Island

Tugen Hills

6 Kampi Ya
4 Samaki
5
Council
Barrier 2

7

Ol Kokwe
Island

1

To Maralal (170 km)

B4

To Kabarnet & Eldoret

Marigat

To Marsal (170 km)

To Nakuru ◄

E461

Loboi Gate
8
KWS HQ

Road closed

Lake Bogoria
National Reserve ◆

Maji Moto Gate

Lake
Bogoria

Road closed

Bogoria River

Geysers

Laikipia Escarpment

Road closed

1 ▲ ▲ 2

Waseges River

Emsos Gate

▼ To Mugurin (19 km)

N

3 km

3 miles

Where to stay 🛏
Island Camp **1**
Kudu Campsite & Bandas **3**
Lake Baringo Club **2**

Lake Bogoria Spa Resort **8**
Roberts Camp **5**
Samatian Island **7**
Soi Safari Lodge **6**
Tamarind Garden **4**

Camping ▲
Acacia Tree **1**
Fig Tree **2**

Iten, the road turns southeast. From there you will pass the towns of **Kamarin**, **Tambach**, **Chebloch** and **Kabarnet** and finally reach the junction with the B4 in Marigat, where you turn left for Kampi Ya Samaki and Lake Baringo. ►► See Transport, page 117.

Around Lake Baringo

It is an extremely attractive lake with small, wooded creeks, little islands and white pebble beaches, framed by the mountains to the east and west. The Njemps fishermen can be seen on the lake, and the imposing Laikipia Escarpment creates a magnificent backdrop. The lake contains large schools of hippo and crocodile, and the delicious fish, tilapia, is caught here. There are several islands, **Ol Kokwe** being the biggest of them at approximately 1200 ha, while the other islands include **Parmolok**, **Willys Island**, **Devils Island** and many others. The lake's greatest attraction is the huge number of birds. While it lacks the spectacle of its saline neighbours Bogoria and Nakuru, with their huge flocks of flamingos, it more than makes up for this with the sheer variety of birdlife; more than 470 species have been recorded here in total (more than 300 have been recorded in a single day). On **Gibraltar Island** there is a very large colony of the Goliath heron, the largest concentration of these magnificent birds in East Africa. Mammals found locally include Grant's gazelle, waterbuck, mongoose and dikdik, and, recently, a herd of impala and a number of Rothschild's giraffe have been relocated here. The extended area around the lake is very hot and dry.

If you continue driving north past Lake Bogoria you will start noticing large sawn-off tree trunks lying horizontally in the higher branches of many of the trees. This odd sight is in fact a method of honey cultivation (the trunks are hollowed out to the bees' taste); the effort to get the branches up there is quite amazing. The result is the delicious Asilah honey on sale at the roadside.

Kerio Valley → For listings, see pages 115-117.

West of the lakes of Bogoria and Baringo, the good tarred C51 twists and turns up from Marigat and then down from Kabarnet, a descent of around 1000 m in about the same distance, and then rolls through Chebloch Gorge, a deep and narrow gorge with sheer rock walls and over the Kerio River, before climbing up the other side again towards Eldoret via the settlements of Tambach and Iten. If you are driving and heading from Nakuru to western or northwestern Kenya and have the time, this route through the Kerio Valley makes for a much better alternative to the busy main Nairobi–Uganda road. The deep valley covers an area of 66 sq km and is carpeted with lush, semi-tropical vegetation on the slopes, and thorn bush on the dry valley floor. Part of it has been designated a national reserve. It offers stunning scenery and magnificent views and is surrounded by the Elgeyo Escarpment, Tambach Escarpment and the Tugen Hills. Waterfalls splash down, and isolated *shambas* (small farms) of the **Kalenjin** are dotted around the mountainous countryside. The Kalenjin people are very successful in world-class middle- and long-distance running championships (see box, page 114). Apart from the Kalenjin herders and their livestock, there is little else but the unspoilt beauty and quiet. On this western side of the valley, the best place to appreciate the magnificent views is from the **Kerio View** lodge and restaurant (see page 116) near **Iten**. After Iten, the road flattens at the top of the Elgeyo Escarpment and continues through pine plantations to Eldoret in Western Kenya (see page 151), about 30 km. From Marigat to Eldoret it's about 120 km, but allow plenty of time to navigate the bends, stop at the viewpoints and, if possible, lunch at **Kerio**

Born to run

The Kalenjin people have attracted worldwide attention for excelling in world-class middle- and long-distance running championships. They are sometimes referred to as the 'running tribe' having won some 75% of Kenya's distance running races, from the 800 m to the 10,000 m, as well as the marathon, and 40% of international honours in the same races in the past 40 years. The first of these amazing athletes was Kip Keino, who rose to world prominence in the Mexico Olympics in 1968. Despite suffering severe pain from gallstones, he competed in the 10,000-m race. With two laps to go, whilst in the lead pack, he collapsed in pain but, before the stretcher arrived, he returned to the track and completed the race, despite having been disqualified. Just a few days later, he won the silver medal in the 5000 m and the gold in the 1500 m.

In the 1972 Games, Kip Keino won the gold in the steeplechase and silver in the 1500 m. Today he's president of the Kenya Olympic Committee, and his success in Mexico spawned a dynasty of Kenya runners. The reason for their success has been ascribed in part to their 'altitude' training above 2000 m in the Rift Valley – running at altitude is known to have aerobic benefit, and speeds are estimated to increase by 1.6%, plus a diet that contains a high percentage of complex carbohydrates. Most recent successes include the Kenya team picking up 13 medals at the 2007 International Association of Athletics Federations World Championship in Japan and, of course, Kenya's phenomenal success in the 2008 Beijing Olympics. At this, Kenya had their best-ever performance at the Olympics by winning 15 medals in track and field events of which five were gold.

View. Climatic conditions at the bottom of the valleys are arid and hot, while at the top, cool and sometimes misty, which contribute to the diverse range of landscapes.

Kabarnet → *Colour map 3, C6.*

Kabarnet lies on the C51 before it descends into the Kerio Valley. It's a quiet, unimposing town, despite the fact that it is the capital of Baringo district, but has lingering views of the Tugen Hills and back over the Rift Valley and the lakes below. It was established around 1907 as a colonial administrative post and named after a local missionary with the surname of Barnet. 'Ka' is homestead in the Kalenjin language. Its high altitude means it is cool (especially noticeable if you've come from the heat of Marigat), with an Alpine summer feel, and there are great views northwest 1500 m down into the Kerio Valley. It is the hometown of Daniel Arap Moi, ex-president of the Republic of Kenya. In town there are two banks, a post office, petrol station and a good supermarket and covered market. **Kabarnet Museum** ① *Hospital Rd, T053-21221, www.museums.or.ke, 0900-1800, US$5.50, children (under 16) US$2.75*, is housed in the former residence of the District Commissioner and exhibits elements from the local culture and traditions, as well as information on Lake Baringo and its environment. Lush vegetation growing in its broad gardens makes it almost a small botanic park, and there are some mock-up homesteads of the Pokot and Nandi peoples.

For sleeping and eating price codes and other relevant information, see pages 20-24.

● **Where to stay**

Lake Bogoria National Reserve *p111, map p112*

$$$ Lake Bogoria Spa Resort, outside the reserve, 2 km from Loboi Gate, T0710-445 627, www.lakebogoria-hotel.com. An old-fashioned resort with 23 faded but private cosy cottages with a/c and TV, a large cold-water swimming pool and a naturally heated spa pool, which is fed from the hot springs. The thatched restaurant and bar with garden gazebos is a reasonable stop-over for lunch and serves delicious grilled fish from the lake, and the gates to the park are only a 5-min drive away.

$ Kudu Campsite & Bandas, at Maji Moto Gate, T0723-362 546. At the small Maji Moto village just outside the gate, this is a community-run shady campsite, US$3 per person, tents and bedding can be hired, and has simple 2- to 3-bed *bandas*, US$11 per person, and a small open eating area where you can self-cater or basic meals can be organized, and there's a warm stream to bathe in. The last 4-5 km from the lakeside road up to the gate and village is quite steep, though, if you're staying overnight, this is a pleasant early-morning walk back down to the hot springs.

Camping

Acacia Tree, on the western shore is a shady site under acacia trees that is very close to the flamingos. It has pit latrines but no other facilities. Quite unusually there is a small pool here fed by the hot springs; you can dip a plastic bag in and hang it from a tree to make a bush shower. Bring all equipment, food and drinking water.

Fig Tree Campsite, on the southern shore, is pleasant and quiet, and the stream running through the campsite here is just big

enough to get into. Beware of the baboons: secure your property and avoid camping directly under the fig trees as they enjoy the fruit enormously with predictable results. Access to the site is a winding rocky narrow track for 4WDs only. Again, bring everything with you.

Lake Baringo *p112, map p112*

$$$$ Samatian Island, reservations Nairobi, T020-211 5453, www.samatian islandlodge.com. A small, exclusive private island with breathtaking views, luxury accommodation in 7 comfortable, well-furnished and open-plan cottages with 4-poster beds swathed in mosquito nets on the verandas; one is a double-storey cottage for families. There's a stunning infinity pool, massages are available and the food is very good. Rates are all inclusive. Vehicles are left at a site near **Roberts Camp**, and guests are transferred to the island by boat; charter flights can be arranged.

$$$ Island Camp, on Ol Kokwe Island at the centre of Lake Baringo, T0728-478 638, www.islandcamp.co.ke. There is a swimming pool at the highest point of the camp, with very good views, and paths lead down from the pool to the informal dining and bar areas. The 23 en suite tents have a shaded veranda which faces east to catch the sunset. Activities on offer include waterskiing and windsurfing, guided birdwatching walks and champagne bush breakfasts. All meals and boat transfers are included in the rates. Day visitors are welcome, and boats can be hired from Kampi ya Samaki.

$$$ Lake Baringo Club, just south of Kampi ya Samaki, reservations Nairobi T020-445 636, www.sunafricahotels.com. Set in 10 ha of colourful gardens, with a swimming pool and reasonable buffet-style food, there are 48 rooms but they are well overdue a refurbishment (which may have started by the time you read this). Nevertheless, it's a great setting with views over the lake, and crocodiles, hippos and birds are easily seen; birdwatchers will enjoy the boat trips and walks with an ornithologist. Non-guests can use facilities for a small fee.

$$$ Soi Safari Lodge, just north of Kampi ya Samaki, T053-51242, www.soisafarilodge-lkbaringo.com. A double-storey building with a pagoda-style tiled roof, 50 a/c simply furnished rooms with balconies, bar and restaurant overlooking the lake and its imposing islands. Buffet lunches and barbecue dinners are served, and there's a swimming pool, small reptile park and boat trips are available.

$$-$ Roberts Camp, T053-51431, www. robertscamp.com. A lovely spacious set-up near the lake, well shaded by giant acacia trees. Camping is US$5 per person, and tents and bedding can be hired, *bandas* with kitchens are US$40 for 2 people with shared hot showers, and larger en suite cottages sleeping 4-6 are from US$10. Activities include boat rides and bird walks.

The Thirsty Goat Pub and Restaurant prides itself on an astonishing range of ice cold beers, wines, spirits and exotic cocktails, as well as a very good menu that includes vegetarian dishes, and they can organize packed lunches and bush barbecues.

Watch out for hippos in this area and don't approach them; although they seem docile, they can be dangerous. For a small fee you can swim in the pool at the Lake Baringo Club next door.

$ The Tamarind Garden, at Kampi ya Samaki near the council barrier, T0722-649 446. Pleasant and friendly small hotel built of stone and thatch with 12 simple en suite rooms set around a shady courtyard full of plants, a lovely semi-open thatched restaurant and bar with satellite TV and meals like chicken or steak and rice, rates of around US$25 for a double include breakfast and excellent coffee.

Kerio Valley *p113*

$$ Kerio View, T053-44206, 1 km north of Iten and 35 km from Eldoret on the C51, Elgeyo Escarpment, T0722-781 916, www.kerioview.com. Set in an unbeatable location with glorious endless views over the Kerio Valley, accommodation is in 12 simple *bandas*. It is worth stopping for the fantastic food in the double-storey glass-walled restaurant, even if you're not staying. Bring a sweater as it can be cold up here at night, although there is a roaring fire in the main building. There are good-value set lunches and dinners for US$13, plus light meals, and a very long à la carte menu. There's a children's playground, and unlimited hiking includes the 1000-m descent into the valley over 10 km.

$ High Altitude Training Centre, contact through the website, www.lornah.com. Interested athletes may want to visit this high-altitude running centre in Iten, which lies at 2400 m above sea level and offers simple full-board accommodation, a gym, sauna, solar-heated swimming pool, a 400-m dirt track, coaching, and dozens of long-distance running routes across the top of the Elgeyo Escarpment. It was founded by acclaimed Kenyan female long-distance runner Lornah Kiplagat.

$ Sego Safari Lodge, near Chebloch, 31 km after Kabarnet, turn left for 1 km at the signpost, T053-21399, www.segosafari lodge.co.ke. This is a rural budget option on the lower slopes of the valley, still with tremendous views, a small swimming pool, bar with pool table and satellite TV, restaurant for basic meals and 10 simple en suite rooms with hot showers and Masai blankets. It has orange and pawpaw orchards and gets all its milk, meat and eggs from nearby farms. Activities include walks to local homesteads.

Camping

$ Lenlin Campsite, 6 km from Iten towards Kabarnet on the C51, Elgeyo Escarpment, T0722-900 848, www.lelin campsite.com.

Popular with overlanders, this campsite has flush toilets, hot showers and grassy sites with spectacular views down the valley, though it can get cold here at night, plus some simple double rooms. A bonfire is lit at night, and there is a restaurant and bar, though meals need to be arranged with a little notice, or you can bring your own food and asked for it to be cooked.

Kabarnet *p114*
$ Paradise Hotel, on the main road next to the Kobil petrol station, T0726-616 404, www.paradisehotelkenya.com. A faded town hotel with tatty furnishings and predominantly a local conference venue, but nevertheless set in well-tended gardens, with restaurant and bar. You can get decent sandwiches and cakes here if driving through.

◉ Transport

Lake Bogoria National Reserve *p111, map p112*
Several *matatus* a day run between Nakuru and **Loboi**.

Lake Baringo *p112, map p112*
From Nakuru, there are 2 buses daily to **Kampi Ya Samaki**, but *matatus* only reach **Marigat**. The boats for **Ol Kokwa** island, where **Island Camp** is located, may be hired at the jetty north of Kampi Ya Samaki.

Kabarnet *p114*
Buses to **Eldoret** (3 hrs) and **Nakuru** (2 hrs) leave early in the morning. There are regular and quicker *matatus* to Eldoret, Nakuru and **Marigat**.

Masai Mara National Reserve

This is the most popular of Kenya's parks, with very good reason. Almost every species of animal you can think of in relation to East Africa lives on the well-watered plains in this remote part of the country. One of the unique, spectacular and most memorable sights is the annual migration of hundreds of thousands of wildebeest, gazelle and zebra. The landscape is mainly gently rolling grassland, with the rainfall in the north being double that of the south. The Mara River runs from north to south through the park and then turns westwards to Lake Victoria. Most of the plains are covered in a type of red-oat grass with acacias and thorn trees.
▸▸ *For listings, see pages 122-126.*

Arriving in Masai Mara National Reserve → *Colour map 1, B2/3.*

Getting there
Air A large number of visitors choose to travel to the Mara by plane although it is, of course, more expensive. **Air Kenya** operates daily flights from Nairobi to seven airstrips in the Masai Mara, and a daily flight from Nanyuki to the Mara; **Fly 540** operates a daily flight from Nairobi; **Tropic Air, Safarilink** and **Mombasa Air Safaris** all offer daily scheduled flights to the park lodge airstrips. From Nairobi, the flight lasts little more than an hour compared to the five or more hours by road. ▸▸ *See Transport, page 126.*

Road The Mara is 275 km southwest of Nairobi (five hours by road) in the remote southwestern corner of the country right on the Tanzanian border. The main access to the reserve is through the town of **Narok**, 141 km to the west of Nairobi. It is the main trading centre for the Masai people in southwestern Kenya and the last place you can get a cold drink or refuel if travelling there. Narok has two banks (one with an ATM), a post office and a museum, plus countless souvenir stalls. Public buses from Nairobi only go as far as Narok, and the chances of hitching a lift to and through the reserve are slim. From Narok, there is no singular major road into the reserve, which makes it advisable to study your route into the Mara depending on what your destination is once there. None of the access roads to the Masai Mara are in good condition and during the wet season they become quagmires, and a 4WD is essential.

Masai Mara National Reserve

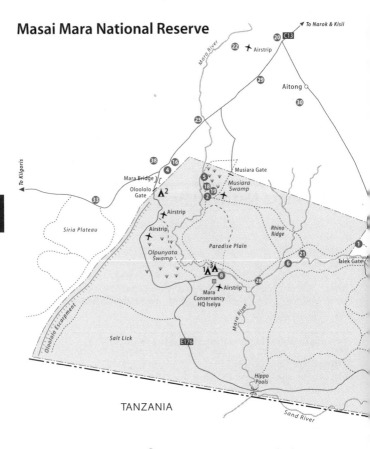

Where to stay

Basecamp Masai Mara **15**
Bateleur Camp **16**
Cottars' 1920s Safari Camp **17**
Enchoro Wildlife Camp **10**
Fig Tree Camp **1**

Governors' Il Moran Camp **18**
Governors' Camp **2**
Governors' Private Camp **19**
Keekorok Lodge **3**
Kicheche Mara Camp **20**
Kichwa Tembo Camp **4**

Kilima Camp **38**
Little Governors' Camp **5**
Mara Explorer **21**
Mara Intrepids **6**
Mara Safari Club **22**
Mara Serena Lodge **8**
Mara Simba Lodge **23**
Mara Sopa Lodge **9**

To get to Narok from the capital take the old Nairobi–Naivasha road (B3 – the more westerly road), which forks to the left at Rironi. This road continues in a northwesterly direction for 6 km then turns left on a sealed tarmac road in a southwesterly direction south of Mount Longonot. From here it is 82 km to Narok. The route is well served by *matatus* and share-taxis. From Narok, if you are driving yourself, there are a number of possibilities for accessing the reserve. Some 15-20 km past Narok, the B3 road reaches **Ewaso Ng'iro**, where there is a crossroads, and from here there are two options.

The first is the most frequently used route, leading to the eastern sector of the park, where **Keekorok Lodge** is located. At Ewaso Ng'iro, turn left on to the C12. Some 40 km ahead the road divides; both tracks lead to the Masai Mara, but to different gates, and converge within the reserve at **Keekorok Lodge**. The one on the right is the main access, leading to **Sekenani Main Gate**; the left route reaches **Ololamutiek Gate**, crossing a collapsed bridge, but it is passable for a 4WD vehicle.

The second option from Ewaso Ng'iro is less used because of its worse condition and abundance of mud after the rains. At Ewaso Ng'iro, go straight ahead along the B3 for 40 km more, up to Ngorengore. At this village turn left on to the C13. From here there are two further choices. The first one is driving straight to **Oloololo Gate** and **Kichwa Tembo Camp**, at the western side of the reserve. The second option is turning left at Aitong to the E177; this track leads to the eastern sector through **Talek Gate**.

If arriving from Kisii from Western Kenya, take the main A1 highway heading south for Tanzania. Past Migori, at Suna, just before reaching the border, there is a left turn off towards Lolgorien and the Masai Mara. This track crosses the Soit Ololol Escarpment and is very steep in places. You'll enter the reserve through Oloololo Gate, at the western sector of the reserve.

There are two **bridges** that cross the Mara River, the New Mara Bridge is along the reserve's main road, the E176, which connects **Keekorok Lodge** with Oloololo Gate. The second bridge over the Mara, lies outside the reserve, northwest of the limits

Loita Hills

To Narok, Naivasha, Nairobi and Ewaso Ng'iro

Talek River

C12

Airstrip 13

23

10 24

Sekenani Gate

12

7

Ololaimutiek Gate

9

3

Sand River

Sand River Gate (closed)

17

Mara Springs Safari
Camp **24**
Mpata Safari Club **33**
Olonana Camp **25**
Rekero Tented Camp **28**
Richard's Camp **29**
Sarova Mara Game Camp **7**
Saruni Camp **30**

Sekenani Camp **12**
Siana Springs Intrepids **13**

Camping ▲
Eluai **1**
Oloololo **2**
Iseiya **3**

shortly after Olocolo Gate. Apart from this main network, there is a web of minor roads in different conditions, some of them passable all the year round and others flooded during the rainy season. Off-track driving over the years has caused wheel-track tangles that are hard to discern from the authorized roads, and the maps available are generally far from perfect.

Tourist information

ⓘ *Daily 0630-1900, US$80, children (under 3-18) US$45, under 3s free, vehicle US$4.*

Entry is per 24 hours or part thereof and covers entry to the national reserve and the Greater Mara region, which also includes a number of group ranches and conservancy areas. The fees are taken at the gates and are paid in US dollars cash. There are now facilities at Olocolo Gate and at the Serena airstrip for accepting Visa credit or debit cards but do not rely on these. In the most part, unless you are self-driving, entry fees are paid at the lodges and camps, or will be part of your safari package if you are on an organized tour.

Safety

If you are exploring the Masai Mara independently in your own vehicle, let someone know where you are going, travel in groups of two or more vehicles if possible, seek advice about the state of the roads, especially in the wet seasons, and remember, in the event of an emergency, mobile phones to do not yet get full coverage in the reserve.

Visiting Masai Mara National Reserve

The greater Mara covers some 1510 sq km ranging between 1500 m and 2100 m above sea level. The reserve receives a high rainfall as a result of both the altitude and humidity of nearby Lake Victoria, 160 km west. It is an extension of Tanzania's Serengeti National Park, a small part of the Serengeti ecosystem which covers some 40,000 sq km between the Rift Valley and Lake Victoria.

Annual migration

If you can, time a visit with the annual migration, which, although it is determined by the times of the rains, generally runs as follows: hundreds of thousands of wildebeest (estimated at 500,000 animals), gazelle and zebra move northwards from the Serengeti Plains in January, having exhausted the grazing there, and arrive in the Masai Mara by about July-August. In the Mara, the herbivores are joined by yet another 100,000 wildebeest coming from the Loita Hills, east of the Mara. Once the Mara's new grass has been eaten, the wildebeests, zebra and gazelles retrace their long journey south to Tanzania in October, where their young are born, and where the grasslands have been replenished in their absence. It is estimated that in four or five months, the wildebeest alone deposit 60,000 tonnes of dung, which fertilizes the grasslands for the next year's migration.

This lengthy trek costs the lives of many old, young, lame and unlucky animals, picked off by predators like lions, leopards and hyenas. One of the highlights of the migration is seeing the animals crossing the **Mara River**. Sometimes thousands of animals will amass on the banks, waiting for an opportunity to cross. Eventually they will choose a crossing point, which can vary from year to year and cannot be predicted with any accuracy. Usually it will be a fairly placid stretch of water without too much predator-concealing vegetation on the far side, although, occasionally they will choose seemingly suicidal places and drown in their hundreds. Below, waiting knowingly in the river, are the enormous Mara crocodiles. First one, then another and then the whole frenetic herd leap into the water.

In places, the river banks have been worn down considerably after centuries of crossings. Most make it to the other side but many hundreds are either taken by crocodiles or drown.

The reserve

The reserve is teeming with herbivores – numbering around 2.5 million – including wildebeest, Thompson's and Grant's gazelle, zebra, buffalo, impala, topi, hartebeest, giraffe, eland, elephant, dik-dik, klipspringer, steinbok, hippo, rhino, warthog and bushpig. There are also large numbers of lion, leopard, cheetah, hyena, wild dog and jackal, as well as smaller mammals and reptiles. In the Mara River hippo and usually sleepy crocodiles can be seen. The number of animals suited to grasslands living in this area has increased enormously over the last 30 years due to woodland being cleared. In addition to the numerous mammals, over 450 species of bird have been recorded, including 57 species of bird of prey. The Masai Mara has a very high density of lion, with about 500 in just over 1500 sq km. Among the rarer mammals found here are the Roan antelope in the southwest sector and the thousands of topi only found here and in the Tsavo National Park. Another shy mammal is the bat-eared fox, sometimes seen peering out of their burrows. The **Oloololo Escarpment** on the western edge of the park is the best place to see the animals, although it is also the hardest part to get around, particularly after heavy rain, when the swampy ground becomes impassable.

The Masai Mara is not a national park but a game reserve, divided into an inner and outer section. The inner section covers an area of 520 sq km, and the greater conservation area is 1510 sq km. The inner section has no human habitation, apart from the lodges. In the outer reserve area the Masai coexist with the game, and evidence of their communities can be seen in the many *manyattas* (villages). The essential difference between a game reserve and a national park is that the indigenous people (the pastoral Masai) have the right to graze their animals on the outer part of the reserve and to kill animals if they are attacked. However, the game does not recognize these designated boundaries, and an even larger area, known as the 'dispersal area', extends north and east contiguous with the reserve, where the Masai people live with their stock. The Masai have never hunted wild animals for food but depend on their cows and, effectively, live in peace with the wildlife. The reserve is controlled by the Narok and Trans-Mara County Councils and not by Kenya Wildlife Services (KWS). At many of the lodges guests are introduced to the cultural side of the Mara, as well as seeing the wildlife, and visits to Masai *manyattas* are on offer, which you can wander round taking as many photographs as you wish. The money generated by these ecotourism initiatives goes directly to the local communities.

There is increasing concern about the impact that the servicing of the requirements of the tourists is having on the finely tuned ecological balance of the reserve. A couple of the identified concerns are the impact that the off-road driving is having on the flora. Many vehicles criss-cross the area causing soil erosion by churning up the grasslands. However, the animals do not appear to be adversely affected by the huge number of visitors to the reserve. Another concern regards the disposal of waste generated by the tourist industry, as some of the predators like hyenas are discovering an easier food source by rummaging through garbage.

☉ Masai Mara National Reserve listings

For sleeping and eating price codes and other relevant information, see pages 20-24.

☉ Where to stay

Masai Mara National Reserve *p117, map p118*

There is an abundance of luxury lodges and tented camps, and some careful thought needs to go into choosing one. However, thanks to the competition, most offer excellent standards and service. All must be booked in advance. At the more expensive, game drives are included in the price, but are an additional expense in some of the less pricey lodges; budget about US$60-80 per person per 2-hr game drive. Night game drives with spotlights are only on offer from the lodges in the Greater Mara area, as vehicles are not allowed out after dark in the reserve itself. Low season is after the long rains, usually Apr-Jun, when room rates drop significantly, but the state of the roads may be at their worst. It's not necessarily a bad time to visit in terms of game viewing, though you may want to consider opting for a flight into the reserve using the money you have saved on accommodation. Always enquire about children policies; some places are very family friendly, while others do not accept children at all. The Masai Mara also offers a number of campsites, really the only option for budget travellers, who may find themselves here if booked on to a budget camping safari, although almost all are accessed on poor roads.

Lodges in the reserve

$$$$ Keekorok Lodge, in the southeast of the reserve, reservations **Wilderness Lodges**, Nairobi T020-650 392, www.wildernesslodges.co.ke, www.keekoroklodge.com. Oldest lodge in the Mara, set in a grassy plain in a good position for the migration, swimming pool, wildlife and local culture lectures, game drives arranged, 101 high-standard rooms, cosy lounge, outside dining room, and an elevated walkway to a bar overlooking a hippo pool.

$$$$ Mara Serena Lodge, reservations Nairobi T020-284 2000, www.serenahotels. com. Well designed, 74 *boma*-style rooms with balconies with a superb view over the Mara River and plains beyond, restaurant overlooking a waterhole, swimming pool, wildlife films, Masai dancing. 2-day packages include return flights from Nairobi or Mombasa, full board and 3 or 4 game drives.

Tented camps in the reserve

A stay in a tented camp, with perhaps a dawn hot-air balloon safari (around US$425: see What to do, page 126), is an unforgettable experience (book well in advance for both). Some tented camps close for a period during Apr-Jun.

There are 4 **Governors' Camps** grouped around the Musiara Swamp near the Oloololo Gate, all different and all expensive, although all meals and game drives are included. They are unfenced but patrolled by Masai guards, just in case the animals get too curious. All the Governors' Camps are consistently rated in the Gold List of *Condé Nast Traveller*'s 'Best Place to Stay in the World'. Rates in the camps vary between US$280 and US$630 per person per night, depending on season, with **Governors' Camp** being the least expensive. Reservations, Nairobi, T020-273 4000, www.governorscamp.com.

$$$$ Governors' Camp, beautiful site by the Mara River. The Mara's original classic safari tented camp was first established in 1972. The 37 tents are very spacious and nicely decorated, with verandas, bar lounge, candlelit dinners, small museum.

$$$$ Governors' Il Moran Camp, in bush along the Mara River. Small and intimate camp hidden under ancient trees, the 10 tents are very private and furnished to a superior standard, with antiques, stunning beds handmade from olive trees, large bathrooms with showers and Victorian baths. You can take dinner at your tent if you wish.

$$$$ Governors' Private Camp, on a bend of the Mara River. A private camp that can only be booked by 1 family/group at a time, up to 16 people (minimum of 4), and usually for a minimum of 3 nights. The food is delicious and served on fine china and crystal, and guests can design their own menus.

$$$$ Little Governors' Camp, access by ferry across the Mara River followed by a short walk with guards. Very special, a splendid site with very high standards. 17 comfortable and tasteful tents with solid floors are tucked around a large watering-hole that teems with animal and bird life. In keeping with safari tradition, lighting is by gas and kerosene lantern or candlelight. Flickering lights at dusk make this an atmospheric place.

$$$$ Mara Explorer, reservations Heritage Hotels, Nairobi T020-444 6600, www.heritage-eastafrica.com. On a bend of the Talek River, this is intended to provide ultra-exclusive sophistication and style for couples. 10 tents where a personal butler is on hand at all times, elephants can be watched from the outside claw-foot bath tubs, lovely riverside dining area, lounge and camp library, and guests can swim at the pool at the nearby Mara Intrepids.

$$$$ Mara Intrepids, reservations Heritage Hotels, Nairobi, T020-444 6600, www.heritage-eastafrica.com. By the Talek River, 30 tents with large 4-poster beds, en suite bathrooms, divided up into 4 different sections each with their own dining areas and mess tents. Swimming pool, elevated viewing platform with bar service, and family orientated with kids' educational activities.

$$$$ Rekero Tented Camp, very close to the confluence of the Mara and Talek rivers, send them an email and they'll recommend the nearest of their agents to you, www.rekero.com. Mobile camp situated for the annual migration, set up seasonally (Jun-Oct, and Dec-Mar), takes up to 20 guests in 9 spacious tents, farmhouse meals, picnics in the bush and sundowners, very good guides for game activities.

$$$$ Sarova Mara Game Camp, reservations, Nairobi T020-716 688, www.sarovahotels.com. Good tents and food, beautiful views, swimming pool, bar with large fireplace, meals can be taken in the restaurant or out in the bush. Large with 75 tents, so rather impersonal but cheaper than many camps and low-season rates start from US$300 for a double.

Greater Mara lodges

$$$$ Mpata Safari Club, Oloololo Escarpment, reservations Nairobi, T020-221 7015, www.mpata.com. A lodge popular with Japanese clientele, with restaurant, library, bar, pool, jacuzzi, very stylish modern decor, very good views, designed by one of Japan's leading architects, 23 cottages with verandas, some with private plunge pool, game drives, walks and visits to Masai villages.

$$$$ Saruni Camp, on the Lemek Koyiaki Group Ranch, to the north of the Mara, near Aitong, www.sarunicamp.com, reservations through **Cheli & Peacock**, Nairobi, T020-604 053, www.chelipeacock.com. Intimate lodge with 6 large and very elegant cottages furnished with colonial antiques, Persian carpets and African art, Italian bathroom fittings, polished wooden floors and large bathrooms with a view, plus 3 luxury tents. Very good mostly Italian cuisine in the dining room, a well-stocked library, and massages on offer.

$$$$-$$$ Mara Simba Lodge, overlooking the Talek River just north of the Talek Gate, reservations Nairobi, T020-434 3960, www.marasimba.com. Family-friendly lodge with 84 rooms arranged in clusters of natural wood and stone thatched *bandas*, some are triples or have interconnecting rooms on the 1st floor, all have verandas overlooking the river. Restaurant and bar, wildlife and ecology talks, swimming pool, room service and evening entertainment.

$$$ Mara Sopa Lodge, near to Ololaimutiek Gate, reservations Nairobi, T020-375 0235, www.sopalodges.com. Well located, this 200-bed lodge is one of the most popular mid-range options in the reserve, with 50 rondavel rooms with balconies/verandas, grand African-style public areas, fine food, friendly staff, excellent swimming pool, balloon safaris and night game drives.

Greater Mara tented camps

$$$$ Basecamp Masai Mara, on a peninsula by the Talek River, reservations Nairobi, T020-577 490, www.basecamp explorer.com. Eco-camp with 12 spacious, comfortable tents shaded by grass roofs, each has its own terrace and a hot shower open to the sky, restaurant, bar, game-viewing tower, Masai entertainment. Makes use of dry toilets, waste recycling, solar energy, etc. Can organize walking safaris. Their separate **Wilderness Camp**, has 5 intimate thatched safari huts perched well apart from each other on an escarpment.

$$$$ Bateleur Camp, reservations **And Beyond**, Johannesburg, T+27-(0)11-809 4300, www.andbeyondafrica.com. On the Mara River, below the location where *Out of Africa*'s final scene was filmed. Romantic and totally private with 9 exclusive tented suites, with expansive bathrooms, ceiling fans, private butler service, decorated with beautiful antiques and framed maps, and there's crystal, bone china and silverware in the restaurant. Walking safaris and day/night game drives are included.

$$$$ Cottars' 1920s Safari Camp, contact through the website, www.cottars.com. An award-winning camp on an unspoilt and remote site near the Tanzania border, the 10 authentic white canvas tents are luxuriously furnished with original safari antiques from the 1920s and have private en suite dressing rooms and bathrooms with old-fashioned tubs. Butlers and beauty therapist for massages and treatments, and game drives in a vintage car.

$$$$ Fig Tree Camp, in a good location on the Talek River, reservations through **Mada Hotels**, Nairobi, T020-605 328, www.madahotels.com. One of the original camps, and one of the less expensive options with doubles from US$360. There are 70 units, some tented camp and some timber cabins, pool, 2 bars and restaurants, a treehouse coffee deck, Masai dancing and wildlife lectures.

$$$$ Kicheche Mara Camp, on the Aitong Plains in the northern Koiyaki Lemek region, reservations Nairobi T020-889 358, www.kicheche.com. 11 comfortably furnished tents, most are secluded and overlook the plains and hills, others are closer together for families/groups and have 4 beds, lounge with comfortable seating, library and games, dining is either alone or with the hosts, good fresh food.

$$$$ Kichwa Tembo Camp, at the base of the Oloololo Escarpment, www. kichwatembo.com, reservations **And Beyond**, Johannesburg, T+27-(0)11-809 4300, www.andbeyondafrica.com. Luxury camp with 40 Hemingway-style safari tents with African-themed decor and private verandas, the main thatched guest areas include a bar/sitting area, indoor/outdoor dining areas, garden with hammocks and a stunning infinity swimming pool.

$$$$ Kilima Camp, in a great position on top of the Siria Escarpment, overlooking the Mara River in the distance, reservations Nairobi T020-208 1747, www.kilimacamp. com. This has 14 very comfortable tents decorated in earthy tones, some sleep a family of 5, bush bar, lounge areas and dining area with great views over the savannah, plus spa treatments, and visits to a Masai *manyatta* within a 30-min walk can be arranged.

$$$$ Mara Safari Club, at the foot of the Aitong Hills, positioned on an ox-bow of the Mara River, reservations **Fairmont Hotels**, Nairobi T020-226 5555, www.fairmont.com/

Marasafariclub. This features 50 luxury tents with 4-poster beds, 10 of which have sunken baths, outdoor showers and platforms for private dining, surrounded by well-cultivated gardens, with a heated swimming pool. Wildlife slide shows, dancing and talks on Masai culture on offer.

$$$$ Olonana Camp, contact through the website, www.sanctuaryretreats.com. A lavish camp on the Mara River, 14 spacious tents, each tastefully appointed with large river-view verandas overlooking a pod of hippos, superb food in the dining room, comfortable sitting area and library, swimming pool.

$$$$ Richard's Camp, on the Aitong Plains, www.richardscamp.com, reservations through Bush Homes of East Africa, Nairobi, T020-600 457, www.bush-homes.co.ke. This small and exclusive tented camp has 6 individually decorated tents, all meals are taken outside, and there is a cosy sitting room with roaring fire. A Victorian bath has been tucked away in the bush where you can bathe by candlelight.

$$$$ Sekenani Camp, near the gate of the same name, reservations Nairobi, T020-270 0781, www.sekenani-camp.com. Intimate, luxurious and very charming, the 15 tents are raised on wooden platforms and set well apart amid lush vegetation; they have polished wooden floors, grand baths and hurricane lamps. A suspension bridge leads to the dining room serving fresh gourmet meals.

$$$$ Siana Springs Intrepids, at the base of the Ngama Hills, reservations Heritage Hotels, Nairobi, T020-444 6651, www.heritage-eastafrica.com. Set in a lush indigenous forest watered by the largest natural springs in the Mara ecosystem known as *Siana* meaning 'the plentiful' in the local language. 38 tents, bar and large dining area, swimming pool, adventure club for kids. Walking safaris, night drives and fly camping along the seasonal streams beneath the Ngama Hills.

$$$-$$ Enchoro Wildlife Camp, close to Sekenani Gate, T0722-655 321, www.enchorowildlifecamp.com. Affiliated to the Youth Hostel Association of Kenya, it can accommodate 50 people in well-furnished en suite permanent tents with hot showers. There's a restaurant for buffets or set meals, and they can organize game drives and visits to Masai *manyattas*. Given that it's on the C12, you could actually get here from Narok by a morning *matatu* going to one of the local villages; ask the camp for full instructions, and they operate regular 2-night/3-day safaris from Nairobi.

$$$-$$ Mara Springs Safari Camp, at the foot of Naunare Hills alongside the forested banks of Sekenani River, 3 km from the Sekenani Gate, reservations Nairobi, T020-224 2133, www.mountainrockkenya. com. Very basic with tents with beds and bedding, some are en suite or share bathrooms with hot showers and flush toilet, from US$55 per person, or pitch your own tent on the well-shaded campsite (**$**). Self-catering in the fully equipped kitchen or meals from the restaurant, and small shop/bar.

Camping in the reserve

The Masai Mara hardly caters for budget travellers apart from a few campsites. However, in reality, these don't work out especially cheap. Camping fees of US$30, children (3-18) US$20, under 3s free, are paid at the gates, but as the campsites aren't fenced, it's mandatory to hire 2 Masai *askaris* (security guards), who you collect from the gate (or they may already be at the campsite) costing KSh2000 (about US$22) each. There are 3 public campsites within the reserve and 5 more private campsites but the latter are generally used by tour operators running camping safaris and, unlike the public campsites which cannot be pre-booked, are often block booked well in advance. Few of the campsites have any facilities, and you'll have to bring everything with you, including water and firewood, and take all rubbish out with you. Baboons and vervet monkeys can be a nuisance, so make

sure everything is secure. Note: you are not permitted to walk more than 25 m from a campsite. In the event of an emergency, there are mobile phone numbers to contact; ensure you get these from the gates.
Eluai Campsite, is near the Mara Serena Lodge airstrip and has no facilities; **Iseiya Campsite**, is near the Park HQ at Iseiya, not far from the Mara Serena Lodge airstrip, and has long-drop toilets but no other facilities, and **Olooolo Campsite** is near the western gate of the same name and has long-drop toilets and very basic cold showers using water from a well (do not drink), but no other facilities.

◑ What to do

Masai Mara National Reserve *p117, map p118*
For details of tour operators that arrange multi-day safaris to the Masai Mara, see Nairobi tour operators, page 77.

A very popular activity in the Masai Mara is a hot-air balloon flight above the plains to watch the big herds from above. Most of the lodges and camps offer this activity, which always works in a similar way. Tourists are picked up around 0530 and driven to the site where the lift-off will take place. The balloon blow-up is part of the experience. Once the balloon rises, passengers have the chance to watch the sunrise high above the plains when the sun comes up and turns the grasslands from blue to gold. Especially during the months of the migration, this is often the highlight of visitors' trips to Kenya. The flight lasts 60-90 mins. Finally, the price usually includes a bush breakfast, made on firewood stoves beneath a tree, frequently served with champagne. If your lodge does not offer this service, they can arrange it and book the day before with one of the lodges that does. Even better, if you know you want to do this before arrival, book it along with

your accommodation or safari. The following lodges have balloons: **Little Governors' Camp**, **Keekorok Lodge**, **Fig Tree Camp** and the **Mara Serena**. Flights cost in the region of US$425.

◒ Transport

Masai Mara National Reserve *p117, map p118*
Air
There are several airstrips in the Masai Mara and flights from **Nairobi** take roughly 1 hr 15 mins but remember they touch down a few times. Fares vary depending on season. Small planes are used so baggage allowance is only 15 kg on these flights. You may have to arrange to leave excess luggage in hotels in Nairobi, and most offer this service for a small fee.

Air Kenya, based at Wilson Airport, Nairobi, T020-391 6000, www.airkenya.com, operates 3 daily flights between **Nairobi** and the Masai Mara, which cost from US$130 each way. It also has a daily direct 1-way flight from **Nanyuki** and **Lewa Downs**, from US$245.

Fly 540, Laico Regency Hotel, Loita St, city centre, Nairobi, T020-243 211, ABC Place, Westlands, Nairobi, T020-445 3252, Jomo Kenyatta International Airport, T020-827 521, www.fly540.com, operates 2 daily flights between **Nairobi** and the Masai Mara, from US$120 each way.

Safarilink, based at Wilson Airport, Nairobi, T020-600 0777, www.flysafarilink.com, operates 2 daily flights between **Nairobi** and the Masai Mara, from US$147 each way.

Mombasa Air Safaris, Moi International Airport, Mombasa, T0734-400 400, www.mombasaairsafari.com, operates a daily circuit between **Mombasa**, **Amboseli**, **Tsavo**, and the Masai Mara airstrips. Flights from Mombasa to the Masai Mara take 2 hrs 45 mins with stops, from US$220 each way.

Contents

Footprint features

Border crossings

Western Kenya

At a glance

⊖ **Getting around** Buses and
matatus link the regional towns,
or you can self-drive.
⊗ **Time required** 3 to 4 days to
drive around the Western Kenya
circuit; 1 day for walking in
Kakamega Forest.
☀ **Weather** Variable; mostly
hot and dry near Lake Victoria,
cooler and wetter in the higher
hills and forests.
⊗ **When not to go** Can be visited
year-round, except for Mount Elgon
National Park, which is very wet
in the rainy seasons (Nov-Dec and
Mar-May).

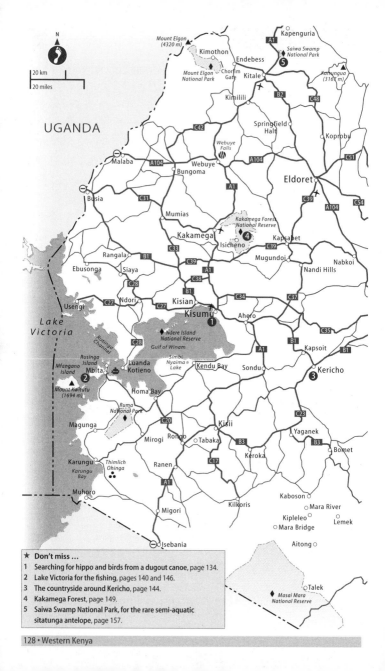

N

Mount Elgon
(4320 m) ▲

Kimothon

Kapenguria ○

A1

Saiwa Swamp
National Park ◆

5

Endebess

20 km
20 miles

Mount Elgon
National Park

Chorlim
Gate

Kitale ○

Karungua
(3167 m) ▲

UGANDA

Kimilili ○

C48

Springfield
Halt ○

B2

Koprobu ○

C42

Webuye
Falls 𝖶

C51

Malaba ○

A104

Webuye ○

A104

Eldoret

○ Busia

C31

Bungoma ○

A1

○ Mumias

C39

Kakamega Forest
National Reserve

Kapsabet ○

A104

C54

Rangala ○

B1

Kakamega ○

Isicheno ○

4

C39

Mugundoi ○

Nandi Hills ○

Nabkoi ○

Ebusonga ○

Siaya ○

C28

C39

A1

C33

C34

C37

Usengi ○

C27

Ndori ○

C27

Kisian

B1

Aheru ○

C38

B1

Lake
Victoria

Kisumu

1

Rusinga
Channel

Rusinga
Island

Mfangano
Island ▲

2

Ndere Island
National Reserve

Gulf of Winam

Simbi
Nyaima ●
Lake

B1

C35

Kapsoit ○

Mbita ⚓

Luanda
Kotieno ○

Kendu Bay ○

Sondu ○

3 Kericho ●

Mount Kwitutu
(1694 m) ▲

Homa Bay ○

Magunga ○

Ruma
National Park ◆

C20

Kisii ○

C23

Mirogi ○

Rongo ○

Tabaka ○

B3

Keroka ○

Yaganek ○

B3

Bomet ○

Karungu ○

Thimlich
Ohinga

Ranen ○

C17

Karungu
Bay

Muhoro ○

A1

Migori ○

Kilkoris ○

Kaboson ○

○ Mara River

Kipleleo ○

Lemek ○

○ Mara Bridge

○ Isebania

Aitong ○

★ Don't miss ...

1 Searching for hippo and birds from a dugout canoe, page 134.
2 Lake Victoria for the fishing, pages 140 and 146.
3 The countryside around Kericho, page 144.
4 Kakamega Forest, page 149.
5 Saiwa Swamp National Park, for the rare semi-aquatic
   sitatunga antelope, page 157.

Talek ○

Masai Mara
National Reserve ◆

Western Kenya is the most fertile and populous part of the country, teeming with market towns and busy fishing villages. This is farm country. The patchworks of maize, sugarcane and tea plantations among the evergreen vegetation and beautiful rolling hills are the mainstay of the local communities, and the produce grown here feeds much of Kenya. To the south of this region is Kenya's share of Lake Victoria, Africa's largest lake, which provides a living for many of the Lou people on its shore, who fish for tilapia and Nile perch from small picturesque dugout canoes, equipped with lateen sails. There are also a number of national parks and reserves in this region. Kakamega Forest National Reserve is the only tract of equatorial rainforest in Kenya that was once linked to the mighty forests of Central Africa. It contains many species of bird, tree and butterfly that are found nowhere else in the country and is a delightful and tranquil place for walking. Saiwa Swamp National Park, near Kitale, is worth a visit to see the rare sitatunga antelope. Mount Elgon National Park, also accessed from Kitale, has good climbing and is home to the famous elephants that enter its caves in search of salt.

Although geographically not far from the Masai Mara to the southeast, Western Kenya doesn't have the big draw card of animal-studded plains and is not that popular with the big tour operators so has few upmarket establishments. But this is to the benefit of the independent traveller. In fact, conditions for budget travellers are perfect: over half the population of the whole country lives here, so public transport is excellent and the main road surfaces tend to be above average; there are numerous cheap hotels and restaurants, and there is plenty to see and do.

Getting around Western Kenya is pretty straightforward. There are flights from Nairobi to **Kisumu**, the region's largest city, where the recently upgraded airport serves as a hub for the region; increasingly there are also flights to the most populous towns, namely **Eldoret**, **Kitale** and **Kakamega**. Several major roads bisect the region. Beyond Nakuru, the main road from Nairobi splits and the **A104** heads in a northwesterly direction to Eldoret and on to the Uganda border at Malaba; this is the route most of the heavy trucks take on their route from Mombasa to the interior. The **B1** heads due west from Nakuru via Kericho to Kisumu. The main **A1** south of Kisumu goes to Tanzania and is good all the way through to Mwanza. Some Tanzanian long-distance buses between Mwanza, Arusha and Dar es Salaam take the route via Kenya, as the roads are better than in the interior of Tanzania. From the border, the Western Corridor of Tanzania's Serengeti National Park is less than 200 km from Kenya, so there is the option of exploring some of Tanzania along with Western Kenya.

All the regional towns are linked by a steady stream of buses and *matatus*, and most (not all) of the roads are in a reasonable tarred condition with only the occasional pothole. Self driving is also a good option in this region; distances between the towns and sights are relatively short and there are plenty of places to stop for petrol and take a break. The towns themselves hold little interest, but driving around the region gives a good opportunity to enjoy the countryside, especially the impossibly scenic hills covered in the brilliant green tea plantations around **Kericho** and **Kisii**.

Kisumu and around

Kisumu, on the shore of Lake Victoria and 310 km northwest of Nairobi, is the principal town in Western Kenya and the capital of Nyanza Province. With a population of just over half a million, it is the third-largest city in the country. It has a tattered charm, a slow, gentle pace of life and a relaxed ambience. Women sit on the side of the road braiding each other's hair while tempting shoppers with their beautifully arranged pyramids of tomatoes or split sundried tilapia fish, and boda boda drivers park their vehicles in the shade and somehow catnap straddled across them while batting away mosquitoes in their sleep. The whole town comes to almost a standstill on Sunday. The sleepy atmosphere is as much due to lack of economic opportunities as to the extremely hot dry weather, which makes doing almost anything in the middle of the day hard work. Unfortunately, the town is not economically prosperous, there is little formal employment, and the poverty rate is among the highest in the country.
►► *For listings, see pages 135-139.*

Kisumu → *For listings, see pages 135-139.* *Colour map 1, A2. Phone code: 057. Population 576,000.*

Arriving in Kisumu
Kisumu Airport ① *T057-202 0811, www.kenyaairports.co.ke*, is 3.5 km to the northwest of the city off the Busia road, and **Kenya Airways** and **Fly 540** have daily flights to and from Nairobi. A smart new terminal building opened here in 2011, and there's a pleasant restaurant to wait at. Kisumu Airport is next to Lake Victoria, and the landing approach offers great views of little boats slicing through the waters below. A taxi from the airport shouldn't cost more than US$8; taxis wait in the car park to meet the planes.

Kisumu is an excellent base for exploring the region, with good bus and *matatu* connections and frequent departures to all the upcountry towns in Western Kenya and the Rift Valley, as well as to Nairobi, which is a six- to seven-hour drive. The main bus and *matatu* stands are north of the main market. The city is the historic western terminus of the Uganda Railway from the Indian Ocean to Lake Victoria; for details of the thrice-weekly passenger services between Nairobi and Kisumu, see box, page 18. The railway station is to the west of town on New Station Road. Despite the hilly terrain, you will have no problem getting around Kisumu itself as there are plenty of taxis and literally thousands of *boda bodas* (bicycle taxis) – so many that it is quite difficult to drive through central Kisumu because of the barrage of bikes. Some *boda boda* drivers have upgraded to motorbikes and new on the scene are motorized three-seater tuk-tuks. ▶ *See Transport, page 138.*

Kisumu

Where to stay	New Victoria 11	Kenshop Bakery 1
Duke of Breeze 4	Royal City 7	Kimwa Annex 2
Imperial 3	Sunset 1	Lakeside Meeting Point 4
Kiboko Bay Resort 5	Vic 8	Laughing Buddha 5
Kisumu 14		Mon Ami 6
Kisumu Beach Resort 5	**Restaurants**	Palms Coffee Shop 8
Milimani Resort 2	Florence 3	Victoria Terrace 7

Lake Victoria

Lake Victoria is one of the most important natural water resources in the sub-Saharan region of Africa. It is the second biggest freshwater lake in the world, with a surface area of approximately 69,500 sq km. The Tanzanian share of the lake is 49%, whilst the Kenyan share of the lake is 6% and Uganda has 45%. The surrounding lake communities in all three countries equal around 30 million people, with a large proportion being totally dependent on the lake for water, food and economic empowerment.

Despite its vast size, Lake Victoria remained one of the last physical features in Africa to be discovered by the 19th-century explorers from Europe. Early charts depict a vague patch of water lying to the north and east of the 'Mountains of the Moon' (today's Rwenzori Mountains in Uganda), but it was not until 1858 that explorers Speke and Burton stumbled on its southern shore near Mwanza in Tanzania, saying "the lake at my feet is the most elusive of all explorers' dreams, the source of the legendary Nile."

Lake Victoria is relatively shallow and has a gentle slope on the shores, hence any slight change in lake level affects a considerably large land area. The lake has a mean depth of about 40 m, with the deepest part at 82 m.

Scientifically, it is puzzling that so many diverse species unique to these waters could evolve in so uniform an environment. Biologists speculate that hundreds of thousands of years ago, the lake may have dried into a series of smaller lakes causing brilliantly coloured cichlids to evolve differently. These fish are greatly sought after for aquariums. One unique characteristic for which cichlids (tilapia being the best known) are noted is the female's habit of nursing its fertilized eggs and young in its mouth. To the people of Lake Victoria, the cichlids have been their livelihood. Lake Victoria is also a home to a predator fish, the Nile perch, introduced into the lake 20 years ago as a sport fish. The lake once had abundant hippo and crocodile but these are reduced.

Background

Kisumu developed during the colonial era into the principal port in the region. The railway line reached Lake Victoria in 1902, five years after plate laying began 1000 km away in Mombasa, opening up trade opportunities. It was briefly called Port Florence. By the 1930s it had become the hub of administrative and military activities on the lake. Kisumu was a difficult place at this time, bilharzia was endemic, malaria and sleeping sickness were common, and the climate was sweltering. However, the area attracted investment from many different quarters, including Asians ending their contracts to work on the railway.

Kisumu and the region of Western Kenya near Lake Victoria are dominated by the Luo people, whose traditional livelihood is fishing. The Luo and the Kikuyu inherited the bulk of political power following Kenya's Independence in 1963, and a prominent Luo, Oginga Odinga, became vice-President under Jomo Kenyatta (a Kikuyu). However, a difference of opinion between them caused Odinga to resign, which resulted in the Luo becoming politically marginalized under the Kenyatta and then the Moi governments. The breakdown of trade between Kenya, Uganda and Tanzania, and the collapse of the East African Community in 1977, also badly affected Kisumu. It has been bypassed by post-Independence development and has had little investment in infrastructure and basic services – the signs are all too visible: warehouses by the docks remain empty, and the port does not have the bustling atmosphere you would expect in such an important town. In addition to this, in recent years, the water-hyacinth problem in Lake Victoria has proved to be an impediment to the local fishing industry and has put a stop to ferry services on the lake. The prolific weed formed great mats, inhibiting even large boats from using the port and it got so bad at the end of the 1990s that people could actually walk across it to reach their marooned boats. Today it is still a problem, and the main bay in front of Kisumu's port, is still covered with it, but 'swamp devils', which regularly chop, shred and remove the weed, have contributed to reducing it. Nevertheless, while the fishing industry may have recovered a little, ferry services are still suspended because of falling water levels (see box, page 132).

Over the years it has also, unfortunately, been a hotbed of ethnic violence, predominantly between the Luo and Kikuyu. The unexplained murder of Robert Ouko in 1990, a Luo politician who at one time served as Kenya's Foreign Minister and administered a report on corruption in the Kenyan government, led to riots where many people died and much property was destroyed. Later, in the build-up to multi-party elections in Kenya in 2002, the nearby area was the scene of outbreaks of ethnic violence in which thousands of people fled their *shambas*, coming into Kisumu or heading up to Eldoret. Then, Kisumu and much of Western Kenya witnessed the worst of Kenya's 2007 post-election violence, when hundreds of people were killed or injured, and many Kikuyu people fled Western Kenya in fear of the lives. Prime Minister Raila Odinga is the son of Oginga Odinga and was born in Nyanza Province, which is a stronghold of his support. On 30 December 2007, when the disputed election results turned to favour Mwai Kibaki (a Kikuyu) and not Odinga (a Luo), the town exploded, and what followed was 10 days of rioting, looting and killing; afterwards, 120 bodies were counted in the city morgue. Most of the violence occurred in Kisumu's slums, but furious mobs stormed Oginga Odinga Street and looted or burnt out shops, supermarkets and even internet cafés. Many of these were Kikuyu-owned; about 90% of the businesses in town were affected.

Places in Kisumu

Kisumu Museum ① *east of the town's main market off Nairobi Rd, T057-202 0332, www. museums.or.ke, 0930-1800, US$5.50, children (under 16) US$2.75*, is set in a lovely garden where paths have been laid out and the trees labelled, and offers a pleasant distraction for an hour or two. Its small yet comprehensive exhibition gallery focuses on displays of material culture of the peoples of the Western Rift Valley and Nyanza Province. This includes traditional clothing and adornment, basketry, fishing gear, agricultural tools and hunting weaponry. There are also a number of stuffed birds, mammals, reptiles and fish. Most impressive is a lion bringing down a terrified wildebeest and a 190-kg Nile perch, thought to be the largest ever caught in Kenya. The ethnographic exhibits centre on the customs and traditions of the tribal groups who lived in this area, and there is a life-size replica of a traditional Luo homestead, which has livestock pens and a granary and local vegetables are grown in the garden. There's also a tiny aquarium, which displays small fish found in Lake Victoria, such as tilapia, a snake pit with some rare species found in Kakamega Forest, and a couple of dead-looking crocodiles in a small pool. Look up from here and you'll see a magnificent collection of weaver bird nests balancing precariously from the branches of a tree that hangs over the crocodile pen. If the branches of the tree get any lower and the crocodiles decide to wake up, the nests will easily be within snappable distance.

The majority of people in Kisumu are Christian (mainly Roman Catholics), but there are a significant number of Muslims. **Jamia Mosque**, on Otieno Oyoo Street, is testament to the long tradition of Islam here and is one of the most striking buildings in the city. Built in 1919, this green and white building has two imams, and calls to prayer can be heard in much of the town. Non-Muslim males may be permitted to enter the enclosure, ask the gateman, and everyone else can admire the gleaming silver domes from the street.

Around Kisumu

Dunga and around

Dunga is a small Luo fishing village, just 4 km outside Kisumu, and is located by following the shoreline road south past the **Sunset Hotel**. It takes about an hour to walk, or get a motorbike *boda boda*. To get back to town, ask around in the village and someone will find a driver and bike. It is a lovely, peaceful place to visit on the shores of Lake Victoria and, given that the views of the lake from the city centre of Kisumu are curiously very limited (only from the tops of tall buildings), this is the best place to come to see the lake itself. **Dunga Swamp** is a belt of papyrus on the lake's edge popular with birdwatchers and is home to more than 100 bird species, including the rare *Papyrus gonolek*, which faces extinction due to the cutting of papyrus reeds along the shores of Lake Victoria. The papyrus yellow warbler is relatively common.

The **Kiboko Bay Resort** (see Where to stay, page 135) at Dunga has great views and a lovely restaurant with tables in the garden to have cold soda or beer and admire the little fishing boats on the lake. The delightful swimming pool, which non-residents can use if they are utilizing the restaurant or bar, sits on a little hill right above the lake. Do not be tempted to swim or even paddle in the lake itself as bilharzia is present. Watching the sun set over the lake is a very pleasant way to end the day, and, remember, being so close to the equator, sunset is between 1800 and 1900 throughout the year. There are hippos here and, once night has fallen, they come out of the water to graze on land. You can negotiate a canoe ride with a fisherman in Dunga, or organize to take a rowing boat out from the resort to nearby Hippo Point where you can see the hippos in the water during the day for about US$25 per boat/per half hour for up to five people. **Kisumu Beach Resort** (see Where to stay, page 136), on the opposite side of the bay, is another nice place to spend the day and enjoy the lake. It has views across the bay to the city and, again, boats can be hired. Note: whether you arrange a boat with the resorts or a local fisherman, ensure there are life jackets – in the morning the lake is usually very calm, but in the afternoons the wind picks up. Additionally, take a hat and sunscreen as you will be relentlessly exposed to the sun and its reflection on the water's surface.

Tiny **Kisumu Impala Sanctuary** ⓘ *on the way up the dirt track to Dunga, 3 km from Kisumu, www.kws.org, 0800-1800, US$15, children (3-18) US$10*, only 1 sq km of marsh, forest and grassland, was created to protect the few remaining impala in the region, decimated over the last century by hunting. The sanctuary was expanded to act as a holding point for captured animals. Nowadays it is home to a lonely old male lion, two leopards, a spotted hyena and several vervet monkeys in addition to several reptiles and birds, but they are all in cages and it is nothing more than a sad-looking zoo. Hippos come up to the sanctuary to graze and, in the past, there have been sightings of the rare Sitatunga antelope. You can get a *boda boda* to the gate and ticket office. A guide takes you around to give you a rather school-child account of the animals and, again, you can hire a boat to take you out to Hippo Point. The boatmen here are particularly knowledgeable about the birdlife.

Ndere Island National Reserve

ⓘ www.kws.org, daily 0600-1800, US$20, children (3-18) US$10.

The reserve covers a small island of just over 4 sq km off the northern shore of Lake Victoria, 30 km from Kisumu. In the local Luo language Ndere means 'meeting place' and, according to legend, Kit Mikayi, mother of the tribe, rested up near here following her long journey south down the Nile Valley. Birdlife teems in the park, from pied kingfishers and swifts to the African fish eagle and the dazzling malachite kingfisher. Hippos and crocodiles are plentiful on the shoreline, and there is also a small herd of impalas. Other animals present include pythons and monitor lizards. Very few visitors make it to Ndere Island, due to its small size and lack of terrestrial wildlife. Bird enthusiasts, however, would find a visit to Ndere Island very rewarding. There is no regular boat service to the park, but both **Kiboko Bay Resort** (see below) and **Kisumu Beach Resort** (see page 136) can organize motor boat trips. This is quite a good way to explore Lake Victoria; the boat takes about an hour to get to the island and there's time to spend on the island itself. From both resorts, boats cost in the region of US$50 per hour for up to five or eight people. It is possible to camp on the island but you have to be completely self sufficient.

◉ Kisumu and around listings

For sleeping and eating price codes and other relevant information, see pages 20-24.

● Where to stay

Kisumu *p130, map p131*
Kisumu is swarming with mosquitoes. If you don't have a net, get a room with one. Cover up and use repellents. A fan is a boon, too.

$$$ Imperial Hotel, Jomo Kenyatta Av, T057-202 2261, www.imperialhotel.co.ke. The 70 smart a/c rooms have made-for-hotel furniture, plush carpets and fittings and satellite TV. The ones on the 3rd and 4th floors have lake views. Facilities include a choice of venues to eat and drink (see Restaurants, page 136), internet access, a very good swimming pool and gym. It's popular, so book ahead; rates are significantly lower Fri-Sun.

$$$ Kiboko Bay Resort, Dunga, 4 km south of Kisumu, T057-202 5510, www.kibokobay. com. This is the nicest accommodation in Kisumu, exceptionally friendly and in a lovely lakeside setting. It is worth coming here for the charming restaurant (see Restaurants, page 136), swimming pool and boat excursions, even if you're not staying. The 12 en suite rooms are set in spacious and comfortable permanent tents on elevated wooden decks under thatched roofs, dotted around manicured gardens. Rates start from around US$100 for a double.

$$$ The Vic Hotel, next to Mega City on the Nairobi Rd, T020-806 6847, www. thevichotelkisumu.com. Newly built with an impressive marble-and-glass lobby, smart and spacious rooms arranged in 2-storey wings with satellite TV, a/c and Wi-Fi, probably the most modern bathrooms in Kisumu, comfortable bar/lounge, restaurant, well-equipped gym and swimming pool. Business orientated and lacking in atmosphere, but excellent service. Doubles start from US$120.

$$$-$$ Kisumu, Jomo Kenyatta Av, T057-202 2833, www.maseno.ac.ke/hotelkisumu. Very large and grand colonial hotel that is now run by Kisumu University. Refurbished with a modern tiled lobby, made-for-hotel furnishings and wall-to-wall carpeting, the former tatty colonial charm has been somewhat lost and it's a shame they didn't refurbish it in the style of its era. However, the 80 a/c rooms are neat with good bathrooms and TV, and there's a decent bar and restaurant (see Restaurants, page 137), lovely swimming pool and car park.

$$ Milimani Resort, off Awour Otieno Rd, signposted from Jomo Kenyatta Av from the **Kisumu Hotel**, T057-202 3245, www. milimaniresort.co.ke. Old-fashioned brick block with car park in a quiet location, a fair distance south of the town centre. The reasonably comfortable rooms are well equipped with fans, nets and TVs but are on the small side. Restaurant, bar and a rather surreal concrete 1960s swimming pool area.

$$ Sunset, Aput Lane, south of town, T057-202 217. A very faded, overpriced and poorly managed 5-storey hotel with threadbare furnishings and unreliable a/c and elevator. But nevertheless worth a mention as the veranda looks over beautiful lawns, all 50 rooms have balconies and views of the lake and sunset. There's a restaurant and bar, secure parking and swimming pool.

$$-$ Royal City, Odera St, T0726-823 128, www.royalcityhotel.co.ke. A fairly new option so everything is quite fresh, with 50+ neat rooms (though small), good hot showers, satellite TV and bathrooms are behind sliding doors. Doubles go from US$45. There's a comfortable bar and a reasonable choice of African, Indian and continental dishes in the restaurant. There's a small shop at reception.

$ The Duke of Breeze, on a side street off Jomo Kenyatta near the **Imperial Hotel**, and next to the Yatin supermarket, T0717-105 444, www.thedukeofbreeze. com. Inexplicably named but decent budget option with 24 large and clean single, double and triple rooms with warm showers, nets and TV. Great rooftop bar and restaurant with city and lake views, ideal to watch the sunset and excellent food including (unusually) salads and stir-fries. A double is US$25.

$ Kisumu Beach Resort, T0733-749 327, 3.5 km west of town on the Busai road, the turn-off is opposite the airport, www. kisumubeachresort.com. Budget resort with beds with mosquito nets in simple tin-roofed *bandas* next to the lake, rustic partially open restaurant and bar, with pool

table, satellite TV and good views across the bay to Kisumu, reasonable African and Indian food, can organize boat trips. Double *bandas* go from US$25, and there's also a shady campsite with hot showers and plenty of space for vehicles, US$5 per person.

$ New Victoria, Gor Mahia Rd, T057-202 1067. Clean and large rooms with fans but check mosquito nets for holes, in an unmissable building brightly painted green and yellow. Triple rooms available, 2nd-floor rooms have pleasant balconies (rooms 205-209 have views of the lake). Good basic food like stews and curries, but Muslim-owned, so no alcohol.

🍴 Restaurants

Kisumu *p130, map p131*
There's little choice of restaurants in Kisumu; the hotels are the best bet. There are plenty of cheap daytime canteens around Oginga Odinga Rd catering for office workers, where you can get a steaming plate of beef or chicken stew with *kachumbari* (spicy tomato relish) and chapatti. Cheap kiosks near the bus stand and market and more in the car park of the Maseno University City Campus sell grilled meat on skewers or tilapia fish with *ugali* (maize dough).

$$$-$$ The Florence, at the Imperial Hotel, see Where to stay, page 135. Open 0630-1000, 1830-2200. This is Kisumu's best and most formal restaurant, offering an elaborate buffet breakfast and dinners of curries, steaks, chicken and pasta, or tilapia fish from the lake, and there's always something for vegetarians. The **Victoria Terrace**, 1030-2200, is a popular bar that serves good-value dishes like grilled fish or burgers.

$$-$ Kiboko Bay Resort, Dunga, see Where to stay, page 135. Open 0700-2300. Very pleasant bar/restaurant with chunky wooden tables inside and plastic tables scattered on the terrace overlooking the lake and in the gardens. You can get a simple toasted sandwich here, and main meals include creamy masala curries and whole baked tilapia fish straight from the lake. Diners can use the swimming pool and pool bar.

$$-$ Kisumu Hotel, Jomo Kenyatta Av, see Where to stay, page 135. Open 0730-2300. Large brilliantly white canteen with CNN on TV, offering English-style cooked breakfasts and very popular school-dinner type fare of pork chops and vegetables or chicken and chips, followed by sponge and custard or fruit salad and ice cream, and there's a comfortable fully stocked bar.

$$-$ Mon Ami, at Mega City on the Nairobi Rd, T057-202 0379. Mon-Sat 1200-2300. Outside seating under a metal gazebo, varied menu including burgers and pizza and some Asian dishes like fried rice, spare ribs and spicy chicken, separate coffee bar that also serves desserts, and the bar has large TV for watching sports.

$ Kimwa Annex, Otuona St. Open 24 hrs. A clean, tiled local canteen with plastic tables that's very popular for huge plates of cheap local fare, served up self-service style from big catering tins, there's also a bar with pool table.

$ Lakeside Meeting Point, Oginga Odinga Rd, opposite Prime Bank, T0717-111 292. Open 0730-1700. Popular and spotlessly clean fast-food joint serving burgers, pies, kebabs, sausages and the like; try the excellent fried chicken and masala chips or Spanish omelette for breakfast. Has some plastic tables on the street.

$ Laughing Budda, Swan Centre, Oginga Odinga Rd. Tue-Sun 1100-2200. Friendly café/bar with snacks and drinks, including excellent milkshakes and herbal teas, sandwiches using home-made bread and treats like chocolate brownies. More substantial are the pastas, Indian curries and vegetarian dishes. Quite often has Wi-Fi, and the bar on the mezzanine level stays open late.

Cafés
Kenshop Bakery, Oginga Odinga Rd. Mon-Sat 0900-1500. Branch of a popular bakery chain, with a few tables, selling very good pies, pastries, bread, pizza slices and ice cream as well as hot drinks and juice, including freshly squeezed sugarcane juice.

Palms Coffee Shop, at the Imperial Hotel, see Where to stay, page 135. Open 0900-2200. A canopied area elevated above the swimming pool with some outdoor tables facing Jomo Kenyatta Av, offering great coffees and freshly baked and surprisingly elaborate cakes and pastries.

☊ Bars and clubs

Kisumu *p130, map p131*
The Duke of Breeze. 0900-2300. On the top floor of the hotel (see page 136) up 4 flights of rickety stairs, great views of Kisumu, an area with couches, good music and food, often shows live sports and holds occasional barbecues, busy on Fri and Sat nights, Wi-Fi.

Shalimar Lounge Bar, at the Imperial Hotel, see Where to stay, page 135. Open 1530-2300. Kisumu's smartest bar on the rooftop, with great city and lake views, serves snacks and a good choice of drinks, including cocktails and imported wine.

◎ Shopping

Kisumu *p130, map p131*
Curios and crafts
The usual range of Kenyan souviners are for sale in Kisumu. *Kisii* soapstone fashioned into chess boards, bowls, pots, candleholders and sculptures, and *kikois* (woven cloth) are a particularly good buy in Kisumu. Street vendors are outside the post office and at a line of stalls opposite the **Kisumu Hotel** on Jomo Kenyatta Av. You will need to barter hard to get a good price.

Markets

Kisumu's main market on Nairobi Rd is one of the largest and most animated in Kenya, and worth a wander to soak up some of the atmosphere. The market bustles every day, although Sun tends to be quieter, and sells everything imaginable: fruit and vegetables, children's clothes, tools, flip-flops, radios, batteries, bags, sheets, etc. There are also second-hand clothes and shoes stalls all over town, and these are well worth a rummage for genuine international brands.

Supermarkets and shopping centres

Nakumatt Nyanza, Mega Plaza, Oginga Odinga St, has a good selection of goods and rather remarkably is one of Kenya's Nakumatt branches that is open 24 hrs. The larger **Nakumatt City**, in the **Mega City**, Nairobi Rd on the left just beyond the museum, Mon-Fri 0830-1800, Sat 0900-1700, Sun 1000-1600, has just about anything for sale and is in a modern shopping centre with a number of other shops, banks and ATMs and coffee shops.

☉ What to do

Kisumu *p130, map p131*
Swimming
Do not swim in the lake as bilharzia is rife, so use the hotel pools at the **Sunset**, **Kisumu**, **Milimani Resort**, **Imperial** or **Kiboko Bay Resort**. Each charge around US$2 for non-guests to use the pool or you may be able to use them for free if you are utilizing the restaurants.

Tour operators

Integritour, downstairs at **The Duke of Breeze**, see Where to stay, page 136, T0700-517 969, www.integritour.com. Useful local tour operator that can arrange visits to the local sights such as Hippo Point with a boat ride, a day trip to Kakamega Forest, Kericho (for the tea plantations and lunch at the **Tea Hotel**, see page 147) or village visits, which perhaps could include a

visit to an orphanage or medical centre run by local NGOs/charities. They are also a good contact if you are interested in volunteering for an NGO in Western Kenya.
Kisumu Travels Ltd, Oginga Odinga Rd, T057-202 4582 www.kisumutravels.com. General travel and flight agent and can also arrange car hire but only with a driver. They may also be able to help in pre-booking train tickets in both Kisumu and Nairobi.

☉ Transport

Kisumu *p130, map p131*
Air
Fly 540, Al-Imren Plaza, Oginga Odinga Rd, T057-202 5331, Nairobi T020-827 521, www.fly540.com, has 2 daily flights in each direction between Kisumu and **Nairobi** taking 45 mins, 1 way from US$79. The early-morning flight at 0750 picks up in **Eldoret** – the plane hardly gets up into the air. It doesn't stop in Eldoret on the way to Kisumu, however.
Kenya Airways, Alpha House, Oginga Odinga Rd, T057-205 6000, www.kenya-airways.com. There are 4-5 daily flights between Kisumu and **Nairobi** taking 50 mins and costing from US$105, 1 way.

Bus and matatu

The main *matatu* and bus stopping point is behind the covered section of the main market. There are regular *matatus* and buses travelling between Kisumu and most major towns in Western Kenya. There are also many leaving for **Nairobi** passing through **Nakuru** and **Kericho** on the B1. Approximate times: **Nairobi**, express 6 hrs or normal 8 hrs, 2 hrs to **Kericho**, 5 hrs to **Nakuru**, 2 hrs to **Eldoret**, 1 hr to **Kakamega**. The offices of **Akamba Bus**, T057-202 3554, www.akambabus.com, and **Guardian Coach**, T0727-544 664, www.theguardiancoach. com, are close to each other in the town centre, on Bank St just off New Station Rd. Both offer good services between Kisumu and Nairobi via Kericho and Nakuru.

The through buses between Nairobi and Kampala in Uganda go via Eldoret on the A104, and those between Nairobi and Mwanza in Tanzania go via Kisii on the A1 south of Kisumu. (See Nairobi Transport, page 80, for more information about these services). You can also get from Kisumu to the Uganda border at **Busia** and the Tanzania border at **Isebania** by frequent *matatu*, from where there is regular transport to the nearest towns over the borders.

Ferry
Low water levels around Kisumu mean that there are no ferry services directly from Kisumu. However, there is a car and passenger ferry between **Luanda Kotieno**, which is 90 km southwest of Kisumu on the Gulf of Winam, and **Mbita** (see page 142). From Kisumu, take the Busia/B1 road about 12 km to Kisian and turn left onto the C27 to Ndori, which is about a 35-km drive, and then on to the lakeshore and ferry jetty at **Luanda Kotieno** at the end of the C28, roughly another 45 km. This route is now fully tarred and the drive from Kisumu to Luanda Kotieno should take about a 1½-2 hrs. The ferry can take about half a dozen vehicles (it's sturdy enough to transport petrol tankers across to Mbita) and takes 45 mins. There are 2 ferries that depart simultaneously from each side at roughly 0700, 1000, 1400 and 1700 (make sure you arrive at the jetties in plenty of time) and cost about US$3 for a passenger and US$6 for a car. From Mbita, another passenger ferry goes to **Mfangano Island** (see page 143). There are regular buses and *matatus* between the main bus stand in Kisumu and Luanda Kotieno. The alternative route to Mbita is via the lakeshore road around the Gulf of Winam and Homa Bay (see page 141).

Train
Kisumu Railway Station, is at the western end of New Station Rd. The thrice-weekly train service to **Nairobi** departs Kisumu on Sat, Tue and Thu at 1830 and arrives in Nairobi at 0800, see box, page 18. It is essential to make reservations in advance and this can be done at the station or through a tour operator. You need to check in at least 1 hr before.

☉ Directory

Kisumu *p130, map p131*
Immigration 2nd floor Reinsurance Plaza, T057-202 4935. **Medical services** Kisumu District General Hospital, is right in the middle of town on Angawa Av, T057-202 0171, but the **Aga Khan Hospital**, Otiena Oyoo St, T057-202 0005, www.agakhan hospitals.org, is Kisumu's private hospital and the best bet if you fall sick. **Police** Omolo Agar Rd, T057-202 4719.

South of Kisumu

The main A1 road heads south to Tanzania via the rambling market town of Kisii. This area receives abundant sunshine and rainfall, and the hillsides feature the terraced fields of subsistence farmers. Another road to the west of here links the simple fishing settlements located on the shores of Lake Victoria, while on the lake itself are a couple of upmarket island fishing lodges. To the southeast of Kisumu, tea is the mainstay of the local economy around Kericho, and the countryside is blanketed with glistening green tea plantations. ▸▸ *For listings, see pages 145-148.*

Kisumu to the Tanzanian border → *For listings, see pages 145-148.*

The main route from Western Kenya to Tanzania, the A1, runs from Kisumu via Oyugis and Kisii, and is in reasonable condition, except for a few patches of potholes. **Migori** is the last town along this stretch, before the Tanzanian border. See page 141 for border crossing information. This small town is a transit stop for people travelling to Musoma and Mwanza in Tanzania. The lakeshore region to the south of Kisumu is an easy enough area to explore by *matatu*. However, there is limited accommodation in this region. Self-drive (in a 4WD vehicle) is probably recommended to get to some of the more remote spots, such as the prehistoric site of **Thimlich Ohinga** and **Ruma National Park**.

Fishing (a male activity) and the smoking of fish (a female activity) are important occupations around this region. **Homa Bay** is the biggest town in the area and here there is a branch of **Kenya Commercial Bank**, a post office and a petrol station. Out on the lake are two islands, **Rusinga** and **Mfangano**. Rusinga is the burial place of Tom Mboya, a great son of Kenya who was assassinated in Nairobi in 1969. On each of the islands there are **fishing camps** providing boats for hire and some accommodation in sublime settings. Much of the business comes from the Masai Mara lodges where, every morning, small planes pick up upmarket safari goers that also want to go fishing.

Kendu Bay → *Colour map 1, A2.*
Kendu Bay is a small town in South Nyanza, now Homa Bay District. It is 70 km or an hour's drive from Kisumu on the Homa Bay–Katito road, off the Ahero–Sondu–Kisii road. The main reason for coming here is to visit the curious **Simbi Nyaima Lake** – a deep volcanic lake, steeped in myths and legends. It has bright green opaque water, is located only a few kilometres from Lake Victoria and, as it is rich in algae, attracts a few hundred flamingos. To get there take the road towards Homa Bay and it is a 4-km walk from Kendu Bay. It takes about two hours to walk around the lake. There are no facilities, so take food and drink. No one knows the source of the lake, and its size is constantly changing. Local people believe it to be unlucky, and the surrounding area is certainly devoid of vegetation. It is not fished and the area is uninhabited. According to one legend, a hungry and tired old woman called Ateku arrived in this area, where she found the villagers celebrating by eating, drinking and dancing. Only one caring female villager gave her food and drink and a bed in which to rest her weary bones. To give thanks, Ateku ordered water to spring from the ground, which later went on to flood the area. Another version of the legend was that the old lady was denied food and lodgings and in wrathful vengeance induced a massive flood that swamped the village.

Border crossings: Kenya–Tanzania

Isebania

Isebania is a small settlement that straddles the A1 road. The border is open 24 hours, the crossing is efficient and quick, and visas for both Tanzania and Kenya are available, but remember that if you've only entered Tanzania and gone back to Kenya, you don't need to buy another visa to re-enter as long as your original one is still valid.

There are money changers on both sides of the border and you can change a small amount of currency to last until you get to the next bank. If coming from Tanzania, the first banks (with ATMs) you'll reach in Kenya are in Migori, 20 km north of the border. If coming from Kenya, the first banks in Tanzania are in Musoma and Mwanza, which are both some considerable distance away.

Once in Tanzania the road is the B6 which is good tar and there are plentiful petrol stations en route. It continues south past the Western Corridor of the Serengeti National Park – it's 195 km from Isebania to the Serengeti's Ndabaka Gate (0600-1600) – and on to Mwanza, which is Tanzania's principal town on Lake Victoria and 325 km southwest of Isebania. There is little accommodation beyond the border, but some places to stay near the Serengeti's Ndabaka Gate, which are useful if you get here too late to enter the park. These include $$$ Speke Bay Lodge, off the main road 15 km from Ndabaka Gate towards Mwanza, T+255 (0)28-262 1237, www.spekebay.com, which has bungalows and permanent tents in a lovely garden on the shore of Lake Victoria, plus a bar and restaurant; and $$-$ Serengeti Stopover, off the main road 1 km west of Ndabaka Gate, T+255 (0)28-262 2273, www.serengetistopover.com, which has 10 simple self-contained chalets with fans and mosquito nets, and a campsite, restaurant and bar.

Homa Bay

About 35 km southwest of Kendu Bay, and 110 km from Kisumu, Homa Bay is an unremarkable ramshackle market town running along two main streets, with a covered market and one reasonable place to stay on the lake – the **Homa Bay Tourist Hotel**, see page 146. Most people rely on fishing here, though, over recent years, water hyacinth has periodically plagued the lakeshore. Above town rises the 1751 m **Mount Homa**, known by the Luo as Got Asego ('famous mountain'), which is the highest of many extinct volcanic plugs that scatter the region. It is possible to climb to the top but it's a scramble through thick thorny bushes, and the only paths are those made by goats. Beyond Homa Bay, the road goes to **Mbita**, a small rural community and a collection point for boats to Lake Victoria's islands (below).

Ruma National Park → Colour map 1, A2.

① www.kws.org, 0600-1800, US$20, children (3-18) US$10.

Ruma National Park is 10 km east of Lake Victoria in the Lambwe Valley in the Suba District, 140 km from Kisumu. The park was established in 1966 to protect the rare roan antelope, found only in this part of Kenya. The land is a mixture of tall grassland and woodlands of acacia, open savannah and riverine forests, interspersed with scenic hills. There are abundant wild flowers. In addition to the roan antelope, other mammals found here include the Bohor reedbuck, Jackson's hartebeest, hyena, leopard, buffalo and topi. Rothchild's giraffe, zebra and ostrich have been introduced in recent years.

Oribi, one of the smallest of the antelope family, are also present. Birdlife is plentiful and diverse, and Ruma is the only protected area in Kenya where the globally threatened blue swallow, a scarce intra-African migrant, is regularly recorded; these arrive around April and depart in September.

This is a delightful park for anyone wishing to achieve isolation on their safari, although there is limited accommodation and the roads are pretty rough. From Kisumu, follow the A1 south onto the C18 Homa Bay turn-off. Continue along the C18 past the Homa Bay turn-off to the north (the C20) and access to the park is on a turn-off to the right soon after the town of Migori. From the Migori Shopping Centre it is 10 km to the park headquarters along a *murram* road. Within the park are also unsealed *murram* roads, which become impassable with black sticky mud, known locally as black cotton, when it rains. A 4WD is recommended and is essential during the rainy season.

Rusinga Island → *Colour map 1, A2.*

About 40 km to the west of Homa Bay on a good dirt road and reached by regular *matatu*, **Mbita** straddles the causeway to Rusinga Island. It is an unexceptional and ramshackle fishing village but provides boat access to other islands in Lake Victoria, including Mfangano (see below); it is also where the car ferry from Luanda Kotieno docks (for details of this service, see Kisumu Transport, page 139).

Across the causeway, Rusinga is an austerely scenic island with high crags dominating the desolate goat-grazed landscape. It is about 16 km long and 5 km across at its widest point, and a single dirt road runs around its circumference. It is easy to walk around or else motorbike *boda boda* taxis provide transport. Inland, foreigners are rare and you are sure of a welcome. Over 80 species of bird are found here, including fish eagles and bee-eaters. On the shores of the island you may see the rare spotted-necked otter, giant monitor lizards or hippos. Lake Victoria is renowned for its glorious sunsets and, after dark, the Luo fishermen from the villages scattered along the lakeside can be seen out on the lake in their beautifully painted boats, lit by paraffin lamps. Boat trips to visit other nearby islands can be arranged locally with these fishermen. The excellent **Rusinga Island Lodge** (see page 146) is a lovely spot and popular with game fishermen in search of Lake Victoria's weighty Nile perch.

The island is rich in fossils and famed for the 1948 discovery by Mary Leakey of one of the earliest austrapithecines remains, the skull of *Proconsul africanus* (*P. heseloni*), a sub-group of *Dryopithecus*. This anthropoid ape lived on the island three million years ago and is believed to be a probable ancestor of the chimpanzee. Aside from the public interest it spurred, the discovery of the skull also ensured the Leakeys' funding for their next expeditions. Louis and Mary, thrilled at the discovery, decided the best way to celebrate would be by having another child. Their third son, Philip, was born in 1949 almost nine months later to the day that the skull was discovered. The skull can be seen in the Nairobi National Museum.

Rusinga Island was also the birthplace of Tom Mboya, an important Kenyan political figure during the fight for Independence. A civil-rights champion, trade unionist and charismatic young Luo politician, he was gunned down in Nairobi by a Kikuyu policeman in 1969, sparking off a crisis that led to over 40 deaths in widespread rioting and demonstrations. There is a school and a health centre named after him, and **Tom Mboya's mausoleum** lies on family land at Kasawanga on the north side of the island, about 7 km by the dirt road from Mbita, or roughly 5 km directly across the island. The mausoleum (open most days to visitors) contains various mementoes and gifts Mboya received during his life. The inscription on the grave reads: *Go and fight like this man, Who fought for mankind's cause, Who died because he fought, Whose battles are still unwon.* You don't have to know anything about the man to be impressed. In any other surroundings his memorial might seem relatively modest, but on this barren, windswept shore, it stands out like a beacon. Mboya's family live right next door and are happy to meet foreign visitors, who rarely come here. A small donation towards the upkeep of the mausoleum is gratefully appreciated.

Mfangano Island → *Colour map 1, A1/2.*
Further along Lake Victoria and slightly bigger than Rusinga Island, Mfangano rises out of the lake to 1694 m at its highest point, and its shore is edged by a narrow line of beaches with black volcanic sand and overhanging giant fig trees. It is much more remote and primitive, with few tourist facilities except for the luxury **Mfangano Island Camp**, see page 146.

A large wooden boat shuttles people between Mbita and surrounding places. It leaves Mbita at 0700 and 0900 to Sena on the east of Mfangano and leaves there again for Mbita at about 1100 and 1400; the journey takes about 1¼ hours. While a road network and electricity supply are the latest arrivals on Mfangano, the people mostly get around by boat, bicycle and motorbike *boda boda* taxi. There's also a network of temporary footpaths that are constantly changing course, so you can walk all over the island. Mfangano's greatest economic resource is the lake, and the islanders fish with floating kerosene lamps to draw in the fish to be netted. Hippos are very much in evidence, as are monitor lizards basking in the sun. There are interesting prehistoric rock paintings here showing signs of aeons of habitation. The rock paintings are in a gently scooped cave on the north coast of the island and are reddish coloured shapes. It is not known who drew them, when or why, although one theory is that they were the work of Twa Pygmy hunters from Congo, and could be 8000 years old. Local people associate the site with supernatural powers and miraculous events and, in some measure, fear them too, which has so far helped prevent the vandalism which has afflicted other rock art sites in Kenya.

Thimlich Ohinga → *Colour map 1, A2.*
ⓘ *Some 55 km northwest of the town of Migori, off the main A1 to the border with Tanzania, www.museums.or.ke, 0930-1800, US$5.50, children (under 16) US$2.75.*
Thimlich Ohinga Prehistoric Site is one of the most significant archaeological sites in East Africa. The name means 'thick bush' or 'frightening dense forest' in the local DhoLuo language. It was declared a national monument in 1983 and consists of dry stone enclosures of what appears to be one of the earliest settlements in the Lake Victoria area. It is an impressive example of a style of architecture whose remnants are found all over the district. The main structure consists of a compound about 140 m in diameter with five smaller enclosures in each and at least six house pits. The drystone walls range from 1 to 4 m high and from 1 to 3 m wide. The materials used were collected locally from the nearby hills. Several parts of the enclosing wall have caved in, and conservation work is urgently required. A giant *Euphorbia candelabrum* towers over the site.

The design of these structures would appear to indicate that the dry stone enclosures were built by a cohesive community, thought to date from about the 14th century, believed to be mostly of Bantu origin. It is believed that the Bantu lived here prior to the arrival of the Luo people. Between them, the early Bantu settlers and later Nilotic settlers built about 521 enclosures in over 130 locations in the Lake Victoria region. They are similar to the 17th-century stone ruins in Zimbabwe. Later settlers appear to have carried out repairs to the stonework between the 15th and 19th centuries. It is unclear as to why the area was abandoned by the Ohingnis in the early 20th century. A similar style of dwelling is used in some places by Luos today.

There is no public transport to get here. If driving you need to follow the A1 road through Migori and after 4 km turn right onto a rough *murram* road at the junction for Muhoro Bay where there is National Cereals and Produce Board depot. Take the first right after the depot for 55 km. This road is accessible by a normal car if it's dry but only in a 4WD if it's wet.

Kisii and the Western Highlands → *For listings, see pages 145-148.*

The Western Highlands are the agricultural heartland of Kenya, separating Kisumu and its environs from the rest of the country. The Highlands stretch from Kisii in the south up to the tea plantations around Kericho, through to Eldoret, Kitale and Mount Elgon. Away from the towns other highlights in this region include the Saiwa Swamp National Park. This is one of the few parks that permits walking, and is an ideal place for a day's hike (see page 157). The Western Highlands have become a major draw for sporting tourists. This is the home of many of Kenya's world-famous runners (see box, page 114). This is probably the finest place on earth for high-altitude athletic training, and many international athletes visit training camps around Iten and Kaptagat. There are good bus and *matatu* connections among most towns and villages and it is an easy region to get around, although the roads around Kisii are in a poor shape.

Kisii → *Colour map 1, A2. Phone code: 058.*
Set in picturesque undulating hills in some of the most fertile land of the country and with abundant sunshine and rainfall, Kisii is a very lively and fast-growing town. It is 120 km south of Kisumu on the junction with the A1 and the road from Kericho and Nakuru. As with so many other towns in agricultural areas, the market here is buzzing and has an excellent array of fresh fruit and vegetables. The town lies on a fault line, so earth tremors are not uncommon. This is the home of the Gusii people and is famous for its **soapstone**, although you may try to buy some in vain as most of what is locally produced is bought up by traders to stock the tourist shops in Nairobi and on the coast.

Tabaka → *Colour map 1, A2.*
This village is the most important producer of soapstone and the centre of carvings in the country. The left turn-off to Tabaka is 18 km west of Kisii off the A1, and the village is 6 km from the turn-off. This road can be fairly dire in the wet. Direct *matatus* come from Kisii. You can visit the quarries and watch the carvers at work, who are members of the **Kisii Soapstone Carvers Co-operative**. The soft pliable stone is fashioned into all sorts of items for practical use such as bowls and plates, as well as tourist items such as animal statues, chess sets and abstract figures, and there are lots of local stalls where you can buy soapstone artefacts. The stone comes in a variety of colours from orange (the softest) to deep red (the heaviest).

Kericho → *Colour map 1, A3. Phone code: 052.*
Perched on the top of a hill, the tea plantations stretch for miles on either side of the road, their bright green bushes neatly clipped to the same height, with paths running in straight lines in between. At 1800 m above sea level, the tea plantations stretch along the

western edge of the Great Rift Valley. The tea bush is an evergreen in tropical climates, so the bushes are harvested throughout the year. An evocative image of this region is the many hundreds of men and women plucking the tea leaves in the plantations with their distinctive white polythene sacks on their backs. The predictable weather (it rains every afternoon here) and the temperate climate, which gives a high ground temperature, make this the most important tea-growing region in Africa. Tea was introduced in Kenya in 1903, and it is now the world's third largest tea-producing nation, after India and Sri Lanka. This is an orderly part of Kenya, very different from the *shambas* further down the slopes, and very English, exemplified by the **Tea Hotel**, with its lovely gardens, which used to be owned by Brooke Bond (see page 147).

Kericho is named after Ole Kericho, a Masai chief who perished in battle at the hands of the Gusii in the 18th century. The town's main purpose is to service the enormous tea plantations, so it has most of the basic amenities on the main road, Moi Highway: branches of the main banks, post office, market, library, village green, the English-style Holy Trinity Church, War Memorial and cemetery. There's also an impressive **Sikh Temple**, which is Africa's largest Gurudwara temple and is dedicated to Baba Puran Singh Ji of Kericho, who was an eminent spiritual Sikh figure. He was born in 1898 in Punjab and emigrated to Kenya in 1916, set up Kericho Wagon Works and was a major benefactor to the town. In the 1970s he went to the UK and became a leading campaigner for getting Sikhs protected under the Race Relations Act there.

For tea tours, where the growing and picking procedures are explained, enquire at the **Tea Hotel**, which has a resident guide who will take you for a walk to the hotel's own estate and explain all about how tea was introduced into the region and the tea-growing process. Tea tasting is included in the excursion and it costs about US$3 per person; they may also be able to arrange a visit to a tea-processing factory around Kericho.

Chagaik Dam and Arboretum

About 8 km to the northeast of Kericho off the road to Nakuru is this exceptionally attractive arboretum. It was established after the Second World War by a Kericho tea planter, Tom Grumbley, and is home to many tropical and sub-tropical trees surrounded by well-tended lawns running down to the lake's edge. The lake is covered in water lilies and fringed with stands of bamboo. It's a good spot for birdwatching and at least one troop of black and white colobus monkeys live in the trees. Trout fishing is available in the Kiptariet River. The **Tea Hotel** will arrange for permissions and equipment hire. The river runs close by the hotel.

◉ South of Kisumu listings

For sleeping and eating price codes and other relevant information, see pages 20-24.

◉ Where to stay

Kendu Bay *p140*
$$$ Kisindi Lodge, turn off the main road about 25 km south of Kendu Bay and 15 km north of Homa Bay and follow signs to the lakeshore, T736-780 078, www.kisindi.com.

A charming new development on a little cliff, with 5 very comfortable thatched en suite huts with patios and great lake views, plus partially open bar and dining area, surprisingly good continental food given the location, no electricity but torches and paraffin lamps are provided. A double is around US$220 with meals. You can walk through the local farms and villages, there's a small swimming pool and massages are offered. The access road is rough but can be negotiated in a normal car or boat transfers from Kisumu can be arranged.

Homa Bay p141
$$ Homa Bay Tourist Hotel, off the main road to the west of the market, T059-22788. Simple resort built in the 1970s occupying a pleasant site on the lakeshore. 21 rooms with fans, mosquito nets, fridges and rather shiny bedspreads, and facilities include a good restaurant serving both local and international food, bar, a spacious lawn with garden furniture, and has its own motorized boat for lake excursions.
$$-$ Hotel Hippo Buck, on the main road about 2 km before town, T0723-262 000, www.hippobuck.com. Not on the lakeshore but reasonably comfortable rooms in a fairly modern white block with balconies, good choice of food in the terrace restaurant, especially fried tilapia fish from the lake, pleasant circular thatched bar in the garden which sometimes has a live band at the weekend. Doubles start from US$40 with breakfast.

Ruma National Park p141
$$ Oribi Guest House, reservations Nairobi T020-600 0800, www.kws.org. Simple guesthouse sleeping up to 5 in 3 bedrooms, everything is provided including towels, lounge with fireplace and veranda, fully equipped kitchen with utensils, caretaker on site and solar power.

Camping
There are 2 camping sites here, **Nyati** and **Fig Tree**. However, there are no facilities. Camping is US$15, children (3-18) US$10.

Rusinga Island p142
$$$$ Rusinga Island Lodge, reservations Nairobi, T020-253 1314, www.rusingaisland trust.com. Stunning and remote luxury retreat with 7 cottages, 1 for families with lovely verandas overlooking the lake, made from stone, wood and grass thatching, and

decorated with traditional fabrics and baskets. Activities include game drives in Ruma National Park, mountain biking, waterskiing, fishing for Nile perch and there's a spa. It's usually accessed by air charter and is a 35-min flight from the Masai Mara or transfers from Kisumu Airport can be arranged.
$$$ Lake Victoria Safari Village, 3 km to the southwest of Mbita, clearly signposted, T0721-912 120, www.safarikenya.net. A lovely rustic resort set in a lush tract of indigenous woodland on the lakeshore where there is a little beach. Thatched rondavels with neat en suite rooms with mosquito nets. There's a rather remarkable 'honeymoon suite' in a 2-storey bright white mock lighthouse, which has an additional stone bath. Shady restaurant and bar, excursions to Ruma National Park, boat trips to the islands and fishing for Nile perch can be arranged with local fishermen, which is much cheaper than the island lodges.
$ Elk Guesthouse, next to the bus stand in Mbita. A very basic local guest house but clean and all beds are fitted with mosquito nets. Does not have a restaurant or bar but there are several cheap eating places nearby.
$ The Viking Guest House, to the right of the bus stand is very similar, although with shared bathrooms, and it also has a bar in a bougainvillea-shaded courtyard.

Mfangano Island p143
$$$$ Mfangano Island Camp, reservations Governors' Camp, Nairobi, T020-273 4000, www.governorscamp.com. Set in a secluded bay surrounded by fig trees, this mostly attracts serious (and wealthy, from US$260 per person) fishermen. There are just 6 rooms made from natural clay and banana thatch, with private verandas and lovely stone bathrooms, very good food, bar and swimming pool. All fishing activities are organized, especially for Nile perch, and are included in the rates. Very high standards here to match the Governors' Camps in the Masai Mara, and most guests arrive here by plane from the Mara. Closed Apr-May.

Kisii p144

There's a very poor choice of accommodation in town; best to move on.

$ Bluu Nile Hotel, 1.5 km north of town on the A1 towards Migori, T0719-671 558. Fairly new and still well kept with 60 simple and clean motel-type rooms with parking, but very bare with no more than TV and mosquito net, reasonable restaurant serving Kenyan fare and plates of chicken or fish with chips or rice.

$ Kisii, in the town centre on the main road opposite the mosque, T058-30134. Probably the best of the budget places in an old wooden building in a compound with secure parking, the rooms are very dated but spacious with OK bathrooms but very basic. There are attractive gardens with thatched huts to sit in and passable food in the restaurant and bar.

$ Mash Park Hotel, on the main road 1 km to the west of town opposite the Caltex petrol station, T058-31910, www.mashpark hotel.com. A reasonably looking modern white block in its own grounds with car park, but poorly maintained basic rooms with unreliable hot water, though most have balconies, some with views of the hillsides. Restaurant and thatched garden bar serving *nyama choma*.

Kericho p144

$$$-$$ Tea Hotel, east of town centre, on Moi Highway on road to Nakuru, T052-30004/5. Built in 1958 by Brooke Bond and set in lush gardens that back directly on to the tea plantations, this is the best hotel in Kericho. Old-fashioned but the 45 rooms in the old colonial building and garden cottages are spacious and some have TVs. There's a swimming pool, and reasonable restaurant with a solid and dependable English-style menu and some Indian dishes. Pleasant campsite (**$**) in the grounds with good hot showers and an electric point for charging batteries. Organizes tours of the tea plantations.

$ Kericho Garden Lodge, Moi Highway, close to **Tea Hotel**, T052-20878. Very basic board and lodgings with singles with shared bathrooms and some doubles with en suite, but reasonably friendly, hot water mornings and evenings, garden bar with *nyama choma*, and satellite TV, parking in the sweeping drive and you may be able to negotiate to camp.

$ Mwalimu, Temple Rd, just to north of Chai Sq in town centre, T052-20601. Basic board and lodgings, corridors are quite dark but the rooms are OK with own bathroom but there's only hot water in the mornings, restaurant and bar, though this gets noisy on weekend nights.

$ New Sunshine Hotel, Tengecha Rd, T052-30233. Probably the best of the basic options with clean rooms and 24-hr hot water, the cheaper ones have inward-facing windows so are dark; the pricier ones are brighter, larger and have TV. Good basic meals in restaurant, bar that is quieter than most.

❶ Restaurants

South of Kisumu p140

Most of the small towns have small *hotelis* (kiosks) selling the likes of *nyama choma*, *ugali*, chips and omelettes and sodas. For more substantial meals, go to the larger hotels. See under Where to stay, above.

❷ Shopping

Kisii p144

There's a branch of **Nakumatt** supermarket on Moi Highway.

❸ Transport

Homa Bay p141

There are regular buses and matatus between **Kisumu** and Homa Bay via Kendu Bay. The bus stand is in the middle of town south of the market. **Akamba Bus**, T059-22578, www.akambabus.com, has 2 daily services, 1 overnight, between Homa Bay and **Nairobi** which take 9 hrs and go via **Kisii**.

Rusinga Island *p142*
There are regular *matatus* between Homa Bay and **Mbita**, which stop on the south side of the causeway to Rusinga Island. You can take a motorbike *boda boda* to the other side.

Ferry
For details of the car and passenger ferry between **Luanda Kotieno** and **Mbita** (see Kisumu Transport, page 139).

Kisii *p144*
Regular buses and *matatus* go to **Kisumu** and **Kericho** and both take 2 hrs. The bus and *matatu* stand is on the main road that runs through town, Moi Highway. There is another *matatu* stand 2 blocks east of the market. Buses to **Nairobi** go via **Kericho** and **Nakuru** and take 7 hrs. Akamba Bus, office also on Moi Highway near the post office, T058-30137, www.akambabus.com, has 2 daily services, 1 of which is overnight.

Kericho *p144*
The bus and *matatu* stand is at the northern end of Isaac Salat Rd and is well organized. There is plenty of transport, both buses and *matatus* run regularly throughout the day for **Eldoret** (3½ hrs), **Nakuru** (3 hrs), and **Kisumu** (2 hrs), where you can pick up onward transport. **Akamba Bus**, on the corner of Moi Highway and Hospital Rd, T052-32092, www.akambabus.com, has 2 daily services between Kericho and **Nairobi** and take 5 hrs. **Guardian Coach**, at the Total petrol station on Moi Av, T0727-545 088, www.theguardiancoach.com, also has a daily service between Kisumu and Nairobi which stops in Kericho.

❶ Directory

Kericho *p144*
Medical services Kericho District Hospital is on (naturally) Hospital Rd, T052-31192. **Police** The main police station is just to the southwest of the Tea Hotel on Moi Highway.

Kakamega and around

To the north of Kisumu is the beautiful Kakamega Forest National Reserve, which will appeal to the nature lover for its walks through the dense canopy of trees and rich ground foliage. It's also home to a number of interesting and unusual primates and small mammals, snakes and reptiles, and butterflies and birds. Further north, the industrial town of Eldoret won't hold the attention of visitors for long, but it is the gateway town to the more remote regions of Northern Kenya and is a major service centre for transport on the A104 to Uganda. ▸▸ *For listings, see pages 152-155.*

Kakamega → *For listings, see pages 152-155. Colour map 3, C5. Phone code: 056.*

This pleasant lively place just over 50 km north of Kisumu (and 30 km north of the equator) is the main town of the Luhya people. Kakamega is famous for being the centre of a gold rush in the late 1920s, which attracted huge numbers of hopeful prospectors. The largest nugget found was named the **Elbon Nugget**, so named by reversing the surname of Dan Noble, a postman, who later bought Nairobi's first hotel, the old **Hotel Stanley**. A major attraction is the Kakamega Forest (below), and the town is the place to buy provisions for an excursion there. Most travellers tend to head straight out to the forest reserve and stay there, which is a much more pleasant alternative to staying in town. About 2 km south of town on the Kakamega–Kisumu road is a curiosity called the **Weeping Stone**. This is an 8-m-high rock upon which a smaller rock is balanced; between the rocks a small trickle of water emanates and continues to flow even during the dry season. Kakamega is well served by public transport, and there's an airstrip 4 km to the southeast of town on the road to Shinyalu; **Fly 540** have recently commenced a scheduled service to and from Nairobi. ▸▸ *See Transport, page 155.*

Kakamega Forest National Reserve → *For listings, see pages 152-155. Colour map 3, C5.*

Western Kenya's 45 sq km Kakamega Forest would not look out of place on the set of a Tarzan movie, with its tangled vines, intermingled branches and a chorus of screeches and mutterings from a whole host of African creatures. Declared a forest reserve in 1966, it is the sole remnant of tropical rainforest in Kenya and one of the last remaining (and fast diminishing) tropical rainforests of East Africa, a remnant of the Guineo–Conglian equatorial belt that once covered all land from the Atlantic to the Rift Valley as little as 400 years ago. Its closest relation, to which it was once joined, is Bwindi Impenetrable Forest on Uganda's western border with the DRC. It is an extraordinarily beautiful forest, with at least 150 species of tree, shrub and vine, including the Elgon teak, 90 dicotyledenous herbs, 80 monocotyledonous herbs of which 60 are orchids (nine unique to Kakamega), and a further 62 species of fern, making a total of 380 different plants in one small area.

Kakamega Forest National Reserve

Where to stay
Forest Rest House **3**
Franka **5**
Golf **6**
Isecheno Bandas **2**
Isukuti Houses **7**
Mago Guesthouse **8**
Rondo Retreat Centre **1**
Udo's Bandas & Campsite **4**

5 km
5 miles

The indigenous trees along the trails are identified with small plaques giving their Latin as well as their local names. Many of these provide a valuable source of fruits and green vegetables for the local people, and about 50 herbs are used for medicines and ritual events. Approximately 20% of the flora and fauna in the Kakamega Forest is not found anywhere else in Kenya.

Arriving in Kakamega Forest

There are two areas in the Kakamega Forest National Reserve that cater for visitors – which one you go to rather depends on where you are staying, and on how easy a journey you want to get there.

Buyangu is in the north and is 12 km from Kakamega on the A1 northeast towards Eldoret. This area is where the reserve headquarters are located and is administered by **Kenya Wildlife Service (KWS)**, T056-30603, www.kws.org, entry fees are paid at the gate, US$20, children (3-18) US$10, vehicle US$3.25. It is much easier to get to than Isecheno (below) if you do not have your own transport as it is a walk of less than 2 km from the main road, which is served by countless *matatus*, between Kakamega and Webuye, but watch out as very few of the drivers seem to recognize the name Buyangu.

Isecheno is towards the south/centre of the forest. From Kakamega take the A1 south towards Kisumu for about 10 km and turn left at Khayega. Carry on down this road for about 7 km when you will reach the village of Shinyalu. Take a right and after about another 5 km you will reach the forest reserve. This route from the A1 is a hilly and potholed dirt road that can be very slippery in the wet. You can pick up a *matatu*, at the stand near the Total petrol station in Kakamega to Shinyalu, then get a motorbike *boda boda* to the forest station; alternatively, negotiate with your *matatu* driver to take you the last 5 km. The Isecheno area is administered by the **Kenya Forestry Service (KFS)**, www.kenyaforestservice.org, and entry fees are paid at the **Isecheno Forest Station** near the entrance, US$8, children (under 16) US$2.

Wildlife and vegetation

There are a number of animals here including the grey duiker, bushpig, bush-tailed porcupine, giant water shrew, clawless otter and a few leopards. There are also several primates including the olive baboon, the red-tailed monkey, the black and white colobus and blue monkey. The forest is also home to the hairy-tailed flying squirrel that can 'fly' as far as 90 m; bush babies and the lemur-like potto can be spotted amongst the branches at night, along with the hammer-headed fruit bat – the largest in Africa with a wingspan of over 1 m and an exceptionally big head.

The forest is also of great ornithological interest as many birds found here are not seen elsewhere in Kenya. Hornbills, woodpeckers, honeyguides, both Ross's and the great blue turaco, grey parrot and the rare snake-eating bird are among the avian residents. In addition, several varieties of barbet, including the double-toothed, speckled and grey-throated, are found here. Butterflies are abundant, and snakes, normally only found in West Africa, can be seen too. Look out for the Gabon viper, a particularly nasty, deadly but fortunately very shy snake that lives in the forest.

Exploring the reserve

The most rewarding way to appreciate Kakamega is to go on a guided walk through the narrow winding paths. At both **Buyangu** and **Isecheno** guides can be hired and cost around US$10 per person for around three hours, and US$15 per person for about five hours. These dedicated local people, who are often self-taught, make excellent and informative guides and know the flora and the fauna intimately; if given the chance, they will reel off every species name in Latin. Birdsong and the occasional whoop of a black and white colobus monkey accompany walks ranging from 1 to 7 km through the peaceful interior. If you wish to see the flowers at their best, plan your visit during the rainy season from April to July, when exotic orchids grow in the junctions of the tree branches. Among the several walks on offer from the KWS headquarters at Buyangu, the most pleasant are 4 km to the small but attractive **Isiukhu Falls**, and 5 km to **Buyangu Hill**, from where the canopy of trees spreads out like a thick green blanket and, on a clear day, a brooding Mount Elgon can be sighted in the distance. On all walks, it is advisable to wear waterproofs, as the rain is heavy, regular and predictable, but it is beautiful walking country.

Border crossings: Kenya–Uganda

Malaba and Busia

There are two border crossings between Kenya and Uganda; both are open 24 hours; and procedures are quick and efficient. **Malaba** is on the A104, 128 km west of Eldoret via Webuye. It is the most commonly used border with trucks and is very busy, so if you are in your own vehicle it may be better to cross at Busia. **Busia** is 153 km west of Kisumu on the B1.

Visas for Uganda and Kenya can be bought at the border in US dollars, pounds sterling or euro cash. Remember that if you go into Uganda and return to Kenya, the Kenyan visa is still valid as long as the date is still valid and you do not need to get another one. However, if you go into Uganda and then into Rwanda or the Democratic Republic of Congo to see the mountain gorillas, for example, and then return to Kenya via Uganda, the Kenyan visa will not be valid and you will have to get another one. This visa agreement is only between Kenya, Uganda and Tanzania.

If you are in your own vehicle you will be badgered constantly by touts trying to 'help', offering to sell relevant forms or escort you through the procedures for a fee. Ignore them; all forms are available inside the border buildings where you will be told what to do. Be wary of petty thieves – lock everything up and make sure anything on the outside of the vehicle is tied down. There are banks with ATMs on both sides of the border at Malaba and Busia.

Once over the Malaba border in Uganda, the A104 road becomes the main A109 to Kampala and the first town is Tororo, 18 km from the border, which has petrol stations, banks, shops and accommodation. About 35 km west of Tororo, the road from the Busia border joins the A109; the route from Busia to this junction is 33 km. In total, from Malaba to Kampala it is 220 km, and from Busia to Kampala, 210 km.

Eldoret → *For listings, see pages 152-155. Colour map 3, C5. Phone code: 053.*

The journey from Kericho due north to Eldoret passes through the **Nandi Hills**, some of the most spectacular scenery in this part of the country, and the **Kano Plains**, bleak mountainous scrubland and ravines. The other approaches to Eldoret are the 156 km along the A104 from Nakuru, which is the main highway and always busy with heavy trucks en route to Uganda, or the much longer but spectacular route via the Tugen Hills and Kerio Valley (see page 113).

Eldoret was originally settled by South African Boers who sailed from the Cape to Mombasa after the Boer War. They then travelled from the coast inland by ox wagon to what was 'plot 64', the number of the farm plot that had a post office on it, which was renamed Eldoret in 1912 ('eldore' means 'stony river' in the Masai language). This pleasant, busy and fairly prosperous highland town is surrounded by fertile countryside growing a mixture of food and cash crops. There is large-scale maize and wheat farming, and cattle keeping of the Ayrshire breed. The airport here is used to transport fresh flowers from the Naivasha region directly to the flower markets of Amsterdam and elsewhere in Europe. Eldoret is home to **Moi University** and the **Moi Teaching and Referral Hospital**, which attracts many European medical professionals on placements. It is a very busy town, with an excellent market, banks, supermarkets, trading stores and, because of the students, dozens of internet cafés. There's no special reason you should stay here, but it's a useful stop en route to Uganda or the Cherangani Hills and Lake Turkana. Again, Eldoret is another Western Kenyan town that suffered during the 2007 post-election violence.

Arriving in Eldoret

Eldoret Airport ① *T053-206 337, www.kenyaairports.co.ke*, is 16 km south of town on the Kisumu road, and **Fly 540** have daily flights to and from Nairobi. A taxi from the airport shouldn't cost more than US$8; taxis meet the planes. There are good bus and *matatu* connections to all the upcountry towns in Western Kenya and the Rift Valley as well as to Nairobi, which is a six- to seven-hour drive. Some long-distance buses stop in Eldoret on the Nairobi–Kampala route. The main bus and *matatu* stands are in the centre of town just off Malaba (Uganda) Rd. Getting around Eldoret itself is easy and there are plenty of taxis; bicycle and motorbike *boda bodas* and *matatus* run up and down Malaba (Uganda) Road, though this is constantly one long traffic jam. ▶▶ *See Transport, page 155.*

◉ Kakamega and around listings

For sleeping and eating price codes and other relevant information, see pages 20-24.

◉ Where to stay

Kakamega *p148*

$$$ Golf, just off the main road, T056-30150/1/2, www.golfhotelkakamega.com. Modern, very pleasant, excellent service and food, the 60 rooms have mosquito nets and TV, there's a swimming pool and facilities for golf, tennis and squash at the **Sports Club** next door. The bar and restaurant is open to non-residents and offers English-style cooking with some Indian dishes. Can arrange tours into the Kakamega Forest. Doubles start from US$125 and include a buffet breakfast.
$ Franka, southwest of the clocktower, T0720-204 880, www.frankahotel.com. Basic and quite small but clean rooms with hot water, bar and restaurant with nice balcony full of plants, a *nyama choma* grill and the popular **Club Franky**, nightclub which is fun but can get noisy at the weekend.

Kakamega Forest National Reserve

p149, map p149

$$$ Rondo Retreat Centre, Isecheno, you can also get here from Kapsabet, take a turn-off for 9 km from the C39 in Chepsonoi,

T056-30268, www.rondoretreat.com. This is a religious centre, open to the public, in a serene location within the forest. Rondo was built in 1948 at the base of what was thought to be the biggest tree in the Kakamega Forest, an Elgon olive tree that still stands today. The original owner left Kenya in 1961, leaving the property to the Christian Council of Kenya. The homestead consists of the main house and 5 cottages of clapboard and colonial-era corrugated iron – 18 rooms in total, with lovely antique decor, beautiful gardens with flowerbeds and fish ponds, very good wholesome food in the dining room, but you need to be on best behaviour here. It's not suitable for children and there is no alcohol or smoking.
$$-$ Isukuti Houses, at the KWS HQ at Buyangu, T056-30603, reservations **KWS**, Nairobi T020-600 0800, www.kws.org. Fairly new pair of houses, each divided into 2 self-catering units with 1 twin bedroom and modern bathroom, veranda, fully equipped kitchen with gas stove and utensils, just need to bring towels, no electricity but hot water is from a wood-burning stove and kerosene lamps are provided. Rates are US$50 per unit.
$$-$ Mago Guesthouse, not in the forest but in the village of Mago on the C39, 23 km south of Kakamega, T0723-352 792, www.magoguesthouse.com. A community-

run guesthouse that supports the adjoining college, with 11 spotlessly clean rooms with modern bathrooms, excellent restaurant and bar run by catering students (the school is run by a chef who used to work at the Kenyan embassy in Paris), 3-4-course lunches and dinners for about US$8. A good place to experience rural village life, and excursions into the forest can be arranged. Rates are from US$45 for a double with breakfast. *Matatus* will drop here.

$ Udo's Bandas and Campsite, just outside the entrance gate at Buyangu, T056-30603, reservations **KWS**, Nairobi T020-600 0800, www.kws.org. 7 twin *bandas* and a campsite next to the stream, bucket showers and long-drop loos, communal cooking area but no utensils, and you need to bring firewood, water, bedding and towels. A small shop sells a few basic supplies such as bread and sodas, and there are small shops and tiny local restaurants in the village. *Bandas* US$30, campsite US$15.

$ Forest Rest House, near Isecheno Forest Station. Run by the Kenya Forestry Service (KFS), this is a small building on stilts, with 4 bedrooms or you can sleep on the veranda if you have a mosquito net, about US$7 per person, bucket showers, long-drops, no electricity and an erratic water supply. Nevertheless it's in a beautiful forest glade where you can also camp. Kerosene lamps are provided, but a torch is essential and you will need to bring all bedding and food (although about 300 m away on the road into the forest is a very small shop/restaurant where you can arrange a plate of good and filling food, but order at least 2 hrs in advance).

$ Isecheno Bandas, Isecheno Forest Station, T0722-619 150. This is run by the Kakamega Environmental Education Program (KEEP) and has 6 very basic *bandas* (Luhya huts) with 3 beds in each, about US$7 per person, separate hot showers and long-drops, and outside kitchen and dining area. You need to bring your own bedding, food and firewood, though meals can be arranged on

request with notice, or again eat at the small shop/restaurant on the road into the forest (above). Again kerosene lamps are provided.

Eldoret *p151*
$$$-$$ Sirikwa, Elgeyo Rd, T053-206 3614. Eldoret's largest hotel, with over 100 rooms in an imposing white block built in the 1960s, located in well-tended gardens with an impressive entrance hall. However, rooms are worn and well overdue for a refurbishment, but there's a relaxed bar, very good food in the restaurant (the generous buffet lunches are great) and a big swimming pool, which non-guests can use for a small fee. A double goes from US$90.

$$ Cicada, off Elgeyo Rd near the **Sirikwa**, T053-206 1081, www.cicada.co.ke. Newly built 5-storey block, so everything is quite fresh and service is excellent, with an underground car park, 56 neat modern rooms with wooden floors, mosquito nets and satellite TV, restaurant serving African, continental and Indian food, bar with balcony and good choice of imported spirits and wine, and internet café.

$$ Eldoret White Castle, Uganda Rd, T053-203 3095. A tall modern tower block with elevators, 120 pleasant, clean rooms with TV, a restaurant (though most food is fried and comes with chips), bar and gym. It's bang in the middle of town with no parking, although you can arrange for an *askari* to watch your car on the street overnight.

$$-$ Klique, Oginga Odinga St, T0732-060 903, www.kliquehotel.com. Another new option, with 43 good rooms with satellite TV and squeaky clean tiled bathrooms, but may be noisy as it's on a busy central street, very good restaurant that serves pizza, sports bar with TVs, sometimes has live music at the weekend.

$$-$ Naiberi River Campsite & Resort, 16 km from Eldoret on the C54 towards Kaptagat, a few kilometres south of Eldoret turn off the A104 at the Shell petrol station, T053-206 2916, www.naiberi.com. A rural resort that's popular with overlanders, set in a peaceful tract of forest, with campsite, dorms and doubles in a log cabin, en suite stone cottages, kitchens, spotless ablution blocks and beautiful gardens with a swimming pool and ponds. Fantastically designed bar with a tunnel, running streams, huge central fireplace and glass roof, and good food on offer including Indian snacks. *Matatus* from Eldoret to Kaptagat can drop at the entrance. A magical spot, highly recommended.

$ Eldoret Valley, Malaba (Uganda) Rd, T053-203 2314. Probably the better of the many basic board and lodgings and handy for the Akamba bus office, but on the main road so can be noisy. Clean rooms with reliable hot water and nets; the restaurant serves decent fried chicken, fish and *ugali*.

$ Eldoret Wagon, Elgeyo Rd, opposite the Sirikwa, T053-200 2270. Basic but clean and secure with some triples, there are new and old blocks so some rooms are better than others, has restaurant, bar, parking and swimming pool. This started life as a members' club for senior railway staff, notice the dining room was built in the shape of a railway carriage with a hooped roof.

❼ Restaurants

Eldoret *p151*

There are a few canteen-type establishments around town but after dark the best choice by far for eating is at the hotels.

$$-$ Mamma Mia's, Ramogi Dr, off Nandi Rd, about 1 km east of town near the Moi University School of Medicine (a bit hard to find – take a taxi), T0731-363 737. Mon-Sat 1200-2200. Popular with students, serves an odd combination of pizzas and Indian food, but both very good especially the chicken tikka, paneer steak and sizzling prawns (when available), plus a fully stocked bar.

$ The Red Bean, corner of Oloo and Elijah Cheriyot streets, off the main road behind Barclays Bank, T056-203 2622. Mon-Sat 0800-2300, Sun 0900-2100. Great super-

modern restaurant with welcoming a/c for freshly made sandwiches, cakes, pastries, soups, milkshakes, fruit juices and excellent lattes, cappuccinos and hot chocolate.

$ Sizzlers Café, Kenyatta St, 2 blocks south of Barclays Bank. 0800-1700. American-style diner, good local food and Western dishes like burgers, old-fashioned ice cream served in cones and milkshakes, good service too.

$ Sunjeel Palace, Kenyatta St, near **Sizzlers Café**, T053-203 0568. Open 1100-2100. Cheap traditional Indian restaurant serving good-value and tasty tandoori, masala and biryiani dishes with good choices for vegetarians and sells beer. Popular with the local Indian community, always a good sign that the food is authentic.

⊕ What to do

Eldoret *p151*

Elgeyo Travel and Tours, Malaba (Uganda) Rd, T053-206 2543, www.elgeyotravel.com. A general travel agent that books flights.

◎ Shopping

Eldoret *p151*

The main **market** around Kimathi Av has a huge selection of fruit and vegetables. There's a large branch of **Nakumatt** supermarket on Oginga Odinga Rd, which is open 24 hrs. Well worth heading for is the **Dorino Lessos Creameries Cheese Factory**, in a green and white building at the end of Kenyatta St next to a car wash, 0800-1600 (to get here, just ask for the 'Cheese Factory'), which sells more than 30 types of delicious cheese, plus yoghurt, excellent ice cream and other dairy products. **Paul's Bakery**, 0730-1500, to the north of town on Malaba (Uganda) Rd, is a good place to stop for fresh bread, pies, cakes, etc. On the main road coming into Eldoret from the southeast look out for people selling fresh mushrooms on the side of the road around the large Shell petrol station at the turn-off to Kabarnet.

🚍 Transport

Kakamega p148
Air

There's an airstrip 4 km to the southeast of town on the road to Shinyalu. **Fly 540**, Nairobi T020-827 521, www.fly540.com, has 1 daily flight in each direction between Kakamega and **Nairobi**, which goes via Eldoret and takes 1 hr 20 mins, 1 way from US$90. Taxis meet the flights.

Bus and matatu

The town is less than 1 hr from **Kisumu** along the very busy A1 and there are plenty of buses and *matatus* travelling this route. The main bus stand is close to the market. **Akamba Bus** has its stand opposite the Hindu Temple, off Mumias Rd, T056-30517, www.akambabus.com, and has 3 daily services, 1 of which is overnight, between Kakamega and **Nairobi** (9 hrs).

Eldoret p151
Air

Some 16 km south from Eldoret on the Eldoret–Kisumu Rd is **Eldoret Airport** www.kenyaairports.com, which although predominantly used for freight is served by **Fly 540**, airport T053-206 3377, Nairobi T020-827 521, www.fly540.com. There are 2 daily flights in each direction between Eldoret and **Nairobi** taking 55 mins, 1 way from US$69. Taxis meet the flights.

Bus and matatu

The *matatu* stand is in the centre of town just off Malaba (Uganda) Rd, and there are a number of *matatus* and buses in all directions throughout the day. The journey direct to **Nairobi** takes 6-7 hrs. The **Akamba Bus** office is on Arap Moi St to the west of the market, T053-206 1047, www.akambabus.com, and has 2 daily services, 1 of which is overnight, between Eldoret and **Nairobi** via **Nakuru** (3-4 hrs); their Nairobi–**Kampala** bus also stops in Eldoret. The other long-distance bus companies that stop in Eldoret on the Nairobi–Kampala route include **Kampala Coach**, on Malaba (Uganda) Rd near Kenya Commercial Bank, T0723-141 534, www.kampalacoach.com. (See Transport in Nairobi, page 80 for more details of these services). Eldoret is roughly 370 km from Kampala via the Uganda border at Malaba and buses take around 8 hrs.

ℹ Directory

Kakamega p148
Police opposite the post office on the Kisumu road, T056-31486.

Eldoret p151
Medical services Uasin Gishu Memorial Hospital, is on Malaba (Uganda) Rd, T053-206 2286. **Moi Teaching and Referral Hospital**, southwest of the centre at the end of Nandi Rd, T053-203 3471, www.mtrh. or.ke, is exceptionally good with a large casualty department. **Police** On Malaba (Uganda) Rd near the National Bank of Kenya, T053-203 2900.

Kitale and around

The busy main A104 heads west of Eldoret and into Uganda, a route heavily used by trucks taking goods over the border. To the north, the small market town of Kitale has an interesting museum and serves as the access point to both the Mount Elgon and Saiwa Swamp national parks. ▸▸ *For listings, see pages 159-160.*

Webuye → *Colour map 3, B5.*

Webuye is an industrial town straddling the main A104 Uganda road and is home to the large **Panafric Paper Mills**, which omits a very unpleasant smell of sulphur dioxide, and some sugar refineries. **Webuye Falls** are about 5 km from the road and provide the water for the mills. You can hire a *boda boda* to take you up there; it's a fairly scenic spot with a short drop of foamy water tumbling over some rocks; behind the main falls, huge stones dominate the countryside, creating a series of smaller falls and rapids.

Kitale → *For listings, see pages 159-160. Colour map 3, C5. Phone code: 054.*

A pleasant, small town, Kitale is in the middle of lush farmland between Mount Elgon and the Cherangani Hills. Originally this was Masai grazing land, but it was taken over by European settlers after the First World War. The town did not really develop until after 1925 and the arrival of the railway. The region is known for its fruit and vegetables, including apples, which are rare in East Africa. Kitale's main attraction for tourists is as a base from which to explore the **Cherangani Hills**, see page 321, or **Mount Elgon** and the **Saiwa Swamp National Park**, see page 157. It's also a stopping-off point on the route to **Lake Turkana** in the north (see pages 319-328).

Arriving in Kitale

Kitale is well served by public transport. There's an airstrip 4 km to the southwest of town on the A1 towards Kisumu, and **Fly 540** have a scheduled service to and from Nairobi. The town is on the B2, just 70 km northwest of Eldoret, and on the A1 heading for Kakamega and Kisumu in the south, and there are regular buses and *matatus*. It is also on the main route to Lake Turkana in the north and, while this road is reasonable until Marich Pass, it rapidly deteriorates beyond there. ▸▸ *See Transport, page 160.*

Places in Kitale

Kitale Museum ① *to the south of town just off the Eldoret Rd, T054-30996, www.museums. or.ke, 0930-1800, US$5.50, children (under 16) US$2.75*, contains ethnographic displays of the life of the people of Western Kenya, with lots of tribal artefacts, and has a section on the evolution of man. The museum also boasts a very comprehensive insect collection as well as birds, reptiles and wildlife exhibits. The museum buildings are set in spacious gardens, and the indigenous trees are labelled. There is an excellent nature trail through local forest – the remnants of a much larger forest that once clothed this area, which is rich in birdlife and monkeys – terminating at some very pleasant picnic sites. There is also **Snake Park**, home to both non-venomous and venomous snakes, in addition to an enclosure containing two crocodiles and another that contains tortoises.

Saiwa Swamp National Park → *For listings, see pages 159-160. Colour map 3, C5.*

ⓘ *T054-29826, www.kws.org, 0630-1800, US$20, children (3-18) US$10. Reached via the sealed well-signposted road, 24 km northeast of Kitale on the Kitale–Kapenguria road. There is a 5-km murram road linking Saiwa to the main road. You can reach here by matatu from Kitale to Kapenguria and beyond and then walk the last 5 km or there may be boda bodas around.*

Kenya's smallest national park, at 2.9 sq km, was established to protect the rare semi-aquatic sitatunga antelope (*Tragelaphus spekei*). The park is a perfect example of how a small area can survive as a complete ecological entity; it encloses the swamp fed by the Saiwa River together with its fringing belts of rainforest. The star of the show, the sitatunga, has splayed hooves, allowing it to walk on the swamp vegetation. There are a sufficient number here to ensure a sighting. Other animals here include the giant forest squirrel, bushbuck, Bohor reedbuck, bush duiker, the de Brazza monkey and both the spotted-necked and clawless otter. There is prolific birdlife, estimated at over 400 species, including the great blue turaco, several varieties of kingfisher and the bare-faced go-away-bird. There is also a very large variety of reptiles, amphibians, butterflies and other insects. There are about three nature trails, totalling 10 km, on duckboards, and there are rest areas and picnic areas along the way. Several tree hides with viewing platforms have been built along the western boundary from where it is possible to view the mammals and birds. The best time to see the sitatunga is in the early morning or evening, as it rests semi-submerged and very well hidden during the heat of the day. The park has three distinctive vegetation types: wetland vegetation with stands of bullrush, reeds and sedges; wooded grasslands containing shrubs and grasses, and indigenous forest, as the national park contains remnants of tropical forest including wild fig and banana trees.

Mount Elgon National Park → *For listings, see pages 159-160. Colour map 3, C5.*
Phone code: 054.

ⓘ *T054-310 456, www.kws.org, US$25, children (3-18) US$15, vehicle S$3.25.*
The brooding flat-topped Mount Elgon, which straddles the border with Uganda, is a distinctive feature of this region of Western Kenya. The name Elgon is said to be derived from the Masai *ol doinyo ilgoon* meaning 'the mountain with the contours of the human breast'. The peak of the extinct volcano, which reaches 4320 m, the second-highest mountain in Kenya with a radius of about 100 km, is estimated to be more than 15 million years old. The Kenya/Uganda border cuts through the caldera, giving half the mountain to Uganda, including the highest peak Wagagai (4320 m), with Lower Elgon Peak (also sometimes called Sudek Peak, 4307 m) in Kenya. The park is governed by KWS on the Kenyan side, and the Uganda Wildlife Authority on the Ugandan side.

The mountain is home to a wide diversity of habitats created by the changing altitude. From the base of the mountain to the top are a number of ecological zones, from mixed deciduous and evergreen forest, which includes wonderful specimens of the *Juniperus procera* more commonly known as the East African cedar, as well as the Elgon teak and the great podos. With increasing altitude the vegetation changes to bamboo forest, and then to Afro-alpine moorlands. Several rivers rise in these peaks, including the Malakis and the Nzoia that feed Lake Victoria, and the Suam and the Turkwell that feed Lake Turkana. The park also contains several beautiful waterfalls, dramatic cliffs and gorges, hot springs and a number of lava-tube caves formed by the action of water on volcanic ash. Some of these are over 60 m wide and attract elephants and other herbivores in search of salt.

Arriving in Mount Elgon National Park

The **Chorlim Gate** into the park is about 25 km northwest of Kitale, and the roads are clearly signposted. Two routes to the gate can be used, either via Endebess, about 15 km from Kitale, or take the tarmac road 11 km past Kitale and turn left onto a *murram* road leading to the gate. Most roads in the park are in good condition but a 4WD is recommended and is essential in the wet season.

Visiting Mount Elgon National Park

Four of the lava-tube caves can be explored. **Kitum** is the largest cave, extending to over 180 m in depth with a width of 60 m and overhanging crystalline walls. This is the cave most favoured by the elephants. Using their tusks, the elephants scrape away at the rock face and pick up the shards with their trunks. At night it is possible to see elephant convoys entering the cave to supplement their diet on the rich salt deposits. Kitum is also home to a large population of fruit bats. **Makingeni Cave** is not far from Kitum and is favoured by buffalo, and both **Chepnyalil** and **Ngwarisha caves** can also be explored. **Endebess Bluff** offers a panoramic view of the surrounding area. Animals likely to be here include colobus monkey, blue monkey, forest elephant (sometimes called cave elephant), leopard, giant forest hog, bushbuck, eland, buffalo, duiker and golden cat.

Climbing Mount Elgon

In a 4WD, it is possible to drive up to about 4000 m – the road passes through forest that is later supplanted by montane bamboo – and then hike over the moorlands, through tree heathers and giant lobelia up to 6 m tall, to Koitoboss peak (4187 m). You need to be accompanied by a KWS ranger, who you pick up from Chorlim Gate, and then drive for about 30 km, or three hours, to the end of the track at Koroborte (3580 m). From here it is then about a three-hour hike to Koitoboss. You can hire the ranger at the gate or in advance at the KWS headquarters in Nairobi (page 45). Make sure you are suitably equipped with warm and waterproof clothing and appropriate footwear. Altitude sickness is less of a problem here than on Mount Kenya, and a night spent en route will lessen any problems; there are some flat areas to camp at the end of the drivable road.

   Note: the highest summit, Wagagai (4320 m), and the vast 40-km wide caldera, are completely on the Uganda side, so a full traverse of the mountain from Kenya is not usually allowed (see below). There are several popular and very well-organized multi-day climbing routes on the Uganda side from the town of Mbale, which is just over 70 km north of the Malaba border – the actual trailhead is a further 20 km north of Mbale at the village of Budadiri. On each route trekkers are accompanied by porters and guides, and campsites and mountain huts are used for accommodation. For more information contact the **Uganda Wildlife Authority** ① *Kampala T+256 414 355 000, www.ugandawildlife. org.* To arrange a trek to the top ascending the Uganda slopes and descending on the Kenyan side (or vice versa) requires prior arrangement and detailed planning with both the Uganda Wildlife Authority, and the KWS in Nairobi (page 45).

◉ Kitale and around listings

For sleeping and eating price codes and other relevant information, see pages 20-24.

● Where to stay

Kitale *p156*
Budget travellers have a good choice of accommodation here.

$$-$ Kitale Club, Eldoret Rd, T054-31338, www.kitaleclub.net. Established in 1924, this old colonial sporting club is said to have been built on the site of the old slave market. It has 36 comfortable rooms, en suite doubles with satellite TV in cottages, or there are simple single rooms with shared bathrooms and hot water in the older run-down buildings. The restaurant serves English fare with some Indian dishes; it's well worth stopping here for a meal. There's also a friendly bar with Mt Elgon views from the veranda, and the swimming pool, tennis, squash, snooker table and an 18-hole golf course, can be used for an extra fee.

$$-$ Mid Africa Hotel, Moi Av, T0727-277 077, www.midafricahotel.com. A neat 5-storey block in the middle of town, with clean double and single rooms with TV, en suite or sharing a bathroom, which are modern and tiled and have reliable hot water. The nicest rooms face the front and have balconies, avoid the ones with only windows facing on to the corridors. There's an excellent and affordable restaurant serving European and Indian food, a *nyama choma* bar on the roof and internet facilities.

$ Alakara, corner of Kenyatta St/Post Office Rd, T054-31554. Secure, friendly staff, and near the bus stands, basic rooms are comfortable enough, but the water supply is intermittent. Restaurant serves fairly simple food but is good value, and breakfast is included in the rates.

$ Karibuni Lodge, about 2 km northeast of town off the Kapenguria road, turn right in town at the Total petrol station and go past the Hospital, T0735-573 798, www. karibunikitale.com. European-run, this is an excellent backpackers' set up with dorm beds, some doubles with or without bathrooms and plenty of camping in the spacious gardens of a homely colonial-style house. All the showers have hot water and meals are taken communally around a large table. Rents out tents and bikes and can organize local excursions to Saiwa Swamp and Mt Elgon.

$ Pinewood Resort, Eldoret Rd, 1 km before town T054-31346, www.pinewood kitale.com. Simple but good set up in an acre of pretty gardens, 2 timber cottages with a bathroom and 3 double rooms in each or camping on green lawns, secure parking, lovely restaurant and bar with satellite TV and pool table, good-value African, Chinese and Indian dishes and pizza, A double is from US$25 with breakfast, camping US$4 per person.

Saiwa Swamp National Park *p157*
You can camp here or stay in Kitale and visit on a day trip. Alternatively, **Sirikwa Safaris**, 23 km north of Kitale on the Kapenguria road, 8 km beyond Saiwa Swamp National Park (see page 326), has accommodation and a campsite and can organize day trips to the Saiwa Swamp and Mt Elgon national parks, and guides and porters are available for multi-day trekking in the Cherangani Hills (see page 321).

Camping
KWS Campsite, T054-29826, www.kws.org. At the main gate of the park in a lovely spot next to a stream, but with no facilities except for 2 thatched cooking *bandas* with barbeques and tables, US$15, children (3-18) US$10. You need to bring all camping equipment, food, water and firewood.

Mount Elgon National Park *p157*
Contact the warden, T054-20329, reservations KWS, Nairobi, T020-600 0800,

www.kws.org. Take drinking water for all accommodation.

$$$ Koitoboss Guesthouse, 500 m before Chorlim Gate. Set on a spacious lawn, house with 3 twin bedrooms and bathroom, hot water comes from wood-burning stoves, dining/sitting room with veranda, fully equipped kitchen with gas stove and fridge, everything is included and there's a caretaker on site. A generator provides electricity 1800-2230. Rates are US$180 for up to 6 people.

$ Kapkuro Bandas, 1 km from Chorlim Gate within the park. In a forest glade, 4 en suite *bandas* with 1 double and 1 single bed, kitchen with gas cooker and hot water comes from a wood-burning stove. Utensils in the kitchen, blankets and lanterns are supplied, but guests need to bring towels and a sleeping bag/sheet if desired.

Camping
There are KWS 3 campsites, all of which are just inside the park near Chorlim Gate: **Nyati**, **Chorlim**, and **Rongai**. Each has water, long-drop toilets and thatched cooking shelters with barbecues and tables, US$15, children (3-18) US$10.

⓻ Restaurants

Kitale *p156*
There are numerous canteen-type places around town serving local fare, and there's a branch of **Kenchic Inn** on the main road opposite the BP petrol station for tasty chicken and chips. For a small town, all the hotel restaurants have surprisingly good food.

⊖ Transport

Kitale *p156*
Air
The airstrip is 4 km from town towards Kisumu. **Fly 540**, T0770-639 429, Nairobi T020-827 521, www.fly540.com, has 1 daily flight between Kitale and **Nairobi**, which arrives mid-morning and departs again early afternoon, and takes 1 hr 10 mins, 1 way from US$110.

Bus and matatu
There are regular buses and *matatus* to and from **Eldoret** along the B2, and **Kakamega** and **Kisumu** on the A1. In Kitale there are various bus and *matatu* stands at the western end of the road to Mt Elgon. The **Akamba Bus** stand is on the corner of Moi Av and Bank St, T054-31732, www.akambabus.com, and has 2 services a day between Kitale and **Nairobi** via Eldoret, 1 of which is overnight, and take 8½ hrs.

⓲ Directory

Kitale *p156*
Medical services Kitale District Hospital, Ravine Rd, T057-20951.

Contents

Footprint features

At a glance

⊖ **Getting around** Car hire
from Nairobi to drive around
Mt Kenya; flights to lodges on
the Laikipia Plateau.
◐ **Time required** At least 3-4 days
to drive around Mt Kenya and visit
the Aberdare National Park; 2-3 days
at a game lodge in the region.
☀ **Weather** Moderate temperatures
year round of 15-25°C but often it's
cloudy and gets cool at night.
✖ **When not to go** Avoid the rainy
season Mar-May as it's wet and cold.

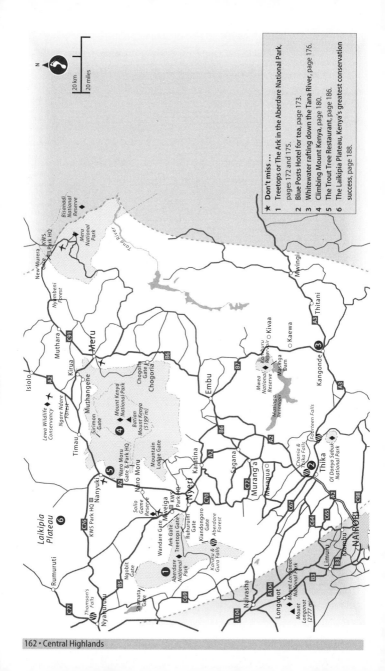

N

20 km
20 miles

★ Don't miss ...
1 Treetops or The Ark in the Aberdare National Park, pages 172 and 175.
2 Blue Posts Hotel for tea, page 173.
3 Whitewater rafting down the Tana River, page 176.
4 Climbing Mount Kenya, page 180.
5 The Trout Tree Restaurant, page 186.
6 The Laikipia Plateau, Kenya's greatest conservation success, page 188.

Isiolo

Bisanadi National Reserve

New Mururi
KWS Park HQ

Meru National Park

Tana River

Nyambeni Forest

Muthara

C91

Meru

Kirua

Muthangene

Mwingi

Thitani

A3

Lewa Wildlife Conservancy

Ngare Ndare Forest

Timau

Sirimon Gate

Mount Kenya National Park

Batian Mount Kenya (5199 m)

Chogoria Gate

Chogoria

B6

Kivaa

Kaewa

Kamburu Reservoir

Masinga Dam

Kangonde

A3

Naro Moru Gate & Park HQ

Mountain Lodge Gate

Embu

B7

Mwea National Reserve

Masinga Reservoir

Fourteen Falls

KWS Park HQ

Nanyuki

A2

Naro Moru

Solio Game Reserve

Nyeri

Kiaritina

Sagana

A2

B6

Laikipia Plateau

C76

Wandare Gate

Ark Gate Treetops Gate

Mweiga

Ruhuruini Gate

Kiandongoro Gate

Aberdare Forest

Karuru & Guru Falls

Aberdare National Park

Murang'a

C72

Maragua

Chania & Thika Falls

Thika

Ol Donyo Sabuk National Park

The Trout Tree Restaurant

C67

C64

C65

NAIROBI

A104

Rumuruti

Thomson's Falls

C77

Nyahururu

B5

Ngobit Gate

Shamata Gate

C69

Mount Longonot National Park

Naivasha

Longonot

Mount Longonot (2777 m)

A104

Limuru

B3

Kabuni

B3

C98

Thomson's Falls

The Central Highlands, to the north of Nairobi and forming the eastern boundary of the Rift Valley, are the heartland of the Kikuyu people who make up the largest ethnic group in Kenya. They used to be known as the 'White Highlands' because – being fertile and well watered – many of the white settlers chose them for their farmland. Thanks to the nutritious volcanic soils of Mount Kenya, this region is now home to much small-scale farming, including coffee, and is very densely populated.

There are a number of towns in the Central Highlands, often referred to as 'upcountry', and these are useful for shops and communications but have few distractions and will not hold the attention of visitors for very long. The real reason people come to the Central Highlands is to visit the Aberdare National Park – home to the famous hotels, the Ark and Treetops – the more remote Meru National Park, and also to climb Mount Kenya. The newest attraction of the region, and one of East Africa's wildlife conservation success stories, is the Laikipia Plateau. Here the many farms and ranches across a vast area have joined forces to protect the wild animals on their land and start tourism initiatives to support their gallant efforts. After the Masai Mara, it's now the best place to view wildlife, including the Big Five, and is home to over 50% of Kenya's rhino. This area is over 9500 sq km and covers not only much of the Central Highlands but also stretches into the Northern Territory and into Western Kenya. It is, however, best accessed from the town of Nanyuki so it is included in this chapter.

Getting there and around

There are a number of towns located along the Kirinyaga Ring Road at the base of Mount Kenya, and the route round the mountain is becoming increasingly popular as a tourist circuit, which is not surprising for it is a really beautiful part of the country. From Nairobi the main A2 heads north, firstly along a dual carriageway through the outskirts of Thika, and then continues northwards through the lush, verdant countryside. Almost every inch of ground is cultivated and you will see terraces on some of the steeper slopes. There are a number of routes to choose from: you can go north to Nyeri and the Aberdare National Park, then clockwise round the mountain via Naro Moru, or anti-clockwise via Embu. The following section will cover the clockwise route around Mount Kenya, taking in Nyeri and Naro Moru, to Nanyuki. It is possible to continue on all the way around the mountain via Meru to Embu and rejoin the A2 at Thika. The towns are linked by a steady stream of *matatus*, and long-distance buses operate services to and from Nairobi. There are also bus and *matatu* links cross-country to Naivasha and Nakuru in the Rift Valley. Main access points to the lodges in the Laikipia Plateau region is from Nanyuki, Isiolo, Nyahuru or Maralal, depending on where the lodges are located.▶ *See Transport in the relevant sections.*

Best time to visit

This area is very high, with peaks in the Aberdares of up to 4000 m, and Mount Kenya, which is 5199 m. You should therefore expect it to get fairly chilly, especially at night. The maximum temperature range is 22-26°C and the minimum 10-14°C. It is also very wet here, with annual rainfall of up to 3000 mm not unusual. But outside of the rainy seasons the sun shines most afternoons and the cloud lifts from the mountains.

Nyeri and around

The region directly to the northeast of Nairobi provides access to one of the highlights of the Central Highlands, the Aberdare National Park, and, if the cloud lifts, affords good views of Mount Kenya to the right of the main A2 road. This is a heavily cultivated area thanks to the rising elevation on the lower mountain slopes, and the market towns have good displays of fresh produce in their markets. Thika can be easily reached from Nairobi for lunch at the Blue Posts Hotel, while the Outspan and Aberdare Country Club make fine country retreats. ▶ *For listings, see pages 173-177.*

Thika to Nyeri → *For listings, see pages 173-177.*

Thika → *Phone code: 067. Colour map 1, A4.*

Directly from Nairobi, the four-laned A2 continues for 42 km up to Thika, which is a growing commuter town for Nairobi; this road can be notoriously busy. It was made famous by the book (and later the television series), *The Flame Trees of Thika* by Elspeth Huxley. It is about her childhood, when her parents came out to Kenya as one of the first white settler families, and their attempts to establish a farm. However, there is little special about Thika – not even many flame trees to brighten it up. It is primarily a market town that was established during the white settler period and is, today, a base for manufacturing activity, with a number of factories around town. You will also soon notice that this is pineapple country, and many hectares are taken up with plantations; the 'man from Del Monte' is the region's largest producer.

The singular attraction is the **Blue Posts Hotel**, a famous colonial landmark (see page 173). A visit is a must if you're in the area. It is nestled between Chania and Thika Falls with shaded tables in sight of the falls, where all you hear is the crashing water, birdsong and the rustling of leaves. There are also easy trails around the base of the falls, thick with flowers and foliage, and teeming with butterflies and dragonflies.

Ol Donyo Sabuk National Park → *Colour map 1, A5.*

ⓘ *27 km southeast from Thika on the Garissa road, T020-206 2503, www.kws.org, 0830-1800, US$20, children (3-18) US$10, vehicle US$3.25.*

This small 21 sq km park, 85 km northeast of Nairobi, is named after the extinct volcano, Ol Donyo Sabuk, 2150 m, which means 'the mountain of the buffalo'. To get here, follow the main A3 Thika–Garissa road for 22 km from Thika to the Makutano junction where there is a signpost to the right. Follow this road 3 km to the village of Donyo and turn right again; it is 2 km to the main gate and car park. Buses and *matatus* run regularly from Thika towards Garissa and you can get off at the Makutano junction. However, from there, transport to the park is irregular. There is a pleasant picnic site at the main gate and a short nature trail further up the hill to another picnic site from where there are views of Thika, Nairobi, the Athi Plains and the Ngong Hills. You can drive 9 km from the main gate to the summit but only in a 4WD. Because of the presence of buffalo, you are not permitted to walk this road without an armed KWS ranger, but this can be arranged at the gate. The top of the volcano is covered in dense forest vegetation and afro-alpine vegetation, including the giant lobelia, and the area is home to 45 species of bird. There is some game including buffalo, monkeys and small antelope but it is difficult to spot them in the heavily wooded terrain. From the top, as well as Nairobi, Mount Kenya and even Mount Kilimanjaro can be seen on clear days.

Sir William Northrup MacMillan, a well-heeled gentleman of St Louis, and an associate of Roosevelt and Churchill, bought the mountain and much of the surrounding land in the early part of the 20th century. This immensely wealthy, 158-kg American came to the protectorate in 1904 and received a knighthood from the British in recognition of his support during the First World War. After his death he bequeathed the mountain to the nation and was buried at the 7-km mark along the road to the summit. It had been intended that his remains would be interred at the summit, but they proved to be too heavy for the hearse, supported on skis and pulled by a tractor, to complete its ascent. Oak trees were planted by the graveside.

Fourteen Falls → *Colour map 1, A5.*

ⓘ *22 km off the Thika–Garissa road about 2 km before the village of Donyo on the way to Ol Donyo Sabuk; follow the directions above. Again you can get a matatu to Makutano junction and walk from there, 0900-1700, US$2, car US$3.*

These falls are particularly splendid during the rainy season and derive their name from the 14 successive falls of water along the Athi River, as this broad plume of water plummets 30 m over a curved multi-lipped precipice. You can negotiate with a local guide (usually a young boy) to lead you down a rocky path from the car park to the base of the falls, where you can get a rowing boat for the best view of the falls. A fine spray hangs in the air and keeps everything cool, and there are lots of birds. The guides also entertain visitors by performing jumps from the top of the falls to the plunge pool below. There are hippos in the river, so take care if you decide to splash around in the shallows.

The Tree Mother of Africa

A Kikuyu born in Nyeri in 1940, Wangari Muta Maathai is the first African woman to win the Nobel Peace Prize. This was awarded to her in 2004 for "her contribution to sustainable development, democracy and peace," and her astonishing work in replanting trees in regions where it was estimated some 30-40 years ago that only 10% of the trees that were being cut down were being replaced.

In 1977, Maathai left her job as professor at the University of Nairobi and founded the **Green Belt Movement** (www.greenbeltmovement.org), on World Environment Day by planting nine trees in her back yard. The movement grew into a programme run by women with the goal of reforesting Africa and preventing the poverty that deforestation caused. Not only did deforestation cause environmental problems, such as soil erosion and water pollution, but lack of trees near villages meant that women had to walk great distances for firewood, and livestock also suffered from not having vegetation to graze on. Maathai believed that if the environment is degraded, a woman's children are the first to be infected and affected. The programme established village nurseries, and women got paid for each seedling they planted. To date, more than 30 million trees have been planted in Kenya, and other African nations have adopted similar programs based on the Green Belt Movement model.

During her numerous environmental campaigns, Maathai met with resistance from the then President Daniel Arap Moi's government, including personally being beaten and jailed. In 1989, she protested against plans to build a 60-storey government building complex in the middle of Uhuru Park in central Nairobi, which also included a large statue of Moi. In his 1989 speech celebrating Independence, Moi suggested that Maathai be a proper woman in the African tradition and respect men and be quiet. The media response to this contributed to the cancellation of the project in 1990. In 1992, she took part in a hunger strike in a corner of Uhuru Park to pressurize the government to release political prisoners. After four days she and other protesters (mostly mothers of those imprisoned)

Sagana and Karatina → Colour map 1, A4. Phone code: 061.

From Thika, the main road (A2) continues north and, just before the small settlement of **Sagana**, it splits, and the A2 heads northwest around the western lieu of Mount Kenya to Nyeri and beyond, while the B6 heads around the eastern lieu of the mountain via Embu. Sagana is where **Savage Wilderness Safaris** has its base for whitewater rafting (see under What to do, page 176). North of Sagana, **Karatina** is 95 km north of Thika and lies on a plateau directly below the southern side of Mount Kenya; the landscape of small-scale farms is ringed by its steeply sloping foothills. Like many areas around Mount Kenya, Karatina was a hotbed for activities by the Mau Mau; Dedan Kimathi, the Mau Mau leader, came from the village of Aguthi, about 25 km to the west of Karatina. In town, there are baskets for sale from the Kikuyu women who sit by the roadside and, as it is often the vendors themselves who make the baskets, they are good value. Worth a visit on market days (Tuesday, Thursday and Saturday), this is one of the biggest fruit and vegetable markets in East Africa, and it attracts buyers from as far away as Mombasa.

were forcibly removed, knocked unconscious and hospitalized. Again Moi responded by calling her "a mad woman" and the incident sparked international criticism. The protest moved to Nairobi's All Saints Cathedral across from Uhuru Park and continued until 1993, when the prisoners were finally released.

In 1998, Maathai began a campaign against the proposed building of housing estates in the Karura Forest Reserve on Nairobi's outskirts. Again, she was persecuted by the government, and, when she and a group of protesters tried to plant a tree in the forest in an area that had been designated to be cleared for a golf course, the group was attacked. Many of the protesters were injured, including Maathai, four MPs, some journalists and German environmentalists. The attack had been filmed, and student protests broke out throughout Nairobi, some of which were violently broken up by the police. Again the event provoked international outrage, and, under pressure, in August 1999, the government announced that they were banning all allocation of public land to development.

Maathai went on to win a seat as an MP in 2002 under the new Kibaki government, and became Deputy Minister of Environment, Natural Resources and Wildlife until 2005. She won the Nobel Peace Prize in 2004 and became a leading international authority on environmental conservation, human rights and women's empowerment issues, and served on the boards of some very powerful and influential organizations. In 2006, she met then US Senator Barack Obama in Kenya and they planted a tree together in Uhuru Park. Maathai died on 25 September 2011 in Nairobi, while receiving treatment for ovarian cancer.

The Norwegian Nobel Committee, in a statement announcing her as the 2004 Nobel Peace Prize winner, said of her, "Maathai stood up courageously against the former oppressive regime in Kenya. Her unique forms of action have contributed to drawing attention to political oppression – nationally and internationally. She has served as inspiration for many in the fight for democratic rights and has especially encouraged women to better their situation."

Nyeri → *For listings, see pages 173-177. Colour map 1, A4. Phone code: 061.*

Nyeri, to the west of the A2 and 154 km from Nairobi, is the administrative capital of the Central Province and lies between the eastern base of the Aberdares and the western slopes of Mount Kenya. The town was founded by Richard Meinertzhagen in 1902 (who, despite his name, was British), as he camped at Nyeri Hill during a revolt against the Tetu (a sub-group of the Kikuyu) who had ambushed an Arab caravan. He was a man with astonishingly accurate foresight and, in 1904, wrote in his diary, "I am sorry to leave the Kikuyu, for I like them. They are the most intelligent of the African tribes that I have met; therefore they will be the most progressive under European guidance and will be the most susceptible to subversive activities. They will be one of the first tribes to demand freedom from European influence and in the end cause a lot of trouble. And if white settlement really takes hold in this country it is bound to do so at the expense of the Kikuyu, who own the best land, and I can foresee much trouble."

During the British colonial period, the land around Nyeri was taken from the Kikuyu and given to white settlers, and the town developed as an army base and important trading centre for farmers. It was here that Dedan Kimathi, the last Mau Mau leader, was captured in 1956 along with 13 other Mau Mau rebels and subsequently executed by the British in 1957, which effectively ended the Mau Mau campaign. After Independence most of the fertile land was returned to the Kikuyu, and, as you drive into Nyeri, you will see the many *shambas* (farms) growing maize, bananas and coffee, as well as many varieties of vegetables. A few famous people have hailed from Nyeri including President Mwai Kibaki, 2004 Nobel Peace Prize winner Wangari Maathai (see box, page 166) and acclaimed runner Catherine Ndereba (known as Catherine the Great in Kenya), who broke the women's marathon world record in 2001 and picked up the silver medal for the marathon at the 2008 Olympics in Beijing.

Arriving in Nyeri

Nyeri is off the A2; the turn-off is 12 km northwest of Karatina, from where it is 14 km to Nyeri along the B5 to Nyahururu (page 104). Another road, the B5, links the A2 further north with Nyeri from Kiganjo. There are regular *matatus* from Nairobi and other main towns in the area. The main street, Kimathi Way, is where you will find banks and the post office, while running parallel Kenyatta Road has more banks and petrol stations. To the southeast of the two is the market and the bus and *matatu* stands.

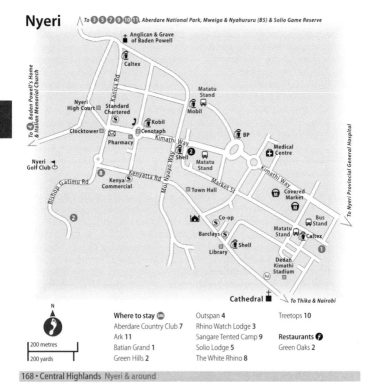

Nyeri

△ To ③⑤⑦⑨⑩⑪, Aberdare National Park, Mweiga & Nyahururu (B5) & Solio Game Reserve

Anglican & Grave of Baden Powell

To ④ Baden Powell's Home & Italian Memorial Church

Caltex

Kanja Rd

Nyeri High Court

Standard Chartered

Matatu Stand

Mobil

Clocktower

Kobil

Cenotaph

Pharmacy

Kimathi Way

BP

Shell

Matatu Stand

Medical Centre

Nyeri Golf Club

Bishop Gatimu Rd

Kenya Commercial

Kenyatta Rd

Moi Nyayo Way

Town Hall

Market St

Kimathi Way

Covered Market

To Nyeri Provincial General Hospital

Co-op

Bus Stand

Barclays

Matatu Stand

Caltex

Shell

Library

Dedan Kimathi Stadium

Cathedral

To Thika & Nairobi

N

200 metres
200 yards

Where to stay
Aberdare Country Club 7
Ark 11
Batian Grand 1
Green Hills 2

Outspan 4
Rhino Watch Lodge 3
Sangare Tented Camp 9
Solio Lodge 5
The White Rhino 8

Treetops 10

Restaurants
Green Oaks 2

Baden-Powell

Lord Baden-Powell was a general in the British Army who distinguished himself in the Boer War during the Siege of Mafeking (1899-1900) in South Africa. It was here that he organized young boys in the town, aged nine to 15, into a disciplined Siege Cadet Corps and put them to non-combat use. It was from this idea that he founded the Boy Scout movement in England in 1907. Guides were soon to follow and, for younger children, Cubs and Brownies. The movement was very successful and is still popular around the world.

Baden-Powell first visited Kenya in 1906 and said at the time that he fell in love with the "wonderful views over the plains to the bold snow-peak of Mount Kenya." He didn't go again until 1935, when he was 80 years old and was carrying out inspections of Scouts at rallies organized throughout the country. He visited his friend and former secretary, Eric Walker, who had built the **Outspan Hotel** (see page 174) and the world-famous **Treetops** (see box, page 172) in Nyeri in the 1920s.

Nyeri was Baden-Powell's great love and he once wrote that "The nearer to Nyeri the nearer to bliss." Baden-Powell spent his final years in his cottage, Paxtu, built for him by Walker in the grounds of the **Outspan** with money collected by Guides and Scouts from around the world. He died in 1941 and his obituary states: "No Chief, no Prince, no King, no Saint was ever mourned by so great a company of boys and girls, or men and women, in every land." He is buried in Nyeri cemetery, and his wife's ashes are buried beside him. Lady Baden-Powell was World Chief Guide until her death (in England) at the age of 88 in 1977.

Places in Nyeri

On the main road you can see a **cenotaph** to those who died during the Mau Mau rebellion. It has the inscription: to the Memory of the Members of the Kikuyu Tribe Who Died in the Fight for Freedom 1951-1957.

It is possible to visit **Lord Baden-Powell's home** ① *US$5, free to scouts and guides, pay at the hotel reception*, which contains a small museum with a display of memorabilia. The cottage, Paxtu, lies in the grounds of the **Outspan Hotel** (see page 174). Baden-Powell's home in England was named Pax, and the name of his 'Kenyan home was a pun on the original (Pax Two). The cottage remains very much as it was when he first had it built, though the old makuti roof has been replaced by an iron one. In the living room are some of the greeting cards Baden-Powell drew for friends. Outside, two big scout movement emblems are surrounded by a tropical garden. See box, above.

After Baden-Powell's death, Paxtu was the home of Jim Corbett, famous hunter/destroyer of several man-eating tigers in India in the 1920s and 1930s. In 1947 Jim Corbett and his sister Maggie moved to Nyeri where he wrote most of his books. In 1952 (when aged 80 years) he received a request to meet Princess Elizabeth and Prince Philip at **Treetops** (see page 172), where he identified animals for the Royals.

About 5 km out of town on the D435 road that leads to the Ruhuruini Gate of the Aberdare National Park is the enormous **Italian Memorial Church**, with its tree-lined drive and manicured grounds. It was built in remembrance of the Italian soldiers and their African recruits who died in East Africa during the Second World War. The walls of the church are lined with the vaults of the fallen soldiers and, in front of the main altar, lies the grave of Amadeo di Savoia, Duce d'Aosta, the commander of the main Italian armies in Ethiopia, who formally surrendered to the Allied army at Amba Alagi, 20 May 1941, and died in Nairobi in 1942. An important mass is held here every year on 4 November, which is Remembrance Day in Italy.

North of Nyeri

Solio Game Reserve → *Colour map 1, A4.*
ⓘ *22 km north of Nyeri and a little north of Mweiga along the B5 towards Nyaharuru.*

This 25,000 ha private reserve features huge stands of yellow acacia trees, higher rolling plains and a vast area of marshland, and incorporates one of the most successful rhino-breeding programmes in Africa. It is presently home to 74 black rhino and 155 white rhino. Formerly a cattle ranch that was fenced as a conservation area in the 1970s by a foresighted American tycoon and nature lover, Courtland Parfet, this was Kenya's first rhino sanctuary. From 1970 it was estimated that Kenya's population of black rhino had dropped from 18,000 to 1500 in 1980 and to only 400 in 1990. This sharp decline was caused by poaching during the 1970s and the early 1980s, both inside and outside the national parks and reserves, with few controls and little enforcement. The outcome of this intensive slaughter was that it left small remnant populations of rhino, sometimes just a single individual, scattered across the country. The then Wildlife and Conservation Management Department (later to become the KWS in 1989), requested Solio to take in some of these remnant black rhinos, and the first five individuals were moved there in 1970. Development of the sanctuary continued and, by 1980, 23 rhino had been moved to Solio where they bred successfully. Meanwhile, other national parks and private ranches in Kenya were made sufficiently secure from poachers to take in rhinos, and Solio became the prime source of rhinos for many of these, including Nakuru, Tsavo and the Aberdare National Parks. More recent relocations from Solio include to the Lewa Wildlife Conservancy and Ol Pejeta Conservancy on the Laikipia Plateau, and to parks and reserves in Uganda. Today, as well as the rhino (rather astonishingly up to 40 at a time can be seen here), most of the plains species can be seen, including two northern species, the reticulated giraffe and the beisa oryx, as well as buffalo, zebra and warthog. Of the cats, lion, cheetah and serval are present but rarely seen but, by contrast, leopard is very unusually common and often seen during the day. You can stay in the reserve at **Solio Lodge**, one of Kenya's newest and most luxurious lodges, or game drives can be arranged from the **Aberdare Country Club**, and the other lodges in the area.➤➤ *See Where to stay, page 173.*

Aberdare National Park → *For listings, see pages 173-177. Phone code: 061.*

ⓘ *T020-237 9409, www.kws.org, gates open 0600-1800, US$50, children (3-18) US$25, vehicle US$3.25.*

The Aberdares are a range of mountains to the west of Mount Kenya, running in a north-south direction between Nairobi and Nyahururu. The national park, established in 1950, encompasses an area of around 715 sq km and is one of Kenya's only virgin forest reserves. The Aberdares come to a peak at about 4000 m and are the third highest massif in the country, with dramatic peaks, deep valleys, enormous spectacular waterfalls cascading down the rock faces, and volcanic outcrops of bizarre proportions. Most of the park features undulating moorlands, and the middle and upper reaches are densely forested with thickets of bamboo, giant heath and tussock grass. There isn't a huge amount of wildlife (comparatively), although birdlife is rich, and the walks around the park offer tremendous views.

Arriving in Aberdare National Park

The park is 165 km north of Nairobi. From Nyeri you can enter the park through three gates: **Ruhuruini Gate**, **Wandare Gate** and **Kiandongoro Gate**. **Outspan Hotel** is the base hotel for **Treetops**; visitors usually come here first and then enter through **Treetops Gate** directly to the lodge. The **Aberdare Country Club** is the base for **The Ark**, which is accessed directly through the **Ark Gate**. From Nyeri follow the B5 towards Nyahururu for 15 km to **Mweiga**, the town close to the **Aberdare Country Club**, and where the **KWS Park Headquarters** (0700-1800) is located. Here you can obtain or reload your Safari Card. Entry

① Aberdare National Park

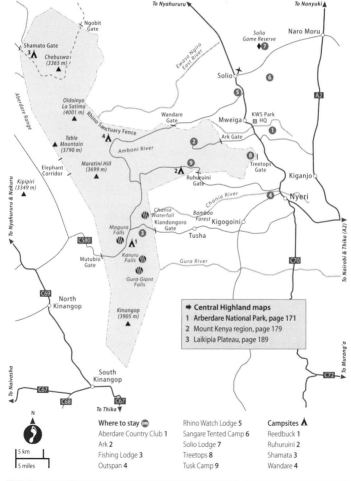

Where to stay 🛏		
Aberdare Country Club 1	Rhino Watch Lodge 5	**Campsites** ⛺
Ark 2	Sangare Tented Camp 6	Reedbuck 1
Fishing Lodge 3	Solio Lodge 7	Ruhuruini 2
Outspan 4	Treetops 8	Shamata 3
	Tusk Camp 9	Wandare 4

Treetops

Originally, Treetops was nothing more than a two-room treehouse sitting on top of a fig tree. Intrepid travellers reached it on foot escorted by armed rangers that protected them from wild animals during the walk. Then guests were left on their own with just a picnic supper and some oil lamps. At dawn, the rangers returned to escort them back, after an exciting and chilling night in the midst of the forest watching the wildlife roaming below their feet. In 1952, Treetops was enlarged for a royal visit from Princess Elizabeth and her husband Philip. A third room was added and a small cabin for the ranger on duty was attached. During their overnight stay, the young princess and her husband witnessed a thrilling fight between two male waterbucks that ended with one killing the other. However, that night would become historical for a different reason as it coincided with the death of the princess's father, King George VI, in London. Although the princess was not aware of the bad news until her next stop at Sagana, the morning she descended from Treetops on 6 February 1952 she had become Queen of England.

to the park is by Safari Card only (no cash), but remember if you are going on excursions to the lodges, they will organize this along with transfers and game drives. There are hiking trails in the park, but because of the wildlife, it is compulsory to be escorted by an armed KWS ranger. If you are not on an organized excursion, this can be arranged at the KWS Park Headquarters at Mweiga for about US$15 per six hours. Trout fishing is popular, especially high up on the moors. A fishing licence is required, which is again organized by your hotel/lodge or obtainable from the KWS Park Headquarters for US$5 per day.

The park is not often visited, primarily because of the weather. It rains heavily and frequently, making driving difficult and seeing the game and mountain peaks almost impossible. Set off early in the day, as it frequently clouds over by late morning and, during the wet season, roads turn into mudslides and are often closed.

Around the park

The Kikuyu call these mountains *Nyandarua* (drying hide); they were the home to Mau Mau guerrilla fighters during the struggle for Independence. Nowadays the mountains are home to buffalo, rhino, elephant, giant forest hog, red duiker, and Syke's and colobus monkeys. The rare, handsome bongo, an elusive forest antelope, is most likely to be spotted near **The Ark**, which is sited close to a swampy glade, waterhole and salt-lick, or up in the bamboo zone. At about 3500 m, where the landscape opens up, is the terrain of lion, leopard and serval cat, but these are rarely seen and most of the lion from the park have been removed to protect the bongo. Birdlife is prolific here, with about 290 species. Among the birds of prey are the crowned hawk eagles, mountain buzzard and the African goshawk. Particularly good walks include trekking up the three peaks, **Oldoinyo La Satima**, 4001 m, **Kinangop**, 3905 m, and **Kipipiri**, 3349 m.

The park is split into two sections, the beautiful high moorland and peaks with sub-alpine vegetation, and the lower Salient, which is dense rainforest and where much of the wildlife lives. The Aberdare Salient is closed to the public and the animals can only be viewed from **Treetops** or **The Ark** (details below). Access to these lodges is prohibited to private vehicles; visitors are obliged to use the hotels' buses.

There are a number of spectacular waterfalls in the park including the **Chania Falls** and the **Karuru Falls**, which have a total drop of 273 m in three steps. The more remote and inaccessible **Gura Giant Falls**, to the south, have a higher single drop of over 300 m. There are a few roads traversing the centre of the national park from Nyeri to Naivasha, giving access to most of the waterfalls.

A major project in recent years has been the building of the **rhino sanctuary** surrounded by a 400 km-long electric fence funded by the KWS and conservation organizations including **Rhino Ark** ① www.rhinoark.org. Other wildlife also live within the fence, including elephant and various members of the cat family. The electricity for the fence is generated locally using waterwheels to harness water from within the forest, a project that also provides power for local people living in the surrounding villages. The fence also protects their livestock and crops from the animals. Various fund-raising activities in support of the project include the 'Rhino Charge' motor rally (see page 25).

◉ Nyeri and around listings

For sleeping and eating price codes and other relevant information, see pages 20-24.

◉ Where to stay

Thika *p164*
$$ Blue Posts Hotel, just north of Thika, towards Murang'a (take the first slip road off the main A2 after the main junction for Thika), T020-260 8702. Established in 1908 as a stopover for white settlers who farmed and lived in central Kenya, this is still a popular hotel with faded colonial charm. The 32 rooms, with satellite TV and veranda, are set in 2 wings and have gloomy old-fashioned furnishings but are comfortable, and there's reasonable food in the restaurant and good service. Doubles start from US$80. The lovely gardens have vast expanse of lawns have very good views over the Thika and Chania waterfalls and are a fine place to sit and have tea and cake in the afternoon.
$ White Line, in the centre of Thika on Stadium Rd, T067-22857. Simple but acceptable board and lodgings, the double rooms have bathrooms, the singles have shared bathrooms and there is sometimes hot water, usually in the evenings, and a bar. There are also some passable board and lodgings type rooms above the **Coconut Grill** restaurant (see Restaurants, below).

Ol Donyo Sabuk National Park *p165*
$$$ Sabuk House, 2 km from the main gate, T020-206 2503, reservations Nairobi T020-600 0800, www.kws.org. A neat house that sleeps 10 in total, and a popular family weekend jaunt for people from Nairobi, with 5 bedrooms and 3 bathrooms, sitting room with fireplace and veranda, fully equipped kitchen with stove and fridge, electricity, and there's a caretaker on site. US$250 per night.

Camping
Turacco Campsite, T020-206 2503, www.kws.org. There's a very basic KWS campsite near the main gate with water and a pit latrine, so you will need to bring everything with you, US$15, children (3-18) US$10.

Sagana and Karatina *p166*
$ Hotel Starbucks, T061-72829, www.hotel starbucks.com. Set back from the main road in the centre of Karatina in a grey/green concrete building, parking spaces outside with an *askari*, 45 simple rooms with TV and nets, canteen-style restaurant and bar with 1st-floor balcony, reasonable African and Oriental food. **The Chicken Inn**, on the ground floor (0600-2200) is a good stop for breakfast, chicken or sausages and chips and fresh juices if passing through.

Camping

Savage Camp, on the A2 just south of Sagana. You can camp in a lovely shady spot next to the Tana River at **Savage Wilderness Safaris'** base for whitewater rafting, which has hot showers and a swimming pool, see What to do, page 176.

Nyeri *p167, map p168*

$$$ Outspan Hotel, Baden Powell Rd, 1 km from Nyeri, well signposted from town, T061-203 2424, reservations **Aberdare Safari Hotels**, Nairobi, T020-445 2095, www.aberdaresafarihotels.com. A wonderful atmosphere and beautiful grounds where peacocks roam. Built in 1926, the cottage was the last residence of Lord Baden-Powell (see page 169) and has 42 spacious rooms, all with TV and many with fireplaces. Also 3 cottages, swimming pool, tennis and squash courts, and golf at the adjacent Nyeri Golf Club, and the restaurant and bar has a wide veranda. Activities include game drives into the Aberdare National Park, a 2-hr guided nature trail along the Chania River, which is great for birdwatching, and in the hotel grounds, Kikuyu ceremonies and songs take place in a typical Kikuyu Village of thatched huts and ceremonial trees.

$$$-$$ Green Hills, Bishop Gatimu Rd, on the top of a hill to the southwest of the town, T061-203 0604, www.greenhills.co.ke. Spread over extensive gardens from where, on a clear day, you can see Mt Kenya, with 92 rooms in a 1970s block but with fresh modern furnishings, balconies and satellite TV. Friendly staff and excellent facilities including 2 restaurants (see page 176), bar, swimming pool, spa, gym and parking. Good-value doubles start from US$80.

$$ The White Rhino, Kenyatta Rd, T061-203 0944, www.whiterhinohotel.com. This colonial hotel is one of the oldest buildings in town. It opened in 1913 and was being refurbished at the time of writing, when 11 rooms were open; they have smart furnishings, satellite TV and balconies, and another 90 rooms are being built on the property. It has a restaurant, bar with *nyama choma* grill, friendly staff and pleasant manicured gardens. It got its name as a white rhino shot by hunters staggered to death on the spot that the hotel now stands.

$ Batian Grand, Gakere Rd, on the east side of town, near the bus and *matatu* stands, T061-203 0743. Best of the basic town hotels in a large modern block with central courtyard and 66 en suite rooms; those looking inwards are much darker than the larger, carpeted ones looking outwards, some of which, on a clear day, have views of Mt Kenya. Hot water, simple restaurant, coffee shop bar with pool table and satellite TV, and secure parking with an *askari*.

North of Nyeri *p170, map p171*

$$$$ Sangare Tented Camp, 27 km north of Nyeri on the road to Naro Moru off the Nyahururu road (B5), but the final access to the lodge is by 4WD, transfers from the **Green Hills Hotel** in Nyeri where you leave your car can be arranged in advance, reservations **Silver Springs Hotel**, Nairobi, T020-272 2451, www.sangaretentedcamp.com. A wilderness camp set on a 2630 ha private ranch and overlooking a small lake that is encircled by yellow acacia trees, 12 en suite tented units with 4-poster beds and rustic African decor, and an attractive cedar wooden cottage is the bar and dining room. Day and night game drives on the property, which is home to plains game, elephant and buffalo, and game drives into the Solio Game Reserve to see rhino and the Aberdare National Park. Rates are full board. Air charters can be arranged from Nairobi.

$$$$ Solio Lodge, Solio Game Reserve, 22 km north of Nyeri on the road to Naro Moru off the Nyahururu road (B5), reservations Nairobi T020-502 0888, www.tamimiea.com. This super-luxury lodge opened mid-2010 and has 6 thatched cottages, beautifully decorated in contemporary African style with fireplaces, stand-alone bathtubs and massive glass windows with views across the plains and

Mt Kenya. There are numerous things to do here including game drives and walks, horse-riding, children's activities, trout-fishing and trips to Aberdare National Park. Doubles from US$1000, but a wonderful all-inclusive experience and a marvellous location for seeing rhino and other species, including elephant, buffalo and plains games. Air charters can be arranged from Nairobi.

$$$ Aberdare Country Club, Mweiga, 15 km north of Nyeri on the Nyahururu road (B5), reservations **Marasa Africa**, Nairobi, T020-557 009, www.marasa.net. Formerly a farmhouse, a charming old colonial country hotel with mountain views, 46 rooms with fireplaces and verandas arranged in garden cottages, with tennis courts, swimming pool, 9-hole golf course, and giraffe, zebra and antelope can be seen in the extensive grounds. Can arrange game drives into the Solio Game Reserve and Aberdare National Park. This is the springboard for excursions to **The Ark** (see below).

$$$ Rhino Watch Lodge, on the Nyahururu road (B5), 6 km north of Mweiga, T0711-585 495, www.rhinowatchlodge.com. Another new lodge in this area with 7 spacious and comfortable chalets modelled on Kikuyu huts with makuti thatch roofs and verandas, some have 2 bedrooms for families, plus 7 simpler tents with stone en suite bathrooms, all set in pleasant gardens with views of Mt Kenya, good food, rustic bar, very close to the Solio Game Reserve for game drives, and trips to the Aberdare National Park can be arranged.

Aberdare National Park *p170, map p171*
As accommodation is limited in the park, an alternative option is to stay at Nyeri or around (see above) and visit on an organized game drive. Remember it gets freezing at night in the park.

$$$$-$$$ Treetops, T061-203 4914, reservations **Aberdare Safari Hotels**, Nairobi, T020-445 2095, www.aberdaresafarihotels. com. Built on stilts, this has 50 small cabin-type rooms with shared bathroom facilities,

a restaurant where meals are served on long bench tables, a rooftop bar and a number of decks from where you can view the animals at night at the 2 waterholes. Transfers are after a lunch at the **Outspan Hotel**. No children under 5. See box, page 172.

$$$ Fishing Lodge, 4 km from Kiandongoro Gate, T020-237 9409, reservations **KWS**, Nairobi, T020-600 0800, www.kws.org. Set in moorlands in the south of the park, 2 timber cottages each with 3 bedrooms and 2 bathrooms, fully equipped kitchen with gas stove, lounge with fireplace and veranda, kerosene lamps are provided, bring firewood and drinking water. A 4WD is recommended at all times of year to get here because of the steep hills. Rates per cottage are US$150-180.

$$$ The Ark, reservations, Nairobi T020-226 5555, www.thearkkenya.com. Wooden lodge with 48 en suite small cabin-style rooms, uniquely shaped to resemble the actual Ark and accessed by a wooden 'drawbridge', designed with decks which provide superb vantage points for viewing the animals visiting the salt-lick and waterhole. A ground-level bunker provides excellent photographic opportunities, and the waterhole is floodlit at night. Transfers are from the **Aberdare Country Club**. No children under 7.

$$$-$$ Tusk Camp, 2 km from Ruhuruini Gate, T020-237 9409, reservations **KWS**, Nairobi, T020-600 0800, www.kws.org. Here is 1 simple *banda* with 2 double beds and 1 *banda* with 4 single beds, sleeps 8 in total. There is an external bathroom with pit latrine and hot shower, fully equipped kitchen with gas stove, caretaker on site, lanterns supplied but guests must bring firewood and drinking water, and a 4WD is essential in the wet. Rates US$100-120.

Camping
There are 4 campsites here, all of which are close to the gates: **Reedbuck**, **Ruhuruini**, **Wandare** and **Shamata**. However, there are no facilities and it can get very cold. Camping is US$15, children (3-18) US$10.

🍽 Restaurants

Thika *p164*

$$-$ Blue Posts Hotel, see page 173. 0700-2200. Lovely place in extensive grounds with views of the Chania Falls, very attentive staff and a wide selection of Kenyan and Western dishes, the buffet lunches (about US$8) are good value. Kids will enjoy the small animal farm (about US$3 entry), pony rides and playground.

$ Coconut Grill, Kenyatta Highway, next to the Tusky Supermarket, T067-22219, 0730-2230. Although there are 39 basic upstairs rooms (**$**) here with hot showers and TV, it's predominantly Thika's entertainment venue with 3 bars, a basement disco and 1st-floor casino with slot machines (both open until 0400), and great restaurant serving Kenyan fare and curries, as well as cooked English breakfasts, fried chicken, fish and chips and stir-fries.

Nyeri *p167, map p168*

If you are staying in a top-range hotel, you will probably eat there. Otherwise, there are many small restaurants around town offering cheap meals like chicken and chips.

$$-$ Green Hills Hotel, see page 174. There are 3 good restaurants here: **Tetu** has buffet breakfasts and lunches and outside tables on the lawns; **Wazalendo** is a fairly smart à la carte restaurant with a kitchen behind a glass wall and a broad menu including steak, prawns and sometimes Nile perch, and the **Pool Bar** serves snacks, and every Sun there are activities, such as a children's puppet show and dancing; it's a popular venue for locals to come and eat, drink and swim.

$$-$ Outspan Hotel see page 174. Open 0700-2200. A good place to stop for breakfast, lunch or afternoon tea – you can admire the gardens and, as long as the clouds are not down, you will get a good view of Mt Kenya and the Aberdares behind. There's also a pub serving good food and, for a small fee, day visitors can use the swimming pool.

$ Green Oaks, Kimathi Way. 0800-2230. Local restaurant with a covered balcony where you can look down on to the street, serving mostly African food, including very cheap *nyama choma*, curries and stews and occasionally has good local fresh trout. Very popular with office workers at lunch time, and there is a TV in the bar that mostly shows European football.

⏾ What to do

Sagana and Karatina *p166*

Savage Wilderness Safaris, Nairobi, T020-712 1590, www.whitewaterkenya.com. Its base is on the Tana River just south of Sagana, which is clearly signposted and offers whitewater rafting on the river as well as climbs of Mt Kenya. A 1-day rafting trip from Nairobi costs US$100 and includes transport from the **Sarit Centre** at 0730, tea and coffee on arrival at the river and a 5-hr rafting trip. Most of the rapids are classed as Grade III but on the last 7 km there are some Grade IV and V rapids. Afterwards there is time to relax at the Savage Camp, have a hot shower or a swim in the pool, plus a BBQ lunch. Longer 3-day, 65-km rafting trips on the Athi River further south, which borders Tsavo National Park, can be arranged for US$410; 2 nights are spent camping on sandbanks, and rates include transfers to and from Nairobi and food. Most of the route is on fairly calm water, though there are some Grade II and III sections of rapids and 2 Grade IV drops. This is excellent for game viewing and birdwatching. There's a minimum of 3 people for the Tana River and 6 for the Athi River.

Nyeri *p167, map p168*

Nyeri is the gateway to the Aberdare National Park and you will come here before you go to the park. If you do not already have a trip arranged, you can organize a 2-hr game drive from most of the hotels. Expect to pay around US$45 per person (minimum 4) exclusive of park entry fees.

Nyeri Golf Club, Kamakwa Rd, T0724-129 289, www.nyericlub.co.ke. First laid out in 1910 and the 2nd oldest golf club in Kenya, this is a fairly tough mountainous 18-hole course; Mt Kenya can be seen from the 6th hole. President Kibaki is a member and the patron. Visitors are welcome for a temporary membership fee, and there's an elegant clubhouse built in the 1930s.

⊙ Transport

Thika *p164*
There are frequent *matatus* from **Nairobi** to Thika from Racecourse Rd and Ronald Ngala Roundabout (45 mins). Note that the Thika Road can get horribly congested and it's a black spot for accidents. In Thika the *matatu* stand is at the end of Commercial St opposite the **White Line Hotel**. From here *matatus* also go to **Nyeri** and beyond north along the main highway, and cross-country to **Naivasha** and **Nakuru**. Getting around town is simple enough as there are plenty of taxis, *boda bodas* and the odd tuk-tuk. If you arrive in town on public transport and want to go to the **Blue Posts Hotel**, you will need to take a taxi, but it's not far.

Nyeri *p167, map p168*
Regular buses and *matatus* ply the route to **Nairobi**, and there are good connections with the main towns in the area. The bus and *matatu* stands are on or around Kimathi Way in the centre of town.

⊙ Directory

Nyeri *p167, map p168*
Medical services Nyeri Provincial General Hospital is to the east of town off Kimathi Way, T061-203 2681.

Mount Kenya and around

The second tallest mountain in Africa, Mount Kenya is about 150 km northeast of Nairobi and is protected in the Mount Kenya National Park, which is a UNESCO World Heritage Site. It's a stand-alone extinct volcano, and the fertile soil on its lower slopes supports the market towns on the road that circles the mountain. Although it's not as popular a climb as Kilimanjaro in Tanzania, trekkers will be well rewarded with the climb up through montane forest and giant bamboo and lobelia to the snow line. ➤➤ *For listings, see pages 184-187.*

Naro Moru → *Colour map 1, A4.*

The A2 road from Nyeri climbs gradually up to Naro Moru, which is little more than a village located at the base of the mountain. It has a few shops, guesthouses and a post office, and is clustered around the railway station that no longer functions as a passenger terminal. Bear in mind before you arrive here that there are no banks in the village. There are no restaurants apart from the one at the **Naro Moru River Lodge**, see page 185, and if you are cooking your own food, you are advised to stock up before you get here. However, the village does receive quite a few visitors, as it serves as the starting point of the **Naro Moru Route** up Mount Kenya (see page 182), and the gate into the **Mount Kenya National Park** is 16 km east of the village, where the KWS Park Headquarters is also located. Along this road and 6 km from the village is the base for the **Mount Kenya Guides & Porters Club** ① *T020-352 4393, www.mtkenyaguides.com*, which can arrange organized climbs (see page 181).

Nanyuki → *For listings, see pages 184-187. Colour map 1, A4. Phone code: 062. Population: 32,000.*

Nanyuki (meaning 'place of red water' in the Masai language) is a small upcountry town, located on the A2 to the northwest of Mount Kenya. It dates back to about 1907 when it was used by white settlers as a trading centre and for socializing. The first settlers arrived to find a few Masai *manyattas* and a great deal of game. The town was established as a trading centre and still has a country atmosphere; today it is home to the Kenyan Air Force as well as a British army base. Despite this, it is a fairly sleepy kind of town and retains some of its colonial character. Nanyuki is usually visited by people planning to use the **Sirimon Route** up Mount Kenya (see page 183). Its good range of shops provides its only interesting diversion. The town serves as the supply centre for ranchers on the Laikipia Plateau (see page 188), as well as the nearby tourist hotels in the foothills of the mountain. On the main road just 1.5 km to the south of Nanyuki there are signposts marking the equator, and more than a few pushy souvenir sellers who will also demonstrate the 'Coriolis Force' – draining water in either a clockwise or anticlockwise direction depending on which hemisphere you're in.

Mount Kenya National Park → *For listings, see pages 184-187.*

The 2800 sq km **Mount Kenya National Park** straddles the equator about 200 km northeast of Nairobi. Mount Kenya, or *Kirinyaga* (the shining mountain), also sometimes referred to as the black-and-white-striped mountain, is the sacred mountain of the Kikuya (Gikuya) people, who believe that it is where their God 'Ngai' lives. The Kikuyu who live on the slopes always build their homes facing this sacred peak. It is actually an extinct volcano that last erupted between 2.8 and 3.2 million years ago, and was gazetted as a National Park in 1949 and a UNESCO Biosphere Reserve and World Heritage Site in 2000; it is managed by the **Kenya Wildlife Service** (KWS). As you drive around the road that circles Mount Kenya you will spend much of the time looking towards the mountain – however, it is often shrouded in cloud. There are some clear days; otherwise very early in the morning or just before nightfall the cloud will often lift suddenly, revealing the snow-capped peaks for a few minutes. Mount Kenya has a vital role in ecosystems in the area. It is Kenya's

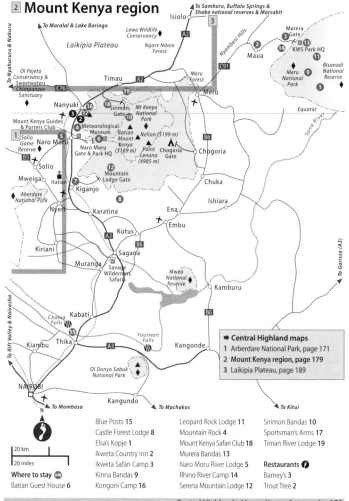

2 Mount Kenya region

Central Highland maps
1 Arberdare National Park, page 171
2 **Mount Kenya region, page 179**
3 Laikipia Plateau, page 189

N

20 km
20 miles

Where to stay 🛏
Batian Guest House **6**

Blue Posts **15**
Castle Forest Lodge **8**
Elsa's Kopje **1**
Ikweta Country Inn **2**
Ikweta Safari Camp **3**
Kinna Bandas **9**
Kongoni Camp **16**

Leopard Rock Lodge **11**
Mountain Rock **4**
Mount Kenya Safari Club **18**
Murera Bandas **13**
Naro Moru River Lodge **5**
Rhino River Camp **14**
Serena Mountain Lodge **12**

Sirimon Bandas **10**
Sportsman's Arms **17**
Timan River Lodge **19**

Restaurants 🍴
Barney's **3**
Trout Tree **2**

most important watershed and its largest forest reserve, and the lower slopes make up the country's richest farmlands. The dramatic landscape includes glaciers, moraines, waterfalls, precarious-looking rock pinnacles and hanging valleys. At the very top is permanent ice in some 11 glacier lakes, though due to global warming these are shrinking fast, and seven glaciers have disappeared in the last 100 years.

The upper base of the mountain is nearly 100 km across; the peak area is formed from the hard core or plug of the volcano, the crater having long since eroded away, and rises steeply on all sides some 450 m above the glaciers and scree slopes. Only experienced climbers can climb the highest peaks of **Nelion** (5199 m) or **Batian** (5189 m) at the summit of Mount Kenya, as this involves the use of ropes, ice-axes, crampons and other specialized climbing gear. The third highest peak is **Point Lenana** (4985 m), which can be reached by any fit walker if they are suitably equipped.

Mountain flora includes a variety of different vegetation over altitudes ranging from 1600 m to 5199 m. From bottom to top, it goes from rich alpine and sub-alpine flora to bamboo forests, moorlands with giant heathers and tundra. Over 4000 m some extraordinary vegetation is found, including the giant rosette plants. Wild animals on Mount Kenya do not normally come into contact with hikers and, because of the dense forest, most species are rarely seen. Nevertheless, the lower forest and bamboo zones are home to elephant, buffalo, eland, bushbuck, waterbuck, zebra, hyena, leopard, colobus monkey and white-throated guenon, and common at higher altitudes is the ubiquitous Mount Kenya rock hyrax. Around 130 species of birds have been recorded in the park.

Climbing Mount Kenya

Fewer people go trekking on Mount Kenya than Kilimanjaro in Tanzania, but those that do rate the experience equally as good and far less crowded than the Kili climb. The Naro Moru, Chogoria and Sirimon Routes are by far the most common routes up the mountain. Other routes have existed in the past, but have now fallen into almost total disrepair and considerable navigation skill and physical strength and stamina are now required to attempt them, as well as special permission from the **KWS**. Experienced climbers should contact the **Mountain Club of Kenya** (see below) for advice about technical ice and rock climbing. These three routes (described here) are best taken leisurely in six days, although they can be done in four. It is an interesting variation to ascend by one route and descend by another. **Point Lenana** at 4985 m is your destination; it is a strenuous hike, but quite manageable if you are reasonably fit and allow sufficient time to acclimatize to the rarefied atmosphere. It is sometimes called the trekker's or tourist's peak. The trek is an excellent opportunity to enjoy the beautiful scenery on the mountain and the snow on the equator.

Arriving at the trailheads There are three towns located along the Kirinyaga Ring Road at the base of Mount Kenya that serve as starting points for the climbs: **Nanyuki** for the Sirimon Route, **Naro Moru** for the Naro Moru Route, both on the western side, and **Chogoria** for the Chogoria Route on the eastern side, see page 197. From these locations, dirt tracks (20-30 km in length and often in very poor condition, necessitating 4WD drive, or walking) lead up to the three main roadheads and park gates at elevations of around 3000 m. Although the higher huts on the mountain can be reached in one day from the main road, it is recommended to take two days unless you are already acclimatized to the altitude.

Best time to visit While Mount Kenya can be climbed at any time of year, the best and safest months are January to March or July to September. Avoid the rainy seasons, April to May and November to December – although, above 3000 m, rain, and higher up, snow, can be encountered at any time of year, even during the driest months (January and February). Temperatures vary considerably depending on altitude and time of day. At 3000 m frosts can occur at night, while daytime temperatures range from 5 to 15°C. Night time temperatures on the summit are well below freezing. Trekkers should be aware that sudden storms, heavy cloud cover and fog can lead to climbers getting lost on the mountain, and it is prohibited to hike alone without a guide.

Information Prior to climbing Mount Kenya it is a good idea to get in touch with the **Mountain Club of Kenya** ① *at the Nairobi Sailing and Sub Aqua Club, behind Langata Shopping Centre, across Langata Rd from the Carnivore Restaurant, Nairobi, T020-501 747, www.mck. or.ke.* It has lots of maps and books in its library, non-members can attend the open night on Tuesdays at the club house, and the website is an excellent resource for information.

Costs The KWS conservation fee is US$55, children (3-18) US$25 per day. For the climb, you pay a fixed minimum for the first three days of US$150/US$70 and then US$55/US$25 per day after that, which includes camping but not huts. Huts cost US$12-15 per person per night and are privately owned by either the Mountain Club of Kenya or the lodges and are paid for as part of an organized trek. Visitors should obtain receipts for payments, which must be shown when leaving. A guide is compulsory on all routes and a tour operator will supply not only guides but porters and relevant equipment. Costs for an organized climb vary widely depending on which route you choose and over how many days, but expect to pay in the region of US$550-650 for a five-day climb, including park entry fees, guides, porters, a cook and food and camping/hut accommodation on the mountain, but excluding tips, transfers from Nairobi and accommodation before or after the climb. The price goes down for larger groups. Many of the tour operators listed under Nairobi can organize climbs (see page 77), and the lodges in the vicinity of the mountain can organize guides and porters, which cost about US$10-15 each per day, plus their daily park entry fees (much reduced as they are both licensed guides and Kenya residents) and the cost of transporting them to the roadheads on each of the trails. Make sure that the agreement is clear before you set off and that the guides are carrying a KWS identity card, which also gives them a discount on park fees. Guides and porters/cooks can be arranged at **Naro Moru River Lodge**, **Mountain Rock Hotel**, **Serena Mountain Lodge**, **Castle Forest Lodge**, or contact the **Mount Kenya Guides & Porters Club** ① *T020-352 4393, www.mtkenyaguides.com*, located on the road to the main gate of the park, 6 km from Naro Moru.

Equipment Take great care over equipment and altitude sickness precautions, otherwise the climb can be sheer misery. Very little camping gear and appropriate warm and waterproof clothing is available locally, so you need to bring everything with you. Alternatively, hire at **Naro Moru River Lodge** (see page 185), although items available cannot be relied on. It is essential to take effective waterproofs, gloves, headgear, warm/windproof clothing, sunglasses or snow goggles, water bottle, first aid kit, head-torch and spare batteries, at least a three-season sleeping bag and a sleeping mat because, above 3000 m, the night temperatures can fall to as low as -10°C, and you may want to consider a light weight trekking pole. As regards clothing, it is important to wear layers as they provide better insulation than bulkier items, and sturdy waterproof hiking boots should be well worn-in. You'll also need a small daypack for things you'll need during the day – porters carry your main pack but tend to go on ahead by some distance. Bear in mind that you won't need much 'stuff' on the mountain – you'll be wearing most of it anyway – and porters are limited to 18 kg including their own things which is a lot to carry; keep it light and leave the bulk of your luggage at a lodge.

Maps and guides *Mount Kenya Map and Guide*, by M Savage and A Wielochowski, is available at **The Stanley** bookshop in Nairobi, see page 73, **Stanfords Bookshops** in the UK, and from **Amazon**. The Mountain Club of Kenya has published the excellent detailed *Guide to Mt Kenya and Kilimanjaro*, listing all the routes, edited by Iain Allan. It is available in the Nairobi bookshops or directly from the club, and you may find it on Amazon.

Naro Moru Route Naro Moru approaches from the west and is the most direct, popular but least scenic route, and includes trekking through a long vertical bog. Opposite the Naro Moru police station is a signposted road that leads to the park entrance. It is possible to drive as far as the Meteorological Station, although inexperienced climbers are less likely to suffer from altitude sickness if they walk the 26 km.

Day 1 Is best spent travelling from Naro Moru to the **Meteorological Station** at 3050 m. A ride can be hired from the **Naro Moru River Lodge** part or all of the way. There are some *bandas* here or some permanent tents.

Day 2 Is to **Mackinder's Camp** (sometimes referred to as Teleki Valley Lodge), located at an altitude of 4200 m, through terrain that is often very wet underfoot. An early departure is recommended as fog and rain are more commonplace during the afternoon. This section includes a very tiring climb through a steep vertical bog and, when you've cleared the bog the route then continues along a ridge on the southern side of the Teleki Valley, gradually descending to the valley floor. This section is much more attractive, with *Senecio* (giant groundsel), heathers, the broad-leafed *Lobelia keniensis* and the feathery *Lobelia telekii*. The camp, a stone building, has about 40 bunks and some tents. It is possible to visit the Teleki tarn from here, taking about 1-1½ hours, if the weather holds out.

Day 3 It is possible to make the final leg to Point Lenana, 4985 m, although it is more comfortable to spend Day 3 in and around the surrounding area known as Mackinder's, getting acclimatized to the altitude. From here, there are some of the best views of the central peaks. Alternatively, climb another 500 m to the **Austrian Hut**, 4790 m.

Day 4 Climb to **Point Lenana**. Most trekkers leave Mackinder's at between 0200 and 0400 to ensure that they reach the summit at sunrise (so a powerful torch is an essential piece of equipment), climbing past the Austrian Hut, 4790 m. From here it is about 30 minutes to an hour's scramble, depending on fitness, to reach Point Lenana.

Day 5 It is possible to descend all the way to Naro Moru (with a lift from the Meteorological Station), but it is more leisurely to return to Mackinder's Camp for a night, and then on to Naro Moru on Day 6.

Chogoria Route The Chogoria approach is from the east between Embu (96 km) and Meru (64 km), and is the most scenically attractive of the routes, although it can be wet. It is a tent route, and you are required to show your tent at the park gates before you will be let in. The Minto's Hut is for porters' use only. Chogoria village, see page 197, is the starting base for the deeply rutted road (4WD essential), which takes you past small, intensively cultivated *shambas* within the lowland forest rising to become bamboo forest. Colobus monkeys can occasionally be seen here. Most trekkers organize the 32-km ride from Chogoria to approximately 6 km beyond the park gate to the roadhead at 3110 m. However, if you walk this stretch you will greatly reduce the possibility of developing altitude sickness.

Day 1 From village to the roadhead by vehicle or on foot and camp there.

Day 2 From the roadhead cross the stream and follow the path going in a southwesterly direction. The route continues along the west side of the Nithi Gorge; it is about a six-hour hike to **Minto's Hut**, 4300 m. En route there are spectacular views of the Gorges Valley. The path leads through dramatic rock fields and, later, through the heather moors to Vivienne Falls, 3650 m, where you can swim in the bracing waters. As you progress upwards, Lake Michaelson can be seen on the valley floor 300 m below Hall Tarns.

Day 3 It is possible to reach Point Lenana, but it may be more comfortable to spend the day getting acclimatized in and around Minto's Hut, located close to Minto's Tarn, 4540 m, which is framed by lofty pinnacles, the scree slopes flecked with giant lobelia and senecio.

Day 4 From Minto's Hut it is about a four- to five-hour climb to **Point Lenana**, via the Austrian Hut, close to the Lewis Glacier. In recent years, the Lewis Glacier has receded significantly, and has left behind steep ice, covered with small stones on the western flank of Point Lenana, which is slippery and loose. Anyone attempting this route during the warmth of the day should take great care.

Day 5 It is possible to descend all the way back to Chogoria (with a lift from the park gate), but it is more leisurely to return to Minto's Hut for a night, and then on to Chogoria on Day 6.

Sirimon Route The Sirimon Gate is 15 km northeast of Nanyuki. This is probably the driest route and goes over much open moorland covered with heather so there is a good chance of spotting wildlife. It's a popular alternative to Naro Moru, and has a gentler rate of ascent, although it is still easy to climb too fast, so allow five days for the trek. Huts on this route can be booked through the **Mountain Rock Hotel** (page 185).

Day 1 From the gate, it's about 9 km or around a two- to five-hour hike through the forest to **Old Moses Hut**, 3300 m, where you can spend the first night.

Day 2 On the second day, you could head straight through the moorland for Shipton's Camp, 4050 m, but it is worth taking an extra day to go via **Liki North Hut**, 3993 m, which is actually a complete wreck and is only meant for porters, but has a good campsite with a toilet and stream nearby. You can also walk further up the hill to help acclimatize.

Day 3 From Liki North Hut, head straight up the western side of the Liki North Valley and over the ridge into Mackinder's Valley. After crossing the Liki River, follow the path for another 30 minutes until you reach the bunkhouse at **Shipton's Camp**, 4200 m, which is set in a fantastic location right below Batian and Nelion. The camp is also within sight of two glaciers, which can be heard cracking.

Day 4 From Shipton's you can push straight for Point Lenana, a tough three- to four-hour slog via Harris Tarn and the tricky north face approach, or take the **Summit Circuit** in either direction, which encircles the main peaks of the mountain between the 4300 m and 4800 m contour lines, to reach **Austrian Hut**, 4790 m, about half an hour below the summit where you can also spend the night. The left-hand (east) route past Simba Col is shorter but steeper, while the right-hand (west) option, takes you on the Harris Tarn trail nearer the main peaks.

Day 5 It is possible to descend all the way back to Chogoria or Naro Moru (see above).

◉ Mount Kenya and around listings

For sleeping and eating price codes and other relevant information, see pages 20-24.

● Where to stay

Nanyuki *p178, map p189*
$$$-$$ Sportsman's Arms, located across the river, 500 m east of town, T062-31448, www.sportsmansarmshotels.com. The best-value hotel in Nanyuki, surrounded by lovely gardens of indigenous trees, built in the 1930s but extended so there are rooms in modern blocks, with satellite TV, and older cottages, with fireplaces, but furnishings are becoming a little worn. Excellent facilities, though, including a gym, very large swimming pool, sauna, tennis courts, internet café, good restaurant and bar, with pool tables and a disco at the weekends.
$ Kongoni Camp, 2 km north of town off the A2, T062-203 1225, www.kongonicamp. com. A fairly new set up in an attractive grove of cedar trees with good mountain views, 5 simple en suite huts, a campsite with hot showers, and the main log cabin building has a restaurant and bar with porch and huge fireplace, serving grills, pizzas, homemade bread and cakes, friendly staff. Can organize the Sirimon Mt Kenya

climb, and an overnight camping trip to the Aberdare National Park.
$ Equator Chalet, Kenyatta Av, T062-318 011. Best of the board and lodgings on the main road, above a supermarket and internet café, the 20 clean rooms surround an internal courtyard that opens on to 2 balcony areas and a roof terrace with mountain views, and have 4-poster beds with nets and modern bathrooms with hot water. Very nice terrace restaurant.
$ Ibis, Lumumba Rd, close to the *matatu* stand, T062-31536. Comfortable rooms with hot water and mosquito nets, fresh tiles and woodwork, ask for a room with Mt Kenya view, above its own bar/restaurant and bright covered courtyard, secure parking.

Mount Kenya National Park
p178, map p179
There are a couple of cheap basic places for board and lodgings in Naro Moru, but for budget travellers it is best to camp at the Naro Moru River Lodge or the Mountain Rock Hotel, see below, which both hire out tents, or stay in Nanyuki. Most lodges will pick up from Nanyuki airstrip.
$$$$ Mount Kenya Safari Club, 15 km east of Nanyuki in the foothills of the mountain,

reservations **Fairmont Hotels**, T020-226 5555, www.fairmont.com. The region's most exclusive and luxurious hotel, with 120 guest rooms in cottages with wooden floors and fireplaces, set in over 40 ha of landscaped gardens. The club was originally established by movie star William Holden (of *Bridge over the River Kwai* fame) and one of the founder members was Winston Churchill. Facilities include horse riding, golf, croquet, a bowling green, swimming pool, spa, several restaurants, lounges and bars, and excursions include trout fishing and day trips to the Aberdare National Park.

$$$$ Serena Mountain Lodge, 5 km inside the park from the Mountain Lodge Gate, T061-203 0785, reservations **Serena Hotels**, Nairobi, T020-284 2333, www.serenahotels. com. Quality Serena lodge situated at 2194 m on Mt Kenya overlooking a waterhole, with similar architecture to the **Ark** and **Treetops** in the Aberdares, and built on stilts, with 41 wooden cabin-style en suite rooms with fireplaces. A close-up viewing bunker is connected to the hotel by a tunnel, post-climb massages and trout fishing on offer, very good guides for walking and climbing excursions, restaurant and bar.

$$$ Batian Guest House, inside the park 500m from the main Naro Moru Gate, 17 km from Naro Moru, T020-356 8763, reservations **KWS**, Nairobi, T020-600 0800, www.kws.org. A former warden's cottage, with 4 bedrooms sleeping up to 8 for US$180 per night. Linen, towels and cooking equipment are provided, and there's a gas cooker and kerosene lamps, but guests need to bring own food, firewood and drinking water.

$$$ Naro Moru River Lodge, 2 km from Naro Moru off the main road, reservations **Alliance Hotels**, Nairobi, T020-444 3357, www.alliancehotels.com, www.naromoru riverlodge.com. At an elevation of 1982 m and overlooking the Naro Moru River, this is a popular place to stay for all budgets and it organizes climbs up the mountain and game drives into the Solio Game Reserve.

19 de luxe cottages with 2 double beds and fireplaces, all elegantly furnished in pine, 12 standard cottages, which are a bit cheaper, 12 self-catering cottages aimed at families, and a campsite (**$**) where you can hire the necessary equipment or sleep in a bunkhouse. Facilities include a swimming pool, tennis and squash courts, 2 restaurants and bar with roaring log fire.

$$$-$$ Castle Forest Lodge, 22 km north of Kutus, on the slopes to the south of Mt Kenya, accessed from Sagana and the C73, T0721-422 908, www.castleforestlodge. com. Set in a natural forest with rivers and falls on either side, the main house was built in 1910 of river stones and wood, and both Queen Elizabeth and former President Jomo Kenyatta have stayed here in the past. A charming old building, with a cosy dining room and bar and a veranda overlooking a waterhole and the valley below. The main house contains 3 double rooms; in the gardens is a bungalow that sleeps 4 and 8 double cottages, each en suite with a fireplace, and 8 km away or a 2-hr walk is a unique isolated bush hut. Can organize climbs, and you can also camp here (**$**).

$$$-$$ Mountain Rock Hotel, 7 km north of Naro Moru on the road to Nanyuki, 1 km off the main road, T062-62625, www.mountainrockkenya.com. Lovely surroundings and 28 simply decorated cottages with fireplaces, welcome on cold evenings, and restaurant and bar. The hotel, which arranges a wide range of activities including horse riding, fishing and birdwatching, is known for its very well-run treks up the mountain on the Naro Moru or Sirimon routes. There's also a quiet, secure campsite (**$**) with hot showers and kitchen area and, if you don't have a tent or equipment, you can hire everything. A double starts from a good value US$80.

$$ Sirimon Bandas, near Sirimon Gate, 9 km along a turning off the main road, 15 km north of Nanyuki, reservations **KWS**, Nairobi, T020-600 0800, www.kws.org.

Managed 2 self-catering furnished cottages, each has 1 room with a double bed, 1 room with 2 single beds, fitted kitchen with gas cooker and lounge; linen, towels, and kitchen utensils are provided but you will need to bring your own food, firewood and drinking water. Each cottage is rented out as a whole for US$80.

$$-$ Timau River Lodge, 20 km north of Nanyuki towards Isiolo, 1 km after Timau, 1 km off the main road, T062-41230, www.timauriverlodge.8m.com. On the forested slopes of Mt Kenya, several simple *bandas* built of cedar logs sleeping 2-4 people and campsites located amongst trees at the top of a very pretty waterfall, where geese and ducks wander around. There is a restaurant and bar with fireplace and pool table, electricity is provided by a generator 1800-2100, kerosene lamps are available at other times. Local guides can take guests on walks through the forest and to local villages.

❼ Restaurants

Nanyuki *p178*
Apart from the hotel restaurants of which in town, the one at the **Sportsman's Arms** is the best, there are few other places to eat in Nanyuki. There's a branch of **Kenchic** on the main road near the Standard Chartered Bank for good chicken and chips.
$ Marina Grill, opposite the post office, Kenyatta Av, T062-32724. 0700-2400. Popular with locals and visiting British soldiers and offers friendly service, an attractive rooftop bar with BBQ and pool table. Convenient for a cold beer and a snack like burgers and pizzas, and has a good selection of desserts. There is also an internet café here.

Mount Kenya National Park
p178, map p179
There are 2 very good options on the road running around the mountain or you can stop at one of the lodges.

$$ Trout Tree Restaurant, 12 km south of Nanyuki on the A2, T062-62059. A trout farm with fantastic 3-course lunches served daily 1100-1600. The very attractive restaurant is constructed around a giant fig tree and overlooks the fish ponds and a patch of lovely forest which is home to curious black and white colobus monkeys. The menu is superb; there's tandoori trout, grilled trout, smoked trout and trout chowder, as well as steaks, fresh salads and vegetables, and strawberries grown on the farm and fresh cream for dessert.
$ Barney's, at the Nanyuki airfield, 5 km to the south of town, T0723-310 064, www.barneysnanyuki.com. 0800-1800. This primarily serves air passengers at the airfield but road travellers can pull in. An excellent and friendly café overlooking the planes parked up on the apron; with outside tables, colourful decor, a full bar, and offering home-made soups, sandwiches, burgers, salads, coffees, milkshakes, and they can make up a picnic hamper for you to take away.

❍ Shopping

Nanyuki *p178*
Nakumatt, supermarket opposite the Town Hall on the main street.
Nanyuki Spinners and Weavers Workshop, 1 km from town on the Nyaharuru road, T062-32062, www.spinnersandweavers.org. The shop here sells hand-woven items and is run by a women's cooperative group that was established in 1977. It's an interesting place to visit, and the group are pleased to give you a full guided tour. The Kenyan Highlands wool is very good for hand spinning, and there is a good selection of rugs, tablemats, sweaters and shawls.
Settlers Stores, on the main street near the Equator Chalet Hotel, is 1 of the oldest shops in town (founded in 1938) and sells hardware and groceries.

⚠ What to do

Nanyuki *p178*
Mount Kenya Safaris 'n Travel, next to
the Marina Grill Restaurant, Kenyatta Av,
T0722-309 525, www.mountkenyasafaris.
com. As well as at the lodges, climbs can
also be arranged here, and they can help
with last-minute bookings to the ranches
on the Laikipia Plateau.
Nanyuki Sports Club, east of Sportsman's
Arms, T062-22623. Opened in 1937, this
is another sports club established in the
colonial years and offers tennis, squash, a
9-hole golf course, swimming and snooker,
but you will need to take out temporary
membership. Quite uniquely, as the golf
course here is laid out on highland ridges,
you are always standing below or above
the ball.
Sportman's Arms Hotel has facilities
that can be used, including the very large
swimming pool, for a small fee by day
visitors, and this is a pleasant place to
come for lunch.

⊖ Transport

Nanyuki *p178*
Air
The airstrip at Nanyuki is 5 km to the south
of town on the Nairobi (A2) road. Even if
you're not flying, it's well worth stopping
here for **Barney's** restaurant (see above).
Air Kenya, Nairobi, T020-391 6000, www.
airkenya.com, has a daily flight between
Wilson Airport, **Nairobi**, and Nanyuki
(50 mins), US$120 1 way. **Fly 540**, Nairobi,
T020-445 3252, www.fly540.com, has a daily
flight on a circuit between Wilson Airport,

Nairobi, Nanyuki and **Meru**, US$115 1 way
from Nairobi; the flight to Meru is US$40
and takes 30 mins. **Tropic Air**, T0722-207
300, www.tropicairkenya.com, is an air-
charter company operating out of Nanyuki.
Destinations include the airstrips on the
Laikipia Plateau, Samburu, Masai Mara
and **Meru**, and they have a daily service to
and from Nanyuki linking the more popular
lodges in these areas. Prices for flights start
at around US$175 per person. Tropic Air also
has 3 helicopters and 2 bi-planes in their
fleet and can organize unique sightseeing
and game-viewing flights to various
destinations. **Safarilink**, Nairobi, T020-600
0777, www.flysafarilink.com, has a daily
scheduled flight between Wilson Airport,
Nairobi, and Nanyuki, US$115 1 way.

Bus and matatus

The bus and *matatu* stage is located
next to the park off Bazaar Rd. There
are frequent buses and *matatus* running
between Nanyuki and **Nairobi**. If you are
heading north to Marsabit and Northern
Kenya you can get buses and *matatus*
from Nanyuki to **Isiolo**.

Car

Nanyuki is 60 km from **Nyeri** and 200 km
from **Nairobi** – a drive that will take you
about 3 hrs.

ⓘ Directory

Nanyuki *p178*
Medical services Nanyuki Cottage
Hospital is located about 1 km out of town
to the southeast off the A2, T062-32666;
it is privately run and has a good reputation.

Laikipia Plateau

This spectacular region is considered the gateway to Kenya's wild northern frontier country but it is only since the early 1990s that the Laikipia Plateau has been recognized as a wildlife area in its own right. With altitudes from 1700 to 2600 m, the plateau covers an area of roughly 9500 sq km – roughly half the size of Wales in the UK – and is second only in terms of size in Kenya to that of combined Tsavo East and West national parks. Wild and sparsely populated, it covers a wide range of landscapes, dominated by acacia bushland, with large areas of open grasslands to the north and south of the district, and dense olive and cedar forests to the east. Much of Laikipia is covered by large privately owned ranches, and most of these were once highly developed and very productive cattle ranches with paddocks, fencing and water-supply systems. During the 1970s, increasing human settlement to the south of the plateau and increasing elephant poaching to the north caused elephant herds to take up more permanent residence on Laikipia and overall game numbers increased. This resulted in internal fences being lost (it's not possible to maintain normal ranch fencing in the presence of large elephant populations), and livestock management systems becoming similar to that used by pastoralists such as the Masai – cattle were herded for grazing during the day and kept in night enclosures, or 'bomas', at night. With burgeoning wildlife populations, cattle ranching became less productive. Over time, in response to increasing demand for wildlife tourism, the ranches began to see the wildlife as an asset to be utilized for financial gain and found innovative ways of accommodating and protecting the wildlife. Today, the numerous tourism initiatives in the region fund what is, without doubt, Kenya's greatest conservation success story over the last 20 years or so; it is an area of beautiful wilderness, where protected game roams freely and safely, while preserving traditional farming methods and ways of life. ➤➤ *For listings, see pages 191-193.*

Arriving on the Laikipia Plateau

This area of wilderness is a sprawling, rather loosely defined area that spreads north from Nanyuki and the northern foothills of Mount Kenya to Maralal, northeast to Isiolo, and west to Nyahururu. Nanyuki is the access point for most ranches and also serves as the supply centre for ranchers on the Laikipia Plateau. The main roads that cross this region are the C76, which connects Nanyuki with Nyahururu, the C77, which runs between Nyahururu and Maralal, and the C78, which joins Maralal with Isiolo. It is important to remember that many of the ranches and the roads therein are privately owned. Some ranches allow access for day visitors with their own transport, others do not. Visitors should always make enquiries in advance. If you are visiting a ranch with your own private transport, it is essential to have a 4WD; you should also ask for directions and preferably a map, in advance. Many ranches and sanctuaries have their own airstrips, which can be used by charter aircraft. Between them, **Air Kenya**, **Fly 540** and **Safarilink** run scheduled services from Nairobi to Nanyuki, and there are some flights to Lewa Downs and Samburu. **Tropic Air**, based at Nanyuki, offers a charter service directly to the lodges, see page 187. Most ranches will arrange to transfer guests directly by air or road from Nairobi or any other destination, as part of their service. Many of the ranches have conservation fees (often included in accommodation rates). These vary from one conservancy to another, usually ranging from US$40 to 100 per person per day. In some, a fee of about US$5 per day is levied on self-driven vehicles. These fees support wildlife security and road infrastructure and maintenance, as well as important aspects of community development. For more information, visit the website of **Laikipia Tourism**, www.laikipiatourism.com.

Visiting the Laikipia Plateau

The region is located on the leeward side of Mount Kenya, forming the arid and semi-arid highlands west and northwest of the mountain. It is dominated by the **Ewaso Ng'iro** and **Ewaso Narok** rivers, and it incorporates the entire Ewaso rivers ecosystems, the **Laikipia National Reserve** and the **Lewa Wildlife Conservancy**. On most ranches cattle share the land with free-ranging wildlife. In recent years this wildlife has become a valuable asset, and many ranches now have lodges, tented camps, guesthouses, homestays and campsites within their boundaries. Some of these are the most luxurious places to stay in Kenya, catering for people on specialist tailor-made safaris and offering a growing wealth of activities and game-watching experiences. Visitors have individually prepared schedules of game-drives and walks and, depending on the lodge, fishing, horse riding and camel treks. Visiting a private ranch in this region is an ideal way of exploring the Kenyan wilderness while getting off the well-beaten paths of the national parks. The real attraction of Laikipia is a wonderful sense of freedom, and game viewing tends to be more intimate and adventurous here.

Wildlife

Centred around the original Laikipia National Reserve, this area has become a sanctuary for elephant, lion, leopard, buffalo and a wealth of plains game, including many endemic northern species such as the Grevy's zebra, gerenuk and reticulated giraffe. It has one of

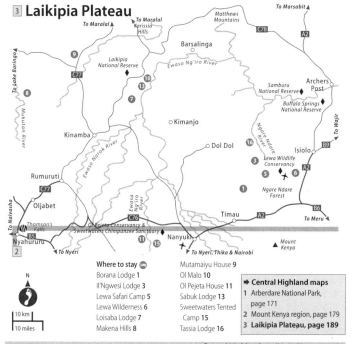

3 Laikipia Plateau

Where to stay 🛏
Borana Lodge 1
Il'Ngwesi Lodge 3
Lewa Safari Camp 5
Lewa Wilderness 6
Loisaba Lodge 7
Makena Hills 8
Mutamaiyu House 9
Ol Malo 10
Ol Pejeta House 11
Sabuk Lodge 13
Sweetwaters Tented Camp 15
Tassia Lodge 16

➡ **Central Highland maps**
1 Arberdare National Park, page 171
2 Mount Kenya region, page 179
3 Laikipia Plateau, page 189

the highest diversity of large mammals in all of Kenya, including significant populations of all the major predators and the Big Five. Almost 6000 elephants migrate through the region each year. Laikipia has also become a focus for many conservation efforts; some ranches have become breeding sanctuaries for rhino, and now the region protects over 50% of Kenya's population of black and white rhino. Wild dog and the sitatunga antelope are also present, and these days the region is widely believed to have an animal diversity second only to the Masai Mara. On Ol Pejeta Ranch, a refuge for chimpanzees rescued from the pet and bush-meat trade has also been established.

Lewa Wildlife Conservancy
① *T064-31405, www.lewa.org, entry by prior arrangement only. To visit here you will need to be staying at Lewa Safari Camp, Il'Ngwesi Lodge, Tassia Lodge or Lewa Wilderness Trails (see Where to stay, page 191).*
The 251-sq-km Lewa Wildlife Conservancy is situated about 15 km southwest of Isiolo on the northern foothills of Mount Kenya on the Laikipia Plateau, approximately 65 km northeast of Nanyuki. It was established in 1995 on what was originally a 180-sq-km cattle ranch called Lewa Downs. The land comprises savannah, wetland, grassland and indigenous forest. The Lewa Downs and later the adjoining state-owned **Ngare Ndare Forest** were fenced to reduce the human/wildlife conflict and loss of smallholders' crops to animals, and today it's home to the Big Five and protects some 100 black and white rhino. The conservancy also protects the threatened Grevy's zebra, holding 20% of the world's population of some 2000 individuals. Lewa Downs also contains an archaeological site where Mary Leakey found prehistoric tools and artefacts, some of which are on display in the **Meru Museum** (see page 196). As it is a non-profit organization, all tourist-generated income goes to pay for security and management of the wildlife. The unique and hugely popular **Safaricom Marathon** (see page 25) is run in Lewa every June.

Ol Pejeta Conservancy and Sweetwaters Chimpanzee Sanctuary
① *The main gate is 14 km from Nanyuki off the road to Nyahururu, T0723-312 673, www.olpejetaconservancy.org, 0700-1900, US$65, children (3-13) US$32, vehicle US$3.20. Accommodation in the conservancy is offered in 5 upmarket lodges or camps (see page 192). Day visitors are permitted by prior arrangement.*
Ol Pejeta Conservancy covers 364 sq km and was established in 1988 on what was a cattle ranch originally owned by Lord Delamere; its later owners included Christina Onassis father-in-law, Roussel, and arms dealer Adnan Khashoggi. It is home to all the Big Five, including East Africa's largest population of black rhino, which is currently put at 85 individuals, and, with a staggering population of over 10,000 large mammals, has the highest ratio of game-to-area of any park or reserve in Kenya. Apart from safaris in vehicles, game walks and horse and camel rides are available, plus visits to the cultural *manyatta* where visitors can meet Masai, Pokot, Samburu and Turkana people and learn a little about traditional ways of life. The **Morani Information Centre** here is visited by over 100 Kenyan schools each year and teaches the students about ecology and wildlife management.
   Sweetwaters Chimpanzee Sanctuary ① *0900-1030, 1530-1630.* This is the only place in Kenya to see (non-indigenous) chimpanzees and was established in 1993 in collaboration with KWS and the Jane Goodall Institute. An initial group of chimpanzee orphans were brought to the sanctuary from a facility in Bujumbura, Burundi, as they needed to be evacuated due to the outbreak of civil war in Burundi. It is now home to 42 rescued chimps, which live in two groups on an island in the Ewaso Ng'iro River and can be viewed

from a boat. Sweetwaters is a member of the **Pan African Sanctuary Alliance (PASA)**, an alliance of 18 sanctuaries in 12 African countries, which between them currently care for over 800 orphaned and/or confiscated chimpanzees.

⦿ Laikipia Plateau listings

For sleeping and eating price codes and other relevant information, see pages 20-24.

⦿ Where to stay

Laikipia Plateau *p188, map p189*
All the places to stay here are very expensive. Expect to pay in the region of US$300-800 per person sharing (rates indicated below are for low season), but most rates are full board and include game activities. Horse and camel safaris are available from most of the lodges and all use local guides. Some are open all year round, while some are closed in the wet seasons: Apr-May and Nov. This is just a selection of accommodation on the plateau, for a full list visit www.laikipiatourism.com or www.www.laikipia.org.

$$$$ Borana Lodge, adjacent and to the west of the Lewa Wildlife Conservancy, www.borana.co.ke, reservations Nairobi, T020-211 5453, www.borana.co.ke. This lodge is situated on a 14,200-ha wildlife-rich, private, working cattle ranch on the edge of the Samangua Valley with panoramic views of Mt Kenya and the plains below. The 8 en suite cottages have been built from local materials, 1 has an extra bedroom for children, the central lounge and dining room is decorated with local art. There's a swimming pool and a hide overlooking a dam which is a popular spot for swimming elephants. From US$540 per person.

$$$$ Il'Ngwesi Lodge, Matthew's Mountains north of the Lewa Wildlife Conservancy, reservations Nairobi, T020-203 3122, www.ilngwesi.com. Constructed with materials from the local area, this community-owned lodge comprises 6 individual thatched *bandas* with open-air showers and good views. There's a large sitting area, a strikingly designed swimming pool and a covered hide overlooking a waterhole. All profits go to the local Masai community and are spent on schools, health, water supplies and cattle dips. From US$300 per person.

$$$$ Lewa Safari Camp, Lewa Wildlife Conservancy, www.lewasafaricamp.com, reservations **Cheli & Peacock**, Nairobi, T020-600 3090, www.chelipeacock.com. Lush green lawns, swimming pool and tented accommodation, with 10 doubles/ twins and 2 family/triple tents, and a main building with a lounge and dining area and veranda with good views over a waterhole frequented by rhino and elephant. Guests get a real insight to conservation and wildlife management here. From US$410 per person.

$$$$ Lewa Wilderness Trails, Lewa Wildlife Conservancy, reservations Nairobi, T020-600 0457, www.lewawilderness.com. This has been the Craig family home since 1924 when the family came from England and began raising cattle here. 9 comfortable thatched cottages with fireplaces and verandas, some have 2 bedrooms for families, plus a swimming pool. There is a cosy sitting room and wholesome and organically grown meals are eaten on a long banquet table in the open-air dining room. From US$420 per person.

$$$$ Loisaba Lodge, T062-31072, www. loisaba.com. A 150-sq-km private wildlife conservancy in the centre of Laikipia Plateau on the Ewaso Ng'iro River, with 7 rooms at the main house with verandas perched over an escarpment and commanding views of Mt Kenya, plus a house sleeping 4 and a cottage sleeping 6 with their own staff, game-drive vehicle and swimming pool. Facilities include swimming pool, tennis court, bocce court and croquet lawn, and the spa has a romantic open-air bubble bath. There are also 'skybeds': wooden platforms set against rocky outcrops and partially covered by a thatched roof, with shower and flushing toilet, which form part of optional walking, horse or camel safaris. From US$390 per person.

$$$$ Makena Hills, T0734-291 710, www.gallmannkenya.org. Situated on the extreme west of Laikipia on the edge of the Great Rift Valley with views of Lake Baringo, this is home to Kuki Gallman – conservationist and author of *I Dreamed of Africa* – who guests can meet if she's home, and it's where the subsequent movie was filmed starring Kim Basinger. There are 6 enormous Arabic desert-style tents with attached dressing room and bathrooms, and facilities include a central reception area with 2 giant fireplaces, front terrace with a camp fire, dining room, bar, shop and swimming pool. Quality organic food is served. From U$$540 per person.

$$$$ Mutamaiyu House, www.mutamaiyu. com, is on Mugie Ranch at the northern end of the plateau, reservations, **Exclusive African Treasures**, Nairobi T020-712 3300, www.exclusiveafricantreasures.com. A magnificent family-owned ranch house built in a grove of ancient, twisting olive trees, with 6 African-style thatched cottages built of local stone, and there's a comfortable lounge with fireplace and a lovely heated cliff-top swimming pool. Among the more unusual activities here are painting safaris with a local artist. From US$260 per person.

$$$$ Ol Malo, halfway between Archer's Post and Loruk, to the west of Samburu National Reserve, T062-32715, www.olmalo. com. A ranch and game sanctuary near the Ewaso Ng'iro River with 4 expensive and exclusive guest cottages and 1 private house sleeping up to 12 spread out along the cliff edge and built out of natural rock and ancient olive wood, with thatched roofs and huge glass windows. You can soak in the bath whilst looking at the animals at the waterhole. There is a dining room, sitting room and swimming pool, and most of the food is home grown. From US$390 per person.

$$$$ Ol Pejeta House, 40 km west of Nanyuki in the Ol Pejeta Consevancy, reservations **Serena Hotels**, Nairobi T020-284 2000, www.serenahotels.com. An imposing former ranch house with vast drawing rooms, spacious verandas and 6 elegantly appointed suites overlooking extensive tropical gardens and 2 swimming pools. **Ol Pejeta** was formerly owned by Lord Delamere and was also one of the holiday homes of the international arms dealer Adnan Kashoggi. An 8-ft basket, which can be winched down by a pulley system, hangs above the main dining room table – it is said that a naked young lady covered in fruit, hidden in the basket, was a treat for guests when Khashoggi owned the ranch! From US$370 per person.

$$$$ Sabuk Lodge, at the northern edge of the plateau on the banks of the Ewaso Ng'iro River, www.sabuklodge.com, reservations **Cheli & Peacock**, T020-600 3090, www.chelipeacock.com. Perched on the edge of the gorge overlooking the river, the 8 thatched cottages have stunning views and each has its own unique design, crafted from local stone and ancient cedar and olive wood, plus there's a swimming pool. The lodge is the starting/finishing point for camel-assisted walking safaris, when guests are guided through completely deserted tracts of wilderness. From US$460 per person.

$$$$ Tassia Lodge, north of **Borana Lodge**, T0727-049 489, www.tassiasafaris.com. This ranch is covered with original cedar forest to the west, it then stretches down the Mokogodo Escarpment onto the plains, with 6 open-sided rooms with views into the valley, extra beds can be provided for children. The comfortable sitting and dining area overlooks a stunning swimming pool, which is built into rocks and surrounded by fig trees. From US$450 per person.

$$$$ Sweetwaters Tented Camp, Ol Pejeta Conservancy, reservations **Serena Hotels**, Nairobi, T020-284 2000, www.serena hotels.com. One of the larger camps, with 39 luxury tents under thatch overlooking a waterhole, floodlit by night, plus swimming pool, restaurant and 2 bars in what was the original homestead. Safaris in vehicles, game walks and horse rides are available, plus night game drives and bush lunches or dinners. One of the cheaper options from US$330 per double room full board, but excluding activities.

East from Nanyuki

Northeast from Nanyuki the road continues around Mount Kenya, turning southeast through Meru and Embu before it joins the A2 again in Sagana, completing its loop around Mount Kenya. The eastern side of the mountain is heavily cultivated, and coffee is grown on the higher volcanic slopes. There are few distractions on this eastern side of Mount Kenya, though the small unassuming village of Chogoria provides access for the Chogoria Route if climbing the mountain, and the Meru National Park lies to the east. Although little visited, this park does offer a couple of upmarket lodges, and in recent years numerous species of wildlife have been reintroduced. ▸▸ *For listings, see pages 198-200.*

Nanyuki to Meru

From Nanyuki, it is 50 km or so east along the A2 to the turn-off that goes on up to Northern Kenya. This is still the A2 and, after 30 km, the first town on this road is Isiolo (see page 329), generally regarded as the gateway town to the north. From there, the A2 continues north via the Samburu, Buffalo Springs and Shaba national reserves to **Marsabit** and eventually the Ethiopian border at Moyale.

Continuing around the mountain on what has become the B6 road, about 30 km on after the turn-off to Isiolo, you will reach the town of Meru. The journey from Nanyuki to Meru is very beautiful and shows the diversity of Kenya's landscape. To the south is Mount Kenya, to the north (on a clear, haze-free day) you can see miles and miles of the northern wilderness of Kenya.

Meru → *For listings, see pages 198-200. Colour map 1, A5. Phone code: 064.*

Meru, a thriving and bustling trading centre, is located to the northeast of Mount Kenya, about 75 km east of Nanyuki and 55 km southeast of Isiolo. It stands in a heavily cultivated and forested area at an altitude of about 3000 m and it can be cold and damp. It's quite a climb up to Meru from either Isiolo or Embu and, in the rainy season, you will find yourself lost in the clouds. However, if you are here on a clear day, you may get good views of the mountain peaks. It is an important coffee-producing region, which is grown in small-holdings on the higher slopes above town in Mount Kenya's rich volcanic soil. From Meru the road to Embu is good; about 5 km to the south of town, the road crosses the equator again, where there is a sign and a few curio stalls. Although it serves as an important trading centre, Meru does not receive many visits from travellers. As it is not close to any of the trails up the mountain, it has not been developed for this. It is, however, the base for visits to the Meru National Park, the entrance of which is just over 80 km from the town. There is a noticeable military presence here and a good range of shops, banks and other facilities. There are two

A real tear jerker

Joy and George Adamson were among the 20th century's most famous champions of wildlife. Their relationship with Elsa the lioness in the 1950s and 1960s is one of the best-known animal stories ever told – immortalized in the book and film *Born Free*. The public image of their lives in the inhospitable bush lands of Kenya was of romantic safaris and tireless commitment. Joy, with her tight blond curls and easy laugh, was a colonial queen and George, with his suntanned chest, khaki shorts and white beard, a legend of the bush. George grew up in India but moved to Kenya as a child and, after working on farms in the Rift Valley, he turned his hand to hunting but had a change of heart about killing lions when he came across one sitting on a rock: "She was sculptured by the setting sun, as though she were part of the granite on which she lay. I wondered how many lions had lain on the self-same rock during countless centuries while the human race was still in its cradle." This passage from his diary was read by Bill Travers, the actor who played George in *Born Free*, at his 1989 memorial service in London. George decided on a career as a game warden and got a job in the remote and unexplored Northern Frontier of Kenya on the border with Somalia and arrested 25 poachers in the first few months.

Joy was born Friederike Gessner in 1910, in what was then the Austro-Hungarian Empire (later to become part of Austria). She set sail for Africa in 1937 and met Peter Bally, a botanist, on the boat between Cairo and Mombasa. They married in Nairobi in 1938 and he renamed her Joy, after the joy that she had bought into his life. Ironically, the marriage was unhappy and didn't last long. Joy met George on safari and seduced him in the Norfolk, the famous hotel in Nairobi, a month later. She shared his passion, respect for the Northern Frontier, an adventurous spirit and a love of wildlife. She was also a fine artist and was commissioned to paint a collection of the tribes of Kenya (which today hang in the Kenya State House and the National Museum). Successful in her own right, her frequent affairs were legendary amongst the tight-knit community of colonial Kenya.

Their safari in 1955 was the one that changed their lives forever. After shooting a dangerous man-eating lioness, George found her three newborn cubs in a cleft of rock and took them home to Joy. When they opened their eyes a few days later, they immediately imprinted on her as their mother. For the first few months, she raised all three, but they grew big and boisterous and two were sent to a zoo in Rotterdam. Elsa stayed and was doted on by Joy, who showered her with affection and attention. The lioness went everywhere with the Adamsons and Joy adored her. Despite their affection for the lioness, they both agreed she must be set free. George taught her to hunt and kill, which involved dragging a carcass behind his Land Rover for Elsa to chase. When she could fend for herself, she was released in the bush but visited the Adamsons almost daily and retained her old friendship with Joy. Elsa's unique rehabilitation became the success it was, when she mated with a wild male and bore three cubs, which she introduced to Joy. Only once before had captive lions successfully been released in the wild but, with no contact, it was never known if they reproduced. Joy took her story to London and the publishing house of Collins. *Born Free* became an instant success and sold over 5 million copies in 12 languages. Her publisher Billy Collins came to Kenya to meet Elsa, where he was seduced by Joy. In January 1961, whilst Joy was away on business with Billy, Elsa became ill from tick-bite fever and died with her feverish head resting in George's lap. Joy returned grief-stricken and buried Elsa next to the Tana River at Meru, causing a worldwide reaction of condolence never before seen for an animal. In 1964 Columbia Pictures started filming *Born Free*, and George was hired as the technical adviser on lion handling. George selected the lions (over 20 were needed) from zoos and circuses, and trained them. Virginia McKenna and Bill Travers, who played the parts of Joy and George (married in real life), refused to use doubles in their scenes with the lions but the crew worked from within cages. After the film was finished, George was able to keep three of the lions and Joy agreed to finance their rehabilitation at Meru Reserve. She had a cheetah cub to set free, so they both set up camps, 15 miles apart, where they lived for over four years, as cheetah and lion cannot share the same territory. Bill Travers returned to Kenya to make a documentary on the Adamsons, but Joy withdrew because she was jealous of the amount of coverage of George. Travers apologized, but she never spoke to him or Virginia McKenna again. An audience of 35 million saw the finished film, *The Lions are Free*. George earned royalties and made money from his autobiography, aptly entitled *My Pride and Joy*. In 1969, Joy moved to Elsamere, her new house on Lake Naivasha, which is today a museum. George's pride of 15 lions was faring well for themselves in the bush and, in 1970, George moved to the isolated wilderness of Kora on the Tana River, where he spent the rest of his life. He re-released Boy, his favourite lion, who played Elsa's mate in the movie, and another young cub that had been found by Bill Travers in a furniture shop at the bottom of the Kings Road in Chelsea. Over the next seven years, George released a further 17 lions and became known as *baba ya simba* (father of the lions). Despite being awarded the Austrian Cross of Honour for Science and the Arts from her country of birth and contributing to wildlife projects throughout the world (and her celebrity status increasing), Joy resented George's obvious contentment at Kora, his activeness, deep concern for his lions and popularity. Her mood was revived when she was given another leopard cub, Penny, in 1977, which she raised and released at her camp at Shaba, and, in 1979, she invited George to come to her camp and celebrate Christmas. At the last minute, he couldn't make it due to problems with his plane. On the 3 January 1980, Joy Adamson was found in a pool of blood, after being stabbed. One of her ex-workers later confessed to her murder in retaliation for being sacked. George buried his wife's ashes at Meru beneath the graves of Elsa and Pippa, a cheetah she had released. Nine years later George was killed by Somali Shifta poachers carrying automatic weapons at his beloved camp in Kora. On the morning of 20 August 1989, after his usual 11 o'clock gin, a 50-year ritual, he rushed in his battered Land Rover to investigate a commotion in the bush. Poachers were ambushing a female German guest and threatening her with rape; George charged forward in the vehicle firing his pistol. George and two of his employees were shot dead in a hail of bullets. He was 81. Hundreds of people came to his funeral at Kora and he was buried alongside Boy. A bottle of gin was placed beneath his coffin and, after the funeral, a wreath was dragged away by a lion – evidence that his pride had visited the grave of the father of the lions.

markets at Meru: one on the main road towards Nanyuki and the other on the opposite side of town. The merchandise on sale is very cheap and includes not just agricultural produce from the farms around Meru, but also baskets and household goods. You are also very likely to see *miraa* for sale, also known as *qat* and *gatty*, which is produced in large quantities around Meru, and is a leaf and twiggy plant that is chewed as a mild stimulant.

Meru Museum ① *on the main road roughly opposite the Meru County Hotel, T064-32482, www.museums.or.ke, Mon-Fri 0930-1800, Sat 0930-1400, US$5.50, children (under 16) US$2.75*, is housed in the oldest building in town, built in 1916, and was formerly a District Commissioner's Office. It has several small galleries, with displays ranging from local geology, stuffed birds and animals, to innovative toys made from scrap materials. The most interesting section of the museum is that related to the customs and culture of the local Meru people: various ethnographic artefacts are exhibited, as well as examples of local timber and stone and tools from the prehistoric site at Lewa Downs. There is a Meru homestead that gives a good idea of how the Meru people live. In the museum shop is a relic of colonial days – a wind-up gramophone made by His Majesty's Voice. This particular model came via Pakistan where the then owner was stationed with the King's African Rifles. There is a small selection of bakelite 78 records, which can be played for KSh10. Outside there is a display of various herbs and other medicinal plants, including an example of a *miraa* plant. A craft shop sells locally produced items.

Meru National Park → *For listings, see pages 198-200. Colour map 1, A5.*

① *T0753-586 195, www.kws.org, Jan-Mar, Jul-Oct US$60, children (3-18) US$30, Apr-Jun, Nov-Dec US$50/25, car US$3.25. To get here take the C91 from Meru to the settlement of Maua, and the park's Murera Gate is 35 km to the west on a good tar road. The park has a well-graded road system of over 600 km, but many roads become impassable in the wet.*

With just a few tourist package tours visiting, Meru National Park is one of the least trampled and unspoiled of Kenya's parks. Some 85 km away from Meru town and 370 km northeast of Nairobi, straddling the equator, the 1810 sq km is mainly covered with thorny bushland and wooded grasslands to the west. There are 13 rivers and numerous mountain-fed streams that flow into the Tana River from the south. Dense riverine forests grow along the watercourses, surrounded by the prehistoric-looking doum palms.

The national park suffered greatly from poachers during the late 1980s, which resulted in the deaths of several rangers and two French tourists, along with the annihilation of the introduced white rhino population. Following these incidents, for many years the option of visiting Meru National Park was effectively withdrawn by all the safari operators. But today the KWS has the security issue well in hand, visitor numbers are steadily increasing and, thanks to gallant efforts by the KWS, there have been huge relocations of animals to the park, which is now home to the Big Five. The most ambitious and successful of these initiatives included the translocation of 56 elephants (nine different families) from the Laikipia Plateau to Meru in 2001; a number of black and white rhino were also moved here in 2006 from other locations in Kenya. The populations of these have steadily grown and Meru is today home to 40 white and 20 black rhino. As well as these, animals include lion, leopard, cheetah, Grevy's and plains zebra, gerenuk, reticulated giraffe, hippo, lesser kudu, oryx, hartebeest and Grant's gazelle and some fairly large herds of buffalo. There are more than 400 species of bird, including kingfishers, rollers, bee-eaters, starlings and numerous weavers, and specials include the Somali ostrich, the red-necked falcon and Pel's fishing owl, which can be heard at night by the Tana River.

The park was opened in 1968 and became famous for its role in the *Born Free* story. The late Joy Adamson hand-reared the orphaned lioness Elsa here, later releasing her into the wild. Elsa died of tick-borne fever and was buried in a forest clearing by Joy. After her death, Joy was also buried at the same site near the Adamson's Falls next to the Tana River, where the grave is marked by a small plaque. For the full *Born Free* story see box, page 194. In recent years, Kenya Wildlife Services has built a three-span Bailey bridge across the Tana River. Funded by the World Bank, the 138-m galvanized steel bridge links Meru National Park to **Kora National Park** to the east and allows for the free movement of animals between the parks. The bridge has been named the Adamson Bridge in honour of George Adamson, who lived in Kora with his beloved lions at Kampi ya Simba.

Bisanadi National Reserve is effectively an extension of Meru National Park on its northeastern boundary, as it can only be reached via Meru's Murera Gate. It covers about 600 sq km, and the area is mainly thorny bushland and thicket merging into wooded grasslands with dense riverine forests of raffia palm along the watercourses. You are likely to see the same sort of wildlife as in Meru National Park, as it acts as a dispersal area during the rains. It is a particularly good place to find elephant and buffalo in the wet season. The reserve is underdeveloped and roads are virtually non-existent, but nevertheless, game drives from Meru's lodges go into this adjoining reserve.

Meru to Thika → *For listings, see pages 198-200. Colour map 1, A5.*

Between Meru and Embu is the village of **Chogoria**, which is the starting point for the **Chogoria trail** (see page 183). This is the only eastern approach up Mount Kenya and it is generally considered to be the most beautiful of the routes. It is also supposed to be the easiest as far as gradients are concerned.

Embu is the final town in the clockwise circuit around Mount Kenya, before the B6 road rejoins the A2 south of Sagana to Thika and Nairobi. This junction is 42 km southwest of Embu. Named after the Embu people who live in this area, it is the provincial headquarters of the Eastern Province. The town is strung out along the main road and it's a busy place, with the bars staying open late. There's nothing to see here, although the old **Isaac Walton Inn** is a reasonable place to stay (see page 199). The surrounding area is densely populated and intensively cultivated. There's another reasonable tarred road that leaves the B6 in Embu and heads southeast for roughly 80 km to **Kangonde**, which is a small town that straddles the main A3 between Thika and Garissa. This is also an alternative route back to Thika, which is about 70 km west of Kangonde, via the Ol Donyo Sabuk National Park (see page 165) and Fourteen Falls (see page 165), but the B6 is a fairly lonely road.

❂ East from Nanyuki listings

For sleeping and eating price codes and other relevant information, see pages 20-24.

◗ Where to stay

Meru *p193*

$$-$ Meru County, on the main road next to the post office, T064-20432. In the town centre in a 4-storey block in its own well-tended grounds, with 40 simple but clean and comfortable rooms and friendly staff. All rooms have hot water but make sure the showers work, and it's worth paying a little more for the ones with TVs and balconies. It has a decent restaurant that serves *nyama choma* and Indian curries, a bar with a patio, and secure parking.

$$-$ Three Steers, roughly 2 km from town off the Nanyuki road, T0723-684 974. Neat motel-style place with spacious and recently refurbished rooms so everything is fairly fresh, tiled floors, modern bathrooms, but with 2 bars and a noisy disco on Fri and Sat, maybe avoid it at weekends. The restaurant serves a wide-ranging menu, including Indian curries and stews, and there's plenty of safe parking.

$ Blue Towers, on Nanyuki road at the junction with the turn-off to Maua and the Meru National Park, T064-30309. Don't be put off by the location at a petrol station, the rooms inside are clean, with TV, tiled bathrooms and hot water. Reasonable breakfast and a buffet dinner with a good choice for around US$7, internet cafe and car park, but no bar, though there are plenty of places nearby to get a beer.

$ White Star, some distance from the town centre on the road to Maua and the Meru National Park, just before the Teacher's College, T063-20989. Simple en suite rooms in a squat block in a compound with parking, you can get basic food here on the attractive leafy terrace but no beer as it is Muslim-owned.

Maua

$$-$ Ikweta Country Inn, 45 km from Meru en route to Meru National Park, T064-21112, www.ikweta.com. A new and welcome hotel in this region and the sister operation to the **Ikweta Safari Camp** in the park (see below), with 38 neat rooms, some with views of the Mboone River, good restaurant, bar and a café in the lovely landscaped gardens full of flowers. Doubles start from US$70 B&B and there are some basic and cheaper rooms (including triples) from US$25 in an annex in the garden. Can organize half- and full-day game drives into the park. You can get to Maua by *matatu* from Meru.

Meru National Park *p196, map p179*

$$$$ Elsa's Kopje, in the middle of the park on Mugwangho Hill, www.elsaskopje.com, reservations **Cheli & Peacock**, Nairobi, T020-600 3091, www.chelipeacock.com. A luxury camp perched on top of a kopje with 9 thatched stone cottages with locally made furniture, 2 have an outside bath with views over the park, and all have their own butler. There's a central dining and lounge area, a stunning infinity swimming pool built into the rocks with sweeping views. Set slightly apart from the camp on a hill, where George Adamson set up a camp after filming *Born Free*, is Elsa's House, with 2 bedrooms and its own swimming pool, ideal for families. Activities include day and night game drives, bush walks and fishing. The camp has its own airstrip, or road transfers can be arranged from Meru airstrip. All-inclusive rates from US$350 per person.

$$$$ Leopard Rock Lodge, about 10 km into the park from Murera Gate, reservations, Nairobi T020-600 0031, www.leopardmico.com. This is a beautiful lodge decorated with exquisite antique furniture and Persian rugs on hardwood floors, built on a 3.5-km frontage on the Murera River and offering luxury full-board accommodation in 15

198 • Central Highlands East from Nanyuki Listings

bandas, each one with 2 bathrooms. Very fine cuisine with a broad selection of wine and champagne, African-style open-air kitchen, small museum with library, jacuzzi and pool bar. A simply stunning swimming pool, which has a perspex wall at one end so it's actually possible to look through the clear wall at the crocodiles in the adjacent river. Most guests fly in. All-inclusive rates from US$450 per person.

$$$$ Rhino River Camp, outside the park on the western edge, it's about a 45-min drive south of the main road and Murera Gate (4WD only), T0732-809 287, www.rhinorivercamp.com. An outstanding Italian-owned lodge with 8 very stylish and large (80 sq m) thatched cottages with canvas walls built on raised platforms among the trees overlooking the Kindani River, lovely swimming pool on a wooden sun deck surrounded by doum palms. The central building has lounge, restaurant, bar and library, good Italian cuisine, massages available, bush walks on the property, and you can borrow mountain bikes to visit the local villages and farms. Rates are full board and include game drives into the park but not park entry fees. From US$200 per person. Again transfers from the Meru airstrip can be arranged.

$$$ Ikweta Safari Camp, outside the park 2 km before Murera Gate, T0705-200 050, www.ikwetasafaricamp.com. Opened in 2011 and sister operation to the **Ikweta Country Inn**, in Maua (see above) and set on a private farm, with excellent rates from US$120 for a double, 10 spacious en suite tents under makuti roofs with decks and simple safari-style furnishings and Kenyan batiks, very large swimming pool, restaurant, bar and lounge, plus a campsite **$**, with flush loos, hot showers and cooking shelter. Offers game drives into the park, so combined with the Country Inn, which you can reach by *matatu* from Meru, this gives an option of visiting the park without your own transport.

$$ Murera Bandas, just inside the Murera Gate near the KWS Park HQ, T0753-586 195,

reservations **KWS**, T020-600 0800, www.kws.org. 4 self-catering *bandas* with 2 bedrooms, each with 1 double and 1 single bed, and en suite bathroom with hot water from a wood-burning stove, BBQ area rather than a kitchen, bring everything you may need, including cooking equipment, drinking water, firewood and food but bed linen and kerosene lamps are provided.

The 4 **Kinna Bandas** are almost identical and are 22 km into the park next to the Bwatherongi River, but only have cold water in the showers. From US$70 per *banda*.

Meru to Thiku *p197*
Chogoria

Most visitors to Chogoria are here to climb Mt Kenya on the Chogoria Route on an organized tour, and spend the first day travelling, either on foot or by 4WD vehicle, the 26 km from the village to the Chogoria Park Gate and KWS campsite at 2950 m (no facilities). The roadhead is a further 6 km into the park from the gate.

Embu

$$ Isaac Walton Inn, Kenyatta Highway, 2 km north of town towards Meru, T068-31128/9, www.izaakwaltoninn.co.ke. The best option in Embu, an old colonial hotel apparently named after an English angler because of the proximity of good fishing spots in the mountain streams nearby. The inn is set in 3 ha of lovely tropical gardens with a swimming pool and views of Mt Kenya on a clear day. There's a comfortable lounge, with a log-burning fire, good bar and restaurant. The 80 rooms in low blocks in the gardens are a little old-fashioned and gloomy but all have modern bathrooms with hot water, TV and a patio. Friendly and helpful staff.

$ Maina Highway Hotel, Kenyatta Highway in the centre of town just south of the post office, T0722-827 700, www.mainahighwayhotel.com. Large, modern concrete block on 7 floors with 95 simple rooms (there's a lift), with hot showers and TV. Excellent views over the town from the roof, restaurant, rates include a cooked breakfast, good security and parking, Muslim-owned, so no bar.

O Shopping

Meru *p193*
There's a branch of **Nakumatt** supermarket on the main road about 200 m south of the museum, which also has a café that is oddly called **Sherlock's Den**, serving the best Western-style snacks in Meru, including burgers and chips and slices of pizza.

O Transport

Meru *p193*
The main bus and *matatu* stands are next to the main market behind the mosque on Mosque Hill Rd, reached from the road going past Barclays Bank. There are several daily buses between Meru and **Nairobi**, which take about 4 hrs, via **Chogoria** (1 hr), **Embu** (2½ hrs), and **Thika** (3 hrs). *Matatus* cover the same route, and also go north to **Isiolo**, which takes about 45 mins, and depart from the main stand near the market as well as opposite the Shell petrol station on the main road just to the south of the Standard Chartered Bank.

Meru National Park *p196, map p179*
Air
The Kina Airstrip in Meru National Park is about 5 km into the park from the Murera Gate. The lodges provide transport to meet the flights. **Air Kenya**, Nairobi, T020-391 6000, www.airkenya.com, has a daily flight between Wilson Airport, **Nairobi**, and Meru (70 mins), US$215 1 way. **Fly 540**, Nairobi, T020-445 3252, www.fly540.com, has a daily flight on a circuit between Wilson Airport, **Nairobi**, Nanyuki and Meru, US$175 1 way between Nairobi and Meru (55 mins) and the flight to/from **Nanyuki** is US$40 (30 mins). The airstrip is also served by charter companies including **Tropic Air**, T0722-207 300, www.tropicairkenya.com, which operates out of Nanyuki (see page 187).

Meru to Thiku *p197*
The road between Nairobi and **Embu** is very busy, and buses and *matatus* are frequent, taking about 2 hrs via **Thika** (1¼ hrs). There are also services north to **Meru** (2½ hrs). The bus and *matatu* stands in Embu are to the east of the junction of Kenyatta Highway, the B6 and the B7 towards Kangonde.

Contents

Footprint features

Border crossings

At a glance

⊖ **Getting around** The best way to explore the parks is to opt for a fly-in or drive-in safari.

⚜ **Time required** 2-3 nights each in Amboseli and Tsavo East/West from either Nairobi or the coast.

☀ **Weather** Fine and sunny most of the year with clear views and moderate temperatures.

✖ **When not to go** Can be visited year-round but the dirt roads in the parks can become difficult in the wet.

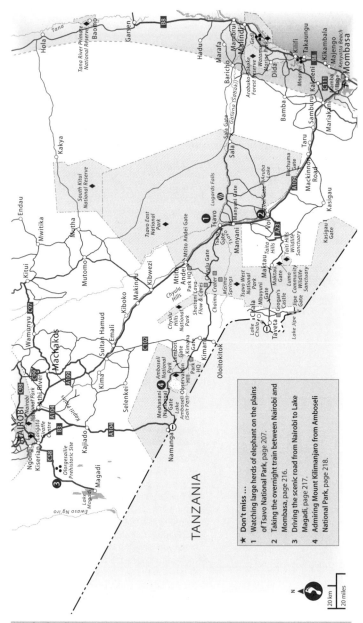

★ **Don't miss ...**

1 Watching large herds of elephant on the plains of Tsavo National Park, page 207.

2 Taking the overnight train between Nairobi and Mombasa, page 216.

3 Driving the scenic road from Nairobi to Lake Magadi, page 217.

4 Admiring Mount Kilimanjaro from Amboseli National Park, page 218.

TANZANIA

N

20 km
20 miles

Southern Kenya is one of the most visited regions of the country. The major game parks in the region are a big draw: Tsavo West and Tsavo East, on either side of the Nairobi–Mombasa road, make up the largest park in the country, and Amboseli National Park is also very popular. Amboseli is probably most famous for its photographs of elephants with snow-capped Kilimanjaro in the background; a picture that, above all, says 'come to Africa'. Another reason for the popularity of these parks is their closeness to the coast; visitors to this region can go on safari and also spend some time on the beach.

There are many points of interest off the Nairobi–Mombasa road leading to the coast. This is one of the most important thoroughfares in the East Africa region, as it runs the length of the country to Nairobi and then to Uganda, where it continues on to Kampala. Hundreds of trucks ply this road each day carrying goods imported through the Mombasa port into the interior of the continent. The Masai Mara Game Reserve in southwest Kenya, contiguous with the Serengeti National Park in Tanzania, is normally accessed via the town of Narok and is therefore included in the Rift Valley section, see page 117.

Nairobi to Mombasa

The region southeast of Nairobi steadily but gently descends for almost 500 km down a long sparsely populated savannah to the coast and is neatly dissected by the Nairobi–Mombasa road and railway line. The land is arid and not especially fertile and, as such, with the exception of the sisal plantations around Voi, supports little cultivation and few major settlements; the ones that do straddle the road and railway line have their origins as railway camps when the 'iron snake' inched its way from Mombasa at the end of the 19th century (see page 18). But the biggest draw to this region are the vast plains that support an extraordinary variety of wildlife. Midway between Nairobi and Mombasa, Tsavo National Park, Kenya's largest protected area, is flanked by several smaller private sanctuaries and is equally accessible from both cities on an organized safari. The road itself that covers the 470 km from Nairobi to Mombasa is in reasonable condition and is regularly resurfaced. The only rough bit can be the last 100 km or so before Mombasa, which is a steady hill where the tar routinely gets chewed up by heavy trucks heading to Nairobi from Mombasa's port. Numerous daily buses ply this route; alternatively there are frequent flights, which take little more than an hour and, thanks to strong competition, are very affordable. If you've got lots of time, you can also take the (very slow) train. ➤➤ *For listings, see pages 212-216.*

Mombasa road ➔ *For listings, see pages 212-216.*

The Mombasa road starts as a continuation of the Uhuru Highway (A109) in Nairobi, passing Nairobi National Park on the right, the turn-off to Jomo Kenyatta International Airport on the left and then passing through a number of industrial areas and housing estates around Athi River. At Athi River is the junction with the A104 to Namanga on the Tanzania border and the main route to **Amboseli National Park**; see page 218 for details of the route down to the park and the park itself. Once in open country on the Mombasa road, the route passes through the **Kapitiei Plains**, which are part of an unfenced region on the southern boundary of Nairobi National Park, where herds of gazelle and antelope can be seen, as well as large-scale cattle ranches. The next section of the route is through semi-arid country broken by the **Ukambani Hills**. The road up this long steep slope is poor, as years of heavy trucks making the laborious climb have dug deep ruts into the road. Just south of the road, by the railway line, is **Kima**, meaning 'mincemeat' in Kiswahili. Kima was so named after a British Railway Police Assistant Superintendent was eaten by a lion in 1900. Charles Ryall, using himself as bait, was trying to ambush a lion which had been attacking railway staff and passengers. Unfortunately the ambush went horribly wrong when he fell asleep on the job.

Further on you will pass through Masai country, which is primarily featureless scrubland, and the town of **Sultan Hamud**. It sprung up during the making of the railway at Mile 250 where it was visited by the then ruler of Zanzibar and named after him. It has hardly changed since that time and, at 110 km from Nairobi, is a pleasant enough place to stop off for a drink and a snack at the petrol station. Just south of **Emali** you can head down to **Amboseli National Park** on the C102, see page 219 for details of this route.

Another good place to break your journey is at **Makindu**, about 60 km from Sultan Hamud, where a Sikh temple of the Guru Nanak faith, built in 1926 by railway workers, still offers spartan but free accommodation and food for travellers (donations gratefully received – see Where to stay, page 212).

The road continues its route passing into more lush pastures with a proliferation of wonderful and rather grotesque baobabs. At this stage the **Chyulu Hills** are visible to the south. The main trading centre at **Kibwezi** is the most important region in the country for sisal growing. Honey production is also much in evidence, and you are likely to be offered some from sellers at the side of the road. From Kibwezi, the road passes through heavily cultivated land to the boundary of Akamba country at **Mtito Andei** – meaning 'vulture forest' – about halfway between Nairobi and Mombasa; it is basically a truck stop with a clutch of petrol stations and a few places to eat, and the **Mtito Andei Gate** to both Tsavo West and East. From here, the road runs through the centre of the parks **Tsavo West** and **Tsavo East** for around 80 km, see page 207 for details. You may spot zebra and antelope from the road, and large troops of baboons may wander across the road so drive slowly.

Chyulu Hills National Park

ⓘ *The turning to the west is in Kibwezi from where it's 9 km to Kithasyo Gate and the park HQ; it's also possible to enter from Tsavo West. T045-622 483, www.kws.org, 0600-1900, US$20, children (3-18) US$10, vehicle US$3.25.*

This 741-sq-km park was established in 1983 as an extension to Tsavo West, which it shares a border with to the south. Described as being the youngest mountain range in the world, the Chyulus are made up of intermingled volcanic cones and lava flows that are considered to be only around 500 years old. Many of the cones are covered with grass and there are extensive forests. This mountain range has no permanent water supply except for a small spring at Ngungani. The park is virtually untouched and there are only a couple of rough roads (4WD only) and, with the exception of the one luxury lodge on a private ranch bordering the park to which most guests fly (see Where to stay, page 212), there's no accommodation, though it is possible to camp at the gate next to the park headquarters if you are self-sufficient. The long mountain range is home to a variety of wildlife similar to that of neighbouring Tsavo, including wildebeest, buffalo, zebra, elephant, mountain reedbuck and eland, but there are far fewer of these in the rough thickets and they are fairly shy. The peak of Kilimanjaro can be seen to the west on a clear day.

Voi → *Colour map 1, A6. Phone code: 043.*

The capital of this region, Voi is a rapidly developing industrial and commercial centre 153 km northwest of Mombasa. According to local history the name of town comes from a slave trader called Chief Kivoi who settled near the Voi River about 400 years ago. The town started to grow at the end of the 19th century when the Kenya–Uganda railway was constructed. This was the first upcountry railhead where passengers would make an overnight stop, but this is no longer offered as you can dine, sleep and breakfast on the train. It has a couple of petrol stations, a bank with an ATM, a post office, a market and supermarkets, and busy bus and *matatu* stages. **Voi Gate** into Tsavo East National Park is around 5 km to the north of town.

Voi to Taveta

The A23 runs westwards form Voi through the Taita Hills for 109 km to **Taveta** on the Tanzania border (see page 210). Buses run between Voi and Taveta and then on to Moshi at the base of Mount Kilimanjaro and, for a short distance, the road goes through Tsavo West, via Maktau and Mbuyuni gates (you don't have to pay the conservation fees if only transiting through the park). The road is initially tar for about 20 km, and then fairly well-maintained murram for the rest of the way. The now-disused railway that follows the road once served as a vital supply line to British forces during the First World War, when

Tanzania was German East Africa. It was on these plains that one of the most eccentric campaigns of the war was fought. Here the British, led by General Jan Smuts, pitted their wits against one of Germany's most charismatic generals, General Paul Von Lettow, in a bizarre battle that featured fleets of Rolls Royces, blown-up railways lines, lack of men, lack of guns and a final surrender that came three months after the rest of the world had signed an armistice. As you drive west, the road crosses a number of 'elephant grids' (they serve the same purpose as cattle grids but are naturally much larger).

Taita Hills Wildlife Sanctuary
The craggy Taita Hills lie to the west of the Mombasa road, where the highest point is **Mount Vuria** at 2205 m and, from the summit, there are excellent views of the plains of Tsavo below. The Taita are in fact three groups of hills, the **Dabida**, **Sagalla** and **Kasigau**. In the foothills, the Taita Hills Wildlife Sanctuary is a 110–sq-km private reserve of thorny savannah that is almost completely surrounded by Tsavo West, and is accessed from the A23, 37 km west of Voi towards Taveta. It is unfenced, except along the northern boundary where an electric fence helps protect the villages and crops along the main road from elephant and buffalo, so the wide variety of game present is the same as that of Tsavo West and includes lion, cheetah, elephant, buffalo, spotted and striped hyena and significant populations of plains game. Prolific birdlife includes the extremely rare Taita falcon, a bird recorded in early Egyptian hieroglyphics. The sanctuary was first established in 1972 by the hotel group Hilton, though the two lodges are today managed by **Sarova Hotels** (see Where to stay, page 213).

Lumo Community Wildlife Sanctuary
Also accessed from the A23, 48 km west of Voi, this is a private 450-sq-km wildlife sanctuary that was formed from the Lualenyi, Mramba and Oza group ranches (hence the acronym: Lumo); it lies adjacent to Tsavo West and the Taita Hills Wildlife Sanctuary. The habitat features woody rolling savannah and remnants of highland tropical rainforest and includes the Mwashoti, Mwakitau and Ndola hills and Lion Rock, which is an important breeding site for lion. It serves as a vital wildlife corridor and dispersal area between Tsavo West and Tsavo East, especially for elephant which follow an ancient migratory route between Lake Jipe in the west to the Galana River in Tsavo East. You can navigate the sanctuary in a vehicle on well-maintained and signposted tracks, and there is one community-owned lodge, the **Lion's Bluff Lodge** (see Where to stay, page 214), which also has a campsite, and you can drop in for lunch.

Voi to Mombasa
From Voi the road runs through the **Taru Desert** for another 150 km down to Mombasa. This area is an arid, scorched wilderness, and there is little sign of life. You will see several small quarries. These supply many of the hotels on the coast with natural stone tiles used in bathrooms and patios. The next small settlement is **Mackinnon Road** with the Sayyid Baghali Shah Mosque as its only landmark.

Another 30 km brings you to the busy market centre of **Mariakani**, a place of palm groves and an atmosphere quite different from upcountry Kenya. If you take the road to the right, the C107, then turn left at the junction with the C106, it leads to the **Shimba Hills National Reserve** (see page 247), which can also be reached from the coastal road south of Mombasa.

For the next 90 km the scenery becomes progressively more tropical, the heat increases, as does the humidity, and the landscape changes to coconut palms, papaya and other coastal vegetation.

Tsavo National Park → *For listings, see pages 212-216. Phone code: 043. Colour map 1, B5/6, C5/6.*

Established in 1948, Tsavo is the largest national park in Kenya and covers 4% of the country's total area. It lies halfway between Mombasa and Nairobi and is bisected by the Nairobi–Mombasa railway and road. It is an Akamba word meaning 'a place of slaughter', which could be a reference to the murderous attacks of the Akamba people in the region by the Masai over the centuries, or else because the area was crossed by caravans of Arab slavers and their captives from the interior to the coast, and many of their victims dropped dead on the way and were eaten by lions. For administrative purposes the park has been split into two sections: **Tsavo East** (13,747 sq km), which lies to the east of the Nairobi–Mombasa road/railway and was made famous by the 'Man-Eaters of Tsavo' – a pair of lions that attacked railway workers – and **Tsavo West** (9065 sq km), to the west of the road. Its beautiful landscape and proximity to the coast make it a popular safari destination. It offers tremendous views, with diverse habitats encompassing mountains, river forest, plains, lakes and wooded grassland. Wildlife includes all the Big Five, plus zebra, giraffe, hippo, crocodile, impala, kudu, eland, jackal, hyena, baboon and cheetah, numerous smaller mammals and over 600 bird species. Because of its open spaces, the animals are fairly easy to spot, and elephants, covered in bright red dust, are often seen wandering along the horizon. Its vastness creates a special atmosphere and, on these endless plains trampled by thousands of animals, it is not difficult to imagine that this is once how all of East Africa looked.

Arriving in Tsavo

Getting there There are no scheduled flights to either Tsavo East or West, although **Mombasa Air Safaris** (see page 242) and **Safarilink** (see page 223) will touch down on request, and there are several airstrips suitable for chartered light aircraft. Most people visit on an organized safari from the coastal resorts. The majority of the access gates lie on the Mombasa road that divides the two sections. As a central point of reference, **Mtito Andei Gate**, which is on both sides of the road and provides access to both, is 233 km southeast of Nairobi and 250 km northwest of Mombasa. Buses from Nairobi to Mombasa pass near the gates, and hitching to them is fairly easy, but since walking inside the park is not allowed, visitors without vehicles may have a very long wait and safari operators with paying passengers will not pick up people. However, it is not an unreasonable option to get the bus to **Voi** and go on a guided game drive with one of the safari lodges there (see Where to stay, page 212). Buses also run between Voi and Taveta on the Tanzanian border and then on to Moshi and, for a short distance, this road actually goes through Tsavo West via Maktau and Mbuyuni gates. If you are self-driving, both Tsavo East and West are fairly easily navigated with a good map as all tracks are clearly defined and junctions are numbered. Bring all your own provisions into the park including petrol and water. You should be able to eat or drink at any of the lodges if you so desire, and there are facilities and shops at the towns on the main road; the biggest of which is Voi. You can obtain and reload Safari Cards at **Voi Gate** (to Tsavo East but accessible from the main road if you are going to Tsavo West) and **Mtito Andei Gate** (to both).

Tourist information ⓘ *T043-30049, www.kws.org, 0600-1900, Jan-Mar, Jul-Oct US$50, children (3-18) US$25, Apr-Jun, Nov-Dec US$60/30, vehicle US$3.25.*

Tsavo National Park

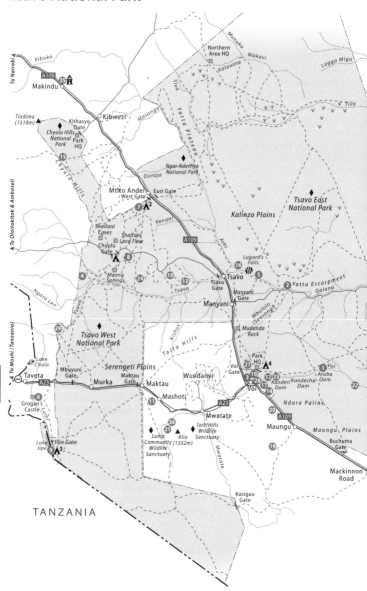

N

|10 km|
|10 miles|

Where to stay
Ashnil Aruba Lodge 1
Bigi Epiya Chapeyu Tented Camp 2
Distarr 3
Finch Hattons 4
Galdessa Camp 5
Grogan's Castle 6
Kamboyo Guest House 7
Kilaguni Lodge 8
Lake Jipe Bandas 9
Lion Hill Lodge 10
Lion's Bluff Lodge 11
Ndololo Safari Camp 12
Ngulia Safari Lodge 13
Ngutuni Lodge 14
Ol Donyo Lodge 15
Patterson's Safari Camp 16
Red Elephant Safari Lodge 17
Rhino Valley Lodge 18
Rock Side Camp 19
Sagala Lodge 20
Salt Lick Game Lodge 21
Satao Camp 22
Sentrim Tsavo Camp 23
Severin Safari Camp 24
Sikh Temple 25
Taita Hills Game Lodge 26
Voi Safari Lodge 27
Voi Wildlife Lodge 28
Voyager Ziwani Camp 29

Camping ⋀
Chyulu 1
Kamboyo 2
Lake Jipe 3
Ndololo 4

To Malindi
Sala Gate
To Mombasa
Samburu
A109

Tsavo East

ⓘ *Park HQ is at Voi Gate just north of Voi on the Nairobi–Mombasa road, where there is a small educational centre. Other gates off the main road are Manyani Gate, 25 km north of Voi, Mtito Andei Gate, 96 km north of Voi, and Buchuma Gate at the extreme southeast corner of Tsavo East. It is also possible to enter the park on the C103 road from Malindi via Sala Gate on the eastern boundary of the park. This route, which runs alongside the Galana River between Manyani Gate and Sala Gate, may be impassable during the rains.*

Tsavo East is the much less-visited side of the park where you will be able to see the wildlife without the usual hordes of other tourists. The landscape is vast scrubland, dotted with baobab trees and frequented by huge herds of elephant. The remoteness of much of the park means it had serious problems with poaching in the past. As a consequence, much of the northern area (about two-thirds of Tsavo East) used to be off-limits to the public in an attempt to halt poaching, which had decimated the elephant population from around 20,000 in 1970 to just 5000 in 1989. In the same period, rhino numbers plummeted from 8000 to less than 50. Today, however, as a result of stringent anti-poaching initiatives, this corner has been well and truly turned and you can be treated to the sight of large herds of 50 or more elephant, which instinctively retreated to the vicinity of the lodges where they are assured of protection. (The present elephant population in the whole Tsavo ecosystem is put at around 11,600 and rhino at about 120.)

The **Kanderi Swamp**, not far from Voi Gate, has the most wildlife in the area. The main attraction is the **Aruba Dam**, built across the Voi River, where many animals and birds congregate. **Mudanda Rock**, about 30 km north of Voi, is a 1.6-km-long outcrop of rock that towers above a natural dam and, at times during the dry season, draws hundreds of elephants. The **Yatta Plateau**, at about 290 km long, is the world's largest lava flow. The **Lugard's Falls** on the Galana River, 40 km northeast of Voi, are pretty spectacular. They are a series of rapids rather than true falls. The rocks have been sculpted into fascinating shapes by the water flow channelled into a gorge so narrow that it is possible to stand with legs spanning the cleft, overlooking the falls.

Tsavo West

ⓘ *There are several entrance gates into Tsavo West. Two are on the Nairobi–Mombasa road: Tsavo Gate and Mtito Andei Gate (which is also the park headquarters). Chyulu Gate in the northwest corner of the park is used by vehicles coming into Tsavo West from Amboseli National Park; 4WD and high-clearance vehicles are required for this route, especially in wet weather. Other entries are at Ziwani Gate, Jipe Gate and Kasigau Gate, all to the south of the park.*

Tsavo West is the more developed part of the park, combining easy access, good facilities and stunning views of Mount Kilimanjaro on a clear day. The savannah ecosystem comprises open grasslands, scrubland, acacia woodlands, belts of riverine vegetation and rocky ridges. The area is made up from recent volcano lava flows, which absorb rainwater that reappears as the crystal-clear **Mzima Springs**, 40 km away, and supports a vast quantity and diversity of plant and animal life.

The main attractions at Tsavo West are the watering holes by **Kilaguni** and **Ngulia** lodges that entice a huge array of wildlife particularly in the dry season. During the autumn the areas around **Ngulia Lodge** are a stopover for hundreds of thousands of birds from Europe in their annual migration. Not far from the **Kilaguni Lodge** the **Mzima Springs** are a favourite haunt of hippos and crocodiles. There is an underwater viewing chamber, but the hippos have obviously decided against being watched by moving to the other side of the pool. Also around the lodges are the spectacular **Shaitani lava flow** and cones, as well as caves that are well worth visiting. You will need to bring a good torch. At the extreme southwest of the park, bordering Tanzania, is the beautiful **Lake Jipe**, see page 212, which is fed by underground flows from Mount Kilimanjaro. Pygmy geese and the black heron are found here along with many other species of bird.

Along the Tanzanian border

Taveta

Taveta is a small town surrounded by sisal estates on the Tanzanian border next to Tsavo West and 109 km west of Voi on the A23. As it's the border crossing, see page 220, it is a thriving point of commerce for the Masai communities on both sides of the border and has an especially large twice-weekly (Wednesday and Saturday) market for a small out-of-the-way place. The **Taveta Military Cemetery**, is to the west of town, next to the District Commissioners Office, and holds the graves of 127 soldiers who died in battles in this region during the First World War (Taveta was invaded by Germany in August 1914). It is believed to be the only place where British and German soldiers were laid to rest side by side. Taveta is actually on a piece of land that juts into Tanzania. The irregular shape of the border here was created in 1881 when Queen Victoria gave Mount Kilimanjaro to her grandson, then the Crown Prince of Prussia and later Kaiser Wilhelm II of Germany, as a wedding present. Consequently, the border was adjusted so that Kilimanjaro fell within the boundaries of the German colony of Tanganyika instead of the British protectorate of Kenya.

Ewart Grogan

Born in Britain in 1874, Ewart Grogan was the first man to walk from the Cape to Cairo – a 3½-year journey that won him the hand of his bride.

In 1896 Ewart sailed for Cape Town, where he was given the task of running a wagon-load of ammunition up to Bulawayo in Southern Rhodesia. He then became Cecil Rhodes's personal escort, when he learnt of Rhodes' vision of 'civilizing' the African continent by building a railway and telegraph line from the Cape to Cairo. After a serious bout of blackwater fever, he went back to England, where he met Gertrude Watt. They fell in love and discussed marriage, but Grogan had little future and no resources, so he returned to Africa and walked from the Cape to Cairo to both prove his worth to Gertrude's father and to survey the route for Rhodes' railway and telegraph line. He was only 25 when he set off. From Cairo he returned to

England and presented the Union Jack, which he had carried with him throughout the journey, to Queen Victoria. Following the publication of his book in 1900, *From the Cape to Cairo*, Grogan became the youngest man ever to address the Royal Geographical Society and he and Gertrude were married later that year. Grogan returned to Africa a prosperous man and acquired 190,000 acres of land around Taveta in Kenya, which he developed for sisal and citrus production. He built his grand house, Grogan's Castle, in the 1930s on a high point near Taveta, overlooking thousands of acres of flourishing sisal plantations. Today it's a hotel (see Where to stay, page 216). Gertrude died in 1943, and Grogan built a children's hospital in Nairobi in her memory called Gertrude's (www.gerties.org), which today is one of East Africa's most important children's hospitals. Ewart died in 1967 in Cape Town, aged 92.

Lake Chala → *Colour map 1, C5.*

Lake Chala is just 8 km north of Taveta, part of the lake being in Kenya and part being in Tanzania. This deep-water crater lake is about 4 sq km and is totally clear, with steep walls, and is filled and drained by underground streams. It is a tranquil, beautiful place to explore on foot, and camping is possible, though you will need to bring all your own supplies. On the Tanzanian western shore is a formal campsite with some permanent tents (www.lake chalasafaricamp.com), which has a bar where you can arrange meals; is accessed from the town of Himo just beyond the Taveta border crossing. Aside from plenty of fish, there are also monitor lizards, baboons, monkeys and common snakes. Unfortunately you can't swim in the lake; a British tourist was killed by a crocodile here in 2002.

Grogan's Castle is an extraordinary construction on an isolated hill 13 km southeast of Taveta on the road to Lake Jipe. It was built in the 1930s by Ewart Grogan (see box, above) as a resort for the sisal estate managers in the area and features both Moorish and art deco touches. It was constructed purely from materials (other than cement and glass) found on his farm. All the walls are 2-ft thick to support the structure, as there are no steel beams; this also keeps the building cool. The floors were made with layers of sisal poles, lime and cement. The roof was originally clay tiles, which Grogan later changed to corrugated-iron sheets imported from Australia. The Tangye engine that drives the generator was built in 1898 and it is still running Grogan's Castle today. It has recently been renovated as a hotel (see Where to stay, page 216) and has spectacular views over Kilimanjaro and Lake Jipe.

Lake Jipe → *Colour map 1, C5.*

About 35 km south of Taveta, the 30-sq-km Lake Jipe also straddles Kenya and Tanzania and is fed from streams from the Pare Mountains on the Tanzanian side and from Mount Kilimanjaro. There are a number of small fishing villages around the Kenyan side on the northern shore, while its southeast shore lies inside Tsavo West National Park where there are some KWS *bandas* (see Where to stay, page 215) and a campsite, and you will need to pay park conservation fees. Again, this is a peaceful place to stop off, and you will be able to see hippos, crocodiles and, if you're lucky, elephant, as well as plenty of birdlife, including storks, egrets, pelicans, spur-winged plovers, ducks and Egyptian geese. A good portion of the lake has become choked with papyrus, which looks nice and is also used by the local people for thatching their houses, but has reduced the fishing on the lake to negligible levels. You can negotiate with a fisherman for a boat ride on the lake.

⦿ Nairobi to Mombasa listings

For sleeping and eating price codes and other relevant information, see pages 20-24.

⦿ Where to stay

Mombasa road *p204, map p208*
Makindu
$ Sikh Temple, in the centre of Makindu. The Sikh temple complex of the Guru Nanak faith offers free accommodation (donations gratefully received). The very clean rooms, sleeping 60 in total, have hot water and are set in simple white blocks in flowering gardens. There's a secure car park and wholesome Indian food in the dining hall (which you pay for). You must be well behaved and polite, and alcohol is not allowed.

Chyulu Hills National Park *p205, map p208*
$$$$ Ol Donyo Lodge, on a private ranch adjoining the park, reservations **Bush and Beyond/Bush Homes of East Africa**, Nairobi, T020-600 0457, www.bush-and-beyond.com and www.bush-homes.co.ke. 6 individual 2- or 4-bedroomed enormous luxury thatched cottages with lounge, open fireplace and a veranda with panoramic views of the plains and Mt Kilimanjaro, some have private plunge pools. There is also the option of sleeping outside on the roof. Stone-and-thatch central dining room and infinity pool overlooking a waterhole,

rates are all-inclusive of food, drinks, day and night game drives and guided bush walks, additional horse riding and mountain biking can be arranged. Most guests fly in by charter flight from Nairobi or the Masai Mara.

Voi *p205, map p208*
The safari lodges around Voi are outside the boundaries of Tsavo East and Tsavo West and therefore park entry fees do not apply, though the options within the parks are better for game viewing.
$$$$ Ngutuni Lodge, 5 km south of Voi and 5 km off the main road in the small Ngutuni Game Sanctuary that borders Tsavo East, reservations **Rex Resorts**, Diani Beach, T040-320 2213, www.rexresorts.com. Very well-designed lodge built of thatch and giant wooden poles with terraces overlooking a waterhole, which is illuminated at night. 48 rooms have 1 double and 1 single and balconies, the food is excellent, and there's a bar and curio shop. This can only be booked as an overnight safari from the coast and rates from US$200 per person include transfers, dinner and breakfast, an afternoon game drive in Tsavo East and a morning game drive in the sanctuary.
$$$$ Rock Side Camp, 29 km south of Voi, on the opposite side of the Nairobi–Mombasa road to Tsavo East, clearly signposted from the village of Maunga and then 10 km from the road, reservations Nairobi, T020-204 1445,

www.rocksidecamp.com. Not a standard safari lodge but a peaceful bush retreat and family-run, with 16 cosy and comfortable wooden en suite *bandas* and 7 bungalows with views of the Taita Hills, swimming pool, bar and restaurant. Activities include walking and birdwatching (84 species have been spotted in a single morning here).

$$$$-$$$ Voi Wildlife Lodge, in town 5 km before Voi Gate, reservations Nairobi, T020-712 5741, www.voiwildlifelodge.com. A large low-lying thatched lodge that has been designed to blend into the surrounding environment on a 10-ha site on the boundary of Tsavo East, with 88 rooms, some designed for the disabled (walkways around the camp are wheelchair friendly), restaurant, 2 bars, 1 on stilts overlooking a waterhole, spa, library, shop and swimming pool. Game drives into Tsavo East and West on offer. If driving past, you can stop here for lunch.

$$$ Lion Hill Lodge, just outside Voi Gate, reservations Nairobi T020-803 0828, www.lionhilllodge.com. Nothing fancy but a good location and, as the name suggests, on top of small hill right on the edge of the park with good views. 8 thatched rooms and 4 tents, simply but comfortably furnished, dining room and bar. The buffet lunches are worth stopping for on the way into the park. Game drives organized.

$$ Red Elephant Safari Lodge, 4 km from Voi and 700 m off the road to Voi Gate, T0727-112 175, www.red-elephant-lodge. com. Budget tourist lodge right on the edge of the park, with 15 smallish but comfortable rooms in mud and thatched cottages with mosquito nets and ceiling fans. The spacious main thatched restaurant and bar has colourful murals on the walls and zebra-striped furniture, simple food but ample portions, splash pool. Can organize game drives into the park and game walks out of the park, and there's African dancing around a fire in the evenings.

$$ Sagala Lodge, 15 km south of Voi and 3 km to the west of the main road, reservations Mombasa T041-548 0070,

www.blueskycorporate.com/Sagala_Lodge. In a pleasant garden setting with 24 simple thatched *bandas* with wooden beds and mosquito nets and nice bathrooms, plus a small swimming pool, restaurant and bar with outside tables under acacia trees, and can organize game drives into the park. Over 150 species of bird has been recorded in the gardens, and there are plenty of walks.

$ Distarr Hotel, between the bus stand and the railway station, T043-30 0277. One of the better basic board and lodgings in Voi but only useful if arriving on a late bus, with clean en suite rooms with hot water and nets, some have little balconies, friendly staff, reasonable restaurant serving fried chicken, vegetable curries and fresh juices.

Taita Hills Wildlife Sanctuary *p206, map p208*

$$$$-$$$ Salt Lick Game Lodge, reservations Sarova Hotels, Nairobi T020-275 7000, www.sarovahotels.com. This is noted for its strange design, basically a group of 96 rooms in huts on elevated stilts that are connected by open-air bridges over a number of waterholes. All rooms and the restaurant and bar have balconies, and the area is floodlit for game viewing at night; there is an underground tunnel and chamber allowing guests to watch wildlife safely at ground level. 2- to 4-day packages generally include transport from Nairobi or Mombasa, sanctuary fees, game drives and full-board accommodation.

$$$ Taita Hills Game Lodge, reservations Sarova Hotels, Nairobi, T020-275 7000, www.sarovahotels.com. This is another rather unusual stone block-type building covered with ivy, with 62 ordinary but comfortable rooms with balconies and wicker furniture, but the decor in the public areas is a little old fashioned. Rates include sanctuary fees and all buffet meals, there's a bar and enormous stone fireplace, plus tennis courts and a pool. If choosing between the 2, which are close together, **Salt Lick** is the better option.

Lumo Community Wildlife Sanctuary
p206, map p208

$$$ Lion's Bluff Lodge, 48 km west of Voi, T0733-222 420, www.lionsblufflodge.com. Built on a bluff with breathtaking views across the plains to Kilimanjaro, this eco-lodge is made from local natural materials, with 12 *bandas* linked by bridges, and verandas seemingly suspended over the savannah. There are handmade, wooden 4-poster beds and an open-sided thatched restaurant and bar. The campsite (**$**) has toilets and showers, water, firewood and a cooking shelter, or you can eat at the lodge, and you can hire tents and bedding. Good family option and extra beds, special meals and children's bush walks can be organized.

Tsavo East *p209, map p208*

$$$$ Galdessa Camp, in a central area near Lugard's Falls, reservations Ukunda, T040-320 2217, www.galdessa.com. An attractive setting in a grove of doum palms on the Galana River, which is excellent for game viewing. The 11 tents are under thatch, comfortably furnished with wooden decks and hot bucket-style showers, plus 3 separate *bandas* which can be booked for exclusive use. The central mess section has a dining area, bar and large, comfortable lounge. Rates include full board, game drives and walking safaris.

$$$ Ashnil Aruba Lodge, in the south of the park overlooking Aruba Dam, reservations **Ashnil Hotels**, Nairobi, T020-356 6970, www.ashnilhotels.com. An affordable mid-range option aimed at overnight visitors from the coast, each of the 40 partly canvas rooms have wide terraces overlooking the Aruba Dam and safari-style decor and 2 have disabled facilities. There's a curio shop, restaurant serving buffet meals and bar, rates are full board, and in the evening are wildlife and cultural talks and African dancing shows.

$$$ Bigi Epiya Chapeyu Tented Camp, in a central area at the foot of the Yatta Escarpment, T0733-743 210, www.epiya-chapeyu-camp.com. A good location on the Galana River with plenty of hippos and crocs, the 18 tents, sleeping 3 or 4, are under *makuti* thatch and are dotted around a spacious riverside area under doum palms. They have simple safari decor and larger than average bathrooms. There's a restaurant and bar with broad wooden deck, good Italian cuisine including home-made pasta and wood-fired pizzas. This is one of the better options for self-drivers (they can mend tyres, for example) and is on the reasonably good track across the park between Manyani and Sala Gates.

$$$ Ndololo Safari Camp, 7 km from Voi Gate, reservations Mombasa T043-30050, www.tsavocampsandlodges.com. Popular for overnight safaris from the coast and professionally run with 20 well-spaced tents on the forested banks of the Voi River. The tents are nicely decorated with handmade olive wood furniture, there's a thatched restaurant, bar and lounge lit by storm lanterns, good food including BBQs, bonfire in the evening where a Masai *askari* tells the story of the 'Man-Eaters of Tsavo'.

$$$ Patterson's Safari Camp, on the Athi River, 8 km from Tsavo Gate, reservations Nairobi T020-202 1674, www.patterson safaricamp.com. There are 20 spacious and shady en suite tents, some sleeping 4 people, with nice views over the sludgy brown river, which attracts a lot of game. It is named after railway worker John Patterson who shot the 'Man-Eaters of Tsavo' when the railway was being built. There's a pleasant thatched bar and restaurant, and a bonfire is lit in the evening.

$$$ Satao Camp, in the south of the park to the east of Aruba Dam, reservations Nairobi T020-243 4600, www.sataocamp.com. A well-run and good-value tented camp with 20 double tents, 2 with disabled facilities, constructed of sisal and *boroti* poles topped with a *makuti* roof, very nice bathrooms with stone features. Overlooks a waterhole with resident hippo, lovely thatched bar and restaurant with atmospheric lighting, very good food, safari chairs out front around a bonfire. Game drives and sundowner trips into the bush on offer, although many animals come right into camp.

$$$ Sentrim Tsavo Camp, 12 km from Voi Gate, reservations, **Sentrim Hotels**, Nairobi, T020-315 680, www.sentrim-hotels.com. Not in as scenic a location as some of the other lodges, this basic tented camp with 20 tents with toilet, shower and fan, is an affordable option within the park. There's plenty of game about and the waterhole here is a favourite with elephant. There's a rustic bar and a mess tent for meals.

$$$ Voi Safari Lodge, 5 km north of Voi Gate, reservations Mombasa, T041-471 861, www.safari-hotels.com. Built on a hillside close to Voi Gate with wide views across the savannah. It's cheaper than other lodges of equivalent standard, but the 52 rooms are small and in need of a refurbishment. There's a swimming pool, the animal hide by the waterhole gives very good close-up eye-level views, and baboons and rock hyrax wander through the hotel and gardens. Not recommended for the unfit or elderly, as there are lots of steps between the buildings.

Camping

Ndololo Campsite, near Voi Gate, about 7 km into the park, T043-30049, www.kws. org, has water and pit latrines, and firewood is available. You pay for camping at the gates: US$25, children (3-18) US$20.

Tsavo West *p210, map p208*
$$$$ Finch Hattons, on the western border of the park, 65 km from Mtito Andei Gate, reservations Nairobi, T020-357 7500, www.finchhattons.com. Award-winning luxury camp that oozes atmosphere. It accommodates up to 50 people in large safari tents, with twin beds, each with minibar, wooden Swahili chest, bookshelves and an antique writing desk, large deck balconies with chairs, tables and daybed. Elegantly appointed bar and restaurant and a comfortable lounge, extensive library of books and an excellent range of classical music including Denys Finch Hatton's favourite selection of Mozart, swimming pool. Dinner is very formal with 6 courses, fine china and crystal glasses.

$$$$ Severin Safari Camp, 40 km from Mtito Andei Gate, reservations Mombasa, T041-211 1800, www.severin-kenya.com. A quality camp with 27 spacious octagonal tents with very high ceilings and mosquito nets, plus 8 self-catering *bandas*, a thatched central area, with good restaurant and bar, firepit for bonfires, with traditional safari chairs overlooking the plains and a floodlit waterhole, lovely spa next to the infinity swimming pool and curio shop. As well as game drives, can organize animal-tracking walks with either a Masai guide or a KWS ranger.

$$$ Kamboyo Guest House, 8 km from the Mtito Andei Gate, T045-622483, reservations KWS, Nairobi, T020-600 0800, www.kws.org. Formerly the warden's house, overlooking its own waterhole and with a rooftop game-viewing deck, a self-catering cottage with 4 bedrooms, 2 bathrooms, lounge, fully equipped kitchen, caretaker on site, generator 1900-2200, otherwise kerosene lamps are provided. You just need to bring food, firewood and drinking water. Must be taken as a unit; from US$200 per night for up to 8 people.

$$$ Kilaguni Lodge, 20 km from the Mtito Andei Gate, reservations Nairobi, T020-284 2333, www.serenahotels.com. Good-quality lodge from the Serena chain, 56 spacious rooms, lots of wooden decks for game viewing, decorated with wooden sculptures of animals, a rock-hewn bar, swimming pool, excellent buffet meals with a wide variety of choice, rates are full board. This was the first lodge to be built in any of Kenya's parks. Mt Kilimanjaro can be seen on a clear day.

$$$ Ngulia Safari Lodge, 25 km from Tsavo Gate and 55 km from Mtito Andei Gate, reservations Mombasa, T041-471 861, www.safari-hotels.com. Slightly cheaper than the others but old-fashioned and the 52 rooms are in need of a refurbishment, but there's a swimming pool and it is in a good location for game viewing. The waterhole, again, is a big draw both for the animals and tourists and they bait leopard in the evening. The lodge is renowned as a haven for bird lovers every year Oct-Dec, who come to be involved in the bird 'ring' of migrating birds escaping the harsh winter conditions of the northern hemisphere. It is the only place in Kenya where this activity takes place.

$$$ Rhino Valley Lodge, about 40 km from both Mtito Andei and Tsavo gates, reservations Mombasa T043-30050, www.tsavocampsandlodges.com. Attractive setting on a rocky outcrop in the Ngulia Hills, with broad views of the waterholes in the valley below. 16 rooms – the 'rock room' is constructed in the rock face like a cave and has a private plunge pool – plus 6 simpler self-catering thatched *bandas* with fully equipped kitchen (from US$110 for a double). Good restaurant and a delightful bar fashioned out of a gnarly tree. As well as game drives, there are guided walks to the top of the hills to watch the sunset.

$$$ Voyager Ziwani Camp, reservations Nairobi, T020-444 6651, www.heritage-eastafrica.com. A Heritage Group's Voyager resort, of good standard and aimed at families and first-time safari goers. At the western boundary of the park, on the edge of a small, secluded dam on the Sante River, which is full of hippos and crocs, with 25 very large and nicely decorated permanent tents and excellent food. Offers game drives and walks with highly qualified naturalists, and there is an **Adventurer's Club** for children.

$$ Lake Jipe Bandas, reservations through the Warden 045-622 483, or KWS, Nairobi, T020-600 0800, www.kws.org. 3 self-catering *bandas* that sleep 5 people in total and share a simple bathroom and kitchen, but no stove and you need to bring your own firewood, drinking water and food. There's no electricity, though kerosene lamps are provided. Bring everything you need with you. Cost is US$50, regardless of the number of people, payable at the park gates.

Camping
Kamboyo Campsite, 8 km from Mtito Andei Gate, and Chyulu Campsite, 1 km from Chyulu Gate. There are no facilities except

water and pit latrines, so you will need to be completely self-sufficient. Another campsite is available on the shores of Lake Jipe. Campers share the outdoor cooking area and ablutions block with guests at the **Lake Jipe Bandas** (see above). You pay for camping at the gates, which costs US$25, children (3-18) US$20.

Taveta *p210, map p208*
$$$ Grogan's Castle, on the road to Lake Jipe, 7 km south of the A23, which is 6 km east of Taveta, T0733-944 234, www.kafafa.com/groganscastlekenya. Set in Ewart Grogan's former house (see box, page 211), which was built in the 1930s and fully restored in 2010, after being derelict for more than 40 years. There are 5 very large rooms where extra beds can be added, featuring high ceilings and Moorish arches, and a self-catering cottage in the grounds that sleeps 4. Amazing views of Kilimanjaro and Lake Jipe from the 2 circular living rooms and meals are taken together on Grogan's original dining table. There's a plunge pool in the spacious gardens.

⊖ Transport

Voi *p205*
Bus
There are buses coming and going all the time between **Mombasa** and **Nairobi**. There are also buses that go through Voi from Mombasa to the border town of **Taveta** and on to Tanzania.

Train
The **Nairobi–Mombasa** train passes through Voi. In theory, from Nairobi it should arrive/depart at 0400, and from Mombasa it should arrive/depart at 2320. It also stops in Mtito Andei about 2 hrs before and after. However, the train is often delayed (see box, page 18).

Taveta *p210*
There are plenty of buses from Taveta to **Voi**, and daily to **Mombasa** via Voi.

East African wildlife

Introduction

A large proportion of people who visit East Africa do so to see its spectacular wildlife. This colour section is a quick photographic guide to some of the more fascinating mammals you may encounter. We give you pictures and information about habitat, habits and characteristic appearance to help you when you are on safari. It is by no means a comprehensive survey and some of the animals listed may not be found throughout the whole region. For further information about East Africa's mammals, birds, reptiles and other wildlife, see the Land and environment section of the Background chapter, page 391.

The Big Nine

It is fortunate that many of the large and spectacular animals of Africa are also, on the whole, fairly common. They are often known as the 'Big Five'. This term was originally coined by hunters who wanted to take home trophies of their safari. Thus it was, that, in hunting parlance, the Big Five were elephant, black rhino, buffalo, lion and leopard. Nowadays the hippopotamus is usually considered one of the Big Five for those who shoot with their cameras, whereas the buffalo is far less of a 'trophy'. Equally photogenic and worthy of being included are the zebra, giraffe and cheetah. But whether they are the Big Five or the Big Nine, these are the animals that most people come to Africa to see and, with the possible exception of the leopard and the

black rhino, you have an excellent chance of seeing them all.

■ **Hippopotamus** *Hippopotamus amphibius*. Prefers shallow water, grazes on land over a wide area at night, so can be found quite a distance from water, and has a strong sense of territory, which it protects aggressively. Lives in large family groups known as 'schools'.

■ **Black rhinoceros** *Diceros bicornis*. Long, hooked upper lip distinguishes it from white rhino rather than colour. Prefers dry bush and thorn scrub habitat and in the past was found in mountain uplands. Males usually solitary. Females seen in small groups with their calves (very rarely more than four), sometimes with two generations. Mother always walks in front of offspring, unlike the white rhino, where the mother walks behind, guiding calf with her horn. Their distribution was massively reduced by poaching in the late 20th century, and now there are conservation efforts in place to protect black and white rhino and numbers are increasing. You might be lucky and see the black rhino in Nakuru, Tsavo and Aberdare national parks.

■ **White rhinoceros** *Diceros simus*. Square muzzle and bulkier than the black rhino, it is a grazer rather than a browser, hence the different lip. Found in open grassland, it is more sociable and can be seen in groups of five or more. Probably extinct in much of its former range in East Africa, it still flourishes in some places.

Opposite page:
Leopard with a kill.
Above left:
Black rhinoceros.
Above right:
White rhinoceros.
Right:
Hippopotamus.

iii

■ **Common/Masai giraffe** *Giraffa camelopardis*. Yellowish-buff with patchwork of brownish marks and jagged edges, usually two different horns, sometimes three. Found throughout Africa in several differing subspecies.

■ **Reticulated giraffe** *Giraffa camelopardalis reticulata*. Reddish-brown coat divided up into polygonal shapes by a network of distinct, pale, narrow lines. Also known as the Somali giraffe, it is native to Somalia, Ethiopia and Northern Kenya, but has been relocated to reserves further south.

■ **Common/Burchell's zebra** *Equus burchelli*. Generally has broad stripes (some with lighter shadow stripes next to the dark ones) that cross the top of the hind leg in unbroken lines. The true species is probably extinct but there are many varying subspecies found in different locations across Africa.

■ **Grevy's zebra** *Equus grevyi*. Grevy's is larger than Burchell's and has much narrower white stripes, which are arranged in such a way as to meet in a sort of star-shaped arrangement at the top of the hind leg. Prefers more arid areas.

■ **Leopard** *Panthera pardus*. Found in varied habitats ranging from forest to open savannah. It is generally nocturnal, hunting at night or before the sun comes up to avoid the heat. Sometimes seen resting during the day in the lower branches of trees.

■ **Cheetah** *Acinonyx jubatus*. Often seen in family groups walking across plains or resting in the shade. The black 'tear' mark is usually obvious through binoculars. Can reach speeds of 90 kph over short distances. Found in open, semi-arid savannah, never in forested country. Endangered in some parts of Africa. More commonly seen than the leopard, but not as widespread as the lion.

Opposite page left:
Common giraffe.
Opposite page right:
Reticulated giraffe.
Top left: Common zebra.
Top right: Grevy's zebra.
Above: Cheetah.
Right: Leopard.

Top: Buffalo. **Bottom:** Elephant.

■ **Lion** *Panthera leo* (see page i). The largest (adult males can weigh up to 200 kg) of the big cats in Africa and also the most common, they are found on open savannah all over the continent. They are often not at all disturbed by the presence of humans and so it is possible to get quite close to them. They are sociable animals living in prides or permanent family groups of up to around 30 animals and are the only felid to do so. The females do most of the hunting (usually ungulates like zebra and antelopes).

■ **Buffalo** *Syncerus caffer*. Were considered by hunters to be the most dangerous of the big game and the most difficult to track and, therefore, the biggest trophy. Generally found on open plains but also at home in dense forest, they are fairly common in most African national parks but, like the elephant, they need a large area to roam in, so are not usually found in the smaller parks.

■ **Elephant** *Loxodonta africana*. Commonly seen, even on short safaris, elephants have suffered from the activities of ivory poachers in East Africa and by 1990 numbers in Kenya were critically just 16,000, down from 170,000 at Independence in 1963. Today, numbers are around 37,000 thanks to better protection by the Kenya Wildlife Services.

Larger antelopes

■ **Beisa oryx** *Oryx beisa*, 122 cm. Also known as the East African oryx, there are two sub-species; the **common Beisa oryx** is found in semi-desert areas north of the Tana River, while the **fringe-eared oryx** is found south of the Tana River and in Tanzania. Both look similar with grey coats, white underbellies, short chestnut-coloured mane, and both sexes have long straight ringed horns. They gather in herds of up to 40.

■ **Common waterbuck** *Kobus ellipsiprymnus* and **Defassa waterbuck** *Kobus defassa*, 122-137 cm. Very similar with shaggy coats and white markings on buttocks: on the common variety, this is a clear half ring on the rump and around the tail; on the Defassa, the ring is a filled-in solid area. Both species occur in small herds in grassy areas, often near water.

Top: Beisa oryx. **Bottom left**: Defassa waterbuck. **Bottom right**: Common waterbuck.

■ **Sable antelope** *Hippotragus niger*, 140-145 cm, and **Roan antelope** *Hippotragus equinus*, 127-137 cm. Both are similar in shape, with ringed horns curving backwards (both sexes), longer in the sable. Female sables are reddish brown and can be mistaken for the roan. Males are very dark with a white underbelly. The roan has distinct tufts of hair at the tips of its long ears. The sable prefers wooded areas and the roan is generally only seen near water. Both species live in herds.

■ **Greater kudu** *Tragelaphus strepsiceros*, 140-153 cm. Colour varies from greyish to fawn with several vertical white stripes down the sides of the body. Horns long and spreading, with two or three twists (male only). Distinctive thick fringe of hair running from the chin down the neck. Found in fairly thick bush, sometimes in quite dry areas. Usually lives in family groups of up to six, but occasionally in larger herds of up to about 30.

■ **Topi** *Damaliscus korrigum*, 122-127 cm. Very rich dark rufous, with dark patches on the tops of the legs and more ordinary looking, lyre-shaped horns.

Top: Greater kudu. **Middle**: Sable antelope. **Bottom**: Topi.

■ **Hartebeest** The horns arise from a bony protuberance on the top of the head and curve outwards and backwards. There are three sub-species: **Coke's hartebeest** *Alcephalus buselaphus*, 122 cm, is a drab pale brown with a paler rump; **Lichtenstein's hartebeest** *Alcephalus lichtensteinii*, 127-132 cm, is also fawn in colour, with a rufous wash over the back and dark marks on the front of the legs and often a dark patch near the shoulder. All are found in herds, sometimes they mix with other plains dwellers such as zebra.

Top: White-bearded wildebeest. Middle: Coke's hartebeest. Bottom: Eland.

■ **White-bearded wildebeest** *Connochaetes taurinus*, 132 cm. Distinguished by its white beard and smooth cow-like horns, often seen grazing with zebra. Gathers in large herds, following the rains.

■ **Eland** *Taurotragus oryx*, 175-183 cm. The largest of the antelope, it has a noticeable dewlap and shortish spiral horns (both sexes). Greyish to fawn, sometimes with rufous tinge and narrow white stripes down side of body. Occurs in groups of up to 30 in grassy habitats.

Smaller antelope

■ **Bushbuck** *Tragelaphus scriptus*, 76-92 cm. Shaggy coat with white spots and stripes on the side and back and two white, crescent-shaped marks on neck. Short horns (male only), slightly spiral. High rump gives characteristic crouch. White underside of tail is noticeable when running. Occurs in thick bush, often near water, in pairs or singly.

■ **Kirk's dikdik** *Rhynchotragus kirkii*, 36-41 cm. So small it cannot be mistaken, it is greyish brown, often washed with rufous. Legs are thin and stick-like. Slightly elongated snout and a conspicuous tuft of hair on the top of the head. Straight, small horns (male only). Found in bush country, singly or in pairs.

■ **Gerenuk** *Litocranius walleri*, 80-105 cm. A curious antelope found in dry bushy scrub in Northern Kenya, also called the giraffe-necked antelope for its long, slender neck and tiny head with large ears and eyes. Is able to stand on its hind legs to reach for food in trees. Seldom needs to drink; gets moisture from fruit and shoots.

■ **Steenbok** *Raphicerus campestris*, 58 cm. An even, rufous brown with clean white underside and white ring around eye. Small dark patch at the tip of the nose and long broad ears. The horns (male only) are slightly longer than the ears: they are sharp, smooth and curve slightly forward. Generally seen alone, prefers open plains and more arid regions. A slight creature that usually runs off very quickly on being spotted.

■ **Bohor reedbuck** *Redunca redunca*, 71-76 cm. Horns (males only) sharply hooked forwards at the tip, distinguishing them from the oribi (see page xiii). It is reddish fawn with white underparts and has a short bushy tail. It usually lives in pairs or in small family groups. Often seen with oribi, in bushed grassland and always near water.

■ **Grant's gazelle** *Gazella granti*, 81-99 cm, and **Thomson's gazelle** *Gazella thomsonii*, 64-69 cm (see page xii). Colour varies from a bright rufous to a sandy rufous. Grant's is the larger of the two and has longer horns. In both species the curved horns are carried by both sexes.

■ **Common (Grimm's) duiker** *Sylvicapra grimmia*, 58 cm (see page xii). Grey-fawn colour with darker rump and pale colour on the underside. Its dark muzzle and prominent ears are divided by straight, upright, narrow pointed horns. This particular species is the only duiker found in open grasslands. Usually the duiker is associated with a forested environment. It is difficult to see because it is shy and will quickly disappear into the bush.

x Bushbuck.

■ **Oribi** *Ourebia ourebi*, 61 cm (see page xiii). Slender and delicate looking with a longish neck and a sandy to brownish-fawn coat. It has oval-shaped ears and short, straight horns with a few rings at their base (male only). Like the reedbuck, it has a patch of bare skin just below each ear. Lives in small groups or as a pair and is never far from water.

■ **Suni** *Nesotragus moschatus*, 37 cm (see page xiii). Dark chestnut to grey-fawn in colour with slight speckles along the back, its head and neck are slightly paler and the throat is white. It has a distinctive bushy tail with a white tip. Its longish horns (male only) are thick, ribbed and slope backwards. They live alone and prefer dense bush cover and reed beds.

Clockwise from top left: Kirk's dikdik; gerenuk feeding; steenbok; bohor reedbuck.

■ **Impala** *Aepyceros melampus*, 92-107 cm. One of the largest of the smaller antelope, the impala is a bright rufous colour on its back and has a white abdomen, a white 'eyebrow' and chin and white hair inside its ears. From behind, the white rump with black stripes on each side is characteristic and makes it easy to identify. It has long lyre-shaped horns (male only). Above the heels of the hind legs is a tuft of thick black bristles (unique to impala), which are easy to see when the animal runs. There is also a black mark on the side of abdomen, just in front of the back leg. Found in herds of 15 to 20, it likes open grassland or sometimes the cover of partially wooded areas and is usually close to water.

Top: Thomson's gazelle. **Bottom**: Common duiker.

Top left: Oribi. **Top right:** Suni. **Bottom:** Impala.

Other mammals

There are many other fascinating mammals worth keeping an eye out for. This is a selection of some of the more interesting or particularly common ones.

■ **African wild dog** or **hunting dog** *Lycacon pictus*. Easy to identify since they have all the features of a large mongrel dog: a large head and slender body. Their coat is a mixed pattern of dark shapes and white and yellow patches and no two dogs are quite alike. They are very rarely seen and are seriously threatened with extinction (there may be as few as 6000 left). Found on the open plains around dead animals, they are not in fact scavengers but effective pack hunters.

■ **Spotted hyena** *Crocuta crocuta*. High shoulders and low back give the hyena its characteristic appearance and reputedly it has the strongest jaws in the animal kingdom. The spotted variety, larger and brownish with dark spots, has a large head and rounded ears. The **striped hyena**, slightly smaller, has pointed ears and several distinctive black vertical stripes around its torso and is more solitary. Although sometimes shy animals, they have been known to wander around campsites stealing food from humans.

Top: African wild dog. **Middle:** Spotted hyena.
Bottom: Chacma baboon.

■ **Warthog** *Phacochoerus aethiopicus*.
The warthog is almost hairless and grey with a very large head, tusks and wart-like growths on its face. It frequently occurs in family parties and when startled will run away at speed with its tail held straight up in the air. They are often seen near water caking themselves in thick mud, which helps to keep them both cool and free of ticks and flies.

■ **Chacma baboon** *Papio ursinus*.
An adult male baboon is slender and weighs about 40 kg. Their general colour is a brownish grey, with lighter undersides. Usually seen in trees, but rocks can also provide sufficient protection, they occur in large family troops and have a reputation for being aggressive where they have become used to the presence of humans.

■ **Rock hyrax** *Procavia capensis*. The nocturnal rock hyrax lives in colonies amongst boulders and on rocky hillsides, protecting themselves from predators like eagles, caracals and leopards by darting into rock crevices.

■ **Caracal** *Felis caracal*. Also known as the African lynx, it is twice the weight of a domestic cat, with reddish sandy-coloured fur and paler underparts. Distinctive black stripe from eye to nose and tufts on ears. Generally nocturnal and with similar habits to the leopard. They are not commonly seen, but are found in hilly country.

Top: Warthog. **Middle:** Rock hyrax.
Bottom: Caracal.

Amboseli and the Tanzanian border

Directly south of Nairobi, the southern part of Kenya is dominated by views of Africa's tallest mountain, Kilimanjaro, with its snow-capped peak. It's best appreciated from the Amboseli National Park, where preferably a few accommodating elephants will amble across the foreground when you take a photo. A steady stream of safari vehicles ply the Nairobi–Namanga road on their way to either Amboseli or Arusha in Tanzania, which is the springboard town for Tanzania's northern circuit parks, including the Serengeti and Ngorongoro Crater. Many people on upmarket holidays may visit parks in both southern Kenya and northern Tanzania, and, for independent budget travellers, the journey from Nairobi to Arusha can be easily done by public transport or there are shuttle services. Once in Arusha, camping and lodge safaris to the northern parks can be arranged; the cheapest and most popular being a three-day safari with one night in the Serengeti and one night near the Ngorongoro Crater. Another option is to climb Mount Kilimanjaro; climbs can be organized in Moshi, 88 km to the east of Arusha. Remember you do not need to buy another visa on your return to Kenya if you have only been to Tanzania. From Nairobi, another road heads due south to Lake Magadi via the prehistoric site at Olorgesailie. ▸▸ *For listings, see pages 221-223.*

Nairobi to Lake Magadi → *For listings, see pages 221-223.*

The C58 is a good tarmacked road that runs from Nairobi to Lake Magadi, which is 107 km from the city and makes for an easy day excursion. To get to it, take the Langata Road out past Wilson Airport and Nairobi National Park. Soon after the park entrance, take a left fork that leads through the village of Kiserian and then climbs up the Ngong Hills before descending to the floor of the Rift Valley. *Matatus* run up and down this road, and Nairobi tour operators can arrange an excursion out here.

Olorgesailie prehistoric site → *Colour map 1, A6.*
ⓘ *On the C58, 65 km southwest of Nairobi, T020-374 2161, www.museums.or.ke, 0930-1800, US$5.50, children (under 16) US$2.80.*
A trip to this important prehistoric site can be combined with a visit to Lake Magadi. The site covers an area of 21 ha and is the largest archaeological site in Kenya. It was discovered in 1919 by geologist JW Gregory and, later in the 1940s, excavated by Kenya's most famous archaeologists, Mary and Louis Leakey. It is believed that a lake covered the present site of the mountain some 100,000-200,000 years ago and that various mammals, including elephants, hippos, crocodiles and giraffes, lived near or in the lake. The abundant presence of game in this area attracted hunters who fashioned stone tools and axes. Fossilized remains of prehistoric animals, some gigantic compared to their descendants, and an abundance of Acheulean hand axes and other stone tools were uncovered here. A small, raised wooden walkway has been built around the display of prehistoric animal remains and tools, enabling the fossils to be exhibited where they were found; a guide is on hand to take you around. You can camp here and there are also eight simple *bandas* (**$**) with shared cold showers and toilets, fireplace and picnic shelter, but you need to bring all bedding and food and drink. It's quite peaceful, and there are small antelope in the area if you go for a walk, but it gets very hot.

Lake Magadi → *Colour map 1, A4.*

ⓘ *At the end of the C58, 107 km southwest of Nairobi, matatus go via Kiserian. There's no recommended accommodation near Lake Magadi, but it's an easy day excursion from Nairobi.*

Some 35 km south of Olorgesailie and located at the base of the Rift Valley is Lake Magadi, a vision in pink. It is only 107 km from Nairobi but the climate – semi-desert with temperatures around 38°C – is very different to that of the capital. As you approach the lake, the views are splendid and you will probably see Masai grazing their cattle. At an altitude of 580 m, this is the second lowest of the Rift Valley lakes. It is 32 km long and 3 km wide and is the most alkaline of all the Kenyan Rift Valley lakes. The high rate of evaporation is the only way by which water escapes from the lake. Several hot springs, mostly at the southern end, bring to the surface a continual supply of *magadi* (soda), which evaporates forming a vast crust of sodium carbonate, which can appear pink in the changing light, although algae in some areas of the lake also turn the salt crust green. A soda ash factory has been built on the lakeshore, and the town of Magadi has grown up around this, which has a few basic facilities including a petrol station and a bank. There is an abundance of birdlife – in particular lesser flamingos, ibis and African spoonbills. The final scenes of the movie *The Constant Gardener*, based on John le Carré's novel, were filmed on the shoreline of the lake, when, in fact, the location in the story was Lake Turkana. Beyond the lake, the **Nguruman Escarpment** rises to 2300 m, forming the western wall of the valley, and stretches south to the Tanzania border, which is then topped by the Loita Hills, which flatten out to the Masai Mara to the west; though there is no road access to the reserve from this direction.

Nairobi to Tanzania → *For listings, see pages 221-223.*

Kajiado → *Colour map 1, B4.*

The road to Kajiado (A104) forks right off the Mombasa highway (A109) shortly after the southern boundary of Nairobi National Park, just east of the Athi River crossing the Athi Plains. Kijiado is the administrative headquarters of southern Masai-land at the southwestern corner of the Kapitiei Plains, which run between Machakos and Kajiado. The town is in the middle of bleak grasslands that show little sign of the abundance of zebra, wildebeest and giraffe that used to roam here. The town is typically Masai and there are many indicators of their preoccupation with cattle.

Namanga → *Colour map 1, B4. Phone code: 045.*

Namanga is the Kenyan border town on the A104; see page 220 for border crossing information. It is the nearest town to Amboseli National Park, and is a convenient stopover between Arusha and Nairobi. Arusha is 130 km to the south, and the drive from Nairobi to Arusha via Namanga takes about five hours. The road to Nairobi (A104) is in good condition, and there are petrol stations in Namanga, as well as shops selling crafts, and lots of Masai street hawkers selling beaded jewellery and red blankets. Prices are high but negotiable.

Amboseli National Park → *For listings, see pages 221-223. Colour map 1, B4/5.*

ⓘ *T045-62251, www.kws.org, 0600-1900, Jan-Mar, Jul-Oct US$75, children (3-18) US$40, Apr-Jun, Nov-Dec US$60/30, vehicle US$3.25.*

The biggest draw of the 392-sq-km Amboseli National Park is its location, with Mount Kilimanjaro providing a stunning backdrop. The whole park is dominated by Africa's highest mountain and at dusk or dawn the cloud cover breaks to reveal the dazzling spectacle of this snow-capped mountain. The downside is that its popularity (it has long been one of the most visited parks in Kenya) and decades of tourism have left well-worn trails, and much off-road driving has made the park look increasingly dusty and rather bleak. Efforts are being made to remedy this, with new roads being built to improve access and a tough policy on off-road driving. Surrounding Amboseli are ranch areas where the Masai share the land with the wildlife (they are not allowed to graze their cattle within the boundaries of the park), and many of the lodges are staffed by the Masai.

Arriving in Amboseli National Park

The main route into Amboseli is along the C103 from Namanga, on the Nairobi–Arusha (Tanzania) road (A104). From Namanga to the **Meshanani (Namanga) Gate** is 57 km or a 45-minute drive down a rough un-tarred road that is routinely graded but, because of the amount of traffic, can often be bumpy. The 240-km journey from Nairobi to Amboseli takes about three hours. The other route from Nairobi is via Emali on the Nairobi–Mombasa road (A109) and then the recently tarred C102 to the park, via either the **Lemboti** or **Kimana (Olkelunyiet) gates** in the east of the park. Many safari operators are now using this route as an alternative to get to the lodges on the eastern boundary of the park. It's also about a three-hour journey (approximately 230 km) from Nairobi. It is also possible to enter the Kimana (Olkelunyiet) Gate via the C103 from the Chyulu Gate in Tsavo West National Park. There are daily flights by **Air Kenya**, **Fly 540** and **Safarilink** from Wilson airport in Nairobi. Buses from the capital reach Namanga but there is no public transport from there to the park gates. The park tracks are signposted and the maps are good, but be prepared for dusty game drives. Both Kilimanjaro and Observation Hill serve as permanent reference

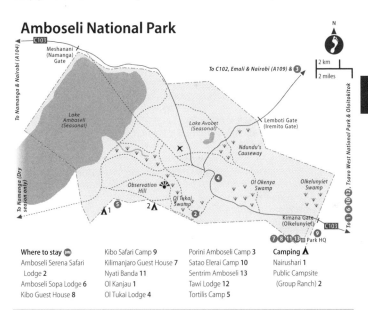

Amboseli National Park

Where to stay
Amboseli Serena Safari
Lodge **2**
Amboseli Sopa Lodge **6**
Kibo Guest House **8**

Kibo Safari Camp **9**
Kilimanjaro Guest House **7**
Nyati Banda **11**
Ol Kanjau **1**
Ol Tukai Lodge **4**

Porini Amboseli Camp **3**
Satao Elerai Camp **10**
Sentrim Amboseli **13**
Tawi Lodge **12**
Tortilis Camp **5**

Camping ▲
Nairushari **1**
Public Campsite
(Group Ranch) **2**

Namanga

Immigration and customs at the border are quick and efficient. Visas for both Kenya and Tanzania can be bought in US dollars, pounds sterling or euro cash, and the border is open 24 hours. If you are on a safari, or using one of the daily shuttle bus services between Nairobi and **Arusha** (see page 81) then the drivers/guides will assist with all border procedures. Remember you don't need to get another visa to return to Kenya if you've only been to Tanzania. Arusha is another two hours' drive or 111 km from the border.

You are advised to take great care if changing money on the black market (which is illegal in both Kenya and Tanzania), as there are many scams practised at the border. There's a branch of **Kenya Commercial Bank**, with an ATM, about 500 m from the border on the Kenyan side or wait until you get to a bank in either Nairobi or Arusha.

Taveta

The border crossing leads to the Tanzanian town of **Moshi**, which is 41 km from Taveta. 14 km from the border at Himo, the road joins the B1 south to Dar es Salaam, but you'll have to go into Moshi first to get transport. Through buses between Moshi and Mombasa cross at Taveta, and there are also plenty of *matatus* from Taveta to Voi and daily buses to Mombasa. Again the border is open 24 hours, visas are available, and there are banks with ATMs in Taveta. If you're not in a vehicle, the two border posts are 4 km apart but you can get a *boda-boda* between them.

points. When rains come harder than usual, some of the roads may be flooded, among them the main access to the **Ol Tukai lodges** from the Namanga road. In this case you will have to turn right towards Observation Hill and drive round the flooded area to the west.

Around Amboseli National Park

Amboseli is in a semi-arid part of the country, and the climate is usually hot and dry. It is fed by an endless underground water supply, filtered through thousands of metres of volcanic rock from Kilimanjaro's ice cap, which funnel into two clear-water springs in the heart of the park. The land is a mixture of open plains, savannah scattered with areas of beautiful yellow-barked acacia woodland, swamps and marshland and clutches of thornbush growing amidst lava debris. To the west of the reserve close to Namanga is the massif of **Oldoinyo Orok** at 2524 m. **Lake Amboseli**, after which the park is named, is usually a parched lake bed. It does hold water during the rains but, even during the wettest years, its depth rarely exceeds 50 cm. The main wildlife you are likely to see here are herbivores, such as buffalo, Thomson's and Grant's gazelle, Coke's hartebeest, warthog, wildebeest, impala, giraffe, zebra and lots of baboons. One of the most spectacular sights is the large herd of elephants here. The elephant population of the greater Amboseli Basin at the base of Mount Kilimanjaro now numbers 1500 in over 50 matriarchal families and associated bull groups. The Amboseli elephants have perhaps the oldest and most intact social structure of any elephant population in Africa. They are also the best known: the **Amboseli Trust for Elephants** (www.elephanttrust.org), which started in 1972, is considered the world's longest study of elephants. There are a few predators, including lion, leopard, cheetah, hyena and jackal, and birdlife is also abundant, with 400 recorded species of which 47 are raptors. Birdwatching is especially good near the swamps and seasonal lakes, where pelicans and Egyptian geese are often spotted; the best time to see Kenya's migratory birds, including African skimmers, red and yellow bishops, goshawks, buffalo weavers and palm nut vultures, is between October and January.

◉ Amboseli and the Tanzanian border listings

For sleeping and eating price codes and other relevant information, see pages 20-24.

◉ Where to stay

Namanga *p218*

$$-$ Namanga River Hotel, 200 m before the border on the right-hand side, T0722-440 089, www.riverhotelnamanga.com. This is a very simple lodge and campsite in a beautiful setting in wonderful gardens, with plenty of shady trees to pitch tents under, or accommodation is in prefabricated wooden huts in the garden. Toilets and (warm) showers are communal. It has an excellent bar and restaurant, for both Kenyan and Western dishes, but choice depends on what ingredients they have. This is primarily used by the cheaper safari operators to save on a night's camping within Amboseli.

Amboseli National Park *p218, map p219*

$$$$ Ol Kanjau, www.olkanjau.com, reservations **Bush and Beyond/ Bush Homes of East Africa**, Nairobi, T020-600 0457, www.bush-and-beyond.com and www.bush-homes.co.ke. The name means 'elephants' in Masai and this is hosted by American naturalists Michael and Judith Rainy, who are working to add wildlife conservation to the traditional pastoral economy of the local community and have been active in Kenya since 1968. A traditional seasonal safari-style tented camp situated just outside Amboseli on the Kisongo Masai group ranch, with just 6 tents and in a good location to spot elephants. Game drives and bush walks with the Masai are on offer. Closed Apr, May and Nov.
$$$$ Porini Amboseli Camp, in the Selenkay Conservation Area, 17 km

north of the Lemboti Gate, reservations **Gamewatchers Safaris**, Nairobi, T0774-136 523, www.porini.com. Small and exclusive camp visited on a 2-night safari from Nairobi with 9 spacious tents, in a spot once favoured by big-game hunters. There's a bar and restaurant, or meals are taken under the shade of an acacia tree; after dinner guests sit around a campfire. The camp is staffed by members of the local Masai community and there are very good walking safaris here as well as game drives into Amboseli. Closed Apr-May.
$$$$ Satao Elerai Camp, 14 km southeast of Kimana Gate, reservations **Southern Cross Safaris**, Mombasa, T041-243 4600, www.sataoelerai.com. Set on community land outside the park, this offers game walks and night drives in addition to game drives in the park, and you can walk with the local Masai as they graze their cattle. Accommodation is in 14 tents and suites, which are nicely designed, incorporate lots of acacia wood and have stone bathrooms and wide verandas. Very good dinners are taken outside under the stars, and there are superb views of Kilimanjaro.
$$$$ Tawi Lodge, 4 km northeast of Kimana Gate, T020-300 943, www.tawilodge.com. More intimate and luxurious than most, the 12 spacious cottages have fireplace, broad wooden deck, contemporary furnishings and Kilimanjaro views from the bed and bathtub. Extras include minibar and butler service, bar and dining room overlooking an active waterhole, swimming pool and massages.
$$$$ Tortilis Camp, www.tortilis.com, reservations **Cheli and Peacock**, Nairobi, T020-600 3090, www.chelipeacock.com. Smart tented camp with16 luxury tents

raised up on a wooden deck and sheltered by *makuti* roofs, large verandas, excellent views of the plains and Kilimanjaro, 2 have adjoining tents for children. Activities include game drives and visits to a Masai village and there's a swimming pool.

$$$ Amboseli Serena Safari Lodge, T045-622 361, www.serenahotels.com. A very attractive design, drawing on elements of Masai traditional dwellings, blending into the landscape, with 96 rooms with hand-painted murals on the walls and wide terraces, and there's a swimming pool. One of the nicest place to stay in the park and near the Enkongo Narok Swamp, which means there is always plenty of wildlife to see. Activities include game drives, sundowners on Observation Hill and visits to Masai *manyattas*.

$$$ Amboseli Sopa Lodge, just outside the park on the road to Oloitokitok on the border with Tanzania, reservations T020-375 0235, Nairobi, www.sopalodges.com. Attractive lodge set in mature wooded gardens, with 83 rooms in well-decorated thatched cottages. Meals are taken in the African-themed dining room or outside on a BBQ patio, there's a pleasant bar area from where you can sometimes spot honey badgers and hyenas, a very large swimming pool, and game drives are on offer.

$$$ Kibo Safari Camp, just outside the park boundary near Kimana Gate, reservations Nairobi T020-455 0532, www.kibosafaricamp.com. A large mid-range and modestly priced tented camp, with 70 fairly simple tents under *makuti* thatch, some for families, with rustic wooden furniture and Masai blankets on the beds, all face Kilimanjaro. There's an open-terraced restaurant and a bar under acacia trees, swimming pool, massages, day and night drives and bush walks.

$$$ Ol Tukai Lodge, reservations, Nairobi T020-444 5514, www.oltukailodge.com. This is a large lodge with 80 rooms in *bandas* that occupy one of the finest viewing points in the park and is set in well laid-out gardens, with swimming pool, good-value food, game drives and Masai dancing in the evening are on offer.

$$$ Sentrim Amboseli, in the southeast of the park near the park HQ, reservations Nairobi, T020-315 680, www.sentrim-hotels.com. One of the cheapest options and principally aimed at the minibus safari market, with 70 basic tents, a little bit too close together, but large with good hot showers and extras including kettle and fridge, swimming pool with jacuzzi, good food in the restaurant, which has a make-your-own-pizza bar.

$$$-$$ Kilimanjaro Guest House, next to the park HQ, 2 km from Kimana Gate, T045-622 250, reservations **KWS**, Nairobi, T020-600 0800, www.kws.org. Self-catering KWS house with 3 bedrooms sleeping 6 and spacious sitting room with veranda, bed linen, towels and kitchen utensils provided, plus gas cooker and fridge, and electricity is by a generator from 1830 to 2200. **Kibo Guest House** is similar except it sleeps 5 in 2 bedrooms and has 24-hr electricity. Both must be taken as a unit at US$150 per night. **Nyati Banda** is a cheaper and more basic option, again, the same set up but sleeps 4 for US$80.

Camping

The campsites in Amboseli National Park are run by Masai communities. Although they are technically just outside the park boundary, they can only be accessed from within the park itself. The public campsite in Amboseli is sometimes referred to as the **Group Ranch**. It is quite large but popular with low-budget camping safari companies so it can get rather crowded and noisy at times. This site is just outside the park boundary, southwest of Observation Hill. There are pit toilets here and a water supply that is not always reliable, so water has to be brought from one of the lodges at times. The special **Nairushari Campsite** is used by higher-budget camping safari companies, located in a secluded site through the southwest corner of the park.

There is firewood here, but bring your own food and water.

⊖ Transport

Namanga *p218*
Plenty of buses and *matatus* go along the A104 between **Nairobi**, **Kajiado** and Namanga. The drive to Namanga takes about 2½ hrs. The shuttle bus between Nairobi and **Arusha** also goes through Namanga (see page 81).

Amboseli National Park *p218, map p219*
Air
The airstrip in Amboseli is in the middle of the park and all the lodges arrange collection. **Air Kenya**, Nairobi, T020-391 6000, www.airkenya.com, **Fly 540**, Nairobi, T020-445 3252, www.fly540.com, and **Safarilink**, Nairobi, T020-600 0777, www.fly safarilink.com, each has a daily scheduled flight between Wilson Airport in **Nairobi**, and Amboseli. The flights take 40 mins; expect to pay around US$100 1 way.

Car
Accessing Amboseli National Park is difficult without organized transport. Most visitors come here as part of a safari package from Nairobi. However, if you get yourself to **Namanga River Hotel** (see Where to stay, page 221), they can arrange hire of a minibus and driver for a group for around US$220 per day, which includes the vehicle and driver's entry fee. Safari operators with paying passengers will not pick up people in Namanga.

Contents

Footprint features

Border crossings

The coast

At a glance

⊖ **Getting around** All-inclusive package holidays with local day and overnight tours; bus, *matatu* or self-drive along the coast road.
⊗ **Time required** 1-2 weeks with 1-2 nights in a nearby game park.
☼ **Weather** Warm, sunny and balmy most of the year.
⊗ **When not to go** During the rainy season in Apr-Jun days are overcast and muggy and it rains in the afternoon.

Tana River National
Primate Reserve

Bodhei

20 km
20 miles

Garsen

Mokowe Lamu
Matondoni Lamu Island
Witu C112 Kipungani Lamu
Airport

Birdlife
Sanctuary

Tana

B8

Hadu

Marafa Depression
(Hell's Kitchen)

Sala   Sala
Gate
Tsavo East   Galana (Sabaki)
National Park

Baricho

Marafa

Mambrui

Malindi

C103

Malindi
Airport

Arabuko-Sokoke
Forest Reserve

Gedi

Malindi
Marine
National
Park

Indian Ocean

6 Watamu

Dida

Watamu Marine
National Park

Bamba

Kilifi

Mnarani
Takaungu

Mackinnon Road
Taru   Samburu

Kaloleni

B8

C111

Mariakani

Kikambala
Majengo

Moi International
Airport

Mamba
Village

Jumba la Mtwana

Mombasa Marine National Park

Kenyatta Beach

Mwaluganje
Elephant
Sanctuary

Mtwapa

Kinango

Likoni

Mombasa

1 2

Shelly Beach

Shimba Hills
National Reserve

Kwale

Tiwi

Tiwi Beach

3

Diani

5

Diani Beach

Ukunda
Airport

Ukunda

Gazi

A14

Chale Island

Lunga
Lunga

Shirazi

Msambweni

Ramisi

Funzi Island

Majoreni

Kidimu

Kisiwani
Island

Shimoni

Wasini Island

4

Kisite-Mpunguti
Marine National Park

★ Don't miss ...

1 Fort Jesus, page 232.

2 Eating dinner on the romantic white-sailed
  dhow Nawalikher, page 237.

3 Shimba Hills National Reserve for views of
  Mount Kilimanjaro, page 247.

4 Wasini Island, page 250.

5 Kitesurfing along Diani Beach, page 259.

6 Watamu or Malindi marine national parks,
  pages 267 and 272.

Kenya's coastal belt possesses a unique climate, a different type of people and a separate cultural history from the rest of the country. The Swahili culture and Kiswahili language have their origins on this coast, stretching down into Tanzania.

Built on a 15-sq-km island and linked to the mainland by causeways and a rickety old ferry, Mombasa is Kenya's second biggest city and is East Africa's main port. It has a history dating back several hundred years, when the Persians, Arabs, Indians and Chinese visited the East African coast to trade in slaves, skins, ivory and spices. Mombasa Old Town has some interesting 19th-century architecture as well as the Portuguese Fort Jesus, which sits in a commanding position overlooking the harbour.

But the idyllic beaches on the Indian Ocean are the real reason to go to the coast. There's a long line of top-class beachside hotels to the south of Mombasa, centred around Diani Beach, and to the north, all the way up to Malindi. More than half of the country's international hotels are based along the coast, and it has long been a package-holiday destination from Europe. Most have been constructed from thatch and local materials and are well spaced out, so despite the coast's popularity, it never gets overly crowded even during the high seasons. The beaches are of fine white sand, and there are plenty of activities on offer, including diving, snorkelling, windsurfing and jet skiing. There are marine national parks aplenty off the coast, protecting the important marine life, and these can be experienced by *dhow*, glass-bottomed boat or, for a closer encounter, through a mask. Here, the colourful coral reefs teem with fish, dolphins and turtles and the aqua blue Indian Ocean provides near-perfect visibility. Away from the beach, there are a number of other attractions in the dense coastal forests and undulating hills, and a safari to one of the closer parks can easily be combined with down time on the beach.

Arriving on the coast

Getting there and around

The gateway to the coast of Kenya is **Mombasa**, although some visitors fly directly from Nairobi to Malindi, Diani or Lamu. There are taxis from Mombasa's **Moi International Airport** (see page 229) to all the coastal resorts, and most hotels and tour operators also provide transport inclusive of a holiday package or, at the very least, can arrange a shuttle bus. The coastal highway runs north of Mombasa all the way to Kenya's northern frontier. It's very easy to drive as far as **Malindi**, and there are regular buses and *matatus*. Services are less regular north of Malindi, although there are daily buses to **Lamu**. To the south of Mombasa, the Likoni car ferry links the city with the coastal road that runs to the border with Tanzania. Once off the ferry there are regular *matatus* to **Ukunda**, the village at the turn-off for the beach road to the resorts along **Diani Beach**, where you can swap *matatus* or take a taxi. Larger buses run daily between Mombasa, Moshi and Dar es Salaam in Tanzania, crossing the border at the extreme south of the coast road at **Lunga Lunga**. Another slower option for reaching the coast is to take the overnight train from Nairobi to Mombasa that runs three times a week. Many people book week-long package holidays to the resorts, but independent travellers may want to consider hiring a car to explore the coast, as the roads from the southern tip of Diani Beach to Malindi are good and most of the resorts accept walk-in guests (often for discounted rates) if they have room, although this would be inadvisable in high season.

Best time to visit

The climate on the coast is markedly different to that in Nairobi and the Kenyan Highlands and, if driving down the main Nairobi–Mombasa road, you will feel the rise in temperature and humidity as you get nearer to the coast. The average temperature is 28-30°C, and days are long and sunny just about all year round. Despite this, there is a down season on the coast during the rainy season from April to June, when it is often overcast and muggy, and many of the resorts and hotels offer discounts and some even close altogether. If you can put up with a few afternoon showers, this is not a bad time to visit, and you are likely to have the beach to yourself, but on the downside, many other facilities such as restaurants and watersports centres also close. By contrast, during high season, especially around Christmas and New Year, the beaches are very busy with European package-holiday makers and room rates are at their premium.

Mombasa

With a history going back 2000 years, Mombasa is the oldest town in Kenya. Although the town is centred on an island about 4 km long and 7 km wide, the more modern parts are now a massive sprawl on the mainland too. It owes its development to its location, for the island forms an ideal natural deep-water harbour. Today goods are sent from the port not only to Kenya but to the rest of East Africa as well.

Mombasa has large communities of Indian and Arabic origin. It has the greatest concentration of Muslims in Kenya and their influence on the culture is strong. There are some ancient, Arab-inspired houses with elaborately carved doorways in narrow streets and passages, and a few other worthy distractions such as Fort Jesus and the city's most famous landmark: two pairs of crossed concrete elephant tusks created as a ceremonial arch to commemorate the coronation of Elizabeth II in 1952. Despite these, Mombasa is not a terribly attractive place, and rubbish here is quite a problem, as is the traffic and pollution. Most visitors do not stay in the town itself – the city's hotels are not especially nice – and instead stay in one of the beachside locations to the north or south of Mombasa and visit on a day trip. It is now linked by causeways to the mainland at three points as well as by the Likoni Ferry.

▶▶ *For listings, see pages 236-243.*

Arriving in Mombasa → *Colour map 2, C1. Phone code: 041. Population: 940,000.*

Getting there

Mombasa is easily accessible. **Moi International Airport** ① *T041-343 3211, www.kenya airports.co.ke,* is 10 km west of the city centre on the mainland. There are many daily scheduled flights from Nairobi on the domestic airlines. Shop around but generally flights are good value; from US$70 one-way with Fly 540, for example. Some of the airlines also have flights between Mombasa and Malindi and Lamu. There are also regional flights between Mombasa and other destinations in East Africa, including direct flights to Zanzibar (Tanzania), and flights via Nairobi to Entebbe (Uganda) and Kigali (Rwanda), operated by both the Kenyan and regional airlines. Mombasa is also served by several direct charter flights from Europe bringing people out on package holidays. Some of the smaller airlines link Mombasa with the airstrips in the parks and reserves on circuits. For example, **Mombasa Air Safaris** flies between Mombasa and airstrips in the Masai Mara and Amboseli.

Arriving at Moi International from Nairobi is quite a pleasant experience as you emerge into the balmy sunny weather. The airport has good facilities: cafés and shops, banks and ATMs, desks for the car-hire companies and tour operators, and stands for various taxi firms that offer transfers into town and further afield to the north and south coast beaches; fares are printed on their boards and are all identical. Pay at the desks, where they'll give you a receipt to show the driver. Depending on your final destination, expect to pay in the region of US$12-15 to the city centre and the railway station; US$20 to Nyali Beach; US$40-60 to the north coast beaches as far as Kilifi; US$80-120 to the resorts around Watamu and Malindi (you can also fly from Mombasa to Malindi, see Transport, page 241); and US$50-60 to Diani Beach to the south, which includes the crossing on the Likoni Ferry. Ignore any individual taxi drivers that try to badger you; these are not registered to operate at the airport. Most hotels and tour operators provide transport inclusive of a holiday package or, at the very least, can arrange a shuttle bus. For those arriving on international flights, visas are processed quickly at immigration. Remember, if you are flying into Mombasa from Tanzania, you will be required to show a yellow fever vaccination certificate.

The overnight train from Nairobi runs three times a week (see page 242, and box, page 18) and there are several bus services a day with various different companies. Although on the coast, there are no boat links to anywhere else in Kenya or to neighbouring countries, and travelling by *dhow* is illegal for foreigners, but cruise ships pull into the port from time to time, and there is the option of seeing Mombasa from the water on the **Tamarind**'s *dhow* (see page 237). ▶▶ *See Transport, page 241.*

Getting around

The city is bisected by two main roads: Moi Avenue, which runs from the industrial area to the west of the island and then becomes Nkrumah Avenue to Fort Jesus in the east, and Digo Road, which crosses it in the centre of the city around the Old Town. Numerous *matatus* run up and down Digo Road going to the Likoni Ferry to the south and Nyali

Beach and other points in the north. Taxis can be found all over town parked on street corners. Tuk-tuks are considerably cheaper for short journeys than regular taxis. You can walk around the centre of Mombasa but the heat and humidity will tire you out quickly if you are too energetic, and the traffic fumes in the city centre are particularly bad.

Tourist information
There's no official tourist office as such but there is a clutch of tour operators along Moi Avenue that can give out information and display a variety of leaflets. They will of course want to book you on to something.

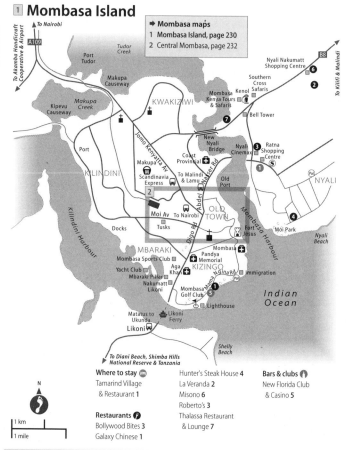

1 Mombasa Island

➡ **Mombasa maps**
1 Mombasa Island, page 230
2 Central Mombasa, page 232

Where to stay 🛏
Tamarind Village
& Restaurant 1

Restaurants 🍴
Bollywood Bites 3
Galaxy Chinese 1

Hunter's Steak House 4
La Veranda 2
Misono 6
Roberto's 3
Thalassa Restaurant
& Lounge 7

Bars & clubs 🍸
New Florida Club
& Casino 5

Safety

Although there's nowhere in the city centre that is considered a no-go area as such, petty theft does occur so don't flash valuables or walk down dark alleyways. Be particularly wary on the crowded Likoni Ferry. Also, by contrast to Nairobi and other towns where streets empty after 1800, on the coast, because of climatic conditions, many businesses close for a siesta in the middle of the day. As such the city stays awake longer, and the streets are still busy in the early evening and shops stay open later. Nevertheless, when they do close and people go home, do not wander the streets; take a taxi.

Background

The seasonal monsoon wind known as the Kazkazi blows down the coast from the northeast between October and April, as it has done for thousands of years, bringing trade to Mombasa. Between May and September this monsoon wind becomes the Kuzi, when it turns through 180° and blows back up the coast towards the Arabian Gulf. The Kazkazi and the Kuzi winds were the key to the foreign exploitation of Kenya and the rest of East Africa for thousands of years: the earliest known reference to Mombasa dates from AD 150 when the Roman geographer Ptolemy placed the town on his map of the world. Roman, Arabic and Far Eastern seafarers took advantage of the port and were regular visitors, and the port provided the town with the basis of economic development and it expanded steadily.

By the 16th century Mombasa was the most important town on the east coast of Africa, with a population estimated at 10,000. A wealthy settlement, it was captured by the Portuguese who were trying to break the Arab trading monopoly, particularly in the lucrative merchandising of spices. The town first fell to the Portuguese under the command of Dom Francisco in 1505. He ransacked the town and burnt it to the ground. It was rebuilt and returned to its former glory before it was ransacked again in 1528. However, the Portuguese did not stay and, having again looted and razed the town, they left.

The building of Fort Jesus in 1593, the stationing of a permanent garrison there and the installation of their own nominee from Malindi as Sultan, represented the first major attempt to secure Mombasa permanently. However, an uprising by the townspeople in 1631 led to the massacre of all the Portuguese. This led to yet another Portuguese fleet returning to try to recapture the town. In 1632 the leaders of the revolt retreated to the mainland, leaving the island to the Europeans. Portuguese rule lasted less than 100 years and they were expelled by the Omanis in 1698. The Omanis also held Zanzibar and were heavily involved in the slave trade. Their rule was supplanted by the British in 1873.

British efforts to stamp out the slave trade and anxiety about German presence in what is now Tanzania, led in 1896 to the beginning of the construction of the railway that was to link Uganda to the sea. The first rail was laid at Mombasa Railway Station on 13 May 1896 and the railhead reached Port Florence (Kisumu) on Lake Victoria on 20 December 1901, having ascended the Great Rift Valley western wall and crested the Mau Summit at some 2700 m above sea level, making it the highest metre-gauge railway in the world. One of the railway camps that was established before the construction of the line across the Rift Valley was at Nairobi. This town grew so rapidly that, by 1907, it was large enough for the administrative quarters to move inland. The climate of Nairobi was considered to be healthier than the coast and, because of its elevation, was too high for malaria-bearing mosquitoes to survive. Meanwhile, with the railway, the importance of the port of Mombasa increased rapidly.

In more recent history, Mombasa was the scene of a terrorist attack in 2002, when a hotel on one of the northern beaches, popular with Israelis and the only Israeli-owned hotel in the Mombasa area, was car bombed by suicide bombers, leaving 10 Kenyans and three Israeli holidaymakers dead. At the same time, an Israeli plane was fired at as it was taking off from Mombasa Airport.

Places in Mombasa

Fort Jesus
ⓘ *Nkrumah Rd, T041-222 5934, www.museums.or.ke, daily 0930-1800, US$9, children (under 16) US$4.50, guides are available for a tip or buy the information booklet at the entrance.*

Mombasa Old Town's major attraction, Fort Jesus dominates the entrance to the Old Harbour and is positioned so that, even when under siege, it was possible to bring supplies in from the sea. There's nothing to see as such in the harbour itself – there may be a few boats but long gone are the days when ocean-going *dhows* docked here. The Portuguese built the fort in 1593 to protect their trade route to India and their interests in East Africa, and it was designed by Italian architect Jao batisto Cairato. The fort was his last assignment as chief architect for Portuguese possession in the east. Today it's hailed as one of the best examples of 16th-century Portuguese military architecture. It's believed that, since the Portuguese sailed under the flag of the Order of Christ, Jesus was an obvious choice of name.

Despite this apparently secure position, the Portuguese lost possession of the fort in 1698 following an uprising by the townspeople who had formed an alliance with the Omanis. The fort had been under siege for 15 months before it finally fell. The British took

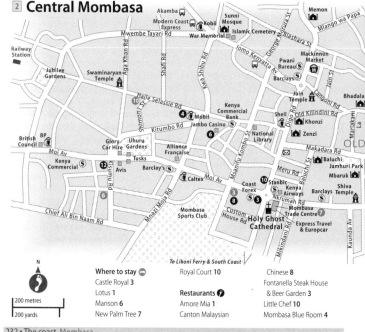

2 Central Mombasa

Where to stay	Royal Court 10	Chinese 8
Castle Royal 3		Fontanella Steak House
Lotus 1	**Restaurants**	& Beer Garden 3
Manson 6	Amore Mia 1	Little Chef 10
New Palm Tree 7	Canton Malaysian	Mombasa Blue Room 4

200 metres
200 yards

control of the fort in 1825 and it served as a prison from then until 1958, when it was restored and converted into a museum.

At the main gate are six cannons from the British ship the *Pegasus* and the German ship the *SS Konigsberg*. The walls of the fort are particularly impressive being nearly 3 m thick at the base, though the fort feels much smaller inside than it looks from the outside. Look out for what is effectively the oldest graffiti in Mombasa, inscribed by early Portuguese sentries. In the late 18th century the Omanis built a house in the northwest corner of the fort in what is known as the **San Felipe Bastion**. The Omanis also raised the walls of the fort, built turrets and equipped it with improved guns and other weaponry to increase its defensive capabilities. Since then, the Omani House has served various purposes, including being the prison warden's house, and today it houses a small exhibition of Omani jewellery and artefacts. You can climb up on to the flat roof for good views of Mombasa. Close to the Omani house you'll see one of the trolleys that used to be the mode of transport around town. Nearby is a ruined church, a huge well and cistern, and an excavated grave complete with skeleton. The eastern wall of the fort includes the Omani Audience Hall and the Passage of the Arches, a passage cut through the coral to give access to the sea.

The **museum** is situated in the southern part of the fort in the old barracks. Exhibits include a fair amount of pottery as well as other interesting odds and ends donated from private collections or dug up from sites along the coast. Also displayed are finds from the Portuguese frigate *Santo Antonio de Tanna*, which sank near the fort during the siege in 1698, and the far end of the hall is devoted to the fascinating culture and traditions of the nine coastal Mijikenda tribes, including a map of sacred forests. The diversity of the exhibits is a good illustration of the wide variety of influences that this coast was subject to over the centuries.

➡ **Mombasa maps**
1 Mombasa Island, page 230
2 **Central Mombasa, page 232**

Recoda **12**
Shehnai **6**

Old Town

While Mombasa's Old Town doesn't quite have the medieval charm of Lamu or Zanzibar, it's still an interesting area to wander around, preferably early morning or late afternoon (out of the midday sun). The Old Town is not in fact that old, as most buildings date from the end of the 19th century, though their foundations and some walls go back many centuries, and you'll get a clearer idea to the age of the town from its 20-odd mosques. The earliest settlement was probably around Mzizima Road, from where pottery dating from the 11th to 16th centuries has been discovered, but there's no other evidence left of this early settlement. However, the Old Town does have a few exceptional houses characteristic of Swahili coastal architecture, with fretwork balconies and ornately carved doors, which were once considered a reflection of the wealth and status of the family; the wealthier the merchant of the house the bigger and more elaborate his front door. Sadly, many of these old houses have been destroyed but there are now preservation orders on the remaining doors and balconies, so further losses should hopefully be prevented.

Leading from Fort Jesus into the Old Town, **Ndia Kuu (Great Way)** is one of the oldest roads in Mombasa; it existed during the Portuguese period and formed the main street of their settlement. Today some of the road's older houses have been restored and now serve as souvenir shops to visitors to the fort. Further north, **Mzizima Road** was the main route between the Portuguese town and the original Arab/Shirazi town. One of the older buildings on the island, **Leven House**, is located just off the top end of Ndia Kuu. It was built around the beginning of the 19th century and took its name from the *HMS Leven*, a British naval survey ship that visited Mombasa in 1824. Officers of this ship came ashore and were given permission to conduct their anti-slaving operations from the house. It was then occupied by missionaries and, later, was the headquarters of the British East Africa Company and a German Diplomatic Mission. In 1997 it was declared a National Monument and now houses the **Mombasa Old Town Conservation Offices (MOTCO)**. Among its most famous visitors were the explorers and missionaries Burton, Jackson and Ludwig Krapf. In front of Leven House are the Leven Steps – here a tunnel has been carved through to the water's edge, where there is a freshwater well. Burton actually mentions climbing up through this tunnel but you do not need to follow his example; there are steps nearby. Close to the Leven Steps and the Fish Market is **New Burhani Bohra Mosque**, with a tall minaret, built in 1902 as the third mosque to have been built on this site. On Mbarak Ali Hinawy Street, to the east of Ndia Kuu, close to the Old Port is **Mandhry Mosque**, built of coral rubble and finished with lime plaster with a white minaret. This is thought to be the oldest mosque on the island, dating from around 1570. Originally it had only one storey but another two storeys were added in 1988 and 1992 because of the need for a madrasa and women's prayer gallery. To the west of here, there are many more mosques and elderly houses in the cramped winding alleyways linking the Old Town to Digo Road, which are wonderfully lively, with market traders selling everything from *kangas* and cell phone accessories to baobab seeds and fried taro roots. It's not a very big area and most of these lanes eventually lead to a main road, so it's not easy to get lost. On Langoni Road, the **Jain Temple** has an intricate icing-sugar exterior in dozens of pastel shades. It was built in 1963 and was the first Jain Temple to be built outside India. Jainism is a Hindu religion closely related to Buddhism, and inside are ornamental painted figurines of deities in niches, each with a drain so they can be easily cleaned and rinsed off. You may be permitted to go inside (mornings only) but ensure you remove shoes and anything made of leather, as the Jain faith is strictly vegetarian.

Nkrumah Road and around

At the eastern end of Nkrumah Road near Fort Jesus is the administrative centre of the British colonial period. The main buildings surround **Treasury Square**, with the handsome **Treasury** itself on the east side, and a small park in the centre complete with well-tended flower beds and benches. To the east of the square on Nkrumah Road, the **Old Law Court** was built in 1902 and has a fine façade. It is now a library and gallery (0800-1800) where there are often local art exhibitions. Near the Law Court and also on Treasury Square is another building of approximately the same age. This was the **District Administration Headquarters**. The roof is tiled and there is a first-floor balcony.

Proceeding west from Treasury Square, on the left is the **Anglican Cathedral**, built in 1903 and with a plaque to mark 150 years of Christianity in Mombasa, celebrated in 1994.

The cathedral itself is a mixture of European and Mediterranean influences, whitewashed with Moorish arches, slender windows, a dome reminiscent of an Islamic mosque, with a cross, and two smaller towers topped by crosses. On the right, just behind the main road and set in lovely gardens with ponds, is the spectacular, modern, Hindu **Shiva Temple**, which is topped with a gold spire and guarded by statues of lions and the Hindu god Ganesh with its elephant head.

Before the intersection with Moi Avenue is the **Holy Ghost Cathedral**, an elegant structure of concrete rendered in grey cement. Cool and airy inside, it has a fine curved ceiling of cream and blue, *fleur de lis* designs and stained-glass windows.

Moi Avenue and around

Mombasa's main road is a two-lane carriageway, about 4 km long that runs from east to west from Digo Road to the port area at Kilindini. Along it are many curio shops and tour operator offices. The most striking building on Moi Avenue is the **Castle Royal Hotel** (see Where to stay, page 236), to the west of the Holy Ghost Cathedral. It was built in 1909 and was completely restored in 2005 after lying derelict for many years. It has a four-storey startlingly white façade and a street-side terrace bar that used to entertain early settlers – it does again today and is a pleasant place from which to watch the comings and goings along Moi Avenue, despite the addition of searing traffic fumes. A little further east, the **Tusks** were built in 1952 to commemorate a visit by Queen Elizabeth (Princess Elizabeth as she was then). They are actually rather disappointing close up and these days are used as an informal notice board to paste fly-posters.

Near the Tusks are the 1-ha **Uhuru Gardens**, which have some handsome trees, a fountain (not working), a café and a brass cannon worn smooth from serving as a makeshift seat. They were established in 1963 to commemorate Kenya's Independence ('Uhuru' means freedom) and today serve as a popular respite area for office workers at lunchtime.

To the north of Moi Avenue, on the corner of Haile Selassie and Aga Khan, is the **Swaminaryan Temple**, an exotic confection in powder blue and pink. In front of the Railway Station are the neglected **Jubilee Gardens**, which were laid out to mark the 60th anniversary of Queen Victoria's reign in 1897. Finally, there is the **War Memorial** on Jomo Kenyatta near the bus company offices, with bronze statues dedicated to the African and Arab soldiers who served with the East African Rifles in the First World War.

Kizingo

Kizingo area, in the southern part of the island around the lighthouse and **Mombasa Golf Club**, is considered to be one of the prime residential areas of the city. It has some very fine late 19th-century buildings whose style has been called **Coast Colonial**. These buildings are spacious and airy with wide balconies and shutters designed to take advantage of every breeze. Hardwoods were used and many of the building materials were imported from Europe and Asia. Along Mama Ngina Drive it is possible to look over the cliffs that rise above Kilindini Channel and out towards the sea.

Mbaraki

To the south of the island at Mbaraki, just to the west of the Likoni Ferry roundabout, is the **Mbaraki Pillar**, which is an 8-m-tall coral stone hollow pillar that is tapered and leans at a slight angle and stands next to a small mosque, which was rebuilt in 1988. It's thought to be about 300 years old but not much is known about it. Theories suggest it might be a tomb, or a house built for a powerful spirit, or even a navigational mark and lighthouse. Old

Portuguese maps show that there was an anchorage at the Mbaraki Creek and, perhaps, the pillar was a shipping mark indicating the entrance and, as it has vertical window slits on all sides, maybe a lantern was placed at the top.

Nyali

Nyali is on the mainland, 8 km northwest of the city centre across the **New Nyali Bridge**, which was built in 2002 to replace an older one; along with the Makupa and Kipevu causeways it is one of the three road crossings on to the island. It was in this area that newly freed slaves settled, and a bell tower is erected in their memory, which can be seen at the junction of the main road north and Nyali Road. Today, Nyali is one of the wealthier suburbs of Mombasa, dominated by large houses where many of Mombasa's expat community live. There are a number of good restaurants here, including the excellent **Tamarind**, as well as the **Nyali Cinemax Centre** and the **Nyali Nakumatt Shopping Centre**, which has a number of shops, restaurants and a very large branch of **Nakumatt** supermarket. Nyali marks the beginning of the main coast road and its strip of north coast hotels and restaurants. ▸▸ *For listings from Nyali northwards, see page 274-288.*

◉ Mombasa listings

For sleeping and eating price codes and other relevant information, see pages 20-24.

● Where to stay

Mombasa *p228, maps p230 and p232*
There is little decent accommodation in Mombasa and very little reason to stay in the city itself. It is much better to stay at a far more attractive beach hotel and visit Mombasa Old Town for the day. For the options closest to Mombasa Island, consider Nyali (see Where to stay, page 274), which is 8 km to the northwest and can easily be reached by public transport.
$$$ Castle Royal Hotel, Moi Av, T041-222 2682, www.castlemsa.com. Lovely white colonial hotel (see page 235) with 60 a/c rooms on 4 floors, nice modern furniture, cool tiled floors, satellite TV, soundproofing and the front ones have balconies. Rates include a generous and varied buffet breakfast and there's a very good terrace restaurant and bar (see Restaurants, below). The best place to stay in the city centre.
$$$ Tamarind Village, adjacent to the Tamarind Restaurant, Cement Silo Rd, Nyali, T041-447 4600, www.tamarind.co.ke. This is a collection of 45 1- to 3-bedroom

self-catering apartments (you can also order food from the restaurant) in a Swahili-style whitewashed building with turrets and curved archways in a lovely waterside setting, with 2 swimming pools, a squash court, gym and pleasant gardens. Each spacious, light apartment has Swahili furnishings, a/c, kitchenette, veranda and satellite TV.
$$ Lotus, Cathedral Lane off Nkrumah Rd, close to Fort Jesus, T041-231 3207, www. lotushotelkenya.com. Good location for the Old Town and Fort Jesus, this has simple clean and quiet rooms with a/c and hot water, a charming central courtyard with wood panels, Oriental arches and tropical plants. There's a relaxed bar with outside tables, and the restaurant serves Western and Indian dishes.
$$ Royal Court Hotel, Haile Selassie Rd, T041-222 3379, www.royalcourtmombasa. co.ke. With a spacious lobby decorated in Swahili style, this 8-storey modern hotel has 42 a/c rooms with satellite TV, Wi-Fi and balconies. It is predominantly aimed at business people but has some of the best standards in the city centre and is good value from US$80 a double. Good rooftop bar/restaurant (see Restaurants, below),

downstairs bar and casino, and a swimming pool on the roof.

$ Manson Hotel, Kisumu Rd, T041-222 2419, www.mansonhotel.com. Located in a tall brick block in a fairly quiet residential area, the 80 rooms have fans, or pay a little more for a/c, balconies, hot water and mosquito nets, but they are old-fashioned and rather dark. Restaurant, TV lounge with pool table, reasonable value and a cooked breakfast is included.

$ New Palm Tree Hotel, Nkrumah Rd, T0736-489 197, www.newpalmtreehotel. com. Rather striking whitewashed old building, reception area has a high ceiling and gallery with comfy sofas, which is a welcome retreat from the busy streets, but the rooms with fan, fridge and TV are very simple and tatty with intermittent hot water. However, there's an internet café, a relaxed bar and restaurant, which serves reasonable local and international food, and it's a short walk to Fort Jesus.

🍴 Restaurants

Mombasa *p228, maps p230 and p232*
In contrast to the dearth of hotels in Mombasa city centre, there is a good selection of places to eat that are accessible by taxi from the nearest beach hotels on the north coast. For cheap eats, there are numerous canteens around the city centre that sell sausage or chicken and chips, samosas and pies, especially popular during the day with office workers. Also look out for the outdoor stalls selling Swahili snacks in the Old Town, along Haile Selassie Rd, and to the southeast of the island along Mama Ngina Dr. At these you might get egg chapatti, as the name suggests, a chapatti cooked with an egg inside it, *kachri bateta*, a potato, tomato, chutney and chilli mix, and *mshikaki*, grilled beef or mutton kebabs. Also look out for fresh coconut juice.

$$$ Hunter's Steak House, Mukamani Rd, near the **Tamarind**, Nyali, T041-231 1156. Open 1200-1500, 1800-late, closed Tue. Secluded international restaurant popular with Nyali's expats, in a rather attractive Mediterranean style with a bar and tables arranged around a well-manicured courtyard, offering a wide variety of seafood and poultry dishes, but best known for its mouth-watering steaks and speciality sauces.

$$$ Roberto's, Nyali Cinemax, Nyali, T0705-185 704, www.robertosmombasa.com. 1030-1500, 1800-2300. Traditional Italian trattoria with murals of Italian village life on the walls and one of the most extensive Italian wine lists in Kenya. The long menu uses imported ingredients and features Italian classic cuisine and is strong on interesting fish dishes, jumbo prawns and wood-fired pizzas. Desserts naturally include tiramisu. They also run a separate ice cream parlour in the complex.

$$$ Shehnai, Fatemi House, Maungano St, T041-222 4801, www.restaurantshehnai.com. 1200-1400, 1900-2230, closed Mon. Superb cuisine, specialities are *mughlai* and tandoori dishes, very professionally run; the quality and taste of food is paramount, elegant furniture, soothing music, pleasant decor, although no alcohol, but there is a terrace bar at the **Jambo Casino** a few doors along if you want to have a drink before or after.

$$$ Tamarind, Cement Silo Rd, Nyali, T041-447 1747, www.tamarind.co.ke. 1230-1430, 1900-2230. This beautiful restaurant has marvellous views overlooking a creek that flows into the ocean, and the Moorish design of the building is well thought out, cool and spacious with high arches, while the food and service are both excellent. It specializes in seafood. It also offers cruises around Tudor Creek on the *Nawalikher dhow*, where you can sip *dawa* cocktails (vodka, lime, honey and crushed ice) and eat lobster, whilst watching the moon rise over Mombasa Old Town and Fort Jesus, and listening to the strains of a traditional Swahili band. The set meals on the *dhow* include seafood hors d'oeuvres to start, followed by grilled lobster or seafood in coconut sauce. There are 2 sailings a day

(Mon-Sat) for lunch (1300-1500; US$40) and dinner (1830-2230; US$70). Reservations essential. This is a memorable eating experience and thoroughly recommended for any visitor to the coast.

$$$-$$ Misono, at the Nakumatt Shopping Centre, Nyali, T041-471 454. Mon-Sat 1230-1430, 1900-2230. Restaurant offering reasonably priced and authentic sushi, sashimi and tepanyaki dishes, the chefs are well trained and offer an authentic 'show' while cooking, the decor has a Japanese feel and diners receive a Japanese greeting at the door accompanied by the sound of a 'bong'.

$$$-$$ Thalassa Restaurant & Lounge, just to the north of New Nyali Bridge, T041-222 7977, www.thalassa-mombasa. com. 1000-2300. Fabulous views over Tudor Creek from this multi-terraced and stylishly decorated venue set in tropical gardens, with a restaurant on a Moorish-style deck with ocean breezes, a bar and lounge which surrounds a swimming pool, ideal for a lunchtime dip. Varied menu from seafood platters to wood-fired pizzas, plus a small selection of Lebanese dishes and a French winelist. A DJ plays in the evening and it stays open after the restaurant closes for dancing.

$$ Canton Malaysian Chinese, in the car park behind the Castle Royal Hotel, T041-222 7977, www.cantonmalay.com. 1100-2300. An upstairs formal a/c restaurant with typical red lantern-style decor, bar with some wine and spirits, authentic food including crispy duck with pancakes and deep-fried crab claws, good choices for vegetarians and lychees for dessert.

$$ Galaxy Chinese Restaurant, Mama Ngina Dr, next door to the Florida Club & Casino, T0726-894 002. Open 1100-1430, 1800-2300. Popular Chinese restaurant – probably one of the best in town – with especially good seafood dishes including excellent ginger crab and a good range of 'sizzling' dishes. Good service, refreshing a/c and great ocean views through a glass wall. There's another branch at Diani Beach.

$$ La Veranda, Mwea Tabere St, behind the Nakumatt Shopping Centre, Nyali, T0733-774 436. Open 0900-late. Good traditional Italian restaurant and bar, home-made pasta with a variety of sauces, pizza oven, homely atmosphere, wide range of drinks including Italian wines.

$$ Rooftop Restaurant, in the Royal Court Hotel, see Where to stay, page 236. Open 1130-1430, 1730-2300. Balcony restaurant with great views of Mombasa's rooftops and pleasant decor of green plants and blue and white linen, with a good range of continental dishes, predominately Italian, plus some creamy Indian curries and tandoori dishes. The casino and bar on the ground floor of the hotel is open until 0600.

$$-$ Bollywood Bites, Nyali Cinemax, Nyali, T041-470 000. Mon-Sat 1800-2300, Sun 1200-1500, 1800-2300. Authentic vegetarian Indian cuisine, modern restaurant decorated in a Bollywood theme, a wide selection of mughlai and tandoori dishes, specialities include Indian ice cream, kulfi, Indian milkshake, faluda, and freshly squeezed juice. Go and see a Bollywood movie at the cinema and eat here for a rather different night out.

$$-$ Castle Royal Hotel, see Where to stay, page 236. Open 0600-1000, 1230-1500, 1900-2300, all day for snacks and drinks. Lovely colonial terrace but rather unfortunately it looks straight at the traffic on Moi Av. Nevertheless a social place for a cold Tusker beer and the food is very good and includes steaks and grills, some pasta, seafood platters for 2, sandwiches and ice cream.

$ Amore Mia, opposite the central police station on Makadara Rd. 0800-1800. Very simple canteen that you wouldn't know was there except for the signboard on the pavement and a few outside tables. They sell snacks, including 18 flavours of ice cream, good coffee, pastries, puddings and delicious skewers of chicken tikka that are grilled over charcoal right on the street and are accompanied by carrot and cabbage salad.

$ Fontanella Steak House & Beer Garden, corner of Moi Av and Digo Rd. Mon-Sat 0900-2200. Nice relaxing courtyard workers' café off the street surrounded by plants, red and white checked tablecloths, attentive service, popular meeting place, very large menu with daily specials, everything from chicken masala, *nyama choma* and fried liver to simple fare such as ice cream, fresh juice and plenty of cold beer.

$ Little Chef, Digo Rd. 0700-2300. Centrally located, very busy canteen with plastic tables serving African food, such as chicken or beef stew with *ugali*, plus burgers, chicken and chips, breezy upstairs balcony bar. You may have to queue at lunchtime.

$ Mombasa Blue Room Restaurant, Haile Selassie Rd, T041-222 4021, www.blueroom online.com. 0900-2200. Established in 1952, this excellent bright, clean and bustling cafeteria seats over 140 people and is something of a Mombasa institution. A family-run, a/c self-service restaurant, it offers Indian snacks, such as samosas, bhajia, kebabs, as well as fish and chips, chicken, burgers and pizzas, and everything is home-made. The delicious ice cream is made with filtered water; in fact they produce ice cream that is suitable for people with diabetes. It also doubles up as a DVD hire shop and has the nicest and quickest internet café in town. Popular with locals and a good place to meet other travellers.

$ Recoda, Moi Av near the Tusks, T041-222 3629. Open 1830-2400. This canteen serves traditional Swahili cuisine and is one of the oldest restaurants in Mombasa (it opened in 1942). The food is basic but cheap with large portions, and it's only open in the evenings and closed during Ramadan. The menu features dishes such as fish with coconut rice and puréed beans, *mahamri* (a staple bread) and *mshikaki* (a type of kebab).

Bars and clubs

Mombasa *p228, maps p230 and p232*
New Florida Club and Casino, Mama Ngina Dr, T041-220 9036, www.floridaclubskenya. com. Restaurant 1000-2400, nightclub from 2100, casino and bars 24 hrs. A branch of Nairobi's raucous Florida clubs, in huge premises, with several bars and dance floors, on the waterfront with ocean views, cabaret live shows at midnight, also casino and restaurant serving *nyama choma* and other snacks. It's popular but it can get crowded so watch your valuables and be aware that it's working girls' territory.

Entertainment

Mombasa *p228, maps p230 and p232*
Golden Key Casino, at the **Tamarind Restaurant**, Nyali, T041-447 1071, www. tamarind.co.ke. 1500-0500. Mombasa's most sophisticated and elegant casino is in a lovely setting on the roof of the restaurant with great night-time views of Mombasa Island from the terrace, with a full range of gaming tables and slot machines, cocktails and snacks.

Nyali Cinemax, located in Nyali opposite Ratna Sq, T041-447 0000, www.nyali cinemax.com. This is an ultra-modern a/c cinema that plays the latest Hollywood and Bollywood releases from around 1400. There are also a couple of restaurants here (listed above), the **Hollywood Bowl**, a 10-pin bowling alley, Mon-Fri 1700-2200, Sat 1200-2400, Sun 1000-2300, and **CasinoMax**, daily 0900-0600. There's also a **Nakumatt** supermarket here.

Shopping

Mombasa *p228, maps p230 and p232*
The souvenirs that you will find in Mombasa are wooden carvings, including Makonde carvings from Tanzania, soapstone carvings and chess sets, baskets, batiks and jewellery. There are lots of curio shops and stalls

around the junction of Digo Rd and Jomo Kenyatta Av; along Moi Av around the Tusks and Castle Royal Hotel; and around Fort Jesus. For *kikois*, *kangas* and other fabrics go to Biashara St, which runs off Digo Rd parallel to Jomo Kenyatta Av. The Indian tailors here can also make up clothes to order from the cloth.

Markets
Mackinnon Market is a lively, bustling and colourful market on Digo Rd and was named after Dr W Mackinnon, a colonial administrator at the turn of the 20th century. The main section of the market is situated in an enormous shed but numerous stalls have spilled out on to the streets. Apart from an excellent range of exotic fresh fruit and vegetables, you will be able to buy baskets, jewellery and other souvenirs. If you are prepared to haggle and bargain in a good-natured manner, you can usually bring the price down quite considerably.

Shopping centres
There are 3 Nakumatts in Mombasa, Mon-Fri 0830-1800, Sat 0900-1700, Sun 1000-1600: **Nakumatt Likoni**, to the south of the island near the Likoni Ferry, also has other shops, ATMs and cafés; **Nyali Nakumatt Shopping Centre**, on the main B8 road on the way to the north coast, has a number of other shops, ATMs, internet café and restaurants and is currently being extended into Mombasa's largest shopping mall, **The City Mall**; and, again in Nyali, there's one at the **Nyali Cinemax** (see Entertainment, above) – this branch is open 24 hrs.

Out of town on the road to the airport is the **Akamba Handicraft Cooperative**, off Port-Reitz Rd, Changamwe, T041-343 2241, www.akambahandicraftcoop.com, 0800-1730. This sells a vast range of curios from animal statues and decorated spoons to walking sticks and wooden bowls. It was established in 1963 with 100 carvers and now promotes and distributes the work of about 3000 carvers. They are presently establishing a nursery of fast-growing neem wood trees to provide renewable resources of wood for the carvers (ebony now is very rare). The showroom is a popular stop for tourists as they are bussed in and out of the airport, or on city tours; you can watch the carvers at work, and reasonably low prices are fixed, with 80% going to the carver, while 20% goes to the cooperative.

⏾ What to do

Mombasa *p228, maps p230 and p232*
Sports clubs
Mombasa Golf Club, Mama Nginga Dr, T041-222 8531, www.mombasagolfclub.com. This 9-hole course was established in 1911 and sits on top of coral cliffs with good ocean views. Day membership is available, and clubs and caddies can be hired.
Mombasa Sports Club, Mnazi Moji Rd, T041-222 4226, www.mombasasportsclub.co.ke. There's an old colonial saying that you can't put more than 3 Englishmen in a foreign country without them forming a club; this is the country's oldest sporting club, established in 1896, the same year the building of the Uganda Railway started; it hosted celebrations of Queen Victoria's Jubilee in 1897. There are facilities here for cricket, squash, tennis, basketball and football, among other sports, and there's a gym.

Tour operators
Mombasa's tour operators act as booking agents for the beach hotels and most can also organize day or overnight safaris to the parks close to the coast such as Tsavo or Shimba Hills, as well as tours of the city and other local attractions. Otherwise, tours can be arranged from the hotels to the north and south of Mombasa, which have arrangements with one of these tour operators. Prices vary depending on where the pickup is and the number of people in the vehicle, but expect to pay in the region of US$50 for a ½-day city tour, US$100 combined with lunch on the Tamarind Dhow

(see page 237), US$110 for a day trip up to Malindi and the Gedi Ruins, and US$180 for a day trip to Tsavo East. Some can also book car hire, train tickets and transfers to the beach. For more Mombasa-based tour operators, visit **Kenya Association of Tour Operators**, www.katokenya.org.

African Quest Safaris, Palli House, Nyerere Rd, T041-231 6501, www.africanquest.co.ke. City tours and day trips to attractions on the north coast, plus longer safaris.

African Route Safaris, 2nd floor, Old Cannon Towers, Moi Av, T041-223 0322, www.africanroutesafaris.com. Offers day tours, 1- to 2-night safaris to Tsavo East and 3-night trips to Tsavo and Amboseli.

Distance Tours, next to the Tusks, Moi Av, T0724-956 579, www.distancetours.com. 1- to 3-day safaris to Tsavo and longer 5- to 6-day safaris from Mombasa to Tsavo, Masai Mara and Amboseli.

Express Travel, Mombasa Trade Centre, Nkrumah Rd, T041-222 8083, www.express travel.co.ke. General travel agent and agent for Europcar. They can organize tailor-made road and flying safaris for a minimum of 2 people.

Kenya One Tours, Nkrumah Rd, T041-202 2311, www.kenyaonetours.com. Good all-round operator offering safaris across the country, plus day trips from Mombasa, overnight safaris to Tsavo and Shimba Hills and fly-in safaris from Mombasa to the Masai Mara.

Mombasa Kenya Tours & Safaris, Nyali Bridge Rd, T0789-586 512, www.mombasa kenyatoursandsafaris.com. City and Mombasa By Night tours, Malindi and Gedi Ruins, and 2- to 3-day Tsavo East and West safaris.

Natural World Mombasa Safaris, Jeneby House, Moi Av, T041-231 2204, www.natural toursandsafaris.com. City tour, Tsavo East day tour, combined Tsavo East, Tsavo West and Amboseli 4-day safaris, and fly-in Masai Mara trips.

Southern Cross Safaris, Nyali Bridge Rd, T020-243 4600, www.southerncrosssafaris. com. Established in 1957, a good all-round

operator with an extensive fleet of vehicles which runs a daily trip to its own camp in Tsavo East, **Satao Camp** (see Where to stay, page 214), and is a specialist for safaris for disabled clients and agents for beach resorts.

Special Lofty Safaris, Nkrumah Rd, T041-222 0241, www.lofty-tours.com. City tours, Mombasa by night tours, half-day trips to Shimba Hills, and 1- to 3-day safaris to Tsavo.

Transport

Mombasa *p228, maps p230 and p232*
Air
Moi International Airport is 10 km west of the city centre on the mainland, T041-343 3211, www.kenyaairports.co.ke. See page 229 for further details, including transport to and from the airport. There are several daily flights between **Nairobi** and Mombasa, which take 1 hr and cost from US$70 1-way, with **Air Kenya**, **Fly 540** and **Kenya Airways**. All tickets can be bought online or directly from desks at the airport. From Nairobi, there are connections to the other destinations in Kenya, see page 79 for details. For more information on international airlines serving Mombasa, see Essentials, page 15.

In addition to Nairobi–Mombasa flights, **Fly 540** has at least 2 daily flights to and from Mombasa and **Malindi** (15 mins) from US$40 1 way, 1 daily flight to and from **Lamu** (45 mins) from US$55 1 way, and 1 daily flight to and from **Zanzibar** in Tanzania (40 mins), which, from US$80 1 way, is especially good value. **Kenya Airways** code shares with Tanzania's **Precision Air**, and has 5 flights a week to and from Mombasa and **Zanzibar**, where there are connections to **Dar es Salaam**. **Mombasa Air Safari** uses small planes and operates a daily scheduled 'Beach to Bush' service from Mombasa, and the airstrip at Diani Beach to **Amboseli**, **Tsavo**, and the **Masai Mara**. It also has daily scheduled flights to **Malindi** and **Lamu**.

Airline offices **Air Kenya**, Diani Airport, T020-391 6000, www.airkenya.com. **Fly 540**, Moi International Airport, T041-2000 5644, www.fly540.com. **Kenya Airways**, Moi International Airport, T041-212 5529, town office, Electricity House, Nkrumah Rd, T041-212 5201-6, www.kenya-airways.com. **Mombasa Air Safari**, Moi International Airport, T041-343 3061, www.mombasaairsafari.com.

Bus
On all buses seats can now be booked and there is no overcrowding with standing passengers anymore. There are lots of bus companies that go to **Nairobi** and their kiosks are on Jomo Kenyatta Av opposite the Islamic Cemetery and near the market. They usually leave early morning and evening, take 9-11 hrs and cost about US$12. **Akamba Bus**, T041-249 0269, www.akambabus.com, is on Jomo Kenyatta Av and their buses depart at 0900 and 2100. Also try **Modern Coast Express**, next to the Kobil petrol station, just south of Akamba, T0729-403 589, www.moderncoastexpress. com. Their Nairobi buses depart in the morning at 1000 and 1030. Buses and *matatus* depart for **Malindi** frequently throughout the day and take about 1½ hrs. They leave Mombasa when full from Abdel Nasser Rd outside the New People's Hotel. There are daily buses to **Lamu**, which also pick up in **Malindi**, 7 hrs, US$10, and include **Pwani Tawakal Bus**, Abdel Nasser Rd, T0722-550 111, which has 3 daily departures from Mombasa to Lamu at 0700, 0930 and 1100, and **Tahmeed Bus**, opposite, T0710-497 979, which depart at 0830 and 1030. The bus will take you to the Mokowe Jetty on the mainland from where you get a ferry across to Lamu (see page 292).

Heading south to **Tanzania**, **Scandinavia Express** is a very good Tanzanian bus company, Arrow Plaza, Jomo Kenyatta Av, T041-490 975, www.scandinaviagroup.com. It runs a daily service at 0800, which takes about 4 hrs to **Tanga**, US$10 and 10 hrs to **Dar es Salaam**, US$18. Their identical daily

service in the opposite direction departs Dar es Salaam at 0800 and arrives in Mombasa at 1800. Other buses to Tanzania also go from Jomo Kenyatta Av. The border is at **Lunga Lunga**, see page 249 for border-crossing information. If not going all the way to Dar es Salaam, then from Tanga there are bus connections on to **Moshi** and **Arusha**.

Car hire
Most of the tour operators listed above can organize car hire.
Avis, airport, T0736-750 006, Moi Av near the Tusks, T041-222 0465, www.avis.com.
Europcar, **Express Travel**, Mombasa Trade Centre, Nkrumah Rd, T041-222 8083, www. expresstravel.co.ke,www.europcar.com.
Glory Car Hire, Moi Av near the Tusks, T041-231 3564, www.glorykenya.com. Also has a branch at Diani Beach.

Ferry
The **Likoni Ferry** docks at the southeast of the island. The 2 ferries cross simultaneously and depart every 15 mins during the day and every hour 1000-0500. They take about 7 mins and are free for pedestrians and cyclists and US$2 for cars. There is always a throng of people waiting to board or disembark from the boat – keep your hands tightly on your possessions and beware of pickpockets and thieves (although if you are in a taxi, you don't need to get out). *Matatus* to the ferry leave from outside the post office on Digo Rd – ask for Likoni. In fact it is possible to get a *matatu* to the Likoni ferry from just about anywhere in the city even if the taxi drivers tell you otherwise. When the ferry docks, the *matatus* for Ukunda (the turn-off to Diani Beach) are located at the top of the slipway from the ferry.

Train
Mombasa Railway Station, T041-433 211, is at the end of Haile Selassie Av at Jubilee Sq. There are services 3 times a week between Mombasa and **Nairobi**. See box, page 18 for full details.

Mombasa *p228, maps p230 and p232*
Cultural centres Alliance Française, Freed Building, Moi Av, T041-222 5048, www.afkenya.or.ke. As well as a library and language courses, they also host art and photographic exhibitions. **British Council**, Jubilee Insurance Building, Moi Av just west of the Tusks, T041-222 3076, www.britishcouncil.org. **Immigration** Mama Ngina Rd next to the police station, T041-

231 1745, www.immigration.go.ke.
Medical services Coast Provincial General Hospital, Kisauni Rd, T041-231 4201. The better option are the private hospitals: **Aga Khan Hospital**, Vanga Rd, T041-222 7710, www.agakhanhospitals.org, or **Mombasa Hospital**, Mama Ngina Rd, T041-231 2191, www.mombasahospital.com, which is the largest and best private hospital on the coast. There are plenty of well-stocked pharmacies in the city centre.

South of Mombasa

The beaches on the south coast are some of the best in the world. The sand – coral that has been pounded by the waves over the centuries – is fine and very white. There are a few well-developed areas, but you don't need to go far to find a quiet spot. The most popular beach is Diani – it is also the most built up and, not surprisingly, is now the most expensive. However, most of the buildings are well designed and local materials have been used so they do not intrude too much. The hotels all have their own restaurants and bars, and most of them arrange regular evening entertainment, such as traditional African dancers and singers or acrobats. They also organize watersports and day trips to sights in the region, including Mombasa city tour, and day trips to Wasini Island and the Kisite-Mpunguti Marine Park, as well as longer overnight safaris to some of the game parks, so it is feasible to stay in one hotel for your entire holiday and take organized local excursions from there. ▶▶ *For listings, see pages 250-259.*

Arriving on the south coast

Once across the Likoni Ferry, the A14, the main Kenya–Tanzania coastal road, heads south on a reasonably good tarred surface and all the turn-offs are well signposted. It runs about 300 m parallel to the coast, although you cannot see the sea from the road. The turn-off to **Tiwi Beach** is about 20 km south of the ferry and the turn-off to Diani Beach is at **Ukunda**, about 25 km. There are plenty of *matatus* running up and down between the township of Likoni where the ferry docks and Ukunda, but these are less frequent south of Ukunda. About 12 km from Likoni is the turn-off to the right to **Kwale** and the **Shimba Hills National Reserve** and **Mwaluganje Elephant Sanctuary**.

Likoni and Shelley Beach → *Colour map 2, C1. Phone code: 040.*

Likoni is a sprawling (and none too clean, with piles of unsightly rubbish everywhere) township on the southern side of the Likoni Ferry and is effectively a creek-side suburb of Mombasa. The road that leads from the ferry is lined with market stalls. **Shelley Beach**, just to the east of the ferry, is the closest beach to Mombasa and can be visited for a day trip if you are staying in the town and are not too bothered by the proximity of the urban sprawl. However, it is narrow and uninviting, and swimming here can be problematic due to excessive seaweed and there is the need to watch carefully over your belongings. There is little coastal development between Shelley Beach and Tiwi Beach.

Tiwi Beach is about 20 km from the Likoni Ferry, 6 km before the Diani Beach turn-off, and 3 km off the main coastal road down a very bumpy track (turn left at the supermarket). Never walk down this road, as muggings can occur. This beach is wider than that at Shelley but not as nice as Diani and, for a number of years, was particularly popular with families and budget travellers. Its popularity has waned in recent years, however, in favour of the hotels at Diani, and **Twiga Lodge**, once a firm favourite on the backpacker circuit through East Africa, is a shadow of its former self.

However, the beach is ideal for children; the waves are smaller than those at Diani, and hundreds of rock pools are exposed when the tide is out, all with plenty of marine life in them. There is also some quite good snorkelling here and it is possible to scuba dive too, although it is prone to large amounts of seaweed in April and May. If you walk up the beach in the direction of Shelley Beach for about 1.5 km you come to the '**Pool of Africa**', a rock pool in the shape of the African continent where you can swim, and even dive through a small tunnel to another pool, aptly named **Madagascar**. Before you go exploring on the beach and reef, check up on the tides (local people will be able to advise) and set out with plenty of time. It is very easy to get cut off when the tide comes in and it turns quite rapidly. Also be sure you have a good pair of thick rubber-soled shoes to protect your feet against the coral and sea urchins. At the south of the beach is the estuary of the Mwachema River and, beyond, the beginning of expansive Diani Beach. It is possible to walk to Diani Beach at low tide but, again, it is important to ensure you check the times of the tides to avoid getting stranded.

The beach itself is the longest commercially used beach in Kenya, with about 20 km of dazzling white sand, coconut trees, clear sea and a coral reef that is exposed at low tide.

① **South coast**

→ **South coast beaches**
1 South coast, page 244
2 Diani Beach, page 246

Where to stay
Amani Tiwi Beach Resort 8
Betty's Camp 1
Coral Cove Cottages 5
Funzi Keys 7
Maweni & Capricho Beach Cottages 4
Msambweni Beach House 11
Mwazaro Mangrove Lodge 9
Pemba Channel Lodge 10
Sable Bandas 13
Sand Island Beach 14
Sands at Chale Island 2
SheShe Baharini 6
Shimba Lodge 15
Shimoni Bandas 3
Shimoni Reef Lodge 12
Travellers Mwaluganje Elephant Camp 16
Twiga Lodge 17

It has acquired a whole string of hotels over the years, although most of these have been sensitively built, often out of thatch and local materials. Diani is the place to come if you want a traditional beach holiday; the climate and scenery are marvellous, accommodation and food is of a very high standard, and activities on offer include windsurfing, kitesurfing, snorkelling, scuba-diving and trips on glass-bottomed boats; there is the additional option of combining time on the beach with a safari to one of the closer national parks and game reserves inland. A number of shopping centres have mushroomed on the 'strip' geared towards tourists, as well as numerous informal souvenir stalls, and other facilities include the golf course and casino at the Leisure Lodge and a number of independent restaurants and nightclubs outside the confines of the resorts. Many of the resorts have also added wellness spas and/or fitness facilities to their ever-growing list of things to do.

Diani is mostly geared to big-spending package tourists from Europe, which generates some disadvantages: intrusive beach touts or 'beach boys' hound visitors, trying to sell curios, camel rides along the beach or trips on glass-bottomed boats, as well as offering themselves as models for photos (some of the Masai who come round are not Masai at all but are of other tribes). Most of the goods are poor quality and hugely overpriced, although you can try bargaining the quoted prices down. Additionally, over the years, Diani has gained a reputation as a pick-up place for European female tourists looking for sex with Kenyan men. Even if no payment for 'company' is exchanged, there are many hopeful young men in the area that seek to befriend a European woman in the hope of a passage to Europe.

Arriving at Diani Beach

The turn-off to Diani is at **Ukunda** village, 25 km south of the Likoni Ferry. After about 1 km there is a T-junction for the road that runs along the back of the resorts on the beach, commonly referred to as the 'Diani strip'; a handful of resorts are to the left, while all the others are to the right. Depending on your final destination, a taxi from Mombasa's Moi International Airport or railway station should cost in the region of US$50-60 for 4-6 people, which includes the ferry crossing. Most of the large resorts at Diani will also collect you, and transfers are usually included in package holiday rates. There is an airstrip at Ukunda, which serves some scheduled flights, including a direct flight to and from Nairobi with **Air Kenya**, although the road trip by taxi is easy enough and shouldn't take more than an hour from Mombasa's Moi International Airport. *Matatus* run frequently from Likoni to Ukunda and cost little more than US$1, though they are crowded so aren't the easiest option with luggage. At the junction in Ukunda, you need to swap *matatus* to another going up and down the beach road. There is also a large fleet of brightly coloured tuk-tuks operating between Ukunda and all along the beach road; you simply flag them down, if the drivers themselves don't drive right up to you. These cost little more than a US$1 for any journey and take up to 3 people. The tuk-tuks have generally replaced the need for car hire here. Rather amusingly, the Diani tuk-tuks have wobbly arms and hands that wave at you as they drive along and some even have giant hats on their roof. Many of the resorts rent out bikes.

Around Diani Beach

At the far north of Diani Beach, just past the **Indian Ocean Beach Club**, is the **Kongo Mosque** (also known as the Diani Persian Mosque). It is rather a strange place, very run-down but not really a ruin, and still has some ritual significance. The mosque is believed to date from the 15th century and is the only remaining building from a settlement of the

Shirazi people who used to live here. There are a number of entrances and you should be able to push one of the doors open and have a look inside.

Jadini Forest ① *T0711-479 453, www.colobustrust.org, Mon-Sat 0800-1300, 1400-1700, US$7.50, children under 12 free*, is a small patch of the forest that straddles the main beach road and used to cover the whole of this coastal area. It is great for birdwatching, and many species of butterflies occupy the clutches of hardwood trees, but it's especially good for spotting primates. The forest is home to troops of baboon, a large population of vervet monkey and the endangered Angolan black and white colobus monkey. There are only an estimated 2000 colobus in Kenya, 400 of which are at Diani. Local group the **Colobus**

② Diani Beach

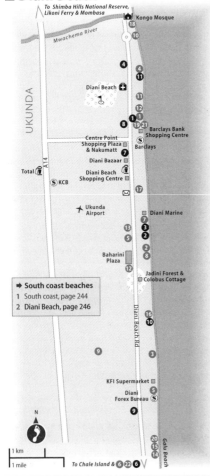

Where to stay 🛏
Alfajiri Villas **1**
Baobab Beach Resort & Spa **3**
Diani Beachalets **5**
Diani Campsite **17**
Diani Marine Villas **7**
Diani Reef Beach Resort & Spa **4**
Diani Sea Lodge **2**
Diani Sea Resort **8**
Forest Dream **9**
Jacaranda Indian Ocean
  Beach Resort **10**
Kijiji Cottages **19**
Kinondo Kweto **6**
Leisure Lodge Beach & Golf Resort **11**
Leopard Beach Resort & Spa **12**
Neptune Palm Beach **15**
Neptune Paradise **14**
Neptune Village **20**
Pinewood Beach Resort **22**
Sands at Nomad **16**
Southern Palms Beach Resort **18**
Stilts **13**
Warrandale Cottages **21**

Restaurants 🍴
African Pot **1**
Ali Barbour's **2**
Bull Steak House **7**
Forty Thieves **3**
Galaxy **4**
Jahazi Bistro **6**
Leonardo's **8**
Nomads Beach Bar
  & Restaurant **10**
Sake Oriental Japanese **11**
Sundowner **9**

Bars & clubs 🍸
Shakatak **5**
Ushago Sports Bar & Grill **12**

Trust is devoted to the conservation of these rare primates and their habitat. Many of the primate species of this area are threatened both by traffic on the main coastal road and by hand-feeding by tourists, which encourages anti-social and unnatural behaviour. The **Colobus Trust** works to build aerial bridges, known as 'colobridges' across the roads to prevent traffic casualties and works to educate tourists against feeding monkeys. Another major problem is that the creatures get electrocuted on the many un-insulated power lines around Diani. The main electricity lines can carry up to 22,000 volts, which can be fatal, whilst the domestic power lines, which carry around 240 volts, can severely stun an animal and cause loss of a limb and/or secondary infections. Trees that allow access to the power lines have been cut back, so the monkeys have reduced contact with them, and the trust sends a team out weekly to keep vegetation trimmed. It has also been involved with rehabilitating vervet monkeys that were kept as pets and releasing them back into the wild at Shimba Hills. It has a centre called **Colobus Cottage** with plenty of information and nature trails, and can give good advice on local wildlife. It also offers a one-hour guided primate walk.

Shimba Hills National Reserve → *For listings, see pages 250-259. Colour map 2, C1.*

ⓘ *On the C106, which branches off the main A14 coast road 12 km south of the Likoni ferry, the main gate is 3 km beyond Kwale, T040-4159, www.kws.org, 0600-1900, US$20, children (3-18) US$10, vehicle US$3.25.*

This small reserve, 33 km southwest of Mombasa, is the largest coastal forest in Kenya after the Arabuko-Sokoke Forest (see page 265) and is an easy day trip from Diani Beach. The 300 sq km are covered with stands of coastal rainforest, rolling grasslands and scrubland. Due to strong sea breezes, the hills are much cooler than the rest of the coast, making it a very pleasant climate. The rainforest itself is totally unspoilt and opens out into rolling downs and gentle hills, and the flora ranges from baobab trees on the lower slopes nearer the coast to deciduous forests on the hills and vestigial rainforest along the watercourses. Two of Kenya's exquisite orchids are found here.

There are a number of Roan antelope, waterbuck, reedbuck, hyena, warthog, giraffe, leopard, baboon and bush pig in the reserve. The altitude and the damp atmosphere also attract countless butterflies and birds around the grassy hills and on the edges of the forest. However, it is famed for being the only place in Kenya where you might see the Sable antelope found in the same habitats as several large herds of buffalo. There are also about 200 elephant in the reserve who favour the refreshing fruit of the borassus palm, which is abundant here, and close-range elephant viewing is virtually guaranteed. The best place to see the wildlife is near the spectacular **Sheldrick Falls** (named after David Sheldrick, the founder of Tsavo East National Park and late husband of Daphne of the David Sheldrick Wildlife Trust in Nairobi, see page 60) and on the **Lango Plains** close to Giriama Point. Picnic sites on either side of the escarpment provide an entrancing view of the Indian Ocean to the east and, on a clear day, the imposing mass of Mount Kilimanjaro rising behind the Taita Hills to the west.

Adjacent is the **Mwaluganje Elephant Sanctuary**, set up to provide access for the elephants between the Shimba Hills and the Mwaluganje Forest Reserve, and protecting 2500 ha of their traditional migratory route. The sanctuary is an innovative concept due to the fact that the local cultures, the Duruma and Digo people, have become involved, along with other local landowners, the Kwale County Council, local politicians and the KWS, and a fee is payable to the local community (US$15, children under 16 US$2, vehicle

US$1.50) from every visitor to the reserve. This has helped to build school classrooms and has improved the water supply in the region. There is only one tented camp in the sanctuary, the **Travellers Mwaluganje Elephant Camp** (see Where to stay, page 254), and you can visit here either on a day tour with lunch or on an overnight trip arranged with the resorts on the coast.

South of Diani → *For listings, see pages 250-259.*

Chale Island → *Colour map 2, C1.*
About 10 km from the southern end of Diani is a small bay and Chale Island, which lies about 600 m offshore and measures just 1.2 km long and 800 m wide. Chale refers to the name of an old warrior of the Digo tribe who is buried on the island and, on certain days of the year, his descendants still come to celebrate religious rituals. During February and March, giant turtles lay their eggs on the beaches. When they are hatched, the baby turtles are helped back to sea by the local people and staff at the only hotel on the island, which is centred around a particularly fine half-moon shaped white-sand beach. Despite being offshore, the forest behind the hotel is home to some wildlife, including vervet monkeys and baboons, and good birdlife. There are also some inland mangrove forests situated on lakes fed by the tides.

Msambweni → *Colour map 2, C1.*
About 50 km south of Likoni is the village of Msambweni, which is home to what is one of the best hospitals on the coast as well as a famous leprosarium. The beach is really lovely here with coral rag-rock cliffs, and there are some ruins in this area that are believed to have been a slave detention camp. **Funzi Island** is a private island, with a luxury lodge, located just off the coast from here at the mouth of the Ramisi River and, again, like Chale Island, it is blessed with swaying palms, mangrove forests and sugar-white beaches.

Shimoni → *Colour map 2, C1. Phone code: 040.*
This is a small fishing village about 75 km south of Likoni whose name means 'Place of the Hole' and is derived from the method of entry to the system of **Slave caves** ① *to the west of the village, take the path opposite the jetty, 0830-1800, US$2.20, children (under 12) US$0.50.* 'Shimo' means cave in Kiswahili and the vast network opens directly on to the beach. There are several caves, once joined together and reputed to extend some 5 km inland. Due to silting, the floor has risen, blocking off access to the further caves, and what you now see is only the main entrance cavern. The next cavern, immediately behind this one, has a freshwater spring in it, but is only accessible via a hole in the roof of the cave. It is said that the caves were used by slave traders to hide the slaves, before they were shipped out to the slave market on Zanzibar. The other story associated with these caves is that they were used as a secret place of refuge by the Digo people during their intermittent battles with various marauding tribes, including the Masai, through the ages. Archaeological findings indicate that these coral caves, with their lovely stalactites, have been inhabited for several centuries. Today they are home to a thriving population of bats.

Shimoni is best known as the take-off point for excursions into the Kisite-Mpunguti Marine Park and Wasini Island (see below) and for deep-sea fishing trips into the Pemba Channel, which is a 35-mile stretch of the ocean that separates Tanzania's island of Pemba from the mainland and is world renowned for its large species of game fish. See What to do, page 259, for fishing operators.

Border crossings: Kenya–Tanzania

Lunga Lunga
The Lunga Lunga border with Tanzania is 106 km south of Mombasa on the A14 and is open 24 hours. Formalities are fairly efficient, and visas for Tanzania and Kenya can be purchased, but only rely on being able to use US dollars cash at this border. You don't need to get another visa to return to Kenya if you've only been to Tanzania, but you will need to produce a yellow fever vaccination certificate to enter Kenya from Tanzania. There are no banks at the border, so you may need to swap a small amount of Kenyan shillings into Tanzanian shillings (or vice versa) with money changers to cover yourself until you reach the next bank. The nearest ones are at Ukunda in Kenya and Tanga in Tanzania.

Once over the border in Tanzania, it is 70 km on the A14 to **Tanga**, which has petrol stations, banks, shops and accommodation. From here, the A14 continues south to **Dar es Salaam**, 423 km from the border. The other option is to turn off the A14 at **Segera**, which is 75 km southwest of Tanga, on to the B1 and head north to **Moshi** and **Arusha**.

There are plenty of *matatus* running up and down the A14 between the Likoni Ferry south of Mombasa Island, Ukunda (for Diani Beach) and the border, but the easiest option is to get a through bus to/from Mombasa, which will take about 10 hours to Dar es Salaam and four hours to Tanga.

Kisite-Mpunguti Marine Park → *Colour map 2, C1.*
ⓘ *The park HQ is 200 m south of the Shimoni jetty, T040-52027, www.kws.org, 0600-1900, US$20, children (3-18) US$10. If you're not on a day tour to Wasini Island (see box, page 250), you can organize small local dhows for trips to the reefs at the park HQ.*

This marine park covers the southernmost part of the Kenyan coastline; the mountains rising straight up in the south over the ocean mark the Tanzanian/Kenyan border. The park covers 40 sq km of turquoise and dark green ocean and four small islands. These have old established trees, including baobabs with their thick gnarled trunks, and a good variety of birds, including brown-headed parrots, sunbirds, palmnut vultures and African fish eagles. Animals include monitor lizards, Sykes monkeys and wild goats. The marine protected areas have a fringing reef, channels, islands and offshore reefs. Hard and soft corals are a common feature, as is a diversity of marine life; it is said to be the best snorkelling in Kenya. Green and Hawksbill turtles and seven species of dolphins are present and are both sighted by visitors on a virtually daily basis. Humpback whales are sighted regularly on their yearly migration in October/November, sometimes as early as July. Every morning, visitors are bussed in from the coastal resorts and the little convoy of *dhows* string out in a line and drop anchor. The water is pure, warm and turquoise in colour, and is so salt-saturated that it is difficult to swim in initially, as it seems to suspend you. There are thousands of fish, in a dazzling array of sizes, shapes and colours, just below the surface. There are also several dive spots here (for dive operators see What to do, page 258), and the reefs are excellent for drift diving. Sting rays and turtles are commonly seen, as are parrot fish, trumpet fish, bat fish, grouper, Napoleon wrasse, clown fish and Spanish dancers. One of the better reefs is **Nyulli Reef**, which lies at 30 m and drops to over 80 m. This reef is spectacularly long, and a large quantity of large pelagics as well as reef fish are found here.

Wasini Island

Wasini Island lies 1 km offshore from Shimoni and falls within the Kisite-Mpunguti Marine Park. At only 1 km wide and 6 km long, it is a wonderful place with hardly any development. A day tour to Wasini Island can be booked directly or through any of the resorts, and is undoubtedly the most popular excursion on the south coast – although it's way too touristy for some, given the busloads. The day begins with a transfer to Shimoni (roughly an hour depending on where you're staying), where you board a traditional *dhow* at around 0900 to explore Kisite-Mpunguti and go snorkelling; with luck, perhaps, joined by turtles and dolphins. Glass-bottomed boats are available for those who do not wish to swim. This is followed by lunch at the famous **Charlie Claw's Restaurant**, which, remarkably, has been serving seafood lunches to tourists since 1978. The menu includes steamed crabs in ginger with claws the size of your fist, along with fresh lime and baked coconut rinds for dipping in salt, followed by barbecued fish and rice steamed in coconut, and a fresh fruit platter and *sim sim* (ginger spiced coffee with balls of sugared sesame seed). Good vegetarian options are available and, for extra, you can add a whole lobster to your meal. There is not much of a beach on Wasini Island, as it gets covered by the incoming tide, so the afternoon is spent lazing on day beds in the restaurant gardens. Alternatively you can visit Wasini Village, where there are remains of an Arab settlement including a pillar tomb with Chinese porcelain insets that have, so far, survived, and the dead coral gardens behind the village, which are above the ocean and can be explored from a boardwalk. At additional expense, there's also the opportunity of diving. The *dhow* returns to Shimoni at about 1600 for transfers back to the resorts.

For more information, contact T040-320 3154, www.wasini.com. Although prices vary by season, expect to pay in the region of US$125, children (3-12) half price, under 3s free, which includes park conservation fees.

◉ South of Mombasa listings

For sleeping and eating price codes and other relevant information, see pages 20-24.

● Where to stay

Room rates vary with the season. Low is Apr-Jun; mid is Jul-Nov; high is Dec-Mar. There's a wide choice of accommodation along the coast and a number of all-inclusive resorts where rates include all meals, usually buffets, and some watersports, which are favoured by package holidaymakers on 1- to 2-week stays. Nevertheless, most of these accept direct bookings and, out of the high season, walk-in guests. A family or group may want to consider renting a good-value self-catering cottage.

Tiwi Beach *p244, map p244*
$$$ Amani Tiwi Beach Resort, www.amanitiwibeachresort.com. At the time of writing this was closed and being rebuilt after a fire – check the website for progress. When it reopens it will have 4-star status with more than 200 rooms, 5 restaurants, several bars, a dive centre and kids' club.
$$$-$$ Coral Cove Cottages, T040-330 0010, www.coralcove.tiwibeach.com. Peaceful and good value, 9 self-catering thatched 1- and 2-bed cottages sleeping

up to 5, furnishings are a little old but very spacious with living room and broad veranda, and on a beautiful white-sand beach, with swaying palm trees in a private cove. A personal house-help can be hired for an additional cost to cook Swahili-type meals and clean, and local people come round daily selling fish and vegetables.

$$$-$$ SheShe Baharini Beach Hotel, reservations Nairobi, T020-856 2025, www.sheshebeach.com. 30 spacious a/c rooms with patios or balconies, some with 4-poster beds, in whitewashed blocks with Moorish design in the gardens or by the swimming pool. There are 2 bars and a good seafood restaurant, which also has a pizza oven and a fairly good selection of wine. Trips on a glass-bottomed boat can be arranged, and you can walk along the beach to the mangrove forest at the mouth of the Mwachema River.

$$ Maweni and Capricho Beach Cottages, T040-330 0012, www.mawenibeach.com. Located on a small cliff overlooking the beach, which is down a flight of steps. There are 26 simple but comfortable 1- to 3-bed thatched self-catering cottages, either sea-facing or in the tropical gardens where there's a small swimming pool. If you don't want to cook, you can hire a cook or eat simple seafood dishes in the **Dhow Restaurant**.

$$ Sand Island Beach, T0733-660 554, www.sandislandbeach.com. 7 quiet and a little remote 1- to 3-bed self-catering low-rise thatched cottages in a grove of palms, 1 sleeps up to 8, 30 m back from the beach, similar set-up to the Coral Cove Cottages above, in that you can hire a cook/maid at extra cost and local people do the rounds with fish and vegetables. Snorkelling equipment available.

$ Twiga Lodge, T0721-577 614. This budget/backpacker place, which hasn't changed much in almost 30 years, has a clutch of very basic and bare rooms, poor and not wholly clean shared bathrooms, and simple beach bar and restaurant serving the likes of fried fish and spaghetti bolognaise. Nevertheless,

it may appeal to some for its 'laid-backness' and you can camp under palm trees right on the beach for around US$3 per person.

Diani Beach *p244, map p246*

This is a far from exhaustive list of places to stay at Diani. For more options visit www.dianibeach.com or www.dianilife.com.

$$$$ Alfajiri Villas, T040-320 2217, www.alfajirivillas.com. An exclusive retreat aimed at families or groups, with 3 beautiful Italian-owned double-storey thatched villas with wide verandas and balconies, 2-4 en suite bedrooms with additional rooms under the *makuti* roof for children, vast beds swathed in mosquito nets, decorated with exquisite objets d'art from around the world, and rim-flow pools almost on the beach. Mediterranean-influenced food with olive oils, parma ham and cheeses flown in weekly from Europe. Very stylish but at a price, full board rates start from US$1400 per villa and include a vehicle for excursions and a butler.

$$$$ Diani Reef Beach Resort & Spa, T040-320 2723, www.dianireef.com. A super-luxurious and comfortable resort with 300 m of beach frontage, all the 300 rooms are a/c with satellite TV, minibars, internet and safes. The hotel has a full range of facilities, including 5 bars, 6 restaurants, 2 swimming pools, kids' club, casino and disco, floodlit tennis courts, squash courts, award-winning spa, a dive school, golf-putting course, and landscaped lagoons with boating facilities and sun bathing islands.

$$$$ Kinondo Kwetu, T040-330 0031, www.kinondo-kwetu.com. In a quiet location on Galu Beach about 2 km south of the large Neptune resort complex, a lovely, Swedish-run, small, family-friendly resort, with 5 cottages and 7 rooms in the main house or a separate villa, beautifully decorated with Swahili decor, rich fabrics, high ceilings and cool stone floors, clover-shaped swimming pool and tennis courts. There's no set place for meals or drinks, which are, rather charmingly, served in the rooms, gardens, beach or boathouse, or even on top of a water tower on the property. As well as the usual watersports, there are sea kayaks for hire, horses for beach rides, a yoga/aerobics instructor and a mini-spa with sauna.

$$$ Baobab Beach Resort & Spa, T040-205 7093-8, www.baobab-beach-resort.com. This is a massive resort on the cliff at the southern end of Diani (to get to the beach you have to climb down the steep steps), popular with British and German package holidaymakers, with almost 300 a/c rooms with views over the gardens, ocean or the 3 swimming pools. Open-air disco, several bars and restaurants, fitness centre and spa, loads of activities from bicycle hire to windsurfing. Rates are full board and meals are mostly buffets, but there is the option to eat in the à la carte restaurant for additional cost.

$$$ Diani Marine Villas, T040-320 2367, www.dianimarinevillas.com. A small, friendly place with a combination of spacious and airy rooms with large Swahili-style beds, including a simple permanent tent under thatch on a wooden deck that sleeps 4, a self-catering honeymoon cottage, with additional hot tub on the roof, and 2 4-bedroom self-catering villas where a cook can be hired. Breakfast is included and restaurants are close by. **Diani Marine** dive centre is based here, and most people stay on a dive package (see What to do, page 258).

$$$ Diani Sea Lodge and **Diani Sea Resort**, T040-320 3438. www.dianisea.com. 2 large resorts next to each other on the beach, popular with German and British package holidaymakers. The 135 rooms in the Lodge are in cottages and have balconies or terraces and a/c, but are simple and small. Better are the 170 a/c rooms at the Resort, which are arranged in blocks with fridge, satellite TV and balcony. Both have buffet restaurants, swimming pools, mini-golf, kids' playgrounds and tennis courts, and diving and watersports can be arranged. Slightly faded but one of the cheapest all-inclusive options and good for families.

$$$ Jacaranda Indian Ocean Beach Resort, T040-320 3730, www.jacarandahotels.com. Moorish-style arched main building with smaller *makuta* thatched-roof buildings in secluded 10-ha grounds with old coconut and baobab trees, with 100 a/c rooms, 3 restaurants, 3 bars including the **Bahari Beach Bar**, which is reputed to have the best view on Diani Beach. Facilities include a 200-m swimming pool, 3 smaller pools, tennis courts and a watersports centre.

$$$ Leisure Lodge Beach & Golf Resort, T040-320 3624, www.leisurelodgeresort. com. Over 200 rooms in standard hotel block with balconies or in villas clustered around private pools, many restaurants, casino, several swimming pools, tennis courts, health club, dive school and windsurfing school. The 18-hole, 72-par championship golf course, home to the **Diani Beach Masters**, is recognized as one of the best golf courses in East Africa.

$$$ Leopard Beach Resort & Spa, T0724-255 280, www.leopardbeachresort.com. A popular luxury resort, set amidst 10 ha of lush tropical gardens, with 70 standard rooms, 20 superior garden rooms, 48 sea-facing rooms, plus some private cottages and villas. Several restaurants and bars, boutiques, diving, disco and live music, and swimming pool. The luxurious spa is set in a lovely patch of peaceful forest where massages etc can be taken outside. Closed end Apr to mid-Jun.

$$$ Neptune Palm Beach, **Neptune Paradise** and **Neptune Village**, T040-320 2350, www.neptunehotels.com. Together these 3 adjoining resorts are the most southerly of the large resorts, more than 2 km south of **Baobab Beach Resort & Spa** and actually on Galu Beach. Between them they have more than 300 a/c rooms with balconies/patios, several bars, restaurants and swimming pools, all set in attractive gardens, all-inclusive rates, activities include watersports, tennis and mini-golf. It's a good family option with a kids' club and a weekly curio market.

$$$ Pinewood Beach Resort & Spa, T040-320 0038, www.pinewood-beach. com. On Galu Beach, almost as far south as Chale Island and therefore on one of the quietest stretches of beach, with 58 rooms and suites incorporating Swahili-style and home-made furniture set in cottages with a/c, minibar, balcony/terrace and internet; the more expensive suites have additional living rooms and kitchens with their own chef for private dining. Facilities include several restaurants and bars, an attractive swimming pool, gym, spa and dive centre.
$$$ The Sands at Nomad, T040-330 0269, www.thesandsatnomad.com. 37 stylish a/c rooms and suites decorated in Swahili style, some have jacuzzis and 4-poster beds. The Nomad Beach Bar and Restaurant is one of the most popular along the 'strip', and there's an additional sushi bar, plus a lovely 5-m-deep pool surrounded by established overhanging trees, a spa, an internet café and watersports centre. Diving the Crab is here (see What to do, page 258), hence the depth of the pool as it's used for diving courses.
$$$ Southern Palms Beach Resort, T040-320 3721, www.southernpalmskenya.com. Quality resort with over 300 rooms arranged in 4-storey blocks, with thatched roofs, a/c, DVD players, minbars, and 4-poster beds, the additional 'day-bed' can be used by children or there are adjoining rooms. Facilities include 4 restaurants, 5 bars, internet café, and there are plenty of activities and entertainment on offer. The highlight here is the vast area of interconnecting swimming pools with 2 swim-up bars.
$$$-$$ Forest Dream, T040-330 0220, www.forestdream.com. A quiet resort with 30 a/c rooms set in thatched cottages in established gardens surrounded by forest where colobus monkeys are regularly seen. However, it's on the opposite side of the road and not on the beach. There's a nice restaurant shaded by palms, a bar, tennis court and very hi-tech swimming pool with underwater music, massage jets and a waterfall/slide that cascades from a huge rock.

$$ Kijiji Cottages, T040-330 0035, www. kijijicottages.com. These are some of nicest cottages for families or groups in the Diani area, well looked after, rates include a cleaner and, for an additional expense, a cook. They have 2-3 spacious en suite bedrooms, broad terraces and are set in gardens, the sea-facing ones cost a little more. There's also an attractive swimming pool.
$$ Warandale Cottages, T040-320 2186, www.warandale.com. Similar set up next to Kijiji, above, and in a handy location near shops and the Leopard Beach Resort & Spa, which you have to walk through to get to the beach, with 6 cottages sleeping 2-6 with verandas, some with sea views, again you can hire a cook/cleaner, and there's a small swimming pool.
$ Diani Beachalets, T040-320 2180, www. dianibeachalets.com. Laid-back and peaceful with a range of budget chalets set in lovely gardens, from fully equipped houses with bathrooms and kitchens suitable for families or groups, to cheap backpackers' *bandas* with shared bathroom and kitchen, the larger units overlook the beach, old furnishings and equipment but they have everything you may need, fishermen come round in the mornings with fresh seafood, and there's a supermarket within walking distance. One of the cheapest options on the south coast; accommodation can work out as little as US$9 per person sharing.
$ Diani Campsite, T040-320 3192, www.dianicampsite.com. This budget/backpacker's place offers 15 simple thatched 1- to 3-bedroom chalets with bathrooms (cold water), some with kitchens, and a grassy campsite (US$4 in your own tent, or you can hire 2-person tents with mattresses and bedding for around US$23), which has a 'camphouse' with cookers, fridges and lockers, plus clean ablution block. There's a restaurant and bar where you can order simple seafood meals and pizzas and the beach is a short stroll away.
$ Stilts, T0722-523 278, www.alibarbours. com. On the opposite side of the main road

from the **Ali Barbour's Restaurant**, and managed by them, in a lush tract of forest inhabited by monkeys and bushbabies. 7 basic cheap tree *bandas*, which as the name suggests are built on stilts, with beds, mosquito nets and balconies, and a campsite, all with shared toilets, showers and solar-heated water. There's a pub and restaurant, which has day beds for lazing around, and the beach is a 5-min walk away.

Shimba Hills National Reserve *p247*
$$$ Shimba Lodge, reservations **Aberdare Safari Hotels**, T0722-200 952, www.aberdare safarihotels.com. A well-designed timber lodge overlooking a waterhole illuminated at night for viewing, which offers similar 'cabin' accommodation to that of **Treetops** in the Aberdare National Park, with small wooden rooms with shared bathrooms and verandas looking straight into the forest. The dining room is open air, there is a pleasant bar and several secluded decks for game viewing well into the night. Optional early-morning game drives and guided walks to the Sheldrick Falls, where there is a natural pool for swimming. Half-board rates are in the region of US$200 for a double, children under 5 are not permitted. Day and overnight visits can be arranged through the Mombasa tour operators or from the coastal resorts.
$$-$ Sable Bandas, T040-4159, KWS, Nairobi, T020-600 0800, www.kws.org. Located 3 km from the main gate to the reserve, this has 4 en suite *bandas* with 2 single beds in each with linen and towels, shared fully equipped kitchen with gas cooker, no electricity but kerosene lamps are provided and there's a caretaker on site. There's also a well-maintained and peaceful campsite here, with excellent views over the surrounding forest. Drinking water, firewood and food must be brought; US$35 per person in the *bandas* and US$15 per person camping.

Mwaluganje Elephant Sanctuary
$$$ Travellers Mwaluganje Elephant Camp, reservations through the **Traveller's Beach Hotel & Club** in Bamburi on Mombasa's north coast, T041-548 5121, www.travellersbeach.com. Set on a small hill overlooking a waterhole in the Elephant Sanctuary are 20 tents, each with 2-3 beds, bathroom and private veranda with views over a well-used elephant trail, restaurant and bar. Although you are very likely to see elephant here, there are much better safari options from the coast and the camp is very run down these days. Again, excursions here are usually arranged from the coastal resorts and include transfers, entry fees and meals.

Chale Island *p248, map p244*
$$$$ The Sands at Chale Island, T040-300 0269, www.thesandsatchaleisland. com. Luxury all-inclusive resort, with 55 rooms centred around a beautiful white crescent-shaped sandy beach, comprising roomy and elegant tented bungalows, or apartments and penthouses in round multi-storey blocks topped with thatch, and a couple of water suites that are actually built over the ocean on stilts and reached by boardwalks, all furnished with African/Arabic antiques. The 2 restaurants offer local and international cuisine, diving and deep-sea fishing are on offer, and there's a swimming pool, spa and gym.

Msambweni *p248, map p244*
$$$$ Funzi Keys, Funzi Island, south of Msambweni, T0733-900 446, www.the funzikeys.com. Very exclusive lodge on a beautifully secluded island, furnished to a very high standard, with 17 enormous stone-and-thatch cottages set along the high-water line and facing west for the sunset, with hand-carved king-sized 4-poster beds, some have jacuzzis, and there's a 45-m rim-flow swimming pool, a perfect honeymoon venue, although there are some family cottages too. Watersports, meals, drinks (except champagne) and transfers are included in

the rates (US$255-725 per person, depending on season). Closed May-Jun.

$$$$ Msambweni Beach House, on Msambweni Beach, reservations Nairobi, T020-357 7093, www.msambweni-beach-house.com. Set in a commanding position on a small cliff with great ocean views, this is a super luxury family-run establishment with 6 spacious rooms in the main house with lovely all-white decor and Swahili furniture, in front of which is a stunning 25-m infinity swimming pool, plus 2 private villas with their own pool, jacuzzi cook and butler. Excellent cuisine including some French and Belgium dishes as well as seafood.

Shimoni *p248, map p244*

$$$ Betty's Camp, T0722-434 709, www.bettys-camp.com. A small, simple and a little overpriced place with no beach as such but overlooking the ocean with either tented rooms under thatch with own shower/toilet or en suite rooms within the main house, can accommodate 10-12 people in total. There's a swimming pool, poolside terrace restaurant and bar open to all, with a good range of seafood, and they can arrange fishing and trips to Wasini Island.

$$$ Pemba Channel Lodge, T0722-205 020, www.pembachannellodge.com. Simple family-run place with 6 *bandas* with veranda and sea views set in tropical gardens, with many trees indigenous to the Shimoni area, and a swimming pool. Attractive, homely lounge, restaurant and bar filled with wicker sofas and overstuffed cushions, marlin trophies and fishing photos adorn the walls. The Pemba Big Game Fishing Club is based here, see What to do, page 259.

$$$ Shimoni Reef Lodge, reservations, Mombasa, T041-447 3969, www.shimonireef lodge.com. Wonderful location, overlooking Wasini Island, with 10 open-plan cottages with ocean views and private verandas, each is on 2 levels and sleeps 4 people. There is a sea-water swimming pool made up of multi levels that is good for kids, an open-air terrace restaurant overlooking the ocean

where seafood is a speciality, diving and snorkelling on offer but is best known for its deep-sea fishing excursions in the Pemba Channel (see What to do, page 259).

$$$-$$ Mwazaro Mangrove Lodge, T0722-711 476, www.keniabeach.de. About 8 km north of Shimoni, there is a sign to Mwazaro Beach, turn right there and the camp is another 1 km. Friendly German-run place, accommodation is in either thatched *bandas* on the beach with sand floors and lit by hurricane lamps, or en suite rooms in the main coral-rag house with solar and wind-powered electricity. The restaurant serves excellent affordable Swahili-style food, there's a comfy lounge and bar where you can play chess or backgammon, and tea is served all day. A guide will take you on an interactive tour to a local fishing village or on a boat tour to a nearby mangrove forest. You can also negotiate to camp here. A lovely remote, laid-back spot and a far cry from the larger holiday resorts.

Kisite-Mpunguti Marine Park *p249, map p244*

$$-$ Shimoni Bandas, at the park HQ 200 m south of the jetty at Shimoni, T040-52027, KWS, Nairobi, T020-600 0800, www.kws.org. In attractive coastal forest with a campsite and 7 simple *bandas* with 2 single beds in each with linen and towels, 3 have en suite bathrooms or share communal facilities with campers, plus a shared fully equipped kitchen with gas cooker, and caretaker on site. Drinking water, firewood and food must be brought; US$35 per person in the *bandas* and US$15 per person camping.

❶ Restaurants

Diani Beach *p244, map p246*

Most of the large resorts have buffet meals for all-inclusive guests and, although these vary in quality, they are usually of a fairly high standard. Some also have specialist restaurants, which are also open to non-guests, and there are also a number of individual places along the Diani 'strip'. If you are on holiday on the south coast and have the cash to splash, ensure you eat at the **Tamarind** in Mombasa (page 237), **Charlie Claw's** on the Wasini Island day trip (see box, page 250), and **Ali Barbour's** (below).

$$$ Ali Barbour's, just north of the Diani Shopping Centre, T0714-456 131, www. alibarbours.com. Dinner from 1900. Diani's most popular restaurant is set in an underground cave that has various chambers that go 10 m below ground level, a stone floor has been fitted and a sliding roof comes across if the weather is bad. Lights have been set in niches in the walls and it's very atmospheric. It does excellent seafood, including an expensive but expansive platter, as well as French food, and has an extensive winelist. Excellent service and a unique experience. Offers free transport from the hotels.

$$$ Sake Oriental, at the Diani Reef Beach Resort & Spa, see Where to stay, page 251. Open 1900-2230. Formal Japanese restaurant with traditional floor seating and sociable teppanyaki tables, authentic food, excellent sushi and some Chinese and Indian dishes. The hotel's **Fins ($$)** restaurant specializes in seafood and Mediterranean dishes and has candlelit tables on a terrace overlooking the beach.

$$$-$$ Nomads Beach Bar & Restaurant, at The Sands at Nomad, see Where to stay, page 253. Open 0700-midnight. Right on the beach on wooden decks and under canvas with good service and atmosphere. It opens early for the good-value buffet breakfast and also does a very popular Sun buffet lunch with live jazz, and the à la carte menu features pizzas, excellent and imaginative pastas, risottos, seafood and grills.

$$$-$ Forty Thieves, next to Ali Barbour's, and under the same management, T0712-294 873. Open 0900-late. Lively bar and restaurant open all day from breakfast serving good food and snacks, the steamed crab and Swahili prawns with coconut rice are especially good and the comfortable lounge-style tables are set under thatch right next to the beach where you can kick off your shoes in the sand. Also good live music and buffet lunch on a Sun and livens up as an evening venue (see Bars and clubs, below).

$$ Bull Steak House, behind the petrol station just north of the **Diani Beach Shopping Centre** T041-200 2600, www. thebullsteakhouse.de. 1700-late. Informal restaurant and bar under a conical thatched roof, plus rooftop terrace, popular with Germans for the very large steaks from 250-g fillets to 1-kg T-bones, good cuts of prime Angus beef, and also pork steaks, lamb, chicken and seafood including whole lobsters. Offers free transport from the hotels.

$$ Galaxy, opposite Diani Reef Beach Resort & Spa, T040-320 0018. Open 1100-1430, 1800-2300. Part of a chain that also has branches in Mombasa, this offers tasty Chinese cuisine, a small menu but with quality items, such as grilled lobster, roast duck and ginger crab, and is set on a nice open terrace surrounded by lush tropical gardens.

$$-$ Jahazi Bistro, at the Pinewood Beach Resort & Spa, see Where to stay, page 253. Open 1000-1730. A good lunch stop on Galu Beach, with tables set in the tropical gardens under swaying palms, extensive menu features crunchy salads, burgers, fish and chips, and excellent thin-based pizzas cooked in an open-air wood-fired oven. Also serves delicious fruit cocktails.

$$-$ Leonardo's, near the Barclay's Bank Shopping Centre, T0720-501 707. Open 0830-2300. Traditional Italian with comfortable garden seating, long menu of fresh pasta and sauces, some seafood including lobster, fresh juices, good strong espresso coffee and is best known for its 24 flavours of home-made ice cream.

$ African Pot, near the Barclay's Bank Shopping Centre, T0722-346 155. Open 1000-2200. Good value, tasty local food, served in the traditional way in (as the name suggests) big earthenware pots, such as *nyama choma* (charcoaled meat), masala curries, *chipati*, *matoke*, *ugali* and pilau rice, all washed down with cold Tusker beer. Good place for a group to share dishes.

$ Sundowner, a 5-min walk from the Diani Beachalets, T040-320 2138. Open 0800-2200. Serves excellent Kenyan food and local beers at low prices, this is one of the best-value places to eat, curries, grilled and fried fish, very good English breakfasts, sometimes has seafood such as lobster, simple decor in outside thatched hut but nice atmosphere.

🍸 Bars, clubs and entertainment

Diani Beach *p244, map p246*
Most of the large resorts put on some kind of evening entertainment for guests, which in Kenya is referred to as 'animation' and is usually a troupe of male dancers putting on a display of acrobatics (at which Kenyans seem to be uncannily good), or perhaps traditional drumming or Masai dancing. Almost all the resorts have nightclubs and many have discos on the beach, which are of varying quality and, in the family resorts, usually feature lots of children running around. Along Diani Beach Rd there are also a couple of independent nightclubs, and there's a **Casino**, at the Leisure Lodge Beach & Golf Resort, 1400-0300, with slot machines, a few gaming tables and a bar.

Forty Thieves (see Restaurants) is probably the nicest place to go dancing next to the beach, and on Wed, Fri and Sat nights the restaurant tables are pushed back for a disco. It also has pool tables, live entertainment, satellite TV, and is a popular night spot for many of the local residents who affectionately call it 'Forties'.

Shakatak, just south of Ali Barbour's, www. shakatak-kenya.com. Bar and restaurant from 1900, nightclub from 2100. This is the biggest nightclub at Diani and has been going strong since 1990. It's German-run with a restaurant and beer garden with German food and German satellite TV. It has a large dance floor and floor shows, and although it's more than a little seedy and tacky, and prostitutes abound, it can be a lot

of fun. The website very generously explains that in Kenya, men over 40 go to nightclubs!
Ushago Sports Bar & Grill, at the southern end of Baharini Plaza (see Shopping, below). 0800-2300, the bar stays open until the early hours. There's plenty on offer here. The popular bar under thatch with comfy couches has plenty of large-screen TVs for watching sports, pool tables and table games like chess and backgammon, and a DJ plays in the evening. The food court has 6 counters offering Swahili, German and Indian snacks, with a central shared seating area, and there's a more formal pizza restaurant, **$**. Finally, there's a swimming pool, kids' playground, internet café and, at the back, a few *bandas* selling Masai curios.

🛍 Shopping

Tiwi Beach *p244, map p244*
If you are self-catering at Tiwi Beach, it's a good idea to pick up provisions at the large branch of **Nakumatt** supermarket near the Likoni Ferry in Mombasa. At Tiwi itself there is only a small shop for basic provisions at the turn-off to the beach, although you will be able to buy fish from the vendors on the beach. The next shops are at Ukunda and Diani, further south.

Diani Beach *p244, map p246*
Curios
There are many curio stalls dotted along Diani Beach Rd and they are usually grouped near the entrance to the resorts. Additionally 'beach boys' wander around selling items, you'll have to be assertive to ensure they leave you alone; as they can be fairly aggressive with their sales tactics. The shopping malls (see below) also have several upmarket curio shops that, among other items, sell *kikoys* and the beautiful beaded leather sandals that are made on the coast.

Shopping malls
There are several shopping malls on Diani Beach Rd, generally open Mon-Sat 0830-

1730, though some of the more touristy shops also open on Sun. The **Barclays Bank Shopping Centre** near the T-junction to Ukunda, has a small supermarket, a shop selling booze and an internet café. On the other side of the junction is the new **Centre Point Shopping Plaza**, which boasts a large branch of **Nakumatt** supermarket. The **Diani Beach Shopping Centre** is to the north of Diani Beach post office and has a supermarket, a booking office for **Wasini Island** (see box, page 250) and a number of top-end jewellery, art and curios shops, including branches of **Kazuri Beads** and **The Kikoy Co. Baharini Plaza** is south of the post office and has a butchery, pharmacy, small supermarket and a couple of boutiques. There's another good supermarket just up from the Diani Beachalets that also sells booze. For fresh fruit, vegetables and fish, you will be able to buy off the vendors who come round all the self-catering places with their stock on their bicycles.

⚙ What to do

Diani Beach *p244, map p246*
Diving and snorkelling
There are over 30 dive sites within a 20- to 25-min boat trip of Diani Beach, which with 15- to 30-m depths, offer excellent visibility and a diversity of marine life. There are also 2 wrecks for experienced divers to explore – the *HMS Hildasay* sank in 1945, while the *MV Funguro* sank in 2002; both lie at a depth of just over 20 m. Expect to pay in the region of US$50-60 for a single dive and US$470-530 for a 4- to 5-day PADI Open Water course. Marine park fees are included in the rates. Almost every resort offers diving through one of the dive schools. Snorkelling, of course, can be done by simply walking into the sea, or from *dhows* and can be arranged at all the resorts. And, if you don't want to get wet, watching the fish through the floor of a glass-bottomed boat is also an option. **Baracuda Scuba Safaris** has its base at **Amani Tiwi Beach Resort**, which is

currently being rebuilt, but for now will pick up from all Diani hotels, T0734-237 692, www.divediani.com.
Diani Marine, at Diani Marine Villas, T040-320 2367, www.dianimarine.com.
Diving The Crab, are at a number of resorts including Baobab Beach Resort & Spa, Southern Palms Beach Resort, and Sands at Chale Island, T0712-387 617, www.divingthecrab.com.
Southern Cross Scuba, again are at a number of resorts including Indian Ocean Beach Resort, Leisure Lodge Beach & Golf Resort, Diani Reef Beach Resort & Spa and Leopard Beach Resort & Spa, T0734-601 221, www.southerncrossscuba.com.

Fishing
Diani Fishing Club, at Diani Reef Beach Resort & Spa, and Pinewood Beach Resort & Spa, T0726-775 047, www.dianifishingclub.com.

Golf
Leisure Lodge Beach & Golf Resort, T040-320 3624, www.leisurelodgeresort.com. This attractive 18-hole par-72 course is open to all guests of Diani Beach hotels and resorts. Expect to pay in the region of US$70 with club hire and, for keen golfers, there are weekly packages. Golfers may spot monkeys around the course.

Tour operators
The most popular excursions from Diani are a day tour to **Mombasa**, **Wasini Island** (see box, page 250), and safaris to **Shimba Hills National Reserve** (page 247), and **Tsavo National Park** (page 207). These can be arranged by all the resorts or the tour operators.
Active Tours & Safaris, Baharini Plaza, T0731-162 355, www.aktivetoursafaris. com.**Beach Air Tours & Safaris**, Barclay's Bank Shopping Centre, T040-320 2440, www.beachairtours.com.
DM Tours & Safaris, Diani Beach Shopping Centre, T040-320 4015, www.dmtours.net.

Diani Tours & Safaris, Diani Beach Shopping Centre, T040-320 2078, www.dianisafaris-kenya.com.
Kenyan Adventures & Beyond Safaris, Diani Bazaar Shopping Centre, T040-320 3764, www.kenyanadventures.net.

Wind- and kitesurfing
With warm water and cross- and side-shore winds, Diani has good conditions for wind- and kitesurfing along the wide uncrowded beach, and the flat water inside the reef is perfect for beginners. Windsurfing costs around US$50 for a half a day, while kitesurfing costs in the region of US$65 for 1 hr's lesson.
H2O Extreme has bases at **Forty Thieves Restaurant** and **The Sands at Nomad**, T0721-495 876, www.h2o-extreme.com.
Kite Kenya at Pinewood Beach Resort & Spa, T0733-787 336, www.kitekenya.com.

Shimoni *p248, map p244*
Fishing
Shimoni is well known as the take-off point for fishing excursions to the Pemba Channel, which separates the Kenya coast from the island of Pemba in Tanzania. It reaches depths of 823 m and is home to 3 varieties of marlin – black, blue and striped – as well as sailfish, spearfish, swordfish, yellowfin tuna, tiger shark, mako shark and virtually every game fish popular with anglers. A gentle north current runs through the channel, acting much like a scaled-down version of the Gulf Stream, and is forced up by the lip in the north of the channel, also referred to locally as the Sea Mountain, which creates rips and eddies that bring nutrients to the surface and concentrate the fish in a very tight area. The fishing season is usually from Aug to the end of Mar. Expect to pay in the region of US$600-800 for a boat with equipment and guides for up to 4 fishermen.
Pemba Big Game Fishing Club based at Pemba Channel Lodge, T0722-205 020, www.pembachannel.com.

Sea Adventures is based at **Shimoni Reef Lodge**, T0721-485 365, www.bigame.com.

⊖ Transport

Diani Beach *p244, map p246*
Air
Ukunda Airport, T040-320 2126, www.kenya airports.co.ke, is used for small planes – usually charters for safaris, but the airstrip is currently being extended to accept the bigger planes on scheduled services. For now, **Air Kenya** has a daily flight from Nairobi's Wilson Airport to **Ukunda**, that departs at 0830, arrives at 0940, departs again at 0955 and arrives back in **Nairobi** at 1115. In Nairobi you can link on to their scheduled services to the airstrips in the parks and reserves. **Mombasa Air Safari** (see page 242) will touch down here on request to pick up passengers for its flights between the coast and the parks.

Bus and matatus
For Diani by *matatu* you have to change at Ukunda village. The fare from **Likoni** to **Ukunda** costs about US$1 and from Ukunda to Diani US$0.40.

Car hire
Most of the tour operators listed above can organize car hire.
Glory Car Hire, at Diani Beach Shopping Centre, T040-320 3076, www.glorykenya. com. Also has a branch in Mombasa.

⊙ Directory

Diani Beach *p244, map p246*
Medical services Diani Beach Hospital, south of **Diani Reef Beach Resort & Spa**, T040-320 2435, www.dianibeachhospital. com. This is a private, modern hospital and 24-hr pharmacy with very high standards and is used to dealing with European patients. It offers numerous cosmetic procedures to holidaymakers.

North of Mombasa

There is a whole string of beaches along the north coast, including Nyali, Kenyatta, Bamburi and Shanzu, with lots of hotels on the seashore immediately north of Mombasa. North of Mtwapa Creek are Kikambala and Vipingo beaches. The major attractions of Watamu Marine National Park, Malindi and Lamu are further north. At these latter places there is much more choice for the budget traveller and anyone who wants to avoid the package tours. There are major historical sites at Kilifi, Malindi and Lamu. The north coast is also the location of the Malindi Marine Biosphere Reserve. This strip along the coast is 30 km long and 5 km wide and was gazetted in 1968; it covers an area of 213 sq km. It lies about 80 km north of Mombasa, and includes the Malindi Marine National Park, the Watamu Marine National Park and Mida Creek. The vegetation includes mangrove, palms, marine plants and various forms of algae that are home to crabs, corals, molluscs, cowrie and marine worms. Coral viewing is popular here, as are boat trips and watersports. ▶▶ For listings, see pages 274-288.

Mombasa to Kilifi → For listings, see pages 274-288.

Nyali, Kenyatta and Bamburi beaches → Colour map 2, C2. Phone code: 041.

Nyali, Kenyatta and Bamburi beaches are well developed and there are lots of hotels. Most of them cater for package tours from Europe and, usually, each hotel caters for a particular nationality. All have facilities, such as swimming pools, tennis courts, watersports, and they tend to look after their guests very well, organizing all sorts of activities and trips. Here the coast is lined with pristine palm-fringed beaches and offshore reefs. Both outer and inner reef walls offer world-class diving, with spectacular coral gardens and drop-offs, and Kenya's best wreck diving on the *MV Dania* (see box, page 265).

Mombasa Marine National Park (10 sq km) was established in 1986 for the protection of the area's coral reefs. It can be accessed by snorkelling or glass-bottomed boat trips from the resorts along the beaches and there are also good diving sites.

Mamba Village ① *Links Rd, Nyali, behind Nyali Beach and the hotels, T041-222 2232, www.mambavillage.com, 0800-1800, feeding is at 1700, US$4.50, children (under 16) US$3*, is the biggest crocodile farm in Kenya and is a habitat for over 20,000 crocodiles of all ages and sizes from newborns to huge, fully grown adults. A film explains some of the conservation efforts as well as the financial side of the venture. However it's fairly run down now, the pools where the crocodiles live are rather dank and the display of 'deformed' crocodiles is not a pleasant sight. Of more interest is the small adjacent **Botanical Garden** and **Aquarium**.

Wild Waters ① *Links Rd, Nyali, next to the Mamba Village, T041-249 1954, www. wildwaterskenya.com, Mon-Fri 1100-2200, Sat-Sun 1000-2200, water slides close at 1800, US$13 per person*, is a water park set in manicured gardens and features 11 slides for adults, another five for children, each named after a Kenyan river. A 300-m 'lazy river' encircles the whole complex and other facilities include fairground rides, bouncy castles, a video game arcade and a food court. There are also a couple of bars here that stay open late.

Bombolulu Workshops and Cultural Centre ① *about 4 km north of Nyali Bridge on the Malindi road, T0723-560 933, www.apdkbombolulu.org, Mon-Sat 0800-1700, Sun 1000-1500, US$7.50, children (under 12) US$4.30, the shop stays open until 1800*, is where you might want to do some souvenir shopping; there's a selection of wooden carvings, leather products, textiles and jewellery. Founded in 1969, the crafts are produced by a

➡ North coast maps
1 Nyali to Kilifi, page 261
2 Kilifi to Malindi, page 262

4 km

4 miles

Where to stay 🛏
Bahari Beach 1
Bamburi Beach 6
Baobab Lodge Resort 7
Indiana Beach
  Apartments 6
Kahama 6
Kenya Bay Beach 2
Mnarani Beach Club 17
Mombasa Backpackers 18
Neptune Beach Resort 2
Nyali Beach 1
Reef Hotel Mombasa 1
Royal Reserve Safari
  & Beach Club 20
Sarova Whitesands Beach
  Resort & Spa 6
Serena Beach & Spa 3
Severin Sea Lodge 2
Sun n' Sand Beach Resort 5
Traveller's Beach & Club 2
Voyager Beach Resort 1

Restaurants 🍴
Fulvio's Pizza 4
Il Covo 2
La Marina 5
Maharajah 2
Minazi@Whitesands 2
Monsoons 10
Moorings Floating
  Restaurant 1
Porini Seychellois 3
Sher-e-Punjab 2
Yul's 2

Bars & clubs 🍸
Casaurina Nomad 6
Pirates Beach 7
Tembo Disco 8

team of 150 local handicapped people (mostly polio victims) and are generally of reasonable quality and good value. There is also a cultural centre with eight traditional homesteads from different ethnic groups, where guides demonstrate traditional dance, music and theatre. You can do a tour of the workshops, and Swahili food is available in the **Ziga** restaurant.

Haller Park

ⓘ *8 km north of Nyali Bridge on the Malindi Rd, T041-548 5901. Open 0800-1700, US$9, children US$4.50.*

This park started out life as the Bamburi cement factory, which began quarrying coral to make lime for the cement around Mombasa in the 1950s. When quarrying stopped in 1971, an effort was made to reclaim the land by reforestation and a nature trail was created. The reclamation scheme was ahead of its time and it attracted the attention of ecologists from all over the world. It was named Haller Park after the Swiss agronomist who turned the lunar quarry landscape into luxuriant tropical forest.

There are all manner of things to do and see, including a fish farm producing tilapia, a luxuriant palm garden, 3.6 km of forest trails with exercise points and equipment along which you can either walk, jog or cycle, a crocodile farm, a butterfly pavilion and a reptile house. Visitors have the unique opportunity of close-up contact with various antelope, monkeys, warthog, giant Aldabran tortoises, bush babies, genet cats and mongoose. Tours of the enclosures are in English, French, German, Italian or Swahili. You can watch the hippos being fed at 1600, and can feed a number of Rothschild giraffes from an elevated platform at 0900 and 1500. Children in particular will thoroughly enjoy this excursion. The **Whistling Pines** restaurant is an excellent place for lunch.

2 North coast: Kilifi to Malindi

➡ **North coast maps**
1 Nyali to Kilifi, page 261
2 Kilifi to Malindi, page 262

Where to stay 🛌
Delta Dunes 9
Hemingways Resort 10
Kilifi Bay Beach Resort 13
Makuti Villas 15
Marijani Holiday Resort 16
Ocean Sports Resort 19
Turtle Bay Beach Club 24

Restaurants 🍴
Savannah Restaurant & Bar 11

Owen and Mzee

One of the newer residents of the Haller Wildlife Park is Owen the hippo. Just before Christmas in 2004, the Sabaki River to the north of Malindi flooded after heavy rains and washed a number of hippo into the sea, which local people tried to coax back. Then the tsunami hit on Boxing Day making the sea swell dramatically and, temporarily, the hippo were forgotten as people were absorbed with rescuing local fishermen. The next day the hippo all made it back to the mainland, except for Owen who was stranded on a reef. He was less than a year old at the time. After a remarkable rescue by the Kenya Wildlife Service that was watched by hundreds of people, he was brought to Haller Wildlife Park. His story is made even more remarkable as,

when he was released into an enclosure already occupied by some giant tortoises, he was adopted by one of them named Mzee (meaning 'old man' in Kiswahili), who is believed to be about 130 years old. Owen arrived exhausted, confused and extremely frightened and immediately ran to Mzee and cowered behind him, as he would have done with his mother. Within days the tortoise and the hippo were eating and sleeping together, and the hippo licked the tortoise's face and followed him everywhere. Owen and Mzee remained inseparable until 2007 when Owen was removed to another enclosure with another hippo. A number of children's books have been written about them, and they have their own website: www.owenandmzee.com.

Mtwapa and Shanzu Beach

Mtwapa is 16 km north of Mombasa's Nyali Bridge and is a small, bustling, chaotic and extremely friendly town; it is the main service point for Shanzu Beach. The main settlement is just north of the road bridge over the creek. The beach itself is sheltered and bordered by palms, and glass-bottomed boat rides out to the reefs are on offer. There are a number of resorts, most interlinked with one another so guests can use all the facilities.

Jumba la Mtwana ① *turn-off 1 km north of the bridge over Mtwapa Creek and it's 4 km to the entrance, www.museums.or.ke, 0930-1800, US$5.40, children (under 16) US$2.70; you can buy a short guidebook to the site or hire a guide*, is one of Kenya's least-known sites. The name means the 'house of the slave', indicating that it may have been a slave-trading settlement in the 15th century, although it was not mentioned in this capacity in either Arab or Portuguese sources. It is a lovely setting and spreads for about 300 m along the beach and 250 m inland with shade provided by baobabs. Many of the houses have been rebuilt and undergone frequent changes and it has been suggested that Jumba la Mtwana could have been a meeting place for pilgrims on their way to Mecca. Within the site, which is spread over several hectares, there are three mosques, a number of tombs and eight houses. The people appear to have been very concerned with ablutions for there are many remains showing evidence of cisterns, water jars, latrines and other washing and toilet facilities. Building with coral rag (broken pieces of coral) was something reserved for the more privileged members of the community, and it is their houses that have survived. Those that belonged to the poorer people would have been built of mud and thatch. There's a lovely little restaurant here, **Monsoons**, see page 281, so it's possible to explore the ruins and then have a lazy lunch on the beach.

Kikambala Beach → *Colour map 2, C2. Phone code: 041.*

Beyond Mtwapa, and 27 km north of Mombasa, the last feasible beach to be reached from Mombasa on a day trip is Kikambala Beach. The turn-off is 8 km north of Mtwapa and the beach is 3 km from the main road. Backed by palms and clutches of thick forest, this is an 11-km long stretch of reef-protected white beach where the sand is so fine in places it squeaks underfoot. There are only a few resorts here, making it much less busy than the strip immediately north of Mombasa. In fact, this is the location of the Israeli-managed **Paradise Hotel**, which was bombed by terrorists in 2002, and it's never really recovered from the subsequent tourist slump. If you go for an isolated walk you may notice the shells of abandoned, once-fashionable holiday cottages with emerald moss growing on the interior walls. Nevertheless, **Sun 'n' Sand** remains popular and is one of the largest resorts on the north coast. The disadvantage is that it's very flat in this area, which means the sea goes out for nearly a kilometre so swimming is only feasible at high tide and it's not the best destination for watersports. On either side of the road for about 40 km beyond Kikambala lie vast sisal estates.

Mnarani Ruins

ⓘ *www.museums.or.ke, 0930-1800, US$5.40, children (under 16) US$2.70.*

These were first excavated in the 1950s and are one of the ancient Swahili city-states that are found along this coast. It is believed that the town was inhabited from the latter half of the 14th century until about the early 17th century, when it was ransacked and destroyed by a group of Galla tribesmen. The inhabitants of the town are thought to have locked themselves into the Great Mosque as they were attacked.

The ruins include one of the deepest wells (70 m) along the coast, two mosques, part of the town wall and city gates and a group of tombs, including a pillar tomb decorated with engravings of a wealthy sharif. Note the tomb of the doctor, which is easily the most ornate. At the ruins of the larger or **Great Mosque** can be seen the *mihrab* (which points towards Mecca), surrounded by carved inscriptions. There are many niches in the walls. To the left of the entrance, the smaller mosque is believed to date from the 16th century. There is a huge baobab tree nearby with a circumference of over 15 m. The ruins are best known for the inscriptions carved into them – many of them remaining untranslated. However, in general, they are much smaller and less impressive than the ones at Gedi.

To get to the ruins, turn left off the main road to the south of Kilifi creek (signposted Mnarani Ruins) and go through Mnarani village. Turn right when you reach the tarmacked road and stop when you can see the creek. There is a signposted path to the left, and the ruins are a few hundred metres down this path and then a climb of about 100 steps. You also get a wonderful view of the creek from the ruins.

Kilifi → *Colour map 2, C2. Phone code: 041.*

The town of Kilifi is situated to the north of Kilifi Creek, 60 km north of Mombasa, while **Mnarani** village is to the south. This popular boating and sailing centre is in an absolutely glorious location – the shore slopes steeply down to the water's edge and the view from the bridge is spectacular. The town has an interesting mix of people with quite a number of resident expatriates. It is an easy-going town with an attractive beach that is fairly untroubled by the hassle of beach boys associated with some of the beaches closer to Mombasa.

On the sea bed

The 80-m ship *MV Dania* spent 45 years plying the waters off the African coast, mainly as a live cattle transporter. In 2002 her life on the waves ended as she was sunk below the ocean just north of Mombasa. But the *Dania* has a new life as one of Africa's finest wreck dives and Mombasa's newest reefs, and the cattle pens and cabins have already become home to all kinds of sea life. The ship now lies in around 30 m of water just off Bamburi Beach and, when she was sunk, landed perfectly upright. She was fully prepared for sinking and had her engines removed and hull cleaned to minimize any environmental impact. The interior was fully cleared for safe penetration by divers, and all potentially dangerous objects, such as wiring and doors were removed, as have all but three of the original brass portholes, allowing divers and marine life to move freely in and out of the control room and the hull with ease. Many artificial reefs have been created around the world from wrecks; some as a result of natural disaster and some, as in *Dania*'s case, intentionally. A variety of materials, ranging from military tanks to naval ships, have been used and, over the years, extensive research has been carried out to monitor and quantify the success of these artificial reefs. The result has been that artificial reefs develop into thriving coral communities, almost indistinguishable from their natural counterparts. The solid structure that an artificial reef provides facilitates the attachment of algae, sponges, benthic organisms and gorgonia to its surface, organisms that would otherwise float around aimlessly, which are vital for coral production. Over time the vessel slowly transforms into a functioning reef; coral is produced, sea turtles and pelagic fish seek refuge amongst the protective overhangs and, as the reef matures, it attracts larger sharks, groupers and moray eels. Artificial reefs also enhance the development of rare coral species that are not often found in natural reefs. In addition to the environmental aspect that artificial reefs bring, coral reefs, both natural and artificial, are also taking on an increasingly important role in supplying compounds for use in medicines. AZT is used in the treatment of HIV-infected patients and its chemical composition is derived from that of a Caribbean reef sponge. Furthermore, 50% of all new cancer drug research is conducted upon marine organisms.

With thanks to Bruce Phillips from **Buccaneer Diving**, www.buccaneer diving.com.

Arabuko-Sokoke Forest Reserve → *Colour map 2, C2.*

ⓘ *The main gate is on the Malindi Rd on the left if heading from Mombasa, 1.5 km before the turn-off to Watamu and Gedi, T042-32462, www.kws.org, 0630-1800, US$20, children (3-18) US$10.* The largest surviving stretch of coastal forest in East Africa, the Arabuko-Sokoke Forest Reserve runs for about 40 km north from Kilifi and is 20 km wide at its widest point. It is home to many species of rare bird and is the most important bird-conservation project in Kenya. There are over 40 km of rough driving tracks and a network of walking paths to explore, and well-trained and knowledgeable local guides are available to take visitors on educational walks. A well-equipped visitor centre is open daily 0600-1600 for information, from where a 4 km nature trail starts.

Over 260 species of bird have been identified in the forest, and Clarke's weaver is endemic to this area: the 16-cm Sokoke Scops owl is only found here and in a small area in eastern Tanzania, in the Usambara Mountains. The reserve also contains rare species of amphibian, butterfly and plant. The forest is home to rare mammals too, such as the very small Zanzibar duiker (only 35 cm high and usually seen in pairs), the Sokoke bushy-tailed mongoose and the rare golden-rumped elephant shrew.

Mida Creek

There is good birdwatching at Mida Creek, which covers 32 sq km of tidal inlet that stretches inland for about 6 km and is a key stopover site for birds migrating from Europe, Asia and the Middle East to eastern and southern Africa. The birds refuel on the variety of invertebrate food items buried in the muddy sandflats at low tide and roost on the exposed sandbanks and on the mangroves at high tide. Young corals and fish also start their lives in these nutrient-rich waters, before the tides sweep them into the Indian Ocean. To reach the head of the creek, leave the Mombasa–Malindi road opposite the entrance to the Arabuko-Sokoke Forest Reserve and make your way down to the creek's shores. The best time for birdwatching is the incoming tide, when all creatures are busy feeding. A telescope is very useful. You are likely to see crab plovers, with their distinctive crab-crunching bills, curlews, sandpipers, stints, terns, spoonbills and flamingos. There is a suspended boardwalk (open sunrise to sunset) that leads 260 m through the mangroves to a bird hide and a small restaurant in a wooden shack. You can also visit by boat on organized excursions from the resorts.

Watamu → *For listings, see pages 274-288. Colour map 2,C2.*

Watamu Village → *Phone code: 042.*

Watamu is known for its spectacular coral reef and three bays: Watamu, Blue Lagoon and Turtle Bay, divided by eroded rocky headlands. Each bay becomes a broad white strand at low tide, and it is possible to walk across to the small offshore islands. Like the southern resorts, Watamu is inundated with seaweed at certain times, but the sand is usually clear from December to April. Most resorts are south of Watamu, on the road that runs down to the KWS headquarters. The setting is attractive, and Turtle Bay is quite good for snorkelling (but watch out for speed boats ferrying fishermen to the large game boats). The water is much clearer here than at Malindi during the wet season. The most exciting way to the reef, 2 km offshore, is to go in a glass-bottomed boat; at low tide and, especially, spring low tide, a number of eroded corals protrude from the surface, which resemble giant Swiss cheeses. Due to the high concentration of plankton in the sea around Watamu, the marine life is superb and it's also an excellent place for scuba-diving. In particular manta rays and whale sharks are common. Watamu is also a good place to hire bikes as an alternative way of exploring the surrounding area, including the Gedi Ruins. There are a number of shops in the village, with reasonable rates.

Bio-Ken Snake Farm

ⓘ *T042-32303, www.bio-ken.com, 0900-1200 and 1400-1700, US$7.50, children (under 12) free.*
Some 3 km north of the village is a research centre primarily dealing with reptiles, especially snakes and snake-bite venom. Bio-Ken is a registered international advisor on the handling of snake-bite victims and holds snake-bite seminars attended by experts from all over the world. There are over 200 snakes at the farm and a variety of species. Bio-Ken also offers a free 'remove-a-snake' service for people in the Watamu area. It also runs a snake-spotting day safari with a picnic lunch for visitors to show snakes and reptiles in

Watamu turtle watch

Watamu has a small but nationally important nesting population of giant green sea turtles along the beaches of the Watamu Marine National Reserve. They are often in danger from human-related activities, including injuries from spear-guns and fishing hooks, nets and lines as well as boat propellers. Watamu Turtle Watch is a volunteer organization that is involved in protecting the turtles' nests to ensure that thousands of turtle hatchlings make it into the sea, and rescuing and rehabilitating injured turtles. It is also involved in projects to tag turtles, providing essential information about their foraging and nesting areas along the coast, as well as conservation initiatives among the local schools and fishing communities to educate about the protection of marine environments. The rehabilitation centre is just south of Watamu village close to the Ocean Sports Resort. As well as seeing turtles close up, the knowledgeable staff will explain about the valuable work they do, and you can ask about volunteer placements if you are interested. Contact T042-233 2118, www.watamuturtles.com, Monday 1400-1600, Tuesday-Friday 0900-1200, 1400-1600, Saturday 0900-1200, US$7 per person.

their natural habitat. There are about 127 different snake species in Kenya. Of these only 18 have caused human fatalities and only another six could kill. Another 10 could cause a lot of pain and the remaining 93 or so are non-venomous and not dangerous.

Watamu Marine National Park → *Phone code: 042.*
ⓘ *T042-31554, www.kws.org, 0800-1800, US$15, children (3-18) US$10.*

The KWS park HQ is some way south of Watamu at the end of the peninsula that guards the entrance to the creek. Unfortunately the road goes a little inland, hiding views of the sea. The park covers 30 km of coastline, with a fringing reef along its entirety, as well as numerous patch reefs. The fringing reef forms several lagoons, some of which are rich in coral and fish species, while part of the beach within the park is a key turtle-nesting ground. It also encompasses **Mida Creek** (see page 266), a diverse and rich ecosystem consisting of mangroves, coral, crustacea, fish and turtles. There are approximately 700 species of fish in the marine park and there are estimated to be over 100 species of stony coral. You go out in a glass-bottomed boat to the protected area and some of the hundreds of fishes come to the boat to be fed. The boats may seem rather expensive but really are well worth it. Trips can be arranged at any of the resorts, or else at the KWS park headquarters. You can also swim or snorkel amongst the fish, which is a wonderful experience, with lots of shells and live corals that are a splendid range of colours. The water temperature ranges from 20-30°C.

Gedi Ruins → *Colour map 2, C2.*

ⓘ *4 km north of Watamu, signposted from the village of Gedi, if you come by* matatu *you will have to walk the last 1 km, T042-32065, www.museums.or.ke, 0930-1800, US$5.40, children (under 16) US$2.70.*

The Gedi Ruins are one of Kenya's most important archaeological sites and are believed to contain the ruins of a city that once had a population of about 2500. It was populated in the latter half of the 13th century, and the size of some of the buildings, in particular the mosque, suggests that this was a fairly wealthy town for some time. However, it is not mentioned in any Arabic or Swahili writings and was apparently unknown to the Portuguese, although they maintained a strong presence in Malindi just 15 km away. It is believed that this was because it was set away from the sea, deep in the forest. Possibly as a result of an attack from marauding tribesmen of the Oromo or Galla tribe, the city was abandoned at some time during the 16th century. Lack of water may have also been a contributing factor, as wells over 50-m deep dried out. It was later reinhabited but never regained the economic position that it once had held. It was finally abandoned in the early 17th century and the ruins were rediscovered in 1884. The site was declared a national monument in 1948 and has been excavated since then. It has been well preserved.

There is a beautifully designed **museum** that includes a restaurant and library. Visitors are made to feel welcome, you can buy a guidebook and map of the site at the entrance gate and there are also informative guides.

The site was originally surrounded by an inner and outer wall (surprisingly thin). The most interesting buildings and features are concentrated around the entrance gate, although there are others. Most that remain are within the inner wall although there are some between the two walls. Coral rag and lime were used in all the buildings and some had decorations carved into the wall plaster. You can still see the remains of the bathrooms – complete with deep bath, basin and squat toilet. There are a large number of wells in the site, some exceptionally deep. The main buildings that remain are a sultan's palace, a mosque and a number of houses and tombs, a water system and a prison. Other finds include pieces of Chinese porcelain from the Ming Dynasty, beads from India and stoneware from Persia – some are displayed in the museum, others in Fort Jesus, Mombasa.

The **palace** can be entered through a rather grand arched doorway, which brings you into the reception court and then a hall. This is the most impressive building on the site. Off this hall are a number of smaller rooms – including the bathrooms. You can also see the remains of the kitchen area that contains a small well.

The **Great Mosque** probably dates from the mid-15th century and is the largest of the seven on this site. It is believed that substantial rebuilding was undertaken more recently. The *mihrab*, which indicates the direction of Mecca, was built of stone (rather than wood) and has survived well. As you leave, note the carved spearhead above the northeast doorway.

A great deal of trade seems to have been established here – silk and porcelain were exchanged for skins and, most importantly, ivory. China was keen to exploit this market and, in 1414, a giraffe was given to the Chinese Emperor and shipped from Malindi. It apparently survived the trip. There was also trade with European countries and a Venetian glass bead has been found here too.

In all, there are 14 houses on the complex that have so far been excavated. Each one is named after something that was found at its site – for example House of Scissors, House of Ivory Box. There is also one named after a picture of a *dhow* that is on the wall.

The tombs are located to the right of the entrance gate and one of them is of particular interest to archaeologists as it actually has a date engraved on it – the Islamic year 802 which is equal to the year AD 1399. This is known as the Date Tomb and has enabled other parts of the site to be dated with more accuracy. There is also a tomb with a design that is common along the Swahili Coast – that of a fluted pillar. Pillar tombs are found all along the coast and were used for men with position and influence.

The site is in very pleasant surroundings – it is green and shady but can get very hot (cool drinks are available at the entrance). There are a spectacular variety of trees including combretum, tamarind, baobab, wild ficus and sterculia, a smooth-barked tree inhabited by palm nut vultures and monkeys because snakes cannot climb up the trunk. You may hear a buzzing noise. This is an insect that lives only for three or four days until it literally blows itself to pieces! There are usually monkeys in the trees above, as well as the noise of many different types of birds.

Kipepeo Butterfly Project
ⓘ *Just inside the entrance to the ruins, T042-32380, www.kipepeo.org, 0800-1700, US$1.50.* This is a community-based butterfly farm established in 1994, which has trained local farmers living on the edge of the Arabuko-Sokoke Forest Reserve, see page 265, to rear butterfly pupae for export overseas. It also produces cloth from silk worms and honey from bees. You can visit the butterfly house to see some of the 260 species. *Kipepeo* is Kiswahili for butterfly.

Malindi → *For listings, see pages 274-288. Colour map 2, C2. Phone code: 042. Population: 81,000.*

Malindi is the second largest coastal town in Kenya after Mombasa. It has a pleasant laid-back atmosphere compared to Mombasa and retains a village feel, especially along the shore road. The streets are also cleaner and the people much friendlier. In the narrow streets of the Old Town are bazaars and shops selling antique furniture and textiles. The beach is excellent and popular and, although seaweed can be a problem (especially before the Spring equinox), it is less so than on the beaches around Mombasa. A great attraction is the **Malindi Marine National Park**, with clear water and brilliantly coloured fish. It is also one of the few places on the East African coast where the rollers come crashing into the shore, there is a break in the reef, and it is possible to surf.

Arriving in Malindi
Getting there **Malindi Airport** ⓘ *T042-213 1201, www.kenyaairports.co.ke,* is 2.5 km from the centre of town on the Mombasa road and is served by a number of airlines. A taxi to the centre costs about US$5 and the resorts to the south will be about US$10.

If you're driving, the B8 road is good all the way; Malindi is 115 km north of Mombasa, which should take around 1½ hours. There are also bus/*matatu* services from Abdel Nasser Road in Mombasa, which fill up and leave about every 15 minutes during the day.
▸ *See Transport, page 287.*

Getting around You can either organize day trips through the hotels, or else try the public transport in the way of tuk-tuks and *boda bodas*. Both these are surprisingly efficient, cheap and easy to find in Malindi at any time of day or night. The main parts of town are relatively safe, even at night, but exercise caution away from the main tourist areas, and take a taxi if going further afield.

Background
The earliest known reference to Malindi is found in Chinese geography, in a piece published in 1060 by a scholar who died in AD 863. The first accurate description of the town is believed to have been written by **Prince Abu al-Fida**, who lived from 1273 to 1331. Archaeological evidence supports the theory that the town of Malindi was founded by Arabs in the 13th century. In any event, locals claim that there was a big Chinese trading influence. This belief is supported by the fact that many of the local people still retain traces of Chinese features.

In 1498 **Vasco da Gama**, having rounded the Cape of Good Hope, stopped off at various ports along the coast. At Mombasa he was not made welcome – indeed attempts were made to sink his ships. At Malindi he found a much warmer reception. The good relations between Malindi and the Portuguese continued throughout the 16th century. The town was governed by Arabs, who were the wealthiest group. The wealth came from the trade with India and the supply of agricultural produce grown in the surrounding plantations.

The town went into a period of decline in the 16th century and, in 1593, the Portuguese administration was transferred from Malindi to Mombasa. Although Malindi continued to suffer as Mombasa expanded and took more trade, the town's prosperity did improve during this period and the use of slaves was an important factor. In the first year of resettlement in 1861 there were 1000 slaves working for just 50 Arabs. Malindi had a bad reputation for its treatment of slaves.

The period under the **Imperial British East Africa Company** (IBEAC) began in 1887, when the Company acquired a 50-year lease from the Sultan of Zanzibar for territories in East Africa. The company administered the area, collected taxes and had rights over minerals found. Bell Smith was sent to the town as officer for the Company and he began to lobby for the abolition of the slave trade. From around 1890, slaves who wished and were able to, could buy their freedom. For those who could not, the company offered jobs, or found paid employment. Relatively few took up the opportunity and the process was a gradual one. With the Protectorate government abolishing the status of slavery in 1907, merchandise trade developed and, in the early 20th century, the most important exports were rubber, grain, ivory, hides and horns.

During the second half of the British period, the foundations were laid for what is now Malindi's most important industry – tourism. The first hotel, **Brady's Palm Beach Hotel**, opened in 1932, and famous visitors included Ernest Hemingway in 1934. In the 1960s, Malindi became a popular place to live for the European population, many of whom were retired farmers from the highlands. The first charter flight from Europe flew to the Kenyan coast in 1972, when there were just five hotels in Malindi, but by 1976 the hotel bed capacity in the town had tripled and hotels had been built at Watamu Beach. Malindi became very popular with Europeans, especially Germans and Italians, and the latter are today estimated to own some 3000 properties and businesses in the area, such as private villas, restaurants and nightclubs, which have not been altogether welcomed by the local people. As a result it is in Malindi that you will find some of the finest espresso coffee, Parmesan and hams to be found in Kenya, but the combination of these European trappings and the old Swahili town gives Malindi a somewhat Jekyll and Hyde character and may not be everybody's cup of tea.

Places in Malindi

Although the history of the town dates back to the 12th century, there are few remains of the ancient town. Two remains that are worth seeing, in the oldest part of the town, clustered around the jetty, are the **Jami Mosque** and two striking **Pillar Tombs**. These are thought to date from the 14th century. Behind the Jami Mosque lies a maze of small streets that form the Old Town district. The oldest surviving buildings are the mosques of which there are nine (including the Jami Mosque) that date from before 1500. Contemporary accounts from the 14th century remark on two-storeyed houses with carved wooden balconies and flat roofs constructed from mangrove poles, coral and zinc mortar. None of these have survived. The smaller dwellings had timber and latticed walls covered with mud and mortar and woven palm frond roofs, called *makuti*. The density of the housing

Malindi

To Garsen, Lamu & Tana River Primate Reserve
Golf & Country Club

N

200 metres
200 yards

St Andrew's

Lamu Rd (B8)

To 8

Air Kenya
Sabaki Centre
Malindi Complex

Galana Centre
Kenya Commercial
Kenya Airways
Dollar
Barclays

Malindi Handicraft Cooperative

Pol

Stanchart Arcade &
Standard-Chartered

District Officer's House
Uhuru Gardens
Fish Market
Blog Cyber
Odinga St
Kobil
Curio Market
Ngala Rd
Kenyatta Rd
Tana Rd
New Burhani Bohra
Jami Mosque & Pillar Tombs
Malindi Sea Fishing Club
Customs House
Football Pitch
Market Rd
Uhuru Rd
Malindi Museum
OLD TOWN

To Tsavo East National Park (C103)

Tourist Rd

Mombasa Rd (B8)

Total

To Airport, Watamu & Mombasa

Portuguese Catholic

Sailfish Club Malindi

Vasco da Gama Cross

Silversands Rd
Malindi District

Silversands Beach

Tourist Rd

Casuarina Rd

To 5 8 11
& Malindi Marine
National Park (5km)

Indian Ocean

Jetty

Where to stay
African Pearl 6
Che Shale 7
Coral Key Beach Resort 2
Diamonds Dream
  of Africa 11
Diamonds Malindi Beach 8
Driftwood Beach Club 4
Eden Roc 9
Kilili Baharini Resort
  & Spa 5
Lawfords 1
Ozi's B&B 12
Sabaki River Camp
  & Cottage 10

Sandies Coconut Village 3
Sandies Tropical Village 20
Scorpio Villas 17

Restaurants
Baby Marrow 9
Baobab 2
Bar Bar 3
I Love Pizza 4
Karen Blixen Café Bar 5
La Griglia & Casino
  Malindi 6
Lorenzo's 8
Oasis Gelateria 10
Old Man & the Sea 7

Bars & clubs
Fermento Bar 11
Star Dust Club 12
Stars & Garters 13

and the materials made old Malindi very vulnerable to fire, and periodic conflagrations (the most recent in 1965) destroyed all the older dwellings. The mosques survived by virtue of having walls of coral blocks and mortar.

The two buildings of note from the British period are the **District Officer's House** in front of Uhuru Gardens, and the **Customs House** behind the jetty. Both have verandas, and neither is in particularly good repair, but the District Officer's House is a handsome and imposing structure.

There are a couple of monuments that date from the Portuguese period, in particular the **Vasco da Gama Cross**, which is situated on the promontory at the southern end of the bay. It is one of the oldest remaining monuments in Africa and was built in 1498 by the great Portuguese explorer, Vasco da Gama, as a sign of appreciation for the welcome he was given by the Sultan of Malindi, and to assist in navigation. The actual cross is the original and is made of stone from Lisbon. You can reach it by turning down Mnarani Road. The small **Catholic church** close to the cross is also believed to date from the Portuguese period and is thought to be the same one that St Francis Xavier visited in 1542 when he stopped off at Malindi to bury two soldiers on his way to India. It is one of the oldest Catholic churches in Africa still in use today and the walls are original, although the thatched roof has been replaced many times.

Malindi Museum ① *close to the Customs House on Casuarina Rd, T042-31479, www.museums.or.ke, 0930-1800, US$5.40, children (under 16) US$2.70*, is housed in an attractive former house of an Indian trader, constructed in 1891. In more recent years it has served as the office for Kenya Wildlife Service and has been the Malindi Museum since 2004. The house is on three floors with cool high rooms, intricate staircases and wooden shutters. There are several very interesting exhibits and everything is very clearly labelled. These include some sacred wooden carved grave posts of the gohu people, which are traditionally used as a link between the living and the dead. Sacrifices are made to them in preparation for harvesting and planting. There are a few boards about Vasco de Gama and his arrival on the coast in the 15th century, and a room of posters dedicated to 'Discover Islam' with information about how Muslim men and women live their lives. On the ground floor are some interesting early photographs of Mombasa, with corresponding modern photos on what the various areas look like today. Also on display is a strange-looking coelacanth, a prehistoric fish that was once thought to be long extinct, but in recent years a few have been found around the coasts of east and southern Africa as well as Indonesia. The massive 1.7 m fish was caught at a depth of about 185 m off the coast of Malindi in 1991 and has fleshy limb-like fins that move like our arms and legs. Scientists believe it could be a specimen that was part of a chain of creatures that evolved and moved to live on land some 360 million years ago. It was identified as an adult female coelacanth, and amazingly was found to be carrying 17 tennis-ball sized eggs, which would suggest that these rare fish are breeding along the Kenyan coast. The museum also doubles up as the town's tourist information office. There is a football pitch opposite the museum where you can watch teams of teenagers in their coloured T-shirts play in the late afternoon.

Malindi Marine National Park
① *KWS HQ, Casuarina Point, 5 km south of Malindi on Casuarina Rd, T042-20845, www.kws.org, 0600-1800, US$15, children (3-18) US$10.*
Situated within the Malindi Marine Biosphere Reserve is this small marine national park. Gazetted in 1968, this is an area of only 6 sq km that offers wonderful diving and snorkelling on the coral reefs off Casuarina Point. This park is popular and with good reason. The water

is brilliantly clear, and the fish are a dazzling array of colours. The fish are very tame as they have been habituated by being fed on bread provided by the boatman. Most of the resorts organize snorkelling and glass-bottomed boat trips, as does the KWS HQ.

To the Lamu Archipelago

After leaving Malindi north on the B8 you cross the **Sabaki River**, which, at approximately 390 km long, is Kenya's second longest river (after the Tana). It is known as the Athi River at its source in the Ngong Hills in Nairobi and in its upper stages, the Galana River in its mid section and, finally, the Sabaki River as it meanders into the Indian Ocean. Birdwatchers are advised to stop here (or you can take a taxi from Malindi) as the tidal mud flats of the river estuary are a vital habitat for migratory waders, gulls and terns, and the coastal scrub and wetlands adjacent to the river mouth are an important habitat at for other waterbirds. Shortly after is the turning for the village of **Mambrui**, which is believed to be about 600 years old. All that remains of the ancient Arab city is a mosque, a Koran school and a pillar tomb, which has insets of Ming porcelain.

At Mambrui is the turn-off from the B8 west to the village of Marafa, which is about 18 km on a poor gravel road. The attraction here is the **Marafa Depression** ① *35 km northwest of Malindi, access is sunrise-sunset when local guides are available for about US$3-4, there's a 3 km (rough) path from the car park*, also known as 'Hell's Kitchen' because of the searing heat that can reach 45°C in the middle of the day. This small shallow canyon is a geological oddity. The rocks are made up of soft and hard sandstone, but as the soft sandstone has eroded away much faster than the hard sandstone, it has left jagged ridges and gullies of exposed sandstone in spectacular colours from off-white to pale pinks and from oranges to deep crimson, and the red oxide in the rocks creates curious patterns. The local name is Nyari, which means 'the place broken by itself' and, according to folklore, a wealthy village once stood here and the people had so many cows that they bathed in milk and refused to share with those in need. As punishment, the gods destroyed their village and left a gaping red and white pit in its place. It is not easy to get to without your own transport, though there are infrequent *matatus* to the village from Malindi or you can hire a taxi for a few hours. The best time to visit is in the late afternoon when the setting sun highlights the rocks' colours beautifully.

Back on the B8, just north of Mambrui and about 20 km from Malindi is the turn-off to the remote and quite wonderful **Che Shale** resort, see Where to stay, page 279, where there is a beautiful and very wide expanse of beach that the resort is now utilizing for kite-surfing. Non-guests are welcome for lunch but you are advised to phone ahead. Further on you will eventually pass **Garsen**, a small town at the crossing of the Tana River where you can get fuel and drinks. From Garsen, the newly tarred C112 road turns back towards the coast and **Witu**, another small old town where you can also get fuel. After Witu the road turns to gravel with a few bumps (though by the time you read this, the final 60 km or so between Witu and Mokowe may have also been tarred). As you drive in this area you may see people of the Orma tribe as well as Somalis, for this is getting close to the border. Both groups are pastoralists, and you will see the cattle that represent their wealth. Finally, about four hours after leaving Malindi, you will get to **Mokowe** and see the Makanda channel, which separates Lamu from the mainland. Here there is a small café and if you are in your own vehicle, you can park it up here and pay for an *askari* to look after your car whilst you visit Lamu. This is also where the buses stop. See also Getting there in the Lamu chapter (page 292).

The upside-down tree

The baobab tree (Adansonia digitata) grows throughout eastern and southern Africa in savannah environments. These huge trees reach heights of about 25 m, have enormous girths of up to 10 m and can live for up to 2000 years. At Ukunda there is one with a girth of 22 m, which has been given 'presidential protection' to safeguard it. The baobab trees store water in their swollen trunk, which enables them to survive during long dry patches. During droughts people open up the pods and grind the seeds to make what is known as 'hunger flour'.

Legend has it that when God first planted them, they kept walking around and would not stay still. So He decided to replant them, upside-down, which is why they look as if they have the roots sticking up into the air.

Tana River Primate Reserve → *Colour map 1, B2.*

ⓘ *On the B8, 50 km north of Garsen, T046-2035, www.kws.org, 0600-1800, US$20, children (3-18) US$10.*

Situated 120 km north of Malindi, the remote and rarely visited Tana River Primate Reserve is located on the lower reaches of the meandering course of the Tana River, covering an area of 171 km of forest, dry woodland and savannah habitat. It has at least seven different types of primate and was gazetted in 1976 to protect the forests and two highly endangered primates, the crested mangabey and the Tana River red colobus monkey as this is the sole habitat of these endangered primates. A number of other animals are present, including Grevy's zebra, the Maasai and reticulated giraffe, buffalo and lesser kudu, and the river has plenty of crocodile and hippo and attracts a variety of waterbirds. The reserve is accessible via the Malindi–Garissa road, but given safety concerns for tourists in the Somali border region, travelling on the B8 between Garsen and Garissa independently is not advised and there is no accommodation in the reserve. However, you can visit this region as guests of **Delta Dunes**, the upmarket lodge at the mouth of the Tana River, see Where to stay, page 280.

---

❿ North of Mombasa listings

For sleeping and eating price codes and other relevant information, see pages 20-24.

❿ Where to stay

Room rates vary with the season. Low is Apr-Jun; mid is Jul-Nov; high is Dec-Mar. There's a wide choice of accommodation along the beach and a number of all-inclusive resorts where rates include all meals, usually buffets, and some watersports. These are favoured by package holidaymakers on 1- to 2-week stays. Nevertheless, most of these accept direct bookings and, out of the high season, walk-in guests.

Nyali, Kenyatta and Bamburi beaches
p260, map p262

There are more than 25 almost back-to-back beach resorts along the 6 km or so strip of coast immediately north of Mombasa. None of them are cheap, and budget travellers have a better choice of accommodation south of Mombasa on Diani Beach.

$$$$-$$$ Sarova Whitesands Beach Resort & Spa, Bamburi Beach, T041-212 8000, www.sarovahotels.com. Quality Sarova property set in 8 ha with 300 m of beachfront and 338 a/c rooms in 5 different categories, with satellite TV and Wi-Fi. The main buffet restaurant has themed nights and boasts that guests on a 2-week holiday can eat a different international cuisine every night, plus 2 speciality restaurants (see Restaurants), 3 bars, **Coco's** nightclub, 4 swimming pools with slides and diving boards, spa, gym, a **Buccaneer Diving** base, and a kids' activity centre and children's café with special buffet meals.

$$$$-$$$ Voyager Beach Resort, Nyali Beach, reservations **Heritage Hotels**, Nairobi, T020-444 6651, www.heritage-eastafrica. com. This is a good, all-round family resort with over 200 a/c comfortable rooms, some with sea views, set in spacious grounds, although the beach here is at its narrowest at Nyali. **Buccaneer Diving** has a base here, and a full range of watersports is on offer, including *dhow* and glass-bottom boat trips, plus a fully equipped boat for fishing, 3 swimming pools, several restaurants and bars and a kids' club.

$$$ Bahari Beach Hotel, Nyali Beach, T041-547 2822, www.baharibeach.net. Set in gardens, the 100 rooms are in whitewashed thatched blocks with a/c, balconies or terraces, there's a large pool, but again only a narrow beach that is covered at high tide. Fairly good-value rates are all inclusive of buffet meals, sodas and beer, and facilities include watersports, a **Peponi Divers** centre and tennis courts.

$$$ Bamburi Beach Hotel, Bamburi Beach, T041-548 5611-7, www.bamburibeach kenya.com. Consistently one of the most popular all-inclusive family places and one of the best value, from US$108 for a double half board in low season. 150 a/c rooms with balconies and satellite TV, 3 restaurants, 4 bars, evening cabaret shows, 2 swimming pools, squash courts, gym, kids' club and a full range of watersports. The beach here is quite narrow but there's a spacious wooden deck above the beach for sunbathing.

$$$ Kenya Bay Beach Hotel, Bamburi Beach, T041-548 7600, www.kenyabay.com. A friendly, laid-back and traditionally built hotel. The 106 comfortable a/c rooms are in 3-storey blocks with balconies or terraces,

and there are some spacious communal areas with stone floors and Swahili-style furnishings. Watersports centre, pool, 3 restaurants, 2 bars and a disco, and Masai dancing and acrobatics in the evening. Good value from US$110 for a double half board.

$$$ Neptune Beach Resort, Bamburi Beach, T041-548 5701, www.neptune hotels.com. Newly refurbished in a not very classy cane and floral decor with 78 a/c rooms, this is the sister resort to the Neptune resorts south of Mombasa and is a very similar set up with the usual resort facilities such as pool, shops, kids' club and games room. **Buccaneer Diving** has a base here. There's a nice informal atmosphere and rates are some of the lowest of the all-inclusive places.

$$$ Nyali Beach Hotel, Nyali Beach, T041-471 551, www.nyali-international.com. This opened in 1946 and was the first hotel to be built on the mainland outside of Mombasa, though obviously it has been refurbished and extended many times since then. It now has 170 rooms with a/c, minibar, satellite TV and balconies or terraces set in 8 ha of gardens. Facilities include 6 restaurants, 5 bars, nightclub, tennis courts, 2 swimming pools and evening entertainment. A kitesurfing centre is based here and 2 free beginners' scuba lessons are included in the room rates.

$$$ Reef Hotel Mombasa, Nyali Beach, T041-447 1772, www.reefhotelkenya.com. Recently renovated, the 160 rooms all have a/c, TV and balconies. Facilities include 3 swimming pools, tennis court, jacuzzi, **Buccaneer Diving** has a base here, and they also rent out sea kayaks and windsurfers. There is a lively nightlife here with 3 restaurants, several bars, a disco and shows.

$$$ Severin Sea Lodge, Bamburi Beach, T041-211 1805, www.severinsealodge.com. This has 188 rooms in the main block with balconies/terraces or in imaginatively designed *makuti* thatched rondavels all of which are a/c and very comfortable. Facilities include 2 swimming pools, tennis courts, watersports and a spa. There is a choice of international restaurants including the **Imani Dhow**, which as the name suggests is set in a *dhow* although it's not in the water.

$$$ Traveller's Beach Hotel & Club, Bamburi Beach, T041-548 5121, www.travellersbeach.com. A consistently popular resort with lots of fun activities, friendly professional staff and a relaxed holiday atmosphere, although the 128 rooms could do with a refurb. Facilities include a gym, spa, indoor and outdoor games, 4 swimming pools, 1 of which you can swim in to reception, watersports, the excellent **Sher-e-Punjab** Indian restaurant (see Restaurants), plus an Italian and buffet restaurants. It also runs the tented camp in the **Mwaluganje Elephant Sanctuary** (see page 254).

$$ Indiana Beach Apartments & Hotel, Bamburi Beach, T041-548 5895, www.indianabeachkenya.com. Unremarkable and simply furnished, the 39 rooms are in a boring white concrete block with balconies, and have a/c, minibar and TV, and some have kitchenettes. But on the plus side there's a pleasant thatched restaurant and bar almost on the beach, a good Indian restaurant, the **Maharajah** (see Restaurants, page 280), 3 swimming pools, a PADI dive school and a gym.

$$ Kahama Hotel, Bamburi Beach, T041-548 5395, www.kahamahotel.co.ke. A neat and bright budget place with 32 a/c rooms and satellite TV, but they don't have balconies. It's 1 block back from the beach, which you reach through the **Kenya Bay Beach Hotel**, B&B rates from US$50 for a double, large swimming pool set in tropical gardens and the lively **Pitcher & Butch** sports bar that does good pub grub like burgers, grilled chicken and steaks.

$ Mombasa Backpackers, 69 Mwamba Dr, Nyali, T0701-561 233, www.mombasabackpackers.com. A neat set-up in a house in a residential area off Nyali Rd and about 500 m south of Nakumatt Nyali Shopping Centre, with dorms and doubles, camping

in the pleasant gardens, swimming pool, kitchen, meals arranged, well run and close to sights and Nyali Beach.

Mtwapa and Shanzu Beach *p263, map p262*

With the exception of the **Serena**, the 4 hotels in a long line next to each other at Shanzu Beach were managed by the UK-based **African Safari Club**, who unfortunately went bankrupt in 2011, so for now the future of these resorts is uncertain.

$$$$ Serena Beach Hotel & Spa, reservations Nairobi, T020-354 8771, www.serenahotels.com. A very pleasant luxury hotel carefully designed to resemble Swahili architecture with about 120 rooms in double-storey cottages, with carved balconies, arranged in winding lanes full of lush vegetation. There's a nice Persian water garden with restaurant, ice cream shop and a number of boutiques, a decent-sized pool with swim-up bar and a wide beach frontage. It's superior to some of the other resorts and popular with a broad range of nationalities.

Kikambala Beach *p264, map p262*

$$$ Royal Reserve Safari & Beach Club, T0733-624 320, www.royalreserve.net. A good family option with 46 a/c 1- and 2-bedroom apartments with kitchenettes and satellite TV, in smart white thatched blocks with balconies/terraces, and a full range of facilities including 2 swimming pools, 1 with swim-up bar, tennis courts, sauna and steam room, mini-golf, kids' club, restaurants, beach bar and disco, and evening entertainment including acrobats.

$$$ Sun 'n' Sand Beach Resort, T0722-204 799, www.sunnsand.info. This is an expansive resort set on 7 ha with 200 m of beach frontage and popular with European package holidaymakers, although the 300 rooms set in 4-storey blocks are well overdue for refurbishment. It has a good range of facilities including 5 restaurants, many bars, nightly entertainment, 3 swimming pools, 1 of which has a 100-m slide.

Kilifi *p264, map p262*

Kilifi Konnection, www.kilifikonnection.com, is an agent for a number of luxury private villas in the Kilifi area, each of a very high standard, with Moorish architecture, staff to cook and clean and their own pool; they can sleep 4-8 people. For families or groups these make a pleasant alternative to the resorts.

$$$$-$$$ Kilifi Bay Beach Resort, Coast Rd, about 6 km out of Kilifi, T041-752 2264, www.madahotels.com. Well designed by an Italian and the best place to stay in Kilifi, the complex accommodates guests in 50 thatched cottages with private balconies. Activities include windsurfing, canoes, snorkelling and diving, bicycles can be hired and free massages are on offer. It has well-tended surroundings, located on cliffs with path down to beach, and there are 2 swimming pools, restaurants and bars.

$$$ Baobab Lodge Resort, Coast Rd, about 3 km out of Kilifi, T041-752 2570, www.mada hotels.com. Also managed by **Mada Hotels** and much cheaper than the Kilifi Bay (above), located on a bluff with good ocean views but not much of a beach, although there's a large shaded swimming pool with swim-up bar and pleasant tree-filled gardens. The 30 a/c rooms are either in a double-storey block or spacious rondavels, and there are 2 bars and a restaurant, evening entertainment and again bicycles can be hired and free massages are on offer.

$$$ Mnarani Beach Club, south side of Kilifi Creek, reservations South Africa, T+27 (0)12-425 1000, www.mnarani.co.za. Overlooking Kilifi Creek, this hotel is among the oldest in the country. It has been beautifully restored, with 84 a/c rooms in natural wood finishes set in cottages in marvellous gardens. Facilities include watersports (sailing, windsurfing and waterskiing), a bar and restaurant overlooking the creek with high standards of food, swimming pool, spa and evening entertainment.

$$ Makuti Villas, on the left on the north side of the creek about 500 m from the bridge, T041-752 2371, www.makutivillas. com. Small hotel with 32 rooms set in thatched blocks in a pleasant tropical garden, with ceiling fans and verandas, and the floors are made from polished river stones. It's clean and fairly basic but good value, and there's a popular bar and restaurant and a large swimming pool.

Watamu *p266, map p262*

Again, as an alternative to the resorts, families or groups of friends may want to consider renting a house or cottage, many of which are very nice, near the beach and sometimes have a pool. Visit www.discoverwatamu.com and check under holiday lets.

$$$$-$$$ Hemingways Resort, about 1 km south of Watamu, T042-233 2052, www.hemingways.co.ke. Watamu's famous fishing club has an enormous stuffed marlin over the reception desk. There are 76 stylish a/c rooms – the ones in the new block are exceptionally spacious and have great sea views – good food and fishermen can get their catch prepared to their liking. An excellent set-up for deep-sea fishing with plenty of boats and fishing guides (see What to do, page 286). Other watersports can be arranged and there's a pool and spa, but not much for children to do.

$$$ Ocean Sports Resort, next door to **Hemingways**, T042-233 2288, www.ocean sports.net. This has recently had a complete refurbishment with 30 rooms in thatched cottages set in gardens with sunny blue and white decor, some sleeping up to 5, plus a 3-bed self-catering unit with staff sleeping 8. There is a bar and restaurant on an especially nice large wooden deck overlooking the beach (see Restaurants, page 282). It's a focal point of Watatmu and well worth dropping in for lunch. Activities include fishing, diving, snorkelling, kitesurfing, boogie-boarding, tennis and squash. Friendly atmosphere recommended, with doubles from US$110.

$$$ Turtle Bay Beach Club, just to the south of Ocean Sports, T042-233 2003, www.turtlebay.co.ke. A good-value and fun all-round family all-inclusive resort popular with British guests, with 145 rooms in 4 ha of grounds, plenty of food and drink on offer as well as lots of activities and entertainment, and it looks after guests very well. Facilities include bike rental, tennis, diving, kids' club, Kiswahili lessons, tuition for windsurfing and sailing, and an enormous swimming pool.

$$-$ Marijani Holiday Resort, to the north of the village, T042-233 2510, www. marijani-holiday-resort.com. A friendly Kenyan/German budget option 100 m from the beach offering 12 spacious rooms with nets, fans, hot water and large 4-poster beds. Some cottages have a kitchen so you can choose bed and breakfast or self catering, and dinner can be arranged with notice. It's set in lovely well-established gardens, which are home to parrots, tortoises, cats and dogs. Bicycles can be rented.

Malindi *p269, map p271*

There's a clutch of basic board and lodgings in the town centre near the bus stand. Most charge little more than US$5 for a bed with or without bathroom but are mostly run-down and pretty grim – far better to stay near the beach. Most of the resorts are on Silversands Beach and line Casuarina Rd on the way to the KWS HQ of the Malindi Marine National Park, which is at Casuarina Point, 5 km south of Malindi (see page 272).

$$$$ Diamonds Dream of Africa, Silversands Beach, Casuarina Rd, 3 km south of town, T042-213 1728, www.planhotel. com. This super luxury and stylish lodge consistently gets good reports, with 35 spacious rooms with a/c, internet, satellite TV and jacuzzis in striking terracotta and white low-rise buildings within an easy stroll to the beach. There's a restaurant, 2 bars, pool, spa and watersports are available to guests at the **Sandies Tropical Beach Resort** (below), which is under the same management.

$$$$ Diamonds Malindi Beach, Silversands Beach, Casuarina Rd, 3 km south of town, T042-213 0714, www.plan hotel.com. A very exclusive boutique hotel with 23 beautifully decorated rooms spread across 8 Arab/African-style 2-level villas set in marvellous colourful gardens on a private beach. Each has a wide balcony or terrace with day beds, a/c, satellite TV and minibar. There's a romantic restaurant with Moorish arches, 2 bars, 2 swimming pools and watersports are available at the **Sandies Tropical Village**.

$$$$ Kilili Baharini Resort & Spa, Silversands Beach, Casuarina Rd, 4 km south of town, T0770-206 500, www.kililibaharini. com. Exclusive luxury and very stylish hotel in thatched villa style, with 29 vast and exquisitely decorated a/c rooms, almost entirely white with some antique furniture and verandas where breakfast is served, several swimming pools, gourmet Italian restaurant, bar, relaxing lounge areas and spa using expensive Italian products.

$$$$-$$$ Lawfords, Harambee Rd, T042-212 1265, www.malindikey.com. This is Malindi's oldest hotel. It opened in 1936 and Ernest Hemingway was once a guest; now it's an upmarket resort, with 60 suites and 10 3-storey villas with very elegant furnishings and works of art on the wall, a/c, Wi-Fi, TV and DVD player and minibars, all set in magnificent gardens full of flowering shrubs and baobab trees. There are 2 superb restaurants serving Mediterranean cuisine, several bars including a whiskey and cigar bar with leather furniture and books, 2 vast swimming pools, 1 in the shape of Africa, and a spa.

$$$ Coral Key Beach Resort, Silversands Beach, Casuarina Rd, 2 km south of town, T042-213 0717, www.malindikey.com. Under the same Italian management as **Lawfords** and a less expensive option, with a very attractive layout, the 150 a/c rooms have wide verandas with comfortable furniture, facilities include a complex of 7 swimming pools, tennis courts, beach bar, restaurant and pizzeria, boutique, and there's a popular disco on Fri night open to all.

$$$ Driftwood Beach Club, Silversands Beach, Casuarina Rd, 3 km south of town, T042-212 0155, www.driftwoodclub.com. Unlike some of the others, this is small and privately owned and one of the older hotels in Malindi. It opened in 1963 and has managed to retain a clubby but informal character, with 15 cosy a/c thatched cottages and 2 pairs of 2-bed villas that share their own pool and are ideal for 2 families, nicely and brightly furnished with *kikoy* fabrics. Facilities include an excellent seafood restaurant, bar, swimming pool, and watersports, including fishing, diving and windsurfing.

$$$ Sandies Tropical Village, T042-212 0444, and **Sandies Coconut Village**, T042-213 0714, Silversands Beach, Casuarina Rd, 3 km south of town, T042-20442, www.planhotel.com. Originally 2 resorts, now joined as 1 all-inclusive resort catering largely for package tours, set in established gardens with lots of *makuti* thatched buildings. Over 140 rooms with high-standard furnishings in either Swahili-style or with a colonial feel. The good facilities include swimming pools, 3 bars, 4 restaurants and a disco on the beach. Diving and watersports are organized for all 4 of the Plan Hotel resorts by **Blue-Fin Diving**, which has a base here, see What to do, page 286.

$$$ Scorpio Villas, Silversands Beach, Casuarina Rd, 2 km from town, T042-212 0194, www.scorpio-villas.com. A good Italian-managed complex with friendly service, the 25 whitewashed villas are set in magnificent tropical gardens around 3 swimming pools, and are furnished with enormous Zanzibar beds and day couches on the verandas where breakfast is delivered if you wish. Restaurant and bar and the beach is a short walk along sandy paths. One of the cheaper options with doubles from US$120 half board in low season.

$$$-$$ Che Shale, 20 km north of Malindi off the B8, T0722-230 931, www.cheshale.

com. This is a real Robinson Crusoe place in a superb and remote location in its own bay with a 5 km white-sand beach. There are 7 lovingly decorated *bandas* under giant palm roofs and right in the sand, with handmade furniture and colourful textiles. Plus there are a clutch of cheaper beach huts from US$45 per person and a campsite (**$**). Restaurant and bar, bonfires are lit on the beach in the evening. A super-relaxing and refreshing and more contemporary set-up than the usual old beach resorts; transfers from Malindi can be arranged. The beach itself is Malindi's premier kitesurfing beach, and they can also organize snorkelling, but it's a long way from the dive sites so you'll have to go into town to organize diving.

$$ Eden Roc Hotel, Lamu Rd, T0720-909 853, www.edenrochotel.co.ke. On a clifftop overlooking the bay in 9 ha of generous grounds containing lily ponds, this is a large hotel that was opened in 1957 by German big-game hunters, and although it has been renovated many times since then, it presently is in a 'need of a refurb phase'. Nevertheless, has 165 rooms that vary in price depending on whether they have a/c or fans, 4 swimming pools, tennis courts, watersports and open-air disco and rates start at an affordable US$90 for a double half board. It has its own beach, although it's a long walk through the gardens and the sea is 100 m away.

$$-$ African Pearl Hotel, off Lamu Rd, about 1 km from town beyond **Eden Roc Hotel**, T0720-673 900, www.africanpearlhotel.com. A simple and a bit unkempt set-up and not on the beach, but friendly and affordable for about US$50 for a double, with 30 rooms in the main building (the 5 rooms on the 2nd floor are the largest and have balconies) and thatched chalets, decent swimming pool, peaceful tropical gardens, good breakfast included but the restaurant is not always functioning, though you can ask to use the kitchen and there's a bar.

$ Ozi's B&B, T042-213 1365. Situated overlooking the beach very close to the jetty,

Ozi's has 16 rooms with nets and ceiling fans and mostly with shared bathrooms; ask for a front-facing room for ocean views. It is simple, but clean and good value and is one of the most popular of the budget hotels; the price includes a very good breakfast and there are restaurants nearby. The downside is you may be woken during the night by the calls to prayer from the nearby mosque.

$ Sabaki River Camp & Cottage, about 8 km north of Malindi, T0714-128 662, www.sabakirivercampandcottage.com. Head north from Malindi, cross the bridge over the river, then immediately turn right to go through the village. Ask here for directions to the home of Rodgers Karabu, which is about 1 km further on. The cottage is on a hill overlooking the mouth of Sabaki River, where thousands of birds, including flamingos, gather; this region has been earmarked as an important bird site for Kenya. Only 2 rooms, they are large and have en suite bathrooms, no electricity and lanterns are used, basic meals can be arranged for US$12 a day. The campsite is located on a breezy dune under cashew nut trees 150 m from the cottage, washing and drinking water is provided in tanks, shower, flush toilet, fireplace and cooking grill. Rooms cost US$30 and camping costs US$7. Good value in a scenic location and very different to the huge resorts.

Tana River Primate Reserve *p274*
$$$$ Delta Dunes, reservations T0718-139 359, www.deltadunes.co.ke. This is a small and remote exclusive camp with just 6 large airy cottages built of mangroves, thatch and driftwood situated in groves of indigenous trees on top of dunes with good ocean views. Situated on the estuary of the Tana River, it is a 3-hr drive from Malindi. Meals are enjoyed in a mess tent, which is home to a resident family of genet cats. Expeditions down the river to the local villages may be arranged, or a 3-hr excursion to the **Tana River Primate Reserve**. It is expensive but you will be very well looked after and the

food is excellent. You can be picked up from the nearby airstrip or from Malindi, and will be taken there by 4WD and boat.

❼ Restaurants

You are not restricted to eating at your hotel and there are a number of other places to try, though you will need a car or taxi in the evening. There are also a number of good restaurants in the resorts where non-staying guests are welcome.

Nyali, Kenyatta and Bamburi beaches
p260, map p262
For more options closer to Mombasa around the Nyali Bridge including the excellent **Tamarind Restaurant & Dhow**, see page 237.
$$$-$$ Il Covo, between **Traveller's Beach Hotel & Club** and **Kenya Bay Beach Hotel**, Bamburi Beach, T041-548 7460, www.ilcovo. net. 1100-1430, 1800-1030, the bar stays open later. Set on 2 storeys with broad wooden decks, good ocean views and just a few steps down on to the sand, this serves Italian cuisine including home-made pasta and pizza, seafood and grills and has a sushi and tepanyaki bar. The bar is fashioned out of a 20-m upturned *dhow* and offers a good choice of cocktails; later in the evening it turns into a very popular disco.
$$ Maharajah, at the **Indiana Beach Apartments & Hotel**, Bamburi Beach, see Where to stay, page 276. Open 1800-2230. Indian restaurant with a very long menu and lots of choice for vegetarians, the decor is a little plain but some of the tables have booth seating that take up to 10 so it's a good place to share dishes, and local Indians eat here which is always a good sign. There's also a snack bar on the beach here (0900-2200) serving light meals, fresh juice and ice cream.
$$ Sher-e-Punjab, Traveller's Beach Hotel & Club, Bamburi Beach, see Where to stay, page 276. Tue-Sun 1200-1430, 1930-2230. An excellent Indian with an established reputation and relaxed atmosphere, with

a long menu of jalfrezi, korma, tikka and biryani dishes and plenty of choices for vegetarians. At Sun lunchtime there's a good-value buffet.

$$ Yul's, next to the **Bamburi Beach Hotel**, T041-548 5950. Open 0900-2300. Popular thatched bar/restaurant under the palms right on the beach with an excellent variety of good food, including seafood grilled over charcoal – try the seafood platter or red snapper in garlic butter – plus pizza, giant burgers, salad, steak, Indian curry and imported Italian coffee. They also make their own ice cream, which is drizzled with flavoured sauces and decorated with fresh fruit. Finally, they also offer watersports such as waterskiing, wake-boarding, banana boats and jet skis, so this is a pleasant place to spend an afternoon.

$ Fulvio's Pizzeria, Malindi Rd, just south of the **Bamburi Beach Hotel**, T041-201 5160. Open 1100-2300. Rustic thatched Italian on the main road behind the resorts so no beach access, but relaxing garden tables and indoor and outdoor bars, plenty of choice of well-loaded pizzas and rich pastas and a good wine list.

$ Minazi@Whitesands, at the **Sarova Whitesands Beach Resort & Spa**, see Where to stay, page 274. Bistro-style restaurant and patisserie with a wood-fired pizza oven that serves light meals, a good variety of coffees, Italian ice creams, milkshakes and smoothies in a nice setting next to the resort's giant lily ponds. Usefully open 24 hrs and serves an early-bird breakfast 0400-0700.

Mtwapa and Shanzu Beach *p263, map p262*

Both the first 2 can organize transport from the resorts further south.

$$$ La Marina Restaurant, about 500 m north of the bridge over Mtwapa Creek, turn right along a dirt track for 1.5 km, T0723-223 737, www.lamarina-restaurant.com. 1100-2200. Right on the creek with tables set outside along a little wharf with good views of the yachts in the marina. Specializes in

seafood and meat open-air grills, plus there are some oriental and vegetarian options. Every evening at 1730 there's an optional short cruise on a *dhow* out on to the creek to watch the sun set while the crew entertain with drumming and acrobatics, and on your return to the restaurant, Masai 'warriors' line the entrance with flaming torches. Expect to pay in the region of US$80 for the unashamedly touristy but entertaining experience and there are considerable discounts for children.

$$$ Moorings Floating Restaurant, on the north side of Mtwapa Creek to the left of the bridge, T041-548 5045, www.themoorings.co.ke. Tue-Sun 1000-2400. A magical floating wooden deck and a marvellous spot to watch the sun sink over the mangroves and baobab trees along Mtwapa Creek, the tables are atmospherically candlelit after dark. It has a fairly short menu but offers excellently prepared seafood, plus steak, chicken and pasta, and has a well-stocked bar with long cocktail list, and a boutique selling *kikoy* items, accessories, shoes and beachwear. It's also possible for groups to organize dinner on a *dhow* up Mtwapa Creek.

$$ Monsoons, at **Jumba la Mtwana**, the turn-off is 1 km north of the bridge over Mtwapa Creek, and it's 4 km to the entrance, see page 263, T0734-663 370. Tue-Sun 1100-1900. To get here you walk past the ruins and on to the beach. A tiny rustic place with a relaxing atmosphere, just 10 tables under thatch and a few day beds on the beach. Don't expect a quick lunch, but the Swahili-style seafood is very good – it's well known for its dressed crab and lobster – and there are a few authentic Italian pasta dishes for good measure.

Kikambala Beach *p264, map p262*

$$ Porini Seychellois Restaurant, off the main road before the village of Kikambala, about 7 km north of the Mtwapa Bridge, T0733-728 435, www.porini-kenya.com. 1200-2230. Set in an open-plan thatched building surrounded by a stunning tropical garden (porini means 'bush' in Kiswahili) where giant tortoises roam, this is a unique restaurant specializing in Seychellois cuisine. The staff wear Seychelles traditional dress and assist diners with washing their hands in clay pots of warm lime water before a feast of spicy grilled meat and chicken, whole fish baked in coconut milk and Creole jumbo prawns, served with fragrant rice and cassava. You can also stay here as it has 3 charming but simple thatched cottages (**$$**) and a swimming pool. The beach is about 2.5 km away.

Watamu *p266*

$$ Ocean Sports Resort, 1 km south of the village, see Where to stay, page 277. Open 0800-late. The original bar here opened in 1952 when it was frequented by the early colonial holidaymakers. Now it's Watamu's focal meeting place and is popular with the region's expats, with especially lovely and relaxing broad wooden decks perched on white sand dunes overlooking the beach. The menu features seafood, steaks and pizzas from the wood-burning oven, and on Sun from 1200 there's a superb and good-value buffet curry lunch accompanied by a live band. Often in a party mood on weekend nights.

$$-$ Savannah Restaurant & Bar, at the T-junction to Gedi Ruins and the main road and opposite the post office, T0726-287 637. Tue-Sat 1600-2400, Sun 1200-2400. A friendly family pub and restaurant with outside tables in tropical gardens and entertainment including a swimming pool, darts and pool table, simple meals like fish or cheeseburgers and chips, plus a good selection of favourite seafood dishes like prawns in coconut sauce or crab salad. Also has 2 simple self-catering thatched bungalows to rent (**$**).

Malindi *p269, map p271*

Most of the restaurants in the hotels are open to non-residents; their set menus and buffets can be good value. Around the main market on Uhuru Rd are some local basic canteens selling Swahili food and chai (tea), and here you can get the likes of beef stew and *ugali*, omelette and chips, pilau rice, or filling chapattis with *maharagwe* (beans) or *na machicha* (a kind of spinach).

$$$ La Griglia, at the Casino Malindi, Lamu Rd, T042-213 0069, www.casinomalindi. com. 1900-2400. Upmarket restaurant and cocktail bar at the back of the casino with an attractive gold and maroon Roman-style decor, outdoor tables under palm trees and Lamu-style furniture. It specializes in Italian food, grills and seafood and there's a good range of gooey chocolate desserts and Italian wines and champagne.

$$$ Lorenzo's Restaurant, at the Mwembe Resort, west of town, 900 m off the main road, T0720-747 180. Open1900-2230. Set in the grounds of an upmarket Italian timeshare resort, this offers superb but pricey Italian cuisine and seafood. The nicely dressed tables with flowers and candles are set under a terracotta roof with open walls overlooking the swimming pool and manmade waterfalls in tropical gardens.

$$$ The Old Man and the Sea, Casuarina Rd, T042-213 1106. Open 1230-2300. Very stylish and the best place to eat in town, named after the Hemingway book, romantic, set in a lovingly restored low Arabic house with stone seats and arches, only a few tables so reservations are essential, impeccable service and gourmet food. Starters include lobster pâté and smoked sailfish, followed by whole crab, or the recommended Indian Ocean seafood platter.

$$ Baby Marrow, Casuarina Rd, south of the Portuguese Church, T0727-581 682. Open 1100-1430, 1800-2230. Lovely setting near the resorts under the arms of an enormous tree, this is very atmospheric with terrace, thatched roof and rustic decor with chunky wooden furniture, all lit up at night by delicate lights in the garden out front, but let down by an average seafood and Italian menu and mediocre service.

$$ Driftwood Beach Club, Silversands Beach, Casuarina Rd, 3 km south of town, see Where to stay, page 279. Open 1230-2200. This is a nice way to spend a lazy day; you can eat here and for a small fee use the pool and sun loungers. The excellent restaurant has an à la carte menu with great seafood, such as tuna sashimi, Thai crab claws or oysters cultivated in Kilifi Creek, plus there's a Fri night barbecue next to the pool and a great curry buffet at Sun lunchtime. Snacks are also served at the bar.

$$ I Love Pizza, Casuarina Rd, T042-212 0672. Open 1230-2300. A good-value and established Italian restaurant that has been going since 1982, serving pizza, pasta, seafood dishes and other food. Located in an atmospheric Arab house, lobsters, crabs, giant prawns combine themselves very well with *pappardelle* or spaghetti, rice or *trenette*.

$ Baobab Restaurant, Casuarina Rd, T042-213 1699. Open 0800-2300. On the seafront with good views, this has red and white checked tablecloths, friendly staff and a wide-ranging menu. You can have breakfast here, snacks and a beer or fruit juice, as well as full meals such as chicken or fish curry, though the quality of the main dishes is inconsistent.

$ Bar Bar, Lamu Rd opposite **Casino Malindi**, T0722-509 809. Open 0730-2230. Informal thatched roadside bar/coffee shop surrounded by potted palms with especially good and generous pizzas using imported Italian meats and cheeses. It's a good spot for an early English or continental breakfast and serves the best cappuccino in town.

$ Karen Blixen Café Bar, Galana Centre, Lamu Rd, T042-200 2525. Open 0700-2300. Imaginatively designed with photos of Karen Blixen and Denys Finch-Hatton on the walls, and tables under umbrellas in the courtyard, this popular and late-night café sells sandwiches, juices, excellent Italian coffees (local residents come here for their shots of espresso), and some light meals at lunchtime.

$ Oasis Gelateria, next door to the **Coral Key Beach Resort**, Silversands Beach, T0720-544 180. Open 1100-2200. Snack bar with tables and umbrellas serving sandwiches and basic meals like omelette and chips, good coffee and delicious fresh mango juice, but it's best known for its 40+ flavours of ice cream (mint, pistachio, orange, cheesecake, vanilla & chocolate – the list goes on). Popular with tourists and Kenyan families.

🎶 Bars, clubs and entertainment

Mombasa to Kilifi *p260*
There are a string of large nightclubs along the north coast, popular with both holidaymakers and locals. These can be fun but men must be prepared to be hounded by prostitutes. Some may close during the week in low season.

Nyali, Kenyatta and Bamburi beaches *p260, map p262*

Mamba International Night Club, at **Mamba Village**, Links Rd, Nyali, behind Nyali Beach and the hotels, T041-222 2232, www.mambavillage.com. 1700-0500. This has a rather staggering 13 bars, large dance floor with stage, restaurant serving burgers and pizza, and can hold thousands of people under an enormous conical shaped *makuti* thatched roof. There's a laser show on weekend nights and music is a mixture of rap, reggae, commercial disco, African music and live bands.

Pirates Beach Bar, just to the south of **Traveller's Beach Hotel & Club**, Bamburi Beach, T041-548 7119, www.pirateskenya. com. 1900-0400. This is another large venue with 5 bars, dance floor on the beach, pool tables, giant TV screens and a restaurant serving basic grills and seafood, which offers snacks like burgers and kebabs late at night. There are also some swimming pools and curly water slides here open 0900-1700.

Tembo Disco, on the Mombasa–Malindi road near the entrance of **Haller Park**, T041-548 5074, www.tembodisco.com. 1800-0600. This is another massive establishment set in a series of *makuti* thatched buildings in tropical gardens with 7 bars and beer gardens with satellite TVs for sports (one of which is open 24 hrs), a *nyama choma* and seafood restaurant, pool hall, pole-dancing club, and the largest open-air disco in Kenya (with a capacity of 3000).

Mtwapa and Shanzu Beach *p263, map p262*

Casaurina Nomad, on the Mombasa–Malindi road, 500 m on the right after crossing the Mtwapa bridge, T041-548 7515, www.casaurina.com. Another large thatched complex, this is open 24 hrs and the restaurant serves up English fry-ups from early morning, and burgers, steaks, fried chicken, *nyama choma* and snacks later in the day and night. There's a large open-air dance floor with good lighting and mixed music, several bars, pool tables and entertainment, such as acrobatics or traditional dancing.

Malindi *p269, map p271*

Most of the resorts have discos – some of them very pleasant in open-air beachside locations – and most open 1-2 nights a week on a 'rotating' system (you'll have to ask where to go on any given night). There is also a particularly dense crop of bars and discos in the northern part of town around the **Galana Centre**, where it's easy enough to walk from one to the next until you find one that suits. Again, they are frequented by prostitutes; sex tourism in Kenya is perhaps at its most acute and brazen in Malindi, which sits very uncomfortably on the traditional Muslim coast.

Casino Malindi, Lamu Rd, T042-213 0069, www.casinomalindi.com. 0900-0500. Fairly upmarket Italian-owned casino with a/c, slot machines and gaming tables and pleasant cocktail bar and restaurant, La Griglia (see page 282).

Fermento Bar, Galana Centre, T042-213 1780. Wed, Fri, Sat from 2200, more nights in high season if there is the demand. Large and expensive bar and disco with karaoke, more upmarket than most with a/c,

reasonable modern decor with banquette seats and potted palms, caters for older Europeans and their companions.

Star Dust Club, Lamu Rd. 2100-late. In a big white building opposite the Galana Centre, this starts fairly late in the evenings but is nevertheless very popular and is open until at least 0400 in season, Sat is the big night. There are 2 dance floors, the outside one has some palm trees in the middle of it and some elevated comfortable lounge areas.

Stars and Garters, Lamu Rd. 1800-late. An informal thatched bar serving plenty of cold beer and *nyama choma*, pool tables, big-screen TV for watching sport, especially English football, and it gets busy when there is an important match on. Turns into a disco on weekend nights.

O Shopping

Nyali, Kenyatta and Bamburi beaches *p260, map p262*

Most of the resorts have shops selling all the paraphernalia you may want on a beach holiday and there are curio stalls clustered around the entrances to the resorts. Additionally, 'beach boys' wander around selling items; you'll have to be assertive with them if you want to be left alone as they can be fairly aggressive with their sales tactics. The principal shopping centre serving the north coast immediately north of Mombasa is the **Nyali Nakumatt Shopping Centre**, on the main Mombasa–Malindi (B8) road opposite **Haller Park**, which has a very large branch of Nakumatt and a number of other shops, ATMs, internet café and restaurants and is currently being extended into the **City Mall**, which will be the largest shopping mall on the coast.

Mtwapa and Shanzu Beach *p263, map p262*

Tusky's Supermarket is on the main Mombasa–Malindi (B8) road, on the right about 200 m after crossing the bridge over Mtwapa Creek. It also has a bakery and fast-food takeaway. At the time of writing a **Nakumatt** was being built at the north end of town.

Watamu *p266, map p262*
There's a clutch of curio stalls in the village near the mosque and on the beach in front of the **Turtle Bay Beach Club. Watamu Supermarket** at the T-junction is one of the better places on this part of the coast for self-caterers; the staff are fluent in a number of European languages, and there's a good selection of fresh produce, meat, fish, imported cheese and hams, and Italian and South African wine. There's a coffee shop next door. **Mama Lucy's Supermarket** is a similar set-up about 200 m north of the T-junction.

Malindi *p269, map p271*
Curios
There are numerous craft stalls at the Malindi curio market near the jetty. In general the quality is reasonably good as are the prices – although you must expect to haggle. During the low season when there are not many tourists about, you may pick up some good bargains. There are also a number of quality shops on the roads lining the Uhuru Gardens and the back streets around here selling very good cloths and items such as bags, clothes and cushions made from *kikoys*. Many of these also sell Swahili antiques, presumably to decorate the Italian villas in the area.
Malindi Handicraft Cooperative, off Kenyatta Rd, T042-213 0248, www.malindi handicrafts.co.ke. 0830-1800. This was established in 1986 and currently represents over 600 artists in the region and is now among the largest producers of crafts in Kenya. There is an excellent selection of crafts here, though there is no bargaining in the shop itself, but you can talk to the carvers themselves and have something custom-made.

Shopping centres and supermarkets
There are no large shopping centres in Malindi but the main market south of Uhuru Gardens is a good place to buy fresh fruit and veg, fish and meat. The numerous Italian supermarkets on Lamu Rd, including ones at the **Galana Centre** and **Sabaki Centre**, sell imported items including wine, salami, prosciutto, olive oil, ricotta and parmesan cheese, as well as everything else that features on the Italian menus at the restaurants around town.

⭘ What to do

Nyali, Kenyatta and Bamburi beaches
p260, map p262
Diving and snorkelling
There are over 25 dive sites within a 10- to 40-min boat trip from the beaches immediately north of Mombasa, which, with 15- to 30-m depths, offer excellent visibility and a diversity of marine life. There is also the artificial wreck for experienced divers to explore – the *MV Dania* (see box, page 265). Expect to pay in the region of US$50-60 for a single dive and US$470-530 for a 4- to 5-day PADI Open Water course. Marine park fees are included in the rates. Almost every resort offers diving through one of the dive schools. Snorkelling, of course, can be done by simply walking into the sea, or from *dhows* and can be arranged at all the resorts. And, if you don't want to get wet, you can watch the fish through the floor of a glass-bottomed boat.
Buccaneer Diving has dive centres at a number of resorts, including **Voyager Beach Resort**, **Reef Hotel Mombasa**, **Neptune Beach Resort**, **Sarova Whitesands Beach Resort & Spa**, and also **Sun n' Sand** on Kikambala Beach, T0728-999 225, www. buccaneerdiving.com.
Peponi Divers, main base at **Bahari Beach Hotel**, Nyali Beach, but will pick up from any hotel, T0722-412 302, www.peponidivers.ch.

Go-karting

Mombasa Go-Kart, on the Mombasa–Malindi Rd, 12 km north of Mombasa, opposite the turning to **Severin Sea Lodge**, T0721-485 247, www.mombasa-gokart.com. Tue-Sun 1600-2200. This is a 500-m bendy floodlit go-kart track; 20 laps cost around US$20. There's also a 10-pin bowling alley, kids' playground and restaurant.

Golf

Nyali Golf and Country Club, across the road from Mamba Village, T0726-414 477. An attractive par-72 18-hole course and, although it's not directly on the coast, it is said to be challenging as the winds influence playing conditions. Players are likely to encounter vervet monkeys (the clubs mascot) on the fairways. Green fees are about US$30.

Kite- and windsurfing

Prosurf Kenya, Nyali Beach Hotel, T0736-912 982, www.prosurfkenya.com. Instructors and equipment for both kite- and windsurfing lessons and courses and also rents out paddle-skis and catamarans. Windsurfers cost around US$50 for a half a day, while kitesurfing costs in the region of US$65 for 1 hr's lesson.

Mountain biking

Bike the Coast, based at Mombasa Go-Kart (see above), T0722-873 738, www.bikethecoast.com. This offers enjoyable off-road, scenic, guided mountain-bike tours around the north coast through local villages and plantations over distances of 20-30 km and taking 1½-2½ hrs. Bikes, helmets, gloves and drinking water are provided. Expect to pay from US$35; for an extra fee they can pick you up from the resorts.

Kikambala Beach *p264, map p262*
Golf

Baobab Golf Course, at Vipingo Ridge, which is a new residential/golf estate at Kikambala to the west of the Mombasa–

Malindi (B8) road, T0733-155 155, www.vipingoridge.com. Opened in 2010, this is the north coast's newest 72-par 18-hole golf course, with a stylish clubhouse and restaurant, as well as a driving range. Visitors are welcome and green fees are about US$65, clubs and caddies can be hired.

Watamu *p266, map p262*
Diving and snorkelling

There are 18 dive sites in the Watamu Marine National Park within a 10- to 20-min boat trip from the beaches. Again snorkelling and glass-bottomed boat trips are available from the resorts.
Aqua Ventures, at Ocean Sports Resort, T042-233 2420, www.diveinkenya.com.
Blue-Fin Diving is based at **Sandies Tropical Village**, in Malindi (see below) but will pick up from all Watamu resorts.

Fishing

Hemingways Resort, see Where to stay, page 277, T042-233 2052, www.hemingways.co.ke. Organizes deep-sea fishing for big game fish in season, which is usually early Jul to mid-Apr with Aug being especially good for sailfish and black marlin. Fully equipped boats cater for 4-6 people and they can take novices; expect to pay in the region of US$400-600 per boat. Can also organize shore fishing in Mida Creek.

Malindi *p269, map p271*
Diving

Blue-Fin Diving, is based at **Sandies Tropical Village**, but will pick up from a total of 21 resorts in the Malindi and Watamu area, T042-212 0444, www.bluefindiving.com. A 4-day PADI Open Water course is US$470, while 2 dives for experienced divers costs US$110.

Fishing

Kingfisher, T0722-624 840, www.kenyasportfishing.net. Offers excursions similar to those at **Hemingway's**, above, and operates out of the **Malindi Sea Fishing Club**, south of the jetty (www.malindiseafishingclub. com). This is a private fishing club that was established in Malindi in 1959 and 1-day membership is included in fishing rates. You can hang your catch on the weighing station and have your photo taken, and the club has a very good bar and restaurant adorned with some impressive fishing trophies.

Sailfish Club Malindi, Casuarina Rd, on the seafront near the Portuguese Church, T0722-362 449, www.sailfishclubmalindi. com. Again organizes fishing charters, and you can record your catch with a photo at the hanging frame on the beach. Also has 9 a/c B&B rooms (**$$**) for fishermen (although not exclusively).

Golf
Malindi Golf and Country Club, north end of town, right fork off Lamu Rd, T042-213 1402. Very unusual 11-hole and 15-tee course spread out on 54 ha. Inexpensive daily membership is available, as well as club hire and caddies.

⊖ Transport

You can organize shuttles from Mombasa's **Moi International Airport** to all the North Coast resorts through the resorts themselves or with the taxi companies in the arrivals hall (see page 229).

Kilifi *p264*
Kilifi is about 50 km from **Mombasa**, and 60 km from **Malindi**. The buses that go between the 2 towns do pick people up here, although only if there is space, as they may be full. It might be easier to get a *matatu*. The bus and *matatu* stand is north of the creek and a little east of the B8 near the market.

Watamu *p266*
Watamu is about 50 km north of **Kilifi**, and 3 km off the main road (B8). Some of the through buses between Mombasa and Malindi stop at **Gede** on the B8, where

matatus continue on to the village centre. The 20 km from Watamu to **Malindi** takes about 20 mins, and there are plenty of *matatus* which cost about US$1.

Malindi *p269, map p271*
Air
Malindi Airport is on the Mombasa road, 2.5 km from the centre of town, T042-213 1201, www.kenyaairports.co.ke, and is served by 4 airlines. From Nairobi, there are connections to the other destinations in Kenya, see page 79 for details.

 Air Kenya, Sabaki Centre, Lamu Rd, T042-212 0411, central reservations, Nairobi, T020-391 6000, www.airkenya.com, as 1 daily flight between Wilson Airport in **Nairobi** and Lamu and Malindi on a circuit, which departs Nairobi at 1400, arrives in Lamu at 1510, departs again at 1605, arrives in Malindi at 1625, departs at 1625 and arrives back in Nairobi at 1735.

 Fly 540, Moi International Airport, Mombasa, T041-343 4822, central reservations, Nairobi, T020-327 4747, www.fly540.com, has at least 2 daily flights between **Nairobi** and Malindi via either Mombasa or Lamu on a circuit, from US$110 1 way. On the same circuit there are flights between **Mombasa** and Malindi (15 mins) from US$40 1 way, and Malindi and **Lamu** (25 mins) from US$45 1 way.

 Kenya Airways, Lamu Rd opposite Barclays Bank, T042-212 0237, at the airport, T042-212 0192, www.kenya-airways.com, has at least 2 daily direct flights between Nairobi and Malindi.

 Mombasa Air Safari, Moi International Airport, Mombasa, T041-343 3061, www. mombasaairsafari.com, has daily flights on a circuit in both directions between **Mombasa** and Malindi, from US$45 1 way, and Malindi and **Lamu**, from US$65 1 way.

Bus
There are plenty of buses throughout the day between Malindi and Abdel Nasser Rd in **Mombasa**, which take about 2 hrs

and cost around US$3. The bus companies all have offices in Malindi around the bus station on Uhuru Rd near the market, but booking is not usually necessary. Non-stop *matatus* are faster, take under 90 mins, cost around US$5, and fill up and leave about every 15 mins during the day. From Malindi to **Watamu**, the 20 km takes about 20 mins, and there are plenty of *matatus* which cost about US$1.

Now that the road has been tarred as far as Witu, the bus from Malindi to **Lamu** takes about 4 hrs and costs about US$8. Again the bus companies have offices around the bus station, and those with services to Lamu include **Pwani Tawakal Bus**, T0722-550 111, which has departures from Malindi to Lamu at 0900, 1130 and 1300, and **Tahmeed Bus**, at 1030 and 1230. However, these times are approximate as the buses come from Mombasa first and take roughly 2 hrs from there to Malindi, where they then take a break of about 30 mins. Check times and try and buy the ticket the day before to guarantee a seat. The buses take you to the jetty on the mainland at **Mokowe**, roughly 220 km from Malindi, from where you get a ferry across to Lamu. Because of security issues in the Kenya-Somali border region, for the last 60 km or so, from Witu to Mokowe, armed police hop on the buses.

Tuk-tuk and boda boda
All over Malindi (and Watamu) are cheap tuk-tuks that cost no more than US$2-3 from one end of town to the other for up to 3 passengers. There are also plenty of bicycle taxis known as *boda bodas* with a single seat on the back that will cost no more than US$1. There used to be car-hire companies in Malindi, and indeed bicycle hire, but with the introduction of what is excellent public transport, they have become defunct.

❶ Directory

Malindi *p269, maps p271 and p270*
Medical services Malindi District Hospital, Casuarina Rd, T042-212 0490. This is a public hospital so in the event of a medical emergency try to get to one of the private hospitals in Mombasa (page 243). There's a well-stocked pharmacy in the **Sabaki Centre**.
Police Kenyatta Rd, T042-212 0486.

Contents

Footprint features

At a glance

⊖ **Getting around** On foot or by donkey and *dhow*. There are no cars.

⚫ **Time required** At least 4 nights to explore Lamu Town and enjoy the beach; longer for the adventurous to explore other islands.

☀ **Weather** Mildly tropical with average temperatures of 30-35°C, but tempered by the sea breeze.

⊗ **When not to go** Can be visited year round; there are only short afternoon showers in the rainy season.

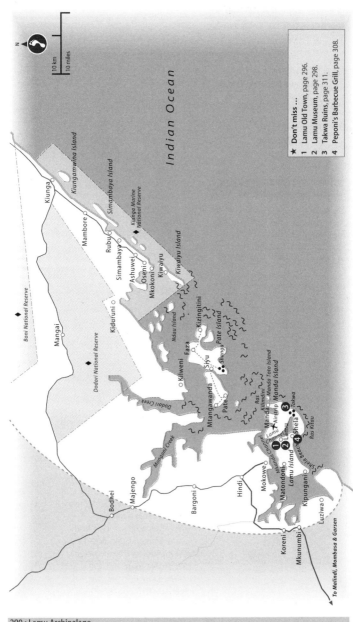

Indian Ocean

★ Don't miss ...
1 Lamu Old Town, page 296.
2 Lamu Museum, page 298.
3 Takwa Ruins, page 311.
4 Peponi's Barbecue Grill, page 308.

N

10 km
10 miles

Kiunga
Kiungamwiha Island
Mambore
Simambaya Island
Rubu
Simambaya
Ashuwei
Osemi
Mkokoni
Kiwayu Island
Kiwayu
Kiunga Marine National Reserve

Boni National Reserve

Mangai

Kidurumi

Dodori National Reserve

Ndau Island
Kizingitini
Faza
Kilweni
Siyu
Shanga
Pate Island
Pate
Mtangawanda

Dodori Creek

Ras
Kilimini
Manda Toto Island
Manda
Manda Island
Airstrip
Takwa

Morigani Creek

Mokowe
Lamu
Matondoni
Shela
Lamu Island
Ras Kitau
Mkanda Channel
Chembe
Mkanda Beach
Kipungani
Braya
Luziwa

Majengo
Bargoni
Hindi
Koreni
Mkunumbi

Bodhei

To Malindi, Mombasa & Garsen

In the extreme north are the intriguing islands of Lamu, which make for a fascinating excursion into the old Swahili way of life. Here visitors can experience the coast's cultural heritage at its most evocative; it is often said that Lamu is similar to how Zanzibar in Tanzania was 30 years ago, before the onset of mass tourism.

The old town of Lamu, known locally as Mkomani, was declared a UNESCO World Heritage Site in 2001 for its cultural importance and for being the oldest, best-preserved and still-functioning Swahili settlement on the East African coast.

In Lamu Town, Shela and the small settlements on the other islands, the alleyways are barely wide enough to pass an oncoming donkey, and the whitewashed walls and Arabic arches contribute to some of the most elegant architecture on the continent. Without the sounds of traffic, the atmosphere is pleasantly peaceful, interrupted only by the low rumblings of electric juicers in the waterfront cafés and the infectious chatter of Kiswahili. The evenings are enchanting, when the dimly lit alleyways are full of warm shadows and fragrant hues. Romantic, traditional white-sailed *dhows* ply the waterfront, there are some wonderful deserted beaches, very atmospheric places to stay and seafood to die for. Whilst embracing tourism, the people of Lamu want to retain the islands' mystic, religious sanctity and cloak of romance, and it should not be forgotten that they belong to another, older Africa.

Getting there

Air Kenya, **Fly 540**, **Kenya Airways** and **Mombasa Air Safaris** have flights to the **Manda Airstrip** ① *T042-632 018, www.kenyaairports.co.ke*. Flying to Lamu is a fantastic way to get a handle on the geography of Kenya's coast: tarmacked roads become dirt tracks criss-crossing each other and leading to tiny rural settlements shrouded in palmy forest, sand spits stretch tentacles out into the blue Indian Ocean and, after less than an hour, the island of Lamu comes into view. Planes lands on the airstrip on Manda Island, just to the north. This is a delightfully simple airport with just a few benches set under *makuti* thatch for waiting passengers and a hand-drawn luggage trolley that takes bags down to the waiting boats to take you across the Lamu Channel. Some of the more expensive hotels will ferry you and your luggage over from the airstrip, otherwise there is always the motorized ferry and *dhows* to meet the planes at the jetty that will take you across for a few shillings.

Lamu is roughly 220 km northeast of Malindi. The B8 road first goes 110 km north of Malindi to **Garsen**, where the newly tarred C112 road turns back towards the coast and the village of **Witu**, after which the road turns to gravel with a few bumps (though by the time you read this, the final 60 km or so between Witu and Mokowe may also have been tarred). For more information about this route, see page 273. Buses to Lamu go fairly regularly but the route is popular so you should book in advance. The trip takes about four to five hours from Malindi and costs US$8. They leave in the morning at between 0900 and 1300, and will have come from Mombasa first with departures approximately two hours earlier, which cost US$10. If possible, sit on the left side of the bus (in the shade) and keep your eyes open for wildlife. Because of security issues in the Kenya-Somali border region, for the last 60 km or so, from Witu to Mokowe, armed police hop on the buses. The bus will take you as far as the jetty at **Mokowe** on the mainland from where you get a ferry, about 7 km, taking about 40 minutes, across to Lamu. The bus companies put their passengers on the same boat and there's plenty of help with your luggage. The bus trip to and from Lamu is long, so ensure you have enough water, although every time the buses stop in the tiny settlements along the way, hawkers are waiting to throw hands through the windows with drinks, bananas and other snacks. If you are in your own vehicle, it is also possible to park it up at the Mokowe jetty, but you will have to pay an *askari* to look after your car while you are on the islands. This is considered reasonably safe to do and is common practice, as Mokowe is effectively Lamu's nearest car park. ▶▶ *See Transport, page 309.*

Getting around

There are no vehicles on the island except for the District Commissioner's Land Rover, a tractor owned by the town council and an ambulance at the hospital, and on Manda Island there's a fire engine at the airstrip. Donkeys, *dhows* and bicycles dominate and everywhere is walkable. The two main thoroughfares in Lamu Town are the waterfront, also known as Kenyatta Road, and the Main Street, which is one block back from the waterfront, also known as Harambee Avenue. The maze of streets mean that it is easy to get lost; just bear in mind that Harambee Avenue runs parallel to the waterfront and the all the streets leading into town from the shore slope uphill slightly.

Safety

In terms of petty crime, as a Muslim society, robbery is not a major problem in Lamu. Nevertheless, always take common-sense precautions: avoid walking around alone after

Travel warning

In September 2011, a British tourist couple were kidnapped at a resort on Kiwayu Island at the far northeast of the Lamu Archipelago near the Kenya–Somali border. The husband was murdered and his wife is still thought to be held hostage in Somalia. Then, in October 2011, a French tourist was kidnapped from a private residence on Manda Island opposite Lamu town and she later died while in captivity in Somalia. It's not clear who was responsible or what the motivation was for these incidents – the perpetrators took the hostages into areas of southern Somalia controlled by Al-Shabaab, a Somali Islamist militia group with some links to Al Qaeda, although some analysts believe it could have been Somali pirates looking for alternative ways of securing hefty ransom payments other than targeting merchant vessels at sea. In response, since October 2011, the Kenyan military has initiated action against Al-Shabaab in the Kenya–Somali border region, and an international navy force continues to monitor the coast against piracy. At the time of writing, both the UK **Foreign and Commonwealth Office** (www.fco.gov.uk) and the **US State Department** (http://travel.state.gov) travel advisories recommend that travellers do not go within 150 km of the Kenya–Somali border, which includes the Lamu Archipelago. Before travelling to the region, get up-to-the-minute advice on the security situation there. A good start is to contact the **Safety and Communication Centre** run by the Kenya Tourism Federation at the KWS complex at the main gate of the Nairobi National Park, Langata Rd, Nairobi, T020-800 1000, www.ktf.co.ke.

dark in secluded areas of town; don't go to remote parts of the island unless you are with a group; and on the beach, stay within shouting distance of other people.

As on the south coast, over the years, the increase in tourism on Lamu has led to an inevitable rise in the number of touts or 'beach boys'. If they accompany you to your hotel, a substantial 'commission' (30%) will be added to your daily rate. To avoid using their services, try and be firm that you don't want their services or carry your own bags to a waterfront restaurant first, have a drink and look for accommodation later. You will have no problem finding a room. Also, be aware that while the presence of touts can be annoying and they can be pretty persistent, they also elicit some aggressive attitudes in some visitors, which does not always go down so well among the local people. In short, some travellers complain bitterly about them, while others actually make firm friends and enjoy their additional helpful local knowledge and services (*dhow* trips for example). It's just a case of your personal attitude and patience on how to deal with the touts.

Tourist office
Lamu Tourist Office ⓘ *on the harbour front to the north of the landing jetty, north of the Donkey Sanctuary, T042-463 3132, www.tourism.go.ke, Mon-Fri 0830-1200, 1400-1630, Sat 0830-1300,* and, next door, the **Lamu Tour Guides Association** ⓘ *T0721-949271, same opening hours.* Both have friendly staff and can organize walking tours of the town and *dhow* trips to islands. A three-hour walking tour of the town costs in the region of US$20 for one to three people.

Background

The town of Lamu was founded in the 14th century, although there were people living on the island long before this. Throughout the years, and as recently as the 1960s, the island has been a popular hide-out for refugees fleeing the mainland.

The original settlement of Lamu was located to the south of the town and is said to be marked by Hidabu hill. There was also another settlement between the 13th and 15th centuries to the north of the present town. By the 15th century it was a thriving port, one of the many that dotted the coast of East Africa. However, in 1505 it surrendered to the Portuguese, began paying tributes and, for the next 150 years, was subservient to them and to the sultanate of the town of Pate on the nearby island, part of the Omani Dynasty that ruled much of the East African coast.

By the end of the 17th century, Lamu had become a republic ruled by a council of elders called the Yumbe, who were, in principle, responsible to Oman. In fact, the Yumbe were largely able to determine their own affairs, and this period has been called Lamu's Golden Age. It was the period when many of the buildings were constructed and Lamu's celebrated architectural style evolved. The town became a thriving centre of literature and scholarly study, and there were a number of poets who lived here. Arts and crafts flourished and trade expanded. The main products exported through Lamu were mangrove poles, ivory, rhino horn, hippo teeth, shark fins, cowrie shells, coconuts, cotton, mangoes, tamarind, *sim sim* (oil), charcoal and cashews. Rivalries between the various trading settlements in the region came to a head when Lamu finally defeated Pate in the battle of Shela in 1813. However, after 1840, Lamu found itself dominated by Zanzibar, which had been developed to become the dominant power along the East African coast. At a local level there were factions and splits within the town's population – in particular rivalries between different clans and other interest groups.

New products were developed for export including *bêche de mer* (a seafood), mats, bags, turtle shell, leather, rubber and sorghum. Despite this, toward the end of the 19th century Lamu began a slow economic decline as Mombasa and Zanzibar took over in importance as trading centres. The end of the slave trade dealt a blow to Lamu, as the production of mangrove poles and grains for export depended on slave labour. Additionally, communications between the interior and Mombasa were infinitely better than those with Lamu, especially after the building of the Uganda Railway.

The airstrip on Manda Island was established in the early 1960s and the first visitors as such were white settlers on day tours, who reputedly flew in for the day with packed lunches as there were no hotels. Then, as places to stay started to open their doors in the early 1970s, it became known as an exotic, remote and self-contained destination and began to attract hippies and other non-conformists, drawn by its undisturbed traditional culture. Since then, budget hotels have become popular with backpackers and, today, there are also numerous top-end places to stay and some luxury villas to rent. Some people argue that Lamu's popularity and increased tourism will ultimately undermine the unique value system and culture of this Swahili settlement. Indeed, there is a sign posted for the benefit of tourists at the airport: "Please remember that Lamu is a conservative Muslim town with a heritage of peace and goodwill. This is our home. Please tread gently here for our children are watching. Please respect this, and enjoy the unique atmosphere of our enduring yet fragile culture."

Lamu's houses

Most of Lamu's houses were built in the 18th century and were constructed out of local materials, with cut coral-rag blocks for the walls, wooden floors supported by mangrove poles and intricately carved shutters for windows. They were traditionally built in an oblong shape around a small open courtyard, with two to three storeys and flat roofs covered with makuti thatch. It was required that a father give his daughters their own living quarters when they married, so he would add another storey to the house or build an adjoining house. When this was across a street, a bridge would be built between the two houses to allow the women to move between them without being seen from the street. In some of the grander houses, the ground floor was occupied by slaves or used as warehouses or workshops, and the family members lived above. To keep them private, the outer walls only had slits for ventilation and all the light came in through the inner courtyard. The main entrance was through a porch with stone seats, a *baraza*, on either side and a wooden carved door, which led into an inner porch and the courtyard. The men of the family would also handle business matters in this area, keeping such things away from the women, who resided in the deeper areas of the home. Staircases started at the front door but, because of the narrowness of the houses, they twisted and turned in many directions before reaching their final destination within the house. Slaves would sleep under the staircases. A *sabule* (guest room) was typically at the top of a staircase, separate from the main family staircase, and had its own bathroom.

In the absence of guests (usually visiting kin or trading partners), the head of the family would often sleep in the *sabule*, particularly when his wife had close female kin staying with her. The living rooms on the main family floor traditionally faced north towards Mecca, and there were no separate rooms as such for sleeping, with beds simply put in curtained alcoves. However, one room was put aside for the husband and wife and the very young children to sleep, and was usually set up a step higher than the rest of the rooms; in some of the grander houses they were very cool and spacious, with wall niches to display pieces of pottery. The kitchen was usually on one of the upper floors, firstly so the smoke wouldn't blow into the sleeping or living areas and, secondly, so women could prepare food away from visitors. There was also a room that was specifically set aside for childbirth; it was additionally used for the laying out of corpses, and for the seclusion of widows.

Lamu Island

Lamu Island is 16 km by 7 km, with a third covered by sand dunes. The best beach on the island stretches for 12 km at Shela. Elsewhere, the coast of the island is covered with crawling mangroves attracting a number of birds. It is possible to walk all over the island, and there are many tracks into the interior. Alternatively, dhows make the short hop between Lamu Town, Shela and Mantondoni. ➤➤ *For listings, see pages 303-310.*

Lamu Town → *For listings, see pages 303-310. Phone code: 042. Colour map 2, B3.*

The town dates back to the 14th century, although most of the buildings are actually 18th century, built in Lamu's Golden Age. The streets are very narrow, and the buildings on each side are two or three storeys high and, as the houses face inwards, privacy is carefully guarded. The streets are set in a rough grid pattern running off the main street called **Harambee Avenue**, which runs parallel to the waterfront and used to open out to the sea, although building from the mid-1800s onwards has cut it off from the quayside. The narrow waterfront stretches the length of the town where cannons still point seawards, touts offer *dhow* rides and white billowing sails occupy every inch of shoreline. The smaller ones serve as local taxis for Manda or the nearby Shela Beach, while the large ocean-going vessels are stacked high with mangrove poles and sand. Muscled sailors with *kikois* hoisted around their waists heave wooden carts from the docks or slumber on deck amongst charcoal burners and grain sacks. Carved doors are one of the attractions for which Lamu has become known. This artesanal skill continues to be taught and, at the north end of the harbour, you can see them being made in workshops by craftsmen and apprentices.

Mosques

There are over 20 mosques on the island, but they don't have minarets and they are usually not very grand affairs and some are little different from other buildings. You can usually pick them out by the pile of sandals outside the doors during prayer time. You will need to seek permission before entering to look around. The oldest mosque in Lamu is believed to be the **Pwani Mosque**, near the fort, which dates back to 1370, and today is just a crumbling ruin, though an Arabic inscription can still be seen on one of the walls. The **Jumaa** (or Friday) **Mosque** is at the north end of town and is the second oldest in Lamu, dating from 1511. Then comes the **M'na Lalo Mosque** (1753), more or less in the centre of town, just a little to the north of the museum and set back from Harambee Avenue. This mosque was built in Lamu's Golden Age and it was followed by **Muru Mosque** (1821) on Harambee Avenue, **Utukuni Mosque** (1823), well into the interior part of the town, and **Mpya Mosque** (1845), in the town centre. **Mwana Mshamu Mosque** (1855) is in the northwest area of the town; **Sheikh Mohamed bin Ali Mosque** (1875), in the town centre, and the **N'nayaye Mosque** (1880) on the northwest fringe of town. Two mosques have been built in the 20th century, the **Riyadha Mosque** (1901), to the south of the town, which is the main centre for the Maulidi Festival (see box, page 299), and the **Bohora Mosque** (1920), which is fairly central, just inland of Harambee Avenue. The **Mwenye Alawi Mosque** (1850), at the north end of Main Street, was originally for women, but it has since been taken over by the men. The small Ismaili community did have their own **Ismaili Mosque**, on Kenyatta Road at the south end of town, but this is now in ruins. Adjacent

Lamu Town

To Mwenye Alawi Mosque & Dhow Boatyard

Wood-carving Workshops

Jumaa

Mwana Mshamu

N'nayaye 8

Lamu Social Hall

Cat Clinic

Swahili House Museum

Utukuni

Murú

MKOMANI

Lamu Tour Guides Association

Whetstone

Donkey Sanctuary

M'na Lalo

Sheikh Mohamed bin Ali

Mwana Hadie Famau Tomb

Mpya

Bohora

Lamu Museum

Jetty

KCB $

Standard Chartered $

House of Liwali Sud bin Hamad

Pwani

Pwani Tawakal

Fort

District Commissioner's Office

Jetty

GARDENI

German Post Office Museum

To Pillar Tomb

Muslim Academy

Riyadha

Air Kenya

TSS

Lamu Book Centre

Ismaili Mosque (Ruin)

LANGONI

Lamu Harbour

Rope Walk

To Shela

Scale

100 metres
100 yards

Where to stay

Amu House **3**
Baytil Ajaib **14**
Casuarina Rest House **4**
Hapa Hapa **5**
Jannat House **8**
Kipepeo Guest House **16**
Lamu Archipelago Villas **6**
Lamu House **13**
Lamu Palace **7**
Petley's Inn **9**
Pole Pole **10**
Stone House **15**
Sunsail **2**
Yumbe House **11**
Yumbe Villa **12**

Restaurants

Bush Gardens **2**
Coconut Juice Café **3**
Hapa Hapa **4**
New Minnaa **5**
New Star **6**
Olympic **7**
Seafront Café **1**
Whispers **10**

to the Riyadha Mosque is the **Muslim Academy**, funded by Saudi Arabia, which attracts students from all over the world.

Lamu Museum
① *Kenyatta Rd, T042-463 3073, www.museums.or.ke, 0930-1800, US$5.50, children (under 16) US$2.75, package ticket for the museum, Swahili House, Lamu Fort and German Post Office Museum US$32, children (under 16) US$16.*

This excellent museum plays an important role in the conservation of old Lamu. It's set in a beautiful whitewashed house built in 1891, which was where the British colonial administrators lived before Independence. Before that, it had housed Queen Victoria's consul – one Captain Jack Haggard, brother of the more celebrated author of *King Solomon's Mines*. It has a fine carved wooden door inlaid with brass studs, the ground floor has a good bookshop and the entrance has some photographs of Lamu taken by French photographer Guillain in the period 1846-1849, as well as a large aerial photo of Lamu Town. In a lobby to the right is a Swahili kitchen with pestles and mortars and vermicelli presses. Also on the ground floor are examples of decorative 18th-century *Kidaka* plasterwork, carved Lamu throne chairs with wicker seats and elaborately carved Lamu headboards. To the rear are displays on the archaeological excavations of the Takwa Ruins (see page 311) on Manda Island, and at Siya and Shanga on Pate Island (see page 312). On the first floor, the balcony has a display of large earthenware pottery. The balcony room has photographs and models of seagoing vessels, mostly *dhows*, and the various types and styles in use. Just behind the balcony room is a display of musical instruments used in festivals and celebrations, including drums, cymbals, rattles and leg rattles. The most celebrated exhibits are the two **Siwa horns**. These are in the shape of elephant tusks, with the mouthpiece on the side. The Lamu horn is made of brass, the horn from nearby Pate is of ivory. They date from the 17th century, are elaborately decorated, and were blown on special occasions such as enthronements or weddings. Local tribes are featured in a side room, and there are displays on the **Oroma** from around Witu, Garsen and southwest of Lamu; the **Pokot** from west of the Tana River, and the **Boni** from the north of Lamu. The jewellery includes nose rings, earrings, anklets and necklaces in bead designs and in silver. There are some illustrations of hand and feet painting, in henna, in black and red. The two end rooms are examples of typical Swahili bridal rooms with furniture and dresses on display.

Swahili House Museum
① *Inland from the museum, www.museums.or.ke, 0930-1800, US$5.50, children (under 16) US$2.75, or you can buy a package museum ticket, see Lamu Museum.*

This is a traditional and fully restored 18th-century Swahili house with period furniture and, although it's quite small, it is interesting and the guides are great. There are three areas on the main floor, and a centre aisle has beds off to the left and right. The beds are wooden with rope and raffia forming the base. The main room has a particularly fine *kikanda* plaster screen on the wall; at one time, all of Lamu's houses were plastered white with this limestone wash as it represented purity. Although historically, when people had slaves in the homes, the areas where the slaves slept weren't plastered. Furnishings include a clock with an octagonal frame and a pointed pendulum case, a style found all along the East African coast. In the kitchen is an *mbuzi* (coconut grinder) and a *fumbu*, a straw implement resembling a large sock, which is used for squeezing the coconut juice from the shredded fruit. There is also a large wooden pestle and mortar, a pasta maker, a

Maulidi

Maulidi is the prophet Mohammed's birthday, and this religious festival has its origins in Egypt from the eighth century. The unique Lamu version is believed to have been developed by Habib Swaleh Jamal Lely, an Arab from the Comoros Islands, who came to Lamu in 1866 and established the Riyadha mosque. It attracts pilgrims from Zanzibar, Somalia, Uganda and the Comoros Islands, when the population of Lamu doubles. Maulidi celebrations take different forms and are normally held in early June. The main religious celebrations take place in and around the Riyadha Mosque, when the central square outside the mosque is partitioned into areas for men and women for traditional dancing accompanied by drumming groups. The best known of these dances is the Goma, which involves lines of men standing together holding long walking sticks known as *bakora*. Swaying to the rhythm of the drums, the men extend the sticks forward or interlink them among their drums. More solemn are the all-night prayer vigils, when the townspeople gather around the mosque for group prayer. On the last day of Maulidi, the men gather at the town cemetery and, following prayers, begin a procession into town. The colourful, energetic procession winds along the seafront towards the centre of town, with the crowds singing and dancing.

During the festival there are also a number of sporting events. These include a donkey race along the waterfront, running the length of the town. For the donkey jockeys, victory in this annual race is a much-coveted title. The race attracts most of the townspeople, who gather along the waterfront or anchor offshore in *dhows* to watch the action. Other events include a swimming race, a cross-country race and football matches. There's also a *bao* competition in the large open square in front of Lamu's fort. *Bao* is probably the oldest-known board game in human history, with archaeological evidence suggesting that the game has been played throughout Africa and the Middle East for thousands of years. The game is based around a basic board of four lines of holes, and involves beads, seeds or stones being placed in the holes, and each player then moving these objects around the board by following a simple set order. The winner is the one who places theirs in a set pattern before the other can.

The annual three-day **Lamu Cultural Festival**, usually held at the end of November, is a similar (though not religious) event and has gained in popularity since it was established in 2001. Like Maulidi, there are *dhow*, donkey and swimming races, plus performances by Taarab musicians, Kiswahili poetry competitions, traditional handicrafts and henna painting demonstrations, a mock Swahili bridal ceremony and a Swahili food bazaar.

water boiler and a flour-grinding stone, as well as other pots and pans. Outside are a well and a garden with frangipani.

Lamu Fort

ⓘ *Harambee Av, www.museums.or.ke, 0930-1800, US$5.50, children (under 16) US$2.75, or again you can buy a package museum ticket (see above).*

Construction of the fort began in 1813 shortly after Lamu's victory at the Battle of Shela and was completed in 1821. The battle was an attempt by the people of Pate, allied with

Alley cat

With their long necks and saucer like eyes, narrow bodies and straight legs, the cats of Lamu are the only cats on earth to bear the same physiques as the cats depicted in Egyptian hieroglyphics. One popular theory suggests that these cats may be the only remaining descendant of a breed of cats that were once found in ancient Egypt and are now extinct in North Africa.

Traders may have carried the cats to Lamu on *dhows* hundreds of years ago. Other breeds of cat have since been brought to the island and, as a result, the local gene pool has been diluted, yet the distinctive-looking Lamu cats still survive among the winding streets. There is a cat clinic to the north of the Donkey Sanctuary where a resident vet treats injured animals.

the Mazrui clan from Oman in Mombasa, to subjugate Lamu, but the attempt failed totally, and victory at Shela signaled the rise of Lamu as the leading power in the archipelago. The fort used to sit on the water's edge, as did Harambee Avenue, but over time another row of houses was built on discarded rubbish, which put the fort 70 m back from the water and the waterfront at where it is today. The construction is of coral blocks, covered with mortar that has a yellowy-orange hue marked by black patches, and inside is a central courtyard surrounded by internal walkways and awnings. It is possible to walk round the battlements, and they afford a good view of the nearby area. It initially served as a barracks for a garrison of soldiers sent by the Sultan of Oman to protect Lamu. Their presence must have been protective, as merchants built houses nearby that date from the same period. Between 1910 and 1984 it served as a prison both under the colonial and Kenyan governments. Now it has a not very good exhibition on the environment, a shop and a library, plus a pleasant café overlooking the busy square at the entrance. It's generally used as a community hall for the local people.

Other places in Lamu Town

In the southwest part of town is a fluted **Pillar Tomb**, thought to date from the 14th century, though it's in danger of collapse. It can be reached by going south, turning inland just after the Halwa Shop, towards the Riyadha Mosque, and continuing on.

Another tomb, the **Mwana Hadie Famau Tomb**, was for a local woman believed to have lived here in the 15th or 16th century. This is situated a little inland from the museum. The tomb had four pillars at the corners with inset porcelain bowls and probably a central pillar as well. Legend has it a hermit took up residence in the hollow interior of the tomb and became a nuisance by grabbing the ankles of passing women at night-time. The solution was to wall up the tomb while the hermit was not at home.

Behind the fort is the **House of Liwali Sud bin Hamad**, a fine example of Swahili architecture. Liwali was a governor appointed by the Sultan of Zanzibar. It is still possible to appreciate how it looked when it was a single dwelling, though it is subdivided now.

On Main Street, just next to the **New Star** restaurant, is the site of the offices of the German East Africa Company. Originally the Germans thought that Lamu would make a suitable secure base for their expansion into the interior (much in the same way as the British used Zanzibar). The agreement regarding British and German 'spheres of influence' in 1886 caused the Germans to turn their attention to Bagamoya, although they opened a post office in Lamu in 1888, which closed three years later. The site is now the missable **German Post Office Museum** ① *Harambee Av, daily 0930-1800, US$2.75, children (under 16)*

US$1.25, or again you can buy a package museum ticket (see above), which has a few faded photographs from the era and not much else. Towards the west of town and south of the Swahili House Museum is the **whetstone** for sharpening knives, said to have been imported from Oman as local stone was not suitable.

Donkey Sanctuary

ⓘ www.thedonkeysanctuary.org.uk.

The Donkey Sanctuary, in the northern part of the town close to the waterfront, is a charity based in the UK, that is concerned with the welfare of donkeys worldwide. In 2008 it celebrated its 21st anniversary in Lamu on 4 July – dubbed by one employee as Independence Day for the donkeys of Lamu. There are an estimated 2200 donkeys on the island, which are used in agriculture but also in carrying household provisions and building materials. They generally plod around town on their own and, in theory, each is owned by someone, although how donkey and owner stay connected is somewhat mystifying. The founder of the trust, Dr Elizabeth Svendsen, first visited Lamu in 1985 while on holiday, and after seeing the poor condition of the working donkeys, established the sanctuary and clinic here in 1987. There is a small enclosure that anyone can visit, where sick donkeys receive free care, and where the donkeys that roam the town can find fodder and water. It's rather endearing here to see a donkey with a cartoon-like criss-cross bandage somewhere on it, covering a minor wound. The twice-yearly de-worming programme on Lamu and the surrounding islands has contributed hugely to the better health of the donkeys, and primitive practices of bleeding a donkey or burning them with hot irons to treat illness is thankfully much reduced. One of the causes of deaths of donkeys on Lamu has been colic, which they can get from eating plastic bags in rubbish dumps. In 2011, a bylaw was passed in Lamu to prohibit shopkeepers giving out plastic bags. This ban came about not just because of the donkeys, but as an environmental initiative on the islands too. (Zanzibar in Tanzania also has a ban on plastic bags.) The donkey awards in March/April are organized by the Lamu Donkey Sanctuary in conjunction with the **Kenya Society for the Protection and Care of Animals** (KSPCA) to promote animal welfare. Prizes are given for the best-cared-for donkey, and a surprising number of local people turn out to proudly parade their well-groomed beasts of burden.

Around the island → *For listings, see pages 303-310.*

Matondoni Village

This is a village of mud and thatched huts of a few hundred people on the western side of the island, about 8 km from town, where you can see *dhows* being built and repaired on the beach. The easiest way to get there is to hire a *dhow* between a group – you will have to negotiate the price and can expect to pay around US$30-40 for the boat. Alternatively you can hire a donkey – ask at your hotel. A third option is to walk, although you should leave early as it gets very hot. The walk will take a couple of hours and is quite complicated. You want to turn off the main street roughly opposite **Petley's** and keep walking west inland. Ask for directions from there; you want to keep going in the same direction as the telephone wires which go to Matondoni – if you follow these you should get there eventually.

Shela

Sticking out on the southeastern tip of Lamu, this village is a smaller duplicate of Lamu town and is the upmarket end of the island. It is a tangle of narrow, sandy lanes, tall stone

Shela stash

In 1915 a man called Albert Deeming was convicted of the murder of a woman and two children in Melbourne, Australia. He was sentenced to death but, before his execution, he prepared a document detailing the whereabouts of 50 kg of gold bars buried on Lamu Island.

In 1901, Deeming had boarded the bullion train from Pretoria to Laurenco-Marques, shot two guards and forced a third to open the bullion compartments. Grabbing as many bars as he could carry, he jumped the train and made his way to the coast. At Delgoa Bay, he sailed by *dhow* to Lamu, but locals were suspicious, and he hid the gold at a small European graveyard at Shela, in the grave of William Searle, a British sailor.

Deeming's belongings were eventually returned to his relatives in South Africa; one of them made a visit to Lamu in 1919, but was unable to locate the grave.

In 1947 the documents passed to a Kenyan farmer, who, with a couple of companions, travelled to Lamu and found the Shela graveyard. Four graves were marked, but none of them had the name of William Searle. Convinced that this must be the graveyard described by Deeming, they began probing the sands. They located a solid object and removed the covering of sand. It was a gravestone with a well-weathered crack. Deeming's instructions were that the gold was in a small wooden box at the head of the grave, at a depth of two feet. Despite extensive excavations they found nothing. They were curious over the fact that an area of sand appeared less compacted than that of its surroundings. Also, when they examined the gravestone, it had some cracks that looked quite recent. They made discreet enquiries in Lamu Town. Four weeks earlier, a party of three Australians from Melbourne had visited Lamu and had spent two days at the Shela sand dunes.

houses, some smaller thatched dwellings and a spacious square ringed with a few market stalls and small shops. Here, in the cool of the evenings, the elders gather to talk and women come out to shop. Also look out for boys washing donkeys on the beach at low tide. In the town are a number of old buildings, including several wonderfully restored houses that you can rent (at a price). The people of Shela were originally from the island of Manda and speak a dialect of Swahili that is quite different to that spoken in Lamu. The **Friday Mosque** was built in 1829 and is noted for its slender, conical minaret. The 12-km **Shela Beach** starts a five-minute walk from the village. Shela is just 3 km or a 40-minute walk from Lamu; go down to the end of the harbour and then along the beach. If you don't want to walk, you can catch a *dhow* taxi.

Southern shores

The southern shores have the best beach, which begins just to the south of Shela: 12 km of almost deserted white sand that backs onto the sand dunes. As there is no reef, the waves get fairly big. Here you can stroll for miles along the deserted shoreline, littered with pansy shells, otherwise known as sand dollars, where foamy waves sweep bare feet and cormorants attempt balancing acts on the sea breeze.

For sleeping and eating price codes and other relevant information, see pages 20-24.

◉ Where to stay

Price varies with the season. Peak periods are Dec and Jan for upmarket travellers and Jul-Sep for families and budget travellers. At other times, there's plenty of scope for negotiation, especially if you plan to stay for more than 1 or 2 days. If you are planning to stay here for a longer holiday and are in a family or group, then it is worth renting a house (with staff). Many are holiday homes of Kenya residents and offer high-quality accommodation at a very modest price. People post details of houses to rent on a notice board at the museum or visit www.lamuretreats.com or www.kenya safarihomes.com. At the lower end of the price range, the hotels in Lamu tend to be hot and suffer from frequent problems with the water supply (expect cold buckets), but nevertheless are still mostly housed in traditional and atmospheric old houses.

Lamu Town *p296, map p297*

$$$ Baytil Ajaib, to the west of the Donkey Sanctuary, T042-463 2033, www.baytilajaib. com. An immaculately restored house with 4 spacious en suite rooms, or a group can rent it as a unit. With verandas and an open courtyard on each floor, supported by gracious columns and arches, where there are comfortable sitting areas with day beds piled with cushions and Swahili and other African artefacts on display. The name means 'House of Wonder' and there are great views over the town and the Lamu Channel. Rates are bed and breakfast or half board and you can discuss menus with the chef.

$$$ Lamu House, near the Lamu Social Hall, T042-463 3491, www.lamuhouse.com. These 2 upmarket houses near the waterfront are the most luxurious place to stay in Lamu Town, with 5 beautiful

and stylish rooms, each decorated with lattice windows, dressing rooms and private terraces, and a lovely whitewashed courtyard with a refreshing plunge pool and day beds. Rates include breakfast and a free *kikoy*, lunch and dinner are US$25 each, and the service is excellent. Can organize day trips or dinner on their *dhow*.

$$$ Lamu Palace Hotel, Kenyatta Rd, T042-463 3104, palacekey@africaonline.co.ke. Located on the harbour front at the south end of town and managed with **Petley's Inn**. Set in an imposing 3-storey block, this has 22 a/c rooms and is very attractively decorated. The pleasant patio restaurant has average and bland buffet set meals, but the à la carte seafood is very good. It's possible to negotiate a better rate off season, Oct-May, and it's one of few places that sells alcohol in Lamu. Friendly and helpful set-up and can organize *dhow* excursions.

$$$ Petley's Inn, Kenyatta Rd, T042-463 3272, reservations through **Lamu Palace**, above. A historic hotel founded in 1962 by an Englishman called Percy Petley who fell in love with Lamu whilst recovering from a safari accident. The hotel has 11 rooms and a swimming pool on the 1st floor. The rooms are very pleasant, in traditional Swahili style, the 2 front rooms have a private terrace. Rooftop restaurant and the 2 bars are popular, and it's one of the few places that serves chilled beers.

$$ Amu House, T042-463 3420, a few streets behind the **Standard Chartered Bank**. This very central and charming place, owned by an American woman, is a reworked 18th-century Swahili house with plaster carvings and niches, pretty Swahili furniture and canopy beds, some rooms have a veranda. Breakfast is included but other meals are only available on request.

$$ Jannat House, north end of town, near Mwana Mshamu mosque, T042-463 3414, www.jannathouse.se. This dates from the 18th century and was built as a merchant's house. The 16 rooms have Swahili furniture, warm (not hot) water and mosquito nets, and it offers Kiswahili language courses. Good food in pleasant garden atmosphere and one of the few hotels with a swimming pool. Rates are bed and breakfast or half board, expect to pay in the region of US$80 for a double but this drops considerably in low season.

$$ Stone House Hotel, near the Swahili House Museum, T042-463 3544, www.stonehousehotellamu.com. This is a quiet, friendly and good-value option, where the small interior coral-walled garden at the entrance provides a nice welcome, and it's one of the best preserved of Lamu's 18th-century houses. It has 12 simple en suite rooms, 4 of which share a bathroom, with Swahili furniture and 4-poster beds, mosquito nets and fans. The small rooftop restaurant has good views and serves seafood and Swahili dishes and fresh juices.

$$-$ Sunsail Hotel, on the waterfront near the District Commissioner's Office, T042-463 2065, www.sunsailhotel.co.ke. 20 double rooms in a fully restored 100-year-old building that was once the sugar depot, with whitewashed walls and an impressive large carved front door. Smart rooms with fans and Lamu beds, tiled bathrooms, restaurant under thatch on the roof with views of the busy jetty, big discounts during low season, very friendly management.

$ Casuarina Rest House, above the Kenya Airways office near the Lamu Museum, T042-463 3123. Another popular budget option in a great location on the waterfront, with 10 clean and spacious rooms, 6 have their own bathroom, while 4 have shared bathrooms, mosquito nets and fans in a building that used to be the Police Station, and it's well run and friendly, with a large rooftop area, and breakfast is included.

$ Hapa Hapa, to the rear of the Hapa Hapa restaurant on Harambee Av, T042-463 3145. Fairly simple but spacious, with clean shared bathroom, some rooms look out over the Lamu Channel, no fans though so ask for one of the top rooms, which catch the sea breezes.

$ Kipepeo Guest House, on the waterfront to the north of Lamu House, T042-463 3569, www.kipepeo-lamu.com. This imposing white 4-storey block run by a German woman has 7 simple but comfortable doubles, with or without tiled bathrooms, and offers some of the best views of the Lamu Channel from the rooftop terrace. You can self-cater in the kitchen or breakfast is available for US$3. Groups can hire a whole floor (with the kitchen) and fit in as many as they like to a maximum of 10 from about US$110.

$ Lamu Archipelago Villas, on waterfront at southern end, T042-633 247. Good location, 12 rooms in an imposing white building, some with their own bathrooms, includes breakfast, fans, nets, efficiently run, though rooms are a little grubbier than others in town.

$ Pole Pole, just inland, north end of town, T042-463 3344. This is one of the highest buildings in Lamu, with good views from the roof, but is quite run down now. It offers very basic board and lodgings with mosquito nets and fans, some of the 15 rooms have bathrooms with cold water, although this cannot be relied upon. Nevertheless cheap from about a negotiable US$8.

$ Yumbe House, near the Swahili House Museum, T042-463 3 101, info@yumbehouse.com. This is a basic but wonderful hotel full of atmosphere and excellent value and is consistently popular with backpackers. It's a traditional house of 4 storeys and is airy and spacious, clean, friendly, has a good water supply and the price includes breakfast. The garden courtyard is especially pretty.

$ Yumbe Villa, located near the fort, see Yumbe House, above, for contact details. This is the annex of Yumbe House where you'll stay if that's full and is another traditional house with Zidaka niches in the ground floor walls, and clean and tidy rooms with traditional Lamu beds, mosquito nets, en suite shower and toilet, some have fans and fridges.

Shela *p301*

In recent years there has been much restoration work going on in Shela (left to its own devices Shela would probably be far more dilapidated than it is today), and there are now some wonderful places to stay. By comparison, Lamu Town is definitely the poorer cousin. Some of the houses are now very luxurious and are popular with wealthy Europeans: Princess Caroline of Monaco, for example, owns a house in Shela.

$$$$ Kizingo, T0733-954 770, www.kizingo.com. This is a small peaceful eco-lodge situated at the end of Shela Beach with 6 thatched cottages (set well apart from each other), verandas, hammocks and unrivalled sea views. Room rates include all meals as well as afternoon tea with home-made cake and boat transfers from Manda Island. Fine wines from South Africa, Chile and Italy and cocktails are extra. Supports a local turtle conservation project, and activities include visiting the turtles that come on to the beach to lay their eggs, fishing, snorkelling, and bird and bush walks. Guests can also hire bikes to explore the local villages. Closed May-Jun.

$$$$ Shela House, T0715-577 896, www.shelahouse.com. This is a collection of 4 luxury houses in the village: **Shela House, Beach House, Garden House** and **Palm House**. The decor is very luxurious, with lots of dark wood and cream walls, floors and furniture, and each house has 3 staff including a cook, and you can self-cater or full-board meals are available. **Shela House** is on 3 floors around an open courtyard, the house well and an ancient gardenia, and has 5 bedrooms, nursery room and a day room and terrace; there are also hammocks on the rooftop. **Beach House** has 4 doubles, and 1 triple room, a swimming pool, bar area and low comfortable *baraza* seats, and a rooftop terrace. **Garden House** has a ground-floor dining and seating area, and 3 bedrooms, 1 for children, and a shaded rooftop *baraza* and open terrace with sun beds. **Palm House** is designed around an open courtyard, with 2 doubles and 1 twin room with private balconies. There is a panoramic view from the covered rooftop, with a bar, sun beds and *baraza* lounging area. Rates vary from US$570-2200 per house per night depending on the number of people (Beach House can sleep up to 14) and must be booked for a minimum of 3 nights.

$$$$-$$$ Peponi's, Shela Beach, T0733-203 082, www.peponi-lamu.com. Facing the channel that runs between Lamu and Manda, this has 24 cottages with verandas, hammocks and swinging chairs in a really wonderful setting with about 500 m of private beach. There is an excellent restaurant (see under Restaurants, below) as well as a bar. The hotel provides full watersports facilities, probably the best and most extensive on the island, and organizes excursions. Very efficiently run and booking well ahead is advised. Closed mid-Apr to end of Jun.

$$$ Baitil Aman Guesthouse, in the middle of the village, T042-463 3584, www.baitil aman.com. This 18th-century house took over 7 years to restore and now features some particularly fine examples of Zidaka niches in the walls and some splendid carved wooden doors. There are just 8 rooms with mosquito nets, fans and outdoor seating areas. Rates are bed and breakfast, dinner is US$20 extra per person, which is served in the dining room or on Swahili mats on the rooftop terrace. The name means 'House of Peace'. Low season rates start from US$100 for a double.

$$$ Banana House, in the village, 50 m back from the beach, T042-463 2044, www.bananahouse-lamu.com. This is run by a friendly Dutch woman as a holistic place to stay, it offers daily yoga sessions and guests are required to wash their feet in a small pool before entering the house barefooted. There are 6 en suite rooms, plus 1 more for children that shares a bathroom with parents, and the top-floor suite is a vast 200 sq m area. There's also a 2nd-floor restaurant, attractive sitting areas with hammocks and day beds, and 1 lounge area has an interesting wall embedded with hundreds of coloured bottles.

$$$ Fatuma's Tower, in the village, T042-463 2213, www.fatumastower.com. Another nicely restored house, this has 5 doubles plus a ground floor 3-bedroom family apartment, furnished in local antiques and fabrics, with several balconies and terraces for relaxing and a small plunge pool with a waterfall in the garden. On the 1st floor is a bright white yoga hall, which lets light in through slit windows, where yoga classes are held in the early evening and massages are available. You can either self-cater, a cook is provided, or lunch and dinner are US$20/25 respectively.

$$$ Kijani Hotel, on water's edge between Peponi's and Shela Beach, T0725-545 264, www.kijani-lamu.com. Here are 10 en suite rooms in a collection of restored old Swahili houses, with fine gardens, traditional furniture, white archways, verandas, 2 small swimming pools, seafood, Swahili dishes, and a touch of Italian cuisine in the Kijani restaurant, excellent standards. Room rates are bed and breakfast, half or full board and include boat transfers from the airport. Fishing, snorkelling and guided tours of Lamu Town are available. Closed May-Jun.

$$$ Mtende House, reservations Langata Link Holiday Homes, Nairobi, T0722-360 111, www.holidayhomeskenya.com. Another well-restored 18th-century house, sleeping up to 6 on 3 floors, with excellent views. The top floor features a covered rooftop with hammocks and day beds. There is a lovely outside area for al fresco dining, fully equipped kitchen, and staff includes houseboy and cook. Other similar houses for rent in the village are Zahir House, which sleep 8, and Bahati House, which sleeps 10. Rates start from around US$180 per night depending on the season but, shared among a group, they represent excellent value.

$$$ Shella Royal House, in the village, reservation Wilderness Getaways East Africa, Nairobi, T020-387 6636, www.wildernessgetawaysea.com. Here there are 2 houses, 1 with 3 storeys and 1 with 4 storeys, with 13 spacious and airy rooms, all but 1 are en suite, with traditional furnishings and whitewashed walls, and a lovely roof terrace with day beds for relaxing. Rates are half board and Swahili dinners feature plenty of fish and seafood. They also have a *dhow* for excursions, some tents and can arrange overnight camping trips to the other islands.

$$ Shella Bahari Guest House, on the beach, close to Peponi's, T042-463 2046, www.shellabahari.co.ke. A similar set up to the nearby Stop Over with 5 spacious rooms, big beds, nets, fans, Swahili furniture. The rooms open out on to a broad balcony that is right above the water at high tide, and the ones at the back without a view are cheaper. The top room here is the best and very private, with its own balcony and hammock, and there's a small restaurant where you can discuss what you want for dinner beforehand.

$$ Shella Pwani Guest House, very close to Peponi's and the jetty, above the shop selling *kikoys*, T042-463 3540. Has 4 double rooms and 1 triple, the top double room is the best, though all have bathrooms (cold water), fans and mosquito nets, set in an old house with some nice traditional plasterwork and well managed. There is a small dining room downstairs, where it is possible to organize meals that include seafood and Swahili dishes and the rooftop terrace has fine views.

$$ Stop Over Guest House, on the beach, reservations through Lamu Homes, Nairobi T020-263 8719, www.lamuhomes.com. A nice renovation with 5 clean rooms and a rooftop 'penthouse' that can sleep 4, simply furnished with fans and mosquito nets, good views of the sea and plenty of sea breezes. The 3 rooms on the 1st floor can be rented as an apartment with access to kitchen facilities on the same floor. On the ground floor is a restaurant serving Swahili dishes, fresh juices, soft drinks and seafood.

Southern shores p302

$$$$ Kipungani Explorer, reservations Heritage Hotels, Nairobi, T020-444 6652, www.heritage-eastafrica.com. One of the Heritage Group's highest standard 'Explorer' resorts, this lodge, with just 13 *makuti* thatched cottages made from local palm leaf mats, is located at the southern tip of Lamu Island. All are extremely spacious and comfortable and each has a veranda. It organizes various excursions and snorkelling trips, and there is a sea-water swimming pool, good restaurant and bar where non-guests can visit for lunch. Boats to get there depart from **Peponi's**. The property has an extremely close bond with the people of neighbouring Kipungani Village, who will show you their ancient boat-building and mat-weaving techniques. Closed mid-Mar to 1 Jul.

✿ Restaurants

You will find lots of yoghurt, pancakes, fruit salads and milk shakes as well as good-value seafood. If you are looking for the traditional food that you find in upcountry Kenya, such as *ugali*, beans, curries, chicken and chips, there are a number of places that do these, mainly on Harambee Av – particularly at the southern end of town. One of the highlights of eating in Lamu is the availability of fresh and cheap fruit juices, and a pint of juice goes for little more than KSh100. They are made to order as attested to by the constant rumblings of electric blenders in the restaurants. There's a wide variety of fruit, including orange, mango, lime, pineapple, pawpaw, avocado, banana, tamarind and coconut. They do tend to add sugar, so you must tell them beforehand if you want your juices natural. Restaurants close fairly early, usually about 2100, so if you want a beer after dinner, the only choices are the terrace bar at the **Lamu Palace Hotel** and the downstairs and rooftop bars at **Petley's**. In Shela, you can get a single malt on the terrace at **Peponi's**, and, elsewhere on the island, the **Kipungani Explorer** and the **Kizingo** resorts have bars. Bear in mind that Lamu is a predominantly Muslim society, so during Ramadan – the

month of fasting – many of the restaurants and cafés will remain closed all day until after sunset and it is considered highly impolite to eat and drink (and smoke) in public until after dark. Stomach upsets are fairly common, so stick to bottled water and avoid ice. If you are self-catering, the fresh produce market near the fort has everything you may need, including fresh seafood, though the catch comes in early in the morning so get there before 0900.

Lamu Town *p296, map p297*
$$$-$$ Moonrise Restaurant, at Lamu House, northern end of waterfront see Where to stay, page 303. Open 0800-2200. A terrace overlooks the waterfront, and there's a lovely atmosphere with candlelit tables in the evening. The inventive menu of outstanding seafood is considered the best on the island – examples are white snapper carpaccio, shrimp soup, aromatic ginger crab, seared tuna steak or calamari tempura. Pasta and risotto dishes are also available. Excellent service, an extensive wine list and beers are served in buckets of ice.
$$ Bush Gardens, on the waterfront near the fort. 0700-2100. A very good seafood restaurant; specialities include lobster cooked in coconut sauce, poached monster crab, jumbo prawns and oysters, good fresh juices, cheaper briyanis and stews. It is friendly but service can be extremely slow, especially when full. Tables are set outside under *makuti* thatched roofs.
$$ Lamu Palace Hotel, southern end of waterfront, see Where to stay, page 303. Open 0800-2300. This is a pleasant restaurant looking out over the waterfront, with some tables on a very attractive terrace surrounded by plants, serving seafood, grills, Indian food and alcohol including wine. Set meals at dinner are rather bland but presented nicely; the à la carte dishes although more expensive are far superior. Towards the back of the restaurant is an extremely comfortable bar and lounge area.

$$ Stone House Hotel, near the Swahili House Museum, see Where to stay, page 304. Open 1900-2130. This small but lovely rooftop restaurant is open to non-hotel guests and has enchanting views of the narrow alleyways and Lamu's *makuti* rooftops. Tables are set in open Arabian archways. With low lighting and sea breezes, it's quite romantic. There's a short but neat menu of pasta, seafood and Swahili dishes, and vegetarians are catered for.

$$-$ Hapa Hapa Restaurant, on the water-front close to **Bush Gardens** (above). 0800-2100. One of the most popular restaurants with tourists, this has a long menu of pasta and pizza, good fruit juices and snacks, lots of fish including an overloaded seafood platter and jumbo prawns, occasionally barracuda, shark and tuna. Very simple decor under thatch but a lively place with excellent food. Breakfasts are good here too; try the banana or mango pancakes with honey.

$ Coconut Juice Café, Harambee Av, southern end, 0800-2000. A 2-storey cafeteria and, as the name suggests, it serves specialist juices that are freshly made, with combinations of lime, peanut, avocado, papaya, mango, coconut and banana, and you can also ask them to blend them with their home-made yoghurt. Also serves basic local and fairly greasy meat and fish dishes.

$ New Minnaa, just off Harambee Av, to the southern end. Upstairs daytime cafeteria, very popular with local people and cheap, with clean plastic tables that are continuously cleared, serves local stews, biryanis, fried fish, chapattis and local specialities, such as *mkata wa nyama* (a kind of pizza) or *maharagwe* (beans in coconut sauce). If you are hankering after Nairobi-style chicken and chips, this is the place to come.

$ New Star Restaurant, Harambee Av, southern end, near the **German Post Office Museum**. Another cheap local canteen serving dishes like rice and beans, *ugali* and beef stews but under a tatty *makuti* roof and in a fairly grubby environment. It does open very early for breakfast though, from 0530.

$ Olympic Restaurant, south of the town also on the waterfront, 0800-2100. A *makuti*-roofed eating area with only a handful of tables – to find it look out for the blackboard of specials outside – but worthwhile for the excellent cheap food. If you're lucky and prepared to wait for about an hour, you might get grilled red snapper with tamarind sauce and coconut rice, prawn biryani or crab served with fresh limes and salad. Also good juices and fruit pancakes for breakfast. Very friendly.

$ Seafront Cafe, on the waterfront east of the **German Post Office Museum**. 0800-2200. Another *makuti*-thatched tourist restaurant that stays open later than most, and with shorter waiting times for food, this sells the usual fare, including good fish curries with coconut rice, an excellent crab soup and seafood salads served with a chapatti, plus juices and milkshakes. Ask about the catch of the day.

$ Whispers, Harambee Av, T0722-611 282. Open 0900-2100, may close in the afternoon if it's quiet, though it stays open during Ramadan. Set in a lovely coral rag-built house with tables outside in the beautiful tropical-garden courtyard, this is a high-quality café with juices, cappuccino, ice cream, spaghetti, pizzas, sandwiches and home-made cakes. They serve wine.

Shela *p301*

$$$ Barbecue Grill, at Peponi's, see Where to stay, page 305. Open 1200-1600, 1900-late. Excellent and open to non-residents, the food is of a very high standard and is probably the best on the island. The beautiful dining room has cool white arches and Swahili copper pots and furniture, or there are tables on the terrace shrouded with bougainvillea. Service is excellent and discreet. Superb seafood, including oysters, lobster and crab, and the giant prawns cooked in chilli and lime are to die for. Alternatively choose the Swahili menu, which is a variety of dishes served on a copper platter to share. The friendly bar serves a full range of alcohol, including

New Year's Day dhow race

The people of Lamu are fiercely proud of their maritime tradition, and there is an annual *dhow* race on New Year's Day at Shela Beach. This event is an important event on the island, and winning the race is a great honour among *dhow* captains. Like the annual donkey race, it brings the island to life, and the shorelines throng with supporters. Individual *dhows* are brightly decorated, and festivities on race day last well into the night. Local captains and their crews compete on a course that tests their skills and prowess, and race day is one of showmanship and celebration. Until recently *dhows* were built entirely without nails – sewn with coconut cord and pegged by wooden dowels. All *dhows* have eyes painted on the bows for protection and to see dangerous rocks. A poignant, well-used Kiswahili proverb, 'You cannot turn the wind, so turn the sail,' originates from the sailors of Lamu.

cocktails and international spirits, and is popular with Shela's expat community.

$ Stop Over Restaurant, at the hotel of the same name, see Where to stay, page 306. Serves simple, basic but good-value food, including pancakes for breakfast, grills and some seafood, such as fantastic grilled prawns with coconut rice, fresh fruit juices, and it also has a great location right on the beach, which is just as well as food takes a long time to appear.

◎ What to do

Lamu Island *p296, map p297*

Watersports can be organized from **Peponi's** in Shela (see Where to stay) and include wind-surfing (with instruction), waterskiing, snorkelling, sailing and scuba diving (Nov-Mar). They also have their own modern fully equipped boat for deep-sea fishing, and offer day trips with a picnic lunch and drinks from US$200 for 4 people.

Taking a *dhow* trip is almost obligatory, and drifting though the mangroves is a wonderful way to experience the islands. You can organize this through all the hotels or the touts; take your time to shop around and find a *dhow* captain you like. Prices vary; expect to haggle hard, but generally it's around US$8 per person for half a day and US$12 for a full day per person for groups of 4-5 people. The boats aren't big enough for more than 5. If you are a solo traveller, ask around the budget hotels to see if you can tag along with another group. There are a number of options, but whatever you arrange, make sure you know exactly how much you'll be paying and what that will include, and don't hand over any money until the day of departure, except perhaps a small advance for food or a deposit to hire snorkelling equipment. The most popular trips are the slow sail across to **Manda Island** with a barbeque lunch on the beach there, and perhaps a visit to the Takwa Ruins, or a sail down the Lamu Channel to the southwest corner of Manda Island around Kinyika Rock to snorkel on the reefs. *Dhows* can be hired for trips to **Pate**, and full-moon trips can also be arranged. During the day, take a hat and sunscreen, as there is rarely any shade on the *dhows*. Also remember, *dhows* without motors are dependent on the tides, so departure and return times are obviously arranged around the tide times.

Around both Lamu and Shela you may be approached by ladies, usually in the restaurants, who offer to do henna tattoos on your hands and feet.

◎ Shopping

Lamu Town *p296, map p297*
Books
The museum has a very good collection of books on Lamu, its history and culture.

Lamu Book Centre has a reasonable selection as well as the local newspapers, and there are a couple of second-hand book stalls along the waterfront.

Souvenirs

Boys walk around selling hand-built model *dhows*, which are not too easy to carry around, so get them at the end of the trip. Other items to buy include carved chests, cloth, especially *kikoys*, jewellery (silver in particular), plus all manner of carved wooden curios. There are a few stalls on the waterfront and some shops, silversmiths and tailors along Harambee Av, and to the north of town are some wood-carving workshops where you'll see mostly chests and furniture being made, including the distinctive 4-poster beds. You can get things made for you, but be prepared to bargain, and there is the question of getting it home. **Baraka**, Harambee Av, T042-463 3264. This is Lamu's best and most beautiful gallery adjoining the **Whispers Restaurant**. It sells high-quality but expensive carvings, Lamu chests, jewellery and clothing, and there are pieces on display from across Africa.

☉ Transport

Lamu Island *p296, map p297*
Air

Check-in time is 30 mins before take-off from the Manda airstrip. Allow plenty of extra time to arrange a boat transfer or *dhow* taxi to get to Manda; the crossing itself takes about 15 mins from Lamu town and about 30 mins from Shela.
Air Kenya, Baraka House, near Whispers Restaurant, T042-463 3445, Nairobi, T020-391 6000, www.airkenya.com, has a daily flight between Wilson Airport in **Nairobi** and Lamu, which departs Nairobi at 1400, arrives in Lamu at 1550, departs again at 1610, and arrives back in Nairobi at 1800, 1 way from US$152. **Fly 540**, airport, T042-463 2054, Nairobi, T020-445 3252, www.fly540.com,

has 2 daily flights between Jomo Kenyatta International Airport in **Nairobi** and Lamu via **Malindi**, 1 way from US$170. **Kenya Airways**, Nairobi, T020-642 2000, www.kenya-airways. com, also has 1 daily flight between Jomo Kenyatta International Airport in **Nairobi**, and Lamu via **Malindi**. Mombasa Air Safari, Moi International Airport, Mombasa, T041-343 3061, www.mombasaairsafari.com, has daily flights on a circuit in both directions between **Mombasa** and Malindi, from US$45 1 way, and **Malindi** and Lamu, from US$65 1 way. **Safarilink**, airport T042-463 2211, Nairobi T020-600 0777, www.flysafarilink. com, has 1 daily flight between Wilson Airport in **Nairobi** and Lamu, which departs Nairobi at 1345, arrives in Lamu at 1530, departs again at 1600, and arrives back in Nairobi at 1800, 1 way from US$140.

Bus

The buses from **Malindi/Mombasa** stay overnight at **Mokowe** and return to Malindi and Mombasa at around 0700 and 1300 – check the times with the bus that you arrive in Lamu on. Allow plenty of extra time for the ferry from the main jetty to Mokowe; for the early buses you need to be at the jetty before sunrise; there are boats waiting from 0600 and plenty of people waiting for them. **Pwani Tawakal Bus**, on Main St near the fort in Lamu, T0722-550 111, T042-463 3380; **Tahmmed**, no office but cell phones for Lamu, T0722-935 373, T0721-623 282.

❶ Directory

Lamu Town *p296, map p297*
Medical services Lamu King Fahd District Hospital, T042-463 3425, located at the southern end of the town to the south of and inland from the fort, which does malaria tests but other than that is poorly equipped and busy, so anyone with serious medical conditions should try to get to Mombasa. **Immigration** At the District Commissioner's Office near the jetty.

Other islands

Apart from Lamu Island itself, the archipelago is made up of a multitude of tiny islets and two other main inhabited islands – Manda and Pate. These have far fewer facilities for visitors than Lamu – although the airstrip is on Manda – but can be explored with local dhow operators or on more formal organized tours.➤➤ *For listings, see page 314.*

Manda Island → *For listings, see page 314. Colour map 2, B3.*

This island is just to the north of Lamu and has the airstrip on it. It is very easy to get to and is a popular day trip to see the ruins at Takwa. The island is about the size of Lamu but has only a small permanent population – partly because of a shortage of fresh water and thus, cultivable land. About a fifth of the island is made up of sand dunes and sandy flat land with just thorn bushes and palms. Another three fifths of the island are mangrove swamps and muddy creeks. The island is separated from the mainland by the narrow Mkanda Channel and the main port is **Ras Kilimdini**, which is located on the northern side of the island.

Arriving on Manda Island
Access to Manda Island and the towns is by way of motorized ferry to the airstrip as well as by *dhow*. However *dhow* is the easiest, as it will take you closer to the ruins, otherwise you will have to walk across the island. The *dhow* will cost about US$30-40 for a group of four to five people. See page 309 for how to organize a *dhow* from Lamu. It takes about 1½ hours and is dependent on the tides. You may have to wade ashore through the mangrove swamp.

Places on Manda Island
The **Takwa Ruins** ① *www.museums.or.ke, 0930-1800, US$5.50, children (under 16) US$2.75,* are ruins of another ancient Swahili town that is believed to have prospered from the 15th to the 17th centuries, with a population of 2000 to 3000 people. It was abandoned in favour of the town of Shela on Lamu, probably because salt water contaminated most of the town's supplies of fresh water. The ruins consist of the remains of a wall that surrounded the town, about 100 houses, a mosque and a tomb dated from 1683. As with many of the other sites on the coast, the remains include ablution facilities. The houses face north towards Mecca as does the main street. There is a mosque at the end of the street that is thought to have been built on the site of an old tomb. The other feature of the ruins is the pillar tomb, which is situated just outside the town walls. The ruins have been cleared but little excavation has been done here. The creek that Takwa is located on almost cuts the island in half during high tide.

Pate Island → *For listings, see pages 303-310. Colour map 2, B3.*

Pate Island is about three times the size of Lamu and located about 20 km to the northeast. Unlike both Lamu and Manda, it does not have a large area taken up by dunes. The island is divided into two parts – indeed it may have once been two islands, but the channel dividing them is so shallow that only the smallest boats can go down it. The land is very low-lying and the towns are situated on shallow inlets that can only be reached at high tide. The only deep-water landing point is at **Ras Mtangawanda** in the west of the island, but, as it is not a sheltered harbour, it has never had a major settlement. Although it is fairly easily accessible, it does not receive many visitors.

Arriving on Pate Island

To get to Pate Island, there's a motorized public ferry that departs usually daily from the Lamu jetty about one hour before high tide – you'll need to check locally when this is. The reason for this is the Mkanda Channel is only accessible by boat at high tide. The ferry not only carries passengers but goods from Lamu to Pate, so it's a long and uncomfortable ride, and you may find yourself wedged between boxes and many other people. You will also need plenty of food and water. However, they do pull a blue tarpaulin over the boat to protect against the sun. After two to three hours, it stops at near deserted **Mtangwanda** on Pate Island, which is the nearest point to Pate Town. It takes about an hour to walk to **Pate Town** from here. After a further four to five hours the ferry stops at **Faza**, and then goes on to **Kizingitini**, which takes about another hour. Again, you'll have to check locally when the ferry returns from these places on its run back to Lamu, as times are determined by high tide in the Mkanda Channel. Sometimes much smaller *dhows* link the points on Pate Island but, again, are dependent on the tides. Generally, when visiting Pate Island the best thing to do is to get off the ferry at Mtangwanda, walk to Pate Town and then walk through Siyu to Faza, from where you will be able to get the ferry back to Lamu. Alternatively a group can organize a *dhow* in Lamu to explore for a few days, but there is nowhere to stay as such, though camping is possible if you have a tent.

Pate Town

The town of Pate is only accessible from the sea at the right tide – and you will have to walk from the ferry's landing place at Mtangwanda. It is in the southwest corner of the island and is one of the old Swahili towns that dot the coast. The town shows strong Arabic and Indian influences, and was once most famous for the silk that was produced here. The old stone houses are crumbling, and tobacco has been planted amongst the ruins. The main ruins are those of **Nabahani**, which are found just outside the town. Although they have not yet been excavated, you should be able to make out the town walls, houses, mosques and tombs.

The age of the town is disputed; the earliest remains that have been found are from the 13th century, although, according to some accounts, the town dates back to the eighth century. The town was reasonably prosperous up to 1600, although by the time the Portuguese first arrived, it had begun to decline. The Portuguese did not have much success and by the 17th century had withdrawn to Mombasa. The final decline of Pate was the war with Lamu. There had been an ongoing dispute between the two islands. Over the years the port at Pate silted up, so Lamu was used instead by the bigger *dhows*, and the tensions increased. The situation reached a climax in 1813 when the army from Pate was defeated at Shela and the town went into a decline from which it has never recovered.

Siyu

The channel on which Siyu is sited is so silted up that only the smallest boats can reach Siyu. It is therefore necessary to approach the town on foot – either from Pate (about 8 km) or from Faza (about 10 km). Unless you are happy to get lost and therefore walk for hours, you would be advised to take a guide, as the route (particularly from Pate) is complicated. Siyu is a stone-built town dating from about the 15th century. It became most well known as a centre for Islamic scholarship and is believed to have been an important cultural centre during the 17th and 18th centuries. At one time it is said to have had 30,000 inhabitants. Today there are probably fewer than 4000 people living in the town, and the inhabited part is slightly apart from the ancient ruined area. A creek separates the residential area from the **fort**, built by Seyyed Said, believed to date from the mid-19th century when the town was occupied by forces of the Sultan of Zanzibar. The fort has some impressive canons and has been partly renovated. The town is fairly dilapidated and outside the town are coconut plantations. It is a small fishing village that has a thriving crafts industry – you will be able to see leather goods being made, and doors, furniture and jewellery.

About one hour's walk from Siyu there are the **Shanga Ruins**, but they are almost impossible to find without the help of a local guide. Ask around in Siyu for someone to show you the way. There have been excavations in recent years that show signs of unearthing impressive remains. There are buildings from the 13th and 14th centuries and many artefacts have been found dating back to the eighth and ninth centuries. There is a pillar tomb, a large mosque, a smaller second mosque, about 130 houses and a palace. The whole town was walled with five access gates and, outside the wall, is a cemetery containing well over 300 tombs. If you are visiting the islands by *dhow* and would rather not walk, you can ask your boatman to take you to Shanga direct.

Faza

Faza is about 18 km from Pate Town and 10 km northeast of Siyu. Although the town of Faza is believed to date from the 13th century and possibly as early as the eighth century, there is little in the way of ruins left here. Today it's a ramshackle place of mud thatched huts crammed together, with piles of rubbish everywhere. In 1990, there was a huge fire that destroyed most of the houses in the town, so the huts are the replacement. However, the town is important in that it is the district headquarters of Pate Island and some of the mainland. It therefore has a number of modern facilities that are not found elsewhere on the island – such as post office, school, telephone exchange, a police station (where the police force has nothing to do) and some simple shops and restaurants.

The original town is believed to have been completely destroyed in the 13th century by the nearby town of Pate, rebuilt and destroyed again in the late 16th century, this time by the Portuguese. It was again rebuilt and joined forces with the Portuguese against Pate. However, its significance declined until recently when, being the district headquarters, it resumed its position of importance.

Close to where the ferries anchor are the ruins of the **Kunjanja Mosque**. Although no more than a pile of rubble, you can still see some of the mihrab, which points to Mecca and which is a beautiful example with fine carvings. There are some splendid Arabic inscriptions above the entrance. Outside the town is the tomb of Amir Hamad, the commander of the Sultan of Zanzibar's army who was killed here, in action, in 1844. Faza makes an interesting place to walk around. From Faza you could, if you wanted, walk on to the other villages on the island, all within 40 minutes of Faza: Kisingitini, Bajumwali, Tundwa, and the closest, Nyambogi.

◉ Other islands listings

For sleeping and eating price codes and other relevant information, see pages 20-24.

● Where to stay

Manda Island *p311*

There is no fresh water on Manda Island; it is brought over from Lamu daily. Consequently water is used carefully at the lodges and water conservation is encouraged.

$$$$ Manda Bay, reservations Nairobi, T020-211 5453, www.mandabay.com. An exclusive resort offering watersports and *dhow* safaris, all the 16 spacious and comfortable cottages with their own bathrooms and verandas are constructed with local materials in traditional coastal style, with palm-thatch roofs and woven matting covering the floors. Meals, seafood and Italian, are relaxed and casual, served in the dining room, on the beach, or on a *dhow*. Rates are full board and include soft drinks, beer and wine. Closed mid-May to mid-Jul.

$$$$ The Majlis, reservations Nairobi, T0773-777 066, www.themajlisresorts.com. A luxury resort with 25 very spacious a/c rooms spread over 3 beachside villas built of white coral stone and timber, an eclectic mix of decor with antiques and modern hand-crafted furnishings, sculpture and art, open-sided restaurant with a 14-m-high thatched roof, excellent choice of food, including Italian and sushi, several bars, 2 swimming pools and a spa. They organize activities for children, plus deep-sea fishing and snorkelling by *dhow*.

$$$ Diamond Village, T0720-015001, www.diamondbeachvillage.com. Very comfortable and affordable *bandas* on the beach with thatched roofs, 1 for families that sleeps 4-8 people, and the others with a double bed downstairs and a single bed mounted in the roof. Because of the lack of water, toilets are pit latrines. There is also a rather unique treehouse in the arms of a baobab tree, which has a wooden deck all the way around the trunk. Very good food in the open-air restaurant. A rather special feature of the lodge are the giant clam shells that act as bird baths and attract a colourful array of birds at both dawn and dusk.

Camping

Camping is available at a pretty site at the Takwa Ruins for around US$8 per tent, though there are no facilities and you will need to be completely self sufficient. Bring plenty of water as none is available on the island.

Pate Island *p312*

Every few years a lodging house opens in Faza, but the lack of visitors forces them to close sooner or later. Private accommodation, though, is easy to find; you can ask around to stay at a family house or people may also approach you. Again, in Siyu, it is possible to rent rooms in local houses – there are no formal guesthouses. It's possible you may get offered food by your hosts and other than that there are only basic provisions available from small shops and stalls.

● Transport

Pate Island *p312*

For details about getting to Pate from Lamu by ferry and *dhow*, see page 312.

Contents

Footprint features

Border crossings

At a glance

⊖ **Getting around** Self-drive (a 4WD is essential); tours; flights to Samburu, Buffalo Springs and Shaba game reserves. Public transport is very limited.

✪ **Time required** To get to Lake Turkana and back, allow at least 1 week; 2 nights in a lodge in Samburu.

☼ **Weather** Mostly very hot with temperatures that can be in excess of 40°C.

✖ **When not to go** Can be visited year-round but the climate is harsh.

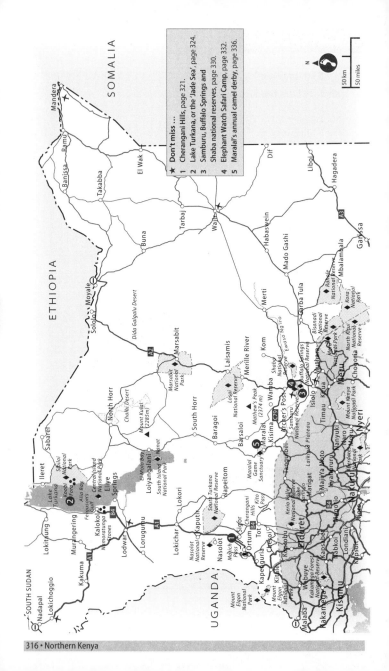

SOMALIA

ETHIOPIA

SOUTH SUDAN

UGANDA

Don't miss ...
1 Cherangani Hills, page 321.
2 Lake Turkana, or the 'Jade Sea', page 324.
3 Samburu, Buffalo Springs and
   Shaba national reserves, page 330.
4 Elephant Watch Safari Camp, page 332.
5 Maralal's annual camel derby, page 336.

N

50 km
50 miles

Mandera
Ramu
Banissa
Takabba
El Wak
Dif
Liboi
Hagadera
Garissa
Mbalambala
Kora National Park
North Kitui National Reserve
Bisanadi National Reserve
Rahole National Reserve
Garba Tula
Mado Gashi
Habaswein
Tarbaj
Wajir
Buna
Moyale
Solai
Dida Galgalu Desert
Marsabit
Marsabit National Park
North Horr
Chalbi Desert
Mount Kulal (2285m)
Sabarei
Ileret
Koobi Fora
Sibiloi National Park
Lake Turkana
Allia Bay
Central Island National Park
Ferguson's Gulf
Eliye Springs
El Molo Bay
Loiyangalani
South Island National Park
South Horr
Baragoi
Logi National Reserve
Laisamis
Merille River
Kom
Mathew's Peak (2374m)
Barsaloi
Wamba
Shaba National Reserve
Buffalo Springs
Samburu National Reserve
Archer's Post
Isiolo
Timau
Kiura
Meru
Choyeta
Mount Kenya National Park
Nyeri
Nanyuki
Naro Moru
Maralal
Maralal Game Sanctuary
Kisima
Rumuruti
Nyahururu
Maji'ya Moto
Laikipia Plateau
Aberdare National Park
Thomson's Falls
Marigat
Kabarnet
Eldama Ravine
Nakuru
Lake Bogoria National Reserve
Lake Baringo
Kerio Valley National Reserve
Kapenguria
Ortum
Sigor
Tot
Cherangani Hills
Kapsowar
Iten
Eldoret
Kakamega
Kakamega Forest National Reserve
Webuye
Kitale
Mount Elgon National Park
Mount Elgon National Reserve
Malaba
Kisumu
Kapsabet
Londiani
Kericho
Kipson
Tabkoi
Nasolot National Reserve
Nasolot
Marich Pass
Kito Pass
South Turkana National Reserve
Lokori
Kapeitom
Lokichar
Kaputir
Lodwar
Loruguru
Kalokol
Namoratunga Stones
Kakuma
Lokitaung
Murangering
Lokichoggio
Nadapal
Lokichar
Merti
Shaba National Reserve
Ewaso Ng'iro
Ng'iro
Buffalo Springs
A1
A2
A3
B4
B9
C77
C27

This is a vast area of forested and barren mountains, deserts and scrubland, occasionally broken by oases of vegetation and the huge Lake Turkana. Northern Kenya accounts for almost half of the country and yet only a fraction of the population live here. The people who do inhabit the area – the Samburu, Rendille, Boran, Gabbra, Turkana and Somali – are semi-nomadic peoples that cross between their villages in the region using ancient migration routes, existing as they have done for generations, hardly affected by the modern world. The main reason tourists come to Northern Kenya is to see the wonders of Lake Turkana – the Jade Sea – and, in spite of the barren environment, there are also plenty of national parks. Just north of Isiolo you will find Samburu, Buffalo Springs and Shaba national reserves, all three along the banks of the magical life-giving Ewaso Ng'iro River and which jointly cover an area of some 300 sq km. Further north still are the less-visited parks at Maralal, Losai and Marsabit. Travelling in the northern regions can be rough and uncomfortable; the roads are far from good, distances between places are vast, there are very few facilities, and it's a long way from the comfort of the game lodges and beach hotels in the rest of the country. Unfortunately, these days, there are also safety issues in the region, as well as an ongoing refugee crisis that has spilled over the borders from Somalia and newly proclaimed South Sudan. What's more, decades of prolonged drought have given rise to conditions of acute poverty (see page 320).

Arriving in Northern Kenya

The main road through Northern Kenya is the A2 – or **Trans-East African Highway** – that passes through **Isiolo**, **Marsabit** and on to **Moyale** at the Ethiopian border (see page 345 for border crossing information). From Isiolo it is obligatory to travel in a convoy on this road, which has always been in a terrible condition. However, the 138-km stretch from Isiolo to **Merille River**, which is more or less midway between Isiolo and Marsabit, is now a two-lane tarmac road (as of mid-2011). Nevertheless, the road deteriorates after that, so a 4WD is still essential. In the extreme north, there are very few defined roads around **Lake Turkana**. The eastern and western shores of the lake are accessed completely separately, and are physically separated by the vast uncrossable **Suguta Valley** south of the lake. The eastern shore is reached via **Maralal** and Marsabit, with the central point of access being the small oasis town of **Loiyangalani**. The western shore is accessed via **Kitale** on the A1, and the central point of access is **Lodwar**. There are airstrips on both shores for chartered aircraft.

Turkana and much of the north is best visited as part of a professionally organized safari. Most operators offer an eight- to nine-day tour heading up the Rift Valley to stop at Lake Baringo, going on to **Maralal** and then to **Lake Turkana** via Baragoi and South Horr. The return journey goes via **Samburu National Reserve** and **Buffalo Springs National Reserve**. Some go via the **Marsabit National Park** crossing the Chalbi Desert. Most use open-sided 4WD trucks, not built for comfort but they are sturdy and reliable. If you have a bit more money to spend, some companies arrange flying safaris, and there is a scattering of upmarket lodges. See page 77 for tour operators specializing in the region; **Gametrackers** are particularly recommended.

Driving yourself is a possibility if you are experienced in wilderness driving (a 4WD is imperative), though this is not exactly trouble free. You will need to bring a number of tools in case of breakdown or getting stuck in the sand, such as a jack, sand ladders, a shovel and a rope, and a GPS is a good idea. You'll need plenty of fuel too, as it is in particularly short supply. Driving at night is not only foolish, but illegal.

This barren region is in sharp contrast to the green, fertile land of the Central Highlands. Much of Northern Kenya is desert scrub where only the hardiest of vegetation is able to survive; prolonged drought over the last few decades has exacerbated the already formidable conditions, and the nomadic people and their herds continue to suffer. The plains routinely reach dangerously hot temperatures by midday of 50°C with no hint of wind.

Kitale to Lake Turkana

If you are coming up into Northern Kenya from Kitale, you travel a glorious route through the highlands, close to the Saiwa Swamp National Park (see page 157). Continuing through the northern gorges of the Cherangani Hills will bring you to the desert plains through the Marich Pass. This is a dramatic deep rocky cleft at an altitude of 3000 m carved by the Moruny River between the heavily wooded Cherangani Hills, opening out to the arid plains of the Lake Turkana basin below. The views are incredible, looking down onto the plains from the lush highlands, and the first glimpse of Lake Turkana doesn't disappoint. Volcanic in origin, Lake Turkana is the most northerly of the Kenyan Rift Valley lakes, crossing over the border of Ethiopia. Its dry, arid and lunar-like shores feature low white gravel dunes and sparsely populated vegetation of ragged doum palms, stripped to ribbons by sudden, violent storms that blow day and night. Its extreme terrain and remote location makes it one of the wildest and least touched regions of East Africa. ▶▶ *For listings, see pages 326-328.*

Arriving at Lake Turkana

Seeing the western side of Lake Turkana by road involves a long rough trip. The most direct route north is along the **A1** road, which goes from Kitale via Kapenguria to Lodwar and Lokichoggio and on to the South Sudan border in the extreme northwest of Kenya (see page 323). Note the A1 is surfaced from Kitale to Lodwar (302 km), but the heavy traffic has completely broken up the tarmac north of the Marich Pass, so it's now a long and uncomfortable ride of about eight hours between Kitale and Lodwar by bus or *matatu*. You can also approach Lodwar from Eldoret or Kabarnet via Iten, and then on through the upper Kerio Valley and Cherangani Hills joining the Kitale–Lodwar road near Kapenguria. The third route is via the unmade road from Lake Baringo through the Kito Pass, across the Kerio Valley to Tot. See under Cherangani Hills, page 321, for details of these routes. The other option is to fly, and there are now daily scheduled flights from Nairobi to airstrips at Lodwar and Lokichoggio, which mostly transport aid workers to the border region with South Sudan. However, after a day or two of arduous road journeys to get to the northwest, the option of flying back may be very tempting. ▶▶ *See Transport, page 327.* For access to the lake from the eastern side, see page 335.

Kapenguria → *For listings, see pages 326-328.*

Kapenguria is a small dusty town 40 km north of Kitale on the A1, lying in the foothills of the Cherangani Hills and surrounded by grazing land and some fields of millet and sorghum, which the local Pokot people cultivate. To get here you will first pass the turn-off to the tiny **Saiwa Swamp National Park**, which is on the right of the main road 24 km north of Kitale. As it's more often visited as part of a tour of Western Kenya along with nearby Mount Elgon National Park, it is included in the Western Kenya chapter, page 157. However, both these parks can be easily combined with a trip towards Lake Turkana via Kitale.

Kapenguria has a special place in Kenya's history as it is where the six most influential leaders in the struggle for Independence were detained and tried in 1952 for their activities during the Mau Mau Rebellion. These were Jomo Kenyatta, Kungu Karumba, Fred Kubai, Paul Ngei, Bildad Kaggia and Ramogi Achieng Oneko, and they became known as the 'Kapenguria Six'. The **Kapenguria Museum** ① *near the council offices, T054-62050, www.museums.or.ke, 0930-1800, US$5.50, children (under 16) US$2.75*, tells the story and

Travel warning

Draw a line across the map of Kenya starting at Kitale in the west, through Lake Baringo and Isiolo, all the way to the Tana River Delta in the east. The area above this line is referred to as Northern Kenya. These days, it is generally known as a lawless place. The pastoralists in the region are largely nomadic and depend on livestock (cattle, sheep, goats and camels) for their livelihood. They rely on access to pasture and water but such resources are scarce and under increasing pressure, and the region has witnessed a lean period of droughts over the last decade. Violent conflicts involving pastoralists associated with competition for these basic resources have become widespread and severe and, in some areas, herdsmen have lost up to 80% of their herds through drought. Today, many of the nomadic communities are severely malnourished and rely upon food aid – it is only through this emergency relief that the people have survived.

Added to this, there are gangs of armed bandits, mostly cattle rustlers, who are capable of attacking and destroying entire villages and their occupants, and of robbing vehicles on the main roads throughout the region. Because of Kenya's porous borders with Sudan and Somalia, they have been able to get automatic weapons, and a vicious cycle of revenge killings has emerged.

The problems in Sudan and Somalia, and the influx of refugees into Kenya from these countries, have also contributed to the tension and increased pressure on resources. The vast refugee camps, which were built from 1992 along the Sudanese and Somali borders, each for around 90,000 people, are today impossibly overcrowded and some now house up to 250,000. The United Nations has identified Northern Kenya as a "rapidly developing emergency", with an estimated 2.4 million people currently receiving food aid.

There is a high military presence in the north; vehicles usually travel in convoys and are, in some cases, escorted by armed guards; road blocks are common, and vehicle searches are a part of everyday life. Anyone travelling here should exercise extreme caution and get local on-the-ground advice. In particular, the area north of Isiolo into the far northeast towards the Somali border, including the town of Garissa, has a combination of dangerous desert travel, overcrowded refugee camps and frequent bandit raids, which makes this region very risky for travellers. The national reserves of Samburu, Buffalo Springs and Shaba are not affected by these safety issues.

is housed in the former prison where the six were detained. Displays in the museum include books, documents and photographs about African resistance to colonial rule and you can visit the tiny cell where Kenyatta was held. While they were incarcerated, the Independence movement gathered momentum and was predominantly led by Tom Mboya and Oginga Odinga who kept up the pressure for the release of the detainees: KANU's election slogan in the 1961 election was Uhuru na Kenyatta (Independence and Kenyatta). Kenyatta was released in 1961, after KANU won the election, and the other five were released soon afterwards. Kenyatta became the first president of newly independent Kenya in 1963. The museum also has some ethnographic exhibits and, outside, is a mock-up of a Pokot homestead.

From Kapenguria, the A1 continues north towards Lodwar and, after 67 km, it traverses the **Marich Pass**, which is a deep, rocky cleft carved where the Moruny River emerges from the Cherangani Hills onto the dry plains of the Lake Turkana Basin. Once through the pass, the road levels out into the endless scrub, where you'll see nothing but a few lonely

Turkana goat herders. You can either stay on the A1 to Lodwar, 195 km north of the pass, and perhaps stay overnight here at the **Marich Pass Field Studies Centre** (see Where to stay, page 326) or there's the option of exploring the Cherangani Hills.

Cherangani Hills

These wild, thickly forested hills are miles away from the popular tourist circuit, with fine mountain landscapes. They are the fourth highest mountain range in Kenya and include rolling hills as well as dramatic mountain peaks that form the highest, most breathtaking and spectacular escarpments of the Rift Valley. Unlike most of Kenya's mountains and ranges, the Cherangani Hills are not volcanic in origin. They are centred upon a forested escarpment and surrounded on three sides by sheer cliff faces. There are occasional sightings of lammergeyers here, drifting on the thermal currents. The **Pokot**, who have inhabited the hills for around 1000 years, claim they took over existing irrigation systems, which zigzag all over the escarpments. The waterways make this area a lush land of agriculture, with back-to-back *shambas* (small farms) everywhere. The hills are criss-crossed by walking paths, and ease of direction and undemanding slopes make this excellent country for relaxing hill walking. The paths cross open farmland, pass through sheltered valleys and wind their way up to forested peaks. All the main routes cross the 3000 m contour, with decreased oxygen supplies. Car engine performance may be adversely affected by the altitude, and it is essential to carry extra supplies of fuel as consumption is heavy.

Arriving in the Cherangani Hills

There are two approaches from the Kapenguria–Lodwar road (A1). One route, known as the Cherangani Highway, is one of the most terrifying and challenging roads in Kenya and you will need a 4WD. Turn off the A1 at Kapenguria east to **Cheptongei** and then head down through indigenous forests to **Iten** in the Kerio Valley (page 113). From Iten you can continue west on the C51 through the scenic valley to Kabarnet, or east to Eldoret. The other way is from the A1 at Sigor in the Western Cherangani Hills; turn on to the B4 and to the village of **Tot**; from here you can stay on the B4 and go via the steep **Kito Pass**, which then drops down to Lake Baringo. However, this route involves travelling along a track through the northern face of the Cherangani Hills and the streams may flood the road in heavy rains when this route is only manageable with a 4WD. Alternatively at Tot, you can turn south on to the C52 and go along the **Elgeyo Escarpment**, again to the Kerio Valley near Iten. The best way to appreciate the Cheranganis is to walk. Both **Sirikwa Safaris** and the **Marich Pass Field Studies Centre**, see Where to stay, page 326, organize Pokot guides on guided multi-day treks, which can include ascents of the highest peaks: **Mount Sekerr** (also known as Mtelo Mountain or Sigogowa, 3326 m) and **Mount Koh** (2608 m). Also ask at these places for information on road conditions, if you are considering driving yourself into the hills.

North to Lodwar and beyond

Nasolot National Reserve → *Colour map 3, B5/6.*

ⓘ *36 km north of the Marich Pass to the west of the A1, the gate to the reserve is 6 km from the main road, www.kws.org, 0600-1900, US$20, children (3-18) US$10.*

Nasolot National Reserve covers 92 sq km, ranging in altitude from 750-1500 m, and the boundary to the east is the seasonal Weiwei River. The habitat is predominantly thicket and dry bushland, with many succulents and acacias bordering the seasonal streams and rivers that criss-cross the reserve. There are elephants in the reserve but they are well camouflaged by the flora, though you are quite likely to spot their dung. Other mammals include the greater and lesser kudu, warthog and bushbuck. The birdlife is rich and varied and includes the white-crested turacos, Abyssinian ground hornbills, superb starlings and Abyssinian rollers.

A good road bisects the reserve and leads to the **Turkwell Dam**, a hydroelectric dam at the head of a gorge harnessing the waters of the Turkwell River. The dammed waters have formed a large artificial lake that stretches westwards between the hills, home to a large variety of birdlife. There are no formal camping facilities at Nasolot, though camping is permitted virtually anywhere in the reserve. Again, both **Sirikwa Safaris** and the **Marich Pass Field Studies Centre**, see Where to stay, page 326, can organize safaris here.

South Turkana National Reserve → Colour map 3, B6.
ⓘ 50 km north of the Marich Pass to the east of the A1 road.
South Turkana National Reserve is remote, rarely visited and has no tourist facilities or roads, though the main road passes its western boundary and the Kerio River borders it to the southeast. Dense thorn bush and riverine forest make up its 1000 sq km area. The local Turkana kill wild animals for food, unlike the other groups in this region, meaning there is little game left in the reserve, though elephant migrate through here to the Kerio Valley.

Lodwar → Colour map 3, B6. Phone code: 054.
The principal town in the northwest of the region and 302 km north of Kitale is Lodwar, the administrative centre of the Turkana District. Lodwar began life as a formal town only in the 1930s when the first European and Indian traders arrived. It was an important colonial outpost, as local tribal disputes were common. Jomo Kenyatta was held here briefly in 1959 whilst in detention (see page 319). It has been said that Kenyatta was taken to Lodwar from Kapenguria so that the Mau Mau would be unable to rescue him, given the distance and the fierce nature of the Turkana tribesmen – even today the Turkana that have migrated to the towns in the southern areas of Kenya are known for their ferocity, and are often employed as *askaris* (watchmen/guards). Lodwar is not nearly as isolated as in the past, due to the opening of the surfaced road from the highlands and an airstrip, but it is still very much a backwater town and poverty is very acute here. Take good care of your possessions and be prepared for aggressive begging. There is a branch of **Kenya Commercial Bank** with an ATM, a post office, a small supermarket and a Kobil petrol station in town. Like Lokichoggio (below), NGOs have a big presence in Lodwar.

If you haven't seen the Turkana people before now on the route north from Kitale, you will see them in Lodwar. They come into town to trade goats and chickens at the market, and you may often see them sitting under the shade of the few trees along the dusty streets. Like the Masai, they are a tall, handsome and striking-looking people and wear similar colourful fabrics and beads. Both men and women often shave their heads, sometimes leaving a mowhawk-style tuft of hair, and ceremonial scars on faces and arms are common. Given Lodwar's proximity to the borders, you may also see fairer-skinned Ethiopians, as well as Sudanese and Somali women in full chador.

To South Sudan
North of Lodwar the A1 continues the 121 km to **Kakuma** on a good tarred road. This is the site of a very large refugee camp administered by the **United Nations Commission for Refugees** (UNHCR) and the government of Kenya. It was set up in 1992, predominantly

Border crossings: Kenya–South Sudan

Lokichoggio

It is now possible to cross the border between Northern Kenya and newly proclaimed (July 2011) South Sudan. From Loki, the A1 road continues over the border to **Juba**, the capital of South Sudan. At the north end of Loki, beyond the dry river bed, the Kenyan military has set up a border checkpoint (0600-1800). Here, you will have to get a Kenyan visa if coming from South Sudan, and get stamped out of Kenya if going to South Sudan. About 30 km beyond Loki the A1 reaches **Nadapal**, the South Sudanese checkpoint; 'no-man's land' lies between the two. You'll need to have arranged a visa for South Sudan before arrival here, as they are not issued at the border (though this may change). Although there is public transport as far as Loki, the only cross-border traffic are trucks, many of which are transporting aid into South Sudan. However, this too is likely to change rapidly, as local trade between the two countries increases. In the mean time, Kenyan police are providing armed escorts for civilian vehicles travelling between Loki and Nadapal, from where it's another 375 km to Juba. Once in South Sudan, the road is in a reasonable condition as it was retarred and de-mined in 2008. Nevertheless, before attempting this route, get up-do-date local information; in reality, the only travellers likely to go to this border region are those working for the many NGOs operating here. The other option to get to Juba is to fly; both **Kenya Airways** and **Fly 540** have scheduled flights from Nairobi (see Nairobi Transport, page 80, for contact details).

to house refugees during the conflicts in southern Sudan. It's a vast settlement of tents, thatched huts and mud abodes, and is a very harsh place to live with frequent dust storms and temperatures of over 40°C. Because of the semi-arid environment (again like Lodwar), agriculture is not possible, so people rely on hand-outs from the aid agencies. Once (non-Kenyan) people are admitted to the camp, they are not permitted to move around the rest of Kenya so, it has been argued, for more than 20 years Kakuma has represented not only a place of exile and safety, but also, effectively, a prison. Now the civil war has ended in Sudan, and the new country of South Sudan has been proclaimed (July 2011), people are starting to trickle back; but at its height the camp accommodated 70,000 people.

Beyond Kakuma, **Lokichoggio** (sometimes spelt Lokichogio or Lokichioki) is another 95 km further on. More commonly known simply as 'Loki', it is the last town on the A1 in Kenya's northwestern Turkana District, 216 km northwest of Lodwar and about 30 km from the border with South Sudan (see box, above). Loki is a sprawling, hot and dusty settlement of breeze-block buildings and shipping containers – not really a town as such, as it has grown haphazardly around the airstrip that started life in the 1970s to serve missionaries in the remote Turkana region. When the Sudanese civil war intensified from 1986, leading to an influx of refugees into Northern Kenya, the international community intervened to provide food relief and medical supplies, and Loki became the service point. Today it is the main base monitoring the situation in South Sudan, and there are more than 40 international NGOs here as well as a very large hospital. The airport is used by the United Nations, UNICEF and the World Food Program, but also has passenger flights (see Transport, page 328). The local people are mainly Turkana nomads who trade their livestock in town, in contrast to the oddly placed community of international relief workers, missionaries and hospital staff. There is a post office and a branch of **Kenya Commercial Bank** with an ATM.

Lake Turkana (western shore) → *For listings, see pages 326-328. Colour map 3, A6.*

The largest lake in the country, Lake Turkana runs about 250 km from the Ethiopian border in a long thin body of water that is never more than 50 km wide. It stretches into the Ethiopian Highlands, where the Omo River enters its waters. Giant Nile perch are reported to grow up to 180 kg in the lake, but Nile tilapia are a more commercial option as they are more palatable and are either dried or frozen before being marketed all over Kenya. The lake also supports a huge number of hippos and the largest population of Nile crocodiles in the world, estimated to be 20,000 strong. Villagers along the lakeside often encounter crocodiles, but believe there are enough fish in the lake and that they don't pose too much of a threat. Nevertheless, you may come across a lone fisherman on the lakeshore carrying a line in one hand and a rock in the other to throw at any crocodile that may get too close. There is also a profusion of birdlife here, including herons, egrets, plovers, cranes and kingfishers, as well as many European migratory species.

Count Sammuel Teleki Von Szek is believed to have been the first white man to see the lake in 1888. In honour of his patron, Von Szek named it Lake Rudolf, after the Austrian Archduke. President Jomo Kenyatta changed the name to Lake Turkana in 1975. This lake used to be far larger than it is today. Around 10,000 years ago it is believed the water level of the lake was about 150 m higher and it was considered to be one of the sources of the Nile. At that time it supported a far greater number and diversity of plant and animal life. Now a combination of factors, including evaporation and major irrigation projects in southern Ethiopia, have brought the water level to its lowest in memory. As a result, the water is far more alkaline than in the past. This is likely to be further exacerbated by the completion of the Gilgel Gibe III Dam, which is presently being constructed upriver on the Omo River in Ethiopia and is due to be operational by 2013. The purpose of the dam is to provide electricity not only for Ethiopia, but also for parts of Northern Kenya and South Sudan. Environmentalists believe that this dam could further reduce the seasonal floodwaters to Lake Turkana and again reduce the water levels significantly (possibly by another 10 m). This would lead to a further increase in the water salinity, to a level where it may no longer be drinkable. It could also drastically

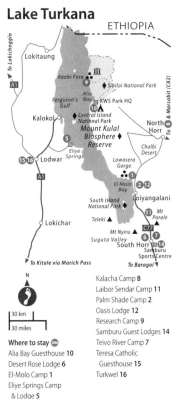

Lake Turkana

Kalacha Camp **8**
Laibor Sendar Camp **11**
Palm Shade Camp **2**
Oasis Lodge **12**
Research Camp **9**
Samburu Guest Lodges **14**
Teivo River Camp **7**
Teresa Catholic
    Guesthouse **15**
Turkwel **16**

Where to stay
Alia Bay Guesthouse **10**
Desert Rose Lodge **6**
El-Molo Camp **1**
Eliye Springs Camp
    & Lodge **5**

reduce the number of fish in the lake, which the people around Lake Turkana depend on for sustenance and their livelihoods.

Do not be fooled by the lake's calm appearance, the waters are highly unpredictable; storms build up out of nowhere and are not to be dismissed lightly as they are capable of sinking all but the most sturdy craft. The climate up here is extraordinary. It can easily reach 50°C during the day with not a cloud in sight, then out of nowhere a storm will break, whipping up a squall on Lake Turkana. For most of the year the area is dry, but when the rains do come, the rivers and ravines become torrential waterways sweeping over the parched plains. It is quite a sight and can leave you stranded until the water levels drop.

Arriving at Lake Turkana

From Lodwar, the nearest access point by public transport to the western shore of the lake and Central Island National Park is at oppressively hot **Kalokol**, a small village lying just a few kilometres from the lakeshore. Several *matatus* run daily from Lodwar to Kalokol. The 56-km tarmacked road is potholed but the journey shouldn't take much more than an hour. From Kalokol it is a one-hour walk or 4 km to **Ferguson's Gulf** on the lake; you will need to walk out to the abandoned fish-processing plant. The local boys will offer to be your guide. You are advised to walk either in the early morning or evening as it gets extremely hot. Plenty of water and a good sense of direction are both vital. Note that there is nowhere to stay here and only a few very basic food stalls, so to see the lake you'll need to plan a fairly long (and hot) day trip from Lodwar.

Ferguson's Gulf

The 4-km walk beyond Kalokol eventually takes you to the Ferguson's Gulf area on the lakeshore, which is the most accessible part of Lake Turkana, although with a bleak beach scattered with bits of abandoned fishing boats, it is not the most attractive. However, the lake is fringed with acacias, doum palms and grass, in contrast to the moonscape appearance with a mass of volcanic lava around Teleki's Volcano at the south of the lake. There are loads of birds, particularly flamingos, and it is the only place in Kenya where, in the springtime, black-tailed godwits and spotted redshanks can be seen. Birds of prey can also be spotted, and the number of hippos and crocodiles make swimming exciting. If you intend to swim, ask the local people where to go.

En route to or from Kalokol and about 15 km before the village look out for the standing stones of **Namoratunga**, which are of spiritual significance to the Turkana. Although they are only 50 m from the road they are hard to spot and resemble sacks of charcoal. There are 10 cylindrical stones about 1 m high, although some have fallen over. Nothing is known about them; the Turkana themselves don't know what their original purpose was. In the past the lakeshore may have come right up to the stones. The name is derived from a Turkana legend that some visitors came across a group of dancers at the site and laughed at them, turning the dancers to stone.

Eliye Springs

Eliye Springs is on the lakeshore 65 km to the east of Lodwar and the turn-off is about halfway along the Lodwar–Kalokol road. The last 10 km is very sandy and a 4WD is essential. It is a far more pleasant place from which to see the lake, with palm trees and the warm water bubbling up from the springs. There is a fairly new lodge here (the **Eliye Springs Camp & Lodge**, see Where to stay, page 327), which can organize transfers from

Lodwar (most usefully from the **Fly 540** flights from Nairobi), and can also arrange fishing on the lake and boat trips to Central Island National Park (below).

Central Island National Park
ⓘ www.kws.org, 0600-1900, US$20, children (3-18) US$10.
This was established as a 5-sq-km national park in 1983 in order to protect the breeding grounds of the Nile crocodile. Formed as a result of volcanic activity, the island is an old volcano with three immense crater lakes that lie in the basins of a series of volcanic vents. Researchers suspect that there is still a tiny active volcano situated on the tip of the island. The crater lakes are connected through subterranean ducts with the main lake, and are renowned for their differing shades of jade, green and blue at various times of the day. The island is a favourite haunt for breeding crocodiles as well as migratory and resident birds. If you arrive around April-May, you can witness crocodiles hatching and sprinting off down to one of the lakes. The island has black lava sand beaches. It was designated as a UNESCO World Heritage Site in 1997 and is approximately a 45-minute boat ride from Ferguson's Gulf. It is possible to negotiate with a local fisherman to take you out on his craft, but remember that the lake's unpredictable squalls are a real danger, and there are crocodiles. The **Eliye Springs Camp & Lodge** can also organize local boats for a cost of around US$20-30 per person depending on how many people are in the boat (they can take about 8 people); alternatively, you can opt for the more expensive but safer option of hiring their speed boat at around US$180 for four people.

◉ Kitale to Lake Turkana listings

For sleeping and eating price codes and other relevant information, see pages 20-24.

◉ Where to stay

It makes sense to stay in **Kitale**, where there is a good choice of budget accommodation (see page 156), before travelling to Lodwar. Unless you are driving and camping, there are very few places to stay anywhere north of Kitale, so careful planning is required.

Cherangani Hills *p321*
$$$-$ Sirikwa Safaris, on the A1, 23 km north of Kitale, 8 km beyond Saiwa Swamp National Park, T0737-133 170, www.sirikwa safaris.com. This is the lovely home of the Barnley family, set in a well-tended English-style garden in the foothills of the Cherangani Hills. The farmhouse has 2 double guestrooms with fireplace, plus there are 3 furnished permanent tents and a campsite with barbecue, firewood, hot showers and flush loos. Excellent home-

cooked meals are available. Day trips to the Saiwa Swamp and Mt Elgon national parks can be arranged, and guides and porters are available for multi-day trekking in the Cherangani Hills with overnight stays in local villages. Discuss with them what you would like to do.
$$-$ Marich Pass Field Studies Centre, on the A1, 103 km north of Kitale, 1 km north of the Sigor–Tot junction at Marich Pass, T0722-139 151, www.gg.rhul.ac.uk/ MarichPass. This is a lovely forested spot on the banks of the Moruny River and is primarily an educational establishment catering for university groups, but independent travellers are welcome. There are 19 *bandas* sleeping 2-3 people with or without bathrooms, 4 larger cottages that sleep up to 6, dorms sleeping 5-25 people, and a campsite with plenty of space for vehicles. The ablution block has toilets and cold showers, and hot bucket showers can be arranged. The restaurant offers buffet meals and packed lunches for excursions,

and beer and soft drinks. Plenty of walks with Pokot guides can be arranged here, giving an insight into Pokot culture, or you can explore the Cherangani Hills to the south over several days. Again, discuss what you want to do.

Lodwar *p322*
Lodwar has only a couple of basic board and lodgings places.
$ Teresa Catholic Guesthouse, just south of town, 2 km off the main road. This centre sheltered in a surprisingly green compound of neem trees is owned by the Catholic Diocese of Lodwar and primarily provides basic accommodation and meals to missionaries working in the region but they will take travellers of both sexes. It has 30 simple rooms, beds have mosquito nets, well-maintained and some are self-contained with showers and toilets, while others share bathrooms. Breakfast and dinner are provided with notice.
$ Turkwel Hotel, in the centre of town near the bus stand. Best in town, rooms come with a net, fan and bathroom, for slightly more you can hire a larger self-contained cottage with a full breakfast included in the price. The restaurant serves some Western dishes, such as simple chicken and chips, and the bar is popular with Lingala music playing into the small hours, which can get quite noisy.

To South Sudan *p323*
Lokichoggio
$$ Hotel California, reservations **Afex Group**, Nairobi, T020-302 7000, www.afex group.com. This compound is primarily used for NGOs in Loki and, while there are similar set-ups in town, it is the most organized and easiest to contact. You need to pre-arrange a visit with the **Afex Group** office at the Jockey Club at the Ngong Racecourse in Nairobi (see page 77). They also run similar camps in South Sudan. There are 16 en suite rooms (8 of which have a/c), 28 tents with showers and toilets and another 30 tents with shared

facilities. There's also a lively restaurant and bar – the focal point for workers in Loki – which serves excellent food and treats like cappuccinos and wine (remember everything is flown in). It also has a pizza oven. Pool tables, gym, volleyball court, internet access and DSTV are also available. The compound has generators, boreholes for water and plenty of parking and security.

Lake Turkana (western shore) *p324, map p324*
$$$-$ Eliye Springs Camp & Lodge, Eliye Springs. Follow the main sandy road straight to the lake, where the palm leaves are on the road, T0725-151 083, www.eliyesprings resort.com. This new lodge and campsite presently offers the only accommodation on the eastern side of the lake and has 6 large en suite thatched rooms with neat furnishings and verandas facing the lake, plus 10 Turkana huts which share bathrooms and a cooking shelter with campers (there are staff to light fires, etc), and 2-man tents with bedding can also be hired. There's a comfortable restaurant and bar under thatch, though meals depend on what's available, but expect plenty of fish. Activities can be organized, including fishing, boat trips to Central Island National Park and visits to the local Turkana village. Everything is set right on the sandy lakeshore with a few gnarly neem trees for shade and security is provided for vehicles.

⊖ Transport

Kapenguria *p319*
Regular *matatus* run between **Kitale** and Kapenguria – or more precisely Makutano, the extension of Kapenguria on the A1; the town itself lies a little to the east of the main road. The Kitale–Lodwar buses can also drop/pick up here but, given that they go when full from both places, you will not be able to pre-book or guarantee a seat. If you're driving, then fill up with fuel in Kapenguria (Makutano); although there is

another petrol station just before the Marich Pass at Ortum, it's still a fair distance north to Lodwar.

Lodwar *p322*
Air
Fly 540, T0770-639 429, Nairobi T020-827 521, www.fly540.com, has 1 daily flight between **Kitale** and Lodwar and **Nairobi**, which arrives mid-morning and departs again early afternoon, 2 hrs, 1 way from US$130.

Bus
The main bus and *matatu* stand is to the east of town on one of the roads that leads from the A1 beyond the Kobil petrol station. There are several daily buses that go between **Kitale** and Lodwar, taking around 8 hrs. 3 regular bus companies operate this route: **Eldoret Express**, **Dayah Bus** and **Fomoco Bus**. Most buses tend to travel later in the day from Kitale and depart at around 1500, while from Lodwar to Kitale there are both day buses, which depart at about 0700, and night buses, which depart from about 1800. However, they only go when full in both directions so enquire in plenty of time at the bus stands. There are also a few *matatus* that work the route, though whether they reach their final destination depends on the number of passengers. It is wise to take water and food for the trip, as breakdowns and delays are common. It is also possible to hitch a ride on a truck on this route – a small payment is expected.

Lokichoggio *p323*
Air
Lokichoggio Airport is to the east of town, T054-32266, www.kenyaairports.co.ke. **ALS**, Nairobi, T020-600 9864, www.als.co.ke, runs a daily scheduled flight from **Nairobi**'s Wilson Airport to Lokichoggio (1½ hrs), which may also touch down at the airstrip in **Lodwar** on the way there or back. Some of the flights also continue on to **Rumbek** in South Sudan, so the airport has immigration facilities.

Bus
Matatus go between **Lodwar** and Lokichoggio and take around 3 hrs.

Lake Turkana (western shore) *p324, map p324*
Occasional *matatus* go between **Lodwar** and Kalokol and take 1½ hrs. The petrol station at Lodwar is the last place to buy fuel and food on the way to the lake.

Isiolo and around

Isiolo is an interesting little frontier town on the A2, 83 km northeast of Nanyuki, and is very different from the rest of the Central Province towns around Mount Kenya. It is a small town north of Meru inhabited mostly by the descendants of Somali people who were resettled there after the First World War. It is also the nearest town from which to explore the national reserves at Samburu, Buffalo Springs and Shaba, all grouped together 40 km to the north. These national reserves are the most accessible of the northern wildlife sanctuaries.
▶▶ *For listings, see pages 332-334.*

Isiolo → *For listings, see pages 332-334. Colour map 4, C2. Phone code: 064.*

There's a busy goat, cattle and camel market here, in addition to the fruit and vegetable market, though security problems with nomadic bandit groups operating to the north up to the Ethiopian border have disrupted livestock raising, leading to a fall in prosperity. Petrol is available, and there is a branch of **Barclays Bank**, with an ATM, and a post office (the last town to have these facilities until you reach either Maralal or Marsabit). It is also the last place to buy a good supply of provisions in the small supermarkets. The social life of the town revolves around drinking and chewing *miraa* (the large and quite unsavoury *miraa* market is south of the BP petrol station). There is also a large Muslim presence in town, which has a scattering of mosques. George Adamson, who was later to become internationally famous along with his wife, Joy, for hand-rearing Elsa, the lioness featured in *Born Free*, was a game warden in Isiolo prior to becoming a celebrity. The town is also closest to the entrance of the **Lewa Wildlife Conservancy**, situated about 15 km to the southwest, see page 190.

For travelling to Lake Turkana's eastern shores the best route is likely to be from Isiolo, but for any travel north from here on the A2 towards the Ethiopian border at Moyale vehicles congregate at the police post 3 km north of town to form a convoy, which is then accompanied by armed guards. However, in saying that, in the last couple of years it has been less of a necessity for private vehicles to join this convoy (mostly trucks carrying livestock and grain) and the police may well organize another convoy for smaller vehicles later in the day or allow you to go it alone. *Matatus* still cover the short distance to Archer's Post (below).

Archer's Post

About 35 km drive north of Isiolo, this is a very small and hot outpost bordered by the Samburu and Buffalo Springs National Reserves to the west and the Shaba National Reserve to the east. It was named after a British colonial administrator, Geoffrey Archer, who was posted here in 1911. The road from Isiolo has recently been tarred; this has improved the fortunes of the town, which is now fully electrified; electricity is presently being extended to the lodges in the reserves (formerly run on diesel-powered generators). There are a couple of small shops and cafés, as well as curio sellers hoping to catch the traffic into the reserves. The Samburu people inhabit this region, and you are very likely to see some magnificently dressed and adorned people in Archer's Post, especially the warriors with their intricate hairstyles, ochre-painted skin and purple robes. Always ask before you take photographs; you may be permitted to for a small fee.

Samburu, Buffalo Springs and Shaba → *For listings, see pages 332-334.*
Colour map 4, C2/3.

ⓘ *T065-62053, 0630-1830, entry to each reserve is US$20, children (3-18) US$10, plus vehicle US$3.25. Note these reserves are not administered by KWS but by the Samburu County Council, www.samburucouncil.com.*

Just north of Isiolo and around 325 km north of Nairobi are the Samburu, Buffalo Springs and Shaba national reserves, some of the more remote and least visited of Kenya's game parks. They are located in Kenya's hot and arid northern region; when you see a camel train walking single file along a dry riverbed, you know you're in a pretty parched area. The three reserves cover around 440 sq km in total and are separated by the Ewaso Nyiro River, which provides water for the animals including the local goats and sheep, and some relief from the equatorial sun. They are some of the most pleasant national parks in Kenya, are not too crowded and are usually visited on a combined safari of all three. There are a number of lodges and campsites in the reserves, but think carefully when to go – daytime temperatures regularly reach 40°C between January and October, even when it rains.

Arriving in Samburu, Buffalo Springs and Shaba
A couple of hours' drive north of Nanyuki, they are accessible by road via Isiolo and Archer's Post. There are airstrips in both Samburu and Buffalo Springs reserves. Samburu and Buffalo Springs are contiguous reserves, while the separate Shaba, which is often also included in safari itineraries in this region, is a short drive to the east. At Archer's Post the entrance to Shaba is at the right side, while the main gate to Samburu, **Archer's Post Gate**,

Samburu & Buffalo Springs National Reserves

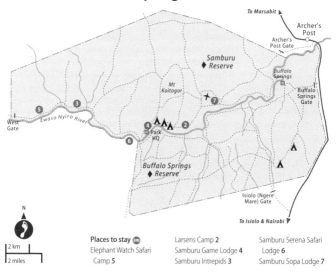

Places to stay 🛏	Larsens Camp **2**	Samburu Serena Safari
Elephant Watch Safari	Samburu Game Lodge **4**	Lodge **6**
Camp **5**	Samburu Intrepids **3**	Samburu Sopa Lodge **7**

is found 5 km on the left. Samburu also has another gate at its western end, but it is seldom used. Access to Buffalo Springs is either through Samburu or 20 km north of Isiolo, where there is a detour left leading to **Isiolo Gate**, formerly known as Ngare Mara Gate. Some 10 km ahead, 3.5 km before Archer's Post, a second detour leads to the **Buffalo Springs Gate**. Most people visit on an organized safari.

Samburu National Reserve

This reserve was opened in 1965 in the hot, arid lowland area just to the north of Mount Kenya. Vegetation is made up of a narrow stretch of palms and woodland along the Ewaso Ng'iro River, away from this is acacia woodland and hot, dusty scrubland. This desolate landscape is the face of the less hospitable Africa, but is the preferred habitat for some mammals well adapted to this harsh environment, some of them rarely seen in milder climates. Among these are Grevy's zebra, reticulated giraffe and Beisa Oryx, whose natural habitat is north of the equator. There are also elephant, cheetah, vervet monkey, and hippo and crocodile habituate the river. The long-necked gerenuk, also known as the 'giraffe-necked antelope', is an unusual animal that spends much of its time on its hind legs reaching up to the withered bushes. Leopards are regularly spotted. The birdlife is unusually prolific in this park, and large flocks of guinea-fowl can be seen in the afternoons coming to drink at the riverbanks. Doves, sandgrouse and the pygmy falcon are frequently seen. The area north of the Ewaso Nyiro River is very attractive, with plains and low hills that are rocky in places. The dry watercourses are fringed with acacias, and the blue-grey mountains fringe the view in silhouette. After a downpour, the arid countryside turns green overnight, and soon flowers and sweet-smelling grasses are abundant.

One of the highlights of the area are the 'Singing Wells'. Samburu warriors bring their cattle to these watering holes on a daily basis during the dry season. Some of the wells are up to 10 m deep. The warriors strip off, descend to form a human chain and chant traditional Samburu songs as they pass water up by hand for the cattle.

Buffalo Springs National Reserve

Buffalo Springs is south of the river from Samburu; a bridge over the Ewaso Ng'iro River linking the two reserves was built in 1964. Elephant, zebra, giraffe, oryx, cheetah and crocodile can be found in the riverine forest of acacia and doum palm. In the park is a crater, made when an Italian bomber mistook buffalo for targets in the Second World War. It is now a spring and is reportedly safe to swim in. Unlike Samburu, Buffalo Springs has populations of the common zebra as well as the Grevy's zebra – it's an unexplained phenomenon why the common zebra is not found on the north side of the river.

Shaba National Reserve

To the east of Archer's Post is Shaba National Reserve, which is to the south of the Ewaso Ng'iro River. It is home to a number of gerenuk, gazelle, oryx, zebra, giraffe, cheetah, leopard and lion, which roam around acacia woodlands, bushlands and grasslands. Shaba got its name from the volcanic rock cone in the reserve. The riverine areas are dominated by acacia and doum palms. The martial eagle can often be spotted here, alert for its prey the guinea-fowl, or the occasional dik-dik. Joy and George Adamson (see box, page 194) who hand-reared lions and leopards and returned them to the wild, had a campsite in Shaba Reserve. Joy's last project was the release of Penny the leopard, who subsequently mated and reared a cub in the eastern part of the reserve. It was here that Joy was murdered in

1980, and there is a simple memorial plaque commemorating Joy's life and work erected by Samburu County Council at her campsite under the shade of umbrella acacias, adjacent to a swamp in eastern Shaba. The reserve was the location of some parts of *Out of Africa* and *Born Free*, and also the US TV show *Survivor Africa* in 2001.

⊙ Isiolo and around listings

For sleeping and eating price codes and other relevant information, see pages 20-24.

⊙ Where to stay

Isiolo *p329*
Plenty of board and lodgings, but those preferring more comfort should move on to the reserves, or else stay around Nanyuki (page 178), which is 83 km or 1 hr's drive to the southwest on the (good) A2.

$$-$ Bomen Hotel, Kanisani Rd, T064-52225, www.bomenhotel.com. Easily the best bet in town, it's also worth stopping here to eat. Dated and aimed at the local conference market, but with 47 well-furnished rooms, with TV and reliable hot water, in a white block set in an attractive and leafy walled compound, with secure parking, good restaurant, bar with pool table, internet access, friendly staff, rates include a generous buffet breakfast. Independent travellers without their own vehicles should head here, as with a bit of negotiation, you can arrange a vehicle and driver for a day's safari to the reserves.

$$-$ Gaddisa Lodge, 3 km east of town, follow the road past the post office, T0724-201 115, www.gaddisa.com. Set in spacious grounds behind a stone wall and gate, this offers secure parking and has a very large, refreshing swimming pool (though unfortunately there's not always water in it), restaurant and bar, and the simple en suite rooms in concrete cottages have large beds and mosquito nets. Good drinking water comes from a well and rates include breakfast and dinner. Run by a Dutch woman who can arrange guided excursions to local villages.

$ Rangeland Hotel, 10 km south of town on the Nanyuki/Meru road, T064-52340, www.rangelandhotels.com. This is a curious set-up, which is predominantly a local country *nyama choma* spot and a conference venue in a pleasant garden setting with acacia trees, but it also has 8 basic en suite garden cottages and, popular with overlanders, a very good campsite on springy lawns with a cold shower and toilet. There's also a bar serving some snacks and limited hot meals and, by the time you read this, a proper restaurant may be up and running.

Samburu *p331, map p330*
$$$$ Elephant Watch Safari Camp, reservations Nairobi T020-804 8602, www.elephantwatchsafaris.com. Eco-friendly camp on the banks of the Ewaso Ng'iro River with 6 tents draped with colourful cloth and unusual furniture, including huge sofas, woven local mats and special beds and furniture made from trees knocked over by elephants. The bathrooms are partially open-air and built around trees with sun-heated hot water. Very good gourmet food, and the whole area is lit by torches at night. This camp is owned by the Douglas-Hamilton family, who have been involved in elephant conservation since the 1970s – Dr Iain Douglas-Hamilton, the founder of **Save the Elephants** (www.savetheelephants.org) has without doubt played a major role in reducing elephant poaching in Kenya.

$$$$ Samburu Intrepids, reservations **Heritage Hotels**, Nairobi, T020-444 6651, www.heritage-eastafrica.com. 30 luxurious tents raised on wooden decks overlooking the Ewaso Ng'iro River, with large 4-poster beds. The family units are 'double' tents with a shared lounge. There's a swimming pool, and activities include camel safaris and visits to Samburu villages. Education is a focus, and there are special activities for children with Samburu guides and nightly talks and slide shows on wildlife and culture in the lounge.

$$$ Larsens Camp, reservations Wilderness Lodges, Nairobi, T020-650 392, www.wildernesslodges.co.ke. By the river, with 20 well-furnished tents in very elegant colonial style, the dining tent is open and tables are adorned with silver and fine china. There is an animal-viewing platform in a tree, champagne breakfasts or picnic lunches can be set up on a sandbank in the river and, as well as game drives, bird walks around camp can be arranged.

$$$ Samburu Game Lodge reservations Wilderness Lodges, Nairobi, T020-650 392, www.wildernesslodges.co.ke. This, the first lodge in the reserve, built in 1963, was renovated to very high standards in 2006, situated on a bend in the river. A wonderful place to stop off for a drink at the **Crocodile Bar** even if you don't stay. Relaxed atmosphere in a beautiful setting, swimming pool, shop, open-sided dining area, a wide range of accommodation along the river bank in 61 cottages and *bandas*, each with 4-poster beds with mosquito nets, 1 with wheelchair access.

$$$ Samburu Serena Safari Lodge, reservations Nairobi T020-284 2000, www.serenahotels.com. Located on the south bank of the river, west of **Samburu Game Lodge**, this lodge is outside the reserve, though it must be accessed from the inside. Unfortunately it was badly damaged when the Ewaso Ng'iro River burst its banks during unprecedented floods in 2010 and is presently being rebuilt. Check with **Serena** for progress.

$$$ Samburu Sopa Lodge, reservations Nairobi, T020-375 0235, www.sopalodges. com. In the middle of the park on a raised hill with good views and overlooking a waterhole, the 30 cottages have 2 bedrooms and verandas, and the public areas are nicely

decorated in Samburu colours, local stones and natural materials. Swimming pool, game drives, visits to Samburu villages and wildlife talks on offer.

Camping

The Samburu campsites are scattered along the Ewaso Ng'iro River near the **Samburu Game Lodge** and the West Gate. All sites are flat, cleared spaces under trees with no facilities except for pit latrines. Those nearer to the lodge tend to be more secure. At **Butterfly Public Campsite**, it is possible to walk to the lodge for a cold drink and a look at the crocs. This is not advisable after 1900 as the lodge gates are locked and leopard bait is laid. Another site is the **Vervet Campsite**, also near the lodge and popular with camping safari companies. In all the campsites baboons can be a real nuisance, so guard your belongings. Camping costs US$12 per person and is paid at the gates on entry.

Buffalo Springs *p331, map p330*

There is no formal accommodation in Buffalo Springs and most people stay at the lodges in Samburu and visit on game drives.

Shaba National Reserve *p331*

$$$ Sarova Shaba Game Lodge, reservations, Nairobi T020-271 4444, www.sarovahotels.com. This, the only accommodation in Shaba, has 85 rooms in chalets, a little dated these days but nevertheless comfortable. There's a restaurant, bar, petrol station, a magnificent swimming pool that curves around a natural rock formation, and a game-viewing deck from which you can watch and feed crocodiles. As well as game drives, bird walks and massages are on offer.

🍴 Restaurants

Isiolo *p329*

$ Bomen Hotel, see Where to stay, page 332. Open 0700-2200. Has the widest choice and the best food – if there's a conference on, you can pay to eat their lunch and dinner buffets – and is the best bet for a beer in the evening, with an attractive outdoor terrace. There's also a *nyama choma* spot in the car park.

$ Roots Restaurant, on the main road opposite the Caltex petrol station. The best of the cheap restaurants and open most of the time, simple fare includes *nyama choma*, some Somalian dishes, it has a fully stocked bar and a TV for watching football.

☉ Transport

Isiolo *p329*

The bus and *matatu* stand is on the main road (A2) south of the market. There are daily buses that go when full to **Nairobi** (6 hrs) stopping at **Nanyuki**, **Nyeri** and other towns, and many *matatus* also link the towns on this route. Regular *matatus* run to **Meru** and other nearby Central Province towns on the eastern side of Mt Kenya.

A bus runs between Isiolo and **Maralal** via **Archer's Post** and **Wamba**, leaving each town on alternate days at 1100-1300 depending on passenger numbers and taking 5-8 hrs. If you are driving this route yourself, ensure you have enough fuel to get to Maralal, 217 km away.

Isiolo is an important transport hub for travel north to **Marsabit** and **Moyale**, and northeast to **Wajir** and the very remote town of **Mandera** close to both the Somali and Ethiopian borders in Kenya's far northeast, although travel to northeastern Kenya is currently not recommended on grounds of safety. For many years the only way to get to **Marsabit** (8 hrs) and **Moyale**

(9 hrs from Marsabit) was to arrange a lift on a truck; you can still do this, but you may have to travel in the back on top of the cargo and it is a hot, dusty journey – by the day's end your hands may well hurt from holding on so hard, and you can expect to be totally ingrained in red dirt. Trucks usually leave in convoy at 0530 from the police post, but double check the night before. However, now that the road is partly tarred (the 138-km stretch from Isiolo to Merille River, which is more or less midway between Isiolo and Marsabit), there is a daily bus from Isiolo to **Marsabit**. It leaves at around 2000 and in theory should take 8 hrs, but be prepared for delays because of frequent punctures. From Marsabit, again there is the option to hitch a ride on a truck, and 1 daily bus (see page 347). If you are driving this route, there are a number of petrol stations in Isiolo and it is advisable to fill up for the 500-km journey as there is no guarantee of fuel in Marsabit. Make sure you have enough food and water too, as there is little or nothing between Isiolo and Marsabit.

Samburu *p331, map p330*

Matatus run the 35 km from **Isiolo** to **Archer's Post**. The daily buses between Isiolo and Marsabit pass through Archer's Post but they do so at night and are likely to be full of passengers doing the complete journey.

Air Kenya, Wilson Airport, Nairobi, T020-391 6000, www.airkenya.com, has daily flights between Samburu and **Nairobi**, US$205 1 way, departs Nairobi 0730, arrives in Samburu 0820, departs at 1110, arrives in Nairobi 1215. It sometimes also stops at **Nanyuki**, lengthening the journey time.

Isiolo to Lake Turkana

Exploring the lake from the east is far more exciting than the west, and you pass through a number of national reserves. Driving here takes skill and nerves of steel, and you will need a 4WD vehicle. Few of the roads are surfaced, and the main A2 road is tricky to say the least. Avoid the rainy season as some routes become impassable. Some public transport is available, though it is not as reliable as on the western side. The following route is taken: north from Isiolo to Archer's Post on the A2 road, also known as the Trans-East-African Highway, then looping west along the C79 to Wamba and Maralal, before travelling north along the secondary road to Baragoi, South Horr and the eastern side of Lake Turkana, including the remote Sibiloi National Park. ►► *For listings, see pages 339-342.*

Arriving at Lake Turkana

There is only one bus that runs up and down between Maralal and Isiolo every other day and there may be the odd *matatu*. There are also buses and *matatus* running between Maralal and Nyahururu (see page 334), where you can hop on to a bus to Nairobi. But Maralal is really the end of the road as far as public transport is concerned and nothing else except trucks head north from here to South Horr. Without your own transport, going north to the lake requires putting the word out (and paying) and waiting, possibly for several days, for a lift. Again, as with the western side of the lake, if you're not self-sufficient there is hardly anywhere to stay. The much better option for independent travellers to visit the eastern side of the lake is an 8- or 10-day tour from Nairobi with **Gametrackers** ⓘ *Nairobi, T020-222 2703, www.gametrackersafaris.com*. These camping trips, using rugged trucks, head up the Rift Valley to Maralal and then to Lake Turkana via Baragoi and South Horr, then cross the Chalbi Desert to Marsabit National Park; the return journey goes via Samburu National Reserve.

Wamba and the Mathew's Mountains → *Colour map 4, C2.*

Wamba is a small town on the C79, 103 km northwest of Isiolo and 65 km from the Samburu National Reserve. Northeast of Wamba are the **Mathew's Mountains**, where the peaks are covered in cycads and podocarpus forest. The best view of the mountains is to be seen from the road going up to **Kitich Camp**. The highest peak in the range is **Mount Warges** at 2688 m. Other peaks are Mathew's Peak at 2374 m, Mathew's South Peak at 2284 m, Lolokwe at 1852 m, Lesiolo at 2475 m and Poror at 2581 m. These mountains offer pleasant walking opportunities in the shade but views tend to be restricted by the flora. The Ngeng River has a couple of big rock pools suitable for swimming. Guides and *askaris* are needed to visit this area, or you can explore from the two luxury lodges (see Where to stay, page 339), which lie in lush forest at the southern end of the mountains, near Wamba. After the severe ivory poaching crisis of the mid-1970s and early 1980s, there were no recorded elephants remaining in the Mathew's Mountains; today there are several hundred. Other large mammals present include buffalo, giraffe, Grevy's zebra, eland, lesser kudu and several other species of antelope. The forests are also a favourite habitat for leopard, which is often seen in the vicinity of the lodges.

Maralal → *Colour map 4, C1. Phone code: 065.*

High up in the hills, Maralal looks down onto the Lerochi Plateau and lies on the C77 160 km from Nyahururu. It is the last place of any size on the rough road north to the

Maralal International Camel Derby

The annual Maralal International Camel Derby has been operating since 1990, and is held over the first weekend of August each year. The Amateur Camel Race is on the Saturday morning and the Professional Camel Race is on the Sunday. The races can be hilarious events for amateurs and exciting for professionals, and even if you've never sat on a camel before, you can join in. The derby is centred at Yare Camel Camp (see page 340), and transport to and from Nairobi for the weekend is usually arranged. The amateur event is 12 km around Maralal town, starting and ending outside Yare Camp. It takes about one hour if you have a compliant camel. There is a small entry fee in addition to hiring the camel and handler, which is about US$30. In the amateur race the handler runs alongside the camel to coax it along, but not so in the professional race, when the rider must have sufficient experience to handle a camel independently over the distance of 42 km. Apart from having lots of fun, the aim of the derby has also been to promote an interest in better camel breeding among the people of northeastern Kenya and for them to understand the benefits that such animals can bring to these desert and arid land inhabitants. The Kenyan national herd of over one million animals is rapidly growing, and there is an ongoing overflow from Somalia, which has estimated herds of 5.6 million camels, many of which have filtered into Kenya.

eastern shore of the lake. The town, with two wide tree-lined dusty streets and ramshackle wooden shops, has a 'Wild-West' atmosphere. Only a few visitors come to Maralal on their way to Turkana or for camel trekking at **Yare Camel Camp**. Many rural Turkana and Samburu people who have lost their livestock through drought have moved into the town, and the poverty (and begging) can be rather disturbing. However, the traditionally garbed Samburu certainly brighten up the surroundings, with their skins, blankets, beads and hair styles, and at the lively market you can buy Samburu handicrafts, such as the colourful necklaces made of thousands of beads, or sandals made of tyres. There is also the small **Maralal Game Sanctuary** that can be accessed from the **Maralal Safari Lodge** (see Where to stay, page 340). It covers the cedar-clad hillside above the town, and in the thorn scrub lower down there are a few Grevy's zebra, impala, eland, buffalo, baboon and warthog; elephant pass through seasonally. Much of this wildlife can be seen from the comfortable terrace of the lodge; the only permanent water in the sanctuary is a small waterhole just a few metres away. Maralal was, until his death in 2003, home to Wilfred Thesiger, explorer and travel writer, who spent a number of years here in his later life looking after orphaned children.

The town itself has a few basic amenities, and if you are heading north, Maralal is the last town with a bank. Both the **Kenya Commercial Bank** (with ATM) and the post office are near the market and bus stand, and there are also several petrol stations in town.

Baragoi → *Colour map 4, B2.*

From Maralal the road climbs north into the mountains and is awful in parts, particularly as there are a fair few steep climbs and descents and it's littered with large rocks. It takes from three to six hours (depending on conditions) to cover the 103 km to Baragoi, the next settlement on the route up to the eastern shores of Lake Turkana. About 20 km north of Maralal, there is a track to the left to the village of **Poror** and, after about 6 km, you come to the edge of the rim of the **Losiolo Escarpment**, also known as 'World's End' because of its dramatic views. Here the wall of the Rift Valley plunges more than 2000 m into the Suguta Valley and is the longest sheer drop in Kenya's part of the Rift Valley. About 40 km before Baragoi the scenery changes dramatically, as the road drops off the pine-clad mountainous ridge down to a lunar landscape of solidified lava rocks on the desert floor, where it is blisteringly hot.

Baragoi is a small settlement in this wilderness area. The locals jokingly say that the road is the 'International dividing line' between the Samburu and Turkana, and you will notice the design differences in their homesteads – the dome shape of the Turkana contrasts with the flatter wider Samburu *manyattas*. Livestock is paramount in this region; you may notice that some of the herders are armed to protect their flocks from rustlers. There are a few general stores here, and you should be able to get petrol (sold out of drums) and get punctures repaired (which you may well need to). However, at present, there is no electricity or running water in Baragoi and local people rely on digging wells for water in a nearby dry riverbed that skirts the town.

South Horr → Colour map 4, B2.
The nearest village to the southern end of Lake Turkana, South Horr is set in a beautiful canyon and is an oasis of green between two extinct volcanoes (Mount Nyiru and Mount Porale). The Samburu regard Mount Nyiru as being a place sacred to N'kai, their god, at the flat top of the mountain where there is a plentiful supply of water and they take their cattle there to graze during the dry season. If you want to climb the mountain, the shortest approach is via Tum, and an early morning start allows the ascent to be made in the mountain's shadow. On the summit a great pile of rocks marks the grave of a famous *laibon*, and there are excellent views of Lake Turkana and the Sugutu Valley. There are some great walks in the mountain forests all around you; you could either hike (it's a good idea to take a guide) or go on a camel trek, best arranged from the **Desert Rose Lodge** in Baragoi (see Where to stay, page 340). You should be able to buy fuel if necessary at the **Samburu Sports Centre & Guest Lodges** in the village, see Where to stay, page 340.

Lake Turkana (eastern shore) → For listings, see pages 339-342. Colour map 4, A1/B1.

The region around the eastern shores of Lake Turkana has been made into one of Kenya's four biosphere reserves, the 7000-sq-km **Mount Kulal Biosphere Reserve**. The area includes many different types of environments ranging from mountain forest about 2400 m above sea level to desert, with grasslands, dry evergreen forest, woodlands, bushlands and saltbush scrublands in between. It covers most of Lake Turkana, its volcanic southern shores, the **South Island National Park** and the **Chalbi Desert**. The latter is a shimmering and seemingly endless expanse of sand, stretching for 300 km from the south of North Horr to the shore of the lake of which it was once part. Even today, perhaps once in every decade, in one of the torrential downpours that occur during a rare rainy season, it will again come into flood to form a vast but shallow lake.

Loiyangalani
Once at Loiyangalani, 270 km north of Maralal, the barren lava beds at the southern end of Lake Turkana peter out into the waters of the lake itself. One of the biggest villages on the eastern lake shore, Loiyangalani is a collection of huts with thatched grass and galvanized-iron roofs that stretches along the lakeshore with the imposing mountains

forming an impressive backdrop. There is a life-giving spring here, but the surrounds are flat stony plains, scattered with the bleached bones of livestock carcasses. In Samburu, Loiyangalani means 'a place where the weak seek refuge', but the seeming tranquillity here is somewhat marred by the fact that the surrounding region suffers from occasional and sometimes violent incidents of cattle rustling and spats among the communities that live in this harsh and barren land. Loiyangalani has only a few hundred homesteads, but it is inhabited by seven ethnic groups – the Turkana, Samburu, El Molo, Dassanach, Gabbra, Borana and Rendile. Of these, the El Molo people constitute Kenya's smallest ethnic group; they are believed to be of Cushitic origin from the northeast but their numbers are dwindling. They are hardy fishermen who mainly fish the lake for Nile perch and, occasionally, hunt crocodiles and hippos; the name El Molo is derived from a Samburu expression *loo molo onsikirri*, which means 'the people who eat fish'. They are thought to number about 4000 but, because of intermarriages with the Turkana and Samburu, their ancestry is questionable and the number of 'pure' El Molo is thought to be very few.

There are few facilities in Loiyangalani, but you will be able to get punctures repaired and may be able to buy diesel from drums – the truck drivers sell it to villagers for use in boat engines and motorbikes.

South Island National Park

South Island covers 39 sq km and features two extraordinary much-eroded tertiary volcanic mountains: **Teleki** and **Mount Kulal**. It was established as a national park in 1983 for the protection of the Nile crocodiles' breeding ground, and is also home to several species of venomous snake, including vipers, puff adders and cobras. It is also an important breeding ground for hippos, and is home to a flock of feral goats. The terrain of South Island is rugged, access is difficult and there is no permanent human settlement on the island, making it one of Kenya's most inhospitable parks. To get there from the mainland, you will need to hire a boat and guide from Loiyangalani, but be aware that few local fishermen venture there and it's a 30-km round trip by boat, which can be a dangerous endeavour given the violent swells in the lake.

Sibiloi National Park

ⓘ *125 km north of Loiyangalani, T054-21223, www.kws.org, 0600-1900, US$20, children (3-18) US$10, vehicle US$3.25.*

Lying on the eastern shores of Lake Turkana in the far north of Kenya, just 30 km from the border with Ethiopia, this is one of the least well known or visited of Kenya's national parks, despite its large size of 1570 sq km. It is now designated a UNESCO World Heritage Site, although it has few tourist facilities because of its isolated geographical location. It is scorchingly hot and arid (especially December-March) and very strong winds blow in the early morning and evening. Rainfall is less than 250 mm per year and, in some areas of the park, it hasn't rained for several years.

Arriving in Sibiloi National Park Sibiloi is very remote and only fully equipped 4WD expeditions should attempt the drive there; a convoy of at least two vehicles is highly recommended. It is about 125 km from Loiyangalani along a rough track through the desert to North Horr and then northwest to Alia Bay, the KWS park headquarters, which has some official buildings, an airstrip, a basic guesthouse and a campsite (see Where to stay, page 342). You will need to bring all your own supplies, and it must be stressed that sufficient supplies of fuel and water and spare tyres must be carried by any travellers who visit this area.

Visiting Sibiloi National Park The landscape of the park features grassy plains with yellow spear grass and doum palms on the lakeshore, extending to dry semi-desert intercepted with sandstone outcrops and empty sandy riverbeds inland. Within the national park is **Central Island**, which contains the world's largest crocodile population of about 12,000. Despite the fact that this park is windblown and arid, it has a surprising variety of wildlife, including the reticulated giraffe, Grevy's zebra, Grant's gazelle, oryx, hartebeest, topi, ostrich and gerenuk, although these are rarely seen. Birdlife is prolific, with over 350 recorded species. Sibiloi National Park extends well into Lake Turkana, in the process encompassing a large portion of Lake Turkana's huge population of Nile crocodile.

Within the park stands a petrified forest, which serves as a reminder that seven million years ago, this area was lush and densely populated. The national park was originally established by the National Museum of Kenya to protect the unique prehistoric archaeological sites. In 1960-1970s the Leakeys made many remarkable fossil finds of humans from 10,000-12,000 years ago. These finds included *Homo Habilis* and *Homo erectus*, which dated man's origin to three million years ago. **Koobi Fora palaeontological site** is located here, as is a small museum near the park headquarters, which houses the remains of prehistoric elephants among other things. This is generally unstaffed and only open when there are researchers in the area, but there are some simple *bandas* to sleep in (see Where to stay, page 342). Over 4000 fossil specimens have been found in this area. Important finds include the homanid remains, the shell of a giant tortoise believed to be over three million years old, the fossilized remains of the elephant's forebear – the behemoth with massive tusks, and crocodile jaws measuring over 1.5 m (which equates to an overall length of over 14 m). The discovery of these fossils has resulted in a greater understanding of the environment one to three million years ago.

◉ Isiolo to Lake Turkana listings

For sleeping and eating price codes and other relevant information, see pages 20-24.

● Where to stay

Wamba and the Mathew's Mountains
p335
$$$$ Kitich Camp, 34 km northwest of Wamba on a rough road towards the village of Parsaloi, alternatively fly in, reservations www.kitichcamp.com or Cheli & Peacock, Nairobi, T020-600 3090, www.chelipeacock. com. A peaceful and remote spot with 6 comfortable and spacious en suite tents and bush outdoor showers in an attractive forested setting beside a seasonal river where elephant and buffalo are often spotted. There are game walks with the Samburu, birdwatching and a natural pool nearby is suitable for swimming. One of the owners is Italian, and the food is very good,

house wines are included and there's a bar and sitting room with fireplace. Kitich means 'place of happiness' in Samburu.
$$$$ Sarara Camp, north of Wamba in the Mathew's Mountains, access is by charter flight, T0722-805 893, www.sararacamp. com. This was the first tourist lodge to be wholly owned and run by the local Samburu people, with the assistance of the Lewa Wildlife Conservancy. It is on the **Namunyak Wildlife Conservation Trust**, an area of 85,000 ha; Namunyak means 'place of peace' in Samburu. The conservancy was set up in 1995 to promote wildlife conservation and to assist the local community to benefit from tourism, in return for protecting the wildlife species living on their land. The camp has 6 luxury tents, each with its own veranda with views of the mountains, flush loo and open-air bush shower. The lounge/ dining *banda* overlooks a natural swimming

pool and waterhole frequented by elephant. Activities on offer include game drives and bush walks, and the rare opportunity to see a Samburu singing well ceremony. You can get here by chartering a plane from **Tropic Air** in Nanyuki (see page 187).

Maralal *p335*

$$$ Maralal Safari Lodge, in the Maralal Game Sanctuary, 3 km out of town towards Baragoi, T065-2060, www.angelfire.com/jazz/maralal. An old-fashioned country retreat with thatched cottages, verandas and fireplaces. There's a bar and restaurant, swimming pool, terraces for game viewing and birdwatching, and also a souvenir shop. The lodge is by a waterhole, which attracts a wide range of wildlife. It's the best place to eat in town, even if you're not staying.

$$-$ Yare Camel Camp, 2 km south of town on the road towards Isiolo/Nyahururu, T0722-33674, yarecamelcamp@yahoo.com. This camp is set in a grassy compound with good views of the surrounding hills, with excellent camping facilities, lots of toilets and hot showers, US$3 per pitch or you can hire tents and bedding for around US$10 for 2 people. There are also 15 charming *bandas*, some are triples, all a/c and roomy from US$40; with breakfast and dinner from US$65. There's a bar/restaurant and games room, with a dart board, table tennis and a pool table. A number of camel safaris (led by Samburu guides) can be organized here, from a 30-min ride for US$5 to an all-day ride/walk with a packed lunch for US$30. There is also the option to go on an overnight trip for US$100, which includes food, cooking equipment and tents (not sleeping bags). Visits to Samburu *manyattas* can also be arranged for around US$5 per person, which includes a fee to take photos.

Baragoi *p336*

$$$$ Desert Rose Lodge, reservations Nairobi, T020-386 4831, T0722-322 745 (lodge), www.desertrosekenya.com. To get here, turn left 18 km to the north of

Baragoi and it's 15 km along a very steep sandy track (4WD only). Alternatively, the lodge has an airstrip and they can arrange air charters. On the southern slopes of Mt Nyiru, this is a remote and secluded lodge with 5 sympathetically designed luxury guesthouses, a notable feature being the open-air bathrooms. Fantastic views, a stunning rock swimming pool, bar and restaurant and wooden decks. There are a number of walks around the lodge, and leopards can sometimes be spotted, as well as abundant birds; nearby is a unique waterfall that provides a rock slide. Profits from the lodge have been used to build the local primary school and medical centre. A typical 4-day package here including return flights from Nairobi, a scenic flight from the lodge, camel trekking, accommodation, all meals and drinks costs in the region of US$3900 per person but comes down considerably for a group of up to 5 people. They can also organize tailor-made camel trekking from 2 days to 1 week.

South Horr *p337, map p324*

$ Samburu Sports Centre & Guest Lodges, in the village, T0720-334 561, www.safarisportscamp.com. This is a mission and well-worth aiming for because of the excellent facilities, but best behaviour is expected and no drinking or smoking is permitted. It is involved in both promoting sports among the local Samburu (there's a soccer pitch and volley ball and basket ball courts) and teaching vegetable gardening – you can buy fresh vegetables here when available. There are 12 comfortable *bandas* (US$15 per person), a modern kitchen, campsite under the shade of neem trees, spotless flush toilets and cold showers, restaurant, cold soft drinks and fuel can be bought, and you can use the satellite internet.

Both the Samburu community-run options below, which are suitable for self-sufficient overlanders, have been recently established by an NGO based in Maralal, the **Ndonyiro**

Community Conservation Alliance (NCCA), T0721-565 383, www.nomadicjourneys.com, as initiatives to provide the Samburu with alternative livelihoods other than livestock-keeping during the prolonged drought in northern Kenya. They are well worth supporting if you're driving up the long road to Loiyangalani; however, be aware that you may get a lot of constant 'attention' from your hosts.

$ Laibor Sendar Camp, 20 km north of Teivo River Camp (27 km from South Horr). Located at the base of a giant sand dune, which is ideal to climb for a view of sunset over the desert and of both the peaks of Mt Kulal on Turkana's South Island to the north and Mt Marsabit in the east. This is a Samburu-run set-up with 2 bandas and 3 traditional Samburu huts, each with 2 beds, a campsite, an eating and cooking shelter, and long-drop loos (no showers). A short camel ride or a visit to a Samburu *manyatta* can be negotiated.

$ Teivo River Camp, formerly known as **Kurungu Campsite**, about 7 km north of South Horr. This is in a nice sheltered spot surrounded by trees, and is run by the local Samburu who can sell you trinkets and may put on a display of dancing if you're prepared to pay. The camp has limited solar-powered lighting, 3 basic thatched *bandas* with 2 beds in each (US$4 per person), a campsite (US$2.50 per person), bucket showers, flush loos, and firewood is available. You need to pay extra for an *askari* for security.

Lake Turkana (eastern shore) *p337, map p324*
Chalbi Desert
$$$ Kalacha Camp. This is situated in the Chalbi Desert, on the edge of a permanent oasis and is managed by **Tropic Air** in Nanuyki (see page 187), which also provide the only way to get here by air transfer, T0722-207 300, www.tropicairkenya.com. It has been set up as a community-based project for the Gabbra people of this area,

providing them with a further source of income. The oasis provides water for vast numbers of their livestock, including cattle, sheep, donkeys and camels. A very simple camp, built using local materials, including *dhom* palm trunks for the poles and leaves woven into mats for the roofs and walls. The 4 *bandas* have twin beds, flush toilet and cold shower. The mess area is a circular building designed around a small kidney-shaped swimming pool. You need to bring your own food and drink, including plenty of drinking water, but the 4 members of staff will help prepare meals and there's a fridge run on paraffin.

Loiyangalani
These places to stay used to be on the lakeshore but are now some metres back, given that the lake has shrunk in recent years.
$$$ Oasis Lodge, T0729-954 672, www.oasis-lodge.com. Primarily a fishing lodge run by an unfriendly German, with 24 wooden cottages with electricity, but very run down these days with nothing more than foam mattresses and a trickle of water in the bathrooms (if at all) and, from around US$200 for a double full board, very overpriced for what you get. However, there's little other choice and there are good meals based on fresh fish from the lake, and there's a swimming pool. They can organize fishing and boat trips to South Island National Park and you can negotiate with a guide here for about US$20 per person to take you on very interesting trips to the nearby El Molo village. Can arrange flights from Nairobi.

$ El-Molo Camp, located next to and run by **Oasis Lodge**. A scruffy campsite but it does have a swimming pool (which may or may not have water in it), cold showers and long-drop loos. You'll need to hire an *askari* to watch your vehicle.

$ Palm Shade Camp, also adjacent to **Oasis Lodge**. The best place in Loiyangalani in a pleasant fenced spot in a clutch of palm trees where you can camp (on grass!) or there are 4 simple thatch-and-reed *bandas* with mattresses and mosquito nets, plus clean long-drop toilets and showers, and a simple kitchen with water and fireplace. You may be able to negotiate with the women to cook you a plate of goat stew or fish from the lake, and they can arrange beers and sometimes fresh bread. The camp is fed by a spring, so the water is good, and they will allow you to fill up your own water containers. As in the other places on the lakeshore here, camp away from the palm trees – they can be very noisy at night when the wind whips through them. **Gametrackers** also have a campsite in the region but you can only stay there if you are on one of their (recommended) tours.

Sibiloi National Park
$$ Alia Bay Guesthouse, near the KWS Park HQ at the entrance, warden T054-21223, Nairobi T020-600 0800, www.kws.org. This very simple guesthouse overlooking the lake is part of the small group of buildings that constitute the park HQ where the warden and other staff also live. It can sleep up to 5 people in 3 bedrooms, beds have mosquito nets, bathroom with cold water, and there's a furnished sitting and dining room. The kitchen is reasonably equipped with eating and cooking utensils, a gas stove and solar-powered electricity. Cost is a flat US$100.
$ Research Camp, reservations Nairobi T020-374 2161, www.museums.or.ke. This is located on the Koobi Fora spit in the lake and has 4 dormitories as basic accommodation primarily for researchers, or you can camp. It is run by the National Museums of Kenya and can be booked through them in Nairobi. These are equipped with beds, bedding, mosquito nets and towels, and there's 3 flush toilets and 3 showers and a dining/research *banda*. You need to bring all food and drink but you can cook here over a fire.

Camping
There are 3 campsites near the KWS Park HQ but none has any facilities except pit latrines. The best is **Kampi ya Turkana**, simply because it's on the lakeshore, while the other 2 are further inland.

Isiolo to Moyale

The Trans-East-African Highway (A2) from Isiolo heads north through very dry country to Marsabit and beyond to Moyale on the Ethiopian border. Despite it being a vital transport link to land-locked Ethiopia, it has always been in diabolical condition; in the dry season it's very rocky and bumpy and badly corrugated in patches, and in the wet it becomes a quagmire, as the top soil, known locally as 'black cotton', becomes very slippery and it's easy to get a vehicle stuck in the mud. For many years, local people have attributed the poverty and the lack of infrastructure in northern Kenya to the poor state of this road. However, since mid-2011, the 138-km stretch from Isiolo to the Merille River, which is more or less midway between Isiolo and Marsabit, is now a two-lane tarmac road and, over the next few years, construction is expected to continue. This is good news for self-drivers, but beyond this point, the road is still bad, so while the time it takes to drive from Isiolo to Moyale has decreased (still more than 20 hours), drivers should still be prepared for rough 4WD driving beyond Merille River.

From Isiolo and Archer's Post the road passes through flat desert of red volcanic rock, with the occasional tortured tree jutting incongruously out of the sand. You may see nomadic pastoralists driving their herds, which pick at the sparse vegetation along the way. As you approach Marsabit, the sight of mist-covered Mount Marsabit rises above the horizon and, the closer you get to the town, the greener the vegetation and the cooler the air. But from the relative elevation at Marsabit the rough road flattens out again and travels through an extraordinary unearthly flat plain scattered with volcanic boulders. This is the Dida Galgalu Desert; the name reputedly means 'the plains of darkness' in the Borana language. The last 100 km to Moyale becomes a little easier as you will have left the hard rock, and the road goes over flat sand with thorn bush vegetation lining the road. Once in Moyale, you cross the dusty river bed into Ethiopia, from where it is gloriously smooth tar all the way to Addis Ababa, 775 km away. ▸▸ *For listings, see pages 346-347.*

Getting to Moyale

From Isiolo all the way through to Moyale, vehicles travel in an armed convoy, which departs at 0530 from the police post 3 km to the north of Isiolo. The next fuel is at Marsabit, 277 km away. In Isiolo and at a couple of police barriers along the way, you have to sign a log book, which records all traffic moving on the road. This is a government policy to reduce gun trafficking and cattle rustling. However, in the last couple of years it has been less of a necessity for private vehicles to join this convoy (mostly trucks carrying livestock and grain) and the police may well organize another convoy for smaller vehicles later in the day or allow you to go it alone. Enquire when you get to Isiolo. Without your own vehicle, there are few options; it's either a painstakingly slow and tiresome trip by the one bus that plies the 500-km/two-day journey between Isiolo and Moyale or you can hitch a ride on a truck.

Losai National Reserve → *Colour map 4, B/C2.*

The road travels through this reserve, with the majority of the reserve located west of the road. This is 1800 sq km of thorny bushland, situated in the Losai Mountains southwest of and adjacent to Marsabit National Park and about 175 km north of Mount Kenya. The reserve was gazetted in 1976 to give protection to elephant, greater and lesser kudu, lion and a few black rhino, but none of these remain now thanks to poaching. It is unlikely tourism will develop in the near future as the lava plateau with scattered volcanic plugs is virtually impenetrable even with a 4WD.

Ahmed the Elephant

Marsabit National Reserve used to be famous for its large stocks of elephants, but these have sadly become severely depleted. They included the famous Ahmed, the bull-elephant who was born in 1919 and whose long 3-m-long pointed tusks weighed over 45 kg each and reached the ground. These magnificent tusks added to his legendary status, but they also put his life in grave danger as a target for ivory hunters. The general public developed a deep concern for his safety and during 1972-1973, some 5000 letters calling for Ahmed's protection were sent to the East African Wildlife Society – the body that was in charge of the parks before the Kenya Wildlife Services was formed in 1990. This resulted in President Jomo Kenyatta designating Ahmed as a national monument, and according him 24-hour armed protection. Ahmed died in 1974 of natural causes aged 55 years, and when he died he was 3 m tall at the shoulder, and weighed approximately 5000 kg. His preserved remains can now be seen in the Nairobi National Museum and you can stand next to him for a photo.

Marsabit → *Colour map 4, B3. Phone code: 069.*

Situated at 1000 m above the surrounding plains, Marsabit is permanently green. The hills around the town are thickly forested, making a nice change from the desert that surrounds the area. Marsabit is in Kenya's Eastern Province, 560 km north of Nairobi and 277 km from Isiolo. This is also the administrative capital of the district and a major trading centre. There are three streets in Marsabit, with low-slung concrete buildings painted in vivid green or blue or dirty white, and a number of general stores selling all manner of oddments from car spare parts to cables, pipes, flour and sugar. There are also three petrol stations, a post office, a branch of **Kenya Commercial Bank** (no ATM), and a number of mechanics in town; just ask around. The main inhabitants of the town are the Rendille, who dress in elaborate beaded necklaces and sport wonderful hairstyles. They are nomadic people keeping to their traditional customs and only visiting the town to trade. There is also a fairly large population of Burji people, who mainly arrived in Northern Kenya from Ethiopia during the famines there in the 1970s. Marsabit National Park is nearby.

Marsabit National Park → *Colour map 4, B3.*

ⓘ *T069-2028, www.kws.org, 0600-1900, US$20, children (3-18) US$10, US$3.25 per vehicle.*

Marsabit National Park covers 1554 sq km and contains the cloud-capped **Mount Marsabit**, or Saku, as it's called locally, undoubtedly the most attractive of North Kenya's extinct volcanic mountains. It is a large massif covered with lush, verdant growth that offers a welcome change from the desert that surrounds it. Its altitude stretches from 420 m, where thorny bushland dominates the scenery, to 1700 m above sea level. There are several craters in the forest. The upper reaches are covered in forest, merging into acacia grasslands. The mountain is covered in a thick mist that dissipates by midday, after which it becomes warm and sunny.

A number of birds are found here including 52 different types of bird of prey, and it hosts a wide variety of animals, such as elephant, greater kudu, various species of monkey, baboon, hyena, aard-wolf, caracal and the reticulated giraffe, though it is difficult to see much through the thick forest. It's also home to a large number of snakes, including giant cobras. The volcanic craters are a special feature of Mount Marsabit, several of which

Border crossings: Kenya–Ethiopia

Moyale

Moyale is the only official border post between Kenya and Ethiopia, and it's on the A2, 508 km north of Isiolo. There have been differing reports on the time at which the Kenyan side of the border closes, either at 1800 or 1600, so get there before 1600. The Ethiopian border is closed all day Sunday, as well as on public and religious holidays. It is possible to cross freely during daytime hours into Ethiopian Moyale to do some shopping, or even stay in the Ethiopian part of the town overnight, leaving the car behind on the Kenyan side, prior to completing the border formalities. Driving is on the right in Ethiopia; 'swapping over' takes place on the short stretch of road between the two immigration/customs offices.

Visas for Ethiopia are required by all and must be obtained in advance. This is a long way to come only to be turned away at the border for not having a visa, so it's imperative that you arrange one in advance. In the other direction, Kenya visas are available at the border and can be paid with US dollars cash.

For those in vehicles, customs officials are well used to the process of a **Carnet de Passage**. Nevertheless, ensure you allow a couple of hours for the border crossing as, although the Kenyans give little more than a cursory glance at your paperwork, the Ethiopians are very thorough; checking the chassis and engine numbers against the Carnet, for example.

There is a branch of **Kenya Commercial Bank** with an ATM in Kenyan Moyale. While there is a bank in Ethiopian Moyale, there's no ATM, but it does operate a slow foreign exchange service of sorts. You are likely to be approached by people to change Kenyan shillings, Ethiopian birr, US$ or euros on the black market on both sides of the border. Technically, this is illegal, but if the banks are closed, you may have to change enough to last until you can get to a bank. In Kenya the first place with banks with reliable foreign exchange services and ATMs is Isiolo, and in Ethiopia, it's Awassa (see below).

The main road in the south of Ethiopia is tarred and in reasonable condition, and from Moyale it's 775 km to Addis Ababa. The first settlement of note is **Yabello**, about 210 km, or roughly a four-hour drive or a six- or seven-hour bus ride from Moyale. Yabello is at the junction with the dirt road that goes west to the Omo Valley in southwest Ethiopia. The **$ Yabello Motel**, next to the petrol station, is a reasonable place to stay; some of the rooms have private bathrooms, with hot water, or else you can camp. There are armed security guards and a basic restaurant and bar. The **Hawi Hotel** is another similar option.

Some 420 km from Moyale, and 210 km or a four-hour drive or a six- or seven-hour bus ride north of Yabello, the next reasonably large town is **Dilla**, For travellers on public transport, this is probably the best place to break the two-day journey between the border and Addis Ababa and the most likely place to swap buses (the through bus from Moyale to Addis stops here overnight). For accommodation, try the **$ Lalibela Pension**, or **$ Get Smart Hotel**, which are both just off the main road. Dilla has several petrol stations and two banks. From Dilla it's 90 km north to **Awassa**, the largest town on Ethiopia's main south road that lies on the Rift Valley lake of the same name. This is another option to break your journey and has a good choice of accommodation and facilities. From here it is 275 km to **Addis Ababa**.

contain freshwater lakes. **Gof Sokorte Guda** (Paradise Lake) is a wonderful spot to observe elephant and buffalo in the late afternoon, when they congregate for water. Within the park's boundary is a 'singing well' where the Borana bring their camels and goats to drink. Athletic young men in loin cloths throw up buckets to their neighbours and so on up the human chain to the drinking trough above. This fluid and elegant motion of water accompanied by rhythmic singing of the Borana gives rise to the name.

Moyale → *Colour map 4, A4. Phone code: 069.*

About 250 km north of Marsabit, Moyale is a small transit town that straddles the Kenya–Ethiopia border (see box, page 345). The last 100 km or so of the A2 road become a little easier as the road turns eastward to run parallel with the hills on the border, and the hard rock is replaced by fine red dust. Eventually it turns north again through a narrow pass between the hills, and the clutch of tin shacks that is Moyale appears. On arrival, you sign the arrivals book at the police barrier. The two halves of the town could not be more different: Kenyan Moyale is a dusty impoverished place, with a distinct air of desperation. In contrast, Ethiopian Moyale is a bustling town, with a couple of passable hotels and restaurants and a vibrant market. An illustration of the cross-border differences lies in the fact that residents of Kenyan Moyale often have to buy their water on the Ethiopian side and take it back across the border. Nevertheless, Kenyan Moyale is developing slowly and has recently been supplied with (sporadic) electricity; it has two petrol stations, a post office, basic shops, a police station and a branch of **Kenya Commercial Bank**, which very usefully now has an ATM that accepts Visa. However, try to ensure that you cross the border before nightfall as there are more accommodation options on the Ethiopian side, and it is a far more pleasant place to spend the night. This is where you'll have your first introduction to *injera*, Ethiopia's flat, pancake-like sour bread that's eaten with just about any meal. You can pay for everything in Ethiopian Moyale in Kenya shillings, and there's also a bank but no ATM (see also box, page 345).

◉ Isiolo to Moyale listings

For sleeping and eating price codes and other relevant information, see pages 20-24.

🛏 Where to stay

Marsabit *p344*
There is very little formal accommodation in Marsabit, but locals rent out very basic rooms to truck drivers, usually a simple bed in a tin shack with mud floors. Several of these mostly unnamed board and lodgings can be found on the main road near the Shell petrol station. Overlanders should ask around town for Henry.

$ Henry's Place, south side of town, to the west of the main road. The camp is down the back of a construction yard, past the cows and barns, and has hot showers, clean long-drop toilets, flat ground for camping, plenty of room for vehicles, good drinking water, can organize beers and costs US$5 per person. Henry makes bread for the Marsabit shops, so with a bit of notice you can also arrange basic food here, such as beef stew.

$ Jey Jey's Centre, on the main road in the middle of town. A double-storey unpainted building with bare rooms along straight dark and dirty corridors, each with one small window that opens up to the central courtyard. You can also negotiate to camp here. The Muslim proprietor Jey Jey is affable, is used to foreign travellers and can organize warm bucket baths and plates of reasonable food, such as beef stew or fried chicken with rice or chips and sometimes curries. You can also ask here for a guide to take you to the 'singing wells'.

$ Nomads Rest House, across the road from Jey Jey's, and with very similar board and lodgings, except that the water supply is said to be more reliable.

Marsabit National Park *p344*
$$$-$$ Marsabit Lodge, reservations Nairobi, T020-269 5468, www.marsabit lodge.com. This lodge is wonderfully situated in front of the crater lake, Gof Sokorte Dik, 3 km from town and within the Marsabit National Park. After being closed for a year or more, it is now fully operational. It's still old fashioned, and hot water or choice of food is a bit hit and miss but the friendly staff do their utmost to make the most of what they've got. It has 24 comfortable rooms that lead on to a shared balcony at the back, which has great views, plus a shady campsite (**$**) with simple ablutions. There's a restaurant and bar with a roaring log fire, and game drives and bush walks can be organized. Rates are B&B, full or half board.

Camping
Ahmed and **Absul**, T069-2028, www.kws. org. Both these public campsites are in forested spots near the main gate and park HQ, but there are no facilities except for pit latrines. If you can organize a KWS ranger to go with you, you can also camp on the rim of Paradise Lake, which is beautiful but can be very cold. Camping costs US$5 per person.

Moyale *p346*
There is hardly any choice on the Kenyan side of Moyale and water rarely runs through the pipes. It's best to cross over into the Ethiopian side if at all possible, where there is a better choice of basic board and lodgings. You can pay for everything in Ethiopian Moyale in Kenya shillings.
$ Bismillahi, across the road from the **New Barassa** and behind the Esso petrol station.

This is a large Muslim family compound and upstairs are a row of fairly clean rooms with mosquito nets and netting in the windows, lockable doors and, again, you can organize a bucket of hot water. It's a little quieter than most and you can get a plate of hot food and go across the road for a beer.

$ Koket Borena Moyale Hotel, on the main road near the market. This is the better of the basic board and lodgings in Ethiopian Moyale, set in a secure fenced compound, with rooms that have mosquito nets and private bathrooms with hot water, plus some Borana-style thatched huts and a campsite with reasonable shared toilets and (cold) showers. The restaurant and bar is reliable for a hot plate of food and an icy cold beer, and the management are well used to foreign travellers.

$ Madina Hotel, Kenyan Moyale, central but a bit off the main road to the east of the bank. Another option but not as good as the others, with very simple concrete rooms with bucket baths, dirty toilets, no restaurant, but can organize *askaris* to watch vehicles.

$ New Barassa Hotel, on the main road in Kenyan Moyale, 100 m from the bank. Charging less than US$5, this has about a dozen dark concrete unlockable rooms (but you can use your own padlock), with mosquito nets, set around an earth courtyard There are no showers, but you can have a bucket wash with hot water, and get chapattis and warm tea in the evening, and there's a bar on the street at the front.

⊖ Transport

Marsabit *p344*
It takes around 8 hrs to/from **Isiolo**. The daily bus between Marsabit and Isiolo leaves around 0900 but its departure rather depends on when it has arrived from Isiolo. Going south, it's a bone-rattling journey until the road gets to the new tar around midway at Merille River. The journey from Marsabit to **Moyale** can take up to 9 hrs. The daily bus, in theory, should leave Marsabit for

Moyale around 0800-0900, but again this is determined on when the 1st bus from Isiolo arrives in Marsabit. Before you set off from Isiolo, enquire at the bus stand about the full length of the journey by bus between Isiolo and Moyale. As the A2 on this route is gradually tarred, public transport is expected to improve. The armed convoy usually arrives in Marsabit during the afternoon or early evening in either direction. The convoy leaves again in both directions from the police barrier at around 0530, but check the night before; it's not always deemed necessary for private vehicles these days.

Moyale *p346*

Convoys leave for **Marsabit** and the south at around 0800-0900 and trucks congregate near the police barrier. If you are hitching on a truck, several touts also gather, but try and talk directly to the drivers to negotiate a price. The bus back to Marsabit also leaves with the convoy. If possible, try and organize transport on either the night before. Daily buses depart from the Ethiopian side to **Addis Ababa** and take 2 days, and they usually stop en route overnight at **Dilla** (see box, page 345, for more details). There are other buses between Moyale and the closer towns on the Ethiopian side.

Northeast Kenya

The most remote part of the country is the northeast, a vast empty wilderness with almost no sign that humans have ever been here; the endless blue skies and flat landscapes produce a sense of solitude that is hard to experience anywhere else. The landscape is made up of tracts of desert and semi-desert, barely broken by settlements and with almost no public transport. Its inaccessibility combined with severe security problems around the Somali border make this area unappealing to even the most intrepid travellers – no tour companies operate in this region.

The majority of people living in this area are Somali and, before the creation of country boundaries, pastoralists roamed the area freely. In fact, in colonial days, the area was known as Somali country. As countries in the region gained Independence, Somalis unsuccessfully tried to claim this area as part of Somalia. Shortly after, the area was closed to visitors by the Kenyan authorities who wished to drill for oil. Years of neglect and almost no development leave it one of the poorest areas of the country. These problems have been exacerbated more recently by the civil war in Somalia, resulting in a huge influx of refugees into northeast Kenya. There are a number of refugee camps now set up for them (and for Somali-Kenyans who can no longer support their way of life in this barren area). Somalis are blamed for most of the insecurity in the region.

Garissa → *Colour map 2, A1.*

This town, the administrative centre of the northeast region, is 367 km east of Nairobi on the A3. It is on an alternative route back from Lamu to Nairobi. There are shops for provisions, petrol stations and a branch of **Kenya Commercial Bank** with an ATM. The heat is fierce here and there is high humidity making it an unpleasant climate to stay in for long. The town is mostly populated by ethnic Somalis and, historically, the Somalis claim that much of what was then known as the Northern Frontier District (NFD) had originally been part of Somalia, following the redrawing of the border between Kenya and Italian Somaliland by the British in 1925, a fact much disputed by the Kenyans. The Laikipiak Masai lived in this area as far north as the Juba River and, over the years, have fought incessantly with the Somalis. Travellers are advised not to travel north or east of Garissa towards the Somali border, as there are many incidents of armed robbery with fatalities by heavily armed *shiftas* (bandits) and, more recently, the problem of attacks by Somali Islamist insurgents in the region.

Wajir → *Colour map 4, B5.*

The road to Wajir runs some 300 km from Isiolo, along the most remote route in the country through a vast scrubland that seems to go on forever. The town of Wajir itself is growing, as many rural people have migrated there after a devastating famine hit this area hard in 2006 and many people lost their livestock. The population and atmosphere of the place has more Arab influences than Garissa. The settlement developed around wells that have been fought over by rival clans for generations, water being such a valuable commodity in this area. The **Kolbio border** post is less than 100 km north of here on the A3, where there is a reception centre for Somali refugees who routinely stream over the border into Kenya before being transferred to the massive refugee camp known as **Dadaab**, 75 km from Kolbio towards Garissa. This particular camp has been in existence since 1992 and today houses an estimated population of 250,000 refugees.

Mandera → *Colour map 4, A6.*

This is the most easterly point in Kenya, 370 km northeast of Wajir on the Ethiopian, Somali and Kenyan border. The main line of contact is on the private aircraft that flies in shipments of *miraa*. In the past, trade and communication with Somalia was more important than with Kenya, as Mandera is far closer to Mogadishu, the capital of Somalia, than to Nairobi.

Until recently Mandera was a fairly small border town servicing the local community. Since the Somali Civil War, it has become home to literally tens of thousands of Somalis, putting an impossible strain on resources. The lack of water, always a problem, has become critical. Also, the stability of the place is severely tested by the prevailing conditions and deadly ethnic clashes are common in this region.

Contents

Background

History

Earliest times

There is evidence that the forefathers of *Homo sapiens* lived in this part of East Africa. In the 1960s, **Louis Leakey**, a Kenyan-born European, and his wife **Mary**, began a series of archaeological expeditions in East Africa, particularly around Lake Turkana in the north. During these excavations they traced human biological and cultural development back from about 50,000 years to 1.8 million years ago. They discovered the skull and bones of a two million-year-old fossil, which they named *Homo habilis* and who they argued was an ancestor to modern man. Since the 1970s, **Richard Leakey**, son of Louis and Mary Leakey, has uncovered many more clues as to the origins of humankind and how they lived, unearthing some early Stone Age tools. These findings have increased our knowledge of the beginnings of earth, and establish the Rift Valley as the Cradle of Humankind. Many of the fossils are now in the National Museum of Nairobi. Little evidence exists as to what happened between the periods 1.8 million and 250,000 years ago, except that *Homo erectus* stood upright and moved further afield, spreading out over much of Kenya and Tanzania.

More recently, there have been two significant discoveries. In March 2001 it emerged that a team, including Richard Leakey's wife, Meave, had found an almost complete skull of a previously unknown creature near Lamekwi River in the north. The skull of *Kenyanthropus platyops* has a flat face, much like modern humans, and has been dated at between 3.2 million and 3.5 million years old. This is about the same time as the famous 'Lucy' – *Australopithecus afarensis* – found in Ethiopia in 1974, was living and suggests that modern humans evolved from one of several closely related ape-like ancestors of that period.

A potentially more remarkable find was also announced in 2001. Fourteen fragments of a six million-year-old '**Millennium Man**' were discovered in the remote Tugen Hills west of Lake Baringo. The fossils from four bodies of *Orrorin tugenensis* are among the oldest remains of ape-like ancestors ever found, about twice as old as Lucy. They appear to be more human-like than could have been imagined for a creature that lived so long ago and could be the remains of the oldest known direct ancestor of humans.

In more recent times, from 5000 to 3000 BC, Kenya was inhabited by hunter-gatherer groups, the forefathers of the Boni, Wata and Wariangulu people.

Bantu expansion

Later still began an influx of peoples from all over Africa that lasted right up until about the 19th century. The first wave came from Ethiopia, when the tall, lean **Cushitic people** gradually moved into Kenya over the second millennium BC, settling around Lake Turkana in the north. These people practised mixed agriculture, keeping animals and planting crops. There is still evidence of irrigation systems, dams and wells built by them in the arid northern parts of Kenya. As the climate changed, getting hotter and drier, they were forced to move on to the hills above Lake Victoria.

The Eastern Cushitics, also pastoralists, moved into central Kenya around 3000 years ago. This group assimilated with other agricultural communities and spread across the land. The rest of Kenya's ancestors are said to have arrived between 500 BC and AD 500 with **Bantu**-speaking people arriving from West Africa and **Nilotic** speakers from Southern Sudan, attracted by the rich grazing and plentiful farmland.

The Kenyan coast attracted people from other parts of the world as well as Africa. The first definite evidence of this is a description of Mombasa by the Greek Diogenes in AD 110 on his return to Egypt. He describes trading in cloth, tools, glass, brass, copper, iron, olives, weapons, ivory and rhinoceros horn at Mombasa. In AD 150 Ptolemy included details of this part of the coast in his Map of the World. It was to be another few centuries before the arrival of Islam on the coast and the beginning of its Golden Age.

Arab and Persian settlers developed trade routes extending across the Indian Ocean into China, establishing commercial centres all along the East Africa coast. They greatly contributed to the arts and architecture of the region and built fine mosques, monuments and houses. Evidence of the prosperity of this period can be seen in the architecture in parts of Mombasa, Malindi and Lamu, and, particularly, in the intricate and elegant balconies outside some of the houses in the old part of Mombasa. All along this part of the coast, intermarriage between Arabs and Africans resulted in a harmonious partnership of African and Islamic influences personified in the Swahili people. This situation continued peacefully until the arrival of the Portuguese in the 16th century.

Portuguese and Arab influence

Mombasa was known to be rich in both gold and ivory, making it a tempting target for the Portuguese. Vasco da Gama, in search of a sea route to India, arrived in Mombasa in 1498. He was unsuccessful in docking there at this time, but two years later ransacked the town. For many years the Portuguese returned to plunder Mombasa until, finally, they occupied the city. There followed 100 years of harsh colonial rule from their principal base at Fort Jesus overlooking the entrance to the old harbour. Arab resistance to Portuguese control of the Kenyan coast was strong, but they were unable to defeat the Portuguese, who managed to keep their foothold in East Africa.

The end of Portuguese control began in 1696 with a siege of Fort Jesus. The struggle lasted for nearly 2½ years when the Arabs finally managed to scale the fortress walls. By 1720, the last Portuguese garrison had left the Kenyan coast. The Arabs remained in control of the East African coast until the arrival of the British and Germans in the late 19th century. In this period the coast did not prosper as there were destructive intrigues amongst rival Arab groups and this hampered commerce and development in their African territories.

The Colonial period

The British influence in Kenya began quite casually in 1823 following negotiations between Captain Owen, a British Officer, and the Mazruis who ruled the island of Mombasa. The Mazruis asked for British protection from attack by other Omani interests in the area. Owen granted British protection in return for the Mazruis abolishing slavery. He sent to London and India for ratification of the treaty, posted his first officer to Mombasa together with an interpreter, four sailors and four marines and thus began the British occupation of Kenya. At this time, interest in Kenya was limited to the coast and then only as part of an evangelical desire to eliminate slavery. However, 50 years later attitudes towards the country changed.

In 1887 the **Imperial British East Africa Company (IBEAC)** founded its headquarters in Mombasa with the purpose of developing trade. From here it sent small groups of officials into the interior to negotiate with local tribesmen. One such officer, Frederick Lugard, made alliances with the Kikuyu en route to Uganda.

The final stage in British domination over Kenya was the development of the railway. The IBEAC and Lugard believed a railway was essential to keep its posts in the interior of

Kenya supplied with essential goods, and also believed it was necessary in order to protect Britain's position in Uganda. Despite much opposition in London, the railway was built, commencing in 1901, at an eventual cost of 5 million (US$7.3 million).

Nairobi was created at the centre of operations as a convenient stopping point between Mombasa and Lake Victoria where a water supply was available. Despite problems, the railway reached Nairobi in 1899 and Port Florence (Kisumu) in 1901, and was the catalyst for British settlers moving into Kenya as well as for African resistance to the loss of their lands.

From 1895 to 1910, the government encouraged white settlers to cultivate land in the Central Highlands of the country around the railway, particularly the fertile Western Highlands. It was regarded as imperative to attract white settlers to increase trade and thus increase the usefulness of the railway. The Masai bitterly opposed being moved from their land, but years of war combined with the effects of cholera, smallpox, rinderpest and famine had considerably weakened their resistance. The Masai were moved into two reserves on either side of the railway, but soon had to move out of the one to the north, as the white settlers pressed for more land. Kikuyu land was also occupied by white settlers as they moved to occupy the highlands around the western side of Mount Kenya.

By 1915 there were 21,400 sq km set aside for about 1000 settlers. This number was increased after the Second World War with the Soldier Settlement Scheme. Initially the settlers grew crops and raised animals, basing their livelihood on wheat, wool, dairy and meat but, by 1914, it was clear that these had little potential as export goods, so they changed to maize and coffee. Perhaps the most famous of the early settlers was **Lord Delamere**. He was important in early experimental agriculture and it was through his mistakes that many lessons were learnt about agriculture in the tropics. He tried out different wheat varieties until he developed one that was resistant to wheat rust. The 1920s saw the rapid expansion of settler agriculture – in particular coffee, sisal and maize – and the prices for these commodities rose, increasing settlers' optimism about their future.

However, when the prices plummeted in the Depression of the 1930s, the weaknesses of the settler agriculture scheme were revealed. By 1930 over 50% by value of settler export was accounted for by coffee alone, making them very vulnerable when prices fell. Many settlers were heavily mortgaged and could not service their debts. About 20% of white farmers gave up their farms, while others left farming temporarily. Cultivated land on settler farms fell from 2690 sq km in 1930 to 2030 sq km in 1936.

About one-third of the colonial government's revenue was from duties on settlers' production and goods imported by the settlers. Therefore the government was also seriously affected by the fall in prices. In earlier years the government had shown its commitment to white agriculture by investment in infrastructure (for example railways and ports) and, because of its dependence on custom duties, it felt it could not simply abandon the settlers. Many of the settlers were saved by the colonial government who pumped about £1 million (US$1.46 million) into white agriculture with subsidies and rebates on exports and loans, and the formation of a Land Bank.

Following the Depression and the Second World War, the numbers of settlers increased sharply, so that, by the 1950s, the white population had reached about 80,000. As well as dairy farming, the main crops they grew were coffee, tea and maize. However, discontent among the African population over the loss of their traditional land to the settlers was growing. In order to increase the pool of African labour for white settler development (most Africans were unwilling to work for the Europeans voluntarily), taxes and other levies were imposed. Furthermore, Africans were prevented from growing coffee, the most lucrative crop, on the grounds that there was a risk of coffee berry disease with lots of small producers. Thus, many Africans were forced to become farm labourers or to migrate to the towns in search of work to pay the taxes. By the 1940s the European farmers had prospered in cash-crop production.

As the number of Europeans moving into the country increased, so too did African resistance to the loss of their land and there was organized African political activity against the Europeans as early as 1922. The large number of Africans, particularly Kikuyu, moving into the growing capital Nairobi formed a political community supported by sections of the influential Asian community. This led to the formation of the **East African Association**, the first pan-Kenyan nationalist movement led by Harry Thuku. His arrest and the subsequent riots were the first challenge to the settlers and the colonial regime.

Jomo Kenyatta, an influential Kikuyu, led a campaign to bring Kikuyu land grievances to British notice. In 1932 he gave evidence to the Carter Land Commission in London which had been set up to adjudicate on land interests in Kenya, but without success. During the war years, all African political associations were banned and there was no voice for the interests of black Kenyans. At the end of the war, thousands of returning African soldiers began to demand rights, and discontent grew. Kenyatta had remained abroad, travelling in Europe and the Soviet Union, and returned in 1946 as a formidable statesman. In 1944 an African nationalist organization, the **Kenya African Union (KAU)** was formed to press for African access to settler-occupied land. The KAU was primarily supported by the Kikuyu. In 1947 Kenyatta became president of KAU and was widely supported as the one man who could unite Kenya's various political and ethnic factions.

Mau Mau era

At the same time as the KAU were looking for political change, a Kikuyu group, **Mau Mau**, began a campaign of violence. In the early 1950s the Mau Mau began terrorist activities, and several white settlers were killed, as well as thousands of Africans thought to have collaborated with the colonial government.

The British authorities declared a state of emergency in 1952 in the face of the Mau Mau campaign and the Kikuyu were herded into 'protected villages' surrounded by barbed wire. People were forbidden to leave during the hours of darkness. From 1952 to 1956 the terrorist campaign waged against the colonial authority resulted in the deaths of 13,000 Africans and 32 European civilians. Over 20,000 Kikuyu were placed in detention camps before the Mau Mau were finally defeated. The British imprisoned Kenyatta in 1953 for seven years for alleged involvement in Mau Mau activities, and banned the KAU, though it is debatable as to whether Kenyatta had any influence over Mau Mau activities.

The cost of suppressing the Mau Mau, the force of the East African case and world opinion convinced the British government that preparation for Independence was the wisest course. The settlers were effectively abandoned and were left with the prospect of making their own way under a majority-rule government. A number did sell up and leave, but many, encouraged by Kenyatta, stayed on to become Kenyan citizens.

The state of emergency was lifted in January 1960 and a transitional constitution was drafted, allowing for the existence of political parties and ensuring Africans were in the majority in the Legislative Council. African members of the council subsequently formed the **Kenya African National Union (KANU)** with James Gichuru, a former president of KAU, as its acting head, and **Tom Mboya** and **Oginga Odinga**, two prominent Luos, part of the leadership. KANU won the majority of seats in the Legislative Council but refused to form an administration until the release of Kenyatta.

In 1961 Kenyatta became the president of KANU. KANU won a decisive victory in the 1963 elections, and Kenyatta became prime minister as Kenya gained internal self-government. Kenya became fully independent later that year, the country was declared a republic, and Kenyatta became president. Kenya retained strong links with the UK, particularly in the form of military assistance and financial loans to compensate European settlers for their land, some of which was redistributed among the African landless.

Kenyatta

The two parties that had contested the 1963 elections with KANU were persuaded to join KANU, and Kenya became a single-party state. In 1966 Odinga left KANU and formed a new party, the **Kenya People's Union**, with strong Luo support. Tom Mboya, was assassinated by a Kikuyu in 1969. There followed a series of riots in the west of the country by Luos, and Odinga was placed in detention, where he remained for the next 15 months. At the next general election in 1969, only KANU members were allowed to contest seats, and two-thirds of the previous national assembly lost their seats.

The **East African Community (EAC)** comprising Kenya, Tanzania and Uganda, which ran many services in common, such as the railways, the airline, post and telecommunications, began to come under strain. Kenya had pursued economic policies that relied on a strong private sector; Tanzania had adopted a socialist strategy after 1967; Uganda had collapsed into anarchy and turmoil under Amin. In 1977, Kenya unilaterally pulled out of the EAC and, in response, Tanzania closed its borders with Kenya.

Kenyatta was able to increase Kenya's prosperity and stability through reassuring the settlers that they would have a future in the country and that they had an important role in its success, while at the same time as delivering his people limited land reform. Under Kenyatta's presidency, Kenya became one of the more successful newly independent countries.

Moi

Kenyatta died in 1978 to be succeeded by **Daniel arap Moi**, his vice president. Moi began by relaxing some of the political repression of the latter years of Kenyatta's presidency. However, he was badly shaken by a coup attempt in 1982 that was only crushed after several days of mayhem, and a more repressive period was ushered in. Relations between Kenya and its neighbours began to improve in the 1980s, and the three countries reached agreement on the distribution of assets and liabilities of the EAC by 1983. At this time the border between Kenya and Tanzania was reopened. In 1992 political parties (other than KANU) were allowed. Moi and KANU were returned (albeit without a majority of the popular vote) in the multi-party elections late in 1992. In the 1997 presidential elections Moi was again victorious, with an increased share of the vote. In the elections for the National Assembly, KANU achieved a slender overall majority with 107 seats out of 210.

Modern Kenya

Politics

Daniel arap Moi was elected to the Presidency in October 1978, following the death of Jomo Kenyatta, and began a programme to reduce Kenya's corruption and release all political detainees. Moi, a Kalenjin, emphasized the need for a new style of government with greater regional representation of tribal groups. However, he did not fully live up to his promises of political freedom, and Oginga Odinga (the prominent Luo who had been a voice of discontent in KANU under Kenyatta) and four other former KANU members who were critical of Moi's regime were barred from participating in the 1979 election. This led to an increase in protests against the government, mainly from Luos. Moi began to arrest dissidents, disband tribal societies and close the universities whenever there were demonstrations. This period also saw the strengthening of Kenya's armed forces.

On 1 August 1982 there was a coup attempt, supported by a Luo-based section of the Kenyan Air Force and by university students. Although things initially appeared to be touch-and-go, the coup was eventually crushed, resulting in an official death toll of 159. As a result of the coup attempt, many thousands of people were detained and the universities again closed. The constitution was changed to make Kenya officially a one-party state. Moi decided to reassert his authority over KANU by calling an early election in which he stood unopposed. Inevitably he was re-elected but less than 50% of the electorate turned out to vote.

Subsequent measures have served to centralize power under the presidency and to reduce the ability of the opposition to contest elections. The president acquired the power to dismiss the attorney-general, the auditor-general and judges, while control of the civil service passed to the President's Office. Secret ballots were abandoned, and voters were required to queue behind the candidate of their choice. This severely reduced willingness to be seen voting against the government. Secret ballots were restored in 1990.

In 1990, Dr Robert Ouko, a Luo and Minister for Foreign Affairs and International Cooperation, was murdered. British police were asked to investigate and named Nicholas Biwott, a Kalenjin and Minister for Energy, as being implicated in the killing. Biwott was dropped from the cabinet, but has subsequently returned.

International pressure in 1991 persuaded Moi to introduce a multi-party system. The opposition was fatally split, however, and, in the 1992 elections, Moi was returned as president with 36% of the popular vote. However, the opposition did secure 88 seats of the 188 contested, and the democratic process was significantly strengthened as a result.

The 1997 election was similar, with the opposition split, and Moi returned with 40% of the vote. In the Parliament the opposition made gains, with nine opposition parties securing 103 seats between them, while KANU obtained a slender overall majority with 107.

Moi was re-elected five times over 24 years. His term ended when the KANU candidate, Uhuru Kenyatta (the son of Jomo Kenyatta), who replaced him as head of the party, was beaten at the polls in a landslide victory in the 2002 election by **Mwai Kibaki** of the opposition party, the **National Rainbow Coalition** (**NARC**). Kibaki was previously vice-president (1978-1988) and held numerous cabinet positions. He pledged to attack corruption and established the **Kenya Anti-Corruption Commission** (**KACC**). As a result of this, the IMF resumed loans to Kenya over a three-year period. But some international donors estimate that US$1 billion has been lost to corruption through government departments between 2002 and 2005, and, to date, despite numerous investigations, no high-profile figures have been convicted in court on corruption charges. In 2003, the government also decided to grant immunity to Moi over corruption charges. However, one of Kibaki's profound successes during this period was to provide free education for primary school age children across Kenya, which saw nearly 1.7 million more pupils enroll in school by the end of 2004.

Kibaki instigated a constitutional referendum in 2005, calling for more presidential power with a lesser role for the Prime Minister and cabinet members. However, the final draft of the constitution retained sweeping powers for the Head of State. Some members of his own cabinet and the main opposition party mobilized a powerful campaign that resulted in a majority of 58% Kenyan voters rejecting the draft. As a consequence, Kibaki sacked and reappointed his entire cabinet, and his popularity with the public plummeted.

Kibaki was sworn in on 30 December 2007 for his second presidential term after emerging winner of an election that was marked by accusations of fraud and widespread irregularities that led to civil unrest. His primary contender for President was **Raila Odinga**, son of Kenya's first vice-president under Kenyatta, who went to the polls for the 2007 election on the **Orange Democratic Movement** (**ODM**) ticket. The general and parliamentary election was held on 27 December 2007, which was declared a public holiday for people to vote. The day was peaceful, and people formed orderly queues at the polling stations. The following day was also peaceful, as votes were counted in the constituencies, and early reports from these seemed to indicate that Odinga was well in the lead; the ODM declared victory for him on 29 December. As the polling boxes were delivered and recounted at the Electoral Commission in Nairobi, it began to become apparent that the vote had swung towards Kibaki. A spokesman for the Electoral Commission appeared on television on 30 December and declared Kibaki the winner by about 230,000 votes, though admitted that there seemed to be some discrepancy between the results counted at the constituencies and the recount in Nairobi. Odinga then claimed that at least 300,000 votes for Kibaki were falsely included in the total. Within minutes of the Commission's declaration of Kibaki's victory, rioting and violence, primarily directed against Kikuyus (Kibaki is a Kikuyu), broke out across Kenya. Most noticeably in Odinga's homeland of Nyanza Province in Western Kenya and in the slums of Nairobi, particularly Kibera, which is part of Odinga's Langata constituency. Later in January, the Rift Valley towns of Nakuru and Naivasha were seriously affected. There was some violence on the coast, but it wasn't ethnic-fuelled; the people were simply demonstrating about the injustice of the election result. By the fifth day after the elections, the army and police were out on the streets, attacking and being attacked by demonstrators. By then there was a news blackout in Kenya, which presumably was a move by the government to try and stop the fuel of violence by not allowing news of events happening in other parts of the country to spread. Although the violence was triggered by the elections, long-standing grievances over unequal distribution of land, wealth and power are seen as the real reasons behind the demonstrations, mostly dubbed by the press as 'ethnic' clashes.

The worst of the chaos went on for about 10 days and peaked when about 30 people, including many children, were killed when a church was burnt down near Eldoret, although more incidents broke out sporadically until mid January in the Rift Valley towns. An estimated 700 people lost their lives, although some resources have put this number as high as 1500, and over 200,000 were displaced. Within hours of the crisis, many world leaders including Ghanaian president John Kufuor and South Africa's Archbishop

Desmond Tutu flew in for emergency talks with Kibaki and Odinga. By mid-January, former Secretary General of the United Nations, Kofi Annan arrived in Nairobi to broker peace talks. Eventually, a power-sharing agreement was reached in February 2008, under which Kibaki remained President and Odinga gained the new post of Prime Minister with both of them having equal decision-making powers. A coalition government, with an equal number of ministers for both parties was named in April 2008. Although it is not known which of the two legitimately won the election, this agreement to date seems to have worked. The first positive sign after the agreement was brokered were by-elections for five parliamentary seats which passed peacefully on 11 June 2008. Kenyans also voted in a very peaceful manner on 4 August 2010 overwhelmingly in favour of a new constitution that became law on 27 August 2010. The very high voter turnout of 71% showed the determination of the Kenyan people for change and a new beginning. The outcome of this referendum was welcomed worldwide. However, Kenya has been criticized internationally for not fully investigating the violence over the 2007 elections, although, by 2011, hearings at the International Criminal Court in the Hague had begun; a process that is expected to take a number of years.

Kibaki presently holds his second and final term of office; presidential and parliamentary elections are due to be held in December 2012. This will be the first election under the new constitution.

Domestic politics aside, Kenya has experienced some external challenges in recent years. By 2009, and in the face of worsening and prolonged drought in the north of the country, the Kenyan government stepped up its mobilization of aid and its distribution of food, medicines and water to the millions affected. The Kenyan military and police, alongside the United Nations, UNICEF, the World Food Program and many international NGOs are distributing this aid and are likely to do so for the foreseeable future as the drought continues to cause widespread hardship and, in some regions, famine and malnutrition. From June to September 2011, the Horn of Africa (particularly Kenya, Ethiopia and Somalia) experienced its worst drought for 60 years, and an estimated 10 million people in the region now require food aid; about 2.4 million of these are in Northern Kenya.

Since early 2011 the Islamic militant group Al-Shabaab has controlled much of the region of southern Somalia just over the border with Kenya. This movement describes itself as a combat unit to uphold the principles of Sharia Law, while internationally it has been cited as a terrorist group with some links to Al Qaeda. In August, September and October 2011, Al-Shabaab was suspected of intimidating and kidnapping aid workers in southern Somalia; in Kenya two aid workers at the Dabaab Refugee Camp near the border with South Sudan and three tourists in the Lamu district were kidnapped (there were fatalities among the victims). In October 2011, a joint effort between the Somali, Kenyan and Ethiopian military against Al-Shabaab was initiated.

Economy

Kenya's economy is heavily reliant on rain-fed agriculture and tourism revenues, leaving it vulnerable to cyclical booms and busts caused by the climate and internal stability. Income levels are modest for an African country, although it's not as poor as some of its neighbours, and GDP per capita is about US$1600 per year. Real economic growth is about 5%, which is average for a developing African country. The inflation rate averages about 9% per annum, although it shot up briefly in 2008 to 25% because of increased food and fuel prices caused by the post-election crisis; it returned to single digits in 2009.

The agricultural sector continues to dominate Kenya's economy, although only 15% of Kenya's total land area has sufficient fertility and rainfall to be farmed and only 7-8% can be classified as first-class land. Most families rely on agriculture for their livelihood, and 75% of the labour force is engaged in farming, but incomes in agriculture are low, and the sector generates only 22% of GDP. Kenya's chief exports are tea and coffee, plus horticultural products, such as flowers and vegetables, destined for European supermarkets. Industry contributes 16% of output, but it must be remembered that there is little contribution from mining, which boosts industrial output in many other African countries. Services is the largest sector at 62% of GDP; this includes tourism, Kenya's largest source of foreign exchange, which earns the country about US$800 million per year.

Kenya has been in receipt of structural adjustment loans from the World Bank. Foreign Aid receipts per head are about average for Africa – they would be higher if the international community were more confident about the government's intention to tackle corruption. Some US$8.5 billion of external debt is estimated at being outstanding. Debt service takes up 14% of export earnings and, at present, this is within Kenya's ability to service, providing export revenues can be maintained.

Social conditions

The population in 2011 was estimated at around 41.7 million and it continues to grow rapidly at 2.5% a year. Most people live in the rural areas, with only a quarter in the towns. Overall population density is high by African standards, over double the average. Given that a large proportion of the country is arid, the pressure on the land in fertile areas, particularly in the Central Highlands and around Lake Victoria, is intense.

Literacy rates are good at 85%, and noticeably better than the African average. Primary education runs for eight years with 95% enrolments and, since 2004, primary education has been free. Secondary enrolments are fairly good, with almost 25% of children receiving education at this level, which also improved in 2008 when subsidies for school fees were introduced by the government for secondary education too. Tertiary education opportunities are limited to about 2%, despite the fact that Kenya has expanded its university enrolments substantially since 1980.

Life expectancy at 59 years is much better than the Africa average. However food availability in some areas, particularly in the arid north, which is affected by routine droughts, means that about 30% of the population is considered to be malnourished, which gives cause for concern. Population per doctor is very high, but medical delivery is good, given the low income level. The fertility rate at 4.9 children per woman is about average for Africa, as is the infant mortality rate, which is about 52 per 1000 births.

Culture

People

Kenya has long been a meeting place of population movements from around the continent. This has resulted in there being as many as 40 different ethnic groups living in Kenya and many more sub-groups, with an estimated overall population of 41.7 million people. There are three main groupings based on the origins of these groups. The Bantu came from West Africa in a migration, the reasons for which are not clearly understood. The Nilotic peoples came from the northwest, mostly from the area that is now Sudan. They were mainly pastoralists and moved south in search of better grazing on more fertile land. Finally, there is the Hamitic group, made up of a series of relatively small communities such as the Somali, Rendille, Boran, Ogaden and others, all pastoralists, who spread into Kenya from the north and northeast from Ethiopia and Somalia.

Kikuyu (Bantu) Primarily based around Mount Kenya, this is the largest ethnic group with 23% of the total population. They are thought to have originated in East and Northeast Africa around the 16th century. Land is the dominant social, political, religious and economic factor of life for Kikuyus and this soon brought them into conflict with colonial interests when settlers occupied their traditional lands.

The administration of the Kikuyu was undertaken by a council of elders based on clans made up of family groups. Other important members of the community were witch doctors, medicine men and blacksmiths. The Kikuyu god is believed to live on Mount Kenya and all Kikuyus build their homes with the door facing the mountain. In common with most ethnic groups in Kenya, traditionally men and women go through a number of stages into adulthood, including circumcision to mark the beginning of their adult life, although it is almost unheard of for women to be circumcised today.

It is said the Kikuyu have adapted more successfully than any other group to the modern world. Kikuyu are prominent in many of Kenya's business and commercial activities. Those still farming in their homelands have adapted modern methods to their needs and benefit from cash crop production for export, particularly coffee and tea. They have a great advantage in that their traditional area is very fertile and close to the capital, Nairobi.

Kalenjin (Nilotic) Kalenjin is a name used by the British to describe a cluster of ethnic groups – the Kipsigis, Nandi, Tugen, Elgeyo, Keiyo, Pokot, Marakwet, Sabaot, Nyangori, Sebei and Okiek – who speak the same language but with different dialects and in total make up about 12% of Kenya's population. They mainly live in the western edge of the central Rift Valley and are thought to have migrated from southern Sudan about 2000 years ago. Most Kalenjin took up agriculture, though they are traditionally pastoralists. Administration of the law is carried out at an informal gathering of the clan's elders. Witch doctors are generally women, which is unusual in Africa. In the modern world, the Kalenjin are renowned for their prowess as athletes and are often dubbed 'the running tribe' for their success in long-distance running (see box, page 114).

Kamba (Bantu) The Kamba (more correctly the Akamba) traditionally lived in the area from Nairobi southeast to around Tsavo National Park. They comprise 11% of the total population. Originally hunters, the Kamba soon adopted a more sedentary lifestyle and developed as traders because of the relatively poor quality of their land. Ivory was a major trade item as were beer, honey, ornaments and iron weapons, which they traded with neighbouring Masai and Kikuyu for food. In common with most Bantu people, political power lies with clan elders.

The Kamba were well regarded by the British for their intelligence and fighting ability, and they made up a large part of the East African contingent in the British Army during the First World War.

Kisii (Bantu) The Kisii (also known as Gusii) are based on the town of the same name in the west, south of Kisumu. Traditional practices have been continued, with soothsayers and medicine men retaining significant influence, despite the nominal allegiance of most Kisii to Christianity. They occupy a relatively small area, and population densities are the highest anywhere in Kenya's countryside, with plot sizes becoming steadily smaller with the passing of each generation.

Luo (Nilotic) The Luo live in the west of the country on the shores of Lake Victoria and are the third-largest ethnic group with 13% of the total population. They migrated from the Nile region of Sudan in around the 15th century. Originally the Luo were cattle herders, but the devastating effects of rinderpest on their herds compelled them to diversify into fishing and subsistence agriculture. The Luo were also prominent in the struggle for Independence and many of the country's leading politicians, including Tom Mboya and Oginga Odinga, were Luos.

Luhya (Bantu) The Luhya are based around Kakamega town in Western Kenya, and their extent reaches to Kitale in the north. They make up 16% of the total population and are Kenya's second largest grouping after the Kikuyu. They are closely related to the Kisii and, again, their territory is highly populated. The Luhya are small farmers and are the main cultivators of sugar-cane in the west. In Kenyan politics today, the Luhya vote is important in elections as they represent a sizable number. In the past, both Moi and Kibaki have chosen Luhyas as vice-presidents.

Masai (Nilotic) The Masai (also spelt Maasai) are probably the traditional 'tribe' best known to people outside Kenya; with their striking costume and reputation as fierce and proud warriors, they are resident near many of the game parks and reserves in Kenya and Tanzania. They are thought to number about 850,000. The Masai came to central Kenya from the Sudan around 1000 years ago, where they were the largest and one of the most important tribes. Their customs and practices were developed to reflect their nomadic lifestyle and many are still practised today, though change is beginning to be accepted. The traditional basic Masai diet is fresh and curdled milk carried in gourds. Blood tapped from the jugular vein of cattle is mixed with cattle urine and this provides a powerful stimulant. Cattle are rarely killed for meat as they represent the owner's wealth.

Meru (Bantu) This group arrived to the northeast of Mount Kenya around the 14th century, following invasions by Somalis on the coast. It is not homogenous, being made up of seven different groups of people, accounting for 5% of Kenya's population. Some of the Meru were led by a chief known as the *mogwe* until 1974, when the chief converted to Christianity and ended the tradition. A group of tribal elders administer traditional justice along with a witch doctor, known as a *njuri*, which is the only traditional judicial system recognized by Kenya.

The Meru occupy some of the country's richest farmland, which is used to produce tea, coffee, pyrethrum, maize and potatoes. Another highly profitable crop grown by the Meru in this region is *miraa*, a mild stimulant particularly popular amongst Islamic communities and Somalis.

Swahili (Bantu) The Swahili dwell along the coast and make up about 3% of the total population. Although they do not have a common heritage, they do share a common language, religion and culture. Ancestry is mainly a mixture of Arabic and African. For centuries the Swahili depended largely on trade from the Indian Ocean and played a vital role as middle men between east, central and southern Africa, and the outside world. Today the majority of coastal people are Muslims. The language is Kiswahili, which about 90 million people speak in East Africa.

Turkana (Nilotic) Like the Masai, this group has retained its rich and colourful dress and has a war-like reputation. They comprise about 2.5% of the total population, which makes them the third largest Nilotic group in Kenya after the Kalenjin and the Luo. They are mainly based in the northwest part of Kenya, living in the arid desert region between Lake Turkana and the Ugandan border. This is the most isolated part of the country and, as a consequence, the Turkana have probably been affected less by the 20th and 21st centuries than any other ethnic group in Kenya.

The Turkana are pastoralists whose main diet consists of milk and blood. Cattle, herded by the men, are important in Turkana culture. Camels, goats and sheep are also important and are looked after by boys and small girls. In the dry season some Turkana fish in the lake of the same name.

The traditional dress of the Turkana is very eye-catching and is still fairly commonly worn. Men cover part of their hair with mud which is then painted blue and decorated with ostrich feathers. The main garment is a woollen blanket worn over one shoulder. Women wear a variety of beaded and metal adornments, many of which signify different events in a woman's life. Women wear a half skirt of animal skins and a piece of black cloth. Both men and women sometimes insert a plug through the lower lip. Tattooing is still fairly common. Men are tattooed on the shoulders and upper arm each time they kill an enemy. Witch doctors and prophets are held in high regard.

Music and dance

Drums (*ngomas*) are central to most traditional Kenyan music and dance and a variety of drums are played throughout the country for people to dance to. Other instruments include reed flutes and basic stringed instruments, such as the *nyatiti*, which is similar to a medieval lyre and is usually played by a solo singer. Inland, the colonial period gave rise to *Beni* singing: very long narrative songs with strong elements of social commentary and political criticism. On the coast, the Swahili culture saw the growth of a unique style of music called *Taarab*, which fuses African percussion with Arabian rhythms and is performed by a large group of musicians playing violins, *ouds* and singing in Kiswahili. It is thought to have its origins in the 19th century, when the Omanis traded on the coast. In modern times, these instruments are being replaced by electric guitars and keyboards but the scales of the notes are still distinctively Arabian. Most of the singers are female, and the songs these days are very similar to the music that accompanies Bollywood movies. Since the 1970s, pop music has been popular in Kenya, especially imported West African music, such as *makossa* or highlife, or Congolese rumba; all are very infectious and danceable.

Today, Congolese music (Lingala) is extremely popular and is the type you are most likely to hear on *matatus*, in the streets, in bars and clubs, in fact anywhere and everywhere. Many of the musicians that play this music have actually relocated to Nairobi because of their success there. Also today, thanks to radio, young Kenyans are listening and dancing to, as well as playing, the same sort of chart-topping music as their contemporaries in the rest of the world. Rap has become increasingly popular among young Kenyans, and there are several Kenya-based rap bands. Whilst the style of music is virtually indistinguishable from US-based rappers, the lyrics are most definitely Kenyan and have much to say about life in modern Kenya. The rise of Christianity greatly increased the popularity of gospel and choral music, and many Kenyans sing in church each Sunday.

Acrobatics have become increasingly popular in Kenya, with a growing number of young performers taking to this art, which combines traditional dance with modern gymnastic technique. In Nairobi's poorest suburbs, acrobatics has become a popular form of exercise, entertainment, and a low-cost and accessible form of performance art, and often feature as entertainment in the tourist hotels.

Art

Although Kenya has fewer formal art galleries than many other countries, it has an invaluable artistic wealth easily seen in the many curio and craft markets and shops. There are a few locations in the country with examples of rock art, painted by early man when they still lived in caves. Many of Kenya's tribes have traditionally placed great significance on the decoration of both functional objects, such as pots, baskets, weapons and musical instruments, and also the body. You only have to see a proud Masai or Samburu warrior wrapped in vivid robes and intricate jewellery to see evidence of how important adornment is in these societies. In fact, the Samburu, who pay a great deal of attention to their appearance with their ochre-stained skin and elaborate hairstyles, were named, perhaps a little scornfully, by the other tribes – Samburu means butterfly. For the Masai, the use of decorative beading is very significant, as it is used to emphasise social status and to record stages of initiation and passage.

Wood carving all over Kenya was at first used for decoration of personal items, but today, of course, anything that might be attractive to tourists is carved out of wood; a lucrative trade that employs a number of talented carvers in Kenya. Some of the best carvers are found on the islands of Lamu and produce excellent doors, brass inlaid boxes, picture frames and small replica *dhows*. The Kisii of Western Kenya are well known for their carving in stone, using local soapstone in various shades. Most are small items, such as goblets, chess pieces or ash trays. Sisal baskets, usually produced in Kikuyu areas, are now used as handbags, although they were traditionally carried by Kikuyu women behind the head, with the strap across the forehead.

Painting and drawing in the formal European sense was introduced to Africa by colonialism. Probably the best known artist in Kenya was Joy Adamson, who as well as her work with big cats (see box, page 194) was also commissioned by the Kenya government to paint a series of portraits of Kenya's tribes in the 1940-1950s. Even today these are a great testament to the people of Kenya, especially since many younger people are choosing not to follow their tribal traditions. Today Kenya has a number of young modern artists, and the Nairobi galleries exhibit contemporary art, whilst the curio markets continue to find a steady stream of customers for crafts.

Religion

The Constitution of Kenya guarantees freedom of worship, and there are hundreds of religious denominations and sects in the country. The population in Kenya generally follows three major religious groupings: 45% Protestant, 33% Roman Catholic and 10% Muslim. The remaining people are followers of tribal religions, plus a few Hindus and Sikhs. Most of the Christian population lives in western and central Kenya, while Islam is the main religion for most of the coastal communities and the Somali community. Islam arrived along the East African coast in the eighth century, as part of the trade routes from the Persian Gulf and Oman. Kenya's Christian churches are the outcome of early missionary activities, which assisted in the administration of the country during colonial times. In Kenya today there are still many mission churches, and many international religious groups have a strong presence, including US-style evangelism, which has become very popular in Kenya in recent years.

Although traditional beliefs and practices vary among Kenya's ethnic groups, they share many general characteristics. Almost all involve belief in an eternal creator. For example, the Kikuyu's god is named *Nagi*, who is represented in the sun, moon, thunder and lighting, stars, rain, the rainbow and in large fig trees that serve as places of worship and sacrifice. In many traditional religions, ghosts of ancestral spirits are thought to return to seek revenge on the living, so they too must be paid homage.

Land and environment

Geography

Kenya is 580,367 sq km in area, with the equator running right through the middle. Physically, the country is made up of a number of different zones. It lies between latitude 5° North and 4° 30′ South and longitude 34° and 41° East. The Great Rift Valley runs from the north to the south of the country and in places is 65 km across, bounded by escarpments 600-900 m high. This is probably the most spectacularly beautiful part of the country, dotted with soda lakes teeming with flamingos. To the east of the Rift Valley lies the Kenya Highlands including Mount Kenya, an extinct volcano, which at 5199 m is Africa's second-highest mountain. This is the most fertile part of the country, particularly the lower slopes of the mountain range. Nairobi sits at the southern end of the Central Highlands. The north of Kenya is arid, bounded by South Sudan and Ethiopia. To the west lies Uganda and the fertile shores around Lake Victoria. Further south, the land turns into savannah, and is mainly used for grazing.

The Indian Ocean coast to the east of the country runs for 480 km, and there is a narrow strip of fertile land all along it. Beyond this, the land becomes scrubland and semi-arid. Somalia borders Kenya in the northeast, and this is also a very arid area.

Climate

Kenya's different altitudes mean that the climate varies enormously around the country. Probably the most pleasant climate is in the Central Highlands and the Rift Valley, though the valley floor can become extremely hot and is relatively arid. Mount Kenya and Mount Elgon both become quite cool above 1750 m, and the top of Mount Kenya is snow-covered. Mount Kenya and the Aberdares are the country's main water catchment areas.

Western Kenya and the area around Lake Victoria is generally hot, around 30-34°C all year, with high humidity and rainfall evenly spread throughout the year. Most rain here tends to fall in the early evening. The country is covered in semi-arid bushland and deserts throughout the north and east of the country. Temperatures can rise to 40°C during the day and fall to 20°C at night in the desert. Rainfall in this area is sparse, between 250 mm and 500 mm per annum.

The coastal belt is hot and humid all year round, though the heat is tempered by sea breezes. Rainfall varies from as little as 20 mm in February to 240 mm in May. The average temperature varies little throughout the year but is hottest in November and December, at about 30°C.

Vegetation

Kenya is justifiably famous for its flora and fauna. In areas of abundant rainfall, the country is lush, supporting a huge range of plants, and the wide variety of geographical zones house a corresponding diversity of flora. The majority of the country is covered in savannah-type vegetation characterized by the acacia. The slopes of Mount Elgon and Mount Kenya are covered in thick evergreen temperate forest from about 1000 m to 2000 m; then to 3000 m the mountains are bamboo forest; above this level the mountains are covered with groundsel trees and giant lobelias. Mangroves are prolific in the coastal regions.

Wildlife → *See the colour wildlife section for further information and pictures.*

Mammals

There is much more than the big game to see in Kenya, and you will undoubtedly travel through different habitats from the coast to the tropical rainforests but the big mammals are on the top of most people's 'to see' lists.

Big Nine The 'big five' (**elephant**, **lion**, **black rhino**, **buffalo** and **leopard**) was the term originally coined by hunters who wanted trophies from their safaris, but nowadays the **hippopotamus** is usually considered one of the Big Five, whereas the buffalo is far less of a 'trophy'. Equally photogenic and worthy of being included are **zebra**, **giraffe** and **cheetah**. Whether they are the Big Five or the Big Nine, these are the animals that most people come to Africa to see and, with the possible exception of the leopard, you have an excellent chance of seeing all of them in Kenya.

The **lion** (*Panthera leo*), with weights at around 250 kg for a male, is the second largest cat in the world after the tiger. Lions are unlike other cats in that they live in large prides consisting of related females and offspring and a small number of adult males. Groups of female lions typically hunt together for their pride, being smaller, swifter and more agile than the males and unencumbered by the heavy and conspicuous mane, which causes overheating during exertion. They act as a coordinated group in order to stalk and bring down the prey successfully. Totally carnivorous, they prey mostly on large antelope or buffalo. Visually, coloration varies from light buff to yellowish, reddish or dark brown, and the underparts are generally lighter and the tail tuft is black. They communicate with one another with a range of sounds that vary from roaring, grunting and growling to meowing. Roars, more common at night, can reach sound levels of over 110 decibels and can be heard from distances of up to 8 km.

The **leopard** (*Panthera pardus*) is an equally impressive cat but less likely to be seen as it is more nocturnal and secretive in its habits. It hunts at night and frequently rests during the heat of the day on the lower branches of trees. Well camouflaged, its spots – typically dark rosettes with a tawny-yellow middle – merge into foliage or blend well into less sparse grassland. Its habitat is extremely diverse and it can survive in high mountainous and coastal plains regions as well as rainforests and deserts.

The **cheetah** (*Acinonyx jubatus*) is well known for its running speed; in short bursts it has been recorded at over 90 kph. But it is not as successful at hunting as you might expect with such a speed advantage. The cheetah has a very specialized build: long and thin with a deep chest, long legs and a small head. But the forelimbs are restricted to a forward and backward motion which makes it very difficult for the cheetah to turn suddenly when in hot pursuit of a small antelope. Cheetahs are often seen in family groups walking across the plains or resting in the shade.

The **elephant** (*Loxodonta africana*) is the largest land mammal and, weighing in at up to six tonnes with an average shoulder height of 3-4 m, it is awe-inspiring by its very size. Sociable by nature, elephants form groups of 10 to 20 strong led by a female matriarch, and it is wonderful to watch a herd at a waterhole. Elephants are herbivores and are voracious and destructive feeders, sometimes pushing over a whole tree to get to the tender shoots at the top. Although they suffered terribly from the activities of poachers in the 1970s and 1980s (see Kenya Wildlife Services box, page 10), they are still readily seen in many of Kenya's game areas and are thought today to number about 37,000 country-wide.

The **white rhino** (*Ceratotherium simum*) and the **black rhino** (*Diceros bicornis*) occur naturally in Kenya. Unfortunately, they too have suffered severely from poaching for their horns and, sadly, this is still an issue even today. Their names have no bearing on their colour as they are both a rather non-descript dark grey. The name of the white rhino is derived from the Dutch word 'weit' which means wide and refers to the shape of the animal's mouth. It has a large square muzzle and this reflects the fact that it is a grazer and feeds by cropping grass; its preferred habitat is grasslands and open savannah with mixed scrub vegetation. The black rhino, on the other hand, is a browser, usually feeding on shrubs and bushes, using its long, prehensile upper lip which is well adapted to the purpose; it lives in drier bush country and usually alone. The horn of the rhino is not a true horn, but is made of a material called keratin, which is essentially the same as hair.

The **buffalo** (*Syncerus caffer*) was once revered by the hunter as the greatest challenge for a trophy and more hunters have lost their lives to this animal than to any other. This is an immensely strong animal with particularly acute senses. Left alone as a herd they pose no more of a threat than a herd of domestic cattle. The danger lies in the unpredictable behaviour of a lone bull which, when cut off from the herd, becomes bad-tempered and easily provoked. While you are more likely to see them on open plains, they are equally at home in dense forest. To see a large herd peacefully grazing is a great privilege and one to remember.

The most conspicuous animal in water is the **hippopotamus** (*Hippopotamus amphibius*), a large beast with short stubby legs that can weigh up to four tonnes. However, the hippo is quite agile on land. During the day it rests in the water, rising every few minutes to snort and blow at the surface, and at night it leaves the water to graze. A single adult animal needs up to 60 kg of grass every day and, to achieve this, obviously has to forage far. The banks near a river or waterhole with a resident hippo population will be very bare and denuded of grass. Should you meet a hippo on land, keep well away; if you get between it and its escape route to the water, it may well attack. Hippos need water not only to prevent their skin from drying out, but also to regulate their body temperature.

The **giraffe** (*Giraffa camelopardalis*) may not be as magnificent as a full-grown lion, nor as awe-inspiring as an elephant, but its elegance as a small party strolls across the plains is unsurpassed. Both male and female animals have horns, though in the female they may be smaller. A mature male can be over 5 m high to the top of its head. They are browsers and can eat the leaves and twigs of a large variety of tall trees, thorns presenting no problem. The lolloping gait of the giraffe is very distinctive and is caused by the way it moves its legs at the gallop. A horse will move its diagonally opposite legs together when galloping, whereas the giraffe moves both hind legs together and both forelegs together. It achieves this by swinging both hind legs forward and outside the forelegs.

Although the giraffe itself is unmistakable and easily identified, there are in fact several sub-species that differ from each other. Extending from about the Tana River northwards and eastwards into Somalia and Ethiopia is the almost chestnut-coloured **reticulated giraffe**, which is sometimes considered a separate species. Found further south than the reticulated giraffe is the **common giraffe**, which itself has two sub-species; one is the **Masai giraffe**, which occurs in southwest Kenya (and Tanzania). This has a yellowish-buff coat with the characteristic patchwork of brownish markings with very jagged edges. In most animals there are only two horns, though occasionally animals are seen with three horns. The other form of the common giraffe, known as **Rothschild's giraffe**, occurs west and north of the Masai giraffe and into Uganda as far west as the Nile. It is usually paler and heavier-looking than the Masai giraffe and can have as many as five horns, though more commonly three.

The **zebra** is another easily recognized animal. It forms herds, often large ones, sometimes with antelope. It has a stocky horse-like body, but its mane is made of short, erect hair, its tail is tufted at the tip and its coat is black and white striped. The stripes, which vary greatly in number and width, are a form of camouflage which breaks up the outline of the body. At dawn or in the evening, when their predators are most active, zebras look indistinct and may confuse predators by distorting distance. As with the giraffe, there is more than one sort of zebra in East Africa: **Grevy's zebra** (*Equus grevyi*) and the **common** or **Burchell's zebra** (*Equus burchelli*).

Larger antelope The first animals that you will see on safari will almost certainly be antelope; these are by far the most numerous group to be seen on the plains. Like giraffe and zebra, all antelopes are herbivores but they have keratin-covered horns which make them members of the *Bovidae* family. They vary greatly in appearance, from the tiny dikdik to the large eland and, once you have learnt to recognize the different sets of horns, identification of species should not be too difficult. For identification purposes they can be divided into the larger ones, which stand at about 120 cm or more at the shoulder, and the smaller ones under that height.

The largest of all the antelopes is the **eland** (*Taurotragus oryx*), which stands 175-183 cm at the shoulder. It is cow-like in appearance, with a noticeable dewlap and shortish spiral horns present in both sexes. The general colour varies from greyish to fawn, sometimes with a rufous tinge, with narrow white stripes on the sides of the body. It occurs in herds of up to 30 in a wide variety of grassy and mountainous habitats. The eland will travel large distances in search of food and will eat all sorts of tough woody bushes and thorny plants.

Not quite as big, but still reaching 140-153 cm, is the **greater kudu** (*Tragelaphus strepsiceros*). Although nearly as tall as the eland, it is a much more slender and elegant animal altogether. Its general colour also varies from greyish to fawn and it has several white stripes running down the sides of the body. The male carries very long and spreading horns, which have two or three twists along their length. A noticeable and distinctive feature is a thick fringe of hair that runs from the chin down the neck. The greater kudu prefers fairly thick bush, sometimes in quite dry areas, and usually lives in family groups.

Its smaller relative, the **lesser kudu** (*Strepsiceros imberis*), looks quite similar, with similar horns, but stands only 99-102 cm high. It lacks the throat fringe of the bigger animal, but has two conspicuous white patches on the underside of the neck. It inhabits dense scrub and acacia thickets in semi-arid country, usually in pairs, sometimes with their young.

The **roan antelope** (*Hippotragus equinus*) and **sable antelope** (*Hippotragus niger*) are similar in general shape, though the roan is somewhat bigger, being 140-145 cm at the shoulder, compared to the 127-137 cm of the sable. In both species, both sexes carry ringed horns which curve backwards, and these are particularly long in the sable. There is a horse-like mane present in both animals. The sable is usually glossy black with white markings on the face and a white belly. The female is often a reddish brown in colour. The roan can vary from dark rufous to a reddish fawn and also has white markings on the face. The black males of the sable are easily identified, but the brownish individuals can be mistaken for the roan. Look for the tufts of hair at the tips of the rather long ears of the roan (absent in the sable).

Another large antelope with a black and white face is the **oryx** (*Oryx beisa*). It is a striking creature with a black line down the spine and a black stripe between the coloured body and the white underparts. This is not an animal you would confuse with another. Its horns are long and straight and sweep back behind the ears – from face-on they look V-shaped. It occurs in two distinct sub-species, the **beisa oryx**, which is found north and west of the Tana River, and the **fringe-eared oryx**, which occurs south and east of this river. Both these animals stand 122 cm at the shoulder.

The **common waterbuck** (*Kobus ellipsiprymnus*) is about 122-137 cm at the shoulder. It has a shaggy grey-brown coat which is very distinctive. It can be distinguished by the white mark on its buttocks, which is a clear half ring on the rump and round the tail, and by its rounded ears and white patches above the eyes and around the throat. The male has long, gently curving horns which are heavily ringed. Despite its name, the waterbuck is not an aquatic animal. It does, however, take refuge in water to escape predators, and has a coat that emits a smelly, oily secretion thought to be for waterproofing. They are fairly common and widespread.

The **wildebeest** (*Connochaetes taurinus*) is well known to many people because of the spectacular annual migration through the Masai Mara. It is a big animal about 132 cm high, looking rather like an American bison from a distance, especially when you see the huge herds straggling across the plains. The impression is strengthened by its buffalo-like horns (in both sexes) and humped appearance. The general colour is greyish with a few darker stripes down the side. It has a noticeable beard and long mane. Wildebeest are well known for their distinctive snorts and grunts when alarmed, when they also toss their massive heads about nervously – being the favourite prey of lions they have to be ever on the alert. They occur in herds of 20 to 30 individuals and are often found grazing with zebra.

The four remaining large antelope are fairly similar. Three of these four are **hartebeest** of various sorts and the fourth is called the **topi**. All four antelope have long, narrow horse-like faces and rather comical expressions. The shoulders are much higher than the rump giving them a very sloped-back appearance, especially in the three hartebeest. They have short horns which differ from those of any other animal, as they are situated on a bony pedicel, a backward extension of the skull which forms a base.

One of the hartebeests, **Jackson's hartebeest** (*Alcelaphus buselaphus*; about 132 cm) is similar in colour to the **topi** (*Damaliscus korrigum*; about 122-127 cm) being a very rich dark rufous in colour. But the topi has dark patches on the tops of the legs, a coat with a rich satiny sheen to it and more ordinary looking lyre-shaped horns. Of the other two hartebeest, **Coke's hartebeest** (*Alcephalus buselaphus*; about 122 cm), also called the **kongoni**, is usually considered to be a sub-species of Jackson's hartebeest, but is a very different colour being a more drab pale brown with a paler rump.

Finally, mention must be made of a rare antelope that is present in the Aberdare National Park. This is the **bongo** (*Boocercus eurycerus*), a large and handsome forest antelope, 112-127 cm tall, which can weigh up to 400 kg, making it even bulkier than the greater kudu. It has a striking reddish-brown coat with white-yellow stripes and long, slightly spiralled horns. Its habitat is dense montane forest and bamboo, such as is found on Mount Kenya, and it can live at altitudes of up to 4000 m. However, there are very few individuals left in the wild in Kenya and it is rarely seen.

Smaller antelope The remaining common antelopes are a good deal smaller than those described above. The largest is the **impala** (*Aepyceros melampus*), which is 92-107 cm and is bright rufous in colour with a white abdomen. Only the male carries the long lyre-shaped horns. Just above the heels of the hind legs is a tuft of thick black bristles, which are surprisingly easy to see as the animal runs in graceful leaps. Another two are **Grant's gazelle** (*Gazella granti*), about 81-99 cm, and **Thomson's gazelle** (*Gazella thomsonii*), about 64-69 cm. Thomson's gazelle can usually be distinguished from Grant's by the broad black band along the side between the rufous upper parts and white abdomen, but not invariably, as some forms of Grant's also have this dark lateral stripe. If in doubt, look for the white area on the buttocks which extends above the tail on to the rump in Grant's, but does not extend above the tail in Thomson's. The underparts are white. Thomson's gazelle, or 'Tommies', are among the most numerous animals that inhabit the plains of Kenya. You will see large herds of them often in association with other game.

The last two of the common smaller antelopes are the **bushbuck** (*Tragelaphus scriptus*), about 76-92 cm, and the tiny **Kirk's dikdik** (*Rhynchotragus kirkii*), only 36-41 cm. Both are easily identified. The bushbuck's coat has a shaggy appearance and a variable pattern of white spots and stripes on the side and back, and two white crescent-shaped marks on the front of the neck. The horns, present in the male only, are short, almost straight and slightly spiralled. The animal has a curious high rump which gives it a characteristic crouching appearance. The white underside of the tail is noticeable when it runs. Kirk's dikdik is so small it can hardly be mistaken for any other antelope. In colour it is a greyish brown, often washed with rufous. The legs are noticeably thin and stick-like, giving the animal a very fragile appearance. The snout is slightly elongated, and there is a tuft of hair on the top of the head. Only the male carries the very small straight horns.

A rare and seldom-seen smaller antelope is the **sitatunga** (*Tragelaphus spekii eurycerus*), about 80-120 cm, although in Kenya it is protected in the Saiwa Swamp National Park and is also present on the Laikipia Plateau. Similar in appearance to a bushbuck but with a shaggier coat, it has unique splayed hooves, which allow it to negotiate the vegetated marshy terrain that it favours. The male has long twisted horns. A good swimmer, it is often considered to be a semi-aquatic animal, although in fact it only takes to the water to protect itself from predators.

Other mammals Although the antelope is undoubtedly the most numerous species to be seen on the plains, there are others worth keeping an eye open for. Some of these are scavengers, which thrive on the kills of other animals. These include the dog-like jackals, of which there are two species that you are likely to come across. Both species are similar in size (about 86-96 cm in length and 41-46 cm at the shoulder). The **black-backed jackal** (*Canis mesomelas*), which is the most common and ranges throughout the region, is a rather foxy reddish fawn in colour with a noticeable black area on its back. This black part is sprinkled with a silvery white, which can make the back look silver in some lights. The **side-striped jackal** (*Canis adustus*) is generally greyish fawn in colour, with a variable and sometimes ill-defined stripe along the side. Jackal can be seen in most parks, often near lion kills, but are also common on farmland. The other well known plains scavenger is the **spotted hyena** (*Crocuta crocuta*), which is a fairly large animal, 69-91 cm high. Its high shoulders and low back give it a characteristic appearance. Brownish in colour with dark spots and a large head, it usually occurs singly or in pairs, but occasionally in small packs. The slightly smaller **striped hyena** (*Hyaena hyaena*), 65-80 cm high, is seen less often as it's more nocturnal than the spotted hyena, and quickly returns to its lair at sunrise. Its coat colour varies from grey to light brown with vertical black stripes along the length of the body and dark legs. When hungry, hyenas are aggressive creatures; they have been known to attack live animals and will occasionally try to steal a kill from lions. They always look dirty because of their habit of lying in muddy pools which may be to keep cool or alleviate the irritation of parasites. If camping in unfenced campsites, be very wary of hyena – they have little inherent fear of humans and can get very close and will think nothing of sniffing out and stealing food.

A favourite and common plains animal is the comical **warthog** (*Phacochoerus aethiopicus*). A member of the pig family, it is unmistakable, being grey in colour and almost hairless, with a very large head, tusks and wart-like growths on the face. These are thought to protect the eyes as it makes sideways sweeps into the earth with its tusks, digging up roots and tubers. The warthog often kneels on its forelegs when eating and, when startled, the adult will run at speed with its tail held straight up in the air followed by its young.

In suitable rocky areas, such as *kopjes*, look out for an animal that looks a bit like a large grey-brown guinea pig. This is the **rock hyrax** (*Heterohyrax brucei*), an engaging and fairly common animal that lives in communities; during the morning and afternoon you will see them sunning themselves on the rocks. Perhaps their strangest characteristic is their place in the evolution of mammals. The structure of the ear is similar to that found in whales, their molar teeth look like those of a rhinoceros, two pouches in the stomach resemble a condition found in birds, and the arrangement of the bones of the forelimb are like those of the elephant.

The **caracal** (*Felis caracal*), also known as the African lynx, is roughly twice the size of a domestic cat, with reddish-sandy fur and paler underparts. The graceful cat has very characteristic tufts of black hair at the end of its pointed ears. It is very good at bush camouflage and is scarcely noticed when lying still against the earth, though it is an adept hunter and possesses great speed and lightning reflexes; it can easily snatch a flying bird out of the air. Like a leopard, it often takes prey into a tree to be eaten.

The most common and frequently seen of the monkey group are baboons. The most widespread species is the **olive baboon** (*Papio anubis*), which occurs almost throughout the region. This is a large (127-142 cm), heavily built animal olive brown or greyish in colour. Adult males have a well-developed mane. In the eastern part of Kenya, including the coast, the olive baboon is replaced by the **yellow baboon** (*Papio cynocephalus*; 116-

137 cm), which is a smaller and lighter animal than the olive baboon, with longer legs and almost no mane in the adult males. The tail in both species looks as if it is broken and hangs down in a loop. Baboons are basically terrestrial animals, although they can climb very well. In the wild they are often found in acacia grassland, often associated with rocks, and are sociable animals living in groups called troops. Females are very often seen with young clinging to them. In parts of East Africa they have become very used to the presence of man and can be a nuisance to campers. They will readily climb all over your vehicle hoping for a handout. Be careful, they have a very nasty bite.

The smaller monkey that also makes a nuisance of itself is the **vervet monkey** (*Cercopithicus mitis*), which is the one that abounds at campsites and often lodges. It has a black face framed with white across the forehead and cheeks. Its general colour is greyish tinged with a varying amount of yellow. The feet, hands and tip of the tail are black.

Birds

East Africa is one of the richest areas of birdlife in the world. The total number of species is in excess of 1300, and it is possible and not too difficult to see 100 different species in a day. You will find that a pair of binoculars is essential. The birds described here are the common ones and, with a little careful observation, you will soon find that you can identify them. They have been grouped according to the habitat.

Urban birds The first birds that you will notice on arrival in any big city will almost certainly be the large numbers soaring overhead. Early in the morning the numbers are few, but as the temperature warms up, more and more are seen circling high above the buildings. Many of these will be **hooded vultures** (*Neophron monachus*; 66 cm), and **black kites** (*Milvus migrans*; 55 cm). They are superficially similar, rather nondescript brownish birds. They are, however, easily distinguished by the shape and length of the tail. The tail of the hooded vulture is short and slightly rounded at the end, whereas the black kite (which incidently is not black, but brown) has a long, narrow tail that looks either forked when the tail is closed or slightly concave at the end when spread. Also soaring overhead in some cities you will see the **marabou stork** (*Leptoptilos crumeniferus*; 152 cm). Although this bird is a stork it behaves like a vulture, in that it lives by scavenging. Overhead its large size, long and noticeable bill and trailing legs make it easily identifiable. The commonest crow in towns and cities is the **pied crow** (*Corvus albus*; 46 cm). This is a very handsome black bird with a white lower breast that joins up with a white collar round the back of the neck.

In gardens and parks there are a number of smaller birds to look out for. The **dark-capped** or **common bulbul** (*Pycnonotus barbatus*; 18 cm) can be heard all day with its cheerful call of "Come quick, doctor, quick". It is a brownish bird with a darker brown head and a slight crest. Below, the brown is paler fading to white on the belly and, under the tail, it is bright yellow.

There are a large number of weaver birds to be seen, but identifying them is not always easy. Most of them are yellow and black in colour, and many of them live in large noisy colonies. Have a close look at their intricately woven nests if you get the chance. The commonest one is probably the **black-headed weaver** (*Ploceus cucullatus*; 18 cm), which often builds its colonies in bamboo clumps. The male has a mainly black head and throat, but the back of the head is chestnut. The underparts are bright yellow, and the back and wings mottled black and greenish yellow. When the bird is perched and seen from behind, the markings on the back form a v-shape.

Birds of open plains   Along with the spectacular game, it is on the plains that you will see many of the magnificent African birds. In particular, there are two large birds which you will see stalking across the grasslands. These are the **ostrich** (*Struthio camelus*; 2 m), and the **secretary bird** (*Sagittarius serpentarius*; 101 cm). The secretary bird is so called because the long plumes of its crest are supposed to resemble the old-time secretaries who carried their quill pens tucked behind their ears. The bird is often seen in pairs as it hunts for snakes, its main food source. The ostrich is sometimes seen singly, but also in family groups. There are other large terrestrial birds to look out for, and one of them, the **kori bustard** (*Otis kori*; 80 cm), like the secretary bird, quarters the plains looking for snakes. It is quite a different shape, however, and can be distinguished by its thick-looking grey neck (caused by loose feathers). It is particularly common in Serengeti National Park and in the Masai Mara. The other large bird that you are likely to see on the open plains is the **ground hornbill** (*Bucorvus cafer*; 107 cm). When seen from afar, this looks just like a turkey but close up it is very distinctive and cannot really be mistaken for anything else. They are very often in pairs and the male has bare red skin around the eye and on the throat. In the female this skin is red and blue.

Soaring overhead on the plains you will see vultures and birds of prey. The commonest vulture in game areas is the **African white-backed vulture** (*Gyps africanus*; 81 cm). This is a largish, brown bird with a white lower back, with the characteristic bare head of its family. Because they are commonly seen circling overhead, the white rump can be difficult to see. So look out for the other diagnostic characteristic – the broad white band on the leading edge of the undersurface of the wing. The **bateleur** (*Terathopius ecaudatus*; 61 cm) is a magnificent and strange-looking eagle. It is rarely seen perched, but is quite commonly seen soaring very high overhead. Its tail is so short that it sometimes appears tailless. This, its buoyant flight and the black and white pattern of its underparts make it easy to identify.

Where there is game, look out for the oxpeckers. The commonest one is the **red-billed oxpecker** (*Buphagus erythrorhynchus*; 18 cm). These birds are actually members of the starling family, although their behaviour is not like that of other starlings. They associate with game animals and cattle and spend their time clinging to and climbing all over the animals while they hunt for ticks, which form their main food. There are other birds that associate with animals in a different way; for example, the **cattle egret** (*Bubulcus ibis*; 51 cm), which follows herds and feeds on the grasshoppers and other insects disturbed by the passing of the animals. Occasionally, too, the cattle egret will perch on the back of a large animal, but this is quite different from the behaviour of oxpeckers. Cattle egrets are long-legged and long-billed white birds, most often seen in small flocks. In the breeding season they develop long buff feathers on the head, chest and back.

Birds of dry, open woodland   The two habitats of open plain and dry open woodland form a vast area of Africa, and most of the game parks come into these categories. As well as being quintessentially African, this dry open woodland with acacia thorn trees is an extremely rewarding area for birdwatching. It supports an enormous variety of species and it is relatively easy terrain in which to see them.

The **guinea fowls** live in flocks and if you surprise a group on the road they will disappear into the bush in a panic. There is more than one sort of guinea fowl, but they are rather similar, being a slate grey with white spots.

The tops of the thorn trees are used as observation perches by a number of different species. Specially noticeable is the **red-billed hornbill** (*Tockus erythrorhynchus*; 45 cm), which has blackish-brown back, with a white stripe down between the wings. The wings themselves are spotted with white. The underparts are white and the bill is long, curved and mainly red. As the bird flies into a tree, the impression is of a black and white bird with a long red bill and a long tail. Another striking bird that perches on tree tops is the **white-bellied go-away bird** (*Corythaixoides leucogaster*; 51 cm). This gets its strange name from its call "Go-away, go-away". It is a basically grey bird with a very upright stance. The top of the head carries a long and conspicuous crest. The belly is white and the long tail has a black tip. It is usually seen in small family parties.

The strange-looking, brightly coloured **d'Arnaud's barbet** (*Trachyphonus darnaudii*; 15 cm) is common in the dry bush country. The impression you get is of a spotted bird, dark with pale spots above, and pale with dark spots below. It has a long, dark, heavily spotted tail. Its call and behaviour is very distinctive. A pair will sit facing each other with their tails raised over their backs wagging them from side to side, and bob at each other in a duet. All the while they utter a four-note call over and over again. "Do-do dee-dok". Another brightly coloured bird is the **lilac-breasted roller** (*Coracias caudata*; 41 cm), which is very easy to see as it perches on telegraph poles or wires, or on bare branches. The brilliant blue on its wings, head and underparts is very eye-catching. Its throat and breast are a deep lilac, and its tail has two elongated streamers. It is quite common in open bush country. Also often seen sitting on bare branches is the **drongo** (*Dicrurus adsimilis*; 24 cm), but this is an all-black bird. It is easily identified by its forked tail, which is fish-tailed at the end. It is usually solitary.

There are many different species of starling to be seen in eastern Africa, and most of them are beautifully coloured. Two of the most spectacular are the **golden-breasted starling** (*Cosmopsarus regius*; 32 cm), and the **superb starling** (*Spreo superbus*; 18 cm). Both are common, but the superb starling is the more widespread and is seen near habitation as well as in thorn bush country. Tsavo East is probably the best place to see the golden-breasted starling. Look out for the long tail of the golden-breasted starling, and the white undertail and white breast band of the superb starling. Both are usually seen hopping about on the ground. Another long-tailed bird quite commonly seen in bush country is the **long-tailed fiscal** (*Lanius cabanisi*; 30 cm). Unlike the golden-breasted starling, however, it is a black and white bird that is usually seen perched on wires or bare branches. It can be identified by its very long all-black tail and mainly black upperparts, which are grey on the lower back and rump.

Finally, look out for three birds, which though small are very noticeable. The **red-cheeked cordon-bleu** (*Uraeginthus benegalus*; 13 cm) is a lovely little blue bird with a brown back and bright red cheek patches. They are seen in pairs or family parties, and the females and young are somewhat duller in colour than the males. They are quite tame, and you often see them round the game lodges. In the less dry grasslands you can see the beautiful red and black bishop birds. There are two species, both of which are quite brilliant in their colouring. The brightest is the **red bishop** (*Euplectes orix*; 13 cm), which has brown wings and tail and noticeable scarlet feathers on its rump. The almost equally brilliant **black-winged bishop** (*Euplectes hordeaceus*; 14 cm) may be distinguished from the red bishop by its black wings and tail and rather less obvious red rump. Both species occur in long grass and cultivation, often, but not invariably, near water.

Water and waterside birds The inland waters form a very important habitat for both resident and migratory species. A lot can be seen from the shore, but it is especially fruitful to go out in a boat, when you will get quite close to, among others, the large and magnificent herons that occur here. The king of them all is the aptly named goliath heron (*Ardea goliath*; 144 cm), which is usually seen singly on mud banks and shores, both inland and on the coast. Its very large size is enough to distinguish it, but the smaller **purple heron** (*Ardea purpurea*; 80 cm), which frequents similar habitat and is also widespread, may be mistaken for it at a distance. If in doubt, the colour on the top of the head (rufous in the goliath and black in the purple) will clinch it; also the purple is much more slender with a slender bill.

The flamingos are known to most people and will be readily identified. However, there are two different species that very often occur together. The **greater flamingo** (*Phoenicopterus ruber*; 142 cm) is the larger and paler bird and has a pink bill with a black tip. The **lesser flamingo** (*Phoenicopterus minor*; 101 cm) is deeper pink all over and has a deep carmine bill with a black tip. They both occur in large numbers in the soda lakes of Western Kenya. The magnificent **fish eagle** (*Haliaeetus vocifer*; 76 cm) has a distinctive colour pattern. It often perches on the tops of trees, where its dazzling white head and chest are easily seen. In flight, this white and the white tail contrast with the black wings. It has a wild yelping call, which is usually uttered in flight. Try and watch the bird as it calls: it throws back its head over its back in a most unusual way.

There are several different kingfishers to be seen, but the most numerous is the black and white **pied kingfisher** (*Ceryle rudis*, 25 cm). This is easily recognized, as it is the only black and white kingfisher. It is common all round the large lakes and also turns up at quite small bodies of water. It hovers over the water before plunging in to capture its prey.

Books

History

Anderson D, *History of the Hanged; Britain's Dirty War in Kenya and the end of Empire* Covers the final years of the Mau Mau uprising and looks at the mistreatment of the Kikuyu people, who the British herded into concentration camps where many died.

Fox J, *White Mischief* Looks at the notorious 'Happy Valley' set in 1940s colonial Kenya and investigates the unsolved murder of Lord Erroll, aka Josslyn Hay.

Kenyatta J, *Facing Mount Kenya* Written in colonial times before he became the first president of Kenya, this gives an interesting insight into the history and the culture of the Kikuyu people.

Miller C, *Lunatic Express* Highly readable history of East Africa, centring around the building of the Uganda Railway.

Memoirs

Adamson J, *Born Free* The classic tale of Elsa, the lioness that was raised and set free by Joy and George Adamson in the 1960s. Joy wrote several more books about releasing big cats into the wild in Kenya.

Bryson B, *African Diary* A contemporary look at Kenya through the eyes of renowned travel writer Bill Bryson.

Dinesen I (aka Karen Blixen), *Out of Africa* Written in 1937, this is probably the most famous book there is about Kenya. It is Karen Blixen's account of her life on her coffee plantation in the Ngong Hills and provides a vivid snapshot of colonial life in the last decades of the British Empire.

Huxley E, *Flame Trees of Thika* and *The Mottled Lizard* Stories of the lives of the early pioneers told through the eyes of a young girl growing up on a coffee farm, which she describes as "a bit of El Dorado my father had been fortunate enough to buy in the bar of the Norfolk Hotel".

Maathai W, *Unbowed: A Memoir* Autobiography of 2004 Nobel Peace Prize winner Wangari Maathai, an extraordinary woman who instigated the planting of some 30 million trees in Kenya (see page 166).

From page to screen

One of the greatest wildlife stories ever told was *Born Free*, about Elsa the lioness who was rescued as a cub and rehabilitated back into the wild by Joy and George Adamson, portrayed in the 1966 film by Virginia McKenna and Bill Travers. *To Walk With Lions* (1999) follows George's later life and stars Richard Harris as the formidable man. In the movie *I Dreamed of Africa* (2000), Kim Basinger portrays former Italian socialite Kuki Gallmann's life on a ranch on the Laikipia Plateau and her subsequent work in conservation. *Out of Africa* (1985) is as much a story of Kenya's wildlife and scenic beauty as it is of Karen Blixen's relationship with the aristocratic safari-goer Denys Finch Hatton; it stars Meryl Streep and Robert Redford and won seven Oscars. Adapted from John Le Carré's novel, *The Constant Gardener* (2005) revolves around a British diplomat in Nairobi whose wife is murdered in Northern Kenya while investigating a drugs trial scandal. Starring Ralph Fiennes and Rachael Weisz (who won Oscar for Best Supporting Actress) much of it was filmed in Nairobi's Kibera slum (see page 50).

Markham B, *West with the Night* Marvellous autobiography of Beryl Markham (see box, page 54) who made the first solo east to west Atlantic flight.

Patterson J, *The Man-eaters of Tsavo* Adventurous account of how railway supervisor John Patterson tracked down and shot 2 man-eating lions that had been terrorizing workers during the building of the Uganda Railway.

Thesiger W, *My Kenya Days* Account of the 30 years adventurer William Thesiger spent in Kenya from the 1960s, where he undertook many arduous journeys by camel and on foot into the inhospitable Northern Frontier.

Fiction

Hemingway E, *Green Hills of Africa* Masterly short stories based on the author's African visits in 1933-1934.

Le Carré J, *The Constant Gardener* A powerful story about a British diplomat in Nairobi whose wife is murdered while investigating a drugs trial scandal; later made into a popular movie.

Wildlife and photography

Briggs P, *East African Wildlife* Bradt's comprehensive field guide on the animals you are likely to see on safari, illustrated by photographs and watercolour drawings.

Hosking D, Withers M, *Collins Traveller's Guide – Wildlife of Kenya, Tanzania and Uganda* A good companion to any wildlife-watching trip to the region, covering numerous mammal, bird, reptile and tree species, with a good selection of photographs.

Poliza M, *Kenya* A stunning collection of photographs of Kenya, many of them aeriel, taken by renowned photographer Michael Poliza, and a follow-up of his acclaimed *Africa* book, which showcases Africa's landscapes, wildlife and people.

Contents

Footnotes

Useful words and phrases

Here are some useful words and phrases in Kiswahili. Attempting a few words will be much appreciated by Kenyans.

Good morning	*Habari ya asubuhi*
Good afternoon	*Habari ya mchana*
Good evening	*Habari ya jioni*
Good night	*Habari ya usiku*
Hello!	*Jambo!*
A respectful greeting to elders, actually meaning: "I hold your feet"	*Shikamoo*
Their reply: "I am delighted"	*Marahaba*
How are you?	*Habari yako?*
I am fine	*Nzuri / Sijambo*
I am not feeling good today	*Sijiziki vizuri leo*
How are things?	*Mambo?*
Good/cool/cool and crazy	*Safi / poa / poa kichizi*
See you later	*Tutaonana baadaye*
Welcome!	*Karibu! (Karibu tena!)*
Goodbye	*Kwaheri*
Please	*Tafadhali*
Thank you	*Asante*
Sorry	*Pole*
Where can I get a taxi?	*Teksi iko wapi?*
Where is the bus station?	*Stendi ya basi iko wapi?*
When will we arrive?	*Tutafika lini?*
Can you show me the bus?	*Unaweza ukanioyesha basi?*
How much is the ticket?	*Tiketi ni bei gani?*
Is it safe walking here at night?	*Ni salama kutembea hapa usiku?*
I don't want to buy anything	*Sitaki kununua chochote*
I have already booked a safari	*Tayari nimeisha lipia safari*
I don't have money	*Sina hela*
I'm not single	*Nina mchumba / siko peke yangu*
Could you please leave me alone?	*Tafadhali, achana na mimi*
It is none of your business!	*Hayakuhusu!*
One	*moja*
Two	*mbili*
Three	*tatu*
Four	*nne*
Five	*tano*
Six	*sita*
Seven	*saba*
Eight	*nane*
Nine	*tisa*
Ten	*kumi*

Index → *Entries in bold refer to maps*

Advertisers' index

Credits

Footprint credits

Editor: Felicity Laughton
Layout and production: Emma Bryers
Proofreader: Sophie Jones
Cover and colour section: Pepi Bluck
Maps: Kevin Feeney

Managing Director: Andy Riddle
Content Director: Patrick Dawson
Publisher: Alan Murphy
Publishing Managers: Felicity Laughton,
Jo Williams, Nicola Gibbs
Marketing and Partnerships Director:
Liz Harper
Marketing Executive: Liz Eyles
Trade Product Manager: Diane McEntee
Account Managers: Paul Brew, Tania Ross
Advertising: Renu Sibal, Elizabeth Taylor
Finance: Phil Walsh

Photography credits

Front cover: Hot-air balloon flight over
Masai Mara. Nigel Pavitt / awl-images
Back cover: Hippos in the Mara River.
Nigel Pavitt / awl-images

Colour section

Page i: Brooke Whatnall / Shutterstock.com
Page ii: Nigel Pavitt / awl-images.com
Page v: Nigel Pavitt / awl-images.com
Page vi: Antonio Jorge Nunes /
Shutterstock.com
Page vii: Ludmila Yilmaz / Shutterstock.com
Page viii: Nigel Pavitt / awl-images.com
Page ix: Nigel Pavitt / awl-images.com
Page x: Nigel Pavitt / awl-images.com
(top and bottom)

Printed in India by Replika Press Pvt Ltd

Publishing information

Footprint Kenya
3rd edition
© Footprint Handbooks Ltd
May 2012

ISBN: 978 1 907263 60 6
CIP DATA: A catalogue record for this book
is available from the British Library

® Footprint Handbooks and the Footprint
mark are a registered trademark of
Footprint Handbooks Ltd

Published by Footprint
6 Riverside Court
Lower Bristol Road
Bath BA2 3DZ, UK
T +44 (0)1225 469141
F +44 (0)1225 469461
footprinttravelguides.com

Distributed in the USA by Globe Pequot
Press, Guilford, Connecticut

Every effort has been made to ensure that
the facts in this guidebook are accurate.
However, travellers should still obtain advice
from consulates, airlines, etc about travel
and visa requirements before travelling.
The authors and publishers cannot
accept responsibility for any loss, injury
or inconvenience however caused.

Footprint Mini Atlas
Kenya

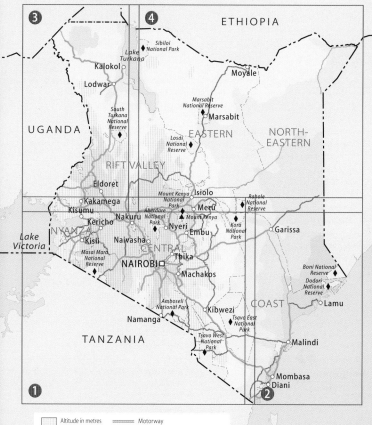

③

④ ETHIOPIA

Sibiloi
National Park ◆

Lake
Turkana

Kalokol ○

Lodwar ○

Moyale ○

Marsabit
National Reserve ◆

◆ Marsabit

EASTERN

NORTH-
EASTERN

South
Turkana
National
Reserve ◆

Losai
National
Reserve ◆

UGANDA

RIFT VALLEY

Eldoret ○

Kakamega ○
Kisumu ○

Mount Kenya
National
Park

Isiolo ○

Rahole
National
Reserve ◆

Nakuru ○
Aberdare
National
Park ◆

Meru ○

Kericho ○

▲ Mount Kenya

Nyeri ○

NYANZA

Kisii ○

Naivasha ○

Embu ○

Korä
National
Park

Garissa ○

Lake
Victoria

Masai Mara
National
Reserve ◆

CENTRAL

Thika ○

NAIROBI □

Machakos ○

Boni National
Reserve ◆
Dodori
National
Reserve ◆

Amboseli
National Park ◆

Namanga ○

Kibwezi ○

Tsavo East
National
Park

COAST

Lamu ○

TANZANIA

Tsavo West
National
Park

Malindi ○

①

②

Mombasa ○
Diani ○

Altitude in metres	Motorway
3000	Principal highway (mainly asphalt)
2000	Principal highway (mainly gravel)
1500	Highway (unsurfaced)
1000	Provincial road (partly-surfaced)
500	Secondary road, track
200	Railway
100	
0	
Neighbouring country	

Indian Ocean

N

100 km
100 miles

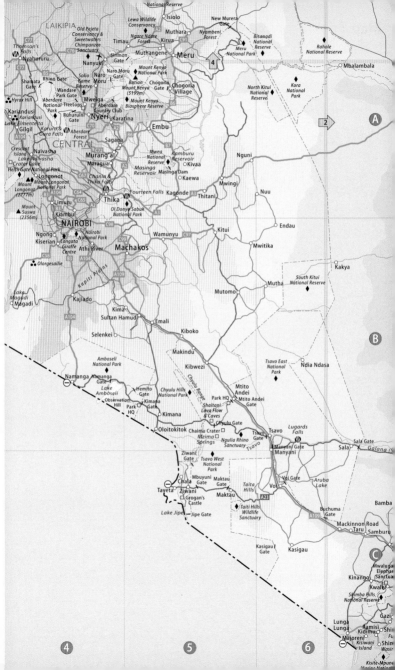

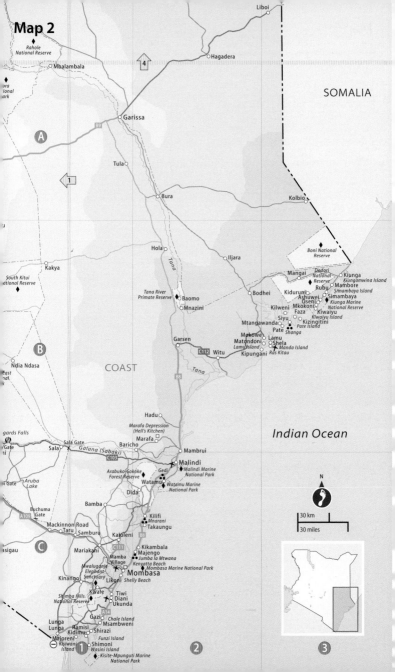

Map 3

ETHIOPIA

SUDAN

○⊖ Nadapal

✈ Lokichoggio

A1

Kakuma

○ Murangering

Lokitaung ○

Todenyang

○ Ileret 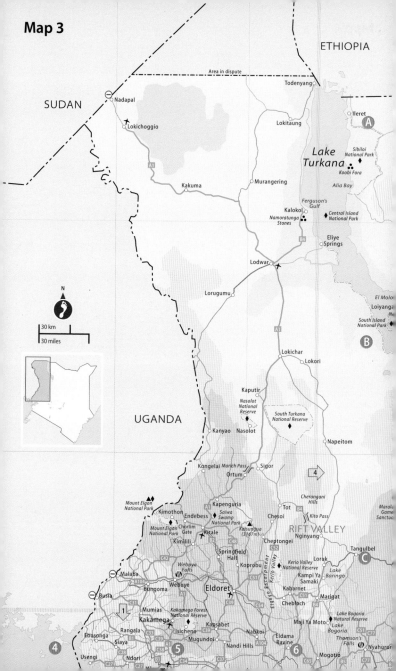Ⓐ

Lake Turkana

Sibiloi National Park ♦

Koobi Fora ♦

Alia Bay

Ferguson's Gulf

Kalokol ●
Namoratunga Stones

♦ *Central Island National Park*

Eliye ○
Springs

Lodwar ○ ✈

B4

○ Lorugumu

El Molo

Loiyanga N(

○ Ⓑ

South Island National Park

N

30 km
30 miles

UGANDA

○ Lokichar
○ Lokori

A1

Kaputir ○

Nasolot National Reserve ♦

South Turkana National Reserve ♦

○ Napeitom

○ Kanyao
● Nasolot

Kongelai *Marich Pass* ○ Sigor
Ortum ○

→ 4

Cherangani Hills

*Marale
Game
Sanctu(*

Mount Elgan ▲▲
National Park

Kimothon ●

*Mount Elgan
National Park*

▲ Kapenguria
*Saiwa
Swamp
National Park* ♦

Endebess ●
Chorlim ●
Gate
● Kitale
*Kaisuggua
(3167m)*

Tot ○

Chesoi ○

B4

Kito Pass

RIFT VALLEY

Cheptongei ○

Nginyang ○

Tangulbel

Ⓒ

Kimilili ●

C45

Springfield ●
Halt

C51

○ Koprobu

Elgeyo escarpment

Kerio Valley

Loruk ○
*Kerio Valley
National Reserve*

○ Kampi Ya
Samaki

*Lake
Baringo*

Malaba ○⊖
C42

*Weboye
Falls*

Bungoma ●

Webuye ●

Eldoret ✈

C39

Kabarnet ○

Marigat ○

⊖ Busia

C31

Mumias ●

*Kakamega Forest
National Reserve*

○ Chebloch

○ Maji Ya Moto
*Lake Bogoria
Natural Reserve*
*Lake
Bogoria* ♦

Ⓒ4

→ 1

Kakamega

● Isicheno
♦

Kapsabet ○

○ Eldama
Ravine

*Thomson's
Falls* ▲▲

Ebusonga ●
Rangala ●
Siaya ●

B1

C34

○ Mugundoi

Nabkoi ○
Nandi Hills ○

Mogotio ○

Nyahururu

Ⓒ5

C57

Usengi ●
Ndori ●

C27
C28

✈

Ⓒ6

Map 4

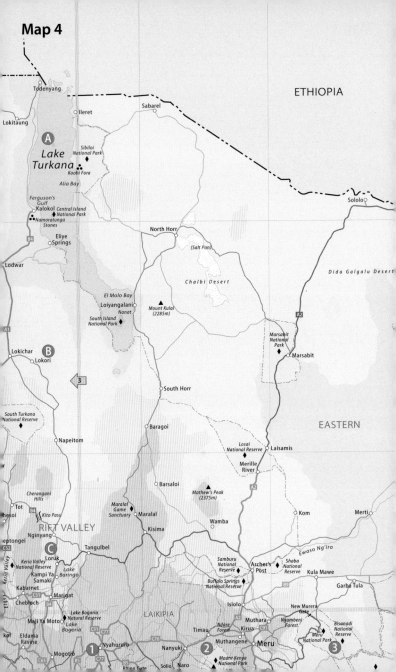

ETHIOPIA

Todenyang
Ileret
Sabarel
Lokitaung
Sololo

A

Lake Turkana

Sibiloi National Park
Koobi Fora
Alia Bay

North Horr

Ferguson's Gulf
Kalokol
Central Island National Park
Namoratunga Stones

(Salt Pan)

Dida Galgalu Desert

Eliye Springs

Lodwar

Chalbi Desert

El Molo Bay
Loiyangalani
Nanat
Mount Kulal (2285m)

Marsabit National Park
Marsabit

South Island National Park

B
Lokichar
Lokori

3

South Horr

South Turkana National Reserve

Baragoi

EASTERN

Napeitom

Losai National Reserve
Laisamis

Merille River

Barsaloi

Cherangani Hills
Tot
hesoi
Kito Pass

Mathew's Peak (2375m)

Kom
Merti

Maralal Game Sanctuary
Maralal

RIFT VALLEY
Nginyang
Kisima
Wamba

C
Loruk
Tangulbel

Ewaso Ng'iro

eptongeli

Kerio Valley National Reserve
Kampi Ya Samaki
Lake Baringo

Samburu National Reserve
Archer's Post
Shaba National Reserve
Kula Mawe

Kabarnet
Marigat

Buffalo Springs National Reserve

Garba Tula

Chebloch

LAIKIPIA

Isiolo

New Murera Gate

Eldama Ravine
Maji Ya Moto
Lake Bogoria Natural Reserve
Lake Bogoria

Muthara
Kirua
Nyambeni Forest

Bisanadi National Reserve

Timau
Ndare Forest
Muthangene
Meru
Meru National Park

Mogotio
1 Nyahururu
Nanyuki
Naro
2
Solio
Mount Kenya National Park
Rhino Gate
3

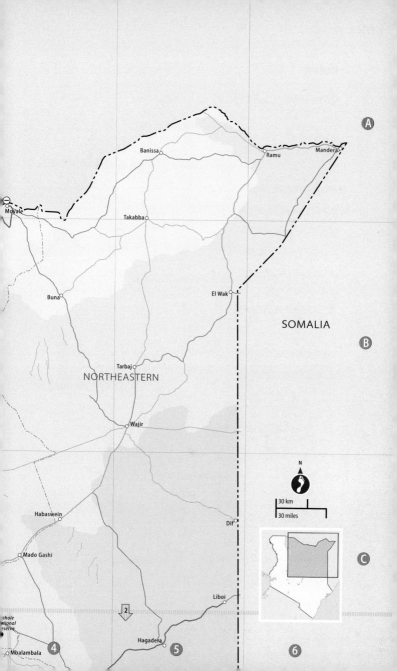

Banissa

Ramu

Mandera

A

Moyale

Takabba

SOMALIA

B

Buna

El Wak

Tarbaj

NORTHEASTERN

Wajir

N

30 km

30 miles

Habaswein

Dif

C

Mado Gashi

Liboi

2

ahole
tional
serve

Mbalambala

4

Hagadera

5

6

Index

Lizzie Williams

Originally from London, Lizzie Williams has worked and lived in Africa since 1995 and has visited 20 African countries. Her first introduction to the continent was backpacking as a 20-year-old around then-Apartheid South Africa, followed by an arduous trip to see the mountain gorillas in Zaire when gorilla tourism was still in its infancy. For several years she led trips across the continent as a tour leader on overland trucks, and has patted a cheetah, walked with a lion, ridden an elephant, fed a giraffe, swum with a hippo and is now something of an expert on African border crossings. For Footprint she is author of *South Africa*, *Namibia*, *Kenya*, *Tanzania*, *Zimbabwe* and *Cape Town, Winelands & Garden Route*, as well as several Footprint Focus guides on these regions.

er guidebooks, Lizzie has written for
nd websites specializing in African travel.
Lizzie lives in Cape Town.

k, as always, personal friends, ex-
rm expats in Nairobi and Mombasa
itality and for constantly keeping me
ng on in the tourist industry in East
tour operators for providing useful
including Karl-Heinz Straus from
e and all at Acacia Africa; Thommo
; John at Gametrackers; and the staff
GLOBE Let's Go Travel. Readers who
s include Jeanne Gallagher, Ben Leed,
Meyer Volnes, Jim van den Hoorn,
lden, Veronique Fortin, Marko Segulin
ul thanks must go to Michael Hodd
compiling *Footprint East Africa*, which
enya Handbook. Finally thanks to
ghton and the rest of the dedicated
king it all make sense.

Distance chart

Diani

850 Eldoret

38 450 Embu

860 630 180 Isiolo

805 255 405 362 Kericho

890 80 490 447 85 Kisumu

365 1135 950 1145 1090 1175 Lamu

1235 385 835 922 532 475 1020 Lodwar

145 925 755 935 880 965 210 1300 Malindi

1173 675 493 313 840 755 1458 1060 1288 Marsabit

820 310 140 40 402 487 1145 962 935 353 Meru

40 810 640 820 865 850 325 1195 105 1133 780 Mombasa

540 310 140 320 265 350 825 695 615 633 280 500 Nairobi

625 225 225 322 180 265 950 610 740 718 365 585 85 Naivasha

695 155 295 252 110 195 1020 540 810 788 292 655 155 70 Nakuru

650 480 310 490 435 520 975 865 765 803 450 610 170 255 325 Namanga

705 325 125 142 280 365 1030 765 820 455 265 665 165 250 170 335 Nyeri

580 355 95 275 310 395 910 735 700 588 190 545 45 130 200 215 120 Thika

Distances in kilometres   1 kilometre = 0.62 miles

Map symbols

- ▢ Capital city
- ○ Other city, town
- 🔁 International border
- ⸬ Regional border
- ⊖ Customs
- ◎ Contours (approx)
- ▲ Mountain, volcano
- ⊐ Mountain pass
- ⤒ Escarpment
- ◠ Glacier
- ▨ Salt flat
- ◌ Rocks
- ❀ Seasonal marshland
- ░ Beach, sandbank
- ◈ Waterfall
- ⌇ Reef
- ═══ Motorway
- ─── Main road
- ─── Minor road
- ≡≡≡ Track
- ⋯ Footpath
- ─── Railway
- ▬■ Railway with station
- ✈ Airport
- 🚌 Bus station
- Ⓜ Metro station

- ---- Cable car
- ╫╫╫ Funicular
- ⛴ Ferry
- ═══ Pedestrianized street
- ⊃ ⊂ Tunnel
- → One way-street
- ▥ Steps
- ⤬ Bridge
- ▲▲▲ Fortified wall
- ▨ Park, garden, stadium
- 🛏 Sleeping
- ⊘ Eating
- ⊙ Bars & clubs
- ▥ Building
- ▣ Sight
- ♰♰ Cathedral, church
- ☗ Chinese temple
- ☖ Hindu temple
- ⊼ Meru
- 🕌 Mosque
- ⊼ Stupa
- ✡ Synagogue
- ℹ Tourist office
- 🏛 Museum
- ✉ Post office
- Ⓟ Police

- Ⓢ Bank
- @ Internet
- ☏ Telephone
- ☖ Market
- ➕ Medical services
- Ⓟ Parking
- ⛽ Petrol
- ⛳ Golf
- ⁂ Archaeological site
- ♦ National park, wildlife reserve
- ✲ Viewing point
- ▲ Campsite
- ⌂ Refuge, lodge
- ▨ Castle, fort
- ⊠ Diving
- ⬈⬆ Deciduous, coniferous, palm trees
- ⊟ Hide
- ♣ Vineyard, winery
- ⚱ Distillery
- ⋈ Shipwreck
- ⚔ Historic battlefield
- ⬚1 Detail map
- ◁1 Related map